LEGITIMACY AND CRIMINAL JUSTICE

LEGITIMACY AND CRIMINAL JUSTICE

AN INTERNATIONAL EXPLORATION

EDITED BY
JUSTICE TANKEBE
AND ALISON LIEBLING

OXFORD
UNIVERSITY PRESS

OXFORD
UNIVERSITY PRESS

Great Clarendon Street, Oxford, OX2 6DP,
United Kingdom

Oxford University Press is a department of the University of Oxford.
It furthers the University's objective of excellence in research, scholarship,
and education by publishing worldwide. Oxford is a registered trade mark of
Oxford University Press in the UK and in certain other countries

First Edition published in 2013

Impression: 1

Published in the United States of America by Oxford University Press
198 Madison Avenue, New York, NY 10016, United States of America

British Library Cataloguing in Publication Data
Data available

Library of Congress Control Number: 2013942170

ISBN 978-0-19-870199-6

Printed in Great Britain by
CPI Group (UK) Ltd, Croydon, CR0 4YY

ACKNOWLEDGEMENTS

This book would not have been possible without generous financial support from the British Academy. This funding provided an opportunity for an interdisciplinary conference on 'legitimacy and criminal justice' held at the University of Cambridge (Cambridge—UK) in May 2012. We are deeply grateful to Deborah Kant, Amy Nivette, and Jo Parsons for their excellent organizational skills which helped so much to make the conference a success. Their diligence and commitment made the conference an enjoyable experience for participants.

We are also highly indebted to the participants at the conference for their insightful comments on, and criticisms of, first and later drafts of papers. We are especially grateful to the discussants: David Beetham, Nicholas Fyfe, Mike Hough, Jonathan Jackson, Andrew M. Jefferson, Susanne Karstedt, Ian Loader, Denis O'Connor, Richard Sparks, Michael Spurr, and Lucia Zedner. Their detailed and constructive comments helped to enrich the discussion and to improve the chapters to follow the conference. We learned a great deal from them.

Bethany Schmidt scrupulously read through all the completed chapters with a fine-toothed comb at our request, formatted them appropriately and made suggestions for edits and corrections. We salute her for her diligent and generous commitment to improving the book, as well as her enthusiastic engagement in the subject.

Finally, we owe our greatest debt to Tony Bottoms. The idea for an interdisciplinary conference on legitimacy was his; he was a co-applicant (together with the editors) for the financial support from the British Academy, and a co-organizer of the conference. We are extremely grateful for his intellectual guidance throughout the process of preparing the book.

Justice Tankebe and Alison Liebling
Cambridge, 2013

TABLE OF CONTENTS

PART IV LEGITIMACY AND CRIME

LIST OF ABBREVIATIONS

AC	Adjustment Center
AI	Appreciative Inquiry
AML	Anti Money Laundering
ANC	African National Congress
BAE	British Aerospace
CAPI	Computer Assisted Personal Interviewing
CCTV	Closed Circuit Television
CDPC	European Committee on Crime Problems
CEP	European Probation Organization
CPS	Crown Prosecution Service
CPT	Committee for the Prevention of Torture
DCRI	*Direction Centrale du Renseignement Intérieur*
DNAT	Anti-Terrorism National Division
DPP	Director of Public Prosecutions
DPRK	Democratic and People's Republic of Korea
DST	*Direction de la Surveillance du Territoire*
ECHR	European Convention on Human Rights
ECOSOC	Economic and Social Council
ECtHR	European Court of Human Rights
EPR	European Prison Rules
ERCSM	European Rules on Community Sanctions and Measures
ESS	European Social Survey
EU	European Union
FCA	Financial Conduct Authority
FCC	German Federal Constitutional Court
FIDH	FIDH
FSA	Financial Services Authority
GDR	German Democratic Republic
GNP	Gross National Product
HMIC	Her Majesty's Inspectorate of Constabulary
HMSO	Her Majesty's Stationery Office
HNW	High Net Worth
HRC	Human Rights Committee
ICCPR	International Covenant on Civil and Political Rights
IMF	International Monetary Fund
IPCC	Independent Police Complaints Commission
IPPC	International Penological and Penitentiary Council
KROM	Norsk Forening For Kriminalreform
LWOP	Life Without Parole
MQPL survey	Measuring the Quality of Prison Life Survey

NATO	North Atlantic Treaty Organization
NFA	National Fraud Authority
NGOs	Non-Governmental Organisations
NPM	New Public Management
NPMs	National Preventative Mechanisms
OECD	Organisation for European Co-operation and Development
OPCAT	Optional Protocol to the United Nations Convention against Torture
PBR	Principles-based Regulation
PCC	Police and Crimes Commissioner
PCCP	Penological Council of the Council of Europe
PI	Polity Index
PPB	Police Professional Body
PTS	Political Terror Scale
PWSL	Prisons Watch—Sierra Leone
RBS	Royal Bank of Scotland
RG	Renseignements Généraux
RUF	Revolutionary United Front
SEC	US Securities and Exchange Commission
SFO	Serious Fraud Office
SHU	Secured Housing Unit
SIAC	Special Immigration Appeals Commission
SPT	Subcommittee for the Prevention of Torture
SSRN	Social Science Research Network
TPIMs	Terrorism Prevention and Investigation Measures
UK	United Kingdom
UN	United Nations
UNSMR	United Nations Standard Minimum Rules for the Treatment of Prisoners
US	United States
USSR	The Union of Soviet Socialist Republics
VPU	Vulnerable Prisoner Unit
WHO	World Health Organisation
WTO	World Trade Organisation

LIST OF CONTRIBUTORS

Professor David Beetham, Emeritus Professor, University of Leeds, UK
Professor Anthony Bottoms, Institute of Criminology, University of Cambridge, UK
Dr Ben Bradford, Centre for Criminology, University of Oxford, UK
Professor Jean-Marc Coicaud, Rutgers University, USA
Professor John Dunn, King's College, University of Cambridge, UK
Professor Manuel Eisner, Institute of Criminology, University of Cambridge, UK
Professor Jacqueline Hodgson, University of Warwick, UK
Professor Mike Hough, Birkbeck University of London, UK
Dr Jonathan Jackson, London School of Economics and Political Science, UK
Dr Andrew M. Jefferson, DIGNITY—Danish Institute Against Torture, Copenhagen, Denmark
Professor Susanne Karstedt, University of Leeds, UK
Professor Michael Levi, Cardiff University, UK
Professor Alison Liebling, Institute of Criminology, University of Cambridge, UK
Professor Ian Loader, Centre for Criminology, University of Oxford, UK
Mr Peter Neyroud, Institute of Criminology, University of Cambridge, UK
Dr Amy Nivette, Nuffield College, University of Oxford, UK
Professor Lawrence Sherman, Institute of Criminology, University of Cambridge, UK
Professor Jonathan Simon, University of California at Berkeley, USA
Professor Richard Sparks, University of Edinburgh, UK
Dr Justice Tankebe, Institute of Criminology, University of Cambridge, UK
Professor Tom R. Tyler, Yale University, USA
Professor Dirk van Zyl Smit, University of Nottingham, UK

LEGITIMACY AND CRIMINAL JUSTICE: AN INTRODUCTION

Justice Tankebe and Alison Liebling

The concept of legitimacy arises from the Latin word *legitimus,* meaning 'lawful', 'appropriate', or 'just'. During the medieval period, legitimacy was widely understood to mean that which conformed to correct customary procedures. Rousseau had it in mind when he argued that the 'strongest man is never strong enough to be master all the time, unless he transforms force into right and obedience into duty' (1968: 52). Authorities who succeed in that transformation are viewed as legitimate; those who do not seek such transformation, or who fail, must draw on coercion to maintain their rule (Reus-Smit 2007). Modern examination of the concept of legitimacy owes much to Max Weber's influential analysis, showing its broad applicability as an analytical tool, and its usefulness in the comparative analysis of various socio-political phenomena (Sternberger 1968).

In the past 20 years, criminologists have become more interested in normative compliance with the law, and especially the concept of legitimacy: that is to say, citizens' recognition of the rightness of the authority of criminal justice officials, and the consequences of this recognition for behaviour. Legitimacy is now an established concept in criminological analysis. A substantial body of empirical research has been conducted, based on surveys in local communities, and on interviews and ethnographic studies in prisons (e.g. Tyler 1990; Sparks, Bottoms, and Hay 1996; Liebling, with Arnold 2004). This work has demonstrated that criminal justice agencies perceived to be legitimate can draw upon 'wellsprings of voluntarism' (Reus-Smit 2007: 169), which promote compliance and active support for legal officials. In the specific context of prisons, there is evidence to show that legitimacy can also generate prisoner well-being through a staff commitment to justice (Liebling, with Arnold 2004).

However, these approaches need supplementing and developing in many ways. First, following Weber (1922/1978) and Raz (2009), political authorities (including criminal justice authorities) virtually always claim to be legitimate authorities. These claims are then responded to by citizens; if citizens identify legitimacy deficits, authorities often adjust their practice (in effect making a revised claim), and so on (Bottoms and Tankebe 2012). Authorities that chronically and persistently fail to adjust their claims to respond to citizens' interests and concerns may soon reach 'critical turning points in which the imperative to adapt is heightened by the immanent possibility of death, collapse, demise, disempowerment, or decline into irrelevance' (Reus-Smit 2007: 166). This interactive and dialogic character of legitimacy has been neglected in the criminological literature to date. Second, and more generally, the burgeoning criminological interest in legitimacy has been primarily empirical and focused on procedural justice in particular. According to this approach, commonplace encounters with legal authorities are 'teachable moments' in which people raise questions 'far beyond those connected with the issue to be decided' (Tyler 1990: 175). The questions raised during these encounters concern the fairness of the procedures employed by legal authorities. The main elements of procedural fairness have been found to include neutrality, consistency, respect, accountability, and participation in decision making. The evidence consistently shows that fair encounters are the main driver of judgements made about institutional legitimacy. Although a great deal of insight into people's normative expectations about power has accrued from the procedural justice approach, there is a need to develop a broader theorization, drawing especially on insights from political theory. The processes of globalization (which often bring people from different cultural backgrounds to live in close proximity to one another) have significantly complicated issues of legitimacy for criminal justice agencies (see, e.g. Nelken 2011). Post 9/11, these general sociological processes have been further confounded by fears of faith-based terrorism. These important developments also remain under-explored in the criminological literature.

In the light of the above, the principal aims of this edited collection are, first, to advance conceptual understanding of legitimacy in the contexts of policing and criminal justice, through an advanced interdisciplinary dialogue drawing on insights from criminology, political science, international relations, and sociology. It is hoped that this will provide impetus for future empirical studies. Part of this agenda must be an improved understanding of the relationship between legitimacy and 'risk management', an increasingly dominant discourse in criminal justice management. Second, the book attempts to develop a better understanding of the implications of analyses of legitimacy for the practical contexts of policing, prisons, and criminal justice. The third aim is to pay attention, in developing the preceding twin aims, to the reality of an increasingly globalized world, and therefore to the growing number of contexts in which criminal justice personnel will encounter ethnically and religiously diverse communities. This will include a focus on the often acute dilemmas posed by perceived terrorist threats to the legitimate authority of criminal justice agencies. Additionally, attention is devoted to the growing importance of international organizations in relation to legitimacy, both in its international and its domestic manifestations.

This edited collection includes 16 substantial new contributions to this important field by some of the best political and theoretical scholars in it, and the results of several recent empirical studies. This collection is divided into four parts. Part I focuses on political science perspectives on legitimacy and criminal justice. It begins, in Chapter 1, with John Dunn, who breaks with the conventional view that legitimacy is a 'factual property of regimes' waiting to be uncovered by observational analysis of behaviour or attitudes of both governors and the governed. A more illuminating approach, he argues, is to view legitimacy as 'a ceaseless process of interactive judgment, necessarily dispersed, by attention and inattention, across the entire population in question.' This view allows Dunn to discuss the relationship between democracy and legitimacy.

In Chapter 2, David Beetham revisits key themes from his seminal book, *The Legitimation of Power*. Beetham's argument is that, despite the socio-structural differences between societies, it is possible to identify 'an underlying structure of legitimacy' common to all. In this chapter, Beetham applies his framework to the global financial crisis. Contrary to his theoretical expectations that the crisis would translate into crisis of legitimacy for banks and financial institutions, Beetham finds a displacement of the legitimacy deficits from these institutions onto democratic governments. The chapter discusses the reasons for this displacement and the implications for theorizing legitimacy.

Jean-Marc Coicaud's discussion in Chapter 3 is directed at the tripartite concepts of legitimacy, justice and crime, and the interconnections between them. His analysis assigns a commanding place to legitimacy for the reason that, to maintain a viable distinction between crime and justice, it is necessary to justify inequalities of power and how those inequalities are organized in society. Legitimacy and legitimation explanations perform the role of justifying these inequalities. Coicaud argues that examining the interconnections between crime, justice, and legitimacy allows us to gauge the degrees of stability and strain or stress in a given society.

Part II of the book focuses on theoretical and methodological issues in the study of legitimacy within the context of criminal justice. Anthony Kronman, following Max Weber, argues that legitimation explanations are an attempt to 'still *a voice within* as well as the sometimes louder but no more pressing *voices without*' (1983: 41). However, the majority of empirical analyses of legitimacy have focused on understanding the 'voices without'. In Chapter 4, Tony Bottoms and Justice Tankebe propose to correct this imbalance by developing more fully what they term 'power-holder legitimacy' or 'self-legitimacy'.

Tom Tyler and Jonathan Jackson's contribution in Chapter 5 poses the questions: What do two decades of evidence tell us about the role of procedural justice and legitimacy in shaping law-abiding behaviour? What are the policy implications of this body of evidence for criminal justice practice? What is the place of consent, vis-à-vis legality and shared values, in people's constructions of legitimate power? In answering these questions, the authors argue for a normative or 'values-based' strategy in responding to the problem of social order.

In Chapter 6, Ian Loader and Richard Sparks seek an improved conception of legitimacy that is sufficiently able to embrace societal expectations of actors and institutions, and how those actors and institutions respond to those expectations. To do this, they draw on the work of Pierre Rosanvallon (2011). Their analysis moves beyond a focus on legitimacy as a mechanism for compliance to a view of legitimacy as a social scientific tool for understanding institutional practices of crime and justice, as well as a means for imagining an alternative and better conception of politics and crime.

Much of what we know about legitimacy draws largely on data from democratic societies. In the final chapter of Part II of the book, Susanne Karstedt offers a comparative analysis of legitimacy in democratic and non-democratic regimes. What emerges from her data is a dual view of legitimacy. On the one hand, it is a highly contextualized and culturally and institutionally particularized concept. On the other hand, procedural justice was found to be a common mechanism through which legitimacy in both democratic and non-democratic regimes can be nurtured and reproduced.

The chapters in the third part of the book are united in their analysis of how criminal justice actors seek to cultivate legitimacy. The first by Michael Levi focuses on white-collar crimes. Levi argues that attempts to explore the implications of legitimacy within organizations often target the behaviour of employees to the neglect of corporate directors. What are the foundations of the legitimacy of financial regulators? How much legitimacy do regulators command, and among what audiences? To what extent and in what ways are the reactions of the state to corporate law-breaking shaped by legitimation concerns? Levi demonstrates that the challenges of legitimacy research in corporate settings are further complicated by global corporation; here, regulators are confronted with a multiplicity of audiences (both 'home' and 'abroad'), with expectations that are often conflicting and contradictory.

Since the 9/11 attacks on New York—and subsequent bombings in London and Madrid—the state has sought to re-assert, re-empower and re-legitimate itself through the promise of security (Loader and Walker 2006). Yet the nature of the response to terrorism can sometimes be counterproductive, by delegitimating rather than re-legitimating the state (Cronin 2009). These issues are the focus of Jacqueline Hodgson's analysis in Chapter 9, drawing on the experiences of the responses of the state to terrorism in France and England and Wales. Hodgson focuses in particular on police discretionary powers, the move towards preventative criminalization and the use of non-criminal interventions for cases that are ordinarily the bailiwick of criminal adjudication. The chapter demonstrates how on each of these issues the state risks undercutting the values that provide the foundation for legitimation.

In Chapter 10, Alison Liebling outlines new challenges to legitimacy evident in high-security prisons, based on a return to Whitemoor prison to repeat an ethnographic study of staff–prisoner relationships with her colleagues Helen Arnold and Christina Straub. Prisoners described a crisis of *identity* and a crisis of *recognition,* based on newly lengthened sentences, restrictions on activities, and an extreme emphasis on risk. A 40 per cent Muslim population, and a 55 per cent Black, minority, and mixed race population, meant that staff did not 'recognize their audience' any more. Long-term prisoners at early stages in their sentences were struggling to survive psychologically, or to find meaning in their environment. The apparent 'legitimacy turn' in criminal justice described by Tankebe (2013) seems to be in reverse in high-security settings.

Jonathan Simon's chapter (11) is partly historical in nature; it discusses the legitimation of mass incarceration in the United States since the 1980s. He demonstrates how legislators, prosecutors, and judges have sought to legitimatize this type of penal arrangement by adopting the view that it is a rational and indispensable social policy. Perceptions of prisoners as dangerous are accompanied by a willingness to sacrifice prisoners' dignity in the quest to procure security. Consequently, argues Simon, a humanitarian crisis continues to build, and in this trajectory Simon foresees a crisis of legitimacy.

In Chapter 12, Andrew Jefferson directs attention to the experiences of legitimation and its challenges in the postcolonial context. Jefferson takes issue with the idea of 'foundations of legitimacy', arguing that this idea suggests a static view of legitimation. He demonstrates that a metaphor of *roots* is more apt because it captures more fully the precariousness inherent in producing, creating, and sustaining legitimacy. Jefferson draws on data from Sierra Leone to illustrate his arguments. His analysis reinforces the centrality of the social context in defining the nature and success of legitimation claims.

In Chapter 13, Dirk van Zyl Smit argues that in research on legitimacy and criminal justice relatively little attention has been paid to the international standards that seek to shape the implementation of punishment in national jurisdictions. Even less attention has been given to the process by which such standards are developed and the role of concerns about legitimacy in that process. Yet an understanding of the development of such standards is an essential precursor of a study of the substantive legitimacy of international standards for punishment. He shows that courts and tribunals, more often than not, have been successful in contributing to a degree of legitimacy for the international standards of punishment that in many cases would have been unthinkable when they were adopted.

Part III of the book concludes with a contribution by Peter Neyroud and Lawrence Sherman, whose central thesis is that for police agencies to establish legitimacy they need to engage in a different kind of dialogue with their audiences; police dialogue should be based on evidence acquired by the application of scientific methods of testing and analysis. The authors argue that such a knowledge-based dialogue demands openness and accountability, as well as attention to cost–benefit estimation.

Part IV considers the theme of legitimacy and crime. The first chapter, by Manuel Eisner and Amy Nivette, argues that in social theory, a major issue in criminological analysis concerns the bridging of the gap between macro- and micro-level explanations of criminal behaviour. The authors demonstrate that legitimacy offers a possible mechanism for bridging that gap. They identify a number of areas that demand careful study if legitimacy is to assume the bridging role the authors assign to it. In the final chapter, Mike Hough, Jonathan Jackson, and Ben Bradford explore the meaning of legitimacy, its constituent elements, and its consequences for compliance and cooperation in different socio-political settings. Their analysis of survey data show that the implications of procedure justice, distributive justice, and effectiveness for legitimacy are culturally variable.

We are grateful to the authors and other participants for attending the conference, for engaging in this continuing and important dialogue, and for developing their contributions in a timely fashion for this volume. We hope it provides an outstanding synthesis of current developments in the field, some theoretical refinement, and much stimulus to further scholarship as well as improved practice.

REFERENCES

Bottoms, A. and Tankebe, J. (2012) 'Beyond Procedural Justice: A Dialogic Approach to Legitimacy in Criminal Justice', *Journal of Criminal Law and Criminology* 102(1): 101–50.

Cronin, A. (2009) *How Terrorism Ends: Understanding the Decline and Demise of Terrorist Campaigns*. New Jersey: Princeton University Press.

Liebling, A. with Arnold, H. (2004) *Prisons and their Moral Performance*. Oxford: Oxford University Press.

Nelken, D. (2011) *Comparative Criminal Justice and Globalization*. Farnham: Ashgate.

Raz, J. (2009) *Between Authority and Interpretation: On the Theory of Law and Practical Reason*. Oxford: Oxford University Press.

Reus-Smit, C. (2007) 'International Crises of Legitimacy', *International Politics* 44: 157–74.

Rosanvallon, P. (2011) *Democratic Legitimacy: Impartiality, Reflexivity, Proximity*. Princeton: Princeton University Press.

Rousseau, J. J. (1968) *The Social Contract*. Harmondsworth: Penguin Books.

Sparks, R., Bottoms, A., and Hay, W. (1996) *Prisons and the Problem of Order*. Oxford: Oxford University Press.

Sternberger, D. (1968) 'Legitimacy' (pp. 244–8) in Sills, D. L. (ed) *International Encyclopedia of the Social Sciences* (vol 9). New York: Macmillan Company.

Tankebe, J. (2013) 'Viewing Things Differently: The Dimensions of Public Perceptions of Police Legitimacy', *Criminology*, 51(1): 103–35.

Tyler, T. R. (1990) *Why people obey the law*. New Haven: Yale University Press.

Weber, M. (1978) *Economy and Society: An Outline of Interpretive Sociology*. (2 vols), Roth, G. and Wittich, C. (eds). Berkeley & Los Angeles, CA: University of California Press.

1

LEGITIMACY AND DEMOCRACY IN THE WORLD TODAY

John Dunn

Anyone who tries to think hard about legitimacy needs in the end to make up their mind about one sharp and intellectually disconcerting issue: is legitimacy, the potent and powerfully orientating category whose operation in the political and social world they hope to understand, best envisaged in the end as a permanent process of judgement, unevenly dispersed across a given population, and constantly shifting in valency, or is it better conceived as a very intimate, consequential but somewhat opaque fact about that social world? For a variety of reasons the balance of professional conviction amongst social scientists construes their subject matter in its entirety explicitly as an immense body of objectively discernible facts about the social world. For many purposes and over many social subject matters, that is a plausible and serviceable perspective. But it is not a perspective which can be articulated successfully in the end, however deftly or insightfully, on the play of legitimacy as a concept through the lives of individuals or societies. In the end legitimacy can only be clearly understood, not as an externally specifiable social fact, but as a process of permanently active judgement, if one conducted with very uneven alertness and imaginative engagement by its full cast of eager or involuntary participants. That is both a clearer way to think about it (it permits clearer thoughts) and a better recognition of what it is that urgently demands understanding. This assessment is congruous with (and perhaps a natural inference from) Tony Bottoms' and Justice Tankebe's (2012: 129) emphasis that legitimacy is inherently dialogic and relational—as they put it, 'more like a perpetual discussion.' It is a natural social scientific impulse to think of the object of study as a phenomenon, a potentially discernible structure of appearances. But that can never be an adequate way to conceive a continuous process of active judging where there can be, and hence is, no phenomenon there to discern until the judgement has been made. What is in question is not an observation, actual or possible, but a less than explicit prediction, hypothesis or guess, masquerading as an observation.

Legitimacy, on this way of seeing it, has an ontological and not merely a perceptual fluidity. It is not a fact of the matter, dispositionally specifiable in advance of the judgement in question, but the act or performance of judging itself. Why does this matter?

Consider what has been happening in Syria now for well over a year. It will not be difficult to see why it not only matters, but locates the bottom line. The friends and foes of President Assad are not in disagreement about an intricate matter of fact. They have been struggling to sustain or break a rickety and ever more odious structure of allegiance.

LEGITIMACY, ALLEGIANCE, AND JUDGEMENT

In essence, a structure of allegiance is a felt and dependable commitment by human agents to recognize, accept, stand by, and actively sustain a specifiable site of authority and the requirements which it, for its own good reasons, chooses to impose. It is a structure of command and obedience fully espoused by those subject to the commands, and espoused because they judge it to hold authority for them, and to be a trustworthy and effective custodian of their fundamental interests as a group of humans living together. Discernibly not the condition which in the early autumn of 2012 obtained over much of the territory of the Republic of Syria.

The paradigm case of legitimacy in action is dutiful obedience to a lawful order of a lawful government, delivered by a person or agency entitled to give such an order, to adjudicate that it is in fact lawful, and to call on appropriate resources to enforce it where it fails to be obeyed. All the elements in this structure can be shaded in an infinite variety of ways; but the elements themselves can reasonably be seen as quite simple. They are best conceived as a nested set of questions. Is the person or agency concerned entitled to issue the order? Do they have clear access to adequate means with which to enforce it? Is their judgment of its legality both positive and well-founded? Is the government or ruler under whose authority they issue their command lawful in the first place (see Finer 1997)?

Articulated answers to these questions, and attempts to show just how those answers bear on one another, have lain at the centre of all the major architectonic accounts constructed across Europe for more than four hundred years of what makes governments legitimate and which of their commands their subjects have good reason to obey (see Carlyle 1903; Skinner 1978; Tuck 1979). Categories devised to focus and validate these answers have since travelled the globe and form key presuppositions for every extant doctrine of right with global pretensions and dispersion.

Judgement operates actively right across this space, and in all human components, active or passive. Every element in these intricate and inherently unstable structures of authorization and interpretation is being judged endlessly by an ever shifting audience, and every human participant judging actively in turn on their own behalf. The principal negative judgements which jeopardize the structures in application are that the government in question is far from lawful, that the agents who claim its authority do not carry whatever authority it does hold, or that their interpretations of these requirements are insincere or mistaken (because, for example, they breach the letter or spirit of the laws it claims to enforce). All such structures are, always have been, and very possibly will always remain permanently in jeopardy in this way simply because of what they are. The dialogue in progress is often one-sided, and all participants quite frequently deaf to what their interlocutors are trying to say, or would like to convey, if they did elect to listen. But whatever its quality, intensity, or acoustic conditions, the relations from which it is composed are themselves simply constitutive.

How exactly should we see democracy as a political category or presumptive form of government as now bearing on these structures in operation? Democratic governments are governments whose rule is authorized by those whom they rule, and in presumption again, so authorized not by a single mythical episode in the penetralia of the distant past, but by a series of iterative occasions over time, one at least of which should always be quite recent. In bare outline, the point of these occasions is to recast every citizen as subject to democratic laws, through some imaginatively accessible and pertinent set of mediations, and hence as part author of the laws to which each is subject. Most of the world's current human inhabitants are subjects (or more politely, citizens) of some state; and even those who are not find themselves physically situated within territories over which at least one state claims lawful authority, and can at least attempt sporadically to enforce it. A very large proportion of the subjects of these states now face rulers who do not present themselves as self-authorized to exercise rule, but as drawing their entitlement to do so directly and actively from the authorization of the subjects themselves. The mediations which purport to provide that authorization vary appreciably from North Korea (the eponymously Democratic and People's Republic of Korea), to Iran, from China to India, and from Switzerland to Singapore or Sweden. You can certainly see them as varying greatly in the imaginative energy with which they attempt to authenticate the authorization; but it cannot be said that the relative energy (which in the DPRK, for example, viewed from the outside, often reaches the level of frenzy) is a clear reciprocal by any conceivable criterion of the plausibility of the authentication itself.

Whether a particular government is indeed lawful, and whether any particular governmental order or law is a valid exercise of whatever authority that government lawfully possesses are, for every person concerned, a matter for political decision (though of course they have not been so thought of by most human beings across the wide expanse of history and geography: that is an analytic perspective of ours upon them, and perhaps also an implicit normative stance towards them). Where national or international courts are called on to adjudicate on such issues, they become also a matter for legal decision; but that cannot blur their fundamental character and should not be seen, even by lawyers or judges, as doing so. Law may be the most persistent and effective human expedient thus far identified for taming the chaos of political decision; but it can never reasonably be envisaged as eliminating or supplanting it.

Legitimacy is a very old imagined presence in the life of human populations, by now often most elaborately articulated, and even effectively enforced, on scales unimaginable to any human being three thousand years ago: the territorial United States of America, the Republic of India, the Russian Republic, the Dominion of Canada, the People's Republic of China. Over the last two and a half centuries a single model or formula for how best to articulate and enforce it has won ever wider sway: the model of what is now called democracy (see Dunn 1992, 2005, 2013; Huntington 1991; Przeworski 2010). How that model can be instantiated remains a focus of intense dispute, and could scarcely cease to be so until it is simply abandoned. Its ineliminably contentious status rests on the scope of its overweening claim: to authorize conclusively a territorial and demographic scope, neither of which can in principle offer a clear and decisive external criterion of their own validity, to authorize extrinsically something which in itself holds and can hold no intrinsic authority. The essence of the claim is to render the essentially arbitrary fully normatively authoritative through something as frail and evanescent as an act of will. But the authority it strains to conjure into existence and keep alive is assumed to hold, *ex hypothesi*, over every active individual will onto which it falls. This is a vast claim, inordinate in its reach and stretched tautly against the limitlessly recalcitrant targets over whom it seeks to cast its spell. Once we see that disenchanted authority must in the end lie at the mercy of those subjects, must be just their own wills reflected back at them, how can there still be authority in the world (Stanton 2011)? Democracy is the modern answer to that question; and it has come in many shapes and sizes.[1]

DEMOCRACY: THE MODERN RECIPE FOR LEGITIMACY

How much difference does it make that this modern answer should have turned out to be democracy? Does it tell us something clear and reliable about the basis of legitimacy and the practical requirements for political order today across the human denizens of the world? Or is its semantic instability and conceptual parlousness itself an index not just of the extremity, but also of the sheer incoherence of what has befallen this antique image of order in the world which the intellectual and economic histories of the last few centuries have refashioned so chaotically and drastically? Impressionable readers of Max Weber (1978) might easily think of authority as an archaic image lingering on in a postmodern world. But however anachronistic the idea of authority may now look and feel, in its democratic guise it has come to be a prominent and load-bearing element in the practical organization of an immense dispersion of collective life (see Kaviraj 2011).

We can be certain that that prominence affects how very many today think and feel and see. No one can yet assess quite how heavy a load it does now bear anywhere in particular, or will or even could bear in the future there or anywhere else. But the question, which it is reasonable to ask with some hope or expectation of an answer, is not one of past, present, or future fact about the social world. It is one of conceptual potential.

What, if anything, is there within the conception of democratic political authorization which could transform (or may have already transformed) the contours of the

[1] Compare the more allegiant accounts of John Keane's *The Life and Death of Democracy*, or, more subtly, David Gilmartin's 'Towards a Global History of Voting', with Dunn's *Setting the People Free* and *Breaking Democracy's Spell*. For a subtle interpretation in relation to a particularly consequential historical instance, see Sudipta Kaviraj's *The Enchantment of Democracy in India*.

age-old discourse of legitimacy that runs, in all its kaleidoscopic variety, through the life of every human society? Most citizens of a state like the (still precariously united) United Kingdom would assume that there must be something, and that the scale of transformation secured must be substantial. My suspicion, like that of Thomas Hobbes three and a half centuries ago, is that there is nothing cognitively determinate and reliable within the concept of democracy with the power to effect such a transformation, and that the antique discourse of legitimacy in all its urgency and indefinition has therefore survived unscathed.

Legitimacy is a presupposition of every actually existing state, and democratic legitimacy at least a less implausible interpretation of what that legitimacy might come from, and what could rationally sustain it than any extant rival. (Just how implausible an interpretation it nevertheless remains is of great importance in relation to the legitimacy of numerous states today and likely to bear differently on different legitimacy pressure points: law, policing, adjudication and sentencing, penality.) Democracy has won the salience it now holds as a default option, always vulnerable in application, but iteratively less vulnerable than any other conception which aspires to answer both questions. In the form in which we now encounter it democratic legitimacy is a conjunction between two structures, one of which is historically prior to, and arguably less strained than, the other. The first structure is that of the state itself, open to interpretations of Alexandrian intricacy, but reducing at its core to a unitary and monopolistic form, uniting a populace, a territory, and a system of government as a continuing entity, irreducible to its constituent parts (see Skinner 1989, 2009). Many glosses have been placed on this structure; but by now the most frequent of these has definitely become holistic and prudential: holistic in the scope of its claims, but prudential in the rationale it tacitly invokes and on which it must largely rely. The passions on which it reckons,[2] and on which it must thus rest most of its weight, may be principally hope or fear; but the balance between the two shifts from state to state and from time to time. Both hope and fear are violent, not calm, passions in David Hume's (2000: 268) terms: powerful, disorientating, and cognitively invasive. Many states openly and shamelessly rest their weight mainly on the adage of the Emperor Tiberius: *oderint dum metuant*—let them hate, provided only that they fear. Those that place it principally on hope, on the quotidian plausibility for a great many of framing their lives within a well protected capitalist economy, need either to intensify their subjects' expectations of economic reward to extravagant and inherently unsustainable levels or shift much of it back instead onto the more insistent pressure of fear. No way of drawing hard and durably on the violent passions can dispense with violence as a leading weapon in its armoury.

The state today has long ceased to place its weight principally on the allegation that any specification of demos or territory, let alone any derivation of its incumbent governors, holds clear validity in itself, and resettled that weight instead on the prudential judgement that humans need some definite way of formatting their lives with one another and sustaining that format against all who threaten it. The key goods sustained on this model are the physical security of its subjects and the specificity and

[2] Hobbes (2012) pt 1, cap 14, vol 2, 216: 'The Passion to be reckoned upon, is Fear.'

reliability of their property rights. Neither of these grounds is evidently better secured by conjoining it with democracy, and the latter was widely, if on the whole inaccurately, assumed to threaten it by critics from ancient Greece to contemporary stalwarts of the American Republican party.

Prudentially secured legitimacy is only as secure as the conviction of those it solicits to accept that it does support their interests in practice. It is therefore weak in face of countervailing sentiments, weaker still in face of sharp dissent over the location of interests, and all but impotent in face of dominant rival claims of right. No modern society has an imaginatively and cognitively compelling rationale for assigning property rights over time in one way rather than another (Dunn 1996). Much of the politics of relatively wealthy capitalist countries centres on the theory and practice of just and prudent taxation: as feebly secured in relation to justice, as it is to prudential political economy. The routine politics of fiscality undermines (and tendentially jeopardizes) the self-evidence of any system of property rights, the assumption that current ownership of anything not already protractedly appropriated by an individual should be seen as resting with anyone in particular. To take something away by force or stealth from an individual without further justification still seems as aberrant, at least outside specialized sub-cultures, as it would in the school playground. But that response fetishizes concrete relations between individuals and things.[3] It does not articulate coherently with any overall understanding of how ownership and control of resources across a human population should and should not persist, or alter in shape, over time. It trades on the normative implausibility of particular acts of appropriation, but wholly fails to carry through to a coherent and compelling answer to the question of who should now own what within the United Kingdom or anywhere else at any time whatever.

CHALLENGES TO LEGITIMACY

The two fiercest challenges to legitimacy within England itself for the last few years (arguably by now the fiercest such challenges within the British Isles as a whole) have been the practice of Islamist terror especially associated with the Al Qa'eda network and the widespread city riots and looting of 2011, triggered initially by the shooting of Mark Duggan. Both of these episodes have prompted very elaborate and intensive repressive responses from the British state, as both quite evidently should have. Both highlighted massive lacunae in state legitimacy which it was imperative for the state to attempt to remedy or finesse. Factual knowledge of each episode, and imaginative conceptions of what prompted it and what forms of action ensued within it could not be concentrated in any conceivable research archive and remain, as they were always fated to do, bewilderingly dispersed across very large components of the national

[3] See Robert Nozick's *Anarchy, State and Utopia*, a work with much deeper critical force than the arbitrariness of its initial assumptions or its relatively perfunctory positive case would suggest.

population. In the former case, unmistakably, they reach very far beyond it.[4] Both episodes took place appreciably closer than Syria; and all too many police officers and penal officials, doctors, and social workers know much about one or other episode from their own angle and could organize their understandings of what they know more instructively through this conception of what legitimacy is and means.

Criminology as a whole must take its bearings perforce from the contours of the criminal law of an existing state, however resolutely it formats its conclusions through a paradigm of social scientific comprehension, and whatever the sentiments or normative judgements which individual criminologists may feel or make about the merits and limitations of that law at any particular time. Underlying, and presupposed by, the criminal law of any state is that state's claim to legitimacy. Criminology as a whole thus deals with deficits of legitimacy in practical observance, however far it also chooses and contrives to deal with deficits of legitimacy under critical interrogation.

In the case of Islamist terrorism the challenge is frontal and categorical and legitimacy is repudiated from the outset. *Commanding Right and Forbidding Wrong* supervenes on the state's demand to be obeyed (Cook 2000). The crescent is simply mightier than the sword or cross, and very blatantly more peremptory than such hazy prudential claims as arise from sharing everyday life in an intricate and highly commercialized urban territory like Bradford or Finsbury Park.

The riots of 2011 may seem a less pressing instance. Who would sanely attempt to analyse decisions on whether or not to shoplift through the category of state legitimacy in any possible application (police, courts, commercial cost-minimizing strategies)? But on the scale at which they occurred, and with the brief hiatus in civic order and commercial security which they represented, it was clear that the very centre of the British state experienced the riots themselves as a more intimate and perturbing air pocket in its legitimacy than the threat of Al Qa'eda itself. Arguably, they were quite right to do so, and not simply because far more of their fellow citizens were directly affected in distressing ways, and because responsibility for re-establishing civic order and normal commercial operation was widely seen as falling more drastically and damagingly on them as claimants to wield the powers of the state. What for most subjects are mainly threats to personal security are as likely to strengthen legitimacy as to impair it. The reasons they do so clearly precede contemporary forms of democratic legitimation.

The claim of the British Government to be obeyed by anyone, citizen or alien, who chooses to menace or harm its subjects, like the duty it acknowledges to defend those subjects against any such threat, both long preceded the coming of democracy to Britain, even as a word in current use. It has never relied upon ratification by presumptive majority choice of its subjects to recognize their duty when asserting its entitlement to demand their obedience or extract resources and exert coercive power to defend them. Britain, like Syria, faces an active struggle for allegiance amongst at least

[4] This is how things must be today in very many national societies. When a French satirical journal publishes a set of deliberately provocative cartoons, the government of France, without clear absurdity, may choose to close French embassies and schools in 20 different countries (see Hugh Carnegy's article 'France on alert over Mohammed cartoons', *Financial Times*, 19 September 2012).

its Muslim subjects. Its prospects in that struggle may be easier to judge because it is an electoral democracy awash with opinion surveys. It is less clear that those prospects must be greatly strengthened by such greater transparency; and it remains reasonable to assume that those prospects would worsen considerably if the demographic balance within the country shifted emphatically towards Pakistan and Bangladesh.[5] To win the struggle, the British state needs to convince over time enough of its Islamist assailants, along with those who sympathize with or shelter them, either that they have misunderstood what Allah requires of them, misjudged the scale of authority over their actions which they should accord him, or simply made an error in supposing him either to exist or to have chosen to communicate imperatively with them at all. The United Kingdom is still the shrunken residue of a confessional state.[6] But today the last two types of judgement are ones it has long repudiated the entitlement to make on anyone's behalf; and its route towards that abandonment was sufficiently painful, tangled and contingent to make profoundly unattractive any positive reassertion of state judgement on religious claims or intuitions. Its tepidly secular assumptions are eirenic and sceptical, not militantly rationalist. The rationale which underlies them and gives them force comes from *raison d'etat*, not from popular choice.

The Islamic terrorist threat is a classic challenge to allegiance, on behalf of a peremptorily higher power. It is not a challenge to the state's entitlement to enforce laws of its own choosing or to choose those laws in the first place. The riots, by contrast, are in the first place attacks on the state as enforcer, adjudicator, and custodian of the property rights of its citizens and of their personal safety as they go about the streets. Right across this space no state at all could afford to develop scepticism over its entitlement to judge and enforce as best it can.

Here what is fundamental is to get into focus what can and cannot be elicited from the specificity of democratic authorization. A comprehensively kleptocratic regime, in which all ownership had been taken and sustained by force, is barely causally conceivable, and some little distance from the substance of even the grossest of existing states. The picture of the Russian state, for example, exhaustively kleptocratic for a brief period, as the USSR decomposed, or of the Republic of the Congo in that guise under Mobutu and ever since, is potently de-legitimatory. But even in these very extreme instances what is actually true of the relation between state and property security for most subjects most of the time overlaps extensively with the democratic politics of fiscal redistribution, as imagined by the Tea Party or the partisans of Silvio Berlusconi. If you suspend the applicability of the category of justice, every regime of coercive redistribution looks to those who lose under it, as St Augustine noted (1871:139), quite close to a giant gang of thieves. For those who do lose under it, the derivation of the predators from the majority electoral choice of their fellow citizens cannot be relied upon to blur this image. They have to accept a great deal of fairly counterintuitive political theory even to be drawn in that direction.

[5] For a despondent assessment of the prospects, see e.g., Christopher Caldwell's *Reflections on the Revolution in Europe*.

[6] From different angles: Diarmaid MacCulloch's *Reformation: Europe's House Divided, 1490–1700*; and J.C.D. Clark's *English Society 1660–1832*.

Whatever legitimacy was conferred upon the politics of radical deregulation and comprehensive marketization by iterative electoral choice across the globe over the last three decades has been more than cancelled since the autumn of 2008 by the convulsive contraction of global credit markets and its knock-on consequences. It is plainly open to irresolvable dispute what approaches to reversing this contraction are causally coherent; but, on any defensible judgement, there is no reason at present to believe that any European government in the autumn of 2012 enjoys the legitimacy to choose and implement an approach which could reasonably be anticipated to succeed in doing so, beyond the scale of the shrinking handful of nation states whose political economy has survived the cataclysm in reasonable order (e.g., Norway, Germany, and Switzerland).

Democracy requires that authority derive clearly and regularly from the equally effective choices of all those directly subject to it. There is no reason at all to believe that any capitalist society can achieve that outcome, or that those who sometimes very conspicuously exercise far greater power over the outcomes than the great majority of their fellow citizens have ever had the slightest intention that it should. There is no reason at all to believe that any rival model of political economy on the scale of territorial states or above it can or will sustain even the notional civic equality embodied in modern democratic constitutions.

CONCLUSION

Most of this train of thought is readily apparent to anyone who considers it carefully. Much must be the stuff of everyday experience in policing, criminal adjudication, prison operation or imprisonment in a society like the United Kingdom. The point of putting it this starkly is to underline something which may be less obvious about the juxtaposition of the political category democracy to this whole domain of experience. In relation to the huge bulk of experience of legitimacy under pressure which any police force, penal service or assemblage of academic criminologists necessarily carries, the thoughts of an academic political theorist, however disconcertingly expressed, can have no real weight. They must speak to what those who perform or interpret professionally the content of this domain already know, not from something the theorist in question can defensibly claim to know better. On the issue of democracy and what it does and does not do to legitimacy, the balance may be a bit different. There the experience of those who have spent decades attempting to grasp the nature of that impact from a variety of angles on a domain which most of their human fellows have had less reason to try to grasp or analyse in any consecutive way might carry a force of its own.

What is clear about the increment of legitimacy which has come to us, or could come for anyone, from the category of democracy is very simple. It is that that increment is far slighter, frailer and more inconstant than we have got into the habit of assuming and constantly assuring one another: not quite the flutter of a butterfly's wing, but at best a delicate and fitful breeze (Dunn 2013). Democracy, as we now spontaneously conceive it, is the benign and trustworthy political order which we ourselves have and live under, and the Chinese, North Koreans or Saudi Arabians conspicuously lack. How can it not be true that legitimacy, in strenuous political, social, and above all economic use, is not completely transformed by the sharpness of that contrast?

There is a very simple model of why it has not been so transformed. The contrast between our regimes and their regimes is above all one of acknowledged and reliably institutionalized accountability (Przeworski et al. 1999). We choose our governors at more or less prescribed intervals and can remove them when enough of us have had more than enough of them. Their governors choose and re-choose themselves, or were chosen long ago by irrevocable divine whim, or sanguinary, and thus far unreversed, armed conquest. When our governors command or coerce us, it is always notionally we ourselves who stand behind and authorize their coercion. That is why, if we are hit with gusto by a police officer in the execution of his or her supposed duty, it is wrong for us to hit back as hard as we can, or even to hit back at all.

At the point of impact, it is hard to believe this. Just what difference should the freest and fairest of elections make to our capacity to believe it, and perhaps even to our duty to believe it? (The ethics of belief is one of the trickiest elements in the vision of a fully rationalized human world.) Just what difference should it make to our capacity to act or refrain from acting accordingly? Very few elections are exhilaratingly free choices; and in a capitalist society none at all can be the free choice of real equals, so the category of democracy itself holds minimal plausibility in active political use. How can the modal Bradford elector sanely conceive themselves the full political equal of the modal Belgravia elector, let alone the political equal within the United Kingdom of foreign citizens like Rupert Murdoch or Roman Abramovich? The state coerces everyone; but its coercive pressure does not fall evenly on all; and the purposes for which that pressure is exerted do not reflect the interests of its subjects in any transparent or equitable way. Democratizing the state is a very partial, historically erratic, and unsteady process—never a free and un-flurried collective decision.

For democracy to legitimate a state comprehensively (rather than provisionally and ultra-hypothetically), it has to be true that the consequent state, the state as it actually decides and coerces, fully registers, and enacts equally, either the wills of every one of its subjects, or at least their several interests judged by some epistemically commanding criterion. We have no such criterion available to us to retreat or advance to. No state at all ever equally reflects the wills of every one of its subjects. The category of democracy simply cannot cover most state decision or action (Dunn 2013).

In the end, all the world is Syria, if often Syria in happier times and Syria under less agonizing interrogation than it had come to be by the autumn of 2012. Viewed from place to place and from time to time, the human world differs extravagantly in how far it deserves legitimacy. But that has no direct and dependable relation either forward or backward in time to the degree to which it evinces legitimacy as social fact: to the extent to which it is experienced and lived in just as it deserves to be, and with loyalty and inhibition aligned within it just as that happy outcome requires.

If you do choose to think of legitimacy as a kind of social fact, you must conceive it as settled patterns of judgement, the patterns of sentiment which go with them and which they sustain, and the habits of acting or refraining from acting, which flow from all of these. Beneath all of them, eddying through, and steadying or disrupting them as they go, there are all the causal elements which affect human judgement, the full chaos of human susceptibility. If you juxtapose all these elements today analytically and cognitively to the power of practical ordering and comprehension which as yet lies within reach of economics as a profession, you can see how heroic it is to predicate legitimacy as a social fact of the current political and economic outcome, not merely throughout the European Union but in any major capitalist state. Democracy is an emphatic normative advance on self-authorizing autocracy; but it is not that kind of advance.

REFERENCES

AUGUSTINE, SAINT A. (1871) *The Works of Aurelius (vol. 1)*, Dods, M. (ed and trans). Edinburgh: T. & T. Clark.

BOTTOMS, A. and TANKEBE, J. (2012) 'Beyond Procedural Justice: A Dialogic Approach to Legitimacy in Criminal Justice', *Journal of Criminal Law and Criminology* 102(1): 119–70.

CALDWELL, C. (2009) *Reflections on the Revolution in Europe: Immigration, Islam and the West.* London: Penguin.

CARLYLE, R. W. and CARLYLE, A. J. (1903) *A History of Mediaeval Political Theory in the West.* Edinburgh: Blackwood & Sons.

CLARK, J. C. D. (2000) *English Society, 1660–1832.* Cambridge: Cambridge University Press.

COOK, M. A. (2000) *Commanding Right and Forbidding Wrong in Islamic Thought.* Cambridge: Cambridge University Press.

DUNN, J. (ed) (1992) *Democracy: The Unfinished Journey.* Oxford: Oxford University Press.

DUNN, J. (1996) 'Property, Justice and Common Good after Socialism' (pp. 121–35), in Dunn, J. *The History of Political Theory and other Essays.* Cambridge: Cambridge University Press.

DUNN, J. (2005) *Setting the People Free: The Story of Democracy.* London: Atlantic.

DUNN, J. (2013) *Breaking Democracy's Spell.* New Haven: Yale University Press.

FINER, S. E. (1997) *The History of Government from the Earliest Times.* Oxford: Oxford University Press.

GILMARTIN, D. (2012) 'Towards a Global History of Voting: Sovereignty, the Diffusion of Ideas, and the Enchanted Individual', *Religions* 3(2): 407–23.

HOBBES, T. (2012) *Leviathan*, Malcolm, N. (ed). Oxford: Clarendon Press.

HUME, D. (2000) *A Treatise of Human Nature*, Norton, D. F. and Norton, M. J. (eds). Oxford: Oxford University Press.

HUNTINGTON, S. P. (1991) *The Third Wave: Democratization in the Late Twentieth Century.* Norman: University of Oklahoma Press.

KAVIRAJ, S. (2011) *The Enchantment of Democracy in India: Politics and Ideas.* Ranikhet: Permanent Black.

KEANE, J. (2010) *The Life and Death of Democracy.* London: Pocket.

MACCULLOCH, D. (2003) *Reformation: Europe's House Divided, 1490–1700.* London: Penguin.

NOZICK, R. (1974) *Anarchy, State, and Utopia*, Oxford: Blackwell.

PRZEWORSKI, A. (2010) *Democracy and the Limits to Self-Government.* Cambridge: Cambridge University Press.

Przeworski, A., Stokes, S. C. and Manin, B. (eds) (1999) *Democracy, Accountability, and Representation*. Cambridge: Cambridge University Press.

Skinner, Q. (1978) *The Foundations of Modern Political Thought*. Cambridge: Cambridge University Press.

Skinner, Q. (1989) 'The State' (pp. 90–131), in Ball, T., Farr, J. and Hanson, R.L. (eds) *Political Innovation and Conceptual Change*. Cambridge: Cambridge University Press.

Skinner, Q. (2009) 'A Genealogy of the Modern State', *Proceedings of the British Academy*, 162: 325–70.

Stanton, T. (2011) 'Authority and Freedom in the Interpretation of Locke's Political Theory', *Political Theory*, 39(1): 6–30.

Tuck, R. (1979) *Natural Rights Theories: Their Origin and Development*. Cambridge: Cambridge University Press.

Weber, M. (1978) *Economy and Society: An Outline of Interpretive Sociology*. (2 vols), Roth, G. and Wittich, C. (eds). Berkeley & Los Angeles, CA: University of California Press.

2

REVISITING LEGITIMACY, TWENTY YEARS ON

David Beetham

It may seem self-indulgent of me to revisit a book I wrote more than 20 years ago (Beetham 1991). However, there are a number of reasons for doing so which go beyond self-indulgence. One is that many of its ideas have been taken up and developed by others, and this is an appropriate moment for me to respond to these developments, as well as to correct a few misunderstandings. These developments have occurred not only within the analysis of state legitimacy, which was the subject of the second half of my book, but also in fields beyond it, such as criminal justice and international institutions; and it will be useful to explore the implications of these analyses for political science more narrowly conceived. In the first part of this chapter, then, I will outline what I see as distinctive about my method of analysing legitimacy. Then I go on to summarize some key developments in legitimacy analysis in the fields of criminal justice, political science and the study of international institutions respectively, and explore their implications for my own analytical framework. Finally, I will test the usefulness of this framework against what is arguably the most significant legitimacy crisis of recent years, that of the international financial sector, and how that crisis has come to be displaced onto the democratic states of Europe and the European Union itself.

THE DISCURSIVE STRUCTURE OF LEGITIMACY

The starting point of my analysis is to insist on the ambiguity of the term 'legitimacy', and how it means different things to the political philosopher and the social scientist. Legitimate power for the philosopher is power which is *rightful* according to rationally defensible standards or principles. Legitimate power for the social scientist is power which is *acknowledged as rightful* by relevant agents, who include powerholders and their staff, those subject to the power and third parties whose support or recognition may help confirm it. This distinction between power which is rightful and power which is acknowledged as rightful is a crucial one, and marks a difference between the reasoned justifications of the political philosopher and the empirical analyses of the social scientist. However, it does not follow from this distinction that legitimacy for the social scientist can simply be reduced to a *subjective belief in legitimacy*, as if this were independent of the grounds on which the claim to legitimacy is based, and of what gives them credibility in a given social and ideational context. Here lies the first distinctive feature of my legitimacy analysis: I argue that the empirical study of legitimacy involves a discursive investigation of the grounds or criteria on which a claim to legitimacy is based, and of the credibility of those grounds to relevant agents in a given social and historical context. As the authors of a forthcoming article referring to my work write: 'Drawing on Beetham we argue that... social science analyses of legitimacy must uncover the "normative expectations" of actors embedded in a social context, and how these actors assess whether their expectations are in fact met' (Cah et al., forthcoming).

If the discursive analysis of legitimacy claims and their credibility to relevant agents in a given social context forms the starting point of my approach, its second distinctive feature is the claim that all legitimacy everywhere conforms to a common threefold discursive structure, comprising rule conformity, normative justifiability, and expressed affirmation or recognition. As I put it, power is acknowledged as legitimate to the extent that:

(1) It is acquired and exercised according to established rules (legality);
(2) The rules of power and its exercise conform to accepted beliefs about the rightful source of authority and the proper ends or purposes of power and standards in its exercise (normative justifiability);
(3) Positions of power and their holders are acknowledged through actions by relevant subordinates which confirm their acceptance or recognition of it (legitimation).

These three levels are not alternatives, since all contribute to legitimacy; together they provide the subordinate with moral grounds for compliance or cooperation with authority. That all are required can be shown by the different negative words we use to express the different ways in which power may lack legitimacy. If there is a manifest breach of the rules, we use the term 'illegitimacy'. If the appropriate normative beliefs lack social anchoring or are not realised in practice, we talk of a 'legitimacy deficit'. If recognition is publicly withdrawn or withheld, we speak of 'delegitimation'.

This threefold framework is a heuristic tool to guide analysis of any particular structure or system of legitimate power, which will have its distinctive form of rules or law, distinctive societal beliefs about the rightful source of authority and purposes of power, and distinctive institutional means for binding in key subordinates through public acts of affirmation or recognition. These distinctions can be usefully illustrated in a comparative table of the major regime types of the twentieth century, set out in Table 2.1. These serve as ideal-types in the Weberian sense, and combinations and variations of each are possible. Each also has its distinctive points of weakness or crisis tendency, which have mostly proved terminal, with the exception of liberal-democracy, though deformations of the latter in an authoritarian direction are well known. Reasons for the survivability of the liberal-democratic type will not be pursued here (see Beetham 2011).

Table 2.1 Legitimating components of different twentieth-century regime types

Regime type	Form of law	Source of authority	Ends of government	Mode of public affirmation
Traditional	Custom/precedent	Heredity/the past	Well-being within traditional order	Assembly of social elite
Fascist	Sovereign decisionism	Leadership principle	National purity/expansion	Mass mobilization
Communist	Codification of collective will	Party monopoly of truth and representation	Building the communist future	Mass mobilization
Liberal-democratic	Constitutional rule of law	The people through competitive election	Individual rights protection and advancement	Electoral endorsement
Theocratic	Sacred texts and canons	Divine will interpreted by the hierarchy	Purifying society's moral order	Various of the above
Dictatorial	Decree	Self-authorization	Restore order and national unity	None

The course of regime breakdown follows a typical pattern whereby a legitimacy deficit in its source of authority becomes compounded by serious performance failure in terms of the expected purposes of rule or standards in its exercise, resulting in a full-blown legitimacy crisis. This leads in turn to acts of delegitimation by relevant agents, with a possible breakdown of legality as its outcome. Of course a long passage of time may occur between these different stages, which may end in a form of rule based largely on coercion and a recognition of impotence in the face of it. As the Arab Spring has taught us, a decisive shift in the mentality of subordination or subalternhood may be needed for the stage of delegitimation to occur, long after a massive legitimacy deficit may have been recognized.

If the preceding summary outlines the distinctive elements in my legitimacy analysis, the main body of the chapter will explore the developments made in that analytical framework by other scholars, both within and outside political science, and my response to these developments. Many of these have involved a concern to operationalize the concept of legitimacy more precisely, so as better to understand its effects on behaviour and its implications for practice. I begin with the field of criminal justice, which deals with the police, courts, prisons, and other forms of punishment.

LEGITIMACY AND CRIMINAL JUSTICE

The subject of legitimacy has become a central concern in the field of criminal justice studies since the early 1990s, which have witnessed an increasingly sophisticated discussion of what makes for the legitimacy of power-holders, both in their own self-understanding and that of those subject to their authority. Although these analyses take their starting point from the political science literature, they move well beyond it in ways that can prove useful in turn for political science. In what follows I will single out four issues which seem to me to be importantly raised by these studies.

LEGITIMACY AND ITS EPISTEMOLOGY

In the account I gave earlier I drew a sharp distinction between the normative–analytical approach of the political philosopher to the subject of legitimacy and its use by the social scientist as a primarily explanatory concept, and I stand by the importance of observing that distinction. However, the two activities turn out to be more closely related than I have given credit for, in two respects. First, the systematic activity of the philosopher in justifying, refining, and improving key principles and values takes place within a *given* normative framework (typically today a liberal-democratic one), whose context-boundedness and historical specificity it is the task of the sociologist of knowledge to identify and explain. It may be from the latter perspective that judgements from the former—for example that the system of Nazi rule was a non-legitimate one when assessed against liberal-democratic criteria—can be seen as inappropriate or anachronistic. Yet the question of what normative frames or standards are appropriate for assessing a given power relation is one which engages, and should engage, both the normative philosopher and the empirical social scientist alike.

It follows, secondly, that the activity of assessing a given power relationship against the normative expectations that those involved can reasonably have of it is one that the normative philosopher and the social scientist can both properly engage in. Both are involved in making judgements, though for different purposes. The idea of a 'legitimacy deficit' is one that can be used both to explain disruptive behaviour or acts of non-compliance *and* to identify where improvements in a given institution or practice are desirable. It is highly relevant in this context that the academic criminal justice community has worked very closely with practitioners in the police and prison services; and that from the standpoint of the practitioners the academic distinction between normative philosophy and empirical social science may seem largely irrelevant to the systematic search for improvement.[1]

LEGITIMACY AND NORMATIVE JUSTIFIABILITY

In this central dimension of legitimacy I have distinguished between being able to show that one's authority is derived from a valid source acknowledged in the society, and that it serves a necessary purpose beyond simply the interests of the power-holders. We could call these rightful authorization and due performance respectively. Yet under 'due performance' there is a further consideration over and above the effective realization of a necessary general interest, and that is conformity to socially expected standards in the exercise of authority. In the criminal justice literature this aspect has been operationalized and given a central place through the concept of 'procedural justice'—the idea that the behaviour of those subject to authority, whether it be cooperation of the public with the police or obedience of prisoners to prison staff, depends on their being treated fairly and with dignity in their interactions with power-holders. It is the quality of these interactions that determines how far those exercising authority are regarded as legitimate, and the extent to which those subject to authority are prepared to cooperate in turn.

In the field of the police and the courts, the idea of 'procedural justice' was first developed by Tom Tyler, and has been subsequently refined in numerous studies, both by himself and others (see Tyler 1990; Tyler and Huo 2002). His starting point was to distinguish between instrumental and normative grounds for obedience, and he succeeded in demonstrating empirically the priority of the latter in explaining compliance and cooperation. Legitimacy as procedural justice in his definition includes both fair treatment in decisions by law enforcement authorities and being treated with dignity and respect in encounters with enforcement officers. It is fair treatment, he shows, that is crucial to perceptions of legitimacy, and to conforming behaviour as a result. 'To the degree that people do regard the police and courts as legitimate,' he writes, 'they are more willing to accept the directives and decisions of

[1] For discussions on this epistemological question I am indebted to a recent conference on Legitimacy and Criminal Justice at the University of Cambridge, and especially to comments by John Dunn.

the police and courts, and the likelihood of defiance, hostility and resistance is diminished' (Tyler 2003: 286).

The centrality of fair treatment to perceptions of legitimacy has also been demonstrated in empirical investigations of order in prisons. In their comparative study of two English prisons, Richard Sparks and Tony Bottoms (2008: 99) came to the conclusion that:

> On a day-to-day level most prisoners accept that someone has to have power over them, on behalf of the State. What then becomes crucial is *the way* that that power is exercised.... Their perceptions of the fairness of the staff in matters such as manner, even-handedness, and the quality of explanations given in case of problems are perhaps the most crucial factors of all in determining whether or not prisoners see the prison operating in a legitimate manner.[2]

Generalizing these insights from police and prison research beyond the field of criminal justice, we can see that the concept of 'procedural justice' or fairness constitutes a special case or example of what I have termed 'socially expected standards in the exercise of power'. Legitimacy deficits in the political field arise not only from inadequate or faulty authorization (e.g., electoral fraud), or perceived performance failure (e.g., widespread economic hardship or physical insecurity), but also from a violation of expected standards in the personal dealings of elected officials (e.g., the expenses scandal among UK parliamentarians). Naturally what these expected standards are varies greatly across time and space. In some countries ostentatious living is something expected or at least tolerated on the part of elected leaders ('But he's a Big Man' a Nigerian taxi driver said to me as his President was buying a second passenger jet for his personal use); whereas in others it can be deeply resented (President Sarkozy celebrating his 2007 electoral victory in a particularly exclusive Paris restaurant). At a more mundane level, people's attitudes to the state can be shaped by the personal treatment they receive at the hands of the most junior official. In the words of Sparks and Bottoms (2008: 100), 'The issue of the subject's interpersonal handling by particular agents of "the system" strongly shapes perceptions of the wider institutions involved.'

DIFFERENT AUDIENCES FOR LEGITIMACY CLAIMS

The idea that there are different audiences for legitimacy claims and their recognition goes back to Max Weber. All rulers, he argued, have to be convinced of their own legitimacy to be able to rule effectively, as do also the key administrative staff on whom the maintenance and enforcement of their rule depends. Yet the quality of obedience on the part of subjects, he also insisted, depended on their own acknowledgement of these claims, and they were therefore important addressees of legitimacy discourse (Weber 1978: 212–6). It is one thing, however, to distinguish the different audiences for legitimacy claims, another to counterpose these to one another as the basis for competing perspectives on legitimacy, such as endogenous vs. exogenous theories, or

[2] See also their book, *Prisons and the Problem of Order*.

power holder vs. subject conceptions.[3] It seems that the latest impetus for this separation or opposition stems from Rodney Barker's book (2001), *Legitimating Identities: The Self-Presentation of Rulers and Subjects*, where he insists that the primary audience for discursive legitimacy claims are power-holders and their immediate staff or coterie. It is this that gives them the self-confidence to sustain their power over their subjects, for whom legitimations are much less important and consequently absorb little 'time, attention, energy or intensity' on the part of their rulers.

This is an old argument, and one I explicitly challenge in my book (Beetham 1991: 25–34). It is also one that much recent criminological scholarship challenges as well. This is because, as expressed in a recent article, 'it is disproportionately the front-line police officers, rather than their managers, who have direct and recurrent encounters with citizens and prisoners, and therefore experience their authority being contested on a day-to-day basis' (Bottoms and Tankebe 2012: 154). As I argue in my book, we should distinguish between the legitimations used by the powerful to reinforce their self-belief, and a legitimate *relationship*, in which the subjects of power acknowledge that rightfulness for themselves (Beetham 1991: 31).

That said, it may be important nevertheless to distinguish between the different perceptions that power-holders and subjects have of their legitimacy. Here the criminal justice literature shows how different audiences may be concerned with different dimensions of legitimacy, and assign differential importance to them. Members of the police, for example, may believe that, provided they act according to the law and in pursuit of their acknowledged purpose (crime prevention and detection), that is sufficient to ensure their legitimacy. Those subject to their interventions, however, may be more concerned with being treated fairly than with legal niceties or the precise scope of authorized police powers. As a consequence, the confidence of the police in their own legitimacy may turn out to be misplaced, and compromise their relations with sections of the wider community.

From this follows a second insight, which is that power-holders' perceptions of their own legitimacy is not a fixed or static matter, but is open to modification in the light of evidence from below. A disjunction between power-holders' and subjects' perceptions may be modified through dialogue with the latter, either directly or through representatives, or by the intervention of those involved in advising on police or prison officer training. This 'dialogic' approach to legitimacy, as it has been termed in a recent article, serves to highlight sites or moments of interaction which may bring about changes in power-holders' perceptions of their own legitimacy, most dramatically, of course, through enquiries into major breakdowns of public or prison order (Bottoms and Tankebe 2012).

A final topic in the discussion of different audiences for legitimacy claims, and the interaction between them, which is raised by the criminal justice literature, concerns the role of third parties who stand outside the direct relation between authorities and those subject to them. Here the issue concerns the expectations for criminal justice held by the wider public, and articulated by politicians and the media, and the impact

[3] This is one fault I find in an otherwise impressive doctoral thesis by Justice Tankebe, *Policing and Legitimacy in a Post-Colonial Democracy: A Theoretical and Empirical Study of Ghana*, chapter 1.

these may have in turn on the mode of policing and discipline within prisons, whether reinforcing or undermining treatment that those subject to it regard as fair. With regard to prisons, Sparks and Bottoms (2008: 99–100) draw attention to the way in which 'wider currents in the political culture constrain and direct the actions of politicians and administrators, and undoubtedly ripple through onto the landings and exercise yards.' With regard to policing, the fact that there are different audiences in the wider society, especially in terms of religion and ethnicity, who may not share the same perception of 'legitimate policing', adds a further complexity to the analysis of multiple audiences and their respective significance.

CONFUSIONS OVER THE CONCEPT OF 'CONSENT'

'Consent' is always a tricky concept, and it might have been clearer if I had avoided using the term as the third component in my analytical framework of legitimacy. When I referred to 'actions expressive of consent' I intended to show how public acts of recognition or endorsement of an authority by relevant agents served to confer or confirm its legitimacy, and in some sense to 'bind in' those taking part as well as to impress those not doing so. Whether such actions can be taken to reveal a subjective state of mind called 'consent' is much more debatable, and would no doubt vary according to the context and type of action. Of the three modes of legitimation I distinguish in Table 2.1, swearing an oath of allegiance has probably the most binding implications for the participants (which is why Sinn Fein MPs refuse to take their seats in the Westminster parliament). It is less clear what taking part in an election precisely commits its participants to, or what it reveals about their subjective state of mind or degree of consent, though it undoubtedly confers legitimacy on the electoral victors. And most notoriously, the mass mobilizations organized by or on behalf of authoritarian regimes tell us little about the state of mind of those participating, though they certainly serve as impressive public endorsements of a regime and help to demoralize its opponents.

So those who seek to develop a richer or more rounded theory of consent in relation to legitimacy are perhaps missing the point of what I was doing. It might be helpful to distinguish between *actions* which express recognition or acknowledgement of an authority on the part of relevant agents, and hence *contribute to* its legitimacy, from consent as a *subjective state of mind*, which *follows from legitimacy* as one of its consequences. Whether such a distinction will remove all confusion from the subject I am not sure; but it is certainly possible to characterize the former as 'acts of recognition or endorsement' without using the term 'consent' at all, as I have done in my earlier summary. And there is a useful parallelism in using the term 'legitimation' to connote such public acts of endorsement, while its opposite, 'delegitimation', connotes public acts of protest, disobedience, and withdrawal of endorsement or recognition, which have a delegitimating effect.

In conclusion, studies of legitimacy within the criminal justice field have succeeded in giving it sharper operational focus and relevance for actual practice, as well as clarifying some key conceptual issues involved. These developments can in turn enrich our understanding of legitimacy as a subject in political science. After all, courts, police, and prisons constitute a central part of the state. And conclusions about the importance of fair treatment and respect can be generalized to other agencies for which the state is ultimately responsible, whether privatized or not. Indeed it extends to politicians themselves, who will forfeit legitimacy to the extent that they simply manipulate their electorates, or fail to treat them with any respect or trust, as research considered in the next section of the chapter will confirm.

LEGITIMACY AND THE NATION STATE

Among the developments in the analysis of state legitimacy over the past 20 years, foremost is the contribution of Bruce Gilley in his book *The Right to Rule: How States Win and Lose Legitimacy* (2009). Like the researchers in the field of criminal justice he sees legitimacy as an important public good with wide ranging benefits. Like them he also seeks to operationalize the concept of legitimacy in a way that enables us to draw clear implications for practice and possible improvement. But where they use a close-grained, almost anthropological, research method, his method is that of identifying quantitative indicators which allow for effective large-scale comparisons between 72 different states and regime types, covering over 80 per cent of the world's population (Gilley 2009, chapter 1).[4]

Starting from the threefold dimensions of legitimacy as legality, normative justifiability, and expressed consent, Gilley identifies nine key attitudinal and behavioural indicators which are available from cross-national survey and other data, and which can be aggregated to measure citizens' perceptions of their state's legitimacy. These are, for legality: citizens' confidence in human rights performance, in the police and in the civil service respectively (World Values Surveys, 1999–2002); for justifiability, three surveys of attitudes towards the existing political system and one behavioural indicator of the incidence of the use of violence in political protests (1996–2000); and for acts of consent, the degree of payment of readily avoidable taxes, and voter turnout in national legislative elections. These are then aggregated into an overall legitimacy score for each state, assessed from the standpoint of its citizens.

The next step, using regression analysis, is to identify which objective features of a country, social, economic or political, most closely correlate with the legitimacy scores, and can be taken as explanatory variables for them. These turn out to be primarily *political* ones. It is a state's performance in three key respects—good governance, democratic rights, and economic development/welfare—that are the chief determinants of citizens' perceptions of its legitimacy. Effective delivery of at least two of these is needed for a high legitimacy score, Gilley concludes, though trade-offs between them and shifts over time are possible.

As with much quantitative analysis of the kind Gilley uses, questions can be raised about his choice of indicators, the method of their aggregation, and possible

[4] For a quantitative and comparative study of legitimacy at a regional level, see John Booth and Mitchell Seligson, *The Legitimacy Puzzle in Latin America: Political Support and Democracy in Eight Nations.*

circularity between cause and effect. Legitimacy turns out to be both a consequence of government effectiveness and a contributor to it, through the level of citizen compliance and cooperation that their recognition of the right to rule brings with it. Nevertheless, this is a path-breaking work in the way in which some of Gilley's conclusions parallel those of the criminal justice literature analysed earlier. Two in particular are worth mentioning here.

First are its implications for practice. A state's level of legitimacy is not something it is fated to endure, but can be improved by policy changes and institutional reform. In particular, poor countries are not necessarily 'trapped in a cycle of underperformance and underlegitimacy from which they cannot escape', as the author's case study of Uganda after 1986 exemplifies. States can enhance their legitimacy either through improving their performance or through shifting it in ways that more closely reflect citizen preferences, and so 'bootstrap their way to virtuous cycles of citizen compliance and state effectiveness' (Gilley 2009: 53–57).

From this stems a second conclusion, that legitimacy is best understood as a dynamic process of interaction or dialogue between states and their citizens, in which performance and legitimacy respond to each other. In the case of Uganda, Gilley writes, the state 'continually evolved in response to dissent and other forms of negative feedback. Indeed institutional change . . . can be seen as in constant dialogue with the demands of legitimacy.' And in terms that further echo much of the criminal justice literature, he concludes that states must learn to trust, respect and respond to their citizens' concerns if they wish to achieve legitimacy (2009: 48–49, 90–93, 132).

Among Gilley's findings that will particularly intrigue political scientists is that some authoritarian states may have higher scores than some democratic ones. For the period in question (1996–2000), Morocco, for example, scored marginally higher than both France and Greece, and Egypt and Jordan above both Slovenia and India. In the light of the subsequent 'Arab Spring', these scores may appear to have been overly generous. However, Gilley covers himself with the observation that 'such states may simply be legitimate for reasons other than their undemocratic nature, and most people might still prefer if they were democratic.' We should remain open to the possibility of legitimate alternatives to democracy, he concludes, but 'even then such claims may be overtaken by events', as indeed they have been in the case of the Arab countries mentioned (2009: 45–46).[5]

Most intriguing of all is the high point on Gilley's legitimacy scale (13 out of 72) achieved by China, a country on which he is himself an expert. Many commentators have pointed out how, since the Tiananmen Square massacre of 1989, China's deficit in democratic rights has been compensated for by successful economic development and effective governance, although corruption by party officials is a source of frequent public complaint. Two further sources of the Chinese state's legitimacy, over and above economic and governmental performance, have been suggested by another expert on legitimacy in China, Heike Holbig, in recent articles.

[5] For the table of legitimacy scores, see Gilley (2009: 15).

One concerns the way in which the Chinese state links its performance to a persuasive legitimacy narrative or discourse. It is not just what a state does, but how it describes what it is doing, that is important for its legitimacy. In the case of China, ideology has always played a central role, especially for rank and file party cadres, and ideological revision has taken place in parallel with rapidly changing economic policies and circumstances. So the party ideologues have had to find ways of integrating new economic elites into their discourse of the working class vanguard, while also emphasizing the state's redistributive role in ensuring social harmony and a common interest. They have had to present the party as an 'ever-innovative organisation capable of learning and adapting to an ever-changing economic, social and political environment', while also deriving authority from a traditional Confucian model of governance. Whether such ideological reformulations or consolidations are sufficient to counter demands for more secure individual rights and greater political participation remains an open question. In terms of my framework, if the perceived source of the party's authority is a kind of self-authorization based on a narrative about its performance capacity and adaptability, then its legitimacy is doubly vulnerable to performance failure (Holbig 2009).

A further source of legitimacy for the Chinese state analysed by Holbig involves what I have called 'third party' recognition or affirmation, in this case by the international community. China enjoys high international status both as leader of the developing nations and as an equal partner of the developed ones through its membership of the G20, WTO, IMF, etc., not to mention its role as a key regional player. This status has only been enhanced since the global crisis of 2008, and China's comparatively successful economic recovery from it. Holbig sees this increasing international recognition as an important resource for China's internal legitimation. 'Explicit acts of recognition by the international community,' she writes, 'represent a direct form of external legitimation that can be readily reproduced in the national discourse' (2011: 178). In particular, this recognition can be used to compensate for the deficit in the public manifestation of consent internally. Generalizing from the Chinese example, Holbig argues that an international dimension of legitimacy should be added to the threefold configuration of legality, normative justifiability, and expressed consent; and she shows how an analysis can follow from this of a dynamic interaction between internal and external legitimation strategies, which may be compensatory, reinforcing, or sometimes mutually contradictory (2011). This process of interaction will also be relevant to the literature reviewed in the following section.

LEGITIMACY AND INTERNATIONAL INSTITUTIONS

When we move from the legitimacy of states to that of international institutions it is clear at once that we are in a completely different domain, whose analysis cannot simply be 'read off' from the national level. Most writers on the legitimacy of international bodies, a subject that has been increasingly studied in recent years, would agree in outline on a number of distinctive features that distinguish it from that of the state. I review three of the key ones in what follows.

THE RELATION BETWEEN POWER AND LEGITIMACY

At the state and sub-state level power is analytically separable from legitimacy, most obviously in the power of coercion, but also in an array of incentives and sanctions available to the relevant authorities. This can make differentiating the respective motives for compliance a complex matter, though all the authors considered in this paper regard the acknowledgement of legitimacy as a, if not *the*, crucial element in obedience. At the level of international institutions, by way of contrast, a power of enforcement rarely exists, and the power that is exercised depends almost wholly on a recognition of its legitimacy to be effective. It follows that it should be easier to detect its presence or absence than in respect of the state, as Thomas Franck explains in a much quoted sentence: 'The international society should be the *best* social system in which to observe a "normative" (i.e. legitimated) social order in its pure form precisely because of the absence of an international government to enforce international laws and contracts' (quoted in Hurd 2007: 11).

Ian Clark, in his book *Legitimacy in International Society*, goes so far as to claim that legitimacy is *constitutive* of international society, and that, as a consequence, 'we can recount an important part of its history in terms of systematic changes in its legitimating principles,' as he indeed proceeds to do (2005: 245–6). Ian Hurd in his book on legitimacy in the UN Security Council argues that 'its power derives from its ability to persuade rather than its ability to coerce,' and that consequently 'it has power when it is seen as legitimate and loses power when that perception recedes' (2007: 12–13). We could add that, unlike in the nation state, power in international society is dispersed between a host of specialized institutions, and each has therefore to be legitimated *separately* as well as on a continuous basis, without any overall coordinating authority.

AUDIENCES FOR LEGITIMACY CLAIMS

Whereas in nation states it is the citizens who constitute the ultimate audience for, and judge of, legitimacy claims, in international society it is the states themselves who form the key subjects. They are at once the authors of the institutions and the agents of compliance and enforcement for their mandates. They authorize the international treaties and the institutions which the treaties establish, through their participation in the founding conventions or treaty revisions and their subsequent ratification. They are called on to comply with the decisions made by those institutions, and to enforce or give them effect as appropriate within their own jurisdictions. They therefore constitute the main audience for legitimacy claims (and counter claims), which are addressed primarily to political elites, though they may sometimes filter down to national publics when elites feel the need of domestic support.

Although all states are supposedly equal, in most international organizations there is a hierarchy of membership, whether constitutionally formalized, as in the UN Security Council, the World Bank, the IMF etc., or informally arranged through the superior resources that more powerful states can bring to negotiations, or the more serious consequences which follow from a withdrawal of their cooperation. The legitimacy of the institutions with a formalized hierarchy is increasingly being called into question as they are seen to diverge from a norm of fair procedure, whether in membership, voting or decision making, with corresponding implications for the acceptability of the decisions that result.[6]

THE DISCURSIVE STRUCTURE OF LEGITIMACY

It will be useful to present the structure of international legitimacy according to the tripartite configuration applicable to the nation state, as this helps to identify the key sites of differentiation between the two levels referred to in much of the relevant literature. To summarize, international institutions, their officials, and decisional outcomes are accorded legitimacy to the extent that they conform to the legal requirements set out in their founding treaties, as authorized by member states (legality, authorization). At the normative level, there is an expectation that they should perform effectively in fulfilling the common purposes for which they were established, and that they should do so according to procedures accepted as fair (normative justifiability). Finally, legitimacy is confirmed to the extent that states comply with decisional outcomes, or refrain from acting in ways which manifestly flout the institution's rules (expressed consent, legitimation). At each of these levels we can identify significant differences between the legitimacy of international institutions and that of the states which authorize them.

As to legality, at the international level, with a few significant exceptions, there exists no authoritative interpreter of the rules, no ultimate court of adjudication. This leaves more room for state actors to interpret the law according to their own interests, as happened notoriously with the interpretation of Security Council resolution 687, which was used to justify the Iraq invasion of 2003 in the absence of a second UN resolution. Moreover, this very absence of interpretative authority has made it possible to ignore legal considerations altogether, as in the NATO bombing campaign of Serbia in 1999. Indeed, Tony Blair's wider justification for 'liberal interventionism' was that legal considerations should not be allowed to stand in the way of urgent humanitarian action to forestall potential threats to international peace, which he claimed special authority to interpret (see Kampfner 2003; Sands 2005).

If normative considerations can be used in this way to trump or subvert legal or procedural ones, this puts correspondingly greater weight on the dimension of normative justifiability in international institutions. At the heart of all international treaties lies a norm of international cooperation and common interest in the realization of

[6] The idea of a hierarchy of membership is developed by Jean-Marc Coicaud in his paper for the Cambridge conference, 'International Legitimacy and International Criminal Justice'. Clark uses the terms 'core' and 'periphery' for a similar purpose.

specific benefits which states could never achieve by acting on their own. Yet this key legitimating norm is itself under pressure from the countervailing norm of state sovereignty which helps to legitimate the participating states domestically. Examples of this tension between the two legitimating principles—between what Clark (2005) calls 'internal and international legitimacy'—occur frequently, as he himself shows, though at times they can also serve to reinforce one another. In a recent study of legitimacy in the European Court of Human Rights (see Cah et al., forthcoming), the authors show how the two competing norms of cooperation and sovereignty are reconciled in the concept of 'a fair compromise between the purposes and performance of human rights courts and the purposes of domestic institutions', and that this provides the social grounding of the legitimacy of the European Convention of Human Rights (ECHR). However, this idea of a 'fair compromise' is perceived and interpreted differently by the political elites of the different member countries. Some, such as the UK, increasingly regard adverse decisions as eroding the court's legitimacy, while others, such as Ireland, see them as compensating for possible parochialism in its internal jurisdiction.[7]

Finally, as to expressed consent, its distinctive feature at the international level works in two opposite directions in regards to its legitimating effects. On the one hand state compliance with the decisions of international institutions, because it is essentially *voluntary*, has a much more legitimating force than at the domestic state level, where compliance may simply be the product of habit or 'dull compulsion' in the face of overwhelming force, and cannot be used as evidence to deduce or enhance legitimacy. Yet by the same token, refusal to comply is much less costly than at the domestic state level, and, if repeated, may serve to delegitimate the institution in question, as US refusals to comply with judgments of the International Court at the Hague or Israeli refusals to comply with UN resolutions about the occupied territories exemplify. This dual character of compliance and consent confirms the key feature of international society identified at the start of this section, that power and legitimacy are inseparable at the level of international institutions, and that, without legitimacy they have no power.

A COUNTER-EXAMPLE: POWER AND LEGITIMACY IN THE INTERNATIONAL FINANCIAL SECTOR

It is odd that whole books can be written about 'international society' or 'international organizations' without mentioning the most dominant player in the international field, which is the financial sector and its banking and investment institutions. Of course these are not inter-governmental ones, and in contrast to the latter wield

[7] The idea of differential impact of institutions at the European level on member state legitimacy is one explored by Chris Lord and myself in *Legitimacy and the European Union*.

enormous power quite independently of any legitimacy. Although they may compete among themselves, collectively the sector exercises massive power through its control of financial resources, and the corresponding dependency of consumers, businesses, investors, and governments on their decisions for their economic well-being and even survival. The recent history of this sector and its institutions raises two questions which challenge the legitimacy analysis of this chapter and the original book on which it is based. First, why does their power need any legitimacy, and, if so, on what grounds and for which audiences? Secondly, how have they survived a legitimacy crisis of epic proportions, without any active process of delegitimation following, but instead have succeeded in displacing the crisis onto our political institutions, whether democratic governments or the European Union itself?

To take the first question, financial institutions naturally require compliance from their employees, but this is mainly ensured through a combination of incentives and sanctions. However, as all writers from Weber onwards agree, those exercising power need first to be convinced of their own legitimacy, in this case through the pursuit of a wider social purpose than simply making money for themselves. Financiers also need to convince governments, legislators, and regulators that their institutional structures, activities and rewards are justified in terms of satisfying a public interest as well as acceptable standards of operation. Beyond that there may be a need for a wider social or public acceptability, though those using their services comply with their requirements not out of any normative considerations, but out of simple self-interest. In this regard, the financial sector may constitute what in my book I describe as a limiting case of a power system which does not need mass legitimacy to achieve its purposes. It also fits Rodney Barker's (2001: 70–71) conception of concentric circles of legitimacy audiences, with power-holders and their immediate staffs at the centre, associates and other elites in the next ring, and the public at the periphery, though I would argue as an exception rather than the norm.

Even so, the fact that legitimacy is necessary to them can be deduced from the great lengths to which the financial sector has gone over the years to construct a legitimating discourse for itself, as well as channels for its effective dissemination. Financial deregulation and 'light touch' regulation were justified by the doctrine of the self-regulating or 'rational' market, bolstered by the whole weight of an academic economics profession devoted to its elaboration. The huge inverted pyramid of casino banking and derivatives trading was justified by the added social value that was being created, together with the fact that, after the repeal of Glass-Steagall, this structure could only with difficulty be distinguished from the normal investment and credit activities which have obvious public utility. Finally, the enormous personal rewards which accrued to financiers were justified on the grounds of the esoteric knowledge, unique skills, and burden of responsibility which their work demanded of them.[8]

[8] These legitimating ideas are explored in John Cassidy's *How Markets Fail: An Anatomy of Irrationality* and Joseph Stiglitz's *Freefall: Free Markets and the Sinking of the Global Economy*. Not everyone would go as far as Stiglitz when he writes of his own economics profession that 'it had moved from being a scientific discipline into being free market capitalism's biggest cheerleader' (p. 238).

One by one these justifications were blown apart by the banking crisis of 2007–8. The free market was exposed as far from self-regulating, and competition between individual banks and traders to maximize profit for themselves and their investors was seen to produce system-wide collapse. Many of the bankers' activities which were claimed to be serving an essential public interest were shown to be, not merely 'socially useless' as the UK's chief regulator publicly conceded, but economically and socially damaging. And the claim of financiers to possess an esoteric knowledge and unique skills justifying their rewards was punctured by the revelation that many of them did not understand the complex instruments in which they were trading, while the few who did were happy to bet against them, while continuing to encourage new investment from others.[9]

According to my model, a legitimacy crisis on this scale is normally accompanied by acts of public delegitimation, the active withdrawal of compliance, expulsion from office or power, and other retributions appropriate to the scale of the disjunction between the legitimating discourse and the reality that has become exposed to public view. Why has this not happened in the case of the banks and financial institutions? Here the people could not act for themselves, as the bankers were both too anonymous and too well protected to suffer any personal violations, while people were too disorganized to follow Eric Cantona's call for a mass withdrawal of savings. So governments had to act on their behalf. To be sure, the chief executives of the bailed out institutions were dismissed, albeit with their gold-plated pensions intact, but this was no different from normal practice in the sector in the event of failure. What was at issue was the failure of a whole system, which brought deep recession and widespread economic distress in its wake. To quote the Governor of the Bank of England: 'The price of this financial crisis is being borne by people who absolutely did not cause it.... Never in the field of financial endeavour has so much been owed to so many by so few.'[10]

What actions might governments have taken that were proportionate to the systemic failure and would have had an appropriate delegitimating force? At one extreme they could have let the banks go bust (most were technically insolvent), set up their own banks, and printed money. Or they could have broken the banks up and forced creditors and shareholders to pay more of a penalty. Or jailed investment traders for reckless risk taking. Or outlawed derivatives trading and banned bonuses and capped salaries across the sector. Or imposed a financial transactions tax, as well as closing down the tax havens which the sector uses to avoid its public responsibilities. Or disbanded the failed ratings agencies. And so on. We can all think of explanations why none of this happened, among which the absence of any inter-governmental structure to control the sector, and the institutional capture of individual governments and legislatures by the financial services industry must bulk large.[11]

[9] Evidence for this is provided in Charles Ferguson's new book, *Inside Job: The Financiers Who Pulled Off the Heist of the Century*.

[10] Speaking to the UK Commons Treasury Select Committee, 1 March 2011.

[11] For institutional capture of government in the UK, see my Democratic Audit paper, 'Unelected Oligarchy: Corporate and Financial Dominance in Britain's Democracy' (2011) and successive updates available at: <http://www.democraticaudit.com>.

However, the cost of not doing any of those options, but instead bailing out the banks and other institutions with public money, and continuing to do so, has been, on the one hand, a rapid return to business as usual, since no serious penalty has been incurred or is in prospect. On the other, the financial crisis has morphed into a sovereign debt crisis, complete with a new discourse of government profligacy; and the legitimacy deficit has been displaced onto democratic governments, which have become the agents of a bank imposed austerity programme. Unlike financial traders, who can hide behind the impersonality of the market, governments cannot evade public responsibility and accountability for their actions, even if these are dictated from elsewhere. Many have simply crumbled under the pressure of public delegitimation, whether through outright collapse, as in Iceland, forced elections leading to electoral wipe-out, as in Ireland and Spain, or the imposition of technocratic rule, as in Greece and Italy. As we can see, this process of public delegitimation has still a long way to run.

In conclusion, my model of a legitimacy deficit intensifying to a legitimacy crisis, then bringing acts of public delegitimation in its train, may need some modest revision in light of the financial collapse of 2007–08. If a legitimacy crisis of such depth does not result in a process of active delegitimation, we can conclude that if for some reason it is aborted, then there is a considerable price to pay. On the one hand, because the power-holders have suffered no public retribution, they will simply continue as before, only with renewed confidence. On the other, the legitimacy crisis may be displaced to another domain, and the active public delegitimation will then be experienced by another set of agents who are simply more vulnerable to it.

This modest revision of my model exemplifies a broader conclusion I have come to in this chapter through reviewing the research on legitimacy that has taken place in many different fields since the publication of the book in 1991. This is that subsequent research has done much to clarify, enrich, and extend the legitimacy analysis contained there, but not fundamentally to challenge or displace it.

REFERENCES

Barker, R. (2001) *Legitimating Identities: The Self-Presentation of Rulers and Subjects.* Cambridge: Cambridge University Press.

Beetham, D. (1991) *The Legitimation of Power.* Basingstoke: Macmillan.

Beetham, D. (2011) 'Legitimacy', in Badie, B., Berg-Schlosser, D. and Morlino, L. (eds) *The International Encyclopedia of Political Science.* Thousand Oaks, CA: SAGE Publications.

Beetham, D. and Lord, C. (1998) *Legitimacy and the European Union.* London: Longman.

Booth, J. and Seligson, M. (2009) *The Legitimacy Puzzle in Latin America: Political Support and Democracy in Eight Nations.* Cambridge: Cambridge University Press.

Bottoms, A. and Tankebe, J. (2012) 'Beyond Procedural Justice: A Dialogic Approach to Legitimacy in Criminal Justice', *Journal of Criminal Law and Criminology* 102(1): 119–70.

Cah, B., Koch, A., and Bruch, N. (forthcoming) 'The Social Legitimacy of the European Court of Human Rights: An Interpretative Analysis'.

Cassidy, J. (2009) *How Markets Fail: An Anatomy of Irrationality.* London: Allen Lane.

Clark, I. (2005) *Legitimacy in International Society.* Oxford: Oxford University Press.

Ferguson, C. (2012) *Inside Job: The Financiers Who Pulled Off the Heist of the Century.* Oxford: Oneworld.

Gilley, B. (2009) *The Right to Rule: How States Win and Lose Legitimacy.* New York: Columbia University Press.

Holbig, H. (2009) 'Ideological Reform and Political Legitimacy in China: Challenges in the Post-Jiang Era' (pp. 13–34), in Heberer, T. and Schubert, G. (eds) *Regime Legitimacy in Contemporary China: Institutional Change and Stability.* London: Routledge.

Holbig, H. (2011) 'International Dimensions of Legitimacy: Reflections on Western Theories and the Chinese Experience', *Journal of Chinese Political Science* 16(2): 161–81.

Hurd, I. (2007) *After Anarchy: Legitimacy and Power in the United Nations Security Council.* Princeton: Princeton University Press.

Kampfner, J. (2003) *Blair's Wars.* London: Simon and Schuster.

Sands, P. (2005) *Lawless World: America and the Making and Breaking of Global Rules.* London: Allen Lane.

Sparks, R. and Bottoms, A. (2008) 'Legitimacy and Imprisonment Revisited' (pp. 91–104), in Byrne, J., Hummer, D. and Taxman, F. (eds) *The Culture of Prison Violence.* Boston MA: Pearson/Allyn and Bacon.

Sparks, R., Bottoms, A., and Hay, W. (1996) *Prisons and the Problem of Order.* Oxford: Clarendon.

Stiglitz, J. E. (2010) *Freefall: Free Markets and the Sinking of the Global Economy.* London: Penguin.

Tankebe, J. (2007) 'Policing and Legitimacy in a Post-Colonial Democracy: A Theoretical and Empirical Study of Ghana', PhD Thesis, Cambridge: University of Cambridge.

Tyler, T. R. (1990) *Why People Obey the Law.* New Haven: Yale University Press.

Tyler, T. R. (2003) 'Justice, Legitimacy, and the Effective Rule of Law', *Crime and Justice* 30: 283–357.

Tyler, T. R. and Huo, Y. J. (2002) *Trust in the Law.* New York: Russell Sage Foundation.

Weber, M. (1978) *Economy and Society: An Outline of Interpretive Sociology.* (2 vols), Roth, G. and Wittich, C. (eds). Berkeley & Los Angeles, CA: University of California Press.

3

CRIME, JUSTICE, AND LEGITIMACY: A BRIEF THEORETICAL INQUIRY

Jean-Marc Coicaud

This chapter argues that taking into account legitimacy can help to understand crime and justice, and, in the process, improve the conditions of possibility for a better system of criminal justice. It is organized into three parts. The first one examines the general meaning of the notions of crime, justice, and legitimacy. The second studies their relations, including what brings them together and what distinguishes them. The third and final part of the chapter focuses on the ways in which upheaval and change can bring about disagreements and conflicts over what constitutes crime, justice, and legitimacy, and their relations.[1]

CRIME, JUSTICE, AND LEGITIMACY

CRIME

At the most general level, a crime is a type of wrong that is especially grave because it involves a serious violation of a value or a set of values central to the identity and integrity of a community and its members (Lamond 2007; Williams 1955). This violation entails at least four aspects. First, in the hierarchy of wrongs, a crime, belonging to the category of the most serious offenses, occupies one of the highest levels (Delmas-Marty 1992). Second, the seriousness of the offense lies not only in its degree but also in its character and, more specifically, in its public character. As such, a crime committed against a person does not bring about a relation limited to the wrongdoer and the victim, as tends to be the case in civil law.[2] Because of its

[1] The author thanks Justice Tankebe and Stuart Green for their comments on an earlier version of the text. He also thanks Thomas Arndt and Derya Berk for their help in researching the article.

[2] This is not to say that the distinction between criminal and civil wrongs, and the nature of the processes used to address them, is a straightforward and static one. It has changed over time and can vary with the nature of the political regime in which it unfolds. On this issue, see, for example Steiker (1997); Robinson (1996).

potential or real negative impact on the sustainability of the community and its members, a crime is not a private but a public matter that concerns the group as a whole. Third, hence the fact that in the case of a crime, the community, i.e. the state, is in charge.[3] The state brings the case on behalf of the individual victim as well as on behalf of the community. It takes on the responsibility of defending the right of the victim but also the rights of the community and its members.[4] Fourth, the criminal nature of the wrong is disclosed by the fact that, once the wrongdoer has been prosecuted and found responsible and guilty for having intentionally committed the crime, the sanction is punishment. In this regard, while compensation can be one of the outcomes of a criminal procedure, it cannot be viewed as a form of criminal punishment per se. For punishment, in principle proportional to the crime, although it may also be rationalized as a matter of deterrence, incapacitation, reform, or rehabilitation[5], is always supposed to be a painful experience and entails a retributive dimension.

For the violation to be recognized as a crime, the value or set of values violated have to be official, that is to say acknowledged as a key component of the life of a group and its members. In modern societies, law is one of the crucial ways through which this happens. In this perspective, wrongdoing that reaches a criminal level not only generates moral and social outrage, but also triggers a chain reaction that, benefiting from the full support of the law, is part and parcel of criminal law and the system of criminal justice in general.[6] It can include police forensic analysis, bringing to trial the suspected guilty party, and carrying, or not, a sentence. Existing to address the criminal act post facto, these steps, as alluded to earlier, can also play a preventive role, by helping to deter deviation from the norm of behavior.

JUSTICE

Among the various possible ways to tackle the issue of justice, we choose here to argue that justice is about what is owed to people (see Scanlon 1998), and what they are entitled to because it is right.[7] Needless to say, such a definition, far from closing the debate on justice, introduces an array of difficult questions. Three especially come to mind. First, what is the nature of this right that is owed to people? Second, how to

[3] While a civil model of handling a wrongdoing (tort law and contract law) puts the victim in charge (it is the complainant who initiates the proceedings against the person who (allegedly) wronged him, and it is for him to carry the case or to drop it), the criminal model puts the community (the state) in charge. See Marshall and Duff (1998).

[4] Incidentally, an act viewed as a crime does not have to necessarily be a violation of the right of an individual. It can be more geared against a core element of the identity of a group, like religion and the beliefs it conveys in a traditional or traditionalist community. Think for instance how in traditional Muslim societies, questioning the will of God is a crime of utmost gravity. See An-Na'im (2011).

[5] For more on punishment and its rationalization, refer to Duff (2001).

[6] On criminal law, see for instance Hart (1958).

[7] My Rutgers School of Law colleague Stuart Green reminded me, in his comments to an earlier version of this article, that criminal law scholars do not generally talk much about 'justice' per se. They are prone to say that justice is done when the offender gets what is 'deserved'. At least this is how a retributivist talks about justice, as justice, in this context, is normally something that is done to an offender.

identify, evaluate, and measure it? Third, how to implement it, i.e. how to ensure that it is realizable and realized enough in concrete terms?

As for the first question—what is the nature of the right that is owed to people?— it can be seen as referring to four elements. First, it refers to the expectations that a human being has about the realization of his/her needs to sustain life.[8] These expectations and needs are associated with the values at the core of the identity of the community and its members, and the range of possibilities and constraints that come with them. Second, it presupposes the ability of identifying with others, of seeing, despite the differences, a human in another and, more specifically, if not the whole of our self in another, at least a crucial part. More to the point, it is on the basis of this identification with others as human beings that derives the idea that they have rights. As such, third, it refers to the pressure that this creates for other fellow human beings not to overlook these expectations and needs. This brings about a sense of responsibility for others that is all the more serious that this takes place in a social environment where the rarity of resources engenders much competition among actors. Fourth, it refers to, at a minimum, not unduly infringing upon others and their existential needs and, more ambitiously, helping them to meet these needs.

Answering the second question—how to identify, evaluate, and measure the right that is owed to people?—begins with factoring in the negative and positive duties towards others that the existential expectations and needs of actors generate in a given context.[9] In this perspective, the former (negative duties, i.e. not infringing upon what is owed to others) is relatively straightforward when infringement amounts to a form of explicit aggression: it is easy to identify, and condemn. But the latter (positive duties towards others, i.e. actively supporting them) is complex. Surely, when for instance this entails taking action to punish a crime, except maybe for the modalities of the punishment itself, it is a somewhat simple matter since the acknowledgement of the existence of a crime makes it clear that punishment has to take place. However, identifying, evaluating, and measuring what is owed to people, that is to say assessing the extent to which people should have access to goods or resources (including which ones), is far more challenging. It calls for the identification and calculation of the fair allocation of goods/resources to individuals. The fact that this is essentially based on the values that shape the identity of the community, that of its members, and the relations, including disparities of status and standing, that they entail, does not fully solve the problem. Indeed, as this state of affairs is always synonymous with inequalities of treatment of actors, such identification and calculation is prone to bring about disagreements and struggles, even in the most stable and just societies.

The response to the third question—how to implement what is owed to others?— rests on the social dimension of justice and the institutions in charge of organizing it, that is of expressing, projecting, and defending it in a variety of ways. In this regard, the social dimension of justice and the role(s) that it gives to justice alludes to the fact that what is owed to people does not and cannot exist in a vacuum. Indeed, the capacity of

[8] On the weaknesses of the concept of need in the context of a theory of justice, see Johnston (2011, ch. 7).

[9] For one of the leading treatments of this question in the content of Western contemporary democratic culture, see Rawls (2005).

an individual to enjoy a right is based upon the duties or responsibility that others feel compelled to respect it and even contribute to its flourishing. This dynamic of rights and duties is one of the aspects of the central function that reciprocity plays in justice (see Johnston 2011) and helps to understand that, in this perspective, justice is as much what is exchanged among actors as what makes possible the exchange. It is a relationship of mutuality and of mutual concern. This explains why it is not enough for the contribution to the rights of others to be a passive or by-standing one. A dose of engagement, if not activism is required. It is required towards other fellow humans but also in support of the institutions that have the mission to secure, via soft (education, ideology, and others) and harsher (force, criminal justice system, and others) means, the realization of justice. Incidentally, the value of active support is one of the elements making legitimacy an important feature.

LEGITIMACY

Legitimacy is the recognition that those who are not in a position of power grant to those in commanding positions to have the right to hold and be in power. It is the process through which power and obedience are justified, transforming the second into consent of the governed (Tyler 2006). In the process, those in power can enjoy without too much worry the perks that can come with power benefiting from a sense of legitimacy (Coicaud 2010b). Yet, it is not as if the recognition of the right to power is without constraints; on the contrary. For the whole purpose of legitimacy, of connecting power with legitimacy, is to put limits on the nature and exercise of power. In this context, three conditions have to be met for the acknowledgement or the justification of the right to power to take place.[10]

First, those in power must deliver services to those who are not in power. These services may vary with the environment but they constitute a requirement that cannot be ignored. Second, the services provided must respond to and reasonably satisfy key needs and expectations of non power-holders. Associated with the sense of possibilities and constraints, and the values (and the expectations connected with them) that are formative of the identity of the context in which the unbalanced relation between power and non power-holders unfolds, these needs and expectations are crystallized in what is viewed as right, including their rights, by actors. Third, in the process, the needs/rights benchmark entails the responsibility and accountability of the institutions and the mechanisms of exercise of power, and of those who are working in them—those in positions of leadership to start with.

One more point comes to the surface here. From the fact that legitimacy tames power by limiting it through the demands it imposes on it, we should not infer that legitimate power is essentially a happy proposition. Although legitimacy eases the tension between power and non-power holders by forcing the former to factor the

[10] This account of legitimacy reflects more the previous work of the author on the topic than how criminal law scholars address the issue of legitimacy (see Coicaud 2002). Stuart Green makes the point that a system of criminal justice is legitimate when it has earned the moral credibility, from the substantive and procedural standpoints, of the community.

latter, it never eliminates entirely the violence inherent to differentiation of power. This gives an unsettling characteristic to the relationships between legitimacy and power, on the one hand, and between legitimacy and justice, on the other. Aiming to keep power under check by taking into account the rights of the non power-holders is the virtue and appeal of legitimacy. It is the generic benefit that derives from legitimacy both for power-holders and non power-holders. The constant challenge is its association and proximity to power. It puts legitimacy in danger of being hijacked, of becoming the captive of the self-serving dynamics of power.

RELATIONS AMONG CRIME, JUSTICE, AND LEGITIMACY

It is all the more the case considering that if the goal of legitimacy is to constrain power and put it as much as possible at the service of justice, it happens that concerns and paradigms of justice are themselves, more often than not, outgrowths of situations of power—of a power hegemony. Think for example about international law. While it is, at least in part, the expression of international justice considerations, it is also built around Western values and norms. As such, owing much to the fact that in modern times European powers and then the United States have dominated the world, it never stops entirely to serve the interests that come with them.

Against this background, the pivotal role that legitimacy plays in the context of the relations between crime and justice is not surprising. Two aspects are particularly important. To begin with, the viability of the distinctions and hierarchies that are part and parcel of justice and crime, and their relations, rests to a large extent on how legitimacy contributes to justify the inequalities of power and their organization in society. In addition, the need of legitimacy increases with the movement by which justice and, consequently, crime get to be understood and applied in expanding terms, following the growth of the culture of human and individual rights. As this movement is a significant feature of criminal justice and its evolution in a democratic environment, the increasing demands that the criminal justice system in a democratic regime has to satisfy to be viewed as legitimate can be less and less overlooked.

JUSTICE AND CRIME AS DISTINCTION AND HIERARCHY, AND LEGITIMACY

Justice and crime are the two opposite but related sides of the same coin. While justice is about, as alluded to earlier, identifying what is right, including the rights of actors, crime constitutes the epitome of wrong. In this perspective, justice and crime are in a fundamental manner a process of distinction and hierarchization.

It is, first, a process of distinction in the sense that it separates right from wrong and determines how this separation can be established in theory, for instance with the help of principles, values, and norms, and in practical terms, on the basis of what takes place in real life, in the context of how actors interact, feel, and how this is endorsed by the institutions of society. But, second, it is also a process of hierarchization, one that creates a hierarchy. For, as a mechanism of evaluation and determination of right and wrong, of good and bad, justice and crime establish what is better (justice) and what is worse (crime), what are high and higher expressions of humanity, and what are low and lower ones. It is on the basis of this general process of distinction and hierarchization that a multiplicity of distinctions and hierarchies are created in the various areas and sub-areas of social life. As a whole, the distinctions and hierarchizations that come with justice and crime are part and parcel of the mechanisms of ordering values, principles, norms, needs, interests, right(s), and ultimately behaviours.

But it does not stop here. For the distinctions and hierarchizations that come with justice and crime are just as well about ordering emotions, both positive and negative ones. Emotions, which recent theories of justice, perhaps more than modern theories of crime (see Karstedt et al. 2011), have been prone to overlook, are indeed an integral element of the dynamics of distinction and hierarchization. While positive emotions are meant to express and convey the humanity of human beings at its best, towards themselves, others, and the environment, negative or criminal ones reveal the *in*-humanity of humanity. Incidentally, in this situation, justice occupies the commanding position vis-à-vis crime since justice is the benchmark against which crime is defined and measured. Crime being the 'dark side' from which justice tries to move away or above which it seeks to elevate people and the world, justice, as an idea and ideal, serves as the reference-point.

Now, in order to be defining and concrete features of society, the distinctions and hierarchizations that justice and crime are, need the support of legitimacy. They need its ability to organize and justify, or validate, the relations of power that come with the distinctions and hierarchizations of justice and crime, and make them part of the daily and accepted reality of the community. The task is fivefold.

First, at a general level, the role of legitimacy is to argue that the inequalities of power existing among the governors and the governed and in the various sectors of activity (economic, social, cultural, and others) between who is in charge and who is not, have three features. One, it has to show that they are connected and create a network of interdependence. Two, it has to make the case that they have a purpose that transcends the imbalances of power (see Weber 2007; Kronman 1983), i.e. generating the organization (order) that is required for society and the well-being of its members to be possible—what we could call a 'systemic service'. Three, legitimacy has to argue that inequalities of power help underwrite the distinctions and hierarchizations associated with justice and crime.

Second, legitimacy has to ensure that the institutions and their leaders involved in the management of the distinctions/hierarchizations of justice and crime are legitimate. These institutions include political institutions, responsible for the overall running of society (in this context overviewing the more specific institutions of criminal justice), and the institutions of criminal justice themselves. In order to be legitimate, the institutions, their members, and their actions have to be in line with (that is to say effectively express, promote, and defend) the principles, values, and norms with which society and its members identify, especially when it comes to justice and crime.

Third, the ways in which the institutional requirement of legitimacy unfolds vary with institutions. For the specific institutions of criminal justice, as a subset of the managing structure of society, they need to be faithful, in their philosophy, form, and acts, to what is viewed as just in terms of substance and procedure. As for the task of the political institutions, it is a much broader one. Literally, it is a systemic and, therefore, a fundamental one. They have a responsibility towards the possibility and functioning of society as a whole, as a well as towards making acceptable the conditions of existence of its members. This calls for, through law making, policy making, and enforcement, among other mechanisms, engineering material (behaviours and other) and immaterial (cultural, psychological, and other) compatibility and convergence (relative homogeneity) among the sectors of society and their members. Compatibility and convergence are particularly important in the strategic domains of the life of society. In this regard, it is understood that each area will have its own idiosyncratic ways of being, handling issues, and relating to others. But such idiosyncrasy has to be within the limits of the framework of compatibility and convergence established by the values and principles that political institutions serve and the key directions they set forth to the public. In an optimal situation, idiosyncrasy should actively contribute to the compatibility and convergence of sectors, not only to maintain society as a system but also to make it vibrant.

Fourth, in modern society, law is a central way of how the distinctions and hierarchizations of justice and crime are looked after. This echoes the fact that law has become the domain in which and through which legitimacy is achieved, as illustrated by the contemporary significance of the notion of 'rule of law'. This indicates that legitimacy may be in some fashion less than law. But, at the same time, legitimacy is more than law since without its support, law lacks credibility and is seen as unable to fulfill its regulatory mission, including at the service of what is right. For unless it is synchronized with the values, principles, norms, and right(s) that are the content of legitimacy and delivers reasonably well, in concrete terms, on their demands, rather than being a facilitator, law is an obstacle. Rather than being a 'plus', it is a 'minus'.

Fifth, while the relationships between legitimacy and institutions, and legitimacy and law are crucial, a situation of full legitimacy requires going beyond law and institutions. One of the most successful versions of legitimacy can be when it has become part of the cultural fabric of society, of its social DNA, so to speak, with good behavior coming as a second nature, as a socialized nature, and deviations emerging only as exceptions. This happens when there is a level of general acceptation among members of society about the distinctions, hierarchies, and inequalities based on the core values of the community and their realization. This exists not only despite, but also in the midst of the disagreements, tensions, and conflicts that can exist, with the role of institutions and law being there to handle these with the objective of not simply preserving stability but of producing further dynamic integration.

TAKING JUSTICE, CRIME, AND LEGITIMACY SERIOUSLY

Interestingly, the significance of legitimacy for justice and crime grows with the expansion of the nature and scope of justice, and, consequently, with the expansion of the nature and scope of crime. Considering how the conception of justice and crime are affected, in fact extended in the democratic context, this is destined to give legitimacy a special place in democracy in relation to justice and crime.

In order to understand this, let us start with the movement by which justice gains relevance. Here, it helps to think about a community where force is the factor that counts most (which therefore makes group-life hardly a community) and where, consequently, what is owed to others is only important to the extent that others have power. In this context, what is owed to others is a matter of balance of power and prudence (others could resist or retaliate if they do not get what is owed to them), not of principle. In other words, justice is not valued (as a principle). The same is true for crime and legitimacy. If what is owed to others has no value from a principle standpoint, violating it (crime) is itself not valued or recognized, this time in negative terms, as a crime (in the context of juvenile delinquency, see Sykes and Matza 1957). As a result, this way of thinking about justice and crime deprives, in a significant fashion, power from being able to find good reasons to make itself legitimate. In the process, it is legitimacy itself that is prone to end up being seen as irrelevant.

This changes when factoring in others, their needs, aspirations, expectations, interests, rights, and emotions becomes part of the equation. With the others' side accounted for, considerations of justice, and of crime and legitimacy, including concerning the conception and exercise of power and their benefits, do matter. In addition, when the others' side becomes more and more of a factor, the characteristics of justice, crime, and legitimacy and their relations are destined to evolve. In particular, the more the nature and scope of justice are expanding, i.e. the more the content of its demands gets thicker and the number of those who benefit from it increases, the more what constitutes a crime is enlarged and targets more people.

This movement does not stop here. It triggers the widening and deepening of the significance of legitimacy. Indeed, if more justice sensibility means and implies more crime sensibility, more justice and crime sensibility means and implies more legitimacy sensibility. Legitimacy applies to more situations and is more constraining in a given situation. If only at this level, more justice and crime sensibility calls for the institutions and actors in position of authority, such as political institutions and their members and, more specifically, the ones of the criminal justice system, to be more mindful of the requirements that come with justice and crime sensibility. Their responsibility and burden of accountability grow with the rise of justice and crime awareness. The more they abide by this, the more their legitimacy; and the less they abide by it, the less their legitimacy. The evolution of democratic culture and, housed within it, of the culture of criminal justice, illustrates this state of affairs at both the national and international levels.

At the national level, in pre-modern and pre-democratic Western societies, concentration of power in the hands of a few and the overall organization of society on the basis of inequality signified the narrow and imbalanced character of what was understood by justice, crime, and legitimacy. Justice was conceived and applied equally among actors of same status, and unequally among actors of unequal status. Not surprisingly, crime followed this logic of stratification, of balanced reciprocity among equals and imbalanced reciprocity among unequals.[11] For example, the gravity of an act committed against a power-holder's interest and right grew with how high the power-holder sat. On the other hand, while lateral criminality, among actors of the same social level, could have severe consequences, much latitude was given to power-holders towards the powerless (Black 2010). The thin character of the rights of those below made it such that few acts perpetrated against them would qualify as a crime. Expressing and keeping under check this organization of justice and crime were among the bare-boned limits that legitimacy imposed on power. In this context, the ability of the powerless to challenge the legitimacy of the powerful was kept to a minimum.

In contrast to this, with the rise and diffusion of democratic values, the notions of justice, crime, and legitimacy have gone through a process of growing specification, densification, and universalization. More and more particular issues fall within the realm of justice debates and demands (specification). A high level of implementation of justice requirements is expected (densification). The beneficiaries of justice are now in principle all members of the community, as eminently illustrated by the fact that in a democratic society, a just law is one that applies equally to all (universalization). With this, crime has also grown in specification (more acts are qualified as criminal), densification (prosecution for crimes is routinely happening in a well-functioning society), and scope (with equality before the law, with the universalization of those benefiting from justice, more perpetrators are treated as criminals). Legitimacy itself has turned more demanding. As all individuals have rights in need of being promoted and protected, the accountability of the various institutions and actors in charge of their promotion and protection entails, more than ever before, the right of asking and challenging. It entails the right of asking and challenging whether or not they are doing a good job for everyone. This includes the rights not only of victims but of perpetrators as well to ask and challenge.

In this regard, as the requirements of democratic values make it less possible to ignore difficult issues, legitimacy is increasingly a debated matter in criminal justice culture (see Bottoms and Tankebe 2012; Lacey 2008; Tyler 2007). Democracy, far from stopping at the doorsteps of its criminal justice system and of how it treats the ones accused of a crime, is also tested and revealed by them. As criminals, too, have rights, democracy has no choice but to ensure that no one, even a perpetrator, experiences a denial of right(s). It amounts to taking to heart the following question: What are the rights of a criminal and how should they evolve in a democratic setting? In the answer to this resides, arguably, in part the evolving fate of contemporary democracy, inside and outside the criminal justice system.

As for the evolution of democratic culture and the reinforcement of justice, crime, legitimacy, and their relations at the international level, changes since the end of World War II have led to the formulation of greater accountability for states vis-à-vis other states and individuals. Wars of aggressions have been made illegitimate (unjust and criminal) by the United Nations Charter and international law has come to condemn a whole set of massive violations of human rights, as war crimes, crimes against

[11] On balanced and imbalanced reciprocity in the context of justice, see Johnston (2011, chapter 1).

humanity, and crimes of genocide. In the post-cold war era, the establishment of ad hoc international criminal tribunals and the International Criminal Court, by increasing further legitimacy and justice demands on states and their political leaders internationally, has confirmed this orientation (see Coicaud 2007, 2010a).[12]

IMPACT OF UPHEAVAL AND CHANGE ON JUSTICE, CRIME, AND LEGITIMACY

What we have seen so far on justice, crime, legitimacy, and their relations has by and large presupposed a sense of stability about each of these notions and their interactions. But this is not always the situation in which they find themselves. As a matter of fact, more often than not, they are caught in the middle of upheaval and change. What happens to them when this is the case? This is what we analyse in this section by focusing on possible scenarios. One can be a positive one, geared towards enhancing the importance of justice, crime, and legitimacy. We have alluded to this earlier. Two others can be more negative. One can amount to the borders between justice and crime getting blurred and legitimacy weakened, bringing about a state of indefinition and confusion. Another one can be all together tragic since, in it, justice, crime, legitimacy, and their relations are turned upside down and lose the meaning that has traditionally led them to be valued as benchmarks of what is right. Ultimately, this shows that there is no absolute or hermetic wall separating these types of scenarios. Although they are markedly distinct, they can mingle, affect one another, and even develop a hybrid identity or transmute based on the context in which upheaval and change take place and how they unfold. In any case, because of space limitations, we only focus here on the first and the third possible scenarios, the most positive and negative ones.

TOWARDS MORE JUSTICE AND LEGITIMACY, AND LESS CRIME

We mentioned earlier that with the development of democratic values, justice, crime, and legitimacy gained in significance. In doing so, we referred to the historical movement by which, with the recognition of more rights for individuals, they became central features of modern social life. That said, having them serve as main points of reference did not happen all at once. It took place over a period of several centuries, from their rise in the West to their spread around the world, and through struggles that continue to this day, within and among nations. In this perspective, each time, the battle for more justice and legitimacy, and less crime, tends to go through four generic phases. While they contain overlapping elements, these phases are enough distinct and prone to happen in sequence to justify the fact that we present them separately. They are: (1) the identification of shortcomings in the organization of order, which become

[12] This is not to say that all is fine with the current international criminal justice picture.

elements of contention; (2) the political character, or 'politicization', of the contestation of the organization of order; (3) the unwillingness to compromise on the challenge and the demands that the political contestation entails; and (4) the integration of the demands for change, leading to the establishment of a new form of stability.

(1) The first step towards the possibility of upheaval and change is the public identification and indication by some that how order is arranged, and how access to goods and resources is organized, is problematic. Four interrelated aspects are important here. They are: who is challenging the established order; what are the modalities of the challenge; what are the area(s) and issue(s) at the centre of the dissatisfaction formulated; and what is the scope or the extent to which the criticism affects the community.

The importance of who goes against the established order relates to whether or not, and if 'yes' to what extent, the actor challenging the status quo has leverage. Leverage can for instance come from standing, status, or numbers. The modalities of opposition are significant because, for example, they can trigger support or rejection among the rest of the members of the community. The area(s) and issue(s) about which there is dissatisfaction matter because some of them are more strategic, that is more 'universalizable', than others. In this regard, the extent to which the area(s) and issue(s) that are the focus of a complaint are 'universalizable' has a bearing on the scope of the impact on the community. Needless to say, this is critical for the next stage, the ability to give the challenge a political character, which is to politicize the fact of going against the established order.

(2) Politicization, the way we refer to it here, is critical for grasping how the organization of order and who is responsible for it, can emerge as a political question as well as a politically contested question, with what this means for the definition and implementation of justice, crime, and legitimacy. This is important because unless the organization of order becomes politically debated and viewed as politically problematic, for instance due to how it structures power and distributes goods and access to goods, the understanding of justice, crime, and legitimacy and that of their relations tend not to be questioned. In the process, it is all the more difficult to change and improve the organization of society that these notions express and sanction.

Politicization presents a double challenge. The first challenge is to show that the manner in which society is organized and the dissatisfactions that come with it are a political problem; a political problem that is produced by how political institutions and their leaders, in conjunction with their allies and the interests they represent, contribute to shape in a biased fashion other institutions (including institutions of criminal justice) and society as a whole. Being successful in doing this leads to the labelling of the problem as political and makes political institutions accountable in connection with it. They can be blamed for allowing the problem to arise and it becomes their responsibility to address it. The second challenge, in part related to the first one, concerns the capacity of actors challenging the status quo to make themselves viewed as political actors/political activists and, more importantly, as legitimate political actors/activists. The ways in which an actor can be referred to as a legitimate political one depends, among other elements, upon the type of society in which this happens and the modalities of the actor's action.[13] At stake in being viewed as a (legitimate) political actor is the crucial benefit of not being considered a criminal. Indeed, it amounts to a form of recognition, which is also a form of decriminalization. The legitimate political actor challenging the order will not be treated as a common criminal. The political label gives credibility to this actor and its action and, at the same time, to their questioning of the legitimacy of the organization of society.

This helps to explain why the qualification or not of a prisoner as a political prisoner is in certain circumstances at the centre of major debates between power-holders and power-challengers. For power-holders, rejecting this qualification is denying legitimacy and that of its actions to the challenger, in fact possibly treating them as criminal, and affirming their own power-holding legitimacy. For power-challengers, political prisoner status can be an acknowledgement of their legitimacy and that of their actions challenging the legitimacy of the regime opposed. This applies at both national and international levels.[14]

The politicization of order—what we could also call the denaturalization of order and its unveiling as socially constructed and politically motivated[15]—can take place in at least two ways. Either there is the feeling that reality does not match the principles of justice and legitimacy, with these principles not being contested themselves. If this is the case, the challenge unfolds within the realm of a given paradigm and calls for improving reality along the demands manifested by these principles. It is about closing the gap between reality and principles. Or, it can be a more radical and challenging situation. That is: it is not only reality that is contested. The principles of justice and legitimacy, and, in the process, what is understood by crime are contested as well, for example, for not being empowering enough. This entails the possibility of a change of paradigm. The movement that in the West went from pre-democratic culture principles and values to democratic culture ones is part of this history and configuration. And within the democratic paradigm itself, the revolutionary struggles that radically challenged liberal-democratic values and their implementation for their formality, as opposed to substantive equality in particular, are another illustration of this state of affairs. They contributed to the emergence of new normative, legal, and political modalities of envisioning, institutionalizing, and organizing the democratic ideals (for instance, socialism and communism).

(3) The third aspect of the struggle for more justice and legitimacy, and less crime, comes with the fact that the politicization of order can be insistent and intransigent. In this case, the challenge simply does not go away. We all have seen situations in which power-holders, at the beginning of a crisis, think that they can ride the storm

[13] Non-democratic regimes are inclined to criminalize most forms of opposition.

[14] In this context the United States, one of the least political societies there is, and one of the most unwilling to recognize as legitimate and political a challenge coming from outside the established political system, would constitute an interesting case study. For instance, domestically, freedom of speech comes with the great difficulty for any relatively radicalized opponent to be treated as a legitimate political activist and the great ease with which a radical activist, especially in the post 9/11 environment, can be labelled 'enemy of the state'. Internationally, for a radical activist, being viewed as a terrorist is certainly more frequent than being qualified as a legitimate political actor.

[15] For the politicization of order as the denaturalization of order, see, for example, Bourdieu (1984).

and come out on the other side still in power, if not altogether victorious. They think that they can successfully deny that there is a challenge, and that if they continue ignoring the problem, it will dissipate. Or, while acknowledging that there is a problem, they try to buy time by counting on challenge-fatigue, by discrediting or even demonizing opponents (labelling them as criminals), or by introducing cosmetic changes, with the goal, once the crisis has subsided, of returning to business as usual. This certainly happens often enough for power-holders to be tempted to see these possibilities as serious options, particularly when they do not want to resort to full repression or bring about the changes requested by the challengers. Nevertheless, when calls for change do not fade away, none of this suffices. For one of the features of political and social transformation is that when a case is successfully made of a question, this case not only manages to stay on the agenda but ends up *defining* the agenda.

Now, for this to happen, it is essential that the challenge of the status quo does not isolate itself from the rest of society. This is especially needed when it has become radicalized. Indeed, isolated radicalization is not a recipe for success. It tends to undermine the cause of the challenge. In contrast, radicalization is more likely to achieve its combat goal if the rest of society rallies or if, in fact, a somewhat radicalization of society as a whole emerges. Ultimately, a point of no return has been reached for the established order when the unwillingness of power-holders to go along with change empties the social environment in which the crisis unfolds of a sense of justice and legitimacy. To some extent the United States, having denied for decades full rights to African-Americans, was running this risk in the 1950s and 1960s. The schizophrenia of pretending to be at the same time a champion of human rights internationally and an officially discriminatory and repressive society towards African-Americans at home had become untenable (see Anderson 2003). Hence, in time, and despite the reluctance of conservative forces, civil rights for African-Americans were made part of the national fabric, and mythology.

(4) Finally, integration is the process through which, by making new rights part of the landscape, justice is expanded and strengthened. In this perspective, a number of actions that were previously seen as non-problematic will now be viewed as unacceptable because they violate the new rights, and what is newly seen as right. While some of them will only constitute civil violations, the most serious of them will be treated as crimes, and sanctioned as such. Needless to say, the regime that succeeds in this integration is prone to enhance its legitimacy. In this regard, integration comes with two characteristics.

First, expansion and strengthening of justice and legitimacy so achieved are not set forever. For any society that does not see itself as static or having reached its final stage, there is the understanding that more changes are likely to be brought in later on. The latest round of change and integration constitutes therefore a temporary equilibrium, what we could call a state of 'socialized instability' (see Coicaud 2001). In this context, socialization enables and makes room for change while ensuring that it does not go out of control to the point of endangering the overall stability of society. This is particularly true in the democratic environment. The nature and dynamics of democratic values, inclusive, geared to (more) individual empowerment and, because of their inspirational and aspirational dimensions, oriented forward and upward, at the same time make this possible and call for it (Allott 2001). Second, integration of more justice and legitimacy considerations, by putting more constraint on crime, is meant to enhance the sense of agency of actors. Once again, this state of affairs, applying to most communities fighting for more justice and legitimacy, and less crime, is magnified in the democratic context. For here, more than anywhere else, as justice and legitimacy are synonymous with empowerment and agency, more justice and legitimacy means more empowerment and agency for actors.[16] It implies for actors an enhanced, although not necessarily more serene, ambition of presence to oneself, others, and the world at large.[17]

This orientation towards an enhanced sense of agency concerns, at a minimum, three categories of actors. To begin with, there are the ordinary members of society, the ones living their daily life and to whom positive and negatives duties are owed. The second category of actors to whom this applies are those who have been made victims, who have been victimized, either by the way in which society is (seen) unfairly organized or by a specific action that has hurt them. In both cases, justice and legitimacy geared towards empowerment and agency have the goal of increasing the capabilities of actors. But it also has the task of bringing justice to the people who have been made victims.

In this specific case, the objective is twofold. To begin with, it is about recognizing to the victim the status of a victim. In addition, it is about prosecuting and punishing the guilty party in such a manner that the victim becomes neither the captive of the crime that has been committed nor of a victim-status. In other words, it is about granting a victim recognition of its victim-status and giving the means to move beyond this status. This is especially important since, when a victim is not offered the means to move beyond such status, the victim ends up being twice a victim. The victim is a victim of a crime, but is also a victim of the unfinished, and unsuccessful, carrying out of justice. This state of affairs, while recognizing the victim as a victim, condemns it to continue being a victim. It does not allow the victim to unlock him or herself from and overcome the status and identity of a victim.

This is all the more contrary to restitution and reconstruction of empowerment and agency as it can run the risk of encouraging, among other things, the development, in the victim, of a victim mentality. This is individually and socially highly counterproductive, toxic and, ultimately, dangerous. For the undermining of sense of agency and responsibility that is part and parcel of a victim mentality can bring an obsessive focus on oneself and one's trauma that has the tendency to hamper the sense of identification and empathy with others. This can pave the way for disaster, as we will allude to in the final part of this section.

[16] In this context, debates on justice can focus on the extent to which fundamental political institutions have a responsibility in ensuring empowerment and agency.

[17] Depression and neurosis are for instance typical pathologies of the democratic culture and the democratic individual, and of the drive of presence to oneself, others, and the world they amount to. They can create much pressure and burden for individuals. It is a case of how the push for empowerment and agency can turn against itself and become counterproductive, generating individual and collective alienation in the process.

In stark opposition, truly rendering justice to the victim by honouring the victim and the human being in the victim is about acknowledging that a crime has been committed and acknowledging the victim status of the individual in a way that gives to this individual the means to no longer be defined by this. It is about giving the victim the resources to transcend the crime and the recognition of this crime, and reclaim, retrieve and reconstruct oneself. This is what real empowerment signifies in these circumstances. Ideally, this entails reconciliation with oneself, others (including at times with the criminal), and the environment despite the crime that has occurred (see further Coicaud 2009). Empowering justice reaches a state that comes close to spirituality, and spiritual elevation, when it allows the victim to become more human, and more of a human being (enhanced sense of agency and responsibility), compared to before the crime happened.

Finally, as for the third type of actors to whom more empowerment and agency come with more justice and legitimacy, it concerns the authors of a crime. Indeed, especially once again in a democratic context, although a key objective of justice and legitimacy applied to a criminal is punishment and retribution, this does not signify that punishment and retribution are meant to make a victim of the criminal. A criminal justice system that transforms a criminal into a victim is not a just criminal justice system. It turns itself criminal. For once the criminal has been sentenced, while he is serving his sentence and once he has paid his debt to society and the victim(s), it is owed to him that he does not become the last victim of his own crime, so to speak. Letting this happen is unjust and illegitimate. Taking justice and legitimacy seriously means that criminals, too, are somehow supposed to be empowered, to become re-empowered agents through the criminal justice process. In principle, the criminal justice system is meant to also help them be reconciled with themselves, others, and the world, even in the case of a death sentence.[18]

Needless to say, more often than not, today like yesterday, stigmatization of crime and criminals is prone to make criminals the last victim of their crime, long after they have served their sentence.[19] They rarely stop being identified with their crime and reminded, during and after their sentence, that by their crime they have put themselves outside the realm of ordinary and valuable human beings. This is especially the case when being identified as a criminal, at times even before a crime has been committed, is being facilitated by economic and racial prejudices (Wacquant 2009; Fagan 2008). In this perspective, for a criminal, belonging again fully to the society of regular people and benefiting from it, from being no less valuable than any other person, is elusive. It has the tendency to no longer be a full right. At best, it is a very conditional one. At worst, it is a luxury that is the source of constant rejection. As such, the criminal joins the ranks of the various outcasts societies produce—like the female prostitute who, because she can be bought by any man, tends

[18] This is in part how we have to understand the ritual of the last words granted to a person about to be executed after have been sentenced to death. The respect that is in principle due to the person about to be put to death is also part of this state of affairs.

[19] To some extent the thinking is: the person has committed a crime, which is bad enough, and it could happen again.

to be seen as valueless and deserving no respect by most of society, including the very men who buy her services.[20]

END OF JUSTICE AND LEGITIMACY, AND TRIUMPH OF CRIME

The preceding scenario presupposes that the power of justice and legitimacy prevails and that, as such, it has the ability to draw clear lines of demarcation and hierarchy between right and wrong. In the process, crime is boxed in, literally. It is well-defined and handled with effectiveness. But this is not always the case. At the other end of the spectrum, there is another configuration in the context of which the notions and values of justice, crime, and legitimacy are turned upside down, coming to mean the contrary of what is traditionally understood by justice and legitimacy (factoring in others' rights), and crime (very serious violation of others' rights).

This scenario, which we can call the end of justice and legitimacy, and the triumph of crime, is not simply theoretical. It happens for example when ideologies of resentment and reactionary extremes colour a moment of history, the political and legal culture of a period, or when they all together take over and become the expressions and producers of new forms of exclusionary governance and society. Think about the various types of radical conservatism that pullulate today in the West and the non-West, in democratic and non-democratic regimes. Think also about the ideologies of crime that came to shape Europe and a significant part of the world in the first half of the twentieth century, in particular with Nazism and fascism.

In this section, in alluding to this inversion of justice, legitimacy, and crime, we wish to touch upon two main points. First, we intend to look into emotions and passions, and values, and what their turning negative signifies for justice, crime, and legitimacy. Second, we want to refer to how justice, crime, and legitimacy turned upside down can be associated with a victim mentality that goes against what justice, legitimacy, and crime are about in a well-functioning society, that is, agency and responsibility.

Until the nineteenth century, in the Western and non-Western worlds, the understanding and analysis of justice did not exclude absolutely the recognition of the existence and importance of emotions and passions. Despite the fact that a deep intellectual and moral commitment to reason and its attributes created much suspicion about them, especially in the West, and especially about the negative ones, their relevance was prone to be assumed and called upon. In this perspective, emotions and passions, particularly emotions and passions seen as positive, were more often than not integrated in the conceptualization and implementation of the possibility of justice, and fully theorized as such. In the West, Aristotle and Spinoza, each in their own way, illustrate this state of affairs. As positivism and rationalism came to dominate the understanding and analysis of human and social life, emotions, passions and, along

[20] The interpretation presenting Mary Magdalene, one of Jesus' most celebrated disciples and the most important female disciple, as a former prostitute at the same time denounces and builds on this reality.

with them, values, lost most of their ability to be viewed as useful tools.[21] This was destined to affect the study of justice. This led it to mainly focus on the interests and rights of individuals and the best way to calculate and distribute them in a rational fashion—'rational' being conceived in opposition to and against emotions and passions. John Rawls' *Theory of Justice* (2005), arguably one of the most celebrated works on justice in the twentieth century, is a testament to this. In his book, the emotive nature of justice is overlooked, if not excluded. The work is essentially about the conditions through which it is possible to secure, intellectually and practically, the rights of actors on an instrumental and rational basis.

Needless to say, the fact that emotions and passions have had the tendency of being dismissed by recent democratic theories of justice is ironic. It is ironic because, as democratic theories of justice, they end up underestimating the democratic ideals and ideas which celebrate, embody, and capitalize on (positive) emotions and passions of connection and inclusion, and that this celebration, embodiment, and capitalization go hand in hand with the development and prevailing of democratic ideals and ideas. This is all the more ironic considering that without the recognition of this reality, one cannot make sense of the fact that the quest for democratic justice and legitimacy since the eighteenth century has generated and taken place through formidable battles of democratic and non-democratic emotions and passions (see Furet 1999; Holmes 1993). These formidable battles, which became more intense with the spread of democracy, continue today.

This shows that, by severing the link existing between justice and emotions and passions, by underestimating the emotive nature of justice, and of legitimacy (and ethics[22]), a double limitation is put in place.

First, this amputates the analysis of justice in a crucial dimension, for it appears particularly challenging to make sense of justice without any reference to emotions. Furthermore, this amputation goes as far as, because of the connection between justice, legitimacy, and crime, damaging the ability to study and understand properly legitimacy and crime. Indeed, underestimating the role and importance of emotions and passions in justice amounts to underestimating the role and importance of emotions and passions in legitimacy and crime. For example, if emotions, and values, of empathy, sympathy, solidarity, identification with others, openness to others, respect for others, and their contrary, are central to justice, they, and their contrary, are equally central to legitimacy and crime, especially in a democratic context.

Second, the severing of the link between justice and legitimacy and emotions and passions hampers the support that can be given to the practical realization of justice and legitimacy, and the containment of crime. This takes place at two levels. To begin with, overlooking the positive and inclusive emotions and passions that enter into the conception of justice and legitimacy, like, in the context of modern democratic justice and legitimacy, the emotions and passions of equality and liberty, is not simply an analytical and theoretical mistake. It also has practical implications. It detracts from

[21] For an analysis of this evolution concerning values, see Coicaud (2002).

[22] The emotive nature of justice and legitimacy applies as well to ethics. Ethics is in a variety of ways underwritten by emotions and passions.

the ability to understand and facilitate in concrete terms what it takes to foster and mobilize positive emotions and passions in support of the implementation of justice; and it detracts from the possibility of making sense and combating the appeal of negative and exclusionary emotions and passions, and the values that come with them, such as hatred, envy, indifference, jealousy, racism, and resentment. Leaving the door open to negative emotions and passions, this can represent major opportunities for crime.

The individual and collective costs associated with these analytic and practical limitations are catastrophic enough not to be minimized. In the worst case scenario, they encourage pathological visions of justice, legitimacy, and crime. In this perspective, justice and legitimacy as a respect for the voice of others is presented as a crime, and the institutionalization of crime, the becoming law of crime, as a path for justice and legitimacy. A few decades ago, that was a key feature of Nazism and fascism's political and legal cultures. Today, radical conservative tendencies connected with racism, anti-Semitism, religious and cultural integrism, which can be part of the landscape of democratic and non-democratic regimes, in the West and the non-West, are not entirely foreign to this. Their tendency to promulgate a closed 'I' and 'we' defined and pursued in opposition to the 'other' is not without being an invitation to the turning upside down of justice, legitimacy, and crime as we know them.[23]

This movement towards the inversion of justice, legitimacy, and crime is all the more dangerous considering that more often than not, especially in the modern democratic environment, negative and exclusionary emotions and passions, and values, come with a sense of paranoia that can enhance the possibility of crime, and the denial of justice and legitimacy. Paranoia has this effect because it allows the paranoiac to bring terror to others without having to take responsibility (i.e. agency) for the wrongs committed. The paranoiac, who for all intents and purposes can also be described as a terrorized actor, can be a terrorist without viewing him or herself as a terrorist.[24] Honest, lucid, and critical reflexivity, which would help to account for its responsibility, is not its forte. The paranoiac is too much the captive of its pathologies for being capable of the distantiation that would allow seeing others and himself in a balanced manner. Ultimately, this conflates with the fact that the paranoiac/psychopath has a very low capacity of empathy and presents himself as a victim.

In this regard, by the twisted mechanism that presents the perpetrator as a victim, the paranoiac perpetrator is no longer a perpetrator, or for that matter, a paranoiac. He is a victim and, therefore, does not have to take responsibility for the crime(s) he commits. In fact, when this state of mind, and psychology, is at work, the very existence of a crime tends to be denied by the perpetrator. Far from presenting himself as an aggressor, he depicts himself, to himself and others, as acting out of self-defence, out of legitimate defence. This can go as far as arguing that the victim of the perpetrator is the real agent of the crime, that the victim is the aggressor, and that, consequently, the

[23] These 'I' and 'we' are all the more closed, egocentric, and self-centered as they are inhabited and structured by a sense of insecurity.

[24] There would be of course much more to say on terror and its relations with justice, legitimacy, and crime.

victim is the author of his own demise. When, adding to this, the perpetrator manages to dehumanize the victim, to present the victim as hardly or not human, justice and legitimacy are at their lowest, and evasion of responsibility and crime at their highest. The worst perpetrator will even push this logic and psychology of crime-denial to the point of presenting his actions as a service rendered to humanity. This sinister state of affairs, which literally is about creating another reality of justice, legitimacy, crime, victim, agency, and responsibility, can unfold at the individual and collective levels. Tragically, it is much more common than one would ever want. Historically, it was one of the defining characteristics of the culture of war, death, and crime that plagued Europe, especially on the Eastern Front (Snyder 2012), and the Far East during pre-World War II and then World War II.[25] We find it more recently as well, in the 1990s, shaping to some extent the mind, psychology, attitude, and actions of perpetrators in the Balkan wars and the Rwandan genocide.

PLASTICITY AND FLUIDITY OF JUSTICE, CRIME, AND LEGITIMACY

The contemporary context and the premium it puts, following the systemic influence of democratic values, on the demands of justice, crime, and legitimacy is geared towards enhancing justice and legitimacy, and combating crime. But this should not lead us to think that this orientation is a sure and secured one. After all, while most favourable to justice, legitimacy, and combating crime, the democratic paradigm is also one in which crime, individual and collective, at home[26] and abroad, has flourished. To speak only about wrong/crime beyond borders, it only suffices to remember the catastrophes of colonialism, imperialism, and totalitarianism, and that these phenomena, each in their own way, cannot be separated from the normative, political, and legal history of democracy and its spread. This unsettling reality is an invitation to draw at least three lessons for justice, legitimacy, and crime.

First, in relation to justice, legitimacy, and crime, there is no firewall separating good and evil; this may be especially true in the modern democratic environment. Indeed, if it is in this context that justice and legitimacy have grown the most, it is in this context as well that they have been amply violated, that, in a variety of ways, crime, individually and collectively, has proliferated. This is particularly the case with the cultures of violence and resentment that have emerged in the democratic world. Hence, the following situation: On the one hand, with more democratic justice and

[25] Nazism, for example, amounted to a disqualification of liberal justice and legitimacy in the context of national and international law. Liberal justice and legitimacy were presented as un-just and illegitimate, as the justice and the legitimacy of the weak, expressions and vehicles of flawed values, laws, emotions, and passions. The Nazi paranoia and its sense of psychological insecurity, led it to obsessively focus on what it felt was owed to Germany and the Germans, and to a large extent regard the denial of others' rights as beyond the criminal, as non-criminal. In this perspective, pathologically absolute rights for oneself meant a totally self-centered and retributive sense of justice in the context of which others, especially those who were viewed as having contributed to the denials of Germany and Germans' rights, did not count and even had to pay for their deeds (see also Schmitt 2006).

[26] Here, an interesting object of analysis would be terror and democracy, for instance the Terror during the French Revolution.

democratic legitimacy come greater rights and empowerment, and greater crime prevention and awareness. On the other, it also comes with a persistence and even inflation of criminal activity, both individual and collective. What to make of this paradox? The expansion of the definition of rights that the expansion of the definition of crime brings, is not enough to answer this question.

Second, the value, emotional, and organizational judgements constituted by justice, legitimacy, and crime can oscillate from one side (justice and legitimacy) to the other (crime) and even create hybrids made of both sides.[27] This is in part due to the fact that the capacity for justice and legitimacy as well as for injustice, illegitimacy, and evil is inherent to being a social human being. Our inhumanity is linked to our (social) humanity. In this perspective, human beings carry as much the possibility and responsibility of justice and legitimacy as the ones of crime, injustice, and illegitimacy. Carrying this possibility and responsibility is why and how human beings are humans. It is at the same time their value and limitation, and their value because of their limitation.[28] It represents the best and worst of human agency, and human burden. More specifically, the ability of actors to opt for good over wrong depends to a large extent upon their capacity to constructively manage fear and insecurity, within and outside. When the defeating power of fear and insecurity is not confronted, it can lead to evil. When affronted and overcome, it can lead to good. Ultimately, actors have to deal with the dynamics of what could be called 'inter-subjective subjectivity' and how some of its key aspects can be summarized in the following statements: peace within comes with peace with others, and war within comes with war with others; and one wants and can do for others (war or peace, and to different extent) what he has wanted and done (war or peace, and to different extent) to oneself.

Third, and finally, even the one that justice and legitimacy are designed to protect the most from crime, the actor victimized, is not immune to losing sight of the demands of justice and legitimacy, and of embracing the possibility of wrong if not crime. Aspects of the Israeli–Palestinian conflict, one case among many, resonate with this issue. Very understandably Israel continues to be traumatized and defined by the holocaust and a history of centuries of crippling prejudices and violence. But it seems as if over time, the most conservative forces of the nation have become the captor, and the victim, of a victim identity and a prejudiced mentality. It seems as if they have fallen into a victim syndrome in the context of which the rights of the other side, the rights of the Palestinians and their violation, are overlooked. This is problematic since, as mentioned earlier, victim status should not and does not put one beyond the realm of right and wrong in such a way that one could always be on the side of right no matter what. Hence, the questions: When does committing wrong to others betray and denature the victim status of the victim, betray and denature a (trans-generational) right owned in the midst of tragedy? And, more generally: How to ensure in history that cycles of victimhood do not generate cycles of perpetration

[27] The ambiguous historical track record of democratic justice and legitimacy can also be viewed, at home and abroad, as an oscillation between humanism and predation, inclusion and exclusion, or a mixture of both.

[28] Trying to be the best human being possible finds its greatest value in the fact that the human being is fundamentally limited.

without responsibility? How to achieve an empowered sense of justice and legitimacy, and security, as the best manner to truly put behind the pursuit of wrong, violence and crime?

CONCLUSION

This chapter has been a brief theoretical exploration of the meaning of justice, crime, and legitimacy and their relations. Obviously, much more work would need to be done on each of these aspects in order to offer a comprehensive theoretical analysis on them. Also, it would be useful to examine the ideas touched upon in this chapter in the context of concrete case studies, at the national and international levels.

At the national level, it would be especially helpful to study these notions and their relations in the environment of stable societies and societies in flux. Concerning the latter, it would be necessary to explore two types of cases, which at times, tend to overlap. First, the case of societies where political institutions and the order they oversee are contested. Second, the case of societies where the transformation of values echoing the evolving composition of the population is introducing pressures on the understanding and implementation of justice, legitimacy, and crime. In this perspective, how the growing ethnic and cultural diversity and pluralism of modern societies tend to render more complex the task of drawing lines of separation and hierarchies between right and wrong, justice, crime, and legitimacy, both in terms of private and public right(s), would certainly be worth studying in greater depth.

Because international criminal justice is still in a nascent stage and raises crucial issues of agency and responsibility within and among states, it would be equally important to concretely examine the notions of justice, legitimacy, crime, and their relations in an international context. Significant changes have taken place in this domain since the end of World War II, and even more so in the aftermath of the Cold War, for instance with the creation of the ad hoc international criminal tribunals and the International Criminal Court. These changes deserve more attention than has been given to them so far. This is all the more the case considering that, as the landscape of international right holders continues to evolve, and as the relations between the national and international realms become more intertwined, there will be the need to do more in terms of addressing individual but also structural violence globally.[29] This will make ever so imperative the task of answering the question of whether or not international criminal justice will be able, including through its relations with national criminal justice, to bring norms of justice, legitimacy and crime, and reality closer together.

On these fronts, more work lies ahead...

[29] By focusing on individual responsibility, criminal justice, nationally and internationally, ignores structural violence and, in the process, also the question of who is responsible for it and who benefits from it. On this issue, refer, for example, to Pogge (2010).

REFERENCES

ALLOTT, P. (2001) *Eunomia: New Order for a New World*. Oxford: Oxford University Press.

ANDERSON, C. (2003) *Eyes off the Prize: The United Nations and the African American Struggles for Human Rights, 1944–1955*. Cambridge: Cambridge University Press.

AN-NA'IM, A. A. (2011) *Muslims and Global Justice*. Philadelphia: University of Pennsylvania Press.

BLACK, D. (2010) *The Behavior of Law*. Bingley, West Yorkshire: Emerald Group Publishing.

BOTTOMS, A. and TANKEBE, J. (2012) 'Beyond Procedural Justice: A Dialogic Approach to Legitimacy in Criminal Justice', *Journal of Criminal Law and Criminology* 102(1): 119–70.

BOURDIEU, P. (1984) *Distinction: A Social Critique of the Judgement of Taste*, Nice, R. (trans). Cambridge: Harvard University Press.

COICAUD, J-M. (2001) 'Legitimacy, Socialization and International Change', in Kupchan, C.A., Adler, E., Coicaud, J-M. and Khong, Y.F. (eds) *Power in Transition: the Peaceful Change of International Order*. Tokyo: United Nations University Press.

COICAUD, J-M. (2002) *Legitimacy and Politics: A Contribution to the Study of Political Right and Political Responsibility*, Curtis, D. A. (trans). Cambridge: Cambridge University Press.

COICAUD, J-M. (2007) *Beyond the National Interest: The Future of UN Peacekeeping and Multilateralism in an Era of U.S. Primacy*. Washington, DC: United States Institute of Peace Press.

COICAUD, J-M. (2009) 'Apology, a Small Yet Important Part of Justice', *Japanese Journal of Political Science* 10(1): 93–104.

COICAUD, J-M. (2010a) 'Deconstructing International Legitimacy', in Charlesworth, H. and Coicaud, J-M. (eds) *Fault Lines of International Legitimacy*. Cambridge: Cambridge University Press.

COICAUD, J-M. (2010b) 'Legitimacy, Across Borders and Over Time', in Charlesworth, H. and Coicaud, J-M. (eds) *Fault Lines of International Legitimacy*. Cambridge: Cambridge University Press.

DELMAS-MARTY, M. (1992) *Les grands systèmes de politique criminelle*. Paris: Presses Universitaires de France.

DUFF, R.A. (2001) *Punishment, Communication, and Community*. Oxford: Oxford University Press.

FAGAN, J. (2008) 'Legitimacy and Criminal Justice', *Ohio State Journal of Criminal Law* 6(1): 123–40.

FURET, F. (1999) *The Passing of an Illusion: The Idea of Communism in the Twentieth Century* (translated by Furet, D.). Chicago: University of Chicago Press.

HART, H. M. (1958), 'The Aims of Criminal Law', *Law and Contemporary Problems* 23(3): 401–41.

HOLMES, S. (1993) *The Anatomy of Antiliberalism*. Cambridge: Harvard University Press.

JOHNSTON, D. (2011) *A Brief History of Justice*. London: Wiley-Blackwell.

KARSTEDT, S., LOADER, I. and STRANG, H. (eds) (2011) *Emotions, Crime and Justice*. Oxford: Hart Publishing.

KRONMAN, A. (1983) *Max Weber*. Stanford: Stanford University Press.

LACEY, N. (2008) *The Prisoners' Dilemma: Political Economy and Punishment in Contemporary Democracies*. Cambridge: Cambridge University Press.

LAMOND, G. (2007) 'What is a Crime?', *Oxford Journal of Legal Studies* 27(4): 609–32.

MARSHALL, S. E. and DUFF, R. A. (1998) 'Criminalization and Sharing Wrongs', *The Canadian Journal of Law and Jurisprudence* 11(7): 7–22.

Pogge, T. (2010) *Politics as Usual: What Lies behind the Pro-Poor Rhetoric*. Cambridge: Polity Press.

Rawls, J. (2005) *A Theory of Justice*. Cambridge: The Belknap Press of Harvard University Press.

Robinson, P. H. (1996) 'The Criminal-Civil Distinction and the Utility of Desert', *Boston University Law Review* 76: 1–25.

Scanlon, T. M. (1998) *What We Owe to Each Other*. Cambridge: The Belknap Press of Harvard University Press.

Schmitt, C. (2006) *The Nomos of the Earth in the International Law of Jus Publicum Europaeum*. New York: Telos Press Publishing.

Snyder, T. (2012) *Bloodlands: Europe Between Hitler and Stalin*. New York: Basic Books.

Steiker, C. S. (1997) 'Punishment and Procedure: Punishment Theory and the Criminal-Civil Procedural Divide', *Georgetown Law Journal* 85(4): 775–1116.

Sykes, G. M. and Matza, D. (1957) 'Techniques of Neutralization: A Theory of Delinquency', *American Sociological Review* 22(6): 664–70.

Tyler, T. R. (2006) *Why People Obey the Law*. Princeton: Princeton University Press.

Tyler, T. R. (2007) (ed) *Legitimacy and Criminal Justice: International Perspectives*. New York: Russell Sage Foundation.

Wacquant, L. (2009) *Punishing the Poor: The Neoliberal Government of Social Insecurity*. Durham, NC: Duke University Press.

Weber, M. (2007) *From Max Webber: Essays in Sociology*, Mills, C. W. and Gerth, H. H. (eds and trans). London: Routledge.

Williams, G (1955), 'The Definition of Crime', in Keeton, G. W. and Schwarzenberger, G. (eds), *Current Legal Problems*. London: Stevens & Sons Limited.

4

'A VOICE WITHIN': POWER-HOLDERS' PERSPECTIVES ON AUTHORITY AND LEGITIMACY

Anthony Bottoms and Justice Tankebe

Legitimacy is now a well-established concept in the literature on criminal justice. However, the research so far completed has focused almost exclusively on what might be called *audience legitimacy*; that is, the legitimacy of criminal justice services as viewed by those they serve (from the general public to convicted offenders). This research tradition has been very fruitful, but we have recently argued that it is incomplete, because it does not examine legitimacy from the perspective of the power-holder (Bottoms and Tankebe 2012). In the same paper, elaborating a point made by Max Weber, we suggested that legitimacy is best viewed as an ongoing *dialogue*, which begins with power-holders making a *claim* to exercise legitimate authority. That claim is responded to by one or more audiences; power-holders might perhaps adjust their claims in the light of audience responses, and so on.

Our aim in this chapter is to develop our earlier discussion by focusing in more detail on the topic of *power-holders' perspectives on issues relating to legitimacy*. Anthony Kronman (1983: 41) has insightfully pointed out that, in dialogues about legitimacy, power-holders may often be 'seeking to still a voice within as well as the sometimes louder but no more pressing voices without'. It is that 'voice within', and how it is related to the exercise of authority, that especially concerns us here.

The chapter contains three main sections. In the first section, we elaborate some aspects of the theoretical approach adopted in our previous paper, focusing in particular on the value of the dialogic metaphor, and its congruity with what we understand to be the ontological status of the concept of legitimacy. We also introduce and clarify a distinction between the concepts of *legitimacy* and *legitimation*.

These preliminary remarks prepare the ground for the other two sections of the chapter, which focus more substantively on power-holders' perspectives on authority and legitimacy. The second section considers issues relating to *power-holder legitimation;* that is, how power-holders seek to legitimate their authority to themselves and to others, and how these legitimating practices might impact on their own understanding of their authority. Then in the third section we address the important question of the *confidence of power-holders in the legitimacy of their own authority*. Here, we summarize a small number of empirical studies which are relevant to an understanding of this topic; these show, we suggest, that both under-confidence and over-confidence in one's own authority can be problematic. We then identify some dangers that can arise through the possession of power, and what can happen to the 'voice within' in such situations.

A DIALOGIC APPROACH TO LEGITIMACY

In this section, we explain some of the central theoretical concepts and approaches that we will be utilizing in this chapter, building on our previous paper (Bottoms and Tankebe 2012). We begin by explaining why we have chosen to regard 'dialogue' as a central feature in the understanding of legitimacy.

WHY A DIALOGIC FRAMEWORK?

Jean-Marc Coicaud (2002: 10) has formulated the following very helpful definition of the concept of legitimacy: 'Legitimacy is the recognition of the right to govern. In this regard, it tries to offer a solution to a fundamental political problem, which consists in justifying simultaneously political power and obedience'. A significant merit of this definition is that it encompasses both the parties necessarily involved in any discussion of legitimacy, namely those who seek to exercise effective political power, and those whom they seek to govern.

As mentioned earlier, almost all the criminological literature on legitimacy has been focused on audience legitimacy. This work—to its considerable credit—is primarily empirical; it has examined, variously through surveys and through ethnographic work, the circumstances under which those without power recognize power-holders as having the right to govern, and the consequences that flow from this recognition. A central and very important set of findings in this literature concerns the importance of *procedural justice* (see for example Tyler 2006a, 2006b; Jackson et al., 2012)—that is to say, citizens are more likely to regard police and other criminal justice power-holders as legitimate when power-holders treat citizens with respect, are willing to listen attentively to their accounts in contentious situations, and so on. These findings, of course, themselves indicate that attributions of legitimacy arise in the context of social dynamics between power-holders and audiences that are 'reciprocal and organic' (Barker 2001: 38).

Within this basic research framework, some research studies have also considered attributions of legitimacy within organizations—that is, examining whether lower-level employees ascribe legitimacy to senior managers. Research of this kind began in commercial organizations, but has now been extended to some police forces (see for example Tyler, Callahan, and Frost 2007; De Angelis and Kupchik 2009); a main conclusion has been that procedurally just practices are associated with positive attributions of legitimacy by employees. These are important findings, but they are distinct from the issues being discussed in this chapter. That is because the research in question treats basic-grade police officers as lower-level employees, ascribing or failing to ascribe legitimacy to their superiors, whereas here we are concerned with the 'inner voices' of such officers as they wield power over other citizens.

From the totality of the procedural justice literature, Tom Tyler (2011: 257) has very interestingly concluded that: 'Every encounter that the public have with the police...should be treated as a socialising experience that builds or undermines legitimacy. Each contact is a "teachable moment" in which people learn about the law and legal authorities'. While this comment was, in its original context, specific to the police, there is no reason to suppose that it does not apply equally to every criminal justice agency.

Yet this conclusion, while clearly correct, places an awesome responsibility on the police and other criminal justice services. Why? Because its message is that *any action by any employee of a criminal justice organization* could potentially contribute (to a greater or lesser degree) to either the enhancement or the diminution of the perceived legitimacy of the service as a whole, in the eyes of a relevant audience. Indeed, in the worst-case scenario, a single incident could severely damage the legitimacy of a whole organization.[1] Given this, it seems clear that researchers interested in legitimacy need to consider the many 'teachable moments' that criminal justice power-holders encounter not only from the point of view of the citizen (asking 'does this officer seem to be acting legitimately?'), but also from the point of view of the power-holder. Relevant questions will then include: 'why did this officer act (or fail to act) in this way on this occasion'?, 'what pressures was s/he under?', 'how could such incidents be avoided in future?, and so on.

The importance of studying legitimacy from the point of view of power-holders as well as of audiences is reinforced by two further considerations to which we have previously drawn attention (Bottoms and Tankebe 2012: 152). First, power-holders cannot and should not be expected to carry out their daily work with reference only to current public opinion and responses; and in any case, some aspects of their work—certainly in the case of the police and prison staff—are necessarily secret, so they cannot be subject to immediate public scrutiny. In other words, as Herbert (2006) has rightly argued in relation to the police, a degree of *self-separation* by power-holders is often both appropriate and necessary in exercising authority responsibly. Secondly, a sense of power-holder self-legitimacy may be important for the stability and effectiveness of those in positions of authority. Unless those who exercise power are convinced that there is an adequate moral justification for their continuation in office, and for their daily actions in (say) a given prison or police command area, they are unlikely to be effective. As Boulding (1967) once put it, the loss of what he called 'internal legitimacy' can sometimes lead to 'disorganization of behavior and an inability to perform an assigned role'.

[1] Examples of this in Britain include (1) the seriously flawed 1993 police investigation into the murder of the black teenager Stephen Lawrence, leading eventually to the conclusion in the official *Macpherson Report* (1999) that the Metropolitan Police Service was 'institutionally racist'; and (2) the 1994 escape of six very high-security prisoners from the Special Security Unit at Whitemoor Prison, until then believed to be escape-proof (see Woodcock 1994).

These various considerations strongly suggest that criminologists' study of legitimacy needs to include empirical research into issues of authority and legitimacy from the perspectives of power-holders. However, they do not yet justify the metaphor of a 'dialogic' relationship.

In adopting and developing the metaphor of 'legitimacy as dialogue', we have been particularly influenced by the following short passage in Weber's (1922/1978: 213) *magnum opus*:

> Experience shows that in no instance does domination voluntarily limit itself to the appeal to [citizens'] material or affectual or ideal motives as a basis for its continuance. In addition, every such system attempts to establish and to cultivate the belief in its legitimacy.

As we pointed out in our previous paper (Bottoms and Tankebe 2012: 128), what Weber is saying in this crucial passage is that, as a matter of empirical observation, those in a position to issue commands (power-holders) never simply anticipate that citizens will obey them—whether that obedience stems from 'material motives' (i.e., anticipated benefits or costs to the citizens), an emotional ('affectual') affinity with the power-holder, or 'ideal motives' (such as philosophical or religious beliefs). Rather, power-holders always also attempt 'to establish and to cultivate [among citizens] the belief in [their] legitimacy'. In other words, for Weber *claims to legitimacy* by power-holders are empirically universal, and they are also ongoing (power-holders attempt not only to claim but also *to cultivate* belief in their legitimacy).

Back in the 1920s, Weber had no systematic empirical evidence to support these assertions. However, subsequent empirical evidence in general strongly supports his position (see for example Kertzer 1988, ch. 3), if not quite to the extent that he claimed (as we shall shortly see, it is not true that '*every* such system attempts to [claim] ... legitimacy' in relation to all audiences). Additionally, when power-holders are making their claims to legitimacy, it does seem to be the case, as Dennis Wrong (1995: 103) has put it, that they usually have:

> A need to believe that the power they possess is morally justified, that they are servants of a larger collective goal or system of values surpassing mere determination to perpetuate themselves in power, [and] that their exercise of power is not inescapably at odds with hallowed standards of morality.

This is the 'inner voice' that is the principal subject of this chapter. It would be a mistake, however, to believe that all power-holders have identical inner beliefs and feelings in relation to the power that has been assigned to them—as we shall show later, there is clear empirical evidence of variation in this respect. That variation, coupled with the inevitably variable reactions of different individuals and different communities in response to the use of power by power-holders, makes for some complex variations in legitimacy dialogues.

LEGITIMATION AND LEGITIMACY

So far, we have spoken only of 'legitimacy', using Coicaud's definition of that term. We now need also to introduce the concept of *legitimation*, which—as will become clear—

is a very important topic when considering power-holders' perspectives on legitimacy.

Rodney Barker (2001) has argued that, contrary to the apparent views of some political scientists, rather more than 'a shift of vantage point' is involved in moving from talk of 'legitimacy' to talk of 'legitimation'. 'Legitimation', he suggests, is 'an observable human activity' in which 'rulers engage'.[2] Its central feature is behaviour by rulers through which they 'claim that they possess a distinguishing, specific monopoly of the right to rule' (pp. 23–4). As such, it is both a *characteristic* (p. 30) and a *characterizing* (p. 2) activity of governments and of other power-holders. By contrast to legitimation, Barker argues that legitimacy is 'not a phenomenon that can be [directly] observed'. Rather, it is a property that is ascribed within a set of human relationships; it 'may be actual to the participants, but is to the observer simply a metaphor or hypothetical state or abbreviation employed by those she studies' (p. 24). For these reasons, Barker asserts, there might be merit in adopting 'a working assumption that there is no such thing as legitimacy' and/or that 'it does not exist as a feasible subject of empirical enquiry' (pp. 25–6). More soberly and less provocatively, he proposes that it is in fact necessary to speak about legitimacy when discussing 'the actions of people engaged in politics, ... but when we do so, we are describing their actions and language, not any independent phenomenon, or independent aspect of the institutions they have created' (p. 26).

In our view, Barker does not help his cause by his tendency to offer extreme statements, such as that perhaps we should work with the assumption that there is no such thing as legitimacy. But if we leave aside the rhetorical flourishes, we can discern that he is making two very important points. First, there is a distinction between *legitimation*, which is (for present purposes, but see n 2) an act by which a ruler seeks to make, enhance or cultivate his/her claim to have the right to rule; and *legitimacy*, which is an attribution conferred on a power-holder by his/her audience(s), acknowledging that he/she does indeed have, in the full sense, the right to rule. Secondly, it is important not to regard 'legitimacy' as an 'independent phenomenon', that is, as an ontological entity that exists independently of the day-to-day flow of relationships between power-holders and their audiences. These, we suggest, are crucial points of clarification, and they will be used as significant underpinnings for the remainder of the argument in this chapter.

THE VALUE OF A DIALOGIC FRAMEWORK

We are now in a position to offer a fuller assessment of the value of a dialogic framework for the study of legitimation and legitimacy in criminal justice contexts. In this

[2] Barker (2001: 107) further claimed that 'if one asks "where, by whom and form whom?"' is the activity of legitimation carried on, the answer in almost every case will be 'amongst rulers, by rulers and for rulers'. However, this account omits the rather frequent occasions when citizens go out of their way to express their support (by word or deed) for those in power. That such actions are legitimations of the power-holder becomes particularly clear when the power-holder is being heavily criticized by one section of the public, and the citizens expressing support are consciously attempting to redress the balance. Considerations of this kind led Beetham (1991) to identify legitimation by audiences as the third of his three 'dimensions of legitimacy' (see later, n 5).

connection, we will initially consider three rather different issues—the multiplicity of power-holders; longitudinal dimensions in the study of legitimacy; and—returning to a theme introduced earlier—the ontological status of the concept of legitimacy.

When discussing legitimation, Rodney Barker (2001: 59) argues that 'four aspects' of this are discernible. They are as follows:

> Rulers are legitimating themselves in their own eyes; at the same time they are legitimating themselves in the eyes of their immediate supporters – administrators, advisers, military leaders; the governing community [= rulers + immediate supporters] is legitimating itself collectively in its own eyes; and the governing community is legitimating itself in the eyes of ordinary subjects.

From the perspective of scholars in criminal justice, such an analysis is seriously inadequate, jumping as it does straight from the totality of the 'governing community' to 'ordinary subjects'. Criminal justice systems are, certainly, sometimes strongly shaped by the elite 'governing community', but even within that elite group the judiciary will, in democratic countries, normally wish to legitimate itself as separate from the legislative and executive branches of government, thus considerably complicating the analysis. Moving lower down the hierarchy, local police chiefs, as partially independent officers, will feel the need to legitimate themselves both upwards (to state or national governing communities) and downwards (to citizens). Going lower down still, police officers engaged in daily routine patrol are lowly actors in the hierarchy of their organization, yet to the citizen they are in possession of enormous power, including the power to arrest and detain; and, as power-holders, they regularly engage in legitimacy dialogues as their authority is challenged by citizens in one way or another. It seems to us that the metaphor of 'dialogue' can be of particular analytic assistance when so many claims to legitimacy are being made by so many different actors, often to different audiences.

We suggested in our earlier paper that a longitudinal dimension is an important element in the characterization of legitimacy as a form of dialogue. Power-holders, we argued, make claims to legitimacy; these are responded to by audiences (not always favourably); power-holders might adjust their claims in the light of the audience response; and so on. We illustrated this process through a reconceptualization of part of James Jacobs's (1977) illuminating analysis of events at Stateville Prison, Illinois, over a fifty-year period (Bottoms and Tankebe 2012: 167–8).

We reaffirm here these previous claims about the value of a dialogic approach in studying legitimacy's longitudinal dimensions. However, we also now want to draw attention to a further strand of relevant research which we did not fully discuss in our previous paper. There is significant evidence, in British national surveys, that those members of the public who have had recent contact with the police tend to have a lower estimation of them (Skogan 1994; Scribbins et al. 2010). For present purposes, the direction of the changed opinion is less important than the fact that contact with the police can and does alter the perceptions of citizens. This has led to a realization that 'the way in which behaviors by the police... are interpreted could easily be colored by the mental frame imposed upon the encounter from the outset' by the citizen's prior experiences (Skogan 2012: 276).[3] Such prior understandings can be derived either from individuals' personal encounters with police officers, and/or from more general community experiences.[4] The concept of a 'dialogue' again fits well with this type of evidence, since in ordinary day-to-day conversations people routinely take into account their previous dealings with the person they are speaking to, and how much (or how little) he/she is trusted by them.

As prefigured earlier, we believe that the metaphor of 'legitimacy as dialogue' is also helpful in drawing attention to the ontological status of the concept of legitimacy. Thinking about legitimacy as a continuous dialogue involving a chain of inputs ('claim/response/revised claim/further response') helps us to see that social-scientific analyses of legitimacy need to stay close to the empirical realities of claims and responses in specific social contexts. (On this point, see also Dunn's chapter in this volume.) Accordingly, Barker (2001: 18) is right to claim that some commentators have fallen into a trap: namely, the trap of assuming that:

> since Weber spoke of the ascription of legitimacy and of belief in legitimacy, the historian or political scientist could most profitably proceed by asking the same question as did rulers and their subjects.... [that is]: '*Is this regime legitimate, does it possess legitimacy*?' (emphasis added).

It is in those final questions that the potential trap lies—because if, *as a social scientist* (rather than simply as a citizen) one asks such questions, one can easily slide into a socially reified conception of legitimacy. Such a process would begin by identifying a set of normative requirements for what might be considered necessary in a 'legitimate regime'; these normative requirements would then be used as criteria for assessing a given set of political arrangements, asking 'are they legitimate?'. Moving down this road can quickly lead to the hypostatization of the concept of legitimacy, pulling it away from its claim/response character. This, we suggest, would be a serious ontological mistake.

If, as we propose, one adopts a dialogic approach to the study of legitimacy, then one must also accept that the circumstances in which claims to (and attributions of) legitimacy are made are potentially very variable. That is so partly because of cultural differences between societies (consider, for example, the likely differences between criminal-justice-related legitimacy dialogues in Japan, Russia, Saudi Arabia, and the United States); it is also partly because any dialogue has an element of unpredictability about it, precisely because of its interactive character. Yet this marked empirical variability, which makes social scientists very 'aware that what makes power legitimate in one society may differ from others, and that the criteria for legitimacy in one may be rejected by another' (Beetham 1991: 6) does not necessarily lead to analytic chaos in

[3] We are most grateful to Professor P. A. J. ('Tank') Waddington, who drew these references to our attention.

[4] Rod Brunson (2007) conducted interviews with 40 African-American young men about both their personal and their indirect experiences of police officers. His analysis showed that in most of the experiences initiated by the police, officers' behaviour was described as 'hostile, combative, and threatening.' These experiences were found to have contributed to an 'accumulated body of unfavorable experiences that collectively shaped young men's views of police.' (p. 95).

the study of legitimacy. A major strength of David Beetham's classic monograph on legitimacy lies in his brilliant insight (so far not falsified) that despite the empirical variability of debates about legitimacy in different countries, there is perhaps 'an underlying structure of [audience] legitimacy common to all societies, however much its [specific] content will vary from one to the other' (Beetham 1991: 22). That common underlying structure is hypothesized to consist of three 'dimensions of legitimacy', namely (in shorthand) 'legality', 'shared values' and 'consent'.[5] This framework greatly simplifies the study of the complexities of audience legitimacy (see more fully Bottoms and Tankebe 2012).[6]

Before concluding this discussion of the dialogic metaphor in the study of legitimacy, we should briefly make three final points:

First, if any readers are still sceptical that dialogue is an appropriate metaphor for discussions of legitimacy, we would urge them to read the dialogue between Angelo (the acting ruler of Vienna) and Isabella (one of his subjects) in Act 2 Scene 2 of Shakespeare's *Measure for Measure*. In that scene, Isabella makes a speech of 'white-hot intensity' in which she attacks what she sees as the 'absurd pretensions' (Lever 1965: lxix) of those office-holders like Angelo who misuse the 'little brief authority' (p. 46) that has been assigned to them. Of special interest for the purposes of this chapter, Isabella's speech forces Angelo to rethink his use of authority: in an aside, the audience hears his 'inner voice' saying, 'she speaks, and 'tis such sense' (p. 47). We shall refer again to aspects of this dialogue in later sections of this chapter.

Secondly, if—as we recommend—one employs the metaphor of dialogue in conceptualizing claims to and attributions of legitimacy, then it is also necessary to bear in mind the everyday observation that there are many different types of dialogue—for example, a rational debate in a seminar, an angry exchange between family members, or a grossly unequal dialogue between an authoritarian boss and an employee. In considering any kind of legitimacy dialogue between a power-holder and an audience, we therefore need to consider how the dialogue is being conducted, and the particular context in which it occurs. It is a major strength of the procedural justice literature to have drawn our attention to a form of dialogue that, other things being equal, is more likely than other forms of dialogue to produce attributions of legitimacy by citizens to power-holders.

[5] In more detail, the three dimensions are: (1) conformity to rules (legal validity); (2) justifiability of rules in terms of shared beliefs; and (3) legitimation through expressed consent (Beetham 1991: 20). A very similar set of dimensions was subsequently independently developed by Coicaud (2002) who, because he originally wrote in French, was initially unaware of Beetham's framework.

[6] As this discussion makes clear, adoption of a dialogic framework means that attributions of legitimacy must primarily be studied empirically. That raises the moral difficulty that the great majority of the population of a given country might regard as legitimate an enactment requiring that all members of a small minority group should be executed. Would such a regime rightly be termed 'legitimate'?. We discussed this problem in our previous paper (Bottoms and Tankebe 2012: 156–9) and concluded that, in such a situation, a social scientist should not describe the regime as legitimate; in effect, therefore, we proposed a normative limit on what can be empirically described as legitimate. This approach is similar to Neil MacCormick's solution to the analogous jurisprudential debate about the meaning of 'law': as MacCormick (2007: 277) put it, 'there are moral minima that have to be satisfied by anything one can acknowledge as law'.

But *thirdly*, although we believe that the characterization of legitimacy as dialogue is in most circumstances an excellent way of understanding its main features, we need to acknowledge that it is not universally applicable. In particular, there are some contexts (such as colonial regimes selling people into slavery, or situations of military detention such as Abu Ghraib) in which the power-holder is effectively interested only in power, and makes no claim to legitimacy *in respect of that particular group of people* (see also Mbembe 2001). Studies have shown that in such situations power-holders typically view the dominated group as 'the other', with 'an impassable social gulf between Us and Them' (Taylor 2009: 7–8). In such situations, a dialogue with the dominated is seen by the power-holder as either impossible or inappropriate; and unfortunately, abuses of power all too often ensue. In other words, these situations constitute a 'limiting case: the example of purely coercive, unlimited, arbitrary abuse of one group over another, where legitimacy is absent' (Beetham 1991: 87). This limitation of the dialogic metaphor needs to be acknowledged, but of course it does not detract from the strength of the metaphor in the great majority of contexts. It is moreover encouraging that the eventual fall from power of dictatorial rulers cannot usually be explained without reference to the absence of a legitimacy dialogue.

POWER-HOLDERS, LEGITIMATION, AND IDENTITY

Thomas Luckmann (1987) has said that 'legitimation is [aimed at] making sense of power ... to those who exercise power; to those who are subject to the exercise of power; or to both'. According to this argument (which is more fully developed by Barker 2001), when engaging in legitimation practices power-holders are not only addressing audiences, they are also speaking to themselves—that is, legitimating themselves in their own eyes as holders of legitimate authority. Barker (2001) suggests that this 'self-legitimation' is not simply a boost to the self-confidence of power-holders; rather, it is connected in some quite deep ways to *a person's identity as a power-holder* (hence the title of his book: *Legitimating Identities*).

Legitimation is often attempted through the use of symbols or ritual. But in her dialogue with Angelo in *Measure for Measure*, Isabella argues that ultimately it is the *power-holder's performance of his office* that legitimates him to his subjects, more than the cultural symbols:

> ... Well, believe this:
> No ceremony that to great ones 'longs,
> Not the king's crown, nor the deputed sword,
> The marshal's truncheon, nor the judge's robe,
> Become them with one half so good a grace
> As mercy does (Lever 1965: 42).

Thus, we have three central issues to address in this section: the use of cultural symbols as legitimation; the performance of the duties of an office as legitimation; and the link between acts of legitimation and self-identity. We will first address separately the first two of these topics, and then argue that the three topics are in fact intimately and reciprocally interconnected.

LEGITIMATION THROUGH CULTURAL SYMBOLS

It is well known that power-holders often use symbols and/or rituals to legitimate themselves in the eyes of relevant audiences. A good example of this is to be found in some actions of Louis Philippe, the so-called 'citizen-king', who ruled France from 1830 to 1848. By way of background, France had experienced considerable political turbulence in the 40 years which followed the Revolution of 1789 and the ousting of the Bourbon monarchy: the revolutionaries' own regime had given way to the imperial rule of Napoleon, and then (from 1815) to the restoration of the Bourbon line. On coming to power in 1830, Louis Philippe:

> .....sought to express his political enlightenment and mark the difference between himself and his Bourbon predecessors by bringing back the revolutionary tricolored flag as the national symbol and the singing of the 'Marseillaise' as the national anthem. Both had been banned by the Bourbon rulers.... Just as the Bourbons had sought the delegitimation of the Napoleonic and revolutionary regimes by these measures, Louis Philippe sought to profit from their continuing symbolic power of legitimation (Kertzer 1988: 43).

This example is taken from the work of the anthropologist David Kertzer (1988), who also attempts more generally to explain the ubiquity of symbolic and ritual displays as modes of legitimation. Interestingly, at the beginning of his argument Kertzer articulates an ontological view of legitimacy very close to our own:

> Authority, the belief that a person has the right to exercise influence over others' behavior, is itself an abstraction, and people can conceive of who has authority and who has not only through symbols and rituals. That the same person one moment has no such authority and at a subsequent moment acquires it must be represented through ritual performances. This is why formal ceremonies of induction are universal for public power holders in government (Kertzer 1988: 24).

Kertzer goes on to quote Ernst Cassirer's (1955: 41) interesting comment that 'in rites of initiation, a man... receives... a new self'. Is this correct? Against this view, it could be argued that becoming a police officer or a prison officer is in principle no different from taking on any new occupational role—say, as a management trainee or as an advice worker. There is, of course, some truth in this alternative view—beginning any job involves a complex interaction between the structural demands of the post and the unique characteristics of the individual (see Archer 2000, ch. 9). But in relation to criminal justice power-holders, Cassirer surely has a point: suddenly acquiring the significant power that is involved in being a police or prison officer (including the power to lock up one's fellow citizens) must feel like 'receiving a new self'. Moreover, as we shall see in the next section, not everyone is comfortable with this new self.

Talk of 'a new self' also raises the issue previously mentioned as to whether power-holders' acts of legitimation might be carried out, at least in part, to legitimize themselves in their own eyes. In an extended discussion of this issue, Barker (2001: 51–2) goes so far as to argue that 'it is for their own self-definition, rather than for their justification in the eyes of their subjects, that legitimation is principally conducted'. *Contra* Barker, we think there is little point in trying to quantify whether 'self-legitimation' or 'legitimation to influence an audience' is the more important in the eyes of power-holders (and empirically testing Barker's claim would raise formidable difficulties). But it seems clear to us that self-legitimation does indeed exist. For those who think otherwise, Barker has a compelling response—namely, that acts of legitimation (such as formal dinners or special small ceremonies) quite often occur within private contexts.

As Kertzer notes, the two key types of cultural legitimation are *symbols* and *rituals*. Perhaps the most readily identifiable symbols in a criminal justice context are police uniforms, which have attracted the attention of a number of researchers (for example Bell 1982; Shaw 1973). In some countries, these are exclusive to the police, so that even the use of imitation uniforms in theatre productions may require a police permit—an exclusivity that helps the uniform to serve as a 'certificate of legitimacy' (Joseph and Alex 1972: 723). Of course, uniforms have a utilitarian value (for example, in crowded spaces they make it easy for members of the public to identify who is a police officer); but they also symbolize status, and as such they separate the police from the rest of society. Thus, a uniform can be seen as 'a forceful barrier, a demonstrative separation between the culture of control and the individuality of the controlled'; or, otherwise stated, a boundary marker to maintain the 'cultural identity' of the police and to help to define their 'institutional specificities' (Young 1991: 67).

Collective ceremonial occasions constitute another avenue where a great deal of symbolism of an identity-forming character takes place. For example, the symbolism at the funeral ceremonies of police officers has been shown to reinforce 'the relative place of the police on the social scale' (Manning 1977: 7). According to Manning, police funeral ceremonies act out the police mission and display their most sacred symbols. They therefore serve to 'recoat moral bonds' among officers, and provide an occasion for officers to see their identity and authority portrayed, confirmed, and justified both to themselves and to their audiences.

LEGITIMATION THROUGH PERFORMANCE IN OFFICE

We have seen that, according to Max Weber (1922/1978: 213), every system of domination 'attempts to establish and to cultivate the belief in its legitimacy'. Rodney Barker (2001: 4) asserts what Weber identified in this passage was 'the desire or need for a very particular form of prestige', namely, 'that particular species of prestige which attaches to government'; and he therefore claims more generally that power-holders' acts of legitimation are primarily motivated by a wish for this prestige.

In our view, Barker's analysis is oversimplified, and an alternative approach can be sketched along the following lines. Anthropologists affirm that human beings always live in groups; and according to ethologists (e.g. Hinde 2007, ch. 2) evolution has resulted in humans having the capacity for both 'selfish assertiveness' and cooperation (or 'prosociality'). Given those facts, human groups always need to find ways not only to allow the healthy self-development of individuals and to encourage social cooperation, but also to discourage acts of harmful selfishness. In other words, all human groups face a problem of *order* or *governance*, and this has been rightly described as:

> A genuinely transhistorical problem rooted in inescapable conflict between the interests and desires of individuals and the requirements of society: to wit, the pacification of violent strife and the secure establishment of co-operative social relations, making possible the pursuit of collective goals (Wrong 1994: 36).

If some form of order or governance is, therefore, a transhistorical necessity for human groups, it makes perfectly good sense for some individuals to seek to serve the general good by becoming leaders in a government or other public service. No doubt, such individuals are partly motivated by prestige, but that is certainly not necessarily their only motivation for becoming a power-holder (Fromm 1964). While this is not the place for an extended discussion of Weber's work, we also consider, *contra* Barker, that this broad understanding of issues of social order was very much in Weber's mind when he wrote about the ubiquity of power-holders' 'attempts to establish and to cultivate... belief in [their] legitimacy'.

There is a little empirical evidence in the field of criminal justice that supports this line of argument. For example, Steve Herbert's (2006) detailed ethnographic study of police officers in Seattle found that officers legitimated themselves through their functions, and saw themselves as 'deeply virtuous, as risk-taking protectors of society' (p. 491). Herbert cites the case of an incident narrated by an officer; it involved a young boy who had been involuntarily threatened when a man angrily confronted the boy's mother. To the officer, the incident demonstrated 'the protector role that he necessarily embraces, even when citizens avoid it'. This was because, when the officer arrived at the scene, he found the frightened mother 'barricaded alone in her room, in no position to protect her son' (p. 491).

It is this kind of expressed motivation that Dennis Wrong (1995) had in mind when he argued that power-holders have a need to view themselves as serving a purpose that transcends simply remaining in power. For criminal justice professionals, we suggest, the primary such purpose relates to the maintenance of a just social order. For them, chronic ineffectiveness, actual or perceived, can have important negative implications for how they view the moral validity of their own authority.

In our earlier paper (Bottoms and Tankebe 2012: 146–7), we argued that effective performance could be a key dimension of attributions of legitimacy by audiences, although of course other dimensions are usually also in play. Empirically, also, evidence from research in contexts involving both police work (Tankebe 2013) and prisons (Liebling with Arnold 2004) shows that lack of security can be grounds for audiences to question the legitimacy of power-holders Thus, it seems that effective performance might often fulfil a dual role in relation to the establishment of legitimate authority: it can both form a foundation for audience legitimacy *and* constitute an important aspect of the self-legitimation of power-holders.

INTEGRATING SYMBOLIC LEGITIMATION, PERFORMANCE LEGITIMATION, AND SELF-IDENTITY

In this section, we have considered both symbolic legitimation and legitimation through good performance in office. We have concluded that both are important in understanding the 'voice within' of power-holders, and indeed—although the evidence for this is limited—that both seem to be related in significant ways to the development of their self-identity.

Taking this argument further, we believe it is likely that, among power-holders, symbolic legitimation, performance legitimation and self-identity are intimately and reciprocally connected. Unfortunately, as far as we are aware there is no empirical evidence to support this claim, so instead we offer a literary example, which, we hope, offers some insight into how the three topics considered in this section might be interconnected in the inner life of a power-holder.

The example comes from a novel by Sarah Blake, set in Massachusetts during World War II, and it concerns one of the novel's central characters—Iris, the postmistress of a small coastal town called Franklin. It is vital to the story that, at that time, the mail was a particularly important form of communication, since telephoning over distance was not yet possible, and in wartime conditions people were beginning to be anxious about loved ones in Europe. The post office in Franklin is situated on the seashore, with a tall flagpole outside it. The town's civil defence secretary is very unhappy about the flagpole, because he believes it could be used by enemy shipping as a navigation aid to plot a course into the town's harbour. He therefore urges the postmistress at least to shorten the pole. But Iris is reluctant:

> She crossed the lobby with the flag in her arms.... One couldn't behave as though the post office was just another building, its flagpole just another piece of wood. It represented something. Order... And here at the very heart of the system... the open mailboxes stretched floor to ceiling, ready for her to fill... Here was the thick chaos of humanity rendered into order. Here was a box for each and every family in the town.... Here, the tangled lines of people's lives unknotted, and the separate tones of voices set down upon a page were let to breach the distance. Hand over hand the thoughts were passed. And *hers* was the hand at the end. (Blake 2010: 76, emphasis in original).

Of course, this is only a fictional account. But this passage very well encapsulates, we believe, how an office-holder can gain a real sense of her own identity ('*hers* was the hand at the end') from the efficient and effective functioning of the part of the system that is her responsibility, believing also that the system as a whole fulfils vital public functions. She further realizes (though she had not really thought about this until the discussion about the flagpole was initiated) that, for her, these important public functions need to be recognized and represented by cultural symbols, which in their symbolism become something more than their material substance ('not just another piece of wood'). Symbol, function, and identity are intimately linked.

For obvious reasons, the discussion in this section has been confined to the power-holder's perspective on legitimacy. But we must always remember that legitimation by power-holders takes place within a dialogue with those over whom the power-holder claims legitimacy. This means that, as Barker (2001: 127) has rightly pointed out, if symbolic legitimation 'involves a style or ritual with which [. . .] subjects cannot associate themselves', (as it easily might, for example, in colonial contexts), this can conflict with what in our judgement should be the power-holder's main aim, namely that of 'the cultivation of legitimate relations between governors and governed'. We shall return to this point in the conclusion to this chapter.

POWER-HOLDERS' SELF-PERCEPTIONS OF THEIR AUTHORITY AND LEGITIMACY

A key concept in power-holders' self-understandings of legitimacy is that of *confidence* in their own legitimate authority, but a little reflection on this concept quickly makes one realize that it is double-edged. Thus, for example, the *Shorter Oxford English Dictionary* (Onions 1973) quotes a comment by Dr Samuel Johnson (eighteenth-century English writer and literary critic) that 'self-confidence is the first requisite to great undertakings', but it also reports that 'self-confidence' can often mean 'arrogant or impudent'. There are some fine lines here, which we will need to explore in this section. As we do so, it will become clear that just as citizens' attributions of legitimacy to power-holders are not an either/or judgement, but a matter of degree, so it is also with power-holders' self-confidence in their authority.

THREE EMPIRICAL RESEARCH STUDIES

There is very little empirical research that focuses specifically on power-holders' perceptions of their own legitimacy and authority. We can however usefully begin to address this topic by considering three such research studies which in one way or another have some relevance to this topic.

The first research to be considered is an ethnographic sociological study carried out in the late 1980s at Albany high-security prison in England (Sparks, Bottoms and Hay 1996). In both 1983 and 1985, Albany had experienced major incidents in which staff had lost control of parts of the prison, and on the second of these occasions some members of staff were for a time trapped by prisoners on an upstairs landing (Sparks, Bottoms and Hay 1996: 103). These incidents led to a severe loss of self-confidence among Albany staff. Shortly afterwards, a new Governor of the prison was appointed; in a later interview, he said that on taking office he quickly realized that staff 'were shell-shocked and . . . physically fearful . . . I saw fear and anxiety in people's eyes, and real twitchiness'. He therefore decided that in order to try to improve matters, he would have to 'start from where we are' (p. 136). This involved creating a new regime at the prison, known as the 'restricted regime' because, in particular, it restricted to two-thirds the proportion of prisoners who were allowed out of their cells for 'association' (unstructured leisure activities in the evenings), with the consequence that prisoners now had to spend one evening in three behind their cell door. Although understandably unpopular with prisoners, this regime did have the desired effect of improving the staff's self-confidence in their ability to keep good order in the prison.[7]

There was however an additional complication. A minority of the residential units at Albany were set aside for so-called 'vulnerable prisoners'; that is, those who for their own protection needed to be kept separate from the main prison, in order to protect them from violent assaults and bullying. Prisoners in this 'Vulnerable Prisoner Unit' (VPU) were well known to be mostly compliant, and neither of the earlier incidents of loss of control had involved the VPU. Nevertheless, in the interests of consistency and equity the Governor decided that the 'restricted regime' would have to be introduced in the VPU as well as the main prison. This decision was firmly supported by most staff, but they recognized that it led to problems as regards the behaviour of a minority of staff. As one officer, who regarded himself as a disciplinarian, put it:

> ... they've had years and years working up on the main wings, and they get down here and think 'fucking hell, I don't believe this ... I shouted at him and he never shouted back'.... Then one thing develops into another you see, and ... the power can go to your head easy.... There's a couple of staff, I've drawn them on one side – and not just me, others have as well – and said 'look, there's no need for that' (Sparks, Bottoms and Hay 1996: 214).

This study, while not systematically questioning officers about their use of authority, nevertheless shows clearly: *first,* that power-holders' lack of self-confidence in exercising authority can severely impair their ability to keep order in a prison; and *secondly,* that when the power dimension of the legitimacy dialogue is stacked heavily in favour of the power-holder, it is easy for 'power to go to your head', i.e. for it to be over-used.

The second study to be considered is also ethnographic, but this time it was more focused on individuals. William Ker Muir (1977) conducted detailed interviews with, and some observation of the work of, 28 police officers with eight or fewer years' experience in 'Laconia', a US city with half a million inhabitants. Muir's analysis was in part explicitly normative, seeking to understand how people become 'good' police officers. His eventual argument was that good officers are those who successfully develop two 'virtues': first, being able to 'grasp the nature of human suffering'; and secondly, knowing how to 'resolve the contradiction of achieving just ends with coercive means' (pp. 3–4).

Central to Muir's analysis is the following empirical finding:

> Every policeman[8] I asked insisted that the critical and recurrent part of his job occurred when he was the object of the threats of others and when he, in turn, had to influence people to do those things they were little inclined to do ... At those times, he had only his authority ... [including the threat to use force] to defend or assert himself (Muir 1977: 54).

[7] The new regime was not merely restrictive, although restriction lay at its heart. The Governor also encouraged the staff to develop good relations with prisoners, and to maintain high standards of 'service delivery' in matters such as food and pre-release programmes.

[8] Muir's fieldwork was carried out in the early 1970s, at which time only male officers undertook patrolling duties in the 'Laconia' police service (as in many other police services at that date).

Using the terminology of this chapter, these 'critical' moments were therefore tense legitimacy dialogues between an officer and one or more citizens, in which the officer was aware of being in theory, 'powerful', but in reality under verbal or physical pressure, and therefore certainly not 'absolutely powerful' (p. 4). According to Muir, whether or not officers ultimately develop the two 'virtues' of policing (see earlier) depends in large part on how they handle these critical incidents, in which their 'basic assumptions about human nature and... conventional notions of right and wrong' were often challenged (p. 4).

In Muir's analysis, four types of police officers emerge from this testing process (pp. 56–7). The four types are separated according to their eventual stance on two matters—the capacity to integrate a degree of coercion into their moral approach; and a realistic as opposed to cynical understanding of the human condition (where realism includes 'an inner understanding of [human] motives', a 'sense of life's rhythms of cause and effect' and an appreciation of the fact that much human experience is in part tragic) (pp. 50–1).[9]

Two categories of officer are unable to integrate coercion easily into their moral stance. One is the *reciprocator*, who 'hates' having to use coercion, but well understands the complexities of the human condition. Such officers prefer a lenient and sympathetic posture when dealing with citizens, and justify their approach by reference to a need to nurture citizens' sense of obligation to them; they are therefore sometimes willing (in the short term) to overlook illegal activity in order to build longer-term relationships. The second category (the *avoider*) is also conflicted about the use of force, but in addition he is unable to recognize and to respond adequately to the needs of citizens because of his 'suspicion and bluntness towards the subtleties of human detail' (p. 56). Thus, he becomes passive, and tries 'to avoid risky situations altogether' (p. 35).

The other two categories of officers have successfully embedded the use of force in an integrated way into their moral compass. One such category is the *enforcer*, but officers in this category have a limited understanding of the human condition—they tend to be aggressive and impatient in their use of coercion, and often unaware and unresponsive to 'changes going on inside the citizen's head and heart' (p. 145). Such officers are therefore ill-suited for communities or neighbourhoods that have historically antagonistic relations with police, because their actions are likely to reinforce prior suspicions, rather than to take advantage of 'teachable moments' to build more legitimate relationships. For this task, the *professional* seems more appropriate. Officers in this final category usually avoided 'the naked assertion of the law'. Rather, 'the law was invoked after careful preparation of a foundation of knowledge, or fearfulness, or both. The professional response characteristically involved *teaching through talk*.' (pp. 144–5, emphasis added). In other words, this last category of officers tried to engage in *dialogues through which they would seek to establish attributions of legitimacy*, and then to use that legitimacy to defuse tensions. According to Muir, this kind of 'professional' police officer comes closest to fulfilling the ideal of the 'good' officer:

[9] These two criteria were adapted by Muir (1977: 49–55) from Max Weber's (1948) classic discussion of the dilemmas for politicians of holding coercive power.

he is not conflicted about the use of force, but he also understands and responds well to the complexities of difficult human situations.[10]

Muir's analysis confirms the findings of the Albany research that problems can arise for power-holders in criminal justice contexts when they have insufficient confidence in their own formally assigned authority (the 'avoider' and the 'reciprocator'), but also when they are over-confident ('the enforcer'). But it adds to the Albany findings some interesting results about individual differences in the use of authority, including significant variations in the ability to come to terms with the need to use force—a key feature of policing.[11] It also raises the hypothesis that these individual differences are developed over time largely out of the experiences of on-street encounters between officers and citizens—a hypothesis that might well underplay pre-existing personality traits,[12] but nevertheless raises important questions for more detailed research in the future.

Before leaving Muir's work, we should note that it has been found to be conceptually very useful by prison scholars, although they have not as yet attempted an explicit empirical replication. In particular, Gilbert (1997) developed from Muir's analysis a detailed set of 'discretionary work style descriptors for [police] officers' in each of the four categories identified by Muir, and he then postulated an adapted set of 'descriptors' for corresponding categories among correctional officers (pp. 54–5). The Muir/Gilbert typology has subsequently been constructively utilized by Alison Liebling and colleagues (2011: 52–53) in their work on English prison officers; and Muir's stress on differing attitudes among officers to the human condition of citizens (prisoners)—that is, 'cynical' vs. 'tragic'—has been found to be particularly salient (Liebling 2011: 491–3).[13]

The theme of individual differences was also prominent in the third piece of research to be discussed here; but this research differs from the other two studies because it was explicitly designed to measure police officers' self-confidence in their own authority

[10] Curiously, however, Muir (1977: 144) appeared to be willing to condone some illegal behaviour by those officers in the 'professional' category: 'Any apparent illegality, if there was one, was always put in an understandable and acceptable light, openly and publicly justified'. On legality as a dimension of audience legitimacy, see Bottoms and Tankebe (2012: 137–41).

[11] This point is, of course, of particular interest in view of Weber's (1922/1978: 56) famous assertions that within the modern state 'the use of force is regarded as legitimate only so far as it is either permitted by the state or prescribed by it'; and that such a claim by the state 'is as essential ... as its character of compulsory justification and of continuous operation'.

[12] In the language of contemporary psychology, Muir's explanatory model is primarily 'situationist'; thus he speaks of 'the dynamic process by which the recurrent use of coercive means produces the perspectives and passion to which the professional political model is sensitive' (p. 58). However, there is now 'a wealth of evidence [which] suggests that in seeking to explain [coercive behaviour] ... we need to move beyond the question of whether it is a product of people's dispositions *or* the situation in which they find themselves, to understand instead how these elements combine' (Haslam and Reicher 2012: 139, emphasis in original).

[13] This highlighting of the 'human' dimension over the 'coercive' dimension differs from Muir's original research and it is interesting to speculate why this might be so. Possibly, the work of prison officers involves more sustained contact between officers and law violators than is the case for the police, hence magnifying the importance of differing perceptions of the human condition. Conversely, as we have seen, Muir postulates that the four categories in his typology arise directly out of tense on-street encounters in which the dilemma whether to use force is a constant reality; such encounters are perhaps far less frequent in the more controlled environment of a prison.

and legitimacy, and to examine the conditions that might have shaped these views. The research was a small survey of 181 frontline officers in Accra, Ghana, with a good response rate (82 per cent) (Tankebe 2007). As regards demographic factors, the study found that officers' views of their legitimacy did not differ by gender or by educational level. However, officers differed in their assessments of self-legitimacy according to their length of service; specifically, officers with at least ten years' service were more likely to report more positive views of their own authority (although this relationship was relatively weak statistically). The analysis further showed that the nature of social relations among officers of the same rank, as well as between those at different ranks, shaped views about authority and legitimacy. In particular, officers with the least confident view of their legitimacy were officers who reported strained relationships with colleagues, and who perceived themselves to have been treated unfairly by senior officers. Thus, and congruently with assessments of audience legitimacy (see earlier discussion), procedural justice appears to be a component of self-legitimacy. Finally, and in agreement with some findings reported in the previous section, a perception that the police organization was effective in tackling crime was associated with an increased confidence in self-legitimacy.

As we indicated at the beginning of this chapter, there has to date been a marked dearth of empirical research into criminal justice power-holders' perspectives on their own legitimacy and authority. The three research studies summarized earlier in this section are no more than indicative of the kinds of research that might usefully be pursued in this field in the future.[14] But, on an optimistic note, perhaps even from these three preliminary pieces of research one can begin to see how studies of officers' self-understandings of their authority and legitimacy might in the future be relevant in answering some of the questions that we posed earlier in relation to so-called 'teachable moments'. Those questions were, it will be recalled: 'why did this officer act (or fail to act) in this way on this occasion?', and 'what pressures was s/he under?'

ETHICAL FAILURES BY POWER-HOLDERS

The Oxford philosopher J. R. Lucas (1980: 4–5), in his book on the concept of justice, elaborated a point originally made by Aristotle and suggested that we can best discover what justice is by adopting 'a negative approach', that is, learning about justice by focusing on its opposite (injustice). As Lucas strikingly put the matter: 'If I talk only about justice, I am in danger of relapsing into platitudes: it is when I get hot under the collar about some specific piece of unfairness that my eloquence has an edge to it.'

In a similar manner, perhaps we can gain a better understanding of healthy self-understandings by power-holders through a consideration of what unhealthy self-understandings look like.[15] To begin to address this issue, we can return to Isabella's

[14] It is, however, interesting that they represent three different methodological approaches (a survey; an ethnographic interview study; and an ethnographic sociological study). A similar mixture of methodologies seems likely to pay dividends in the future.

[15] This discussion is limited to normal governmental contexts, and does not include situations of gross abuse of power, as discussed at the end of the first section of this chapter. There is a large literature on these extreme situations, and it is not practicable within the scope of this chapter to enter this territory.

dialogue with Angelo, the temporary ruler of Vienna, in *Measure for Measure*. Towards the end of the discussion, Angelo asks Isabella why she is applying her harsh words to him. She replies:

> Because authority, though it err like others,
> Hath yet a kind of medicine in itself
> That skins the vice o'th'top. (Lever 1965: 47)

Here, Isabella is claiming that power-holders (including Angelo), although they have faults like other people, often find that the very possession of authority provides them with a kind of medicine, or palliative, which covers over ('skins') their vices (Lever 1965: 47). In other words, the possession of power is potentially very corrosive, and power-holders might often be tempted to cover over their vices with the language of authority itself.

Four hundred years later, some remarkably similar conclusions have emerged from the findings of modern psychology. Terry Price's (2006) important book, *Understanding Ethical Failures in Leadership,* draws on broad reviews of the psychological literature, and on selected case studies, to argue that ethical failures in leadership are frequently not *volitional* (that is, based on a deliberate decision to flout the rules, usually motivated by self-interest), but are instead *cognitive* (that is, based on self-justifying exceptionalism—'because I've been put in authority here, I'm entitled to this special treatment/entitled to do this unusual act'). Elaborating this last point, Price (2006: 1) comments that 'the collective nature of the ends to which leaders are committed' provides a special set of cognitive conditions within which they act; or, otherwise stated, a set of conditions that are especially conducive to ethical failure if due diligence is not constantly exercised by the power-holder. Thus, he argues, leaders are probably:

> more inclined than the rest of us to think about their behavior in ways that purportedly [justify] deviations from generally applicable moral requirements. Whether leaders understand their behavior as being distinctive by way of [their] *personal characteristics*, the *extraordinary situations* they face, or the *special norms* to which they are subject, they can appeal to these potentially justifying features to ground the exceptions they make of themselves (p. 8, emphasis added).

Examples of this kind of exceptionalism can, unfortunately, be found in the context of policing. For example, and considering the italicized words in the quoted passage, some officers might wish to justify breaches of laws or of accepted professional standards by reference to their special personal qualities, or the exceptional dangers they face, or the special role of the police service as the 'thin blue line' that ultimately defends society. Hence the phenomenon known as 'noble cause corruption', whereby, for example, an officer might 'doctor' or even completely invent evidence to secure a conviction against a suspect who the police consider to be 'obviously' guilty, but where the legitimate evidence is thin. Another example would concern issues of integrity, where there might be a tendency for some officers to be tempted to accept special 'favours' in various situations, and then to justify their behaviour on the grounds of their special role. Issues of this kind were recently considered, for England and Wales, in a thematic report by Her Majesty's Inspectorate of Constabulary (HMIC) (2011).

Although the report found no evidence of widespread corruption, it also sounded some warning notes; for example:

> The significant variation between [different] forces and authorities in relation to defining and applying standards was stark. This inconsistency made little sense to us... The Police Service needs to undertake work to identify the standards and values expected of its entire workforce, providing clarity on where the boundaries lie. (HMIC 2011: 18).

Unfortunately, where there is no clear official guidance on the appropriate boundaries in relation to these 'integrity' issues, then the scope for justifications of malpractice based on cognitive exceptionalism will be considerable. Not surprisingly, there is also evidence in the HMIC report suggesting that, where malpractice of this kind is observed by the public, it reduces audience legitimacy.

As a final sobering thought in relation to such issues, Bass and Steidlmeier (1999: 188) have identified *authentic transformational leaders* in organizations as persons who are 'inwardly and outwardly concerned about the good that can be achieved for the group, organization, or society for which they feel responsible'. In other words, they are altruists, fully conscious of—and concerned about—the collective good of their local communities. Yet the lesson of Terry Price's analysis that such public commitment does not necessarily protect such leaders from ethical failures, emanating from situations in which power-holders might 'mistakenly believe that their behaviour is justified in the end because the importance of "the good that can be achieved for the group, organization, or society for which they feel responsible" outweighs the moral cost of deviating from applicable moral requirements' (p. 137). As Price puts it, Bass and Steidlmeier's analysis, like 'all theories that lean heavily on the volitional account of ethical failure... underestimates the complexity of the moral psychology of leaders' (p. 9). As we try to develop, within criminology, a better understanding of power-holders' perspectives on authority and legitimacy, it is vital that that complexity is fully taken into account.

CONCLUSION

In this chapter, we have tried to address a topic which scarcely yet exists in the criminological literature, but which, we have suggested, badly needs to be developed if the study of legitimacy in criminal justice contexts is to be taken forward in an optimum fashion. In doing so, we have worked within the dialogic framework for the study of legitimacy that we identified in our previous paper (Bottoms and Tankebe 2012). We hope that, within that framework, we have raised some worthwhile issues for future research and discussion, but we cannot claim to have achieved more than that.

We have agreed with Herbert (2006) that criminal justice power-holders require an element of *self-separation* in performing their tasks, as well as a responsivity to the shared values of their audiences in the communities that they serve. In discussing power-holders' perceptions of their own authority and legitimacy, we have noted the double dangers of under-confidence and over-confidence—if self-confidence is severely lacking, the officer cannot credibly claim authority, but by contrast there is a danger that over-confidence can lead to an overweening sense of power, especially where the audience perceives itself as powerless (as in the VPU at Albany Prison). In addition, we have drawn attention to Price's (2006) important work on those ethical failures by power-holders that are cognitive rather than volitional in character, and can therefore lead to malpractice even by successful and altruistic leaders who are neither over-confident nor under-confident.

We have also discussed legitimation practices by power-holders, and we have seen how symbolic legitimation, performance legitimation, and perceptions of self-identity as a power-holder can work reciprocally and appropriately together. In that sense, legitimation practices should be regarded as a natural and indeed valuable element in healthy power-holding. We have also noted, however, that symbolic legitimation, if taken to extremes and beyond the values that power-holders share with their audiences, can be alienating to audiences, and damage legitimacy.

The latter finding usefully reminds us that, while this chapter has focused on power-holders' perspectives on legitimacy, power-holders are only one party to the legitimacy dialogue. Any sensible power-holder, in making his or her continuing claims to legitimacy, will therefore always take account of the responses of audiences, and, where appropriate, adjust his/her legitimacy claim accordingly.

The preceding summary makes it clear that to exercise well the responsibilities of a criminal justice power-holder can be a difficult matter. It involves confidence but not over-confidence in one's own authority (which in turn will normally require effective performance in office); awareness of the dangers of both flamboyant acts of legitimation and of cognitively-motivated malpractice; and appropriate sensitivity to the shared values of the community or communities within which he or she has been given power. But this is, clearly, only a broad-brush sketch; refining it will require much more empirical research and professional reflection.

REFERENCES

ARCHER, M. S. (2000) *Being Human: The Problem of Agency.* Cambridge: Cambridge University Press.

BARKER, R. (2001) *Legitimating Identities: The Self-Presentation of Rulers and Subjects.* Cambridge: Cambridge University Press.

BASS, B. M. and STEIDLMEIER, P. (1999) 'Ethics, Character and Authentic Transformational Leadership Behavior', *Leadership Quarterly* 10: 181–217.

BEETHAM, D. (1991) *The Legitimation of Power.* London: Macmillan.

BELL, D. J. (1982) 'Police Uniforms, Attitudes and Citizens', *Journal of Criminal Justice* 10: 45–55.

BLAKE, S. (2010) *The Postmistress.* London: Penguin Books.

BOTTOMS, A. E. and TANKEBE, J. (2012) 'Beyond Procedural Justice: A Dialogic Approach to Legitimacy in Criminal Justice', *Journal of Criminal Law and Criminology* 102(1): 119–70.

BOULDING, K. (1967) 'The Legitimacy of Economics', *Western Economic Journal*, 5: 299–307.

Brunson, R. K. (2007) '"Police Don't Like Black People": African-American Young Men's Accumulated Police Experiences', *Criminology and Public Policy* 6: 71–102.

Cassirer, E. (1955) *The Philosophy of Symbol Forms*, (vol 2). New Haven: Yale University Press.

Coicaud, J-M. (2002) *Legitimacy and Politics: A Contribution to the Study of Political Right and Political Responsibility.* Cambridge: Cambridge University Press.

De Angelis, J. and Kupchik, A. (2009) 'Ethnicity, Trust, and Acceptance of Authority among Police Officers', *Journal of Criminal Justice* 37(3): 273–79.

Fromm, E. (1964) *Beyond the Chains of Illusion: My Encounter with Marx and Freud.* London: Continuum.

Gilbert, M. J. (1997) 'The Illusion of Structure: A Critique of the Classical Model of Organisation and the Discretionary Power of Correctional Officers', *Criminal Justice Review* 22: 49–64

Haslam, S. A. and Reicher, S. (2012) 'Tyranny: Revisiting Zimbardo's Stanford Prison Experiment' in J. R. Smith and S. A. Haslam (eds *Social Psychology: Revisiting the Classic Studies.* London: Sage.

Herbert, S. (2006) 'Tangled Up in Blue: Conflicting Paths to Police Legitimacy', *Theoretical Criminology* 10: 481–504.

Hinde, R. (2007) *Bending the Rules: Morality in the Modern World.* Oxford: Oxford University Press.

H.M. Inspectorate of Constabulary (2011) *Without Fear or Favour: A Review of Police Relationships*. London: Home Office.

Jackson, J., Bradford, B., Stanko, E. A., and Hohl, K. (2012) *Just Authority? Trust in the Police in England and Wales.* Oxford: Routledge.

Jacobs, J. B. (1977) *Stateville: The Penitentiary in Mass Society.* Chicago: Chicago University Press.

Joseph, N. and Alex, N. (1972) 'The Uniform: A Sociological Perspective', *American Journal of Sociology* 77: 719–30.

Kertzer, D. L. (1988) *Rituals, Politics and Power.* New Haven: Yale University Press

Kronman, A. T. (1983) *Max Weber.* London: Edward Arnold.

Lever, J. W (ed) (1965) *Measure for Measure* (The Arden Shakespeare). London: Routledge.

Liebling, A. (2011) 'Distinctions and Distinctiveness in the Work of Prison Officers: Legitimacy and Authority Revisited', *European Journal of Criminology* 8(6): 484–99.

Liebling, A. with Arnold, H. (2004) *Prisons and their Moral Performance: a Study of Values, Quality and Prison Life.* Oxford: Oxford University Press.

Liebling A., Price D., and Shefer, G. (2011) *The Prison Officer* (2nd edn) Abingdon: Willan Publishing.

Lucas, J. R. (1980) *On Justice.* Oxford: Clarendon Press.

Luckmann, T. (1987) 'Comments on Legitimation', *Current Sociology* 35: 109–17.

MacCormick, N. (2007) *Institutions of Law*. Oxford: Oxford University Press.

Macpherson, W. (1999) *The Stephen Lawrence Inquiry: Report of an Inquiry by Sir William Macpherson of Cluny*. Cm 4262-I. London: The Stationery Office.

Manning, P. K. (1977) *Police Work: The Social Organisation of Policing.* Cambridge, Mass.: MIT Press.

Mbembe, A. (2001) *On the Postcolony*. Berkeley: University of California Press.

Muir, W. K., Jr (1977) *Police: Streetcorner Politicians.* Chicago: University of Chicago Press.

Onions, C. T. (ed) (1973) *The Shorter Oxford English Dictionary on Historical Principles* (3rd edn). Oxford: Clarendon Press.

Price. T. (2006) *Understanding Ethical Failures in Leadership.* Cambridge: Cambridge University Press.

SCRIBBINS, M., FLATLEY, J., PARFREMENT-HOPKINS, J., and HALL, P. (2010) 'Public Perceptions of Policing, Engagement With the Police and Victimisation: Findings From the 2009/10 British Crime Survey', *Home Office Statistical Bulletin 19/10*. London: Home Office.

SHAW, L. (1973) 'The Role of Clothing in the Criminal Justice System', *Journal of Police Science and Administration* 4: 414–20.

SKOGAN, W. G. (1994) *Contacts Between Police and Public: Findings from the 1992 British Crime Survey*. London: HMSO.

SKOGAN, W. G. (2012) 'Assessing Asymmetry: The Life Course of a Research Project', *Policing and Society* 22: 270–9.

SPARKS, R., BOTTOMS, A. E., and HAY, W. (1996) *Prisons and the Problem of Order*. Oxford: Clarendon Press.

TANKEBE, J. (2007) 'Policing and Legitimacy in a Post-Colonial Democracy: A Theoretical and Empirical Study of Ghana'. PhD Thesis, Cambridge: University of Cambridge.

TANKEBE, J. (2013) 'Viewing Things Differently: The Dimensions of Public Perceptions of Police Legitimacy', *Criminology* 51: 103–35.

TAYLOR, K. (2009) *Cruelty: Human Evil and the Human Brain*. Oxford: Oxford University Press.

TYLER, T. R. (2006a) 'Psychological Perspectives on Legitimacy and Legitimation', *Annual Review of Psychology* 57: 375–400.

TYLER, T. (2006b) *Why People Obey the Law*. (revised edn) New Haven: Yale University Press.

TYLER, T. (2011) 'Trust and Legitimacy: Policing in the USA and Europe', *European Journal of Criminology* 8: 254–66.

TYLER, T., CALLAHAN, P., and FROST J. (2007) 'Armed, and Dangerous(?): Motivating Rule Adherence Among Agents of Social Control', *Law and Society Review* 41(2): 457–92.

WEBER, M. (1948) 'Politics as a Vocation', in Gerth, H. H. and Mills, C. W. (eds) *From Max Weber: Essays in Sociology*. London: Routledge and Kegan Paul.

WEBER, M (1922/1978). *Economy and Society: An Outline of Interpretive Sociology*. (2 vols), Roth, G. and Wittich, C (eds). Berkeley and Los Angeles, CA: University of California Press.

WOODCOCK, J. (1994) *Report of the Enquiry into the Escape of Six Prisoners from the Special Security Unit at Whitemoor Prison, Cambridgeshire, on Friday 9th September 1994*. Cm.2741. London: HMSO.

WRONG, D. (1994) *The Problem of Order: What Unites and Divides Society*. Cambridge, MA: Harvard University Press.

WRONG, D. (1995) *Power: Its Forms, Bases and Uses*. (revised edn) London: Transaction Publishers.

YOUNG, M. (1991) *An Insider Job: Policing and Police Culture*. Oxford: Clarendon Press.

5

FUTURE CHALLENGES IN THE STUDY OF LEGITIMACY AND CRIMINAL JUSTICE

Tom R. Tyler and Jonathan Jackson

INTRODUCTION

Twenty years ago, when one of us published *Why People Obey the Law* (Tyler 1990), a central part of the argument was that legitimacy plays an important role in shaping people's law-related behaviour. The influence of the perceived legitimacy of the police and law on everyday compliance was shown to be both distinct from, and larger than, judgements about the likelihood of being caught and punished.

The argument that legitimacy matters was striking at the time, because the general intellectual climate was focused not on values but on the gains and losses assumed to motivate the rational actor. Scholars and practitioners were well aware of the limits of deterrence models. But given the presumed centrality of costs and benefits to people's calculations about their law-related behaviour, they also felt that there were no clear alternative approaches. Drawing upon the literature in psychology, it was possible to build upon a tradition that placed greater emphasis upon the role of values—rather than rational choice—in shaping behaviour (Tyler 2011).

Today the limitations of rational choice models are more widely recognized (Caplan 2007; Green and Shapiro 1994). Empirical research has demonstrated that deterrence calculations have, at best, a weak relationship to law-related behaviour. In the case of American drug use, one study found that only approximately five per cent of the variance in citizen drug use can be explained by citizen judgements of the likelihood of being caught and punished by the police and courts (MacCoun 1993). This conclusion is typical of the findings of studies of compliance with the law, in which deterrence is generally found to have a small influence on most people's behaviour.

More general reviews of deterrence research conclude that the relationship between risk judgements and crime is 'modest to negligible' (Pratt et al. 2008: 383), and that the 'perceived certainty [of punishment] plays virtually no role in explaining deviant/criminal conduct' (Paternoster 1987: 191). Studies of the effect of the death penalty suggest that the argument that capital punishment deters crime 'still lacks clear proof' (Weisberg 2005: 163). A recent methodological critique concluded that the econometric literature on capital punishment, imprisonment, and deterrence has not yet provided '...*any* causal evidence on the deterrence question' (Charles and Durlauf 2013: 46).

Studies of punishment also suggest that it is ineffective in deterring the *future criminal conduct of those being punished.* The widespread punishment of minor crimes does not generally lower the rate of subsequent criminal behaviour, as would be predicted by models of specific deterrence (Harcourt 2001; Harcourt and Ludwig 2006). Studies of more severe punishment, like imprisonment, find that more severe punishments are not related to lower rates of later criminality (Lipsey and Cullen 2007; Lynch and Sabol 1997). In fact, studies of juveniles suggest that incarceration increases the likelihood of later criminality (McCord et al. 2001).

Taken together these various critiques of instrumental models suggest that they have striking limits. Given these findings today, giving serious consideration to the importance of legitimacy seems very reasonable.

LEGITIMACY, PROCEDURAL JUSTICE, AND PROCESS-BASED POLICING

The findings reported in *Why People Obey the Law* were important because they showed a robust association between legitimacy and compliance with the law. The primary empirical method for operationalizing legitimacy was to measure both obligation and trust and confidence. The predictive power of legitimacy on compliance was then determined using a panel study, in which respondents were asked about both their personal contacts with the police and courts, and their everyday behaviour in relationship to the law.

Since that early work, legitimacy has been linked to a variety of positive effects on important law-related behaviours. Numerous studies, which have conducted in an increasing number of different countries, support this basic argument, with legitimacy explaining variation in compliance with the law (Sunshine and Tyler 2003; Tyler 2006; Tyler and Fagan 2008; Jackson et al. 2012a), as well as the willingness to defer to the decisions of police officers and judges (Tyler and Huo 2002), to continue to accept decisions over time (Tyler et al. 2007), to cooperate with legal authorities (Tyler et al. 2010; Jackson et al. 2012b), and to believe that the criminal justice system has a rightful monopoly over the use of force in society (Jackson et al., 2013). Studies also show why people view the police and courts as legitimate. People focus on the fairness of the manner in which authorities exercise their authority (i.e. on procedural justice), with such procedural justice judgements distinct from—and typically more important than—evaluations of the favourability or fairness of outcomes.

What is striking in these studies is the degree to which performance issues are not central to public evaluations (Benesh 2006). Legitimacy is primarily an issue of procedural justice, although performance has some influence. For example Tyler (2001) analysed several surveys of public views of the courts and found that issues such as delay and cost, while often mentioned in critiques of the courts by journalists and public figures, exerted a minor influence on public trust and confidence in the courts—a finding replicated in a study of the California courts (Rottman 2005). Similarly, Sunshine and Tyler (2003) found that judgements of police performance in fighting crime and estimates of the risk of being caught and punished for wrongdoing (which is an index of whether the police can present a credible threat to wrongdoers) were weak predictors of legitimacy.

Several aspects of these findings are significant for public policy. The first aspect is the powerful nature of procedural justice. Studies of personal experiences suggest that the fairness of procedures can be five or six times as important as the nature of the outcome (Tyler and Huo 2002), and that this effect is strong even when those outcomes are negative. When people do not get what they want or feel they deserve, they still care about the procedures involved. Second, studies make clear that legal authorities can enforce the law and still build legitimacy. Tyler and Fagan (2008) found that even when delivering negative outcomes, police officers could build legitimacy by acting in fair ways.

Third, it is possible to implement procedural justice-based improvements in realistic and do-able ways. For example, the police in Queensland altered procedures in drink-driving stops, increasing their legitimacy in the eyes of those who were stopped by the police (Mazerolle et al. 2013). Similarly, the administrative offices of the government in the Netherlands trained those handling grievances to use fair procedures. This reduced time to close cases, lowered costs, increased citizen satisfaction, and heightened staff morale (Van der Velden 2009). Other agencies have increased legitimacy by soliciting citizen feedback about policies and practices by re-contacting those who request help to see if their problems have been dealt with; and/or other similar approaches. The changes involved are not costly or difficult.

Fourth, these approaches do not put officers at risk. Using evidence collected in observer-based studies of police-citizen encounters in Indiana and Florida to explore the role of police coercion in motivating citizen compliance, McCluskey (2003: 100) found that for initial requests by the police for compliance '[s]urprisingly the coercive power that police bring to bear on a citizen in the form of commanding, handcuffing, arresting and so on, has a minimal impact on citizen's compliance decision.' At later points in the interaction, McCluskey found that 'the higher the level of coercive power displayed by police, the less likely targets are to comply.... For every one unit increase the index of coercion citizens are about twice as likely to rebel against the self-control request' (p. 108). This led him to conclude that '[t]hough coercion may be a central component of the police role, it appears to serve little to enhance compliance when first asked or when requests are repeated by the police (p. 173). This accords with the idea that '[t]he best officers are those who use less, not more force' (Terrill 2001: 232). In contrast to the general ineffectiveness of coercion, McCluskey found that when the police use procedures that are fair, compliance increases substantially. Identifying three distinct aspects of procedural justice—ethicality, information seeking, and decision making—and showing that each independently contributes to the general increase in initial compliance that results from procedural justice, McCluskey (2003) described people as 'seekers of justice' (p. 173).

Finally, while the target for many of the procedural justice programmes has been the general public, there is also evidence that these approaches are helpful in dealing with people involved in more serious crimes. It is important to ask whether 'hardcore' criminals are sensitive to issues of procedural justice, as well as whether they engage in value-based behaviours. Tyler and Huo (2002) focused upon the respondents within their general population sample that were young, minority males. They then explored the basis of the reactions to personal experiences with legal authorities among the members of this group. Their results indicated that this group was as focused upon issues of procedural justice in making acceptance decisions as was the general minority population and, beyond that, people in general.

Tyler and Casper (Casper, Tyler, and Fisher 1988; Tyler, Casper, and Fisher 1989) analysed the results of a panel study of defendants (who were generally young, minority, and male) arrested for felonies. They found that the evaluations of the procedural justice of the case disposition process made by these defendants had a strong influence upon their satisfaction with their experiences, and was the primary factor in shaping their generalization from their personal experience to their overall views about the legitimacy of the law and the legal system.

Other studies suggest that procedural justice plays an important role in shaping the attitudes and behaviours of 'criminals'. Research has shown that the procedural justice of prisons is related to inmate behaviour (Bottoms 1999; Gray 2007; Sparks, Bottoms, and Hay 1996), that the justice of criminal procedures influence recidivism (for drug courts see Gottfredson, et al. 2007; McIvor 2009; for post-release meetings with prior offenders, see Papachristos et al. 2009; Taxman et al. 1999), that procedural justice shapes the reactions of domestic violence suspects (Paternoster et al. 1997), and that issues of quality of treatment by peers and authorities are central to the actions of the members of juveniles and the members of gangs (Bourgois 1995; Crawford 2009; Emler and Reicher 1995; Hinds 2007, 2009).

LEGITIMACY AND THE EXERCISE OF LEGAL AUTHORITY

The argument that legitimacy matters (and that procedural justice drives legitimacy) is becoming increasingly popular. Several factors motivate this heightened influence on the policies and practices of legal authorities. One is the increased recognition that improvements in the objective performance of legal actors have not been translated into increasing legitimacy, meaning that legitimacy needs to be addressed as an issue in and of itself. Second, budget pressures make enacting deterrence and performance-based models more challenging. Finally, in the US the continuing racial gap in legitimacy has been recognized, but it has been seen as politically difficult to enact policies designed to aid one racial group. Crucially, procedural justice is a strategy that is colourblind. It argues for treating everyone fairly. But doing so addresses the primary concerns of minority groups about legal authorities.

If the legal authorities viewed legitimacy as another core goal of their policies and practices, then those policies and practices would be viewed from an enlarged lens that moves beyond issues of legality and effectiveness. For the police, legitimacy provides a way to think about policies such as racial profiling, zero order policing, aggressive street stops, and undercover surveillance of Muslims. For the courts, legitimacy is a way to consider the value of restorative justice conferences, drug courts, problem solving courts, mental health courts, and other alternatives to traditional adjudication. For corrections, legitimacy creates a conceptual framework through which one can assess indeterminate sentencing, actuarial risk assessment, three strikes laws, 'supermax' prisons, and policies such as solitary confinement. All of these policies and practices would be evaluated not only through reference to their legality and effectiveness, but also in terms of their influence on legitimacy.

RECONCEPTUALIZING LEGITIMACY

Given the strong theoretical, empirical, and practical case for the value of legitimacy, now seems a good time to 'take stock'. Like Bottoms and Tankebe (2012) we believe that it is important to re-examine and expand the way we think about and operationalize legitimacy. Such an enterprise will help us move beyond the framework drawn from the existing empirical literature in the 1980s and 1990s.

In early studies into police legitimacy, felt obligation to obey legal authorities was operationalized through survey questions like: 'People should obey the law even if it goes against what they think is right' and 'You should obey the police, even if you disagree with the reasons for the action.' Trust and confidence was measured using items such as: 'On the whole Chicago police officers are honest' and 'The basic rights of citizens are well protected by the Chicago courts.' These items were combined into one index of legitimacy. Capturing both authorization and motive-based trust, this index accords with the idea that to find an authority to be legitimate is to feel that it is one's duty to obey the instructions of police officers and judges (one grants legal institutions the authority to dictate appropriate behaviour) and that those authorities have one's best interests at heart (one believes that the power is being exercised in ways that are normatively justified).

When thinking about reconceptualizing the concept of legitimacy, it is important to ask why legitimacy influences behaviour. From a psychological perspective, legitimacy is a motivation to act based on positive and intentional beliefs about the right to power and influence. In particular, when one recognizes the legitimacy of an institution, one believes that the institution has the right to prescribe and enforce appropriate behaviour, and that one has a corresponding duty to bring one's behaviour in line with that which is expected. Kelman and Hamilton (1989) refer to legitimacy as 'authorization' to reflect the idea that a person authorizes an authority to determine appropriate behaviour within some situations, and then feels obligated to follow the directives or rules that authority establishes. As they indicate, the authorization of actions by authorities:

> ...seem[s] to carry automatic justification for them. Behaviorally, authorization obviates the necessity of making judgments or choices. Not only do normal moral principles become inoperative, but – particularly when the actions are explicitly ordered – a different type of morality, linked to the duty to obey superior orders, tends to take over. (Kelman and Hamilton 1989: 16)

Legitimacy is typically framed as a value that leads the person holding it to feel a responsibility and obligation to defer to the law and the decisions of legal authorities. Psychologists have a key mechanism through which people take on values—internalization (Kelman and Hamilton, 1989). Internalization is typically linked to discussion of morality, i.e. how people take on social and moral values, and is central to the work of, among others, Freud, Weber, and Durkheim. Hoffman (1977: 85) writes:

> The legacy of both Sigmund Freud and Emile Durkheim is the agreement among social scientists that most people do not go through life viewing society's moral norms as external, coercively imposed pressures to which they must submit. Though the norms are initially external to the individual and often in conflict with [a person's] desires, the norms eventually become part of [a person's] internal motive system and guide [a person's] behavior even in the absence of external authority. Control by others is thus replaced by self-control [through a process labeled internalization].

The obligation to obey an element of the legitimacy scale reflects the internalization of the value that it is morally or ethically just to obey the police and the law, e.g. that it is appropriate to obey authorized authorities. The second aspect of legitimacy is trust and confidence in the authorities. This reflects an assessment of their character and motivation (Tyler and Huo 2002). If people feel that the authorities are sincere, benevolent, and concerned about their welfare, then they trust them to act in ways that benefit the people over whom they exercise authority. This is an endorsement of the moral validity of power. Citizens trust that power-holders exercise their power in ways that encapsulate subordinate interests.

What forms of law-related behaviour does legitimacy shape? Extant findings show that people tend to cooperate, comply, and accept the state's monopoly of the use of force when they believe that agents of the law are rightful holders of authority and when they view the legal system as conferring upon them an appropriate and reasonable duty to obey. Feelings of trust and confidence in the police and courts—and a willingness to defer to their instructions—generate the belief that authorities have the right to define appropriate behaviour; encourage the perception that authorities are justified in expecting feelings of obligation and responsibility from citizens; and strengthen identification with the goals, motives, and moral purpose of legal authorities.

Legitimacy is thus a quality that is possessed by an authority, law, or institution that leads others to feel obligated to accept its directives. It is 'a quality attributed to a regime by a population' (Merelman 1966: 548). When people ascribe legitimacy to the system that governs them, they become willing subjects whose behaviour is strongly influenced by official (and unofficial) doctrine. They also internalize a set of moral values that is consonant with the aims of the system. And—for better or for worse—they take on the ideological task of justifying the system and its particulars (see also Jost and Major 2001).

As Kelman (1969: 278) puts it:

> It is essential to the effective functioning of the nation-state that the basic tenets of its ideology be widely accepted within the population... This means that the average citizen is prepared to meet the expectations of the citizen role and to comply with the demands that the state makes upon him, even when this requires considerable personal sacrifice.

Widespread voluntary cooperation with the state and the social system allows authorities to concentrate their resources most effectively on pursuing the long-term goals of society. Legitimacy activates self-regulatory mechanisms: people defer to, and cooperate with, legitimate authorities because they feel it is appropriate to do so. Hence, the authorities do not need to provide incentives or sanctions to all citizens to get them to support every rule or policy they enact.

BROADENING OUR CONCEPTION OF LEGITIMACY: CONSENT, LEGALITY, AND SHARED VALUES

Yet, while the support for the core argument that legitimacy promotes compliance is strong, two related aspects of this literature are noteworthy. First, the magnitude of legitimacy effects is often, at best, moderate in strength. While typically more important than deterrence judgements, legitimacy assessments have a modest impact. In particular, evaluations of the morality of behaviour are often found to have a stronger influence upon behaviour. Second, the operationalization of legitimacy has been narrow, reflecting the limited manner in which legitimacy has been theoretically framed. Ironically, while legitimacy has been recognized as central to governance since at least the writing of Plato, the empirical study of legitimacy effects has been limited until recent years.

An obvious need for future research is to assess the impact of legitimacy using better measures. This requires better conceptual models from which to draw empirical indicators of legitimacy. Fortunately, several recent bodies of scholarship are contributing to this effort. We first turn to Bottoms and Tankebe's (2012) argument for a conception of legitimacy that draws more upon the political science literature. While their argument is theoretical, it is important to consider its implications for empirical research on legitimacy. We will focus particularly upon their elaboration of the Beetham/Coicaud threefold conceptualization of legitimacy as not just *consent*, but also *legality* and *shared values* (Beetham 1991; Coicaud 2002).[1]

Consent refers to the agreement of the members of the public with decisions made by authorities. As Bottoms and Tankebe (2012: 114) state, consent '... precludes the

[1] Bottoms and Tankebe (2012: 137) argue that only consent is constitutive of legitimacy, and that legality and shared values are '... explanatory variables seemingly influencing audience legitimacy'. This raises an interesting definitional ambiguity. Is legitimacy defined by what constitutes it, or does it also include what shapes it? And is legality and shared values constitutive only of power-holder legitimacy, and consent constitutive only of audience legitimacy?

use of external means of coercion; where force is used, authority itself has failed'. Interestingly, they note that Raz (1986: 135) recognizes pre-emptive consent, in which citizens agree '...in advance to treat the appropriately enacted laws and the appropriately formulated orders of the State as superseding and replacing his/her own judgment'. This discussion of consent raises two important issues for empirical research.

The first is how to measure truly free consent. How do we distinguish free consent from pragmatic or strategic consent (from people without the power to resist)? If we ask someone whether they 'should obey the police even when they think the police are wrong', then agreement is typically used to reflect the view that the police are legitimate. But it could also reflect the view that it is dangerous to defy the police, or that one has little choice but to be obedient and comply. Hence, at least some of the questions used to measure obligation may be ambiguous in meaning.

The classic response to this methodological problem is to ask about feelings of duty and obligation (without reference to the content of any particular decision or rule) in anonymous or confidential interview situations, in which people can respond without concern for the power of authorities. For example, Round five of the European Social Survey (ESS) (Jackson et al. 2011, 2013; European Social Survey 2011, 2012; Hough et al. 2013a, 2013b) asked individuals (in personal interviews in a person's home) whether they believe that it is their duty to do what the police tell them to do (even when they do not understand or agree with the reasons). In such a situation, it seems unlikely that the prospect of police force or intimidation from officers is forefront in many people's minds. People seem to be reporting whether they feel a general sense of duty to obey, not whether they would feel intimidation by officers in a particular situation.

Moreover, the use of the word 'duty' seems to lift us above the sentiment that one would comply because one has little choice. Obligation involves a social, legal, or moral tie—it is a constraining power of a promise, contract, law, or sense of duty. Asking people whether it is their 'duty' to obey the police seems to capture a positive sense of obligation (something that one is expected or required to do out of moral or legal obligation) rather than a negative sense of obedience out of fear of reprisal or a sense of powerlessness. And importantly, a note to the ESS interviewers (to clarify the questions to respondents if necessary) and translators of the questionnaire (to ensure comparable and appropriate meaning across different languages) defined duty as 'a citizen's moral duty to the state.' Such measures of perceived obligation thus seem to reflect pre-emptive consent—in this sense the research seems well designed to reflect the theoretical framework.

Second, the finding of widespread and significant procedural justice effects on legitimacy is particularly relevant in this discussion. People who fear reprisal or intimidation from officers are unlikely to believe that the police wield their power in just ways. They are unlikely to believe that the police would give them voice (including them in decision-making processes), would be neutral when they make decisions (acting on the consistent application of rules based on proper procedure rather than on personal opinions or prejudices), would treat them with respect and dignity, and act out of a sincere desire to do what is right.

Importantly, study after study has shown strong positive associations between procedural justice and felt obligation (Tyler and Huo 2002; Sunshine and Tyler 2003; Tyler 2006; Tyler and Fagan 2008; Jackson et al. 2012a, 2012b). Looking across the empirical evidence, felt duty to obey seems to be rooted in positive connections to authorities (established by experience or expectations of procedural justice) rather than dull compulsion or some kind of fear of reprisal if they did not acquiesce. For example, a recent survey of 1,000 young males from various black and ethnic minority communities in London found that around half of the variance in felt obligation to obey the police was explained by perceptions of police effectiveness and procedural fairness, and by far the biggest statistical effect was from perceived procedural fairness (Jackson et al. 2012a; see also Jackson et al. 2013). Among this population of young men from ethnic minority backgrounds, who typically have a more fractious and adversarial relationship with the police, those who felt an obligation to obey the police seemed extremely unlikely also to fear reprisal or feel a dull compulsion to obey. When they said they felt obligated to obey the police, they also tended to believe that the police are procedurally just; it is unlikely that they were also worried about retaliation, force, or intimidation from officers because a procedurally just police force does not impose its will in unfair ways, whether by force or intimidation.

The converse of the finding just outlined was that the more people felt that the police were procedurally unfair, the less likely they were to feel obligated to obey. In such instances, a felt lack of obligation seems to be the rejection of the authority of a seemingly unjust police force. Extant empirical evidence suggests that people who do not feel obligated to obey the police—who tend also to believe that the police are not procedurally fair—precisely because they believe that the police act in ways that preclude true legitimacy (e.g., when they do not treat people with dignity, make unfair decisions, use force, or intimidation). Feelings of duty and obligation thus seem to fall away when the police do not seem to wield their power in fair and just ways.

Finally, it is important to recognize that people never give total pre-emptive consent. Legitimacy always has limits. Tyler (2005) points out that while people often express a general sense of obligation to obey authorities and laws, their responses also reflect the view that there are limits. People recognize that 'there are times when it is perfectly all right for people to disobey' and that 'it is important for people to learn when to question authority'. Hence, pre-emptive consent always has a scope, as we would hope it would. For example, Kelman and Hamilton (1989) discuss the damage which occurs when people in organizations uncritically obey orders that are morally questionable.

Shared values are the 'shared beliefs and values of a given society' or 'those moral beliefs to which people appeal for the ultimate rationales of action' or 'core values'. A theoretical framework for the influence of shared moral values on both cooperation and compliance has recently been tested (Jackson et al. 2012a, 2012b; see also Robinson and Darley 1995, 1997). In this work, people who felt aligned with the moral values of the police (Sunshine and Tyler 2003) also tended to accept the authority of the police and courts, cooperate with the police, and comply with the law (Jackson et al. 2012a,

2012b). That procedural justice was an extremely strong predictor of moral alignment is consistent with the idea that wielding one's power in fair and just ways provides a justification for the possession of power in the eyes of citizens (as well as a motivation for citizens to act based on group identification).

Identification may thus be another mechanism (alongside internalization) by which legitimacy shapes law-related behaviour. According to the group engagement model (Tyler and Blader 2000, 2003), authorities convey a sense of respect and inclusion to subordinates when they wield their power in fair ways. Pride and status encourages identification with the group, and identity judgements then shape attitudes, values, and cooperative behaviour. Pride, respect, and group identification—activated by the use of fair procedures—may consequently encourage not just a felt obligation to obey the rules of the group, but also a (connected) sense of shared moral values and purpose. The status and identity information conveyed by procedural justice may combine with the activated sense of shared moral values to strengthen one's *identification* with the group. Moral alignment may strengthen the motivation to accept legal authority and abide by the rules of the group because (a) the goals accord with one's moral values, (b) the interests of the group become one's own interests, and (c) people value the social connection they have with the police and the community that the police represent.

Moral alignment can be seen as a constitutive element of legitimacy, because it embodies a sense of normative justifiability of power and authority in the eyes of the citizens. When officers wield their power in fair and just ways, this seems to imbue them with a sense of appropriate moral purpose and values in the eyes of citizens, in turn generating and sustaining the moral validity of the power and authority of the role and institution (Jackson et al. 2012a, 2012b). Operating within an appropriate ethical and normative framework (principally by wielding power in fair, just, and neutral ways) thus seems to validate power possession in the eyes of citizens (Hough et al. 2013a, 2013b). How individual officers act shapes the legitimacy of their role—specifically the moral right to exercise power.

There is, however, a difficulty with viewing moral alignment (shared moral standpoints) as an aspect of legitimacy in diverse multicultural societies. If the people within a political entity do not share a common set of moral values, then it will be harder for government authorities such as the police or the courts to represent shared values, and harder for them to invoke values as a source of authority. It will also be harder for legal authorities to enforce laws that do not reflect moral values, shared or not. When the police are trying to enforce laws against using drugs or illegally downloading music and films, they will have difficulty drawing upon a shared value structure because many people do not view such behaviours as immoral. As with parking violations or speeding, many people do not view breaking such laws as wrong, and adopt a more instrumental 'try to catch me' attitude toward their behaviour.

But the extremely strong association between trust in police fairness and moral alignment suggests that procedural justice is a central way in which authorities demonstrate their moral values. Moral alignment may not depend too strongly on consensual views among different communities. Procedural justice sits above diverse value positions—two parties in an interaction (indeed, in an argument) do not have to agree with each other on the specific issue at hand to treat each other with respect and dignity, allow each other a voice, and develop a sense of mutual trust. Fair treatment and fair decision making may demonstrate to citizens that police officers respect their views and values, and are thus working to a broad set of appropriate moral standards that recognize the worth of citizens and give the officers a rightful claim to power and authority. Wielding authority in a fair manner may thus communicate to individuals that police power is based on shared norms of conduct and shared moral positions. How the police treat people and make decisions may communicate to citizens that they are group exemplars of morality in society.

Bottoms and Tankebe (2012) also discuss the possibility that *procedural justice* and *effectiveness* are constitutive parts of legitimacy rather than a causal factor shaping legitimacy. This raises an interesting question. Are assumptions, inferences, or expectancies about fairness (and effectiveness) part of legitimacy? Or are they best seen as judgements that shape legitimacy? Tankebe (2013) includes in his composite scale of legitimacy measures such as 'The police would treat you with respect if you had contact with them for any reason' (a measure of procedural justice), 'People usually receive the outcomes they deserve under the law' (a measure of distributive justice), and 'How well do the police enforce road legislation to improve traffic flows?' (a measure of effectiveness). The question is whether these measures reflect judgements of actions of and therefore the trustworthiness of the police, which involve assessments of, and assumptions about, the intentions and abilities of the police to do what they are trusted to do, e.g. to be fair, to be effective, etc. Or do they reflect a psychological state of legitimacy—judgements of the right to power, to prescribe behaviour, and enforce laws?

Distinguishing between judgements of trustworthiness and judgements of legitimacy remains an important and ongoing challenge in this area of research. From the perspective of Hardin (2006), to find the police trustworthy is to assume that they have the intentions and competence to be effective and fair (Jackson and Bradford 2010). Thus viewed, trust in the police is the belief that the police can be relied upon to act competently (be effective), to wield their authority in fair ways (be procedurally just), and to provide equal justice and protection across society (be distributively fair). If one trusts police officers, one takes a leap of faith; one predicts future and current behaviour in the presence of risk and uncertainty. One does not know whether police officers are *currently out there* fulfilling their function; one does not know whether police officers will fulfill their function *in the future*. But one nevertheless trusts officers to fulfill their function because one makes certain assumptions about the intentions and capabilities of individual police officers. From this perspective, perceptions of procedural justice are judgements of trustworthiness. They are not direct judgements about the moral right to power. How police officers wield their authority (i.e., how they behave) legitimizes the institution in the eyes of citizens. But procedural justice does not constitute legitimacy.

A useful distinction for future research is thus between power and moral authority (legitimacy) and abilities and intentions (trust). From this perspective, legitimacy is a belief about the moral right of the police to possess and exercise power and influence, while trust is a belief about how individual police officers perform their roles. In the words of Hawdon (2008: 186): 'The role is legitimate; the individual is trusted.' In future research, we would suggest that measures of trust focus on the intentions and capabilities of individual officers, i.e. whether the officers can be trusted to fulfil specific institutional functions, like being effective, fair, dependable, and having appropriate priorities (see, for example, Stoutland 2001; Flexon et al. 2009). By contrast, measures of legitimacy should focus on the authority that the institution (the role) confers onto individual officers and, conversely, the moral validity that actions of individual officers confer back to the institution and role (an appropriate sense of legality, lawfulness, and the embodiment of right and wrong).

DIALOGIC APPROACHES TO LEGITIMACY

The most important part of Bottoms and Tankebe's (2012) paper is the idea that legitimacy is dynamic and interactive, involving claims to legitimacy from power-holders and audience reception of those claims. It certainly makes sense to study legitimacy over time as a dynamic interaction among power-holders and subordinates. For example, one common comment about street stops is that a person who has been stopped repeatedly views an interaction differently to person who has not been stopped repeatedly. It may well be that, over time, the dynamic of such stops changes for both parties, in part based on the officer's changing sense of authority and power, and in part based on the citizen's reception of the officer's claims to power and authority.[2]

Understanding this dynamic requires longitudinal approaches of the type proposed by Bottoms and Tankebe. Longitudinal work would capture the officers' sense of power and authority, the moral values expressed in their actions, and the lawfulness of what they do. Such work would also capture the citizens' sense of duty to authority, judgement of the moral values expressed in their actions, and perceptions of the lawfulness of those actions. It may be that citizen's judgement of the moral values expressed by officers and their perceptions of the lawfulness of police actions constitute what Bottoms and Tankebe (2012: 125) call '...a positive *recognition* by citizens of the power-holder's *moral right* to exercise that power'.

However, the degree to which we move beyond procedural justice is ultimately an empirical issue. Studies of procedural justice show the striking degree to which people react to procedural justice. No doubt there is a larger framework that contains procedural justice and other elements relevant to legitimacy. Prior studies, for example, often find that distributive justice also shapes perceptions of legitimacy. And, as noted,

[2] Interestingly, a recent study of street stops by Tyler, Fagan and Geller (2013) suggests that this is not, in fact, what happens. They divided respondents into groups based upon the number of prior stops that they had experienced. They found that the influence of procedural justice upon legitimacy was almost identical among those with no prior stops and those with over 10 prior stops.

Tankebe (2013) suggests that lawfulness may constitute legitimacy; procedural justice may be wrapped up with other aspects of policing. But, ultimately this depends upon whether these other aspects of policing (like legality) are important to people when they assess legitimacy.

BUILDING A SELF-REGULATORY MODEL

If we accept the traditional view that a key goal of legal authorities is to motivate compliance with the law, then the benefits of studying legitimacy are clear. Legitimacy motivates compliance at least as much as, and often more than, considerations of the risk of being caught and punished for wrongdoing. However, it is also possible to suggest a broader change in the way we think about the relationship between law, legal authorities, and the public. The model we propose is the *self-regulatory model.*

As has been noted, crime-control policy typically assumed that compliance is motivated by the threat or use of force. Such an approach has a number of problems. Within a given situation, it generates anger and resistance; it produces compliance but does not encourage willing acceptance. Hence, people often revert to their prior behaviour when the authorities are not present.

Framing interactions with legal authorities as force-based creates a negative tone and provides no basis for building trust or creating a positive relationship. Hence, the authorities at best are not creating a positive social bond that could be called upon in future situations, and at worse are undermining existing trust and feelings of connection. All of this means that deterrence strategies contain within them the dynamics to undermine people's relationships with legal authorities and their commitment to shared values such as legitimacy and morality. As authorities seek to maintain social order over time, they are inevitably drawn into increasing surveillance of and intrusion into the lives of people, whose behaviour is ever more motivated largely or even solely by their instrumental calculations about risk.

Further, as a necessary concomitant of this strategy, authorities must demonstrate their credibility by citing, fining, and incarcerating ever greater numbers of people for longer times, strategies that themselves have been shown to be ineffective as producing long-term increases in compliance. In part because of the widespread belief that crime is deterred by the threat and/or the experience of punishment, a massive number of American citizens have been convicted and sentenced to serve time in American prisons. Today the US is a world leader in the proportion of citizens it holds in prison. The US has the highest prison population rate in the world, 756 per 100,000 national population in 2007—much higher than those in equivalent countries such as England and Wales (153 per 100,000), France (96 per 100,000), and Germany (89 per 100,000) (Walmsley 2008).

An alternative approach focuses upon building the willing acceptance of decisions and widespread voluntary deference to regulations and laws in everyday life by enhancing the legitimacy of the law and of legal authorities. This legitimacy is built by designing and implementing laws and the policies and practices of legal authorities through fair procedures.

The focus of concern needs to be broadened to include not just compliance—motivated by concerns about costs and gains—but willing deference to the law and the decisions of legal authorities. The legal system benefits when people voluntarily defer to decisions and continue to defer over time. In the context of personal experiences with police officers or judges, the legal system is more effective if people voluntarily accept the decisions made by legal authorities. Absent such acceptance, legal authorities must engage in a continuing effort to create a credible threat of punishment to assure long-term rule-following/decision acceptance.

These types of voluntary deference are not effectively motivated by the risk of punishment because while threats can sometimes compel obedience, they do not motivate voluntary deference. Thus, a force-based strategy creates long-term problems because 'citizens who acquiesce at the scene can renege' (Mastrofski et al. 1996: 283). If citizens fail to fully agree with legal restrictions, further police intervention will eventually be required. Hence, the legal system is also concerned with its ability to gain long-term compliance, not just immediate compliance. Willing deference leads to long-term acceptance, rather than short-term compliance.

The value of cultivating legitimacy lies in the fact that it enables the effective exercise of social authority. While authorities can exercise power directly through the promise of rewards or the threat of punishment, such approaches to deterrence are expensive, inefficient, and psychologically naive. They may be especially problematic during instability or crisis, when authorities need the support of the people at a time in which they lack control over resources. An organization or society whose governance is motivated only by incentives and sanctions is at risk of disintegrating during times of trouble or change. If a system enjoys widespread legitimacy, authorities can appeal to members based upon their shared purposes and values, providing the system with much-needed stability.

Legitimacy is thus a highly desirable feature of social systems (see also Tyler 2006 ; Tyler and Huo 2002). It has many appealing features as a possible basis for the rule of law. On the face of it, felt obligation to institutions appears to be an all-purpose mechanism of social coordination, insofar as people feel obligated to obey whatever laws or decisions authorities make, within some specific social realm. A focus on legitimacy follows from a shift from compliance to willing deference, since those citizens who feel an obligation to obey can be motivated in ways besides the threat or use of punishment.

COOPERATION

Beyond deference, legal authorities are increasingly focusing upon the benefits of active public cooperation with the police, the courts, and the law (Sampson et al. 1997). The legal system—and particularly the police—needs voluntary help from the public (Tyler and Fagan 2008). Studies of crime and policing make clear that the police benefit when members of the community voluntarily work with them to manage social order in their community. First, the police need community members who are familiar with the neighbourhood and its residents to report crime and criminals to the police. Second, the police need community residents to join them in town meetings and neighbourhood watch organizations to identify and deal with community problems.

The shift from compliance to cooperation first requires us to expand the scope of our instrumental model—a model that can potentially involve both costs and benefits. While the legal system is based upon highlighting the cost of rule-breaking, law and legal authorities also offer benefits that can strengthen social capital. For example, Tyler and Huo (2002) found that the primary reason for people having contact with the police and courts is having gone to them for help. Legal authorities can create benefits by their performance in resolving disputes and maintaining social order. Unlike the relationship of the police to regulation, in which they are primarily the dispensers of punishment, when we consider cooperation we can also see the police as a group able to provide people with desirable outcomes by helping them to solve problems and address problems in their communities. The police can provide desirable rewards such as high performance in solving crime, maintaining order, or addressing public problems. Members of the public can—and should—have an active interest in police success that does not rest on sanctions directed at them.

A focus on cooperation also suggests the potential value of considering values beyond legitimacy. One value of great importance is the already noted issue of moral alignment—the belief that the police, the courts, and the law enforce shared community values that reflect the person's sense of what is right. A large proportion of the psychological literature shows that an important human motivation is the desire to act in accordance with one's values about what is morally right and wrong. Tyler and Blader (2005) show that employees in a management setting are motivated by the assessment that their organization acts in ways consistent with their own moral values. When people feel aligned with the moral values of an authority in a group setting, they will act in ways that support the group that the authority represents. Institutions can encourage cooperation by activating ethical motivations such as these, motivations that lead people to adhere to group rules and to act on behalf of the group (Tyler 1990; Tyler and Huo 2002).

Across the social sciences, there has been a widespread recognition that it is important to understand how to motivate cooperation on the part of people within group settings. This is the case irrespective of whether those settings are small groups, organizations, or communities (Tyler 2011). Studies in management show that work organizations benefit when their members actively work for company success. Within law, research shows that crime and problems of community disorder are difficult to solve without the active involvement of community residents. Political scientists recognize the importance of public involvement in building both viable communities and strong societies. Those in public policy have identified the value of cooperation in the process of policy making—for example, in stakeholder policy making groups. Hence it is important to ask whether the actions of legal authorities can aid in the production of social capital that might more generally engage cooperation.

Recent discussions of legal authority focus on a broader conception of the relationship between community residents and legal authorities. This broader framework suggests a new, wider conception of citizenship. Rather than concerning a simple deference to authorities, citizenship is increasingly seen as connected to the willing and active cooperation with authorities in creating and maintaining order in the community. For example, Tyler and Fagan (2008) identify two distinct forms of cooperation that benefit the police. The first is cooperation in solving particular crimes, for instance by reporting crime in the community. The second is cooperation in co-policing the community, by working with the police in discussions about community issues and problems, and through general willingness to work with the police (for example, by joining neighbourhood watch and helping to patrol areas in one's community). Tyler et al. (2010) make a similar distinction in their study of anti-terror policing in the Muslim American community. They note that the same two types of cooperation are valued by legal authorities: reporting potentially dangerous actions and generally working with the police to help police the community against terror threats.

Both of these forms of cooperation are essentially voluntary. Non-cooperation risks little or no sanction. In particular, *not* reporting threats to the community is something that is virtually undetectable. People's willingness to do so is therefore linked to a broader loyalty or sense of duty to the community and its authorities. Such cooperative behaviours are therefore general civic activities akin to the more traditionally studied forms of political participation. The issue that is being raised in respect to crime, in other words, is the same type of issue raised with regard to any matter affecting a community. How can citizens be motivated to become involved in deciding how to manage their community and in engage in behaviours oriented toward doing so? The powerful influence of procedural justice, legitimacy, and moral alignment on public cooperation with legal authorities is just one example of a broader set of motivations based on social connections rather than material interests (Tyler 2011). Studies demonstrate the importance of several types of normative commitment to motivating cooperation with legal, managerial, and political authorities.

One issue motivating cooperation is identity. Individuals cooperate with organizations when those organizations serve the social function of providing individuals with a favourable identity and a positive sense of self (Blader and Tyler 2009). Pride and respect within the group are important. If people feel pride in the group and believe that they are accorded respect, then their motives will be transformed from the personal to the group level. If individuals identify with the group that the police represent (i.e. the society and nation) then they merge their sense of self with the group. Defining themselves in terms of their group membership, they will be more willing to act cooperatively on behalf of that group. The goals of the police then become one's own goals.

Moreover, the actions of legal authorities can have an impact on people's views about government (Tyler et al. 1989). Because the actions of legal authorities generalize to views about society and government it should be possible to develop strategies of law enforcement that are more socially beneficial by building identification with government and society, as well as the type of supportive values that lead to feelings of obligation. For example, the police might be able to help build government legitimacy that would lead people to pay their taxes. Further, they might build the type of connections that lead people to work willingly and enthusiastically in their communities in many other ways ranging from shopping in stores to going to local restaurants. In other words, rather than being viewed as a (necessary) cost that has negative implications for society, the legal system could generate supportive attitudes and values that would resonate more broadly through society.

Legal authorities can produce the benefits of building public support, benefits which include success in fighting crime and also general support for the community. People are more likely to come to and revisit communities in which they feel that they will be well treated by the representatives of government they are most likely to encounter—the police. This benefits communities economically because people more willingly come to them to work, to shop, as tourists, and for entertainment and sporting events. Hence, the police play a central role in creating the reassurance that makes a community inviting and desirable to the general public. In other words, the law provides a framework for building vibrant, successful communities. If people feel reassured by the presence of the police, and believe that they will be protected and, if they need it, helped, then they will be encouraged to engage in their communities socially and economically. When people engage in such behaviours they build social capital and the sense of efficacy that has broad social value.

If people engage in their communities, they will come to know others and know how to work with them when problems arise in the community. They build trust in others and develop the belief that others can and will join together to address issues when they arise. By providing a framework of reassurance the police are creating the climate that allows the community to develop valuable psychological and sociological characteristics. Underlying these comments is the question of how legitimacy, trust, and values such as collective efficacy are related. It may be that strong government and legitimate institutions help foster collective efficacy (LaFree 1998; Sampson 2002; Kochel 2011). Work in the UK suggests that people infer the moral values of the police partly from the strength of the values and social ties they experience in their community (Jackson et al. 2012a; Hough 2013; Bradford et al. 2013). We would argue that to some extent both of these propositions are true; a feedback loop may exist between collective efficacy and institutional legitimacy.

CONCLUSION

A value-based perspective on human motivation suggests the importance of developing and sustaining a civic culture in which people more willingly abide by the law because they feel that legal authorities are legitimate and thus ought to be obeyed. For this model to work, society must create and maintain public values, and psychological social capital must be created. Political scientists refer to this set of values as a 'reservoir of support' for government and society (Dahl 1956). But however labelled, a value-based model is consistent with a social psychological understanding of how authorities can effectively regulate citizen behaviour, maintain social order, and promote an effective, well-functioning society—by developing and maintaining a culture of supportive social values that will be internalized by the citizenry (Tyler 2011).

As we have noted, such values include feelings of obligation and responsibility to the state. They also include judgements about the degree of moral alignment that people feel with the police, the courts, and the law. And, they include broader types of social connections to society, such as identification with authorities and institutions. All of these values provide an alternative basis for the effective operation of the legal system, separate to a crude and simple instrumental discourse about 'the war on crime' in which weapons of deterrence and incapacitation are deployed in instrumental ways.

REFERENCES

Beetham, D. (1991) *The Legitimation of Power.* London: Macmillan.

Benesh, S. C. (2006) 'Understanding Public Confidence in American Courts', *Journal of Politics* 68(3): 697–707.

Blader, S. and Tyler, T. R. (2009) 'Testing and Expanding the Group Engagement Model', *Journal of Applied Psychology* 94: 445–64.

Bottoms, A. E. (1999) 'Interpersonal Violence and Social Order in Prisons', in Tonry, M. and Petersilia, J. (eds) *'Prisons', Crime and Justice: A Review of Research*, xxvi, Chicago, IL: University of Chicago Press: 205–82.

Bottoms, A. and Tankebe, J. (2012) 'Beyond Procedural Justice: A Dialogic Approach to Legitimacy in Criminal Justice', *Journal of Criminal Law and Criminology* 102(1): 119–70.

Bourgois, P. (1995) *In Search of Respect: Selling Crack in El Barrio.* Cambridge: Cambridge University Press.

Bradford, B., Huq, A., Jackson, J., and Roberts, B. (2013) 'What Price Fairness When Security is at Stake? Police Legitimacy in South Africa', *Regulation and Governance* doi: 10.1111/rego.12012.

Caplan, B. (2007) *The Myth of the Rational Voter.* Princeton: Princeton University Press.

Casper, J. D., Tyler, T. R., and Fisher, B. (1988) 'Procedural Justice in Felony Cases', *Law and Society Review* 22: 483–507.

Charles, K. K. and Durlauf, S. N. (2013) 'Pitfalls in the Use of Time Series Methods to Study Deterrence and Capital Punishment', *Journal of Quantitative Criminology* 29: 45–66.

Coicaud, J-M. (2002) *Legitimacy and Politics: A Contribution to the Study of Political Right and Political Responsibility*, Curtis, D. A. (trans). Cambridge: Cambridge University Press.

Crawford, A. (2009) 'Criminalizing Sociability Through Anti-Social Behaviour Legislation: Dispersal Powers, Young People and the Police,' *Youth Justice* 9(1): 5–26.

Dahl, R. (1956) *A Preface to Democratic Theory.* Chicago: University of Chicago Press.

Emler, N. and Reicher, S. (1995) *Adolescence and Delinquency: The Collective Management of Reputation.* Oxford: Blackwell Publishers.

European Social Survey (2011) 'Trust in Justice: Topline Findings from the European Social Survey', *Ess Topline Results Series Issue 1.* By Jackson, J., Hough, M., Bradford, B., Pooler, T. M., Hohl, K., And Kuha, J. European Commission.

European Social Survey (2012) 'Policing by Consent: Understanding the Dynamics of Police Power and Legitimacy', *Ess Country Specific Topline Results Series Issue 1 (UK)*. By Jackson, J., Hough, M., Bradford, B., Hohl, K., And Kuha, J. Economic And Social Research Council.

Flexon, J., Lurigio, A., and Greenleaf, R. (2009) 'Exploring the Dimensions of Trust in the Police Among Chicago Juveniles', *Journal of Criminal Justice* 37: 180–9.

Gottfredson, D. C., Kearley, B. W., Najaka, S. S., and Rocha, C. M. (2007) 'How Drug Treatment Courts Work: An Analysis of Mediators', *Journal of Research in Crime and Delinquency* 44(1): 3–35.

Gray, J. (2007) 'Fair Decision Making and Legitimacy: The Effects of Treatment on Compliance and Outcome Satisfaction in a Sample of Incarcerated Males', PhD Diss, University of Southern Illinois.

Green, D. P. and Shapiro, I. (1994) *Pathologies of Rational Choice Theory*. New York: Yale University Press.

Harcourt, B. E. (2001) *Illusion of Order: The False Promise of Broken Windows Policing*. Cambridge: Harvard University Press.

Harcourt, B. E. and Ludwig, J. (2006) 'Broken Windows: New Evidence From New York City and a Five-City Social Experiment', *University of Chicago Law Review* 73(1): 271–320.

Hardin, R. (2006) *Trust*. Cambridge: Polity Press.

Hawdon, J. (2008) 'Legitimacy, Trust, Social Capital, and Policing Styles: A Theoretical Statement', *Police Quarterly* 11: 182–201.

Hinds, L. (2007) 'Building Police-Youth Relationships: The Importance of Procedural Justice', *Youth Justice* 7(3): 195–209.

Hinds, L. (2009) 'Youth, Police Legitimacy and Informal Contact', *Journal of Police and Criminal Psychology* 24: 10–21.

Hoffman, M. (1977) *Empathy and Moral Development*. New York: Cambridge University Press.

Hough, M. (2013) 'Procedural Justice and Professional Policing in Times of Austerity', *Criminology and Criminal Justice* 13(2): 181–97.

Hough, M., Jackson, J., and Bradford, B. (2013a, forthcoming) 'The Governance of Criminal Justice, Legitimacy and Trust', in Body-Gendrot, S., Lévy, R., Hough, M., Snacken, S., and Kerezsi, K. (eds) *The Routledge Handbook of European Criminology*. Oxon: Routledge.

Hough, M., Jackson, J., and Bradford, B. (2013b, this volume, ch 16). 'Legitimacy, Trust and Compliance: An Empirical Test of Procedural Justice Theory Using the European Social Survey', in Tankebe, J. and Liebling, A. (eds) *Legitimacy and Criminal Justice: An International Exploration*. Oxford: Oxford University Press.

Jackson, J. and Bradford, B. (2010) 'What is Trust and Confidence in the Police?', *Policing: A Journal of Policy and Practice* 4(3): 241–8.

Jackson, J., Bradford, B., Hough, M., Kuha, J., Stares, S. R., Widdop, S., Fitzgerald, R., Yordanova, M., and Galev, T. (2011) 'Developing European Indicators of Trust in Justice', *European Journal of Criminology* 8(4): 267–85.

Jackson, J., Bradford, B., Hough, M., Myhill, A., Quinton, P., and Tyler, T. R. (2012a) 'Why do People Comply with the Law? Legitimacy and the Influence of Legal Institutions', *British Journal of Criminology* 52: 1051–71.

Jackson, J., Bradford, B., Stanko, E.A., and Hohl, K. (2012b) *Just Authority? Trust in the Police in England and Wales*. Oxon: Routledge.

Jackson, J., Huq, A., Bradford, B., and Tyler, T. R. (2013) 'Monopolizing Force? Police Legitimacy and Public Attitudes towards the Acceptability of Violence', *Psychology, Public Policy and Law*.

Jost, J. T., and Major, B. (2001) 'Emerging Perspectives on the Psychology of Legitimacy' (pp. 3–32), in Jost, J. T. and Major, B. (eds) *The Psychology of Legitimacy*. Cambridge: Cambridge University Press.

Kelman, H. C. (1969) 'Patterns of Personal Involvement in the National System: A Social-Psychological Analysis of Political Legitimacy' (pp. 276–88), in Rosenau, J. (ed) *International Politics and Foreign Policy*. New York: Free Press.

Kelman, H. C. and Hamilton, V. L. (1989) *Crimes of Obedience*. New Haven: Yale.

Kochel, T. R. (2011) 'Can Police Legitimacy Promote Collective Efficacy?', *Justice Quarterly* 29(3): 384-419. DOI: 10.1080/07418825.2001.561805.

LaFree, G. (1998) *Losing Legitimacy: Street Crime and the Decline of Social Institutions in America*. Boulder, CO: Westview.

Lipsey, M. W. and Cullen, F. T. (2007) 'The Effectiveness of Correctional Rehabilitation: A Review of Systematic Reviews', *Annual Review of Law and Social Science* 3: 297–320.

Lynch, J. P. and Sabol, W. J. (1997) 'Did Getting Tough on Crime Pay?', Washington DC: The Urban Institute.

MacCoun, R. (1993) 'Drugs and the Law: A Psychological Analysis of Drug Prohibition', *Psychological Bulletin* 113: 497–512.

Mastrofski, S. D., Snipes, J. B., and Supina, A. E. (1996) 'Compliance On demand: The Public's Response to Specific Police Requests', *Journal of Research in Crime and Delinquency* 33(3): 269–305.

Mazerolle, L., Antrobus, E., Bennett, S., and Tyler, T. R. (2013) 'Shaping Citizen Perceptions of Police Legitimacy: A Randomized Field Trial of Procedural Justice', *Criminology* 51(1): 33–63. doi:10.1111/j.1745-9125.2012.00289.x.

McCord, J., Widom, C. S., and Crowell, N. A. (2001) 'Juvenile Justice', New York: National Research Council.

McIvor, G. (2009) 'Therapeutic Jurisprudence and Procedural Justice in Scottish Drug Courts.' *Criminology and Criminal Justice* 9(1): 29–49.

Merelman, R. J. (1966) 'Learning and Legitimacy', *American Political Science Review* 60: 548–61.

Papachristos, A. V., Meares, T. L. and Fagan, J. (2009) 'Why Do Criminals Obey the Law? The Influence of Legitimacy and Social Networks on Active Gun Offenders.' *John M. Olin Center Research Paper* No. 373, Yale University Law School.

Paternoster, R. (1987) 'The Deterrent Effect of the Perceived Certainty and Severity of Punishment: A Review of the Evidence and Issues', *Justice Quarterly* 4(2): 173–217.

Paternoster, R., Brame, R., Bachman, R., and Sherman. L. W. (1997) 'Do Fair Procedures Matter? The Effect of Procedural Justice on Spouse Assault.' *Law and Society Review* 31(1): 163–204.

Pratt, T. C., Cullen, F. T., Blevins, K. R., Daigle, L. E., and Madensen, T. D. (2008) 'The Empirical Status of Deterrence Theory: A Meta-Analysis' (pp. 367–96), in Cullen, F. T., Wright, J. P., and Blevins, K. R. (eds) *Taking Stock: The Status of Criminological Theory*. New Brunswick: Transaction Publishers.

Raz, J. (1986) *The Morality of Freedom* (2nd edn). Oxford: Oxford University Press.

Robinson, P. H. and Darley, J. (1995) *Justice, Liability, and Blame*. Boulder, CO: Westview.

Robinson, P. H. and Darley, J. (1997) 'The Utility of Desert', *Northwestern University Law Review* 91: 453–99.

Rottman, D. B. (2005) 'Trust and Confidence in the California Courts', available at: <http://www.courts.ca.gov/documents/4_37pubtrust1.pdf> accessed 24 July 2013.

Sampson, R. J. (2002) 'Transcending Tradition: New Directions in Community Research, Chicago Style', *Criminology* 40(2): 213–30.

Sampson, R. J., Raudenbush, S. W., and Earls, F. E. (1997) 'Neighborhoods and Violent Crime', *Science* 277: 918–24.

Sparks, R., Bottoms, A. E., and Hay, W. (1996). *Prisons and the Problem of Order*. Oxford: Clarendon Press.

Stoutland, S. (2001) 'The Multiple Dimensions of Trust in Resident/Police Relations in Boston', *Journal of Research in Crime and Delinquency* 38(3): 226–56.

Sunshine, J., and Tyler, T. R. (2003) 'The Role of Procedural Justice and Legitimacy in Shaping Public Support for Policing', *Law and Society Review* 37(3): 513–48.

Tankebe, J. (2013) 'Viewing Things Differently: The Dimensions of Public Perceptions of Legitimacy', *Criminology* 51(1): 103–35.

Taxman, F. S., Soule, D., and Gelb, A. (1999). 'Graduated Sanctions: Stepping into Accountable Systems and Offenders', *The Prison Journal* 79(2): 182–204.

Terrill, W. (2001) *Police Coercion*. El Paso, TX: LFB Scholarly Publishing.

Tyler, T. R. (1990) *Why People Obey the Law*. Princeton: Princeton University Press.

Tyler, T. R. (2001) 'Public Trust and Confidence in Legal Authorities: What do Majority and Minority Group Members Want From the Law and Legal Institutions?' *Behavioral Sciences and the Law* 19: 215–35.

Tyler, T. R. (2005) '*A Deference-Based Perspective on Duty: Empowering Government to Define Duties to Oneself and Others*', in Finkel, N. J. and Moghaddam, F. M. (eds) *The Psychology of Rights and Duties*. Washington, DC.: American Psychological Association.

Tyler, T. R. (2006) 'Psychological Perspectives on Legitimacy and Legitimation', *Annual Review of Psychology* 57: 375–400.

Tyler, T. R. (2011) *Why People Cooperate*. Princeton: Princeton University Press.

Tyler, T. R. and Blader, S. (2000) *Cooperation In Groups: Procedural Justice, Social Identity, and Behavioral Engagement*. Philadelphia: Psychology Press.

Tyler, T. R. and Blader, S. (2003) 'Procedural Justice, Social Identity, and Cooperative Behavior', *Personality and Social Psychology Review* 7: 349–61.

Tyler, T. R. and Blader, S. (2005) 'Can Businesses Effectively Regulate Employee Conduct?: The Antecedents of Rule-Following in Work Settings', *Academy of Management Journal* 48(6): 1143–58.

Tyler, T. R., Casper, J. D., and Fisher, B. (1989) 'Maintaining Allegiance Toward Political Authorities: The Role of Prior Attitudes and the Use of Fair Procedures', *American Journal of Political Science* 33(3): 629–52.

Tyler, T. R. and Fagan, J. (2008) 'Legitimacy and Cooperation: Why Do People Help the Police Fight Crime in their Communities?' *Ohio State Journal of Criminal Law* 6(1): 231–75.

Tyler, T., Fagan, J. and Geller, A. B. (2013). 'Street Stops and Police Legitimacy: Teachable Moments in Young Urban Men's Legal Socialization' *Yale Law School, Public Law Working Paper*. Available at: <http://ssrn.com/abstract=2289244> accessed 24 July 2013.

Tyler, T. R. and Huo, Y. J. (2002) *Trust in the Law: Encouraging Public Cooperation With the Police and Courts*. New York: Russell-Sage Foundation.

Tyler, T. R., Schulhofer, S., and Huq, A. (2010) 'Legitimacy and Deterrence Effects in Counter-Terrorism Policing: A Study of Muslim Americans', *Law and Society Review* 44(2): 365–401.

Tyler, T. R., Sherman, L. W., Strang, H., Barnes, G. C., and Woods, D. J. (2007) 'Reintegrative Shaming, Procedural Justice, and Recidivism: The Engagement of Offenders' Psychological Mechanisms in the Canberra RISE Drinking-and-Driving Experiment', *Law and Society Review* 41(3): 553–86.

Van der Velden, L. (2009) 'Conflicts Between Citizens and Government Organisations: Towards a Pro-active, Solution Driven Approach', Ministry of the Interior and Kingdom Relations: The Hague, the Netherlands.

Walmsley, R. (2008) *World Prison Population List* (8th edn). London: International Centre for Prison Studies.

Weisberg, R. (2005) 'The Death Penalty Meets Social Science: Deterrence and Jury Behavior Under New Scrutiny', *Annual Review of Law and Social Science* 1: 151–70.

6

UNFINISHED BUSINESS: LEGITIMACY, CRIME CONTROL, AND DEMOCRATIC POLITICS

Ian Loader and Richard Sparks

> If legitimacy in the broadest sense implies absence of coercion, democratic legitimacy implies something more: a tissue of relationships between government and society [...] In these respects, legitimacy is an 'invisible institution' as well as a 'sensitive indicator' of the society's political expectations and the response to those expectations. A broader, more searching definition of legitimacy is therefore an essential component of any effort to expand the meaning of democracy.
>
> (Rosanvallon 2011: 9)

INTRODUCTION

In this chapter we seek to recover and re-explore the central importance of the concept of legitimacy for criminological analysis.[1] We treat the idea of legitimacy as a *political* construct with critically important applications to the contemporary analysis of crime control. We begin by noting what we see as the problematic disconnect between two important bodies of work on legitimacy in criminal justice: one focused on the situational deployments of penal and policing power, the other on more macroscopic analyses of the emergence of late-modern (or 'neoliberal') penality. What falls between these preoccupations, we suggest, is a closer analysis of the institutional arrangements for deliberating, debating, and deciding on what it is that criminal justice institutions are being called upon to do.

This perspective suggests that legitimacy in criminal justice is properly thought of as a problem of comparative political analysis and requires attention to the impact

[1] We wish to thank the editors of this volume, along with Ben Bradford, Nicola Lacey and Lucia Zedner, for their helpful comments on an earlier version of this chapter. The usual disclaimer applies.

of competing demands and allocations of powers and resources and to variations in the legitimation problems of crime control institutions in the circumstances of the societies in which they arise. It also however demands that much closer attention be paid to the interface between such questions of legitimacy and the ideas and practices of democracy—and hence to understanding legitimacy as a 'sensitive indicator' of societal troubles and political responses to them, as Rosanvallon suggests. In what follows, we use Rosanvallon's work to spell out one way in which this interface may be explored with respect to relations between crime control authorities and subjects. We also point to a number of boundary situations at each of which the relationship between legitimacy and democracy is acutely in question. These include the special implications of transitional justice and conditions of post-conflict reconstruction, and the legitimation problems raised by new developments in surveillance technology, privatization and the internationalization of crime control. In conclusion we begin to examine the potential of the concept of legitimacy as an 'unfinished' ideal and its position in the critical appraisal of contemporary crime control dilemmas.

LEGITIMACY AND CRIME CONTROL: THE MISSING MIDDLE

The concept of legitimacy has in recent decades attracted much interest and wielded growing influence over the study of criminal justice. Crudely put, one can identify two leading kinds of contribution. We will be very brief in sketching each of these since the first is a key topic for this volume as a whole and the second has been discussed at length elsewhere, including by us (e.g., Loader and Sparks 2007, 2010, 2012a).

The first is a body of work on 'procedural justice' instigated chiefly by Tom Tyler. Its organizing question is why people obey the law and more precisely why they feel motivated to comply with the demands of authorities for reasons other than immediately utilitarian ones such as seeking their own short-term benefits or avoiding penalties. The main initial focus of this programme of work is on the situational deployment of police power during interactions with citizens but much of the most interesting work has subsequently concerned a wider range of contexts and parties—such as in Valerie Braithwaite's research on tax avoidance/compliance (e.g., Braithwaite 2011). These bodies of work have shown that individuals are commonly more concerned with the fairness of these encounters than with their outcomes per se. Certain key features of such encounters—such as politeness, neutrality, and respectfulness—are claimed to be a vital ingredient of police legitimacy and of people's normative—rather than instrumental—compliance with the law (e.g., Tyler 2003, 2011). These claims have—over the last two decades—been supported by an impressive body of empirical research on policing mainly in studies carried out in the United States. They have also shaped prisons research (see Sparks et al. 1996; Liebling with Arnold 2004; Sparks and

Bottoms 2007) and in both police and prison contexts have exercised considerable appeal upon forward-looking practitioners.[2]

This 'process-based' approach to legitimacy has recently begun to be explored in a more comparative fashion (Tankebe 2009; Tyler 2011; Jackson et al. 2012). One potential source of frailty in the procedural justice model to date has been that it might simply not 'travel' very well beyond the borders of the United States to places where the location of policing in political culture is either much more contested (as in great swathes of Latin America or southern Europe) or for that matter more consensual, as has sometimes been argued for Japan. It has also lately received more probing, though nonetheless sympathetic, examination of its theoretical foundations in important articles by Bottoms and Tankebe (2012) and Jackson et al. (2012). We return to these debates shortly.

Elsewhere in the criminological forest a great deal of important work has taken place on changes in the intensity of political discourse around criminal justice and its attendant controversies, and especially the heating up of penal questions in some countries in recent decades. Observers of these transformations have focused upon a range of issues including the shift that they discern in the direction of public attention towards penal issues (such as sentencing and releasing prisoners) in the media (Newburn and Jones 2005; Simon 2007); the rise of a more demotic and emotionally charged use of crime and punishment in electoral politics (Beckett 1997; Pratt 2007); the mobilization of victims' groups and other lobbies, and on occasion their appropriation by political actors and ideologues for ulterior purposes (Dubber 2006; Barker 2007; Newburn 2007).

There are some major differences of views among contributors to these debates. For some the 'new punitiveness' is associated with a broad set of structural transformations that expose people in general to experiences of insecurity and risk, and politicians in particular to allegations of impotence in the face of turbid and confusing events that escape their willed direction (Garland 2001). This interpretation—mainly directed towards American and British experiences—views what has occurred in the last quarter of the twentieth century and since as a transformation in penal values and practices ushered in by a yet wider set of economic, social, and technological changes summarized by Garland, echoing Giddens, Bauman and others, as 'the coming of late modernity'. In that context the clamorous politics of vindication around criminal victimization and the punishment of offenders is understood as the state 'acting out' in response to rising crime rates and the exposure of the limits of its own sovereign capacity. For others the major motor of change lies in the transition towards

[2] No doubt this division of the field into two tendencies is a simplification for the sake of present argumentative convenience. For example, much of the research on prisons mentioned here has been greatly influenced not just by Tyler's approach but by the views proposed by David Beetham in *The Legitimation of Power* (1991). Beetham's approach has proved particularly helpful to studies whose focus falls on the dynamics of legitimacy in particular institutional settings (see further Sparks and Bottoms 2007). In this chapter we go on to consider some arguments of the French political theorist Pierre Rosanvallon which we find useful in thinking about the positioning of crime and punishment in contemporary democratic politics broadly considered. We suspect it may prove quite feasible to show a relatively high degree of consonance, both formally and substantively, between Beetham's model and Rosanvallon's—but this is not developed here.

a 'neo-liberal' view of the relationship between economy and society, and the disruptions consequent on the global dominance of market forces.[3] On this view the recent agitations of the penal realm flow from the need to re-cast it in ways more congenial to the political project of neo-liberalism, and to stabilize its otherwise shaky and divided social order in the face of a range of disturbances that it itself provokes (Wacquant 2009). Thus the extension of the penal state is the correlative consequence of the reining back of the social state, a transfer of functions from the (supporting, providing) 'left hand' to the (dominating, penalizing) 'right hand' of the state. This position envisions the punitive upsurge as a strategic response to the destabilizing effects of the withering of the social state and the deregulation of markets. It betokens a new vision of authority that presents penal severity as 'a healthy necessity, a vital reflex of self-defence by a social body threatened by the gangrene of criminality' (Wacquant 2008: 11).

Space forbids us from giving a fuller exposition of these important arguments. Neither, certainly, do we wish to overdraw the differences between them. Suffice to note for the time being that they are certainly by implication concerned with what we might choose to call problems of legitimacy, whether that is understood as relating to the exposed limits of state sovereignty or the struggle between contending accounts of the proper balance between the social and penal functions of government. On occasion this is made explicit by some contributors, notably for example Wacquant (2012: 67) when he suggests that the imposition of 'stern tutelage' on stigmatized groups 'offers a prime theatrical stage onto which governing elites can project the authority of the state and shore up the deficit of legitimacy they suffer whenever they forsake its established missions of social and economic protection'. Much of this work, whatever its internal disagreements or differences of emphasis, deals with the penological consequences of fairly drastic forms of social change, and often with the requirements upon political actors to buttress their authority in the face of limits upon their capacity to deliver security. Such concerns have long antecedents. Their precursors include, for example, the focus on the social and political uses of 'law and order'—and hence on crime politics as a form of legitimation work used to shore up ebbing political authority—explored with such eloquence and force by Stuart Hall and colleagues in *Policing the Crisis* (1978). Even so, legitimacy has rarely been an explicit organizing topic for work in these traditions, and has sometimes been introduced only in order for its possibility to be questioned or denied.

In our view, both the work in the procedural justice tradition and the more macroscopic surveys of penal social relations in the contemporary world have considerable virtues, as well as attendant shortcomings. We want to suggest that these shortcomings are in a certain sense symmetrical, with the result that each tends to illuminate delimited dimensions of the problem rather than the space between them. Yet it is this

[3] Some versions of these arguments have also, like the procedural justice ones, been open to criticism on grounds of a certain lack of comparative sensitivity and thus of over-predicting the scale and reach of 'penal transformation' or 'the new punitiveness' (see, for example, Tonry, 2007b). We have some sympathy with this critique, though not the theoretical incuriosity that sometimes goes with it. We certainly take the view that local adequacy in an intensely interactive and inter-connected world is a key requirement for contemporary theoretical work—a view that we develop further later in the chapter.

space—the space of politics, of claims-making, and stance-taking, of discourse and debate, of assertion and contestation, the space in short of arguments and public reasons (Fossen 2012)—that the relevance of the concept of legitimacy primarily resides.

The work on procedural justice has made it clear why legitimacy should be a key concern of criminology. Legitimacy is in this sense about the right to govern with acknowledged authority—a solution to the fundamental political problem of how to justify power and obedience (Pitkin 1966; Coicaud 2002). To study legitimacy is to address the question of what it is that sets consensual authority apart from naked power or dull compulsion. The procedural justice rendition of this problem is that legitimacy is acutely at issue in respect of police and prisons (as coercive arms of the state) and most sharply experienced during encounters where coercive force always has the potential to be deployed. The deployment of police power can have fateful material effects. But it also carries a heavy symbolic charge. It is a 'teachable moment' (Tyler 2012) which cannot help but communicate a message about an individual's place in the order of things and hence either affirm or challenge their status identity. This is why such encounters matter especially to minority groups whose membership of a political community is not secure or cannot be taken for granted. The empirical research aimed at testing these insights supports the view that being treated fairly and with respect by police and justice authorities matters deeply to people (more so than the outcomes) and that procedural fairness is a vital ingredient in building and sustaining legitimate (police) authority.[4] If, as Bottoms and Tankebe (2012: 139) have recently argued, legitimacy is a matter of ongoing dialogue, that dialogue most crucially takes place between power-holders and audiences *in situ*.

These are indeed great strengths and it is not part of our purpose in this chapter to seek to underplay the importance of the research that is being undertaken under the sign of procedural justice. But we also think it important that the question of legitimacy in crime control is not *reduced* to process or procedure, as if these somehow exhausted the theoretical and practical import of the idea. To explain why, we need to identify some of the limits of the procedural justice paradigm:

(1) Notwithstanding Bottoms and Tankebe's use of the term 'audience legitimacy', the procedural justice paradigm is not primarily about *audiences* at all. It gravitates instead to those who have direct experience of the police and to the effects of that experience. People in these circumstances might more appropriately be called the subjects or, in some versions, users or 'consumers' of these powers and services. In this regard the term 'audience' can itself be a source of error unless clarified quite stringently. We are all subjects of policing and penal powers, not just their witnesses. The point is rather that the procedural justice paradigm arguably has less to say about how legitimacy is generated and sustained (or not)

[4] This research simultaneously insists upon but also complicates the force of the word 'procedural'. It has been clear from the outset of this literature that there is more at stake here than the correct application of procedures, properly so-called, and that not all legitimacy-supporting conduct by officials is necessarily procedurally exact—sometimes it is the judicious use of discretion, and the personalization of the encounter, that is perceived as fair.

among those who principally experience policing and criminal justice through others, or through local rumour or gossip, or by means of media representation, and, thus crucially, as citizens, or taxpayers, or other kinds of involved onlookers (Smith 2007). Where do *their* beliefs about order, control, and justice, and the meaning of legitimate police authority, come from? How forcefully are they held? What demands do they give rise to?[5] This question arises, we suggest, in an interesting way in the recent extension by Jackson et al. (2012) of the procedural justice approach, undertaken in the context of a study of Londoners, to include a notion of 'moral alignment' between police and publics. To the extent that such questions of alignment (or its absence) condition the practice of policing and its reception by citizens, we are back in the realm of political culture, claims-making, and public reasons (Fossen 2012) and no longer only concerned with encounters or 'procedure'.

(2) Work in the procedural justice tradition is focused on the agents of police/penal power and the situations in which their power is deployed. This is a great strength. But it risks bracketing off—and treating as beyond the purview of the concept of legitimacy—a host of wider contextual and comparative aspects of the criminal question. These might include the reach of the criminal law and conceptions of criminal responsibility; the purposes and powers of policing and the arrangements for determining their priorities and bringing them to account; the uses and scale of imprisonment; the balance that is struck between penal and social modes of regulation and the processes by which such a balance is struck; the ideologically charged character of crime control; and the relation of all these factors to the wider patterns of resource ownership and distribution. All of this, we think, speaks to questions of the legitimacy of a range of governing authorities in responding to problems of order and security. What arrangements exist, here or there, for deciding on these matters and how should we evaluate their claims to do so democratically, or efficiently, or equitably? Questions of these kinds remind us that we cannot continue to raise the problem of legitimacy in criminal justice for very long without considering a series of legal, constitutional, philosophical, and political problems. We might bracket these for purposes of designing specific research projects, but we cannot disregard them indefinitely.

(3) Work on procedural justice has until recently (Tyler 2011; Jackson et al. 2012) had a rather placeless and timeless quality. It has, as it were, been lifted out of the political cultures within which crime control takes place. It is true that almost all the work on procedural justice in policing has hitherto been done in the US—some have indeed suggested it has a particular resonance in and affinity with the US given the historic centrality of the assertion of individual rights against state agents in that country (Tonry 2007a). The applicability of the position is now also

[5] One attendant difficulty here arises from the dominance of survey methodology within work on procedural justice (and public sensibilities towards order and authority more widely), and the limited capacity of surveys to fully 'get at' the question of what is 'going on' when someone reports that the police are doing a good or a bad job, or indicates respect or disrespect for the police, or expresses an opinion about crime problems and what to do about them (Loader and Mulcahy 2003: ch. 1; Smith 2007: 34–40).

being tested in the UK and elsewhere in Europe. But this is not quite the same thing as thinking about the legitimacy of police in ways that take as central the theoretical task of *situating* it in the political and mundane cultures of particular times and places.[6] There are also many social and cultural dynamics of the present to take into account in terms of globalization and implications for sovereignty; the mobility of people and the accentuated sensitivity of borders (Aas 2011; Bosworth 2012); the shifting loci of power and emergence of new centres of social steering and authority (commercial, international); developments in surveillance and investigative technologies (Nellis 2012); and the advent of new media and their impact upon political agency. Legitimacy may be an antique problem of politics, as Bottoms and Tankebe (2012) among others note. Our analysis of it must however be situated in and alive to the contours of the world we inhabit now lest it also become an archaic one.

(4) Work on procedural justice has exercised considerable appeal for police and prison managers—sometimes indeed it seems designed to do exactly this. It tells tough-minded cops and hard-pressed prison managers that fairness is beneficial *for* crime control, or *for* order in prisons. It gives reform-minded police and prison managers a credible language in which to talk to their hard-nosed and dubious colleagues and to explain to them why more forceful policing or more highly controlled prisons do not always achieve their ostensible objectives. It plays a significant part in internal conversations about the direction of change in these institutions. This has produced demonstrable benefits on the ground. Yet it may also sometimes come at a cost. The risk is of making legitimacy into a category of administrative practice (rather than a tool of critical social science) in ways that render it a measurable property of institutions and regimes (a police 'confidence target') rather than a 'ceaseless process of interactive judgement' between subjects and authorities (Dunn, this volume; Fossen 2012). The capacity of legitimacy to inform and influence the shape and dynamic of these processes is a large part of its appeal as a concept. But do we need to think harder and develop a more capacious institutional imagination about what it means to conceive of legitimacy as a perpetual dialogue: Between whom? On what terms? In what settings?

One of the strengths of recent work on the political sociology/economy of penal change is, conversely, that it attends closely to many of these wider issues. It aims precisely to understand the heating up of the crime question and its effects in these very terms. Here, as we have noted earlier, the analytic focus has been, variously, on the shifting contours and loci of sovereignty, the unfettering of capital, the decline of the social state, and the production of social anxieties—and on how 'crime' has featured as a political resource for dealing with legitimacy problems of democratic governments, or for underpinning the political project of neo-liberalism. It is in response to these wider problems of legitimation that authorities have seen the appeal of 'governing through crime' (Simon 2007).

[6] This thicker understanding of place, circumstance, and institutional context has been, we would argue, one of the distinctive contributions of work in the sociology of prisons to the (re)conceptualization of legitimacy in criminal justice (Sparks et al. 1996; Liebling with Arnold 2004; Sparks and Bottoms 2007).

Yet, we suggest, too much of this work also stands aloof from the institutional processes that link macro-level economic and social change with the changing politics of order in particular political cultures and with institutional variation across those cultures (cf. Lacey 2011). There is also (and we are just as willing to indict some of our own work on this point as to criticize that of anyone else) a certain reluctance to indicate what kinds of politics and which institutional configurations might address crises of legitimation in more just or socially inclusive ways. The emphasis has been more on critical analysis and the erection of defensive barriers to protect against the heat of the penal upsurge than on sketching the outlines of alternative futures. Some of the frustrations evinced by some otherwise not entirely unsympathetic observers (perhaps most trenchantly Tonry 2007b) perhaps speak to the fact that they find so little by way of explicit clarification on how to begin to navigate a path away from a world in which crime and punishment figure so pervasively and pathologically in efforts to build political capital and sustain governmental legitimacy.

So what is missing? How might we redirect work on legitimacy (or supplement the forms of analysis we have discussed in this section) in ways that can illuminate more broadly the contemporary politics of crime and punishment? What work can the idea of legitimacy do (and what are its limits) in the project of building a better—by which we mean, more democratic and deliberative—politics of crime and its regulation? This chapter is concerned with these questions. Answering them, we think, requires recovering and putting to use legitimacy as a *political* concept (Fossen 2012: 9). It means altering the starting point from which legitimacy is taken to be important for the study of crime and justice. Work on procedural justice has mobilized the idea of legitimacy with a view to finding better answers to the question of why people comply with the law. We think instead that one needs to explore the question of legitimacy with a view to asking how we can improve the quality of democratic governance in the field of order and security. This orients enquiry not only to the police and prisons but to the range of social and political institutions that act upon (or may act upon) crime. It also helps us to keep in mind the inseparable connection between empirical discovery and normative judgement that the concept of legitimacy carries with it, and reminds us that the critical promise of the idea of legitimacy lies—to recover a term of Mathiesen's (1974)—in its 'unfinished' quality, the way it brings us back time and again to the gap between how things are and how they might be.

We return to this question in the conclusion. We must first put some more flesh on our claim that the idea of legitimacy can be reoriented in ways that illuminate both the extant realities of democratic politics in the realm of crime control and the unfulfilled promise of such a politics within that realm.

LEGITIMACY AND THE COMPARATIVE ANALYSIS OF CRIME AND PUNISHMENT

The perspectives we have so far mentioned (the Tyler-instigated procedural justice literature on one hand; the more ambitious accounts of late-modern/'neo-liberal' crime control and its discontents on the other) sometimes seem to fall all-too squarely on one side or other of an all-too familiar micro-macro division. Perspectives that focus too exclusively on the former (procedural/micro) side of this division stand at risk of treating legitimacy as a self-contained, even self-explanatory, product: legitimacy is sustained by legitimacy-sustaining behaviour. On the other hand there is a risk of evacuating the question of legitimacy properly so-called in some of the more sweeping interpretations of penal/criminological transformations: legitimacy is sustained by legitimacy-sustaining ideological work. The former position predominantly settles its gaze upon interactions, encounters, and practices, especially on the deployment of authority by power-holders. The latter tends to emphasize the symbolic, even perhaps epiphenomenal, nature of legitimacy.

To suggest that there is something unsatisfactory here (about the division, rather than rejecting the insights of either body of work) is not simply to advocate some kind of middle way. Rather it is to propose a distinct re-focusing on the institutional character and composition of criminal justice policies and practices. What arrangements exist in any given time and place for debating, deliberating, and deciding on what it is that such institutions are being called upon to do? How are resources distributed by them and to them? Do these matters stand wholly or mainly within the domain of executive action, relayed and implemented by experts and practitioners? Or do they have an active place in public discourse and debate? What parts of criminal justice belong to central government and which are delegated to regional or municipal levels, and what if any differences does this make to the probity, integrity, or efficiency of these agencies or to their democratic accountability? This set of questions concern what we may call the *institutional architecture* of criminal justice and its relation to contests over legitimacy.

A distinct but related set of questions concern what we have elsewhere termed the temperature of the criminal question (Loader and Sparks 2010). How *hot* are these matters taken to be? What is seen to be at stake when they are discussed? How far are they understood to be matters of ideological import, around which adherents of different parties mark out their differences? In other words, to what extent do the politics of crime and punishment become a privileged battle-ground for disputing rival claims to authority and social leadership (for hegemony in one relevant diction); and what substantive principles and arguments are in contention on such occasions?

It is not going too far in anticipating our conclusions to suggest that arguments about the proper scope and conduct of crime control and punishment (including those about the effectiveness, propriety, and proper organization of the services that deliver them) cannot but be bound up with debates about the citizen's (and, increasingly, non-citizen's) relationship to the state; or about the devolution or concentration of these powers of sovereignty; or about the accountability of office holders and so on. They are properly political questions in other words and have regard to the scope of democratic politics and its futures. In our view, several current discussions of legitimacy in criminal justice advance the argument some way in this direction (see, for example, Bottoms and Tankebe 2012: 105) but not perhaps as far as we would like to see it pressed.

Bottoms and Tankebe's analysis, though much more sophisticated than most prior contributions, remains committed to: (1) the basic problematic concerning which conditions (principally the tri-partite division of legality, shared belief and consent) favour the acceptance by subordinates of the exercise of legitimate power by office-holders ('audience legitimacy') and (2) the nature of the justifications offered by power-holders for their uses of authority ('power-holder legitimacy'). In other words, they see themselves as providing a correction to the preoccupations of most political science approaches with governing elites by emphasizing 'the significant role in social order played by more junior power-holders (such as frontline police and prison officers), who are in direct contact with citizens and often exercise a significant degree of local power on a daily basis' (Bottoms and Tankebe 2012: 132). As such, they are concerned to provide students of policing or of prisons with a better conceptual apparatus for understanding power relations and this is very important in a middle-range kind of way. But Bottoms and Tankebe also freely acknowledge that there are other knotty issues at stake and that the standard framings of the issue by criminologists 'while certainly important, do not go to the heart of legitimacy's central focus, namely the recognition of the right to govern' (Bottoms and Tankebe 2012:133, referencing Coicaud 2002). It is this insight we propose to develop.

Among the most useful aspects of Bottoms and Tankebe's recent theoretical reconsideration of legitimacy in criminal justice is their emphasis on legitimacy as inherently dialogical. It involves, they suggest, a continual dynamic of claim and response, and is thus 'more like a perpetual discussion' (Bottoms and Tankebe 2012: 110) than a single assertion of power or command. This has the enormous virtue of bringing the discussion of legitimacy within criminology into much closer conversation with leading contributions in political and social theory (Dunn, this volume; Fossen 2012). They also suggest (though they seem to regard this part of their paper as more tentative and speculative) that 'the literature on legitimacy needs to be connected more firmly to the literature on justice' (2012: 138) and that understanding legitimacy in terms of dialogue demands transcending the idea that legitimacy has mainly to do with compliance and obedience (2012: 139). Indeed it may have much more to do with change and transformation, than with order and stability.

We propose, in sympathy with the latter view, that discussion of the significance of legitimacy in criminal justice is as important as it is because it goes to questions of the quotient of compulsion and force in ordering relationships; to issues of institutional design and organization (and hence of accountability, accessibility, and so on); and by extension generally to the dilemmas of criminalization and the balances between penal and other modes of social control. The varying institutional arrangements through which these dilemmas are addressed, and crime control is organized and governed, signal the importance of aligning the concept of legitimacy more closely with the practices and ideals of democracy. How though may one best make sense of this connection? Is it possible to develop an account of legitimacy that encompasses more fully the range of social and political institutions that are, or may be, assembled around the criminal question, and the issues at stake in relations between them?

DEMOCRATIC LEGITIMACY AND CRIME CONTROL

One way into these questions can be found in the recent work of Pierre Rosanvallon (2008, 2011). Rosanvallon begins from what he sees of the crisis of two forms of legitimacy that provided democratic regimes with solidity throughout much of the twentieth century, but which have been called into question in what he calls 'an age of distrust' (Rosanvallon 2008). He writes, first, of the 'diminished prestige' of elected office. Once, Rosanvallon argues, elections conferred on the victors a mandate from which to enact their political vision and govern 'freely'. Today, by contrast, elections have become simply the means by which the people choose who is to govern and no longer provide unquestioned authorization for the policies subsequently enacted. Rather, the legitimacy of such policies 'is permanently under scrutiny and must be reconquered day after day and case by case' (Rosanvallon 2008: 117). Secondly, Rosanvallon points to what he calls the delegitimation of selected administrative power. In a better educated, less deferential society people are much less willing to trust in the idea of 'technocrats' who are 'uniquely endowed with the virtues of rationality and disinterestedness' (Rosanvallon 2011: 5): 'The old style—"benevolent" bureaucrats administering a society treated as an underage ward of the state—has become both economically untenable and sociologically unacceptable', Rosanvallon writes (2011: 5). Taken together these developments have made it more difficult for the elected or selected agents of government to sustain the claim that they are acting in the public interest.

Contemporary penal politics supplies plenty of illustrations of these processes at work. In respect of the first, the imperative for politicians to routinely 'renew' their right to govern, and hold together the coalitions of support that keep them in office, make crime and punishment constantly tempting as a site of policy differentiation, legislative hyperactivity, and political theatre—as the aforementioned work on late-modern/'neo-liberal' politicization has demonstrated. In respect of the second, the fall, or absence, of 'Platonic guardians' (Loader 2006) has been a well-documented fact in those democracies where crime politics has become especially emotive and immoderate—in the view of some authors it is a factor helping to explain such punitiveness (Tonry 2007b). So too has been the recurrence of 'scandals' around crime in which one kind of 'bungling bureaucrat' or another is named, blamed, or shamed—whether they be unresponsive cops, interfering (or neglectful) social workers, out-of-touch judges, lax border control agents, and so forth. Often, those doing the blaming are politicians who are themselves seeking to escape blame and to mitigate the political risks that flow from media and popular attention that now surrounds the crime question. A mutually corrosive dance of blame laying and shifting not infrequently ensues. The recriminations that follow the deaths of children under the supervision of social services are one especially tortured and distressing instance of this. But so too in their different ways are the aftermaths of prison escapes, contested cases of police use of lethal force, grisly offences committed by released prisoners, and so on. (See generally Hood 2010.)

Rosanvallon's response to these pathologies is to explore, and fold within an enlarged conception of democracy, what he calls a 'radical pluralisation of the forms of legitimacy' (2011: 8). His purpose is to identify and theorize practices of legitimacy which can supplement or compete with extant mechanisms of election and selection, and thereby generate modes of rule that plausibly give effect to a general interest, rather than to partial or specific ones. His analysis is devoted to three such extensions of democratic legitimacy. Let us outline each and say something about their applicability to our concerns in this chapter.

The first form he calls the *legitimacy of impartiality*. By this Rosanvallon means institutions through which citizens are able to monitor, inspect, scrutinize, and denounce the actions of governing authorities. The legitimacy of such institutions, and their capacity to watch the few on behalf of the many, flows from the idea that no single interest is able to appropriate them. Such bodies are characterized by a structural variable (the fact of independence) and a behavioural variable (the maintenance of distance) that distinguishes these institutions from political office holders and allows them to regulate the activities of others. To undertake such roles (and be vigilant against capture), institutions of impartiality need to be 'open to social input and attentive to the aspirations and demands of citizens' (Rosanvallon 2011: 88); subject to formalized rules (for example surrounding appointment of members) that prevent takeover by partisan interests, and have their structure and function transparent and subject to 'permanent open debate' (2011: 103).

A range of such institutions now operates in the crime control and criminal justice field—ombudsmen, inspectorates of police, probation and constabulary, independent police complaints commissions, prison monitoring boards, information and surveillance commissioners, lay visitors, commissions of inquiry, and so on. The scope, independence, powers and impact of such agencies of oversight and redress have, arguably, increased over recent decades with attendant gains to the accountability and transparency of policing and criminal justice. They have become part—with their analogues in other domains of public policy—of a set of 'power-monitoring and power-controlling devices' that John Keane (2009: 12) calls 'monitory democracy'. As such, their role is today frequently interpreted within the frame of a liberal fear of democratic politics and pervasive distrust of politicians—what Rosanvallon (2008: 8) terms 'an anxious and pessimistic view of democracy'. In criminology, we have argued (Loader and Sparks 2010: ch. 4), that they are frequently treated as a means of 'insulating' criminal justice from political competition, mass media, and public opinion. Rosanvallon acknowledges the temptation of such an account, but he also highlights its limits. These institutions of 'counter-democracy' have, he argues, a 'dark side' which he calls 'the problem of the unpolitical' (2008: 306).[7] They are, on this view, couched as a defensive rearguard, a means of restraining and humbling power-holders in ways which risk turning a necessary (if insufficient) ingredient of democratic life into a form of cynical anti-politics (Flinders 2011: 44–46).[8] Rosanvallon, instead, proposes

[7] The term 'counter-democracy' is the title and central focus of Rosanvallon's 2008 book. It is arguably unhelpful and is contrary to the gist of the argument, which is to reinterpret several of the forms that are often taken to be restraints on democratic rule within a positive theory of democracy. It is noteworthy that the term counter-democracy does not appear in the later 2011 text.

[8] 'Reactive in essence, these strategies and actions cannot sustain or structure collective projects' (Rosanvallon 2008: 23).

to situate agencies of impartial oversight *within* the boundaries of an expanded concept of political legitimacy—as one of the 'constituent elements of democratic order' (2011: 100). Their overarching task is, he argues, to impose on political power-holders 'an obligation to serve the social interest as defined by some other means than elections' (2011: 101) and hence frame the question of their legitimacy in those wider terms.

Rosanvallon has the same re-interpretive ambition with respect to a second form of legitimacy: *legitimacy of reflexivity*. He uses this term to describe those institutions that help realize the objective of democracy by making the democratic subject more complex in ways that compensate for the failure of electoral majorities to embody the public will. The legitimation work here is done not via the route of detachment, as described, but by multiplying the points of reflection, reconsideration, evaluation, and veto that any democratic society has at its disposal, so as to facilitate a 'reflexive effort of democracy on itself' (Rosanvallon 2011: 123). Rosanvallon locates human rights regimes and constitutional courts as key institutional planks of this 'effort'. He argues that such judicial oversight corrects the shortcoming of representative democracy by requiring members of any current majority to register and respect minority opinion and take account of earlier formations of public will. It thereby operates as a restraint on government and majority opinion in ways that aspire to improve the quality of political deliberation and decision making. Constitutional checks and judicial scrutiny are, Rosanvallon argues, not an illegitimate trumping of the popular will but a vital means of embedding and deepening the idea of democratic legitimacy. It is an argument that has an important bearing on recent debates about the part played by human rights and judicial oversight in moderating the 'popular' will to punish (Tonry 2007b; van Zyl Smit and Snacken 2009; Snacken and Dumortier 2012).

But courts do not possess a monopoly over the practice of social reflection. Rosanvallon argues that a range of forces also contribute to legitimacy understood in this frame. Social movements and NGOs play this role when they denounce failures of government to keep their promises, or to embody a society's principles, or to meet international obligations. The crime and justice field is shaped today by an agonistic politics of this very kind. In Britain, the two-decade long struggle to expose a police cover-up following the 1989 Hillsborough Stadium disaster attests to this (Hillsborough Independent Panel 2012), as does the recent civil society mobilization which followed revelations that the tabloid press 'hacked' the mobile phones of, among others, crime victims. Rosanvallon also emphasizes the 'critical work' that the natural and social sciences undertake in 'preventing governments from arrogantly wrapping themselves in the folds of electoral legitimacy alone' (2011: 148) by bringing to bear knowledge on the issues at hand, and calling on governing agencies to justify their actions by reference to available evidence. The promotion of 'evidence-based policy' in Britain over recent years (and controversies engendered about its scope, meaning, and effects) illustrates well the intimate connections that now obtain between penal politics (and the legitimacy thereof) and knowledge politics (Loader and Sparks 2012a: 27–29).

In respect of these forces, Rosanvallon argues that democracies have only 'scratched the surface' in thinking about new ways of bringing reflexivity into politics (2011: 150) and of new domains of social action in which democratic legitimacy demands it—an issue we will return to. The obligations that societies owe to non-national migrants is one such example; so too is the question of how to develop reflexive participation in the development and deployment of surveillance technology. In this respect, Rosanvallon urges us to conceive of 'hybrid forums' in which scholars, social movements, and citizens can debate contested issues (see also Callon et al. 2011) and of 'citizen-oriented evaluation agencies' which can routinely assess the social value and impact of public policies (Rosanvallon 2011: 150)—and to think about both as vital to the future prospects of democracy. As Rosanvallon puts it: 'democracy can flourish only if it acknowledges the risks of dysfunctionality and equips itself with institutions capable of subjecting its own inner workings to constructive evaluation' (2008: 74–75).

The third and final extension of the idea of legitimacy Rosanvallon calls the *legitimacy of proximity*. By this he means institutions whose legitimation claim rests upon their capacity to attend to the particularity of individuals' lives and to radically immerse themselves in their concrete concerns and suffering in a manner that displays presence, attentiveness, empathy, and compassion. Rosanvallon argues that politics is shaped today by new social demands of precisely this kind. The experience of rejection and humiliation and claims for recognition and the restoration of dignity animate contemporary political life. So too do their accompanying scandals. This is an important insight into modern politics and supplies us with one reason why crime and punishment have the highly-charged centrality in political life which they typically do: simply put, they are fit topics for narrating and responding to in this way.[9] In this regard, the prominence of the crime question is symptomatic of a wider tendency, a point that criminologists (focused on crime and punishment perhaps too exclusively) can easily miss. Rosanvallon argues that, in this altered climate, an ability to engage in what he calls 'empathic representation' (2011: 190) becomes an indispensable political skill. Political office holders (and, one might add, police and criminal justice officials) are required to recognize that single events are no longer isolated cases but may become exemplary symbols, and that the experience of a single victim can be made to 'stand-in' for the circumstances, fears, and hopes of many (other or potential) victims. The legitimacy of power-holders thus greatly depends on the display of 'compassionate sincerity' (2011: 190) and the knack of grasping and articulating the public issue in an individual's private trouble. Legitimacy in this environment is a fragile entity. But Rosanvallon warns that legitimacy-seeking activity organized as a response to victimhood all too often amounts to a 'kind of social exorcism' (2011: 200), a symbolic politics which names and empathizes with suffering so as to make it more

[9] Consider in this regard the police-related events of a single recent month in the United Kingdom (September 2012) and the intense (not to say contrasting) reactions and calls for empathy (and action) they provoked. In that month: an independent inquiry found that South Yorkshire Police had deliberately doctored evidence and lied in a bid to denigrate the 96 victims of the Hillsborough Stadium disaster of 1989; two female officers in Greater Manchester had a hand-grenade propelled at them and were shot dead having been deliberately lured to their deaths by a false call to investigate a burglary (the streets of Manchester were later lined by tens of thousands of citizens, and many hundreds of off-duty police officers, at their funerals); an official report revealed that Greater Manchester Police (and social services) carelessly missed several opportunities to stop the sexual grooming of young girls in Rochdale, and it was alleged that a police officer was sworn at and insulted (he claimed to have been called 'a pleb') in Downing Street by a Cabinet Minister, who was subsequently compelled to resign his ministerial post.

tolerable, while leaving its sources untouched. The politics of proximity can, Rosanvallon argues, 'be fully democratic only if it is incorporated into a durable strategy for achieving a more just society' (2011: 201).

The idea of the legitimacy of proximity is intended as a guide to how this might be done. Interestingly for our purposes, Rosanvallon situates procedural justice—its appeal, its promise, and its limits—in this context. Fostering institutions whose encounters with citizens are shaped by procedural fairness is, he argues, a means of making individuals feel that their concrete experience matters, that their voice has been heard, and that they are being valued. Such fairness is therefore crucial in sustaining the 'flow of legitimacy' under the conditions that Rosanvallon describes. The fact that procedural recognition is a public good that 'everyone can share equally' (2011: 186) is also a clear asset in these conditions. So too is the fact that this good is likely to be experienced most affirmatively by individuals and social groups who feel their sense of belonging is precarious and cannot be taken for granted. But the insights of procedural justice also need to be kept in mind when we move—in ways that we have indicated we ought to—into trickier terrain relating to the distribution of resources and the hard choices allocative decisions necessarily involve. These choices too, Rosanvallon argues, 'are legitimate only if compatible with the "democratic method" of attention to particularity' (2011: 186). Here Rosanvallon calls for new 'institutions of interaction' (2011: 215) such as permanent public commissions of experts and citizens, which can oversee and judge political institutions, improve information exchange, and debate government proposals. Effective democratic governance today requires, in his view, new combinations of three basic elements: organized political representation, immediate social expression, and expert knowledge. These need to be assembled, and to interact, in forums that facilitate two essential properties of democratic politics: the clash of values and platforms, and the building of consensus. In an 'age of distrust', this is what democratic legitimacy demands: 'government decisions will not be seen as legitimate unless they have been developed, debated, and tested in forums of this type. Citizens will come to understand that democratic government means organizing this kind of interaction in as open and cooperative a way as possible' (2011: 216).

The three 'emerging figures of legitimacy' (2011: 219) that Rosanvallon describes advance our argument in several ways. First, they focus analytic and empirical attention in the right place. Rosanvallon reminds us that legitimacy inheres in institutions and relationships (not only in either procedures or outcomes or discourses). Legitimacy has to do with the tissue of relations that obtain between governors and governed (or, in Bottoms and Tankebe's (2012) formulation, 'power-holders' and 'audiences') and hence with the accountability, transparency, and responsiveness of the range of authorities that are assembled around the crime question in any given place or time. Secondly, Rosanvallon's work provides the basis for a dynamic and non-prescriptive framework within which one can investigate the presence, operation, and mix of legitimacy sustaining (or corroding) institutional practices in ways that are attuned to variations in political culture. It may as such offer theoretical orientations for comparative empirical study of legitimation processes and judgments in the domain of crime and justice. Thirdly, Rosanvallon offers a bridge between empirical enquiry and normative judgement. His work invites us to attend closely to the shape of the existing architecture assembled around the crime question in different political cultures, but also to imagine the kinds of institutions that are wholly or partially absent in given societies, but which may be pressingly needed if their crime control arrangements are to make good a claim of democratic legitimation. In this way, Rosanvallon offers one means of giving effect to the idea of legitimacy as a tool of social critique and normative reconstruction. Finally, we have here a frame of reference which cuts through, and exposes as false, any stark choice between 'insulationism' (Loader and Sparks 2010: ch 4) and 'democratization'.[10] Rosanvallon reminds us that a critique of, and alternative to, insulationism does not have to take the form of (penal) populism, and that extending the scope and depth of democratic politics in respect of crime and justice requires one to build upon and reinterpret, rather than jettison, what is of value in the insulationist position. In fact, he argues that populism is best understood as a pathological extension, not of democratic politics, but of unpolitical counter-democracy (2008: 267–73). Rosanvallon's point is that we need—in a democratizing rather than fearful spirit—to attend to the appropriate mix of impartial, reflexive, and proximate institutions, whether in empirical studies of actually existing legitimation contests or in the deployment of legitimacy as a regulative ideal guiding the construction of a better politics of crime.

In our view, we can by these means extend the analysis of legitimacy and crime control in ways that move beyond (but without ever seeking to deny the immense value of) the paradigms of procedural justice and late-modern/'neo-liberal' politicization. Rosanvallon's analysis remains, however, very much focused on relations between governments and citizens within settled liberal democratic states. But the world today is full of new (and other) things—not just democratic states and their citizens. It is a world in which people strive to build democratic states (and effective, responsive police and justice systems) following armed conflict or periods of authoritarian rule. It is a world of mass mobility in which millions move across borders and reside legally or illegally, freely or in detention, within societies of which they are not citizens. It is a world where power, authority, and crime control capacity are located in international and transnational bodies—most obviously the European Union, but also the Council of Europe, the International Criminal Court, and so on. It is a world where commercial actors—from local firms to global multinationals—play an increasing role in practices of security and detention. It is a world where crime control is not only or mainly delivered by human but also by non-human actors—from access control systems, to CCTV, to drones, to sophisticated surveillance and tracking systems.

To mention all this is not in any way to argue that state crime control has ceased to matter, or that we can sideline the issues we and others have raised about its legitimacy (or lack thereof). But it is to suggest that the criminological conversation about legitimacy has today to concern itself not simply with the 'how' of legitimacy (whether that is located in fair procedures, or in some wider frame of reference along the lines we have suggested), but also with the 'who' or 'what' of legitimacy (Fraser 2008: 15)—a

[10] Or, in the discourse of political theory, between legal and political constitutionalism (Bellamy 2007), or, more crudely, between liberalism and democracy.

point made recently by Mary Bosworth (2013) in the context of immigration detention. This means thinking afresh and with an enlarged political imagination about which actors in today's world count as subjects to which questions of legitimation ought properly to apply. We do not have space (nor yet the expertise!) to fully attend to this question in what remains of this chapter. But we do at least need to ask whether our extension of the concept of legitimacy to arrangements for deliberating, debating, and deciding about matters of crime control, and our use or Rosanvallon's work as our preferred means of enacting such a reformulation, itself needs to be reformulated. How, if at all, can the figures of legitimacy that Rosanvallon describes be made to have some analytic purchase in sites of transitional or inter- and trans-national justice, or exercise some leverage over the involvement in the criminal question of market actors and security technologies? By way of conclusion, let us try to find a route into these questions.

CONCLUSION: LEGITIMACY AND 'THE UNFINISHED'

One such route lies in thinking about how the idea and ideal of legitimacy can be connected to the theory and practice of 'the unfinished'. This term was introduced into the criminological lexicon by Thomas Mathiesen in the 1970s (1974) and has exercised a sporadic influence over criminological praxis ever since. Mathiesen developed his idea to theorize and inform the work of KROM—the Norwegian prisoners' organization with which he was deeply involved. In this context, the notion of the 'unfinished' was intended to enable KROM (and by extension radical penal politics more generally) to navigate a course between 'being "defined out" as irrelevant and "defined in" as undangerous' (1974: 23). This required a message whose relation to the existing order of things was that of competing contradiction: the message had to be a genuine alternative to the present in respect of goals and/or means and it had to be brought into actual competition with prevailing structures. The way to accomplish this, Mathiesen argued, was to ensure that the alternative took the form of, and was constantly maintained as, a 'sketch'—an unfinished outline of future possibilities that one mobilizes in the present while always resisting pressure to 'finish the drawing' (1974: 11).

Our concerns in this chapter are not so directly political, or immediately tied to a specific practice, as those of Mathiesen. But we do think that a close affinity can be established between the idea of legitimacy and the kind of analytical and political work which Mathiesen proposed. The promise of legitimacy in this regard lies in its capacity to interrogate and unsettle existing arrangements of police and penal power (using a language that institutions cannot help but recognize, thereby creating space for immanent rather than external critique) and to guide and regulate the search for alternative and better ways of arranging and doing things. With this in mind, we can return to the questions left hanging at the close of the previous section. The issue they point towards is that of 're-scaling' legitimacy so that it may inform analysis of the diverse range of sites in which power and authority is exercised in the field of crime and justice today—sites that extend beyond and below the police and criminal justice agencies of the nation-state. In recent years, this re-scaling has begun to take place in debates about justice (not only in its 'home' discipline of political theory but also in criminology and legal studies) and we have become accustomed to thinking about ideas such as global, transitional, transnational, and inter-generational justice.[11] Such re-conceptualization has been attempted rather less often in respect of legitimacy—perhaps because that term seems so entrenched within modern state-society relations. But there is no necessary reason for thinking that the idea of legitimacy is trapped in that lineage, and cannot do any useful work in new settings of crime control and criminal justice. Habermas, for instance, has made a powerful case for 'loosen[ing] the conceptual ties between democratic legitimacy and the familiar forces of state organisation' and pressed the claims of deliberative democracy as a model for doing so (Habermas 2001: 111).

Bottoms and Tankebe's (2012) re-casting of legitimacy as a 'perpetual discussion' between 'power-holders' and 'audiences' is a valuable point of departure in this regard (just as it undoubtedly is in the more familiar criminal justice settings for which it was coined). But if that formulation is to become our guide it is going to be necessary to expand our operative sense of where power is held and exercised (to encompass international institutions and policy networks, corporate actors, and so on). We also need to think harder about the range of 'audiences' subjected to, or affected by, the actions of such power-holders and the governance structures within which they operate. And we need to analyse and imagine the kinds of inclusive dialogue that democratic legitimacy might conceivably require across different crime and justice sites: between what actors—states, NGOs, non-citizens, etc.? In what deliberative settings? With what transactions between 'weak' and 'strong' publics? With what connections to decision making and makers? (see generally Brunkhorst 2002; Dryzek 2012: Part III).

This is a formidable as well as an exciting agenda. It is also an agenda in respect of which there is material to draw upon and extend—both theoretically and empirically. There is an established literature on legitimation problems, and how they may be addressed, in the world's most developed post-state polity—the European Union (EU), some of which touches on the EU's expanding justice and home affairs capacity (e.g. Eriksen 2011). There is a large and vibrant literature on international and transitional justice, and on the challenges of building and sustaining effective police and justice systems in post-conflict settings, that could fruitfully be brought into closer conversation with the extant debates on legitimacy. The literature on private security has at least started to grapple with the questions of human rights, accountability, and democratic governance that accompany the pluralization of policing and the commercialization of detention (Stenning 2009; Sklansky 2011). There is also evidence that private security actors experience a need to legitimize their commercial practices to themselves (and others) in non-market terms (Thumala et al. 2011). There are examples in several fields of science and technology of public involvement in decisions

[11] One can point to other concepts within democratic theory whose Westphalian presuppositions have been challenged and that are now being re-cast in a transnational frame. The 'public sphere' is a case in point (Fraser 2008: ch. 5).

about technological development and deployment that could be extended to surveillance technology (Callon et al. 2011). We might in respect of these developments—picking up on the argument proposed in this chapter—begin to think about the institutions of impartiality, reflexivity, and proximity that have been developed (whether partially or prefiguratively) or may yet be created in order to foster the democratic legitimacy of both international and non-state institutions and networks of crime control and coercive power. There is, in short, plenty that remains analytically and politically 'unfinished'. Its exploration will require, in our view, a closer conversation between criminology and the relevant resources of political analysis and international relations than has been established hitherto.[12]

In respect of this agenda, as well as in relation to more established legitimation problems that beset the crime control apparatus of modern nation-states, there is a second aspect to our recovery of Mathiesen's notion of the 'unfinished'. One concern of this chapter has been to remind readers of certain costs (there have, we know, been major benefits as well) that attend any transformation of legitimacy into a category of administrative practice—as witnessed in both police forces and prisons in Britain over the last two decades. Against this backdrop, we have sought to recover and extol the virtues of legitimacy as a critical social scientific idea and a future-oriented political ideal—one that in both of those guises has a role to play in the 'unfinished' project of democratization. To think about legitimacy in this way is to conceive of it as a tool for the conceptual and empirical analysis of existing institutional practices of crime and justice, and as the basis for grounded but experimental theorizing about what a better politics of crime and justice might look like or could plausibly be enacted. The value of legitimacy here lies in the way it fixes our gaze on the gap between the world as it is and the world as it might be. As such, legitimacy remains, in our judgement, an indispensable resource for criminology understood as civic social science. It is a resource that enables criminologists to combine closely-observed social analysis of the practices of claims-making, stance-taking, dialogue, and judgement that surround extant institutional efforts to address the criminal question with the patient task of 'imaginative persuasion' that remains required if one is to continue, little by little, the 'very partial, historically erratic and unsteady process' (Dunn, this volume) of rolling back the boundaries of unaccountable power (wherever it may be found) and extending those of democratic authority.

REFERENCES

Aas, K. F. (2011) 'Crimmigrant Bodies and Bona Fide Travellers: Surveillance, Citizenship and Global Governance', *Theoretical Criminology* 15(3): 331–46.

Barker, V. (2007) 'The Politics of Pain: A Political Institutionalist Analysis of Crime Victims' Moral Protests', *Law and Society Review* 41(3): 619–64.

[12] We have made this point on other occasions (Loader and Percy 2012; Loader and Sparks 2012b). All that is necessary to add here is the claim that the concept of legitimacy may offer one route through which to advance in concrete and manageable ways such inter-disciplinary dialogue.

Beckett, K. (1997) *Making Crime Pay*. New York: Oxford University Press.

Beetham, D. (1991) *The Legitimation of Power*. Basingstoke: Macmillan.

Bellamy, R. (2007) *Political Constitutionalism*. Cambridge: Cambridge University Press.

Bosworth, M. (2012) 'Deportation and Immigration Detention: Globalising the Sociology of Punishment', *Theoretical Criminology* 16(3): 123–40.

Bosworth, M. (2013) 'Can Immigration Confinement be Legitimate? Understanding Confinement in a Global World', in Aas, K. F. and Bosworth, M. (eds) *The Borders of Punishment*. Oxford: Oxford University Press.

Bottoms, A. and Tankebe, J. (2012) 'Beyond Procedural Justice: A Dialogic Approach to Legitimacy in Criminal Justice', *Journal of Criminal Law and Criminology* 102(1): 101–50.

Braithwaite, V. (2011) 'Resistant and Dismissive Defiance towards Tax Authorities' (pp. 91–115), in Crawford, A. and Hucklesby, A. (eds) *Legitimacy and Compliance in Criminal Justice*. London: Routledge.

Brunkhorst, H. (2002) 'Globalizing Democracy without a State: Weak Public, Strong Public, Global Constitutionalism', *Millennium* 31: 675–90.

Callon, M., Lascoumes, P., and Barthe, Y. (2011) *Acting in an Uncertain World: An Essay on Technical Democracy*. Cambridge, MA: MIT Press.

Coicaud, J-M. (2002) *Legitimacy and Politics*. Cambridge: Cambridge University Press.

Dryzek, J. (2012) *Foundations and Frontiers of Deliberative Governance*. Oxford: Oxford University Press.

Dubber, M. (2006) *Victims in the War on Crime: The Use and Abuse of Victims' Rights*. New York: New York University Press.

Eriksen, E. O. (2011) 'Governance between Expertise and Democracy: The Case of European Security', *Journal of European Public Policy* 18(8): 1169–89.

Flinders, M. (2012) *Defending Politics: Why Democracy Matters in the Twenty-first Century*. Oxford: Oxford University Press.

Fossen, T. (2012) 'Taking Stances, Contesting Commitments: Political Legitimacy and the Pragmatic Turn', *Journal of Political Philosophy* DOI: 10.1111/jopp.12003.

Fraser, N. (2008) *Scales of Justice*. Cambridge: Polity.

Garland, D. (2001) *The Culture of Control*. Oxford: Oxford University Press.

Habermas, J. (2001) *The Postnational Constellation*. Cambridge: Polity.

Hall, S., Critcher, C., Jefferson, T., Clarke, J., and Roberts, B. (1978) *Policing the Crisis*. London: Macmillan.

Hillsborough Independent Panel (2012) *Report of the Hillsborough Independent Panel*. London: Stationery Office.

Hood, C. (2010) *The Blame Game: Spin, Bureaucracy and Self-Preservation in Government*. Princeton: Princeton University Press.

Jackson, J., Bradford, B., Hough, M., Myhill, A., Quinton, P., and Tyler, T. (2012) 'Why do People Comply with the Law: Legitimacy and the Influence of Legal Institutions', *British Journal of Criminology* 52(6): 1051–71.

Keane, J. (2009) *The Life and Death of Democracy*. London: Pocket Books.

Lacey, N. (2011) 'Why Globalisation Doesn't Spell Convergence: Models of Institutional Variation and the Comparative Political Economy of Punishment' (pp. 214–50), in Crawford, A. (ed) *International and Comparative Criminal Justice and Urban Governance*. Cambridge: Cambridge University Press.

Liebling, A., with Arnold, H. (2004) *Prisons and their Moral Performance*. Oxford: Oxford University Press.

Liebling, A. (2007) 'Why Prison Staff Culture Matters', in J. M. Byrne, D. Hummer and F. S. Taxman (eds) *The Culture of Prison Violence*. Boston: Allyn and Bacon Publishing.

LOADER, I. (2006) 'Fall of the "Platonic Guardians": Liberalism, Criminology and Political Responses to Crime in England and Wales', *British Journal of Criminology* 46(4): 561–86.

LOADER, I. and MULCAHY, A. (2003) *Policing and the Condition of England: Memory, Politics and Culture*. Oxford: Oxford University Press.

LOADER, I. and PERCY, S. (2012) 'Bringing the "Outside" In and the "Inside" Out: Crossing the Criminology/IR Divide', *Global Crime* 13(4): 213–18.

LOADER, I. and SPARKS, R. (2007) 'Contemporary Landscapes of Crime, Order and Control: Governance, Risk and Globalization' (pp. 78–101), in Maguire, M., Morgan, R., and Reiner, R. (eds) *The Oxford Handbook of Criminology* (4th edn). Oxford: Oxford University Press.

LOADER, I. and SPARKS, R. (2010) *Public Criminology?* London: Routledge.

LOADER, I. and SPARKS, R. (2012a) 'Situating Criminology' (pp. 3–38), in Maguire, M., Morgan, R. and Reiner, R. (eds) *The Oxford Handbook of Criminology* (5th edn). Oxford: Oxford University Press.

LOADER, I. and SPARKS, R. (2012b) 'Beyond Lamentation: Towards a Democratic Egalitarian Politics of Crime and Justice' (pp. 11–42), in Newburn, T. and Peay, J. (eds) *Policing: Politics, Culture and Control*. Oxford: Hart.

MATHIESEN, T. (1974) *The Politics of Abolition*. London: Martin Robertson.

NELLIS, M. (2012) 'Implant Technology and the Electronic Monitoring of Offenders: Old and New Questions about Compliance, Control and Legitimacy' (pp. 159–80), in Crawford, A. and Hucklesby, A. (eds) *Legitimacy and Compliance in Criminal Justice*. London: Routledge.

NEWBURN, T. (2007) '"Tough on Crime": Penal Policy in England and Wales', *Crime and Justice* (vol 36). Chicago: The University of Chicago Press.

NEWBURN, T. and JONES, T. (2005) 'Symbolic Politics and Penal Populism: The Long Shadow of Willie Horton', *Crime Media Culture* 1(1): 72–87.

PITKIN, H. (1966) 'Obligation and Consent—II', *American Political Science Review* 60: 39–52.

PRATT, J. (2007) *Penal Populism*. London: Routledge

ROSANVALLON, P. (2008) *Counter-Democracy: Politics in an Age of Distrust*. Cambridge: Cambridge University Press.

ROSANVALLON, P. (2011) *Democratic Legitimacy: Impartiality, Reflexivity, Proximity*. Princeton: Princeton University Press.

SIMON, J. (2007) *Governing Through Crime: How the War on Crime Transformed American Democracy and Created a Culture of Fear*. New York: Oxford University Press.

SKLANSKY, D. (2011) 'Private Policing and Human Rights', *Law & Ethics of Human Rights* 5(1): 2–26.

SMITH, D. J. (2007) 'The Foundations of Legitimacy' (pp. 30–58), in Tyler, T. (ed) *Legitimacy and Criminal Justice*. New York: Russell Sage.

SNACKEN, S. and E. DUMORTIER (eds) (2011) *Resisting Punitiveness in Europe? Welfare, Human Rights and Democracy*. London: Routledge.

SPARKS, R. and BOTTOMS, A. (2007) 'Legitimacy and Imprisonment Revisited: Notes on the Problem of Order Ten Years After', in Byrne, J., Taxman, F., and Hummer, D. (eds) *The Culture of Prison Violence*. London: Allyn and Bacon.

SPARKS, R., BOTTOMS, A. and HAY, W. (1996) *Prisons and the Problem of Order*. Oxford: Oxford University Press.

STENNING, P. (2009) 'Governance and Accountability in a Plural Policing Environment: The Story So Far', *Policing* 3(1): 22–33.

TANKEBE, J. (2009) 'Public Cooperation with the Police in Ghana: Does Procedural Fairness Matter?', *Criminology* 47(4): 1265–93.

Thumala, A., Goold, B., and Loader, I. (2011) 'A Tainted Trade? Moral Ambivalence and Legitimation Work in the Private Security Industry', *British Journal of Sociology* 62 (2): 283–303.

Tonry, M. (2007a) 'Introduction' (pp. 3–8), in Tyler, T. (ed) *Legitimacy and Criminal Justice*. New York: Russell Sage Foundation.

Tonry, M. (2007b) 'Determinants of Penal Policies', in Tonry, M. (ed) *Crime, Punishment and Politics in Comparative Perspective*. Chicago: University of Chicago Press.

Tyler, T. (2003) 'Procedural Justice, Legitimacy, and the Effective Rule of Law', *Crime and Justice* (vols 3–30). Chicago: University of Chicago Press.

Tyler, T. (2011) 'Trust and Legitimacy: Policing in the USA and Europe', *European Journal of Criminology* 8(4): 254–66.

Tyler, T. (2012) 'Legitimacy and Compliance: The Virtues of Self-Regulation' (pp. 8–28), in Crawford, A. and Hucklesby, A. (eds) *Legitimacy and Compliance in Criminal Justice*. London: Routledge.

Van Zyl Smit, D. and Snacken, S. (2009) *Principles of European Prison Law and Policy: Penology and Human Rights*. Oxford, Oxford University Press.

Wacquant, L. (2008) 'Ordering Insecurity: Social Polarization and the Punitive Upsurge', *Radical Philosophy Review* 11(1): 9–27.

Wacquant, L. (2009) *Punishing the Poor*. Durham NC: Duke University Press.

Wacquant, L. (2012) 'Three Steps to a Historical Anthropology of Actually Existing Neoliberalism', *Social Anthropology* 20: 66–79.

7

TRUSTING AUTHORITIES: LEGITIMACY, TRUST, AND COLLABORATION IN NON-DEMOCRATIC REGIMES

Susanne Karstedt[1]

AUTHORITARIAN REGIMES IN AN AGE OF DEMOCRACY

In their most recent rendition of the Index on Political and Civil Liberties Across the World 2013, Freedom House reported that since 2006 democracy, and political and civil rights were in continuous decline globally. Even if the Arab Spring in 2011 had challenged authoritarian rule, and notwithstanding its successes, there had been severe setbacks in the region, which on balance amounted to rather less than more political and civil rights. Marking the seventh consecutive year in which countries in decline outnumbered those with gains this represented the longest continuous global backsliding since the first publication of such a report in 1972. It now seems to threaten the gains in freedom that were made since the start of the 'third wave of democratization' in the 1980s, and after the Cold War.

When Francis Fukuyama (1992) declared the 'end of history' with the global triumph of democracy after the fall of the Berlin Wall, in hindsight this might rather have signified the beginning of the end of a 'third wave of democracy' (Jaggers and Gurr 1995; Huntington 1993) that had started in the 1980s in Latin America, and spread to Europe and Asia. He did not however forecast an end to dictatorships and authoritarian rule. With nearly a decade of non-democratic regimes on the rise at the start of the twenty-first century, the direction of change seems to have turned and is now heading towards non-democratic regimes. In 2012 the 16 countries that exhibited

[1] I am deeply grateful to Michael Koch, MA, University of Bielefeld for the collection of data, analyses, and graphics. His excellent advice and patience are invaluable. I express my gratitude to the Regulatory Institutions Network, Australian National University that hosted me as Visiting Fellow from January to April 2013. I thank all RegNet colleagues for ideas, support, and comments which very much improved work on this article, in particular John Braithwaite and Peter Drahos. Finally I thank the young researchers from the Centre for Independent Social Research, St. Petersburg, Russia for their comments.

gains in freedom, were outnumbered by the 28 that showed declines. The types of institutions of freedom that were mainly affected are those that are seminal for the functioning of contemporary democracies. While competitive elections and political pluralism only slightly declined or even improved between 2008 and 2012, the losses for freedom of the press and expression, freedom of assembly and of non-governmental organizations, independent judiciary, and equal protection under the law were quite substantial (Freedom House 2013: 2). These are losses which directly affect criminal justice systems, both in terms of their functioning as well as in terms of their legitimacy.

The global landscape of democracies and mixed or autocratic regimes presents a checked pattern according to the most widely used indicators of which the Freedom House Index is just one. Like democracies, contemporary authoritarian and autocratic regimes come in many shapes: common categorizations differentiate between civilian, military, and 'royal' dictatorships (Cheibub, Gandhi, and Vreeland 2010), or monarchies, personal, and military rule in non-democratic regimes (Brooker 2009; Schedler 2006). Contemporary analyses of authoritarian regimes recognize the diversity of their institutions (Gandhi 2008). Importantly authoritarian regimes need to be seen in perspective and within the context of an 'age of democratization' rather than being simply juxtaposed to a homogenous bloc of democracies. It is the competitive nature of 'hybrid regimes' that defines the regional spread and types of authoritarian regimes after the Cold War (Levitsky and Way 2010).

Given their undeniable and continuous global presence, non-democratic and authoritarian regimes pose pressing questions: What accounts for their success and ongoing stability, in particular as transitional democracies often fail miserably (Esty et al. 1998)? How do they muster support and legitimacy from their citizens, given the spread of new information technologies? In which ways do they elicit support for control, and often heavy-handed action by police and the authorities? Their obvious strength, stability and survival seem to testify to successful policies of securing the legitimacy of their governments and regimes, and the continuous support of sufficiently large groups of their citizenry (e.g. Case 1993). Different types of authoritarian regimes will vary according to the institutions and mechanisms that elicit and foster legitimacy among the population, and ensure cooperation with authorities and compliance with norms. Legitimacy of criminal justice therefore should differ among authoritarian regimes as much as it does between established democracies. This raises questions for established and transitional democracies: What kind of support and legitimacy do authoritarian regimes muster, and does it differ from what democratic processes generate (and what we might think of as 'legitimate legitimacy')?

It cannot be ignored though that citizens assign legitimacy to authoritarian governments, and their criminal justice apparatus. Certainly one indication of this is that they willingly cooperate with criminal justice institutions, particularly with the notorious secret services and police in these countries. For example, tens of thousands of citizens as 'informal informers' submitted information on their fellow citizens to the Staatssicherheit (Stasi) the secret service of the former communist German Democratic Republic (Fulbrook 1997; Bruce 2010; for Romania's Securitate see Deletant 2006). Even if we have to concede some level of coercion in engaging them, many of them seem to have willingly and voluntarily obliged to the request for a range of reasons. Similarly, German citizens collaborated with the Gestapo, the secret police of the Nazi regime in Germany (Gellately 1990, 2001; Rees 1997; Mann 1987). Besides collaboration with these institutions of coercive control, citizens in non-democratic countries cooperate with the police and authorities and invest them with confidence. In contemporary China, the police seem to enjoy a rather high level of trust and confidence among its citizens, in urban as well as in rural areas (see for an overview Sun et al. 2012; Michelson and Read 2011). Citizens seem to be not much less willing to cooperate than in democracies. It is however telling that we think of citizens *cooperating* with criminal justice institutions in democracies, but as *collaborators* when it comes to authoritarian states.

As Bottoms and Tankebe (2012) stress the 'dialogic' and 'interactive' nature of legitimacy they implicitly refer to its characteristic as being voluntarily granted. Obliging to the demands of the power-holder for acceptance of authority and compliance with rules, is an act of volition on the part of citizens (or subjects) and cannot by definition be an act of mere coercion by the power-holder. Authoritarian and non-democratic regimes are traditionally seen as enforcing obedience and compliance by their citizens. However, as Johnson (2011) points out, observers tend to underrate the level of voluntary compliance and obedience that they could and can muster. Democratic regimes on the other hand certainly give more space to and allow for considered, discursive, and also discordant responses from the audience of citizens, and withdrawal of legitimacy is (mostly) not threatened with coercive responses.

Could it be that the 'dialogic nature' of legitimacy in contemporary societies actually disadvantages democracies? During the past decades, democratic governments and institutions have quite dramatically and across the board lost the trust and confidence of citizens, not the least criminal justice institutions.[2] Besides evidence from cross-national surveys, other signs of a loss of legitimacy of democratic institutions are decreasing voter turn-out in local, regional, and national elections, rapidly decreasing membership of established political parties, and the rise of fringe and protest parties. 'Dialogic legitimacy' might turn out to be a double-edged sword, as dialogue equally facilitates legitimizing as well as delegitimizing content. In addition, contemporary democratic institutions are geared towards a 'healthy' distrust of governments, bureaucracies, and their representatives, and actually designed to balance trust with 'institutionalized distrust' (Braithwaite 1998). They are based on 'pragmatic dissent' (Mann, 1970; Muller and Seligson 1994) among the citizenry and between citizens, governments and institutions, rather than on consensus. Police actions that citizens feel to be unfair and illegitimate caused riots across the world; in London and in Tunisia in 2011; in India (Braithwaite 2013); and in China on a large scale (Financial Times 2010; Göbel and Ong 2012). Obviously these had wider repercussions on regime legitimacy and stability in Tunisia than in the UK, but their impact on regime stability in democratic India and non-democratic China does not differ dramatically, given the evidence available.

[2] See for a comprehensive overview Jackson et al. 2012.

This chapter aims at transcending the prism of democracy through which legitimacy has been studied. Do contemporary authoritarian regimes actually differ in terms of the legitimacy of their criminal justice systems from democracies? Do they generate considerable levels of legitimacy notwithstanding the low accountability of authorities and the level of coercion many of them exert? Or do democracies have 'comparative advantages' (Karstedt 2006) in generating legitimacy for their criminal justice institutions, and eliciting support and cooperation from their citizens? Is procedural justice, fair decision making, and respectful treatment universally and across regime types a decisive mechanism in enhancing legitimacy and cooperation with criminal justice? These questions will be addressed by exploring the legitimacy of criminal justice in authoritarian regimes in two steps. After briefly reviewing seminal conceptualizations, I will first provide some historical evidence on legitimacy of police and courts in authoritarian regimes, mainly from Nazi Germany and the former East-German Democratic Republic. In a second step I will analyse legitimacy of criminal justice for a cross-national sample of 140 democracies and autocracies based on two different typologies of democratic and non-democratic regimes for the beginning of the twenty-first century; for this study the period from 2004 to 2008 was chosen.

LEGITIMACY IN NON-DEMOCRATIC REGIMES: A CONCEPTUAL FRAMEWORK

DEFINING NON-DEMOCRATIC REGIMES AND THE AUTHORITARIAN STATE

The 'short' twentieth century had been an age of totalitarianism (Linz 2000: 1); in particular its European manifestations have shaped scholarly engagement and analysis of totalitarian and authoritarian states until recently. However, the rise and continuous presence of non-democratic regimes and authoritarian states have encouraged a more global, comparative and also differentiated perspective on contemporary non-democratic regimes (e.g. Levitsky and Way 2010; Gandhi 2008; Schedler 2006). This was a significant step towards leaving the prism of democracy aside, through which many of these regimes had been analysed during and since the 'third wave of democratization'. The then dominant 'transition paradigm' classified many of the non-democratic regimes as en route to fully democratic regimes, and optimistically defined them as 'illiberal democracies" (Zakaria 1997) or 'semi-democracies' (Case 1993). As Esty et al. (1998) already noted in the 1990s, these transitions were not a one-way road, and a number of transitional countries were at risk of overall state failure. More than a decade later, and in the face of 'durable authoritarianism' that 'survived' the third wave of democratization (Brownlee 2007) terminology has switched towards defining them as authoritarian and non-democratic regimes, however qualifying them in a number of ways, and thus accounting for their institutional diversity. Across the globe, these new regimes that emerged from the Cold War, 'combined electoral competition with varying degrees of authoritarianism'; they are characterized by electoral manipulation, abuse of state resources, and high levels of coercion (Levitsky and Way 2010: 3). These are so-called 'hybrid regimes', and defined as 'competitive authoritarian' states (Levitsky and Way 2010: 3), or 'electoral authoritarianism' (Schedler 2006). According to Levitsky and Way (2010: 3), 33 regimes could be counted as such in 1995, 'exceeding the number of full democracies in the developing and post-communist world'. Brooker (2009) differentiates between 'monarchical and personal rule', 'military' and 'one-party rule'. Institutional settings vary widely between these types, but also within different types of dictatorships, and account for their stability and survival (Gandhi 2008). Accordingly they differ in the role of coercion and the power (and violence) their criminal justice institutions can and do wield.

The diversity of contemporary non-democratic regimes poses challenges when comparing them to democratic governments. However, two characteristics of non-democratic and more circumscribed 'authoritarian regimes' seem to be useful for this task. 'Low accountability' refers to the lack of regular, free, and fair elections of national, regional, and local governments as well as to a deficiency in rule-governed mechanisms of accountability of other institutions in society. 'High coercion' refers to the unrestrained exercise of power and even violence by governments and institutions. Taken together these two attributes combine into a lack or absence of the rule of law defined as legal mechanisms that restrict the arbitrary exercise of state and governmental power (Krygier 2011). As such they become particularly visible in the system of criminal justice: as unrestrained powers of civil and military police, restraints of the independence of courts and direct government intervention into both.

Contemporary conceptualizations and theorizing privilege the combination of 'high accountability' and 'low coercion' of democratic regimes as seedbeds of legitimacy of their institutions and incentives for cooperation by their citizens. Both characteristics capture institutional designs that allow for the 'dialogic' and 'interactive' nature of legitimacy (Bottoms and Tankebe 2012), and that elicit voluntary compliance with rules and laws among the citizenry rather than enforced obedience as in authoritarian states. On the opposite extreme of the scale, 'low accountability' and 'high coercion' in a similar vein circumscribe a range of institutional settings through which non-democratic regimes seek to consolidate, claim legitimacy, exert control, and solicit compliance (see e.g. Brooker 2009: 144). This institutional space in non-democratic regimes is defined by different levels of accountability and coercion, and by specific mechanisms and institutional designs that allow for making officials accountable or target coercion against specific groups (e.g. by special courts).

Authoritarian regimes have a range of 'dialogic mechanisms' at their disposal, when they open up routes for citizens to express grievances, and to make lower-level representatives in the state bureaucracy accountable for their decisions. One important dialogic route are letters directed to the highest authority, and to the leader himself, thus assigning ultimate legitimate power over lower-level bureaucrats to him, and trusting in his willingness to recognize and rectify wrongful decisions. Both Markovits (2010) and Niethammer (1991) describe these routes and their usage by citizens of the former German Democratic Republic (GDR). This route of 'upward' communication is complemented by 'downward' and direct intervention into courts, bureaucracies, and other institutions, thus taking 'short-cuts' that are not available in the complex bureaucracies of democracies, and their independent institutions. Occasional corruption scandals, often orchestrated from above and including the sacrifice of lower level bureaucrats as well as of high-ranking officials allow citizens to express their discontent and grievances (Holmes 1993). The regime can (re-) establish itself as responsive to the demands of citizens, and enhance its credentials of justice and legitimacy (Karstedt 2003; Mica 2012 for Romania; Brooker 2009).

LEGITIMACY: AN EMPIRICAL AND NORMATIVE CONCEPT

As it turns out, legitimacy is not a privilege of democracies: neither are contemporary non-democratic regimes exclusively based on coercion, nor is compliance fully voluntary in democracies. Legitimacy emerges as a janus-faced concept, both empirical and normative, and comprising both the *process* of justification, and the *outcome* as 'justified'. Legitimacy implies the process through which citizens arrive at believing that the rules and decisions of a power-holder should be obeyed, the power-holder has a right to issue these decisions, and rightly expects compliance with these (Sunshine and Tyler 2003). It also refers to the outcome of this process in terms of acceptance and compliance with rules. For the power-holder this implies legitimizing her claim to the right of holding power, and the acceptance of this claim. This of course, is an empirical definition of legitimacy, and one that is based on an interactive process in which shared beliefs about legitimacy are developed and put into practice. The 'output' of this process can be measured in terms of acceptance of decisions and compliance with rules, or trust and confidence in authorities, whilst the process itself will be analysed in terms of its motivational and interactive determinants that generate legitimacy (or not) (see MacCoun 2005). It is this empirical definition of legitimacy that has been promoted by Tom Tyler and his colleagues.

However, legitimacy as a concept is also imbued with normative meaning, both in terms of its outcome and in terms of the process that generates it. What is held as 'legitimate' within a social group is deeply embedded and shaped by its culture, social structure, and political institutions, and changes with these contexts. This is the legacy of Max Weber, and his ideal types of 'legitimate domination' perfectly illustrate this point. Each one derives its specific legitimacy from a set of norms, values, and institutions, which are then used as the standard for evaluating power-holders, decisions, and rules, and also the process through which legitimacy is generated (see Beetham 1991; Coicaud 2002). The Weberian notion of legitimacy thus implies the *empirical analysis* of its *normative embeddedness* and its context-specific realizations. As David Smith (2007) points out, the contemporary vision of legitimacy both in terms of process and outcome is mainly informed by standards of legitimacy in democracies, particularly the US. As such, it has an often unrecognized and un-acknowledged normative underpinning, according to which neither every shared belief counts as 'legitimate' nor does any route to power.[3]

The dual nature of the concept—both empirical and normative—and the ensuing tensions between empirical analysis and implicit normative standards raise a number of unsettling questions for our sense of what constitutes legitimacy in contemporary criminal justice, and makes it difficult to approach the question of legitimacy in non-democratic regimes. The empirical understanding of legitimacy, in particular when based on procedural justice and fair treatment, opens up space for the manipulative use of apparently fair procedures by the authorities in order to achieve acceptance of unequal outcomes from citizens without jeopardizing their overall legitimacy (MacCoun 2005: 188). The legitimacy of power-holders might not be affected at all in the eyes of the majority of citizens, if minority groups are differently and unfairly treated by the authorities, in particular by criminal justice agencies (Karstedt 2011; see MacCoun 2005 for an overview of differential treatment; in different countries Tyler 2007). The empirical conceptualization of legitimacy 'makes it possible to say that a political system such as Nazi Germany... though clearly evil, can still be legitimate.' Torture might be regarded not only as 'entirely normal' but also as a perfectly legitimate practice in a belief system shared by the citizenry and the power-holders (Smith 2007: 35), both in democratic and non-democratic regimes.[4]

From an empirical perspective, legitimacy as an outcome exists and can be observed in both democratic and non-democratic regimes, though the interactive processes, the motivational basis, and the mechanisms that generate it might differ considerably. From the normative point of view, however, we hesitate to assign 'legitimacy' to non-democratic regimes, to civilian and military dictatorships, or (most outlandish) to warlords in non-sovereign spaces. The normative notion of 'democratic' legitimacy to which we intuitively subscribe, relies on the demands not only for fair procedures but also for accountability of authorities, restraint of power holders by rule of law, and openness rather than manipulative efforts on the part of the authorities. In contrast, as non-democratic regimes do not meet these normative expectations, any observed legitimacy of non-democratic regimes and their institutions, trust in their authorities and governments, or the motivational basis of legitimacy generating processes appear as being 'normatively illegitimate' and mistaken by those who grant it to power-holders (MacCoun 2005: 188). In addition, as the empirical concept clearly requires *voluntary* acknowledgement of legitimacy, non-democratic regimes are seen as lacking, preferring to use coercion in order to achieve acceptance of and compliance with decision, rules, and laws.

The normative as well as the empirical concepts of legitimacy are thus based on the juxtaposition of 'high accountability/low coercion democracies' and 'low accountability/high coercion authoritarian regimes' as outlined in the previous paragraph.

[3] International law establishes norms of what kind of routes to power are acceptable and consequently which regimes are recognized internationally.

[4] The debate about torture and the position of the US government after the terrorist attacks of 9/11 demonstrate that such shared beliefs are not restricted to authoritarian regimes. Smith (2007) reports numerous examples of illegitimate and illegal practices by the police in democracies, including torture, which seem to be supported within the police as well as by the population.

Both rely on the assumption that voluntary acknowledgement of legitimacy is only possible in the former and absent in the latter. In this way the empirical concept of legitimacy is imbued with normative content which gives preference to the democratic process of generating legitimacy. However, from a Weberian point of view, legitimacy is generated as a shared belief of citizens and power-holders in the context of different cultural and institutional settings, each requiring and producing its own type of legitimacy. In order to explore legitimacy of criminal justice in non-democratic, authoritarian regimes, and contrast them with democratic regimes, we need to rely on his concept of legitimacy which acknowledges the normative content in different realizations of legitimacy (see also Beetham 1991).

LEGITIMACY IN AUTHORITARIAN AND TOTALITARIAN REGIMES: EVIDENCE FROM HISTORY

Drawing on the history of Europe in the twentieth century and the totalitarian state, historians have defined authoritarian states as relying on high levels of coercion, and in particular on spreading fear in order to achieve compliance and cooperation by citizens. In both processes criminal justice agencies, the police as well as secret police and special courts were important actors and institutions. However, historical evidence from Nazi Germany (Gellately 1990, 2001; Mann 1987), the former Soviet Union (Fitzpatrick and Gellately 1997; Brooker 2009), Fascist Italy and Franco's Spain (Dunnage 2004; Cenarro 2004) shows that these regimes actually relied on consent and voluntary cooperation with criminal justice institutions, including the most dreaded ones.[5] As Johnson (2011: 601) concludes from his analysis of three Special Courts in the Rhineland under the Nazi regime that were in charge of so-called political crimes, '... most people did not live their lives in fear and dread; rather most ordinary German citizens freely gave their consent to a regime they thought was acting in their best interests, and those of other members of the "People's Community"'. Authoritarian states do not use coercion indiscriminately, but in a selective and targeted way against specific groups (see Karstedt 2011), and this in turn secures consent from a majority.

Authoritarian states thus muster a complex web of institutions that use coercion and voluntary cooperation in a selective and balanced way. Where the rule of law is absent or weak in authoritarian states, space is opened up for a range of institutions that operate and take over functions of the established branches of criminal justice. This 'hybrid' system of justice provides mechanisms of direct intervention and manipulation of the justice system. This is the space of party courts and tribunals

[5] As Johnson (2011) points out, two perspectives have shaped historians' views of the relationship between coercion and voluntary engagement and compliance, in particular for the Nazi regime. From the perspective of the totalitarian state coercion, fear and threat dominate (e.g. Evans 2005). More than two decades of research, in particular on the Gestapo have provided evidence for a high level of voluntary commitment and cooperation of citizens under the Nazi regime, as does Johnson's own research.

('party moots', Mica 2012), secret police units under direct control of the party and its organization, or 'tribunals' and 'committees' established in neighbourhoods and work places and vested with quite extended powers in deciding upon conflicts and cases (see also Brooker 2009). While party courts and tribunals are often tasked to channel 'registered dissatisfaction' (Mica 2012: 142), and cautiously and selectively apportion blame to party cadres and officials, neighbourhood and work place committees and tribunals explicitly seek to involve citizens in (criminal) justice and legal matters. As Inga Markovits (2010: ch. 6) explains in her history of a lower court in communist Germany, the courts had to involve such committees, and seek advice as well as information from them, e.g. in divorce but also in criminal cases. Legitimacy is thus claimed for a range of institutions, and cooperation from citizens is sought in realms and ways much closer to everyday life than the formal procedures and practices of rule-of-law justice can provide. These institutional practices generate involvement and channels of communication, as well as opportunities for voluntary cooperation.

Historical research on legitimacy of regimes and their branches of criminal justice have to rely on files from the police and courts, as e.g. for the Gestapo (Mann 1987; Gellately 1990, 2001; Rees 1997) or local courts and police in Rhineland cities (Johnson 2011) in Nazi Germany. The narrative of a court in communist Germany from 1945 up to the fall of the wall by Inga Markovits (2010) is exceptional, as is the case study analysis of party tribunals in Romania under the Ceausescu regime (Mica 2012). Further evidence of cooperation with the secret police and security forces of communist Germany—Stasi—are provided from files that have been preserved (Fulbrook 1997). The role of coercion versus willing support is gauged by indicators of general regime legitimacy. Goetz Aly and his colleagues (2007a) collected an array of indicators of voluntary support for and legitimacy of the Nazi Regime, ranging from names for children, in particular the usage of Adolf (Hitler's given name), leaving the churches, participating in saving schemes (e.g. for a Volkswagen after the war), and phrasing of obituaries for soldiers killed in battle. Death sentences against Germans before the People's Court (Volksgerichtshof), which was in charge of so-called 'political crimes' indicate levels of coercion targeting the majority population. These indicators complement Johnson's (2011) data on similar special courts at the local level.

Cooperation with the Gestapo as indicated by reports and denunciations was initially strong (Gellately 1990, 2001; Mann 1987). The Gestapo mostly relied on such denunciations, as they only had a limited number of agents and officials; during the first years of the Nazi regime they displayed a high level of caution regarding those denunciations from the population that were seemingly caused by private conflicts, revenge, and other issues. However, after the beginning of the war, denunciations levelled off sharply until the end of the war (Mann 1987). This development coincides with all other indicators of support and legitimacy among the population that were collected by Aly and his colleagues; all of these rapidly decreased after the beginning of the war in 1939, with a further steep decline in 1941 after the start of the war against the Soviet Union (Müller 2007). As the Germans voluntarily gave consent to and cooperated with the regime, they also withdrew it where they could do so without getting into trouble.

In October 1942, Hermann Goering, a member of the highest leadership echelon of the Nazi regime tried to stem the erosion of support and legitimacy for the regime and the war with a speech that combined promises of welfare with increasing threats against those who were withdrawing support. After this speech, death sentences issued by the People's Court against Germans increased considerably; 90 per cent were issued after this date (Schlüter 2007; Aly 2007b). The evidence that Johnson (2011) provides from court files corroborates this trend. Until the end of the 1930s Germans were hardly prosecuted for overtly showing a lack of support, however Jews were, and also severely punished. Cooperation with the Gestapo thus seems to have been determined by the general legitimacy of the regime and by the course of the war itself. Whether decline was further accelerated by the exponential increase of death sentences against Germans toward the end of the war, cannot be decided, but seems plausible.

In the German Democratic Republic, the courts were initially designed to reflect the values and practices of the 'working class', and as such explicitly geared towards ensuring legitimacy among this majority group of the population. Thus fresh judges were recruited from these social groups and received fast-track legal training. The lower courts also were obliged to cooperate with committees in neighbourhoods and factories, which were under the control of the party, and even to hold court sessions and meetings there, which were not always well received (Markovits 2010: chs. 2 and 5). The court was thus operating in a local landscape of competing types of justice institutions, including those set up by the party. In the course of the four decades of its existence, however, the court prevailed. It did so by developing and providing procedures which were seen as just and fair, and the citizens entrusted the court with their conflicts rather than the committees. They became increasingly reluctant to offer and divulge information on private lives and individuals in family as well as criminal court cases; turn-out for such committee meetings decreased considerably over the years and made them dysfunctional in the end. In their rejection of justice by the collective they opted for a more rule-of-law based system, and insisted on their privacy as individuals.

The judges acquired some of the characteristics of these committees in the way they tried to solve conflicts and establish 'order' rather than applying the law. They thus subscribed to and strengthened the prevailing attitudes of the public and the parties that were more outcome-oriented rather than focused on procedure, and expectations and delivery of justice converged in what Markovits (2010: 190) terms 'warm' or 'maternal' justice. When the rule of law finally arrived in 1990, the disappointment was famously expressed as 'We wanted justice, and got the rule of law' (Rechtsstaat). Summing up four decades of development as represented in the narrative from a lower court, increasing rule- and procedure-oriented decision making obviously ensured legitimacy of the court. What counted as fair and just among the population was increasingly informed by individualized and 'liberal' conceptions of law and justice rather than based on notions of the collective, or in favour of working class members. However, this process coincided with strong outcome rather than procedure orientations throughout the period, and citizens' demands of what they saw as 'substantive'.

Uprisings, riots, and protests necessarily signify the culmination of withdrawal of legitimacy and support for a regime; they are expressions of a crisis of legitimacy of a regime and its institutions. Mica (2012) describes two protest incidents under the Ceauşescu regime in Romania, in 1977 and 1987, and the ways in which the regime tried to salvage and re-establish legitimacy and support. The ramified system of justice allowed for special party 'moot courts' or tribunals held in the workplace, and thus for multiple pressure on those who had participated in the protests, including what Mica calls 'workplace bullying'. Besides the severe sentences handed down to selected protesters, the 'party moots' indeed provided a space for dialogue, requests for accountability, and the attribution of blame to higher ranking managers, bureaucrats, and party officials, resulting in dismissals and criminal prosecutions. Collective 'condemnation' of protests and protesters was negotiated and traded in for admissions of guilt by officials. Confronted with a visible crisis of legitimacy, even one of the most ruthless authoritarian and dictatorial regimes of Eastern Europe used 'dialogue' to re-establish and re-assure basic levels of legitimacy and support.

The particular nature of dialogic and interactive legitimacy is perhaps best epitomized by the complaint system in non-democratic states. They all give space and a direct route for citizens to complain to the highest authorities thus overriding the lower bureaucratic levels and officials. Contemporary leaders in non-democratic states make ample use of popular television shows and internet websites where selected complaints are forwarded by scrutinized citizens, and leaders can demonstrate their concern for citizens and 'fairness' in deciding these matters.[6] These accounts of legitimacy of (criminal) justice and its institutions in authoritarian regimes demonstrate that the mechanisms that ensure legitimacy and cooperation function within this context: fairness, dialogic measures, and balanced outcomes seem to ensure and repair legitimacy and support, even if issued in institutional contexts other than criminal justice. It is however important that these simultaneously single out and target specific groups that are excluded, persecuted, and severely punished. Authoritarian regimes are divisive and exclusionary (see Karstedt 2006, 2011), and cooperation of one group is sought at the expense of the exclusion of others.[7] As Johnson (2011) and Markovits (2010) both point out, legitimacy in authoritarian regimes is outcome-oriented and based on *substantive* rather than *procedural* justice. As long as justice meets the substantive interests of the majority population in authoritarian states, deficiencies in procedural justice are accepted[8] (see Brooker 2009 on the Soviet Union; Rajah 2012 on Singapore). At least in war-time Germany legitimacy of criminal justice seems to have been tightly linked to overall regime legitimacy, and finally to its decay. In contrast, Markovits does not find signs of decreasing legitimacy of the court even as the legitimacy of the 'system' evaporated

[6] President Putin of Russia makes ample use of such TV shows and websites, which also conflate state and (his) political party complaints routes; he builds on a system of consumer complaints that was popular in the former Soviet Union; personal communication from Elena Bogdanova, Centre for Independent Social Research, St. Petersburg; see Bogdanova 2013.

[7] See for post-independent Singapore Rajah 2012. In her analysis of the 'rule by law' she observes similar exclusionary mechanisms.

[8] Rajah (2012) terms this pattern 'paternal' in contrast to Markovits, for whom it is 'maternal'.

in the end. In addition, collaboration with the Stasi, the secret police, seemingly did not significantly subside until the very end of the GDR in 1989 (Bruce 2010). From the historian's perspective, ensuring legitimacy, support, and cooperation for justice can be achieved in and by non-democratic regimes, and is not a privilege of democracies. The level of cooperation with secret police and its continuous support is certainly one of the most disturbing features of legitimacy in past and contemporary authoritarian regimes.

MEASURING REGIME TYPE AND LEGITIMACY IN CONTEMPORARY SOCIETIES

The 'third wave of democracy' and the 'transition paradigm' intensified efforts to develop indicators of democracy and to measure progress towards full democracy that had begun in the previous decade. The most prominent and widely used among these are the Polity Index (Marshall and Jaggers 2010) and the Freedom House Index, which both use a range of different indicators of institutional and structural characteristics of democracies (for an overview see Karstedt 2006). Both indices rate countries on a continuous scale rather than providing discreet and mutually exclusive forms of governance. The Polity Index comprises two 'institutional indicators' of democracy and autocracy respectively. Both are based on key qualities of the competitiveness of political participation, to which the regulation of participation is added for autocracies, the openness and competitiveness of executive recruitment and constraints on the chief executive. Each institutional indicator is measured on an additive 11-point scale; combining the two scales results in a continuous scale which ranges from −10 indicating autocracies, to +10, indicating full democracies.[9]

In contrast more recent classifications of democratic and non-democratic regimes are based on typologies of mutually exclusive forms of governance. The indices by Cheibub, Gandhi and Vreeland (2010) and Geddes, Wright, and Frantz (2012) were explicitly developed to capture and classify authoritarian regimes and dictatorships (see also Levitsky and Way 2010). Cheibub and his colleagues' classification is based on the electoral process and the origins of power, and they identify three types of democracies—semi-presidential, presidential, and parliamentary, and three types of non-democratic regimes—military, civilian, and royal dictatorships. Geddes et al. identify four types of authoritarian regimes according to the type of power-holder: party-based, personal, military, and monarchy regimes. Both classifications represent the source of power, institutionalized accountability, and potential level of coercion, and thus what can be called Weberian types of legitimate domination. All indices cover most of the world's countries.

[9] See for a detailed account of the construction of the Polity Index Marshall and Jaggers 2010; <http://www.systemicpeace.org/polity/polity4.htm> accessed 15 October 2012.

For the purposes of this study, two indices were selected and are used, depending on the availability of data on legitimacy.[10] The Polity Index (PI) was used with the classifications 'autocratic' (–10 to –6), 'mixed' (–5 to +5), 'nearly democratic' (+6 to +9) and 'fully democratic' (+10), based on the mean value for 2004 to 2008.[11] The classification by Cheibub, Gandhi, and Vreeland (CGV) was used for contrasting democratic regimes (all three types) with the three different types of dictatorships—civilian, military, and royal, based on the predominant type during the period between 2004 and 2008.[12] This resulted in classifications of 133 countries according to the Polity Index and 128 according to the CGV Index of democracies versus dictatorships. Based on the Polity Index 24 per cent of these are classified as fully democratic, 32 per cent as nearly democratic, 28 per cent as mixed, and 16 per cent as autocratic. The CGV Index classifies 58 per cent as democratic (all three types), 23 per cent as civilian, 13 per cent as military, and 6 per cent as royal dictatorships. The classifications of both indices are in agreement in most of the cases, and consequently result in near-identical distributions.

According to the most recent data available for the Polity Index (2011) and using our classification, regime types show a distinct regional clustering across the globe. As Figure 7.1 shows 63 per cent of all states with mixed and 10 per cent of all states with autocratic regimes are located in Africa. Most of the autocratic states are located in Asia, where also a quarter each of mixed and nearly democratic regimes is found. Europe is the home of the majority of full democracies (56 per cent). 'Nearly democratic' regimes are most evenly distributed across the globe. Using our sample of 128 countries, the CGV classifies the majority of African and Asian mixed and autocratic regimes as civilian dictatorships (30 countries), 16 as military, and 8 as royal dictatorships. Military dictatorships have the strongest presence in Africa, and Asia has a 40 per cent share in civilian and military dictatorships. Most of the 'royal dictatorships', which mainly comprise the Arab Kingdoms, are located in Asia. Europe and the Americas have a small share in civilian dictatorships, but none in military or royal ones. Most regimes types are regionally clustered, and thus also define the regions in many ways.

Do these classifications mirror the pattern of high accountability/low coercion for democracies and low accountability/high coercion for non-democratic and authoritarian regimes, which were identified as delineating the distinct institutional spaces where legitimacy is generated in democratic respectively non-democratic regimes? High accountability was measured by a Rule of Law indicator, which is included in the World Bank's Worldwide Governance Indicators. It is based on a range of measurements, and captures perceptions of the extent to which agents have confidence in and abide by the rules of society, and in particular the quality of contract enforcement,

[10] The classification by Geddes et al. (2012) was not used as it resulted in very uneven coverage of data on legitimacy of criminal justice.

[11] This classification closely follows the Polity Index classification in 'autocracies' (–10 to –6), 'anocracies' (–5 to +5) and 'democracies' (+ 6 to + 10) (<http://www.systemicpeace.org/polity/polity4.htm> accessed 15 October 2012).

[12] Countries with a regime change during this period are excluded from analyses with the CGV classification.

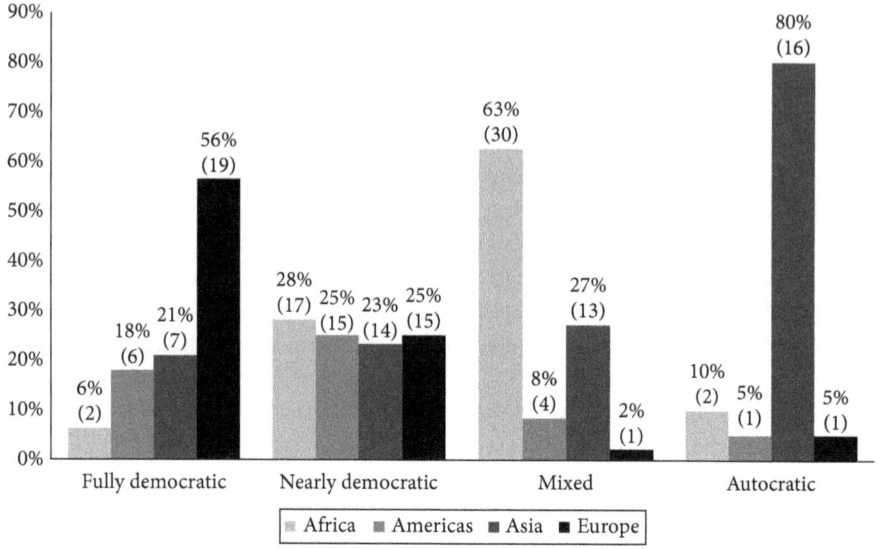

Figure 7.1 Global and Regional Distribution of Regime Types (Polity Index 2011; 163 countries; own classification)[13]

property rights, the police, and the courts, as well as the likelihood of crime and violence; countries are ranked from 0 (lowest) to 100 (highest).[14] Coercion was measured by the Political Terror Scale which combines information from the US State Department Country Reports and reports from Amnesty International. It comprises state-sanctioned/unlawful killings, disappearances, torture, and political imprisonment. The two rankings were combined resulting in a scale from 1 indicating 'no state violence' to 9 indicating 'pervasive state violence'.[15] For both scales the mean value for the period between 2004 and 2008 was calculated, and a dichotomy of 'high' versus 'low' was achieved using the median as cut off point. This resulted in four categories from high rule of law/low state violence to low rule of low/high state violence which are indicative of democracies and autocracies respectively.

Both our typologies of democratic and non-democratic regimes show a remarkable fit with this classification (Table 7.1). For the Polity Index, 30 out of 32 (94 per cent) fully democratic countries are classified as 'high accountability/low coercion', the two exceptions being Israel and the US as 'high rule of law/high state violence' countries during this period. As can be expected, the 43 nearly democratic regimes are fairly evenly divided among 'high accountability/low coercion' (13 countries; 30

[13] *Source*: Marshall, Monty, and Jaggers (2010); UN Statistics Division (2012); own computations.

[14] Version 11 was used <http://info.worldbank.org/governance/wgi/index.asp> accessed 3 November 2012.

[15] Political Terror Scale (PTS) by Mark Gibney, Linda Cornett, and Reed Wood, version 2010, available at <http://www.politicalterrorscale.org/> accessed 31 October 2012. The PTS is combined from two sources, the US State Department and Amnesty International country reports; both are ranked from 1 (no state violence) to 5 (has expanded to the whole population) and provided separately. Here a sum scale was constructed that ranked from 1 to 9; see also Landmann and Carvalho 2010.

per cent), including e.g. Croatia, Latvia, Ghana, South Korea), and 20 countries (47 per cent) being classified as authoritarian with 'low accountability/high coercion' (including e.g. Russia, Paraguay, and Nepal). Among the 37 'mixed' and more autocratic countries, 26 (70 per cent) classify as low accountability and high coercion, thus exhibiting the pattern typical of autocracies, as do 12 out of the 21 countries (57 per cent) that are autocracies. These patterns reflect the larger range on the Polity scale that the latter three types cover, and presumably also different types of authoritarian regimes. This is corroborated by using the CGV typology of 'dictatorships'. Among the 29 'civilian dictatorships' four out of five (23; 79 per cent) fall into the autocratic category of low accountability and high coercion, as do 11 out of 16 military dictatorships (69 per cent). Two of the civilian dictatorships, Malaysia and Namibia are situated at the opposite end of the scale, with high accountability and low coercion, as are two of the military dictatorships (Burkina Faso and Singapore[16]). In contrast, the 'royal dictatorships' reflect a more democratic pattern. Only one of the eight countries included in this group, Swaziland, has the autocratic pattern of low accountability and high coercion, while four Arab Kingdoms fall into the democratic category of high accountability and low coercion (Kuwait, Oman, Qatar, and United Arab Emirates). Contemporary autocratic states thus can vary considerably in the mechanisms through which they generate legitimacy in general and for their criminal justice systems in particular.

Measuring legitimacy on the aggregate level of countries or regimes is particularly difficult. Research on legitimacy and procedural justice has generated a wealth of conceptualizations, and tried to distinguish between legitimacy, trust and confidence, and satisfaction with authorities, process and outcome on the individual level, which can hardly be translated into aggregate measurements (see Smith 2007). Indicators of legitimacy on the aggregate level are thus not built on attitudinal data, but use structural and institutional indicators instead that signify outcomes rather than processes (see Gilley 2006). In this analysis, both structural and attitudinal indicators will be used, with one structural and overarching indicator of regime legitimacy in conjunction with attitudinal indicators that directly target the criminal justice system, and the civil service as decision makers and power-holders. The selection was partially guided by achieving coverage of as many countries as possible and in particular of non-democratic regimes.

Originally termed 'Political Legitimacy' and developed for the State Failure Index, the structural indicator of regime or political legitimacy is based on several components that measure fragmentation, discrimination, and exclusion mainly along divisions of ethnicity, and general effective authority over groups and territory. As such it provides a measure of the stability and general acceptance of state and government power. We have defined it here as 'inclusionary legitimacy', as it indicates the extent to which all groups are included; legitimacy is based on widely shared beliefs rather than those of the elites; and authority is accepted throughout

[16] The classification of Singapore is a result of the CGV decision rule to classify a dictatorship as 'military dictatorship' if it has a head of state that has or had a leading position in the armed forces. In 2003, a former general became the head of state in Singapore.

Table 7.1 Patterns of Accountability and Coercion for Democratic and Non-Democratic Regimes (2004–8)

	Polity Index: Democratic and Non-Democratic Regimes				Total	CGV: Dictatorships			Total
Accountability and coercion	Fully democratic	Nearly democratic	Mixed	Autocratic		Civilian dictatorship	Military dictatorship	Royal dictatorship	
low accountability/ high coercion	0 (0%)	20 (47%)	26 (70%)	12 (57%)	58	23 (79%)	11 (69%)	1 (13%)	35
low accountability/ low coercion	0 (0%)	6 (14%)	2 (5%)	2 (10%)	10	2 (7%)	1 (6%)	0 (0%)	3
high accountability/ high coercion	2 (6%)	4 (9%)	4 (11%)	3 (14%)	13	2 (7%)	2 (13%)	3 (38%)	7
high accountability/ low coercion	30 (94%)	13 (30%)	5 (14%)	4 (19%)	52	2 (7%)	2 (13%)	4 (50%)	8
Total (%)	32 (100%)	43 (100%)	37 (100%)	21 (100%)	133	29 (100%)	16 (100%)	8 (100%)	53

Marshall, M and Jaggers, K. (2010) Polity IV Project: Political regime characteristics and transitions 1800–2010, Polity level 2011 (<http://www.systemicpeace.org/polity/polity4.htm>) last accessed 15 October 2012. Cheibub, J. A., Gandhi, J. and Vreeland, J. R. (2010) 'Democracy and Dictatorship Revisited': Regime type 2004–2008 (<https://sites.google.com/site/joseantoniocheibub/datasets/democracy-and-dictatorship-revisited>) last accessed 15 November 2012. Kaufmann, D., Kraay, A. and Mastruzzi, M. (2011) The Worldwide Governance Indicators project: Rule of Law 2004–2008, variable ranges from 0 = low accountability to 100 = high accountability (<http://info.worldbank.org/governance/wgi/index.asp>) last accessed 3 November 2012. Gibney, M., Cornett, L., & Wood, R., (2012): Political Terror Scale 2004–2008 (<http://www.politicalterrorscale.org/>) last accessed 31 October 2012; own computations.

the country rather than restricted to particular regions or parts. The scale ranges from 0 (no inclusionary legitimacy, highly fragmented) to 3 (inclusionary legitimacy, no fragmentation).[17]

As targeted and attitudinal indicators of legitimacy of the criminal justice system 'confidence in the police' and 'confidence in the justice system' of citizens of the country were used. This measure throws a wide net over the different dimensions of trust, satisfaction, and legitimacy that have been identified at the individual level. It is deemed to approximately capture essential characteristics of legitimacy: it concerns expectations as to the future performance of authorities, of what they are obliged to do, and what is justifiable that they should do, and what can be rightly expected from them. These data were retrieved for the period between 2004 and 2008 from the World Value Survey (2005), the European Value Survey (2008), the Arab Barometer (2006), and the African Barometer (2005, 2008) and measured as the proportion of citizens, who either had 'a great deal' or 'quite a lot' (or equivalent response categories) of confidence in the police and the justice system. 'Confidence in the civil service' and the overall 'respect for individual human rights' were included as additional indicators of legitimacy in terms of acceptance of decisions of power-holders and a sense of shared values in decision-making processes.[18] Analyses are based on 79 countries for confidence in police and the justice system, 68 countries for confidence in the civil service, and a small number of 39 countries for which data on public perceptions of respect for individual human rights are available.

Legitimacy of criminal justice and the civil service are based on public perceptions of their efficiency and fairness in decision making and action. Efficiency of the criminal justice system is perceived largely in terms of combating crime, in particular violent crime. Perceptions of fairness and even-handedness should be severely affected by the level of corruption within the police, the justice system, and the civil service, or the lack of efforts by the government to control corruption. In order to control for these conditions the homicide rate[19] was used as a proxy for perceived efficiency, and

[17] The Political Legitimacy Indicator was constructed by M. G. Marshall and B. R. Cole, and includes indicators of Regime/Governance Inclusion from the Minorities at Risk Database 2010, and the Elite Leadership Characteristics Database 2010: Factionalism, Ethnic Group Political Discrimination, Political Salience of Elite Ethnicity, Polity Fragmentation, and Exclusionary Ideology of the Ruling Elite. The Political Legitimacy Score is calculated as the sum of these indicators, with high values indicating a lack of legitimacy; scores of 4 and 5 were recoded as 3. For the purposes of this study the scale was reversed with 0 indicating a low level of inclusionary legitimacy and 3 the highest level. Marshall, Monty G and Benjamin R. Cole (2011): State Fragility Index, Political Legitimacy Score (<http://www.systemicpeace.org/inscr/inscr.htm> accessed 3 November 2012).

[18] Sources for 'confidence in police' and 'confidence in justice: World Values Survey <http://www.worldvaluessurvey.org/> accessed 10 November 2012; European Values Survey <http://www.europeanvaluesstudy.eu/> accessed 10 November 2012; Arab Barometer <http://www.arabbarometer.org/> accessed 10 November 2012; African Barometer <http://www.afrobarometer.org/> accessed 10 November 2012; if two waves were available during the period, the mean was calculated. Sources for 'confidence in civil service': World Values Survey <http://www.worldvaluessurvey.org/> accessed 10 November 2012; European Values Survey <http://www.europeanvaluesstudy.eu/> accessed 10 November 2012. Source for 'respect of individual human rights': World Values Survey <http://www.worldvaluessurvey.org/> accessed 10 November 2012.

[19] Source: World Health Organisation (2012) 'WHO Mortality Database': Homicide rates 2004–2008 (<http://www.who.int/healthinfo/mortality_data/en/index.html> accessed 15 November 2012).

the level of control of corruption[20] as a proxy for perceived fairness of decision making. Both are highly unevenly distributed among the different regime types, with democracies having significantly lower levels of lethal violence and corruption (see Karstedt 2006, 2013). Analyses (ANOVA, and comparisons of mean (t-tests)) are based on both regime classifications, the Polity Index and the CGV Index as far as possible. However, due to small numbers and uneven distribution of e.g. homicide data for the CGV Index, preference had to be given to analyses with the Polity Index in a number of instances.

CONTEXTUALISING LEGITIMACY OF CRIMINAL JUSTICE IN CONTEMPORARY AUTOCRACIES

Democratic and non-democratic regimes significantly differ with regard to the extent of inclusionary legitimacy. Figure 7.2a shows that, using the Polity Index classification, fully democratic countries are most inclusive in terms of their legitimacy base, and significantly differ from all other regime types.[21] Mixed regimes are least inclusionary with regard to their sources of legitimacy; as this group includes a considerable number of failing or weak states, fragmentation of the sources of legitimacy might account for higher instability of regime. In contrast, autocratic regimes achieve medium levels of inclusivity, close to 'nearly democratic' regimes. As the CGV classification of non-democratic regimes shows this is mainly owed to high levels of inclusive legitimacy in 'royal dictatorships'. Figure 7.2b demonstrates that these muster the highest level of inclusionary legitimacy, on par with democracies, whilst military and civilian dictatorships have the lowest levels. The countries included in this group are mainly kingdoms in Arab countries, many of them small and with a very homogenous citizen base, which gives them a head start in achieving inclusionary legitimacy for the government in general. Military and civilian dictatorships often emerge in and rule over a highly fragmented population, where ethnic and civil strife are common and regime legitimacy is particularly contested.

Legitimacy of both criminal justice institutions—the police and the justice system more generally—is strongly linked within all regime types (based on the Polity Index; $r > .75$; $p < .000$), and both are related to confidence in the civil service ($r > .5$; $p < .00$). Legitimacy of these institutions and their representatives, as well as decision making by the authorities are interrelated, and this applies to fully democratic, nearly democratic or mixed and autocratic regimes. Consequently, a consistent pattern emerges

[20] The Control of Corruption Indicator is included in the World Bank's Worldwide Governance Indicators (Daniel Kaufmann, Aart Kraay, and Massimo Mastruzzi). It reflects perceptions of the extent to which public power is exercised for private gain, including both petty and grand forms of corruption, as well as 'capture' of the state by elites and private interests, and efforts to curb corruption. Percentile ranks among all countries from 0 (lowest) to 100 (highest). Version 11 was used <http://info.worldbank.org/governance/wgi/index.asp> accessed 3 November 2012.

[21] The figures are based on ANOVAs; due to small numbers, all reported significance levels have to be interpreted with caution.

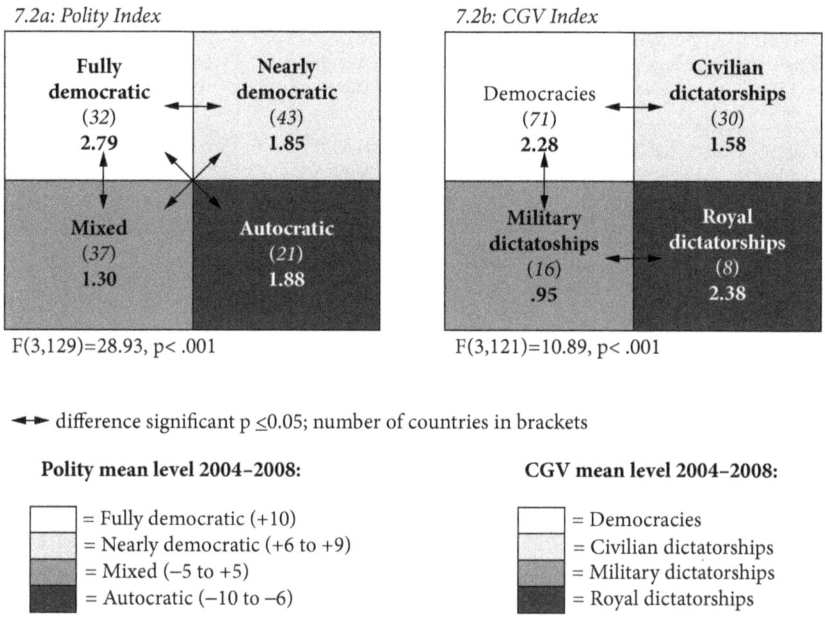

Figure 7.2 Inclusionary Legitimacy in Democratic and Non-Democratic Regimes (mean)[22]

for confidence in all three institutions across regime types. As Figures 7.3a to 3c demonstrate, 'nearly democratic' countries of which many are in a transition, have throughout the lowest levels of citizens' confidence in police, justice and the civil service. Confidence in police is highest in full democracies, followed by mixed and autocratic regimes. This rank order is reverted for confidence in justice, which has the highest mean level for mixed and autocratic regimes, and equally and more distinct for confidence in the civil service, where mixed and autocratic regimes have a mean level, which exceeds the one of democracies by 10 per cent (54 per cent vs. 44 per cent). These differences are mostly not significant with the exception of the lower levels in nearly democratic countries.

The pattern of high levels of confidence in justice and the civil service in mixed and autocratic regimes is repeated when the CGV classification of democracies and dictatorships is used (Figures 7.4a–4c). Both military and royal dictatorships exceed democracies in terms of levels of confidence in the police, and all types of dictatorships do in terms of confidence in justice and the civil service. These are small numbers, however it is the pattern that counts here. At least it can be said that democracies do not necessarily and by default enjoy higher levels of legitimacy of these vital institutions than non-democratic regimes.

The CGV classification includes many of the 'nearly democratic' countries in the overall category of democracies; as these are those with the lowest levels of legitimacy, the overall mean level of democracies is decreased in contrast to the three

[22] *Source*: Marshall and Jaggers (2010); Cheibub, Gandhi, and Vreeland (2010); Marshall and Cole (2011) (see also Table 7.1). Score reversed, 0 = no inclusionary legitimacy, 3 = high inclusionary legitimacy.

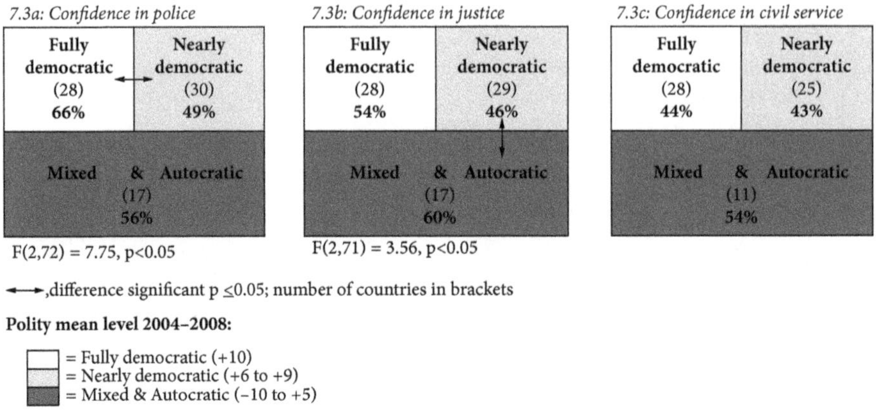

Figure 7.3 Confidence in Police, Justice and the Civil Service in Democratic and Non-Democratic Regimes (mean percentage confident, Polity Index)[23]

dictatorships. However, the spread around the median (at about half of all countries are above and below this level) does not considerably differ between full democracies and non-democratic regimes. If for each regime type quartiles of confidence in police and the justice system are calculated, the range within each quartile as well as the overall range are fairly similar between fully democratic and non-democratic regimes.

Democracies have a significantly more inclusive base for legitimacy than the other regime types, however they hardly differ from 'royal dictatorships' in this regard (see Figure 7.2b). As noted earlier, half of the royal dictatorships included in this study fall into the 'democratic' category of 'high accountability and low coercion'. Democracies do give more space to open debate and to the expression of discontent among citizens, which in turn might impact on general public opinion as expressed in these surveys. Citizens in democracies are also fairly similar to those in mixed and autocratic regimes when assessing the respect for individual human rights by the authorities in their country (67 per cent and 65 per cent respectively), in contrast to those who live in 'nearly democratic' countries (46 per cent). In sum, autocratic regimes are not at a disadvantage when generating legitimacy for criminal justice and decision-making authorities.

The surprisingly high level of respect for individual human rights that citizens in mixed and autocratic regimes, and in all types of dictatorships attribute to the authorities might also explain their confidence in justice. The courts are more distant from

[23] *Source*: Marshall and Jaggers (2010); World Values Survey (2005): *Confidence in Police, Justice and the Civil Service*, 1 = A great deal, 2 = Quite a lot, 3 = Not very much, 4 = None at all: percentage of 1 and 2 (<http://www.worldvaluessurvey.org> accessed 10 November 2012), European Value Survey (2008), *Confidence in Police, Justice and the Civil Service*, 1 = A great deal, 2 = Quite a lot, 3 = Not very much, 4 = None at all: percentage of 1 and 2 (<http://www.europeanvaluesstudy.eu/> accessed 10 November 2012), Afrobarometer (2005 & 2008): *Trust in Police and Justice*, 1 = A lot, 2 = Somewhat, 3 = Just a little, 4 = Not at all: percentage of 1 and 2 (<http://www.afrobarometer.org> accessed 10 November 2012). Arab Barometer (2006): *Trust the police & Trust the courts*, 1 = A great deal of trust, 2 = Quite a lot of trust, 3 = Not very much trust, 4 = None at all: percentage of 1 and 2 (<http://www.arabbarometer.org/> accessed 10 November 2012).

7.4a: Confidence in police

Democracies (57) 59%	Civilian dictatorships (13) 54%
Military dictatorships (3) 60%	Royal dictatorships (2) 76%

7.4b: Confidence in justice

Democracies (56) 49%	Civilian dictatorships (13) 57%
Military dictatorships (3) 56%	Royal dictatorships (2) 69%

7.4c: Confidence in civil service

Democracies (54) 44%	Civilian dictatorships (8) 50%
Military dictatorships (3) 59%	Royal dictatorships (2) 57%

Number of countries in brackets; significance levels not calculated

CGV mean level 2004–2008:

= Democracies
= Civilian dictatorships
= Military dictatorships
= Royal dictatorships

Figure 7.4 Confidence in Police, Justice and the Civil Service in Democratic and Non-Democratic Regimes (mean percentage confident, CGV)[24]

the government than the police, and as Markovits (2010) has shown for the former GDR, they keep this distance and adhere to their traditional and professional values, as well as to procedures of 'doing justice'. Consequently citizens would tend to perceive higher levels of procedural justice in the courts, which in turn might account for higher levels of confidence. In addition, in Europe as well as in Latin America regional Human Rights courts have an impact on local courts and the justice system; citizens in mixed and autocratic regimes therefore might see the courts as a place where the wrongs and unfair treatment at the hands of the other agencies might be atoned (see Osiel 1995 for Latin America; Ellmann 1995 for South Africa).

Citizens' confidence in police and the justice system might be affected by levels of crime and violence, and their assessment of overall fairness of decision making severely eroded by rampant corruption. Democracies are the least violent if measured by the mean homicide rate (2.67), closely followed by mixed and autocratic regimes (3.01 and 3.10). 'Nearly democratic' countries have a fourfold level of homicides (12.48).[25] How does this impact on the confidence in police, justice, and the civil service in different regimes? As Figure 7.5 shows, only in full democracies do citizens respond to higher rates of lethal violence by significantly withdrawing confidence from the police and the justice system. While democracies seem to be vulnerable to

[24] *Source*: Cheibub, Gandhi, and Vreeland (2010); World Values Survey (2005): *Confidence in Police, Justice and the Civil Service*, 1 = A great deal, 2 = Quite a lot, 3 = Not very much, 4 = None at all: percentage of 1 and 2 (<http://www.worldvaluessurvey.org> accessed 10 November 2012), European Value Survey (2008), *Confidence in Police, Justice and the Civil Service*, 1 = A great deal, 2 = Quite a lot, 3 = Not very much, 4 = None at all: percentage of 1 and 2 (<http://www.europeanvaluesstudy.eu/> accessed 10 November 2012), Afrobarometer (2005 & 2008): *Trust in Police and Justice*, 1 = A lot, 2 = Somewhat, 3 = Just a little, 4 = Not at all: percentage of 1 and 2 (<http://www.afrobarometer.org> accessed 10 November 2012). Arab Barometer (2006): *Trust the police & Trust the courts*, 1 = A great deal of trust, 2 = Quite a lot of trust, 3 = Not very much trust, 4 = None at all: percentage of 1 and 2 (<http://www.arabbarometer.org/> accessed 10 November 2012).

[25] For many of the dictatorships classified by CGV, reliable homicide data are not available for the period.

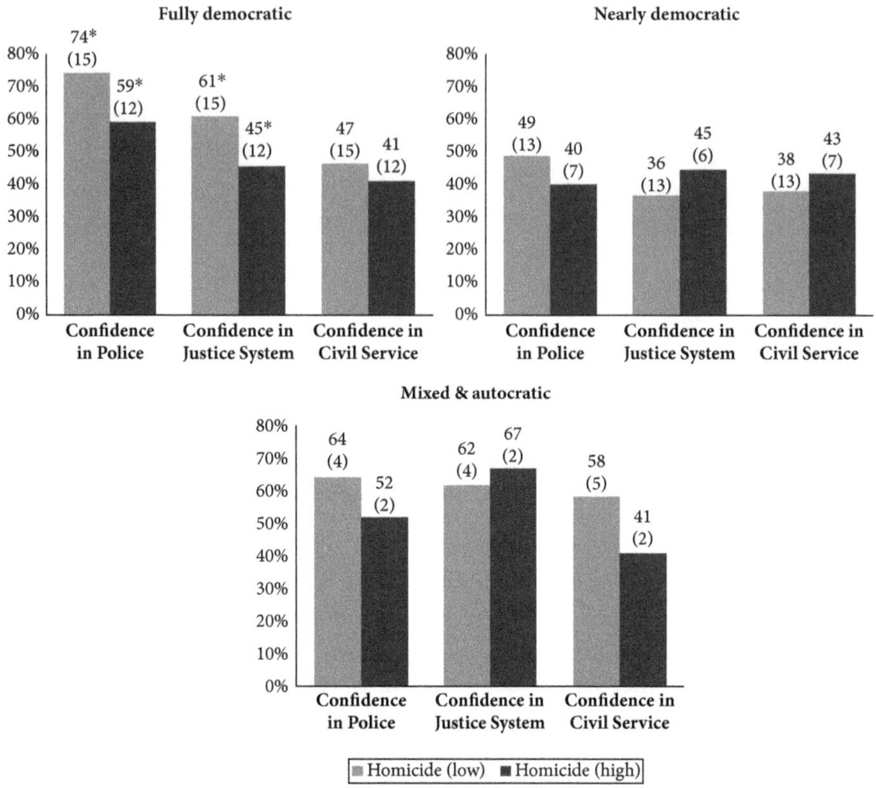

Figure 7.5 Homicide and Confidence in Police, Justice and the Civil Service in Democratic and Non-Democratic Regimes (mean level confident; Polity Index)[26]

**, difference significant $p \leq 0.05$ **, difference significant $p \leq 0.01$*

Number of countries in brackets; mixed and autocratic regimes: significance not calculated

high rates of violent crime, these do not make a marked difference in all other regime types;[27] here they decrease confidence in police, but slightly increase confidence in justice in 'nearly democratic' as well as in 'mixed and autocratic' states. These are states

[26] *Source*: Marshall and Jaggers (2010); World Health Organisation (2012) <http://www.who.int/healthinfo/mortality_data/en/index.html> accessed 15 November 2012.; high and low homicide rates: above/below median within each regime type. World Values Survey (2005): *Confidence in Police, Justice and the Civil Service*, 1 = A great deal, 2 = Quite a lot, 3 = Not very much, 4 = None at all: percentage of 1 and 2 (www.worldvaluessurvey.org), European Value Survey (2008), *Confidence in Police, Justice and the Civil Service*, 1 = A great deal, 2 = Quite a lot, 3 = Not very much, 4 = None at all: percentage of 1 and 2 (<http://www.europeanvaluesstudy.eu/> accessed 10 November 2012), Afrobarometer (2005 & 2008): *Trust in Police and Justice*, 1 = A lot, 2 = Somewhat, 3 = Just a little, 4 = Not at all: percentage of 1 and 2 (<http://www.afrobarometer.org> accessed 10 November 2012). Arab Barometer (2006): *Trust the police & Trust the courts*, 1 = A great deal of trust, 2 = Quite a lot of trust, 3 = Not very much trust, 4 = None at all: percentage of 1 and 2 (<http://www.arabbarometer.org/> accessed 10 November 2012).

[27] High respectively low levels of homicide rates and control of corruption were calculated separately for each of the regime types as above/below the median.

with a high level of coercion, which involves illegal force used by the police on a regular basis, and numerous victims of homicide die at the hands of police forces. The pattern of difference between regime types mirrors the involvement of police in violence; levels of overall state violence as measured by the Political Terror Scale are particularly high in mixed (5.9) and autocratic regimes (4.8), mainly high in civilian (5.8) and military dictatorships (5.9), while the level of royal dictatorships (3.5) is second to the lowest level of democracies (2.2). Consequently, it is rather the justice system, in which citizens trust.

Corruption has a palpable impact on the legitimacy of the police, the justice system, and the civil service in all regime types. Where corruption is better controlled and lower, legitimacy of all institutions generally increases (Figure 7.6). This effect is most pronounced for the police, in whom citizens' confidence increases considerably with higher levels of control of corruption. The impact of fair and controlled decision making without corrupt exchanges is most distinct (and significant) in full democracies, where citizens seem to react sensitively to unfair decision making by the authorities. However those among the 'nearly democratic' countries that manage to control corruption can significantly increase the legitimacy of their police. This pattern is still visible in civilian and military and royal dictatorships: where governments succeed in keeping corruption low and improve fair decisions across institutions, the legitimacy of authorities is generally improved.

STATE IMPARTIALITY AND BUREAUCRATIC AUTONOMY: A FRESH LOOK AT WEBERIAN MODELS?

Given the uneven distribution and small numbers, these patterns should be interpreted with caution. However, a number of important findings emerge. First, it seems that even at the aggregate level of country and regime indicators, procedural justice and fairness in decision making as indicated by control of corruption, are decisive and have a stronger impact on confidence in authorities than perceptions of their efficiency in terms of the control of violence. In particular in non-democratic regimes, police are often involved in the illegal use of violence. Consequently, within these regimes serious violent crime does not have the impact on confidence in police that it has in democracies. However, legitimacy is generated through fair decision making and procedural justice across all regime types as demonstrated by the consistent pattern of decreasing legitimacy where control of corruption is low. This finding points to the *universality* of procedural justice as a mechanism in generating legitimacy for police, the justice system, and other authorities, and both in contemporary democratic as well as non-democratic regimes.

Second, these patterns support the Weberian conceptualization of the normative embeddedness and contextualisation of legitimacy. Fully democratic countries show more 'elasticity' in citizens' confidence in police, the justice system, and other authorities, i.e. legitimacy is more susceptible to potentially negative perceptions of efficiency

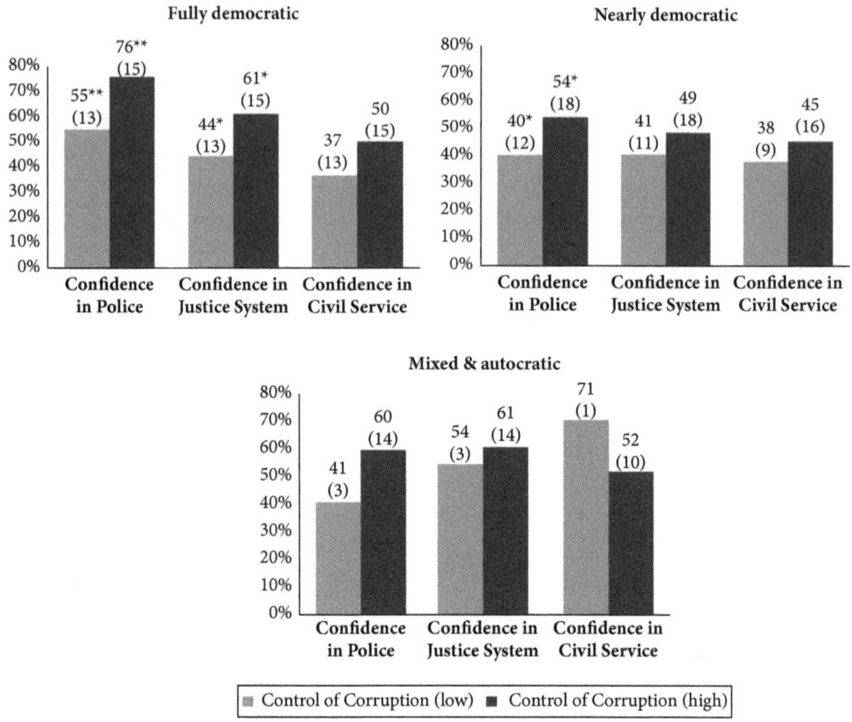

Figure 7.6 Control of Corruption and Confidence in Police, Justice, and the Civil Service in Democratic and Non-Democratic Regimes (mean level confident; Polity Index)[28]

*, *difference significant* $p \leq 0.05$ **, *difference significant* $p \leq 0.01$*mixed and autocratic regimes*: no significance calculated;

Number of countries in brackets; the country with low levels of corruption control and high confidence in the civil service is Azerbaijan.

and fairness in decision making. In democracies, the normative definitions of legitimacy and the ensuing expectations towards authorities and their actions are shaped by anticipations of fair and unbiased decision making. If these are not met, citizens do not hesitate to withdraw confidence and legitimacy. In addition the space for public discussion guaranteed in democracies might accelerate the process of building up as well as retracting legitimacy. This constitutes a comparative disadvantage for democracies, as discontent can quickly ripple through the public. Democracies thus provide

[28] *Source*: Marshall and Jaggers (2010); Kaufmann, Kraay, and Mastruzzi (2011), variable ranges from 0 = low abidance to control of corruption to 100 = high abidance to control of corruption, high and low control of corruption: above/below median within each regime type. World Values Survey (2005): *Confidence in Police, Justice and the Civil Service*, 1 = A great deal, 2 = Quite a lot, 3 = Not very much, 4 = None at all: percentage of 1 and 2 (<http://www.worldvaluessurvey.org> accessed 10 November 2012), European Value Survey (2008), *Confidence in Police, Justice and the Civil Service*, 1 = A great deal, 2 = Quite a lot, 3 = Not very much, 4 = None at all: percentage of 1 and 2 (<http://www.europeanvaluesstudy.eu/> accessed 10 November 2012), Afrobarometer (2005 & 2008): *Trust in Police and Justice*, 1 = A lot, 2 = Somewhat, 3 = Just a little, 4 = Not at all: percentage of 1 and 2 (<http://www.afrobarometer.org> accessed 10 November 2012). Arab Barometer (2006): *Trust the police & Trust the courts*, 1 = A great deal of trust, 2 = Quite a lot of trust, 3 = Not very much trust, 4 = None at all: percentage of 1 and 2 (<http://www.arabbarometer.org/> accessed 10 November 2012).

the very processes of generating legitimation, which make them also vulnerable to its loss. These results support a Weberian conceptualization of legitimacy: the culture and institutions of a polity constitute the normative foundations on which legitimacy rests, and is conceived of, expected and realized.

Third, and as a consequence of the preceding, non-democratic regimes can muster levels of confidence in the police equalling those in democracies, and even higher levels in the justice system and the civil service. Democracies are not by default better at generating legitimacy for these institutions. Likewise as in democratic regimes, legitimacy in non-democratic regimes is embedded in a particular cultural and institutional environment, and defined by its normative requirements. If these are met citizens grant legitimacy to power-holders, the police, the courts, and the civil service. Facing an often brutal police force, they have more confidence in justice, which accounts for slightly higher levels of confidence in this institution. However, as the findings indicate contemporary non-democratic regimes are also subject to the *universal* requirements of fair and unbiased decision making by authorities, which transcend the particular pattern of legitimacy that prevails in their polity.

It is an important further finding that the 'nearly democratic' countries consistently have the lowest levels of confidence in police, the justice system, and the civil service. This group includes a high number of countries which recently made the transition to more democratic rule, and as Esty et al. (1998) point out, these are generally conditions of high instability. Nearly half of them (47 per cent) score as 'low rule of law/high state violence' countries and as such are located on the authoritarian end of this classification. More than half (56 per cent) have high levels of state violence, and just one third (30 per cent) are democratic 'high rule of law/low state violence' countries (see Table 7.1 earlier). As many of these countries make the transition from one normative and institutional system to another, legitimacy is subject to conflicting demands and normative assessments. These countries have to cope with the legacy of high state violence and illegal force used by police, as well as corruption throughout their civil service (see Karstedt 2013), while citizens increasingly demand fair and respectful treatment as they are informed by democratic values. This entails an *anomic environment* in which citizens find it hard to summon up confidence in institutions which are deeply tainted by the former regime and do not function according to their now held values, and where power-holders have not yet changed engrained non-democratic cultures and habits of performance.

Finally, our findings confirm a disturbing characteristic of past authoritarian regimes for contemporary ones. Contemporary authoritarian regimes achieve comparably high levels of legitimacy for brutal police forces and biased justice systems, and are capable of soliciting voluntary collaboration of citizens even with such forces and in atrocious actions. Mixed regimes, civilian and military dictatorships have the highest levels of state violence in our sample, and nonetheless their citizens do not have significantly less or even more confidence in the police, the justice system, and the civil service than those in democracies. Evidence from historical authoritarian societies as well as from contemporary non-democratic regimes shows that state violence rather than being pervasive is targeted against specific groups, often vulnerable minorities or groups of political adversaries. State violence 'marks' and defines groups as not belonging, excluded, as non-citizens or as outright enemies, and thus thrives in particular in environments where ethnic fragmentation is high (Karstedt 2011). The majority of the population are mainly unaffected, and are even often supportive of actions against these groups and their individual members. Accordingly, confidence in police and justice remain at high levels as does the willingness of the population to collaborate in these actions.

Our indicator of 'inclusionary legitimacy' reflects the extent to which legitimacy is based on consent from all groups, and widely shared beliefs rather than those of the elites and the majority population. Independent of regime type it is strongly and negatively ($r = -.56$; $p < .000$) related to state violence, and correlates positively with respect for individual human rights as a foundation for shared beliefs and dialogue between power-holders and citizens ($r = .47$; $p < .00$). A socially and normatively fragmented base of legitimacy fosters state violence and its acceptance, while respect for individual human rights coincides with inclusionary legitimacy. However, only small (for confidence in police) or no correlations (for confidence in justice and the civil service) are found for general confidence in authorities. Perceptions of legitimacy of the (majority) population are seemingly unaffected by the fragmentation of the foundations of legitimacy, and might even be enhanced.[29] This is further corroborated by the fact that within regime types, different levels of inclusionary legitimacy do not make a difference; neither in democracies, nearly democratic countries nor in mixed and autocratic regimes are they correlated to confidence in police, justice, and the civil service or do they have a discernible impact on confidence levels (all $p > .10$).

This is only partially true for levels of state violence. While in fully democratic and nearly democratic regimes, levels of state violence are neither related nor have an impact on confidence in police, justice, and the civil service, we find a considerable, and significant impact for mixed and autocratic regimes. Confidence in police decreases by 30 per cent, and in justice by 20 per cent, where state violence is high. These are also the regime types with the highest levels of state violence. As state violence becomes pervasive, it also becomes less targeted and starts to affect majority groups. Legitimacy is consequently withdrawn from criminal justice institutions, which echoes the very same processes under the Nazi regime in Germany.

The legitimacy of these institutions can thrive at the expense of unfair and even violent treatment of targeted groups, and this applies to democratic and non-democratic regimes. As MacCoun (2005) argues, procedural justice in democracies is unevenly distributed, and citizens in democracies tolerate the fact that minority groups receive differential and often less fair treatment (see also Tyler 2007). However, the domination of outcome-oriented perceptions and the prevailing demands for substantive justice in authoritarian states, as shown by Johnson (2011) for Nazi Germany, Brooker (2009) for the Soviet Union and Markovits (2010) for the former GDR, and recently confirmed for China (Liang 2008), might well foster indifferent attitudes towards unfair treatment of minorities and targeted groups among the majority population in authoritarian states that are more engrained and also legitimized than in democracies.

[29] It needs to be taken into account that these indicators are based on survey data, and presumably over-represent the majority population and their attitudes.

These results outline future normative challenges for legitimacy, to ensure procedural justice for all groups in society, and to prevent differential and unfair treatment that seems to be acceptable to majority populations in all regime types. Majority populations need to be convinced that support for and collaboration with the authorities and criminal justice system in such treatment is unacceptable and amounts to 'moral blindness' (Bauman and Donskis 2013). The core groups of societies need to be mobilized against state violence; it is important that they delegitimize a police force that uses illegal force and does not respect individual human rights. Our data show that increasing inclusionary legitimacy and the legitimacy base across all groups in society has the potential to reduce state violence, in which criminal justice actors are heavily involved. Building legitimacy in turn can help in reducing conflict and violence (World Bank 2011: 84), but it is important for whom, for what and in which ways this is done.

These findings and patterns suggest a Weberian, contextualised and culturally and institutionally particularized concept of legitimacy when democratic and non-democratic regimes are compared. However, they also confirm the power of universal mechanisms of procedural justice and fair treatment in generating legitimacy across all contexts and regime types, which might impact and put pressure on contemporary non-democratic regimes in the long run. Taken together, the particular and the universal model of legitimacy conflate—paradoxically—in another Weberian model type: bureaucratic autonomy and impartiality of the state's decision making. Our data lends considerable support to recent conceptualizations of governance and the quality of governance that resurrect the Weberian model of modern bureaucracies as regimes of autonomous and impartial decision making. Francis Fukuyama (2013) has persuasively argued for measuring the quality of governance and government—of which legitimacy is a core element—in terms of the independence and autonomy of bureaucracies that give them space for decision making without pressure and intrusion from power-holders and powerful social groups. Bo Rothstein (2011) in a similar vein has made a case that impartiality should be the core measure of the quality of government on which citizens base their judgements of legitimacy. Impartiality of decision making implies both: the limitations of power and checking institutions, as well as strong institutions that are accountable and deploy power according to rule of law principles (Karstedt 2013). As authoritarian and non-democratic states are a persistent presence in many regions of the world, linking legitimacy to impartial and autonomous decision making might help to explain the conundrum of legitimacy and citizens' support and voluntary cooperation with non-democratic regimes.

REFERENCES

ALY, G. (ed) (2007a) *Volkes Stimme. Skepsis und Führervertrauen im Nationalsozialismus*. Frankfurt: Fischer.

ALY, G. (2007b) 'Ideologie, Skepsis und Angst' (pp 130–45), in Aly, G. (ed) 2007a. *Volkes Stimme. Skepsis und Führervertrauen im Nationalsozialismus*. Frankfurt: Fischer.

Bauman, Z. and Donskis, L. (2013) *Moral Blindness*. Cambridge: Polity.

Beetham, D. (1991) *The Legitimation of Power*. Basingstoke: Palgrave Macmillan.

Bogdanova, E. (2013) 'Complaining to Putin. The Paradox of a Hybrid Regime. Unpublished Paper, Conference on Complaints: Cultures of Grievance in Eastern Europe and Eurasia.' Princeton, 8–9 March 2013.

Bottoms, A. and Tankebe, J. (2012) 'Beyond Procedural justice: A Dialogic Approach to Legitimacy in Criminal Justice', *Journal of Criminal Law and Criminology*, 102 (1), 119–70.

Braithwaite, J. (2013) 'Crime in Asia: Towards a Better Future?', *Asian Journal of Criminology*, forthcoming.

Braithwaite, J. (1998) 'Institutionalizing Distrust, Enculturating Trust' in Braithwaite, V. and Levi, M. (eds) *Trust and Governance*, 343–75. New York: Russell Sage Foundation.

Brooker, P. (2009) *Non-Democratic Regimes* (2nd edn). London: Palgrave Macmillan.

Brownlee, J. (2007) *Authoritarianism in an Age of Democratization*. Cambridge: Cambridge University Press.

Bruce, G. (2010) *The Firm: The Inside Story of the Stasi*. Oxford: Oxford University Press.

Case, W. (1993) 'Semi-Democracy in Malaysia: Withstanding the Pressures from Regime Change', *Pacific Affairs* 66 (1), 183–205.

Cenarro, A. (2004) 'Violence, Surveillance and Denunciation: Social Cleavage and the Spanish Civil War and Francoism 1936–1950.' in Emsley, C., Johnson, E., and Spierenburg, P. (eds) *Social Control in Europe, 1800–2000*. Columbus: Ohio State University Press.

Cheibub, J. A., Gandhi, J., and Vreeland, J. R. (2010) 'Democracy and Dictatorship Revisited': *Regime type 2004–2008* available at: <https://sites.google.com/site/joseantoniocheibub/datasets/democracy-and-dictatorship-revisited> accessed 15 November 2012.

Coicaud, J-M. (2002) *Legitimacy and Politics: A Contribution to the Study of Political Right and Political Responsibility*, Curtis, D.A. (trans). Cambridge: Cambridge University Press.

Deletant, D. (2006) *Ceausescu and the Securitate. Coercion and Dissent in Romania, 1965–1989*. London: Hurst.

Dunnage, J. (2004) 'Social Control in Fascist Italy: The Role of the Police' in Emsley, C., Johnson, E., and Spierenburg, P. (eds) *Social Control in Europe, 1800–2000*. Columbus: Ohio State University Press.

Ellmann, S. (1995) 'Law and Legitimacy in South Africa', *Law and Social Inquiry* 20(2): 407–79.

Esty, D. C., Goldstone, J. A., Gurr, T. R., Harff, B., Levy, M., Dabelko, G. D., and Surko, P. T. (1998) *State Failure Task Force Report*. Phase II Findings. Working Papers. 31 July 1998. University of Maryland.

Evans, R. (2005) *The Third Reich in Power*. London: Allen Lane.

Financial Times (2010) 'The Accuracy of China's "Mass Incidents"'. 2 March 2010, by Will Freeman.

Fitzpatrick, S. and Gellately, R. (eds) (1997) *Accusatory Practices: Denunciation in Modern European History*. Chicago: Chicago University Press.

Freedom House (2013). *Freedom in the World 2013*. Washington DC. <http://www.freedomhouse.org> accessed 20 February 2013.

Fukuyama, F. (1992) *The End of History and the Last Man*. New York: Putnam.

Fukuyama, F. (2013) 'What is Governance?' *Governance* 26(3): 347–68.

Fulbrook, M. (1997) *Anatomy of a Dictatorship: Inside the GDR 1949–1989*. Oxford: Oxford University Press.

Gandhi, J. (2008) *Political Institutions Under Dictatorship*. Cambridge: Cambridge University Press.

Geddes, B., Wright, J., and Frantz, E. (2012) *New Data on Autocratic Regimes*. <http://dictators.la.psu.edu> accessed 30 October 2012.

GELLATELY, R. (1990) *The Gestapo and German Society: Enforcing Racial Policy 1933–1945*. Oxford: Oxford University Press.

GELLATELY, R. (2001) *Backing Hitler: Consent and Coercion in Nazi Germany*. Oxford: Oxford University Press.

GIBNEY, M., CORNETT, L., and WOOD, R., (2012): *Political Terror Scale 2004–2008* available at: <http://www.politicalterrorscale.org/> accessed 31 October 2012.

GILLEY, B. (2006) 'The Determinants of State Legitimacy: Results for 72 Countries', *International Political Science Review* 27(1): 47–71.

GÖBEL, C. and ONG, L. H. (2012) *Social Unrest in China*. European China Research and Advice Network. London.

HOLMES, L. (1993) *The End of Communist Power. Anti-Corruption Campaigns and Legitimation Crisis*. Oxford: Oxford University Press.

HUNTINGTON, S. P. (1993) *The Third Wave: Democratization in the Late Twentieth Century*. Norman: University of Oklahoma Press.

JACKSON, J., BRADFORD, B., STANKO, B., and HOHL, K. (2012) *Just Authority? Public Trust and Police Legitimacy*. London: Willan/Routledge.

JAGGERS, K. and GURR, T. (1995) 'Tracking Democracy's Third Wave with the Polity III Data', *Journal of Peace Research* 32(4): 469–82.

JOHNSON, E. A. (2011) 'Criminal Justice, Coercion and Consent in "Totalitarian" Society', *British Journal of Criminology* 51: 599–614.

KARSTEDT, S. (2003) 'Legacies of a Culture of Inequality: The Janus-Face of Crime in Post-Communist Societies.' *Crime, Law and Social Change* 40 (2–3): 295–320.

KARSTEDT, S. (2006) 'Democracy, Values and Violence: Paradoxes, Tensions, and Comparative Advantages of Liberal Inclusion.' *Annals of the American Academy of Political and Social Science* 605: 50–81.

KARSTEDT, S. (2011) 'Our Sense of Justice: Values, Justice and Punishment.' (pp. 33–58), in Parmentier, S., Walgrave, L., Aertsen, I., Maesschalck, J. and Paoli, L. (eds) *A Sparking Discipline. The Contribution of Criminology to Social Justice and Sustainable Development*. Leuven: Leuven University Press.

KARSTEDT, S. (2013) 'State Crime. The European Experience.' (pp. 125–53), in: Body-Gendrot, S., Hough, M. et al. (eds) *The Routledge Handbook of European Criminology*. Oxford: Routledge.

KAUFMANN, D., KRAAY, A. and MASTRUZZI, M. (2011) The Worldwide Governance Indicators project: *Rule of Law 2004–2008* available at: <http://info.worldbank.org/governance/wgi/index.asp> accessed 3 November 2012.

KRYGIER, M. (2011) 'Four Puzzles About the Rule of Law: Why, What, Where? and Who Cares?' in Fleming, J. E. (ed) *Getting to the Rule of Law*. New York and London: New York University Press.

LANDMANN. T. and CARVALHO, E. (2010) *Measuring Human Rights*. London: Routledge.

LEVITSKY, S. and WAY, L. A. (2010) *Competitive Authoritarianism. Hybrid Regimes after the Cold War*. Cambridge: Cambridge University Press.

LIANG, B. (2008) *The Changing Chinese Legal System, 1978–Present. Centralization of Power and Rationalization of the Legal System*. New York: Routledge.

LINZ, J. J. (2000) *Totalitarian and Authoritarian Regimes. With a Major New Introduction*. London: Lynne Rienner.

MACCOUN, R. J. (2005) 'Voice, Control and Belonging: The Double-Edged Sword of Procedural Fairness', *Annual Review of Law and Society* 1, 171–201.

MANN, M. (1970) 'The Social Cohesion of Liberal Democracies', *American Sociological Review* 35: 423–39.

Mann, R. (1987) *Protest und Kontrolle im Dritten Reich: Nationalsozialistische Herrschaft im Alltag einer Rheinischen Grossstadt*. Frankfurt, New York: Campus.

Markovits, I. (2010) *Justice in Lüritz. Experiencing Socialist Law in East Germany*. Princeton and Oxford: Princeton University Press.

Marshall, M. and Cole, B. R. (2011) *State Fragility Index, Political Legitimacy* available at: <http://www.systemicpeace.org/inscr/inscr.htm> accessed 15 October 2012.

Marshall, M. and Jaggers, K. (2010) *Polity IV Project: Political regime characteristics and transitions 1800–2010, Polity level 2004–2008* available at: <http://www.systemicpeace.org/polity/polity4.htm> accessed 15 October 2012.

Mica, A. (2012) *Scandals and Party Moots. Mass Protest during the Ceausescu Regime in Romania*. Frankfurt: Peter Lang.

Michelson. E. and Read, B. (2011) 'Public Attitudes Toward Official Justice in Beijing and Rural China', in Woo, M., Gallagher, M., and Goldmann, M. (eds) *Chinese Justice: Civil Dispute Resolution in Contemporary China*. Cambridge Mass.: Harvard University Press.

Muller, E. N. and Seligson, M. A. (1994) 'Civic Culture and Democracy: The Question of Causal Relationships', *American Political Science Review* 88: 635–52.

Müller, A. (2007) 'Gesamtstatistik—ein Experiment' (pp. 116–29) in Aly, G. (ed) 2007a. *Volkes Stimme. Skepsis und Führervertrauen im Nationalsozialismus*. Frankfurt: Fischer.

Niethammer, L. (1991). *Die volkseigene Erfahrung: Eine Archäologie des Lebens in der Industrieprovinz der DDR: 30 biografische Eröffnungen*. Hamburg: Rowohlt.

Osiel, M. (1995) 'Dialogue with Dictators. Judicial Resistance in Argentina and Brazil', *Law and Social Inquiry* 20(2): 481–560.

Rajah, J. (2012) *Authoritarian Rule of Law. Legislation, Discourse and Legitimacy in Singapore*. Cambridge: Cambridge University Press.

Rees, L. (1997) *The Nazis. A Warning from History*. New York: New Press.

Rothstein, B. (2011) *The Quality of Government. Corruption, Social Trust and Inequality in International Perspective*. Chicago/London: University of Chicago Press.

Schedler, A. (ed) (2006) *Electoral Authoritarianism. The Dynamics of Unfree Competition*. Boulder, Col: Lynne Rienner.

Schlüter, H. (2007) 'Terrorinstanz Volksgerichtshof.' (pp. 80–95), in Aly, G. (ed) 2007a. *Volkes Stimme. Skepsis und Führervertrauen im Nationalsozialismus*. Frankfurt: Fischer.

Smith, D. (2007) 'The Foundations of Legitimacy' (pp. 30–58), in Tyler, T. (ed) *Legitimacy and Criminal Justice. International Perspectives*. New York: Russell Sage Foundation.

Sun, I., Hu, R., and Wu, Y. (2012) 'Social Capital, Political Participation and Public Trust in Police in Urban China', *Australia and New Zealand Journal of Criminology* 45, 87–105.

Sunshine, J. and Tyler, T. (2003) 'The Role of Procedural Justice and Legitmacy in Shaping Public Support for Policing', *Law and Society Review*, 37(3), 513–47.

Tyler, T. (ed) (2007). *Legitimacy and Criminal Justice. International Perspectives*. New York: Russell Sage Foundation.

UN Statistics Division (2012): 'Composition of Macro Geographical (Continental) Regions' available at: <http://unstats.un.org/unsd/methods/m49/m49regin.htm> accessed 15 January 2013.

World Health Organisation (2012) 'WHO Mortality Database': *Homicide Rates 2004–2008* available at: <http://www.who.int/healthinfo/mortality_data/en/index.html> accessed 15 November 2012.

World Bank (2011) 'World Development Report 2011'. Washington DC: World Bank.

Zakaria F. (1997) 'The Rise of Illiberal Democracy', *Foreign Affairs* 76(6): 22–43.

8

LEGITIMACY, CRIMES, AND COMPLIANCE IN 'THE CITY': *DE MAXIMIS NON CURAT LEX*?

Michael Levi

'Erst kommt das Fressen, dann kommt die Moral.
First you must stuff yourself; then comes morality.'
(Author translation)[1]

INTRODUCTION

Legitimacy is a warm, fuzzy term. It has the enormous advantage that its opposite, *il*legitimacy (like '*un*critical criminology') is on the face of it plainly *un*desirable. It is both an output—in the sense that it is the result of multifarious influences including ideology, inequality, material interests, life experiences, and social conformism—and an input, in that although it is an analytical construct rather than a human/institutional actor, legitimacy has an effect on how we behave, and what we support.

The assertion that legitimacy is obtained to a large measure by *procedural* justice is an important empirical claim, and has generated much fruitful research and policy benefits, because it shifts thinking in the direction of how the policed 'communities' see what is happening to them rather than taking controllers' perspectives as proxies for those of 'society'. Utilitarian majoritarians might quibble at the idea that policed minorities should have any kind of veto right over policing that is for the majority benefit. Most such contentious debates involve ethnic minorities and their beliefs/customs. For example, in the white-collar crime context, if companies believe that they are being 'over-regulated' in relation to harmful externalities, we would not take such complaints as a sufficient basis for abandoning attempts to regulate. However, regulation might be more effective if the businesses were at least partly 'onside', so

[1] Berthold Brecht, 'Wovon lebt der Mensch' in *Dreigroschenoper*.

legitimacy in the eyes of businesspeople is ideally desirable. In this chapter, I will pose some questions for the application of the concept of legitimacy to white-collar crimes committed by corporate and financial services elites and offer some limited empirical data on attitudes and behaviour to illuminate the problems. I will begin by reviewing some relevant research that directly addresses the problems; move to consider attitudes to business legitimacy, regulatory and criminal sanctions, and the implications of recent banking fraud and money laundering scandals.

Historically, like criminology itself, much of the literature on legitimacy deals with the classic areas of street crime and with public order policing. A range of possible assertions could be made about the relationship between crime, policing, and legitimacy. In the particular case of crime in 'the City' (of London, otherwise known as The Square Mile, and its equivalents elsewhere such as 'Wall Street', often juxtaposed in the US with 'Main Street'[2]), are we asserting that:

(1) The behaviour of elites and their policing and accountability to justice (broadly construed) have some demonstration effect on the propensity of others to commit street and household crime?[3]
(2) Inaction (or perceived inaction) against elites makes the public, and non-elite offenders, think that crime control policy and/or 'society' generally is unfair (and if so, so what?), or
(3) Because of the depredations of the rich[4] and the sheltering of their funds in the secrecy havens of the North, less money is available to governments in the Global North and South. Therefore domestic and/or international social welfare cuts may have to be made which increase desperation and criminal conduct among the poor, including the poor in foreign countries who may riot, become engaged in drugs/labour trafficking, terrorism, etc.?[5]

This is quite a diverse set of claims with sometimes ill-specified consequences, and they are not easy to test rigorously. We might expect perceived legitimacy to vary anyway with democratic participation and 'the spirit level' linked to social inequality (Wilkinson and Pickett 2010). Thus, the impact of the impunity of the dozen or so local elites whose rent-seeking led to the insolvency of the Kabul Bank—which $900m fraud cost Afghanistan 5–6 per cent of its GNP in 2012 (Monitoring and Evaluation Committee 2012)—might in absolute financial and social opportunity cost terms be greater than that of elite and non-elite scams in the West (Levi 2012). But the impact

[2] Interestingly, there does not appear to be an equivalent juxtaposition in the UK, though news media sometimes contrast 'the bubble economy' with 'the real economy'.

[3] This is the converse of Oscar Wilde's ironic statement in *The Importance of Being Earnest* that 'if the lower orders don't set us a good example, what on earth is the use of them?... They seem, as a class, to have absolutely no sense of moral responsibility?'

[4] Whether convictable crimes or the 'aggressive tax avoidance' that is probably legal but was condemned as 'morally repugnant' in 2012 by the Conservative Prime Minister and Chancellor of the Exchequer. There is no space here for a detailed examination of the shifts in discourse on tax avoidance in 2012–13 within Europe and the US that led Prime Minister Cameron to make it and the disclosure of 'beneficial ownership' of companies a keynote of the UK's chairmanship of the G8 in 2013.

[5] In a variant of this, Hagan (2012) connects the deregulation of financial services in the Reagan era with both the causes of the global financial crisis and the immiseration of the poor.

on perceptions of legitimacy in Afghanistan might be far less than in the UK or US, since the masses already may have low expectations of their elites. (We might think something similar of Berlusconi's Italy compared with the rapidly forced resignation in 2013 of the French Treasury Minister Jerome Cahuzac who had been in charge of the struggle against tax evasion, after a leak led him to admit he had a large undeclared illicit account in Switzerland.) Sadly, opinion poll data are unavailable to test this, and valid opinion polling in Afghanistan is anyway hardly an easy process.

LEGITIMACY AND RESEARCH ON WHITE-COLLAR CRIME

Although it has been preoccupied with accounting for offending and compliance by the poorer sections of society, the procedural justice literature has not wholly neglected crimes in a business context. In the converse of the classic Chinese proverb that society 'like the fish, rots from the head', Tyler's (2006: 5) Afterword to his classic book asserts that:

> Studies of employees show that they are motivated by their evaluations of the legitimacy of corporate rules (Tyler and Blader 2005). These same studies show that, as in community settings, the legitimacy of policies and rules in work settings is strongly linked to employee evaluations of the fairness of corporate procedures. If companies act in ways that employees experience as procedurally just, their rules are viewed as more legitimate, and are more likely to be obeyed.

With a specific focus on white-collar crime, Tyler (2009: 195) later argued that legitimacy is:

> A key antecedent of successful functioning within organizations. It is important for companies to be able to effectively motivate rule following behavior among employees, i.e., to be able to limit white-collar crime. This chapter compares the utility of two approaches to securing such behavior. Those strategies are as follows: (1) the sanction-based command-and-control model and (2) self-regulation approaches that are linked to activating employee's ethical judgments. Research findings suggest that, while command-and-control strategies influence employee behavior, self-regulatory strategies have a stronger influence. Studies also explore the basis of these ethical judgments, and find that the primary factor shaping them is the procedural justice that employees experience in their workplace. These results suggest that the roots of employee policy adherence and rule following behavior lie in the procedural justice of the organization. Overall, this analysis highlights the important role ethical judgments play in motivating both rule following and policy adherence among employees in work settings and provides practical suggestions for shaping those judgments.
>
> Can businesses effectively regulate the behavior of white-collar employees, and if so, what strategies should they use to best achieve that goal? Recent corporate scandals have evoked a heightened concern among members of the public, government officials, and business leaders about both whether businesses can regulate the conduct of their employees, as well as about how to effectively secure employee adherence with corporate rules and policies. White-collar crime is suddenly on the public agenda.

Partly as a result of its being on the public agenda, it is also on the political agenda (e.g. Labour Party, 2013). However, much depends on what one means by 'white-collar crime', a term which stretches from blue-collar crime to elite malfeasance, with 'organized fraud' being ambiguously located in white-collar and/or in organized crime. Tyler's analysis of legitimacy and adherence to rules by employees is interesting and empirically grounded; and the flurry of criminal and regulatory cases in 2012 and 2013 covering a range of bank misconduct occurring over several years in relation to money laundering, fraud, insider dealing, rogue trading, and terrorist sanctions evasion has reinforced the challenge and importance of corporate discipline. (Though a different perspective would be that given a low objective and perceived likelihood/severity of sanctions or even publicity at the time, corporate leaders had little disincentive to allow or encourage law-breaking of this kind. A control theorist might ask why they should motivate conformity with law rather than maximize corporate or business unit profits, from which they benefited personally by bonuses and continued employment/global marketability.)

But it would be hard to dispute that the more significant problem of legitimacy is the non-adherence or at best partial adherence of global elites to legal rules that are nowadays near-universal (like criminal and regulatory rules against money laundering, financing terrorism, and Grand Corruption) and sometimes patchy and country-specific (like conflict of interest rules, and the criminalization of price-fixing cartels). The effects of this 'extra-legal behaviour' by elites on the behaviour not just of employees but of other citizens, whether they be persistent offenders, occasional offenders or even the rather small subset of people who have *never* offended remain largely to be analysed. It is one thing to show that before and/or after their involvement in crimes, street criminals and 'the Underworld' use techniques of neutralization that involve scaling their harms against suite crimes to diminish their own misconduct in their own eyes and in the eyes of their reference groups;[6] it is another to argue that the relative impunity of elites increases the harm and frequency of those other crimes.

The propensity to commit crime has *prima facie* little connection to the legitimacy of the priorities of the police and indeed of the state in relation to what sorts of offences by what sorts of people to pursue via what means with what resources. Tyler focused on the law-breaking of white-collar *workers* rather than on CEOs and other directors/senior managers. As he notes (2009: 195):

> [T]his chapter does not consider the case in which leaders are creating an unethical climate within their companies so that they can break rules for personal profit. Rather, [it] begins with the assumption that the situation can be one in which the leaders of a company are motivated to encourage their employees to follow rules, and are seeking to understand how best to do so.

This focus on employees is the easier case. However, even there, the validity of data on employee misconduct is more questionable than is indicated in the studies cited in

[6] Al Capone's attributed but unverified reference to the law and other professions as 'the legitimate rackets' and that 'capitalism is the legitimate racket of the ruling class' express this cynicism beautifully. See Maruna and Copes (2004) for an excellent review of techniques of neutralization evidence.

Tyler's text, and he does not consider the mixing of personal and institutional profit that is common in large corporate scandals. Very little of what modest panic there has been about white-collar crimes until recently (Levi 2009) has focused on employees; rather it has focused on director-level 'fat cat' staff and on investment bankers with huge bonuses who work in areas of financial services that are not included in the experiments cited by Tyler, which took place in the 'old economy'. The few studies in financial services have focused more on the culture and biology of masculinity (Coates 2012), rather than on the Tyler obedience issues; while leftist political activists are interested in pointing out the lack of deterrence in traditional ways of regulating business misconduct and juxtaposing attitudes to crimes of the poor and crimes of the powerful (Tombs and Whyte 2007). There are many examples in which financial services sales employees are encouraged to disobey (or, to be more generous, are deliberately not *dis*couraged from disobeying) the law (e.g., Personal Protection Insurance 'mis-selling'—which was arguably systemic fraud—in the UK that occurred for a decade after 2001, and which met with immense reluctance by the banks to compensate their customers—Financial Services Ombudsman 2012); to July 2013, almost £17 billion has been set aside by British retail banks for compensation, and over £9 billion has already been paid out. Mortgage broking deceptions of sub-prime borrowers in the US are a less clear-cut case, for many of these occurred in amoral small firms and some hyper-aggressive larger firms, though these tactics were later adopted by industry leader Countrywide Assurance when it was undercut and found it impossible to get business (McLean and Nocera 2011); a process that repeated itself in the property business in Ireland, after Anglo-Irish Bank began to scoop all the chances to make money (sic!) from property developers because of its easy loan business model (author interviews, 2010). Thus, as in Gresham's Law, the Bad banking drives out the Good. In all of the previously noted cases, the short-run profits this generated contributed significantly to the personal benefits of the directors, as well as to the valuations of the companies and to the apparent prosperity of the economies in which the firms were based. Through derivatives sales to global banks, these vast losses that were at best very negligent spread to other countries.

The argument presented here is not that Tyler is wrong when he asserts that corporate culture and ethics matter, but that his data are derived only from white-collar crimes that are *relatively* non-serious (though still costly compared with other property crimes), i.e. to what might be better termed occupational rather than white-collar crimes. It is moot what level of corporate/individual negligence/recklessness ought to trigger the application of criminal law, in doctrine or practice. It is not obvious that all business sectors or firms within each sector will act in the same way, just as we know from general criminal motivation literature that not all people of similar backgrounds will act in the same way, given the same situational opportunities and pressures.[7]

Early white-collar crime literature focused on the ways in which senior directors and employees alike were sucked into crimes 'for the firm' by differential association models in which they learned to do what was profitable over what was moral (Sutherland 1983, originally 1949). Later, embezzlement *against* the firm's interests was

[7] For a recent re-analysis of older corporate crime data, see Wang and Holtfreter (2012).

explained in a slightly different way (Cressey 1953), though this time law (and/or the desire to be seen as a good citizen by the standards of reference groups) was recognized as legitimate but the neutralization enabled the embezzler to see their conduct as not an example of criminal deception. This capacity for seeing oneself as essentially good (or at least as complying with the norms of one's peers and 'therefore' not being culpable) is key not only, first, to explaining elite involvement in white-collar crimes but also, secondly, to the difficulties that British politicians and global businesses operating in the UK have encountered over tax avoidance in 2012–13, the attribution of personal expenses to business credit cards (or invoices straight to the firm), and Parliamentary expense claims, etc.

There is a comparativist tension in how the literature on legitimacy relates to the learned culture in which public positions are viewed as opportunities for rent-seeking for self, families, and tribe/religious groupings (Wrong 2009): arguably, those who adopt classic meritocratic approaches might be the ones seen as illegitimate even by the poor people in their ethnic or religious group, in Italy as much as in parts of Africa. The demand that the best qualified should alone get the job is not following the expectations from their group. There, the appeal to abstract concepts of Rawlsian justice may work neither for majorities nor minorities. We do not know what different sectors in South Africa think of the allegedly corrupt contracts made by the South African government with BAE, whose not unique alleged kick-backs allegedly were funnelled into the coffers of the African National Congress (ANC), though some may have trickled down into personal bank accounts also. ANC members do not appear to care enough to provoke rebellion, though one of their MPs resigned in protest against the conduct itself and the lack of action against it (Feinstein 2011). Such cynicism about the ends–means relationships and the exercise of power arguably is a reflection of loss of belief in fairness, if that belief ever existed. Meritocratic constructs in which no group is privileged may require a long time to build, and—despite the importance of anti-corruption movements in the 'Arab Spring' and elsewhere—may be hard to sustain.

Tyler (2009: 199) distinguishes between 'compliance with the law and voluntary, willing acceptance of the law', the latter being particularly salient 'in work settings' since it predicts rule following even where there is no perceived detection risk. Of course he (and other authors, e.g. Simpson 2002) are correct in flagging up the limitations of deterrence and cruder forms of rational choice theory in accounting for why people obey the law. Competing accounts for City misconduct range from largely genetic sociopathy that can be more easily 'activated' in rip-off cultures (Babiak and Hare 2007), via 'irrational exuberance' (Shiller 2005), 'animal spirits' (Akerlof and Shiller 2010), and poor decision-making heuristics (Kahneman 2011), affected by excessive concentrations of testosterone in dealing rooms (Coates 2012[8]), to learned corrupt cultures, etc. Where does or might legitimacy feature in this behavioural economics of elites? Can we deduce it independently of their behaviour, and given the opacity of the conduct of individuals—except via civil suits and sometimes criminal prosecutions/Deferred Prosecution Agreements—how are we to be able to infer their

[8] It is intriguing to consider what is the long run optimal proportion of testosterone in a financial services trading room?

individual contributions to those bad outcomes that we *do* come to learn about (Laufer 2006)?

Occupy Wall Street, Occupy London, and movements like Uncut UK seek to strip away the social legitimacy claims of corporations like Amazon, Apple, Goldman Sachs, Google, and Starbucks, stimulating Parliamentary attention by the UK Public Accounts Committee and pressurizing Conservative politicians to condemn 'aggressive' tax avoidance (though not illuminating us as to where the boundary should be drawn). Revelations about Wal-Mart's alleged corporate bribery in Mexico and elsewhere have thrown light on the dark side of that firm's heavily PR-massaged conduct. Global corporations are vulnerable to misconduct allegations in one part of the globe casting their integrity and/or competence in a negative light, thus risking undermining the millions they spend on creating a positive corporate image. This brings us to an important distinguishing feature of this subject area: as with state crime, transnational bribery and elite embezzlement may involve crimes committed by elites in one country against people in another. This is not an issue commonly considered in arguments about procedural legitimacy; nor, for that matter, by many sociological discussions about norms and values.

Whatever our views in the abstract, very few of us in practice regard damage to the interests of people in distant lands who are not related to us as being equivalent to damage to those we know and care about.[9] In the almost 30 years since the gas explosion at Bhopal in 1984, which killed double the number of those in the Twin Towers (but was plainly not intentional and was in no-one's direct interests), there has been only a modest discernible effect on the growth and profits of Union Carbide, later sold to Dow Chemical.[10] The edifice of global capitalism and its financial secrecy havens is central to the sets of corporate and other screening enablers that facilitate a range of crimes (including those by elites) and the laundering of the proceeds thereof. And it is this infrastructure of opacity that is under attack from campaigners such as the Tax Justice Network, Global Financial Integrity, and Global Witness against corporate and individual elite High Net Worth (HNW) malefaction or (contested) immorality.

Not all financial havens—the French term 'paradis fiscaux' has an attractive ring—are in the stereotypical spots from Antigua to Switzerland. What one might term ironically 'not governing through non-crime' also occurs in US states ranging from Delaware to Wyoming. Despite the strong formal commitment of the US government to anti-money laundering policy and enforcement around the world, company registration is a state and not a federal responsibility in the USA, and in financially stretched (as well as earlier, prosperous) times, the states presumably consider that

[9] The exception to this appears to be those mainly of Islamic faith who become inflamed by insults to other members of their group and to the Quran, no matter where in the world those perceived insults occur.

[10] The negative publicity *may* have had an impact upon some staff who left or chose not to work for the company, but this is undocumented. In June 2010, seven ex-employees, including the former Union Carbide India Limited chairman, were convicted in Bhopal of causing death by negligence and sentenced to two years imprisonment and a fine of about $2,000 each, the maximum punishment allowed by law: they were bailed pending appeals in the glacial Indian criminal justice system. An eighth former employee was also convicted, but died before judgment was passed. In 1989, a settlement was reached under which Union Carbide Corporation agreed to pay US $470 million in a full and final settlement of its civil and criminal liability.

they need the income from corporations without performing any of the due diligence functions about customer identification that are normal and universal in opening individual bank accounts.[11] The crime externalities generated mainly though not wholly outside those states are given little consideration, and the President can do little about it. Little surprise, then, that Senate Permanent Sub-Committee on Investigation reviews and a World Bank study (de Willebois et al. 2011) found widespread abuse in both the corporate and the charity sectors in the US; while an international experimental study found setting up corporations for abusive purposes to be very easy (Sharman 2012; Findley et al. 2012). The success of American elites in persuading the public that the vast bail out losses for which they are now paying was due to too much rather than to too little regulation is a stunning ideological achievement. There is no evidence that this has been so successful in the UK or in other parts of the globe, but the practical difference is not clear.

ATTITUDES TO BUSINESS LEGITIMACY IN THE UK

One way of thinking about the 'legitimacy to whom' questions is to delineate the 'stakeholders'. In the case of financial crimes, these comprise a very broad array: in no particular order, they include Politicians, Regulators, Domestic Prosecutors—in England, Wales, and Northern Ireland, these are the Crown Prosecution Service & Serious Fraud Office (SFO) and (for insider trading) the Financial Conduct Authority (FCA), the Insolvency Service, judicial sentencing guidelines, the regulated (who pay fees annually for their own regulation), financial services 'victims', non-financial services 'victims'—corporate and individual, the media, jurors at criminal trials, and the general public. Note also that given globalization of economic activity, stakeholders also include consumers, investors, and workers abroad, plus overseas competitors' regulators and prosecutors, who sometimes may have an interest in tough action or (if corrupt or using poorly drafted law) in *in*action. If legitimacy is seen in terms of responding to stakeholder demands, it is seldom clear what any of the stakeholder list would like to see in terms of action against elites (a term which has been left undefined here). On the one hand, governments appear to want as little done as possible, so as not to 'frighten the horses' and to save the very real costs of prosecution;[12] on the other

[11] There are huge differences across the corporate sector in transparency. It costs $150,000 to apply for a casino licence in Nevada, giving the authorities ample opportunity to conduct due diligence. By contrast, though one can do a lot of harm with a company, checks and costs are minimal in the same state.

[12] The Home Office's resource estimate accompanying the Bribery Bill (now Act) of 2010 assumed that costs were neutral and that there would be an extra 1.25 prosecutions annually in England and Wales by the Serious Fraud Office—therefore very little prosecutorial impact (and an unknown amount of marginal deterrence). In the 2012 financial year, the SFO's budget was cut to just over £30 million. It would be far too crude to juxtapose this to the estimated £52 billion cost of fraud in the UK (NFA 2013)—and not only because the Bribery Act was aimed at transnational bribery and therefore at *uncounted* losses occurring outside the UK—but it is interesting nonetheless. The Labour Party (2013) proposes turning white-collar prosecutions into a profit center by boosting not just prosecutions but also the frequency and size of criminal and regulatory penalties.

hand, they want to appear to act toughly, so as not to give the impression that they are 'protecting their own'[13] and are giving insufficient protection to consumers, investors, and workers. Furthermore, there is an element of global political capital in being seen to act against corrupt elites: capital which was lost when, under pressure from Prime Minister Blair and the Saudis, the SFO dropped charges against BAE over its alleged bribery of Prince Bandar of Saudi Arabia and others. My unsystematic interviews with development aid officials have emphasized the immense loss of prestige for the UK in the Global South that arose from this, as UK pressure on poor countries to act firmly against corruption looked less credible: but it is very questionable whether this loss of legitimacy (in not living up to ethical political claims) affects corrupt *behaviour* among elites and others in the Global South, at least in the short run. There are no obvious ways to assess this impact, other than on giving a stronger evidential base to the pre-existing rhetoric of 'condemning the condemners'.

It is tempting to think in a Golden Age-ist way of '*loss* of legitimacy', but perhaps what C. Wright Mills termed the 'news of higher immoralities' does not come as such a surprise to the populace. In 1993, around the time that the Maxwell £300 million pension fund fraud case was coming up towards trial (and later acquittal by the jury), I was able to add a few questions to the Gallup national representative omnibus poll to test the cultural *zeitgeist* (see Table 8.1). One result was the following, which reflects scepticism towards our elites' integrity claims, even more marked in the older than in the younger generation, and widespread in all socio-economic categories. Even half of the AB social group were prepared to assent to the proposition that one can't get to the top in business without breaking the law. Men were much more sceptical about meritocracy than women, and over a third said it was *certainly* true. No funds have been available to repeat this question, but it would be surprising if the proportion of sceptics

Table 8.1 Public perceptions of the necessity to break the law in order to succeed in business UK public answers to *'You can't get to the top in business without breaking the law'*[14]

	Certainly True	Probably True	Probably Untrue	Certainly Untrue	Don't Know
Total	18	39	18	17	9
Male	34	44	8	4	10
Female	14	37	20	18	10
18–24	13	41	18	19	5
65+	19	41	16	13	11
AB	12	38	18	26	7
C1	16	41	19	17	7
C2	20	41	17	15	8
DE	24	35	17	12	12

[13] A particular issue where the Cabinet are themselves clearly members of the social elite, as they currently are in the UK.

[14] Source: Gallup national sample 1993.

was lower today. So wherever our moral leadership is to come from, there is no obvious perception that the business elites speak from moral authority.

There are no precise equivalents in later public surveys. However, business ethics surveys show some important trends. In 2011 the Edelman Trust Barometer (2012) found only 38 per cent of the UK general public said they trusted business to 'do what is right'—a decline from 44 per cent in 2010 and 49 per cent in 2009.[15] A 2011 survey found business leaders were trusted by fewer than a third (29 per cent) of British adults to tell the truth. Business leaders were ranked thirteenth out of sixteen professions as trustworthy (Ipsos MORI & British Medical Association 2011).[16] This is consistent with findings since the survey was first conducted in 1983. Basran and Webley (2012) researched employee attitudes, including managers/supervisors, but their focus was on small scale financial crimes and was generic: in 2012, among managers/supervisors, only 10 per cent agreed and 77 per cent disagreed that '*It is acceptable to artificially increase profits in the books as long as no money is stolen*'—a fall in disapproval from 2008 (84 per cent disapproved). In a study for the Institute of Business Ethics, Ipsos Mori (2011) found that 31 per cent of AB groups and 24 per cent of C2DE (but a significantly smaller proportion of 55+) considered that business behaved more ethically than a decade ago; while 29 per cent of both socio-economic groups thought business behaved *less* ethically. I am not arguing that these perceptions are empirically correct as measures of business behaviour, nor is it obvious what the operational implications are for anything: but as measures of the social legitimacy of business, they indicate a decline.

REGULATORY APPROACHES AND LEGITIMACY

There has been an episodic shift in regulatory theories between countries and over time, none of which are obviously more effective than any other (Black 2011). In the UK, principles-based regulation (PBR), heavily promoted by the Financial Services Authority (FSA) and the UK government just before the financial crisis, became instantly outmoded. Hector Sants (2009), then chief executive of the FSA (and now head of compliance and government and regulatory relations at Barclays, following their large regulatory fines in 2012), observed that a 'principles-based approach does not work with people who have no principles.' The FSA (Sants 2009)—alongside other UK regulators—moved to 'outcomes-focused' regulation, though the difference between the two is arguably more apparent than real. The US Securities and Exchange Commission (SEC), for example, which regulates mainly through prescriptive and

[15] 1,000 UK adults aged 18 years and above, conducted using online interviews in late November 2011. Respondents were asked: *Below is a list of institutions. For each one, please indicate how much you trust that institution to do what is right using a 9-point scale where one means that you 'do not trust them at all' and nine means that you 'trust them a great deal'.*

[16] 1,026 British adults aged 15 years and above, conducted using face-to-face interviews in June 2011. Respondents were asked: '*Now I will read you a list of different types of people. For each would you tell me if you generally trust them to tell the truth, or not?*'

detailed rules and with an aggressive approach to enforcement, notoriously failed to detect the Madoff fraud, sixteen years from the first warning signs (SEC 2009: 41).

Under the Financial Services Act 2012, the FCA's key aim is to ensure financial markets work well so consumers get a fair deal. To do this, the FCA follows three statutory objectives:

- Protect consumers;
- Enhance the integrity of the UK financial system;
- Help maintain competitive markets and promote effective competition in the interests of consumers.

This replaced the FSA's objectives under the Financial Services and Markets Act 2000, which were:

- To maintain confidence in the UK financial system;
- To promote understanding of the financial system;
- To secure an appropriate degree of protection for consumers;
- To contribute to reducing financial crime.

Note the disappearance of the requirement to 'contribute to reducing financial crime', itself a hard-to-test objective. In a sense, legitimacy lies at the heart of this process of protecting consumers (though Goldman Sachs' alleged derogatory labelling as 'muppets' those unsuspecting corporate clients on whom they dumped their bad proprietary trades—Smith 2012—would not qualify); and of enhancing integrity. There are problems in devising how one would test the assertion that it had contributed to reducing financial crime. Not by referring to the doubling in two years in the NFA's estimated fraud totals to £73 billion in 2012, since most of the sub-categories of fraud in that work are outside the FCA's remit. But on what criteria? What would it take to delegitimate the FCA as a regulator? Much of the media criticism of its predecessor FSA is that they (like their American equivalents) suffered from group-think and timidity in the face of politically mandated 'light-touch' regulation: hence the satirical magazine Private Eye's label of its initials as Fundamentally Supine Authority. They were forced to publish a version of their internal report on the Royal Bank of Scotland, heavily redacted following representations by the lawyers involved (Treasury Committee 2012). Too much (distorted) publicity and City protests, the Chairman of the FSA, Lord Adair Turner (2009), stated that some of the City's financial services activities were 'socially useless'.[17]

It is commonplace to try to account for this in terms of regulatory 'capture culture', as used in financial and industrial regulation. However, given the cultural and ideological power of free market economics, an alternative view might be to attribute it as much to rapture as to capture (Dorn 2010, 2011), though the revolving door of public-private interchange offers economic as well as intellectual incentives not to be too

[17] 'It is hard is to distinguish between valuable financial innovation and non-valuable. Clearly, not all innovation should be treated in the same category as the innovation of either a new pharmaceutical drug or a new retail format. I think that some of it is socially useless activity.' See also his refined comments in a Mansion House speech, available at: <http://www.fsa.gov.uk/pages/Library/Communication/Speeches/2009/0922_at.shtml>.

critical of commercial practices. It is not currently known how much legitimacy within which sub-sets of the population the regulators enjoy or what that constitutes, since institutional evaluations are somewhat bland and commentators may not be confident about their anonymity. Therefore perspectives are refracted through representatives of different bodies and experts.

CRIMINAL SANCTIONING AND LEGITIMACY

In March 1985, a Gallup Poll found that 50 per cent of the British public (compared with 35 per cent in 1969) believe that the courts favour the rich and influential. This popular judgement may be unfair, inasmuch as—at least at that time, and even in the current era—so few rich and influential persons have been prosecuted in the past that the British courts have had little opportunity to discriminate in favour of them (or not). But one may contrast (non)prosecutions in the present era with those of the Savings & Loans (S & L) collapses in the 1980s (which were a specifically American product of deregulation—nowhere else in the capitalist world suffered a similar collapse). In that era, though some well-connected persons escaped prosecution,[18] many powerbrokers and even significant politicians were among the hundreds who went to jail (Nguyen and Pontell 2010). True (and not noted by commentators on the S & L crisis), banking elites did not go to jail, but they had not been involved in the S & Ls, so they had no opportunity to be caught up in that miasma or to be discriminated in favour of. The managerial lines of responsibility were clearer and less complex in S & Ls than they are in global banking, and their losses were much more easily contrasted with the profitability of other firms. However, that was an innocent derivatives-free world in which radical Islam was not even a mote in the eye of international capital, and in which—though the FBI was more focused on a narrow Italian-American construction of 'organized crime'—white-collar crimes were regarded as a threat to America and to the legitimacy of the system. Closing down an S & L was not a cross-national border issue and was considered to create little systemic risk attached, since the federal government both guaranteed and was seen as able to afford the compensation. This, after all, was at the height of American Superpower status.

Legitimacy judgements also impact on trial outcomes, at least in societies in which juries decide on criminal guilt. Most of the discussion of jury decision making in white-collar crimes has focused on its analytical competence or otherwise for dealing with difficult issues (Levi 1983, 1988), but there are also legitimacy-related questions of how verdicts are affected by public beliefs about whether or not (a) the law is justified, (b) the prosecutors and their witnesses have integrity, and (c) the defendant has been unjustifiably singled out for prosecution and is any worse morally than those who are giving evidence for the prosecution. Acquittals under these circumstances are sometimes referred to as 'jury equity verdicts'. (Even where there is no jury trial, public perceptions of the questions

[18] Rightly or wrongly on the evidence before those taking the decisions. The decision not to prosecute is usually immune from appeal, though the NGO Cornerhouse was successful in obtaining a judicial review of the SFO's decision to drop overseas bribery charges against BAE.

posed earlier can be important to how the judgements are received, including public protests.) The separable issue of verdict legitimacy in the eyes of defendants might also be important to some, and may affect recidivism, though there is no evidence of this.

Jury convictions may add legitimacy, unless jurors are depicted as corrupt or populist dupes of the prosecution. The Italian judges and prosecutors are accused by former Prime Minister Berlusconi of bias against him; more defensibly, leading businesspeople and politicians in former Communist regimes of Eastern Europe accuse state-appointed prosecutors and judges of being stooges of the government and of returning verdicts that owe more to politics than to evidence.[19] There has been pressure in the UK (but not in the US, where there are constitutional protections) to replace trial by jury with trial by judge with or without professional assessors, though this has never received a positive Parliamentary mandate outside Northern Ireland at the time of 'the Troubles'. But it is unknown whether professionals or 'Masters of the Universe' would find the judgement of fellow professionals to be legitimate, and they might take the view that professionals were trying to eliminate competitors or were acting on behalf of elite interests in showing that something was being done. Conversely, the public might see acquittals by professionals as elites 'looking after their own'. All of these are hypothetical in the absence of research on verdict legitimacy in cases such as this.[20]

Perhaps this 'simpler age' construction also applies to executives' views of the severity of different penalties. Table 8.2 shows the susceptibility of elites embedded in respectability to social as well as to penal sanctions (Levi 2002). Professional exclusion was viewed more seriously than two years in an open prison (the most likely real world result at the time), and even prosecution without conviction was highly salient. Unfortunately, this study has not been replicated subsequently, so we cannot tell whether or not the findings would differ today. Furthermore, they are unlikely to apply to the probably thicker skinned career fraudsters and corporate raiders/global elites (Levi 2010).

Based on documentary analysis, Barak (2012: 3, 15) tracks the decline in the policing and prosecution of elite white-collar crimes, noting that:

> The federal prosecution of financial fraud in the United States by the end of 2011 had fallen to a twenty-year low... every year since 1999, the number of federal criminal prosecutions has gotten smaller and smaller as the banking oligopoly in the United States has gotten bigger and bigger... the Department of Justice was on track to file just 1,365 prosecutions for financial institutional fraud in fiscal year 2011... the Securities and Exchange Commission filed a record-high 735 enforcement actions, going to trial in 19 cases, settling as many cases as possible with fraudulent defendants who neither admit nor deny wrongdoing while they agree to pay fines worth a fraction of losses to their investors... assigned to the investigative unit of Obama's 2012 Financial Fraud Enforcement Network, there were initially fifteen attorneys, investigators, and analysts as well as ten FBI agents. An additional thirty attorneys, investigators, and support staff from the U.S. attorneys' offices were scheduled to join the unit some time in early 2012.

[19] See the criticisms of the Ukrainian courts in the pre-trial and trial of the former Prime Minister, *Tymoshenko v. Ukraine* (application no. 49872/11) ECHR 136 (2013).

[20] For broader discussions of jury legitimacy and nullification issues, see Hans (2012: 50–3); Hannaford-Agor and Hans (2003).

Table 8.2 UK executive perceptions of the relative severity of alternative sanctions

Sentence	Severity 0–20
5 years' imprisonment	16.3
2 years' imprisonment in an 'ordinary' closed prison	11.5
Being banned from one's profession for life	10.8
2 years' imprisonment in an open prison	9.3
Publicity for one's offending in national press and TV	9.0
Being shunned by former friends and colleagues	7.9
Dismissal from current job	7.8
2 years' probation plus weekend imprisonment	7.3
Being prosecuted by the SFO, but acquitted by the jury	6.5
Being banned from company directorship for 10 years	5.9
£100,000 fine	5.8
240 hours community punishment	3.3
2 years' probation	2.9

My intermittent interviews with US and other knowledgeable public officials (2001–10) suggest that this was attributable mainly to the shift in focus of federal police to counter-terrorist work post 9/11, though there was a brief slurry of investigative activity post-Enron to deal with it and the 'dot.com' bubble, and with corporate elites who flagrantly treated corporate assets as if they were their own personal ones. Hagan (2012) attributes regulatory quiescence to the enduring influence of 'the Age of Reagan', which replaced the 'Age of Roosevelt'; Morgenson and Rosner (2011) to the 'revolving door' between Wall Street, Congress, and the Executive. Whatever the causes—stimulated by the need to raise vast sums for electoral success—there are in essence fewer pressures to seek out criminal sanctions for elites, whereas there is mainly a fiscal bar on prosecuting and imprisoning those who can be constructed as 'the undeserving poor'.

BANK SCANDALS AND THEIR IMPLICATIONS

The era since the Global Financial Crisis has seen a flurry of activity against banks by regulators and prosecutors who were let off the leash of 'light touch' regulation. Considering criminal and regulatory cases together, many major banks have been sanctioned in the UK or, more often, in the US, but barely at all in other financial services centres. To the time of the Standard Chartered penalty in November 2012, US regulators have received almost $3 billion from high-profile money-laundering-related settlements since 2009, compared with $30 million for UK regulators. Other cases are pending that will boost those totals significantly, and indeed the FSA handed down a record-breaking £312 million in fines for misconduct during its last full year as financial regulator, comfortably beating its previous record of £89 million in 2010 (Shoffman 2012). By August 2013, three banks settled penalties in two jurisdictions each over the Libor rate fixing scandal, totalling $1.5 billion (USB), $450 million (Barclays), and $600 million (Royal Bank of Scotland). What effects the publicity given in these cases might have had on public views of banker's integrity or their sense of 'fair justice' is hard to articulate or demonstrate. In principle, one might think of legitimacy aims in two contexts: getting financial institutions and professionals to behave better even when they expect not to be punished for behaving badly (as well as when they do think there is a risk of punishment); and satisfying the public (or at least segments thereof) that the Rich and Powerful are not being treated in an unduly favourable way.

The Department of Justice has brought several cases of money laundering. These included one deferred prosecution agreement (a sort of prosecutorial probation order) against Wachovia in 2010—triggered by its British Deputy Money Laundering Reporting Officer 'whistleblower'—in which authorities said the bank failed to maintain effective anti-money laundering controls and did not stop more than $100 million of Colombian and Mexican drug traffickers' money from being laundered through accounts at the bank. These are analogous to the gross recklessness (at best) displayed by HSBC's Mexican arm, which led to the heavy fine of $1.9 billion in 2012.

The scale of money laundering by prominent international banks may be systemic:

> During the Washington hearing, there was some tacit finger-pointing at London—even though the scale of HSBC's wrongdoing pales next to Wachovia's. Like HSBC, the US bank did not have rigorous systems. As a result some $373bn in wire transfers, versus HSBC's $7bn, were made from 2004 to 2007. More than $4bn in bulk cash was also transported from Mexican banks to Wachovia accounts. Bought in 2008 by Wells Fargo, Wachovia has since paid $160m to settle charges, and nobody in the US has gone to jail (versus 15 in Mexico)...
>
> In 2010, Federal Asset Seizures totalled just $2.5bn, a fraction of the US's estimated $65bn annual illegal drugs market. In the UK in 2009/10, the Serious Organised Crime Agency seized criminal assets worth £318m.[21]

In the period 2001 to 2008, the UK FSA imposed fines against 9 financial services entities for AML compliance breaches. Since then, to April 2013, its fines for breaches of anti-money laundering rules totalled around £24 million. Sometimes it appears that AML breaches are associated with other forms of misconduct. Coutts & Co, a small private bank that handles primarily wealthy individuals, received the UK's biggest-ever fine—£8.75 million—after it failed to conduct proper checks on almost three-quarters of clients that held politically sensitive positions, perhaps because it was expanding fast and paying bonuses to staff that reflected the number of new customers

[21] In 'Money laundering: Taken to the cleaners', *Financial Times* 20 July 2012. See also *Assets Forfeiture Fund and Seized Asset Deposit Fund, Annual Financial Statements Fiscal Year 2011*, US Department of Justice, Washington DC.

they signed up.[22] The small Swiss-based private bank EFG was fined £4.2 million for failing to take reasonable care to establish and maintain effective anti-money laundering controls for high risk customers over a three year period.[23] It is not known what the impact of these sanctions was upon their business and profitability.

A series of major non-American banks—HSBC, Standard Chartered, Lloyds TSB, ING Bank, and ABN AMRO—have been prosecuted or fined by US regulators for stripping the identifiers from transactions in relation to countries like Iran subject to US (and in some cases UN) sanctions. There the motivation for the offending is also profit, but interviews with convenience-sampled compliance officers suggest that the sanctions are or were at the time seen as illegitimate by a significant number of European bankers. Whether the American bankers saw the controls as legitimate and refrained from violations for that reason, or whether they were just aware that their government would act vigorously against them (i.e. there was a credible threat that worked) is unknown. The longevity of institutional awareness is also a significant issue in sustaining reform: in the aftermath of scandal, large sums are spent on compliance, but how long the scrutiny lasts is an open question.

Despite the creation of an impressive appearing set of AML controls in these banks, many big banks seemed comfortable with continued violations of their own rules. The reputational cost, at least as expressed in share prices, is minimal, possibly because banks are already little esteemed, but also because the 'nuclear option' of prosecuting banks or taking away their licenses has been reserved for marginal players: the collateral damage of drastic action being deemed too high (as the bankers doubtless know). It is well known from deterrence research that expected sanction celerity and certainty are more important than severity (Nagin, forthcoming), and it seems plausible that it is applicable to elites also.

A key challenge for behavioural change is how to transmit credible signals that get enough attention at senior operational levels in the hierarchy, though enhancing legitimacy is only part of that process: deterrence and transparency are also salient. At the bank level, 'too big to be prosecuted' typically leads to tough conditions as an alternative to prosecution and probable internal reform in corporations (arguably a good thing); but it also undermines equality of treatment and perhaps legitimacy when small foreign banks get prosecuted and big international banks (e.g. American and British ones) get Deferred Prosecution Agreements or a regulatory fine. Neither proportionality nor individual culpability operate in the same way as they do for 'normal' crimes for gain, and except in some Serious Fraud Office criminal sentencing, there is no sign that cross-crime type consistency is a serious concern. *Prima facie*, one might have expected tax fraud and social security fraud to be scaled along the same dimensions, because they are both offences against the government and taxpayers: but the discourse of 'welfare scroungers' remains a dominant *leitmotif* in the media, political,

[22] 'Coutts fined for laundering violations', 26 March 2012. <http://www.ft.com/cms/s/0/1b88674c-772b-11e1-93cb-00144feab49a.html#ixzz29ahvoAhM>.

[23] See <http://www.fca.org.uk/your-fca/documents/final-notices/2013/fsa-final-notice-2013-efg-private-bank-ltd>.

and criminal justice spheres that, despite the rise in public and political concern about high level tax avoidance and evasion, has prevented them from being treated on a common axis, except to some extent by the Sentencing Guidelines Council.

Levi (2006) has falsified the common view that frauds by elites and by others are neglected in tabloid as well as in broadsheet media, and though this empirical work has not been updated formally to take account of recent scandals, inspection of headlines shows that large fines on household name banks (and celebrity individuals) attract publicity in all news media. Though there are national variations, messages are mixed not (or not just) because of favoritism but because of (1) relatively low staffing resources compared with the high investigative and prosecution costs of cases against major corporate players—a political decision with a small or large 'p'—and (2) regulatory concern about collateral damage which might affect financial stability not just of the Bank itself but also of its depositors and counterparties, generating systemic anxiety in the jurisdiction of sanction and elsewhere. Although the public may be *disenchanted* by the malefactions of the financial services industry, there is not yet evidence in the West that they feel sufficiently threatened or angry enough to withdraw their funds wholesale from mainstream private institutions—and if they did, where could and would they put them safely and with integrity?

CONCLUSION

The conventional legal maxim *de minimis non curat lex* was supposed to set a lower limit to the law's interest in intervening against crime. To suggest, as in my title, that for the *greatest* things the law provides no remedy does not represent a positive principle for which to aim. There may come a day when, aping the gladiators of Rome, hedge fund and wealth management staff reach their air conditioned offices in Mayfair, or less 'entrepreneurial' bankers reach their headquarters in Canary Wharf, directors as well as 'rogue traders' will bow towards the Old Bailey and intone *incarceraturi te salutant*—those who are about to be jailed salute you. But the impact of this hypothetical 'tough on white-collar crime' policy on other criminality and on general social well-being via perceptions of fairness remains unknown. Nor is it clear how we could in practice calibrate sanctions so as to satisfice if not satisfy feelings of reasonable equity between harmfulness, wrongfulness, and punishment.

So where does this leave the issue of legitimacy? Bottoms and Tankebe (2012: 160) propose three avenues for future work on legitimacy: studying power-holder legitimacy, measuring audience legitimacy, and developing longitudinal research on legitimacy (and the dialogic relationships between these three components). They also note the distinction between legitimacy—focused on the present—and trust, focused on expectations about the future. This is directly relevant to this chapter.

First, almost all of the literature assumes a highly unequal power and social status relationship between power-holders and audiences, including offenders. This is not the case for the areas analysed here. The targets of police and regulatory investigation and action may have significantly higher status (though not always more social or legal networked power) than do the authorities. Second, much of the decision making about who is to be deemed criminal and who merely guilty of 'misconduct' or 'mis-selling' takes place in private, hard-to-audit space, with the effects as well as intentions being capable of multiple alternative accounts of culpability and even of harm. Most of the professionals and defendants interviewed by this author over the last four decades would have difficulties in identifying the Serious Fraud Office or its UK predecessors as a frightening adversary—the former Manhattan DA Robert Morgenthau or the US Department of Justice are significantly more alarming—alongside the heavy guideline sentences should they not negotiate a deferred prosecution agreement or plea bargain there. Likewise, formidable are the tough investigating judges from France, Italy, and Switzerland whose roles are at risk of abolition from the 'rationalization' and centralization of prosecution arrangements under greater political control (personal interviews, 2010–11). These variations in approaches to elite misconduct in different advanced capitalist economies may tell us something about legitimacy needs in different countries. Looking at who has been seen as the most 'acceptable' heads of financial services regulators and of the Serious Fraud Office, one inference may be that the UK seldom considers that it needs to legitimate capitalism with a tough approach. But public and media storms may change this. The extraordinary rapidity with which the government's 'independent body' in 2011 stripped the knighthood from the financial folk devil, former RBS CEO 'Sir' 'Fred the Shred'[24] Goodwin, showed the desire to bend before public wrath at 'unjust deserts': but as several outraged commentators noted, there was not a clear rationale for doing so, and other RBS and non-RBS bank directors who allegedly had misconducted themselves had been allowed to keep their titles.[25]

By contrast, looking at the efforts some Swiss have made to take on transnational bribery cases from the developing world as domestic money laundering cases, it appears that the Swiss have a greater need for legitimacy, at least to avoid altogether or defer for many years clamp-downs on their banking and tax secrecy by other OECD countries. The (later retired) proactive Geneva magistrate, M. Bernard Bertossa, a socialist, agreed with amusement to my proposition that if he had not existed, Switzerland would have had to invent him (personal interview, 2002). Time will tell what levels of activism against corrupt public officials will be displayed by an EU-level European public prosecutor. Whilst some might think that legitimacy is institutionally-inscribed, this chapter shows that perceptions of fairness are at least as important a source of legitimacy, but that this finds its criminal justice manifestation dependent on the autonomy of investigators and prosecutors from political decisions and on the activism and competence of those authorities, which includes reforms in corporate

[24] A sobriquet which might have sounded gangster-like applied to an underworld figure, but which resounded positively at the time to shareholders seeking a reduction in 'head count' (like Sweeney Todd, the Demon Barber of Fleet Street?) to generate higher profits.

[25] In 2013, there was similar debate about the titles and entitlement to work in the financial services industry of the former heads of HBOS, whose reckless lending policies resulted in an ill-judged take over by Lloyds, in an agreement brokered by the Labour government, which later spent £20 billion on a bail-out for Lloyds. Under Parliamentary and media pressure, Sir James Crosby (who had also been Deputy Chair of the Financial Services Authority) voluntarily resigned his knighthood (which had never been done before) and took a cut in his generous pension arrangements to reflect his admitted culpability. The other directors did nothing.

transparency and mutual legal assistance. The legitimacy of both the prosecutions and the non-prosecutions of elite businesspeople looks very different in Putin's Russia, Blair/Cameron's England and Wales, and Bush/Obama's USA.

The impacts of low legitimacy in the prosecution and non-prosecution of suspected crimes/misconduct by elites are not always clear. Sometimes, as in Brazil in 2013 and in the Occupy Wall Street movement, resentments tied into dissatisfaction over inequality may generate mass demonstrations and civil disobedience. Sometimes, as in China, the protests are more localized and are not permitted to spread. In an era of hollowed-out states and transnational corporate rule, the formulation of an alternative set of policies and practices is a task of such complexity that it seems beyond the control of individual governments, and protests usually lack a graspable vision of an alternative viable future. So the norm may be that low legitimacy results in low economic performance, and resigned acceptance or enthusiastic embrace of a patron–client spoils system in which white-collar and organized crime merge into a pathological culture of rent-seeking.

REFERENCES

Akerlof, G. and Shiller, R. (2010) *Animal Spirits: How Human Psychology Drives the Economy, and Why It Matters for Global Capitalism*. Princeton, NJ: Princeton University Press.

Babiak, P. and Hare, R. (2007) *Snakes in Suits: When Psychopaths go to Work*. New York: Harper Collins.

Barak, G. (2012) *Theft of a Nation: Wall Street Looting and Federal Regulatory Colluding*. Lanham: Rowman and Littlefield Publishers.

Basran, S. and Webley, S. (2012) *Employee Views of Ethics at Work: 2012 British Survey*. London: Institute of Business Ethics.

Black, J. (2011) *Learning from Failures: 'New Governance' Techniques and the Financial Crisis*, unpublished, London: LSE.

Bottoms, A. and Tankebe, J. (2012) 'Beyond Procedural Justice: A Dialogic Approach to Legitimacy in Criminal Justice', *Journal of Criminal Law and Criminology* 102(1): 119–70.

Coates J. (2012) *The Hour Between Dog and Wolf: Risk-taking, Gut Feelings and the Biology of Boom and Bust*. London: Fourth Estate.

Cressey, D. (1953) *Other People's Money*. New York: Free Press.

de Willebois, E., Halter, E., Harrison, R., Park, J., and Sharman, J. (2011) *The Puppet Masters: How the Corrupt Use Legal Structures to Hide Stolen Assets and What to Do About It*. Washington, DC: World Bank.

Dorn, N. (2010) 'The Governance of Securities: Ponzi Finance, Regulatory Convergence, Credit Crunch', *British Journal of Criminology* 50(1): 23–45.

Dorn, N. (2011) 'Policy Choices in Financial Market Regulation: Market Rapture, Club Rules or Democracy?', in Alexander, K. and Moloney, N. (eds) *Law Reform and Financial Markets*. Cheltenham: Elgar. Chapter summary: available at:<http://ssrn.com/abstract=1946373> accessed 24 July 2013.

Edelman (2012) *2012 Edelman Trust Barometer*, available at: <http://trust.edelman.com/> accessed 24 July 2013.

Feinstein, A. (2011) *The Shadow World: Inside the Global Arms Trade*. London: Hamish Hamilton.

Financial Services Ombudsman (2012) *Annual Review, 2011–12*. London: Financial Ombudsman Service.

Findley, M., Nielsen, D., and Sharman, J. (2012) *Global Shell Games*. Brisbane: Griffith University. Available at: <http://www.griffith.edu.au/business-government/centre-governance-public-policy/research-publications/?a=454625> accessed 24 July 2013.

Hagan, J. (2012) *Who Are the Criminals? The Politics of Crime Policy from the Age of Roosevelt to the Age of Reagan*. New Haven: Princeton University Press.

Hannaford-Agor, P. and Hans, V. (2003) 'Nullification at Work? A Glimpse From the National Center for State Courts Study of Hung Juries', 78 *Chicago-Kent Law Review* 1249–77.

Hans, V. (2012) 'What Difference Does a Jury Make?', *Yonsei Law Journal* 3(1): 36–54.

Ipsos MORI & British Medical Association (2011) *Trust in Professions Index*, available at: <http://www.ipsos-mori.com/researchpublications/researcharchive/2818/Doctors-are-most-trusted-profession-politicians-leasttrusted.aspx> accessed 24 July 2013.

Kahneman, D. (2011) *Thinking, Fast and Slow*. London: Allen Lane.

Labour Party (2013) *Labour's Policy Review: Tackling Serious Fraud and White-Collar Crime*. London: The Labour Party.

Laufer, W. (2006) *Corporate Bodies and Guilty Minds: The Failure of Corporate Criminal Liability*. Chicago: University of Chicago Press.

Levi, M. (1983) 'Blaming the Jury: Frauds on Trial', *Journal of Law and Society* 10: 257–69.

Levi, M. (1988) 'The Role of the Jury in Complex Cases', in M. Findlay and P. Duff (eds) *The Jury Under Attack*. London: Butterworths.

Levi, M. (2002) 'Suite Justice or Sweet Charity? Some Explorations of Shaming and Incapacitating Business Fraudsters', *Punishment and Society* 4(2): 147–63.

Levi, M. (2006) 'The Media Construction of Financial White-Collar Crimes', *British Journal of Criminology* 46(6): 1037–57.

Levi, M. (2009) 'Suite Revenge? The Shaping of Folk Devils and Moral Panics about White-Collar Crimes', *British Journal of Criminology* 49(1): 48–67.

Levi, M. (2010) 'Serious Tax Fraud and Non-Compliance: A Review of Evidence on the Differential Impact of Criminal and Non-Criminal Proceedings', *Criminology and Public Policy* 9(3): 493–513.

Levi, M. (2012) 'States, Frauds, and the Threat of Transnational Organized Crime', *Journal of International Affairs* 66(1): 37–48.

Maruna, S. and Copes, H. (2004) 'Excuses, Excuses: What Have We Learned From Five Decades of Neutralization Research?' in Tonry, M. (ed) *Crime and Justice*. Chicago: Chicago University Press.

McLean, B. and Nocera, J. (2011) *All the Devils Are Here: Unmasking the Men Who Bankrupted the World*. New York: Viking.

Monitoring and Evaluation Committee (2012) *Report of the Public Enquiry into the Kabul Bank Crisis*. Independent Joint Anti-Corruption Monitoring and Evaluation Committee.

Morgenson, G. and Rosner, J. (2011) *Reckless Endangerment*. New York: Times Books/Henry Holt & Company.

Nagin, D. (forthcoming) 'Deterrence in the Twenty-first Century: A Review of the Evidence', in Tonry, M. (ed) *Crime and Justice*, vol 42.

NFA (2013) *Annual Fraud Indicator 2013*. London: National Fraud Authority.

Nguyen, T. and Pontell, H. (2010) 'Mortgage Origination Fraud and the Global Economic Crisis: A Criminological Analysis', *Criminology and Public Policy* 9(3): 591–612.

Sants, H. (2009) 'Delivering Intensive Supervision and Credible Deterrence', available at: <http://www.fsa.gov.uk/library/communication/speeches/2009/0312_hs.shtml> accessed 24 July 2013.

SEC (2009) *Investigation of Failure of the SEC to Uncover Bernard Madoff's Ponzi Scheme—Public Version*. Washington, DC: US Government Printing Office.

Sharman, J. (2012) *Chasing Kleptocrats' Loot: Narrowing the Effectiveness Gap*. U4 Issue August (4), Bergen: Chr. Michelsen Institute.

Shiller, R. (2005) *Irrational Exuberance* (2nd edn). New Haven: Princeton University Press.

Shoffman, M. (2012) 'Record Year for FSA Fines', available at: <http://www.ftadviser.com/2012/12/31/regulation/regulators/record-year-for-fsa-fines-m-in-as649JytgEIKsr-rKkNiH4J/article.html> accessed 24 July 2013.

Simpson, S. S. (2002) *Corporate Crime, Law, and Social Control*. Cambridge: Cambridge University Press.

Smith, G. (2012) *Why I Left Goldman Sachs: Or How the World's Most Powerful Bank Made a Killing But Lost Its Soul: A Wall Street Story*. New York: Business Plus.

Sutherland, E. (1983) *White-Collar Crime: the Uncut Version*. New Haven: Yale University Press.

Tombs, S. and Whyte, D. (2007) *Safety Crimes*. Cullompton: Willan.

Treasury Committee (2012) *The FSA's Report into the Failure of RBS*. Select Committee on the Treasury: UK Parliament.

Turner, A. (2009) 'How to Tame Global Finance', available at: <http://www.prospectmagazine.co.uk/magazine/how-to-tame-global-finance/> accessed 24 July 2013.

Tyler, T. (2006) *Why People Obey the Law*. New Haven: Princeton University Press.

Tyler T. (2009) 'Self-Regulatory Approaches to White-Collar Crime: The Importance of Legitimacy and Procedural Justice' (pp. 195–216), in Simpson, S. and Weisburd, D. (eds) *The Criminology of White-Collar Crime*. New York, Springer.

Wang, X. and Holtfreter, K. (2012) The Effects of Corporation and Industry-Level Strain and Opportunity on Corporate Crime', *Journal of Research in Crime and Delinquency* 49(2): 151–85.

Wilkinson, R. and Pickett, K. (2010) *The Spirit Level: Why Equality is Better for Everyone*. London: Penguin.

Wrong, M. (2009) *It's Our Turn to Eat*. London: Fourth Estate.

9

LEGITIMACY AND STATE RESPONSES TO TERRORISM: THE UK AND FRANCE

Jacqueline Hodgson

INTRODUCTION

The legitimacy of the state's response to terrorism in the UK and in France might be challenged at a number of levels. Whilst the stated aim of both jurisdictions is to deal with terrorism through the ordinary criminal law, the, often exceptional, measures enacted through both criminal law and procedure make the response far from ordinary. Furthermore, the response has included controversial non-criminal measures restricting the liberty of suspected terrorists where it is claimed that the sensitive nature of the evidence prevents prosecution.[1] The justification for these wider police powers, attenuated suspects' rights, broad and ill-defined criminal offences, forms of preventive detention, and the increased role for intelligence, is that we now face a new and different kind of threat, one that merits a new and different response. Britain and to a lesser extent France, have bought into the post 9/11 conception that this is beyond crime; this is a war against terror.[2]

The nature of this new and different threat has often been unclear, defined not by the visible experiences of urban crime and anti-social behaviour, but by (necessarily) secret intelligence sources. Prevention and disruption have been the preferred approach. In France, this was already an established strategy in response to Islamist terrorism in the 1990s; in England and Wales, it slotted snugly within the dominant discourse of preventive criminal justice in the UK.[3] But what is it that is being

[1] The imprisonment in Belmarsh prison of foreign nationals suspected of involvement in international terrorism was successfully challenged in the House of Lords in *A and others v. Secretary of State for the Home Department* [2004] UKHL 56. This led to the creation of the control order under the Prevention of Terrorism Act 2005 (applicable to British as well as foreign nationals) and most recently, the Terrorism Prevention and Investigation Measure—essentially, a slightly modified version of the control order—under the Terrorism Prevention and Investigation Measures Act 2011.

[2] This phrase has fallen out of favour somewhat, but it has been a consistent part of official discourse for a decade. There is a vast literature on the 'war on terror' and its many aspects. For various European accounts, see Wade and Maljevic (2010).

[3] On prevention and precautionary justice see the Themed Section of *Criminal Justice Matters* 81(1) 2010. On prevention and criminalization generally, see Ashworth and Zedner (2012).

prevented? We have heard of known unknowns, of large-scale disasters averted, and varying numbers of extremists and terrorist cells being monitored. This uncertainty as to the nature of the threat has allowed broader and earlier criminalization in order to prevent almost any behaviour that might facilitate, assist, or aid in acts preparatory to terrorism, including the participation or encouragement to participate in a group formed with a view to the preparation of acts of terrorism. Offences are drafted in the broadest of terms, leaving the courts with the task of interpreting them in a way that attempts to provide the necessary precision.

Police powers too have lacked the certainty generally required to justify interference with a person's freedom. Under ss. 44 and 45 of the Terrorism Act 2000, exceptional powers to stop and search did not require any suspicion of criminal behaviour in the usual way.[4] Citizens and vehicles could be stopped and searched quite lawfully for articles that might be used in connection with terrorism—despite the absence of any grounds for suspecting the presence of such articles. Over the course of a decade, hundreds of thousands of people were stopped and searched under these powers, but not a single terrorism conviction resulted, raising serious questions about their legitimacy.[5]

The sheer breadth and imprecision of these measures, which interfere with the rights of citizens in significant ways, calls into question their legitimacy. It is difficult to determine whether the state's response to terrorism has been necessary and proportionate, as the logic of its success is as much in the prevention and so avoidance of criminality, as in the number of those 'brought to justice'. When we add to this the growing use made of intelligence in counter-terrorism law and strategy, the overall picture is murkier still. We are asked to trust the state that these greater infringements of our liberty and into our privacy are necessary to keep us safe from things about which we (are allowed to) know nothing.

The impact of counter-terrorism measures on the wider criminal justice agenda gives further grounds for concern. History shows us that the exceptional has a tendency to become commonplace: measures introduced in very specific circumstances often come to be applied more generally. In France, the increase in police powers in dealing with terrorism, has served to broaden police power more generally, including in ways previously ruled to be unconstitutional (Cahn 2009). As a result, extensive police powers became applicable in the investigation of a variety of offences (including theft), no matter how trivial or serious, simply when committed by a group formed in order to prepare to commit an offence. This problem is compounded when the exceptional nature and context of the measure are used to justify its fast tracking through the Parliamentary process, allowing for only minimal scrutiny and debate. The legislation may be time limited, but this provides little reassurance: once in place, it may be easier to renew than remove.[6]

[4] These have been replaced under the protection of Freedoms Act 2012.

[5] For statistics and discussion of the exercise of these powers between 2000 and 2009, see Lord Carlile's (2009) *Report on the Operation in 2008 of the Terrorism Act* 2000 *and of* Part 1 *of the Terrorism Act* 2006 (especially paras. 140–50); *Gillan and Quinton v. UK* (2010) ECHR 28, [37–47].

[6] The Prevention of Terrorism (Temporary Provisions) Act 1974 was enacted at speed, but was anything but temporary, being renewed for several decades. More recently examples include the Anti-Terrorism

The need to counter this 'new kind of threat' in 'new kinds of ways', has also provided an alibi for greater intrusion into the lives of citizens. The drama and fear of terrorism have been exploited to justify the introduction of wider measures, representing 'opportunistic changes that would not have been sustained outside a period of crisis' (Walker 2006: 1143). In the UK and in France, terrorism has been presented as a reason to increase surveillance measures across the entire population. Across a number of jurisdictions, the Vienna Commission (2007) expressed concern at the use of proactive technologies, with no judicial oversight, which effectively search for reasonable suspicion by cross-referencing databases. Security is used as something of a trump card for the preservation of democracy and freedom, opposition to which is unpalatable, and even unpatriotic in the eyes of some.

All of this is not to argue that the state should do nothing—terrorist acts and threats demand a response. Rather, it is to question the appropriateness, proportionality, and ultimately, the legitimacy of that response. Our own judiciary has warned of the dangers of curtailing the very freedoms that terrorists attack.[7] An excessive state response, or one that is perceived as lacking in legitimacy, can be counterproductive. The Home Office's 'Prevent' strategy was designed to prevent the radicalization of young British Muslims, but in many instances it simply resulted in their alienation. In crude terms, we do the terrorists' work for them if we divide and alienate our own citizens.[8] Cronin (2009: 119) discusses a range of terrorist campaigns, and their success in polarizing populations and delegitimizing the state, often mobilizing support for the terrorist group in the process. Repression can be successful in wiping out terrorist groups, but the extent of the response can itself undermine the legitimacy of the state, as in nineteenth century tsarist Russia or Peru and Shining Path (*Sendero Luminoso*) at the end of the twentieth century (Cronin 2009: 142):

> Long-term repressive measures against suspected operatives may challenge civil liberties and human rights, undermine domestic support, polarize political parties, and strain the fabric of the state itself, thus further undermining its ability to respond effectively to future terrorist attacks. (Cronin 2009: 144)

DEFINING TERRORISM IN LAW

A legitimate response to terrorism needs to be necessary and proportionate. This in turn requires that we define clearly what we understand as terrorism—a task that has

Crime and Security Act 2002, tabled as an emergency measure and received the Royal Assent in little over one month. France too passed *Loi* 2001–1062 *relative à la Sécurité Quotidienne* within a matter of a few weeks in 2001. This did at least contain a sunset clause for 31 December 2003.

[7] In discussing the indefinite imprisonment of foreign nationals in Belmarsh prison in the case of *A v. Secretary of State for the Home Department* [2004] UKHL 56, Lord Hoffman said (at [97]): 'The real threat to the life of the nation, in the sense of a people living in accordance with its traditional laws and political values, comes not from terrorism but from laws such as these. That is the true measure of what terrorism may achieve.'

[8] The Home Office's counter-terrorism strategy has been adjusted to separate out more clearly the need for integration—an objective that was being undermined by anti-radicalization policies.

eluded many. International cooperation is an important strand of counter-terrorism strategy, and the definition and criminalization of terrorism are influenced by a range of conventions and European instruments. Within the EU, this includes the approximation of the definition of terrorism, harmonizing terrorist offences and sharing information.[9] Nonetheless, there is no single definition of terrorism.[10] The definition under section 1 of the Terrorism Act 2000 requires that the act or threat be designed to intimidate the public or a section of the public; or that the act or threat be designed to influence the government or an international governmental organization.[11] Relevant acts are those involving serious violence to the person or damage to property, endangering another's life, creating a serious risk to the health or safety of (or a section of) the public, or seriously interfering with or disrupting an electronic system. There is a requirement that the (threat of) action be for the purpose of advancing a political, religious, racial, or ideological cause.[12] This definition extends to actions, persons, property, the public, and government outside the UK.[13]

Article 421–1 of the French *code pénal* defines an act of terrorism as an offence (e.g., homicide, theft, extortion, or production of explosives) committed by an individual, or a group of individuals, aimed at seriously disrupting public order through intimidation or terror. The requirement to seriously disrupt public order is similar to intimidating the public, but there is no requirement that the action or threats be to advance a specific cause. This aspect is not in the 2002 Framework Decision, nor in most European definitions. It tends to be a feature in the definitions of common law jurisdictions.[14] There are also several 'autonomous' terrorism offences, such as ecological terrorism (Art. 421–2 *code pénal*) and the association of wrongdoers (*association des malfaiteurs*, Art. 421–2–1 *code pénal*) where this relates to the preparation of terrorist offences.[15]

[9] See, for example, the EU Council Framework Decision of 13 June 2002 (2002/475/JHA) on combating terrorism; 'Taking Stock of EU Counter-Terrorism Measures' (Commission Staff Working Paper) 20 July 2010 SEC (2010) 911 final; EU action plan on combating terrorism 15 November 2010 (15893/10). See also Galli and Weyembergh (2012). On the Council of Europe Convention on the Prevention of Terrorism, see Hunt (2006).

[10] Definitions of terrorism vary widely across jurisdictions and agreement on a single definition is riven with difficulties. See Hodgson and Tadros (2013). Cronin argues that like 'war' and sovereignty', the term 'terrorism' does not and cannot be defined in a way that achieves full international consensus. She nevertheless goes on to argue that there are four fundamental aspects to any understanding of 'terrorism': 'a fundamentally political nature, the symbolic use of violence, purposeful targeting of noncombatants, carried out by nonstate actors' (2009: 7).

[11] Where firearms are used, the requirement to influence government or a governmental organization or to intimidate the public is removed (s.1(3) of the Terrorism Act 2000).

[12] This feature is not included in the EU Council Framework Decision of 13 June 2002 (2002/475/JHA) on combating terrorism.

[13] For a recent case demonstrating the breadth of the s.1 definition, see *R v. Gul* (2012), EWCA Crim 280.

[14] Canada, Australia, Hong Kong, and South Africa all adopt this 'ulterior motive' requirement.

[15] These offences exist outwith the terrorist context under Art. 450–1 *code pénal*. Dating back to the nineteenth century when it applied only to the most serious offences, its application was extended to less serious offences under the *Loi sécurité et liberté* of 1981, making it triable in the *tribunal correctionnel* as well as before a jury in the *cour d'assises*. It was abolished from the statute book in 1983, only to be reinstated in 1986 in the context of France's threat from Islamic terrorism. The specifically 'counter-terrorist' version of the offence under Art. 421-2-1 *code pénal* was introduced in the 1994 code.

INTELLIGENCE AND PREVENTION

But it is not only the legal definition of terrorism that is important here: intelligence informs (or is claimed to inform) legal and procedural change, as well as the wider picture of the nature of the terrorist threat. For example, arguments to extend pre-charge detention and questioning in police custody in England and Wales were predicated on the argument that plots are more complex, dispersed, and international in nature.[16] These were not plots that the government could point to, but ones that they claimed were being planned. Similarly, the early intervention of the police, able to stop and search without reasonable suspicion and the almost pre-*actus reus* criminalization of some behaviours are also part of a counter-terrorism response informed by foreign and domestic intelligence as to the nature of the terrorist threat.[17]

In France too, a policy of prevention and disruption dating back to the 1990s saw police officers rounding up large numbers of people, most of who were never charged.[18] Whilst no criminal activity was uncovered, it was nevertheless considered an effective strategy of disruption. In a written answer, addressing the nature of the *association des malfaiteurs* offence, the French Minister of Justice explained that the strategy in the fight against terrorism was to dismantle criminal groups very early on, before any threat has been made or even attempted, rather than to concentrate on individuals or on isolated acts.[19] There were reports of similar actions following the shootings perpetrated by Mohamed Merah and his subsequent death following the police siege in March 2012.[20] The very broad nature of the key offence in French counter-terrorism law (*association des malfaiteurs*, association of wrongdoers) facilitates this, allowing the police to act on the basis of a very low threshold of suspicion.[21] These actions are not evidence-led; they are about gathering intelligence and disrupting groups of people who may or may not be attached to possible networks. One French researcher has likened this strategy to kicking an anthill to see what comes running out.[22]

[16] The requirement for questioning to take place prior to charge in England and Wales reflects the relatively sharp distinction between the police investigation and the prosecution phase, both of which must be kept independent of one another. In France, the *procureur* (public prosecutor) is responsible for the investigation and prosecution of crime, including overseeing the police detention and questioning of the suspect. The suspect may be questioned following her detention, and if the case passes to the *juge d'instruction* (as it would in a terrorism matter), the suspect must be questioned by the *juge* at the outset and this will continue throughout the course of the investigation.

[17] As already noted, this is part of a broader trend in preventive or precautionary criminal justice and conjures images of the science fiction writer Philip K Dick's notion of 'pre-crime'.

[18] See further Hodgson (2006).

[19] Published in the *Journal Officiel Sénat*, 17 February 2001, p. 488. He went on to describe the French approach to the fight against terrorism as being without challenge at the European and International levels.

[20] More than 350 people in France have been stopped in Islamic neighbourhoods since 2007, around 90 were arrested and detained, but not necessarily charged with any offence. See Laurent Borredon and Franck Johannès 'La procédure antiterroriste est dérogatoire par rapport au droit commun', *Le Monde*, 6 April 2012.

[21] A similar offence was adopted in s. 5 of the Terrorism Act 2006—the preparation of terrorist acts.

[22] Laurent Bonelli, quoted by Human Rights Watch (2008).

THE NATURE OF THE THREAT

It is clear that the *modus operandi* of recent attacks is different from non-Islamist terrorism. In contrast to the IRA bombings of the 1970s and 80s in mainland Britain for example, these twenty-first century terrorists are unafraid to die themselves, issue no warnings, and aim at mass casualties. But understanding the precise nature of this new terrorist threat is problematic. The terrorist acts in New York, London, Glasgow, and Madrid appear to have been carried out by Islamic extremists, but we cannot point to proscribed organizations with clear political ends, as was the case with the IRA or ETA. Nor can we identify a clear aim. This is not an attempt to change the course of foreign or domestic policy, or the recognition of a people's right to occupy territory. In Britain and the US, it is characterized as a more fluid and amorphous threat to the values of Western societies, to 'our society', to 'our way of life', to 'the fundamentals of our democracy'.[23]

Yet despite the sometimes vague nature of the threat and the uncertainty as to the identity and motivation of those likely to carry it out, in the five years immediately after 9/11 in particular, Britain (together with the US) employed the rhetoric of war and all that goes with it—a call to unswerving loyalty and a different concept of necessary force.[24] In the UK, speaking after the July 2005 bombings in London, then Prime Minister Tony Blair declared that the rules of the game had changed;[25] in the US, President Bush had already declared a war on terror(ism).[26] Even President Obama, in his first term inauguration speech, continued to talk of America being at war. This rhetoric of war has proved attractive to politicians anxious to show their macho get-tough credentials, but it tends to run counter to rule of law considerations. Employing the politics of fear (see Altheide 2006), it demands an immediate and exceptional response, lacking the accountability and proportionality of ordinary criminal legislation. Kostakopoulou (2008: 321) describes this as a siege mode of democracy supplanting the rights-model of democracy: 'Under such circumstances, officials invoke the existence of an emergency in order to protect the life of the nation and are willing to apply the national security exception even to areas where clearly national security is not at issue.' The rhetoric of war has waned, but still there is a sense that the ordinary legal process and criminal law are not equipped to deal with the imagined terrorist violence.

LEGITIMACY AND TERRORISM LAW

At one level, the states in both Britain and France might claim that their response to terrorism is quite legitimate because legal measures have been enacted through proper

[23] Then Home Secretary Charles Clarke, in response to a question from the Home Affairs Select Committee, Minutes of Evidence, 8 February 2005.

[24] See e.g. Sassòli (2006); Marret (2003: 10). The attack on the World Trade Center was quickly compared in the US to the attack on Pearl Harbor.

[25] 'Let no one be in any doubt, the rules of the game are changing', *The Times*, 6 August 2005, p. 1.

[26] This was subtly modified from a war on terrorism to the more all-encompassing war on terror. See Marret (2003: 10).

and lawful parliamentary processes and the rule of law has been respected. Yet, this fails to capture concerns as to the legitimate nature, scope, and application of legislation—broadly drawn offences and powers that lack certainty and precision; the shift to non-criminal measures to detain and restrict liberty. Legitimacy is not the same as legality, even if legality is a pre-condition for legitimacy.

Drawing on the models of legitimacy developed by Beetham (1991) and Coicaud (2002), Bottoms and Tankebe (2012: 129) suggest a dialogic approach that implies not simply the imposition or the exercise of power and a *de facto* legality, but also an acceptance of that authority and some degree of shared values. In requiring an 'audience response' that may alter over time, this understands legitimacy in dynamic rather than static terms: '... legitimacy should not be viewed as a single transaction; it is more like a perpetual discussion, in which the content of power-holders' later claims will be affected by the nature of the audience response.'

As front line enforcers of the criminal law, the police are central to our view, and often our experience, of its legitimacy. Most obviously, police action will be seen as illegitimate when it is unlawful: enormous damage is done to the credibility of the police as a whole when individual officers have been found to assault prisoners or to falsify evidence.[27] But more commonly, it is *how* the police choose to exercise their power that will determine whether or not they are perceived as legitimate. The exercise of police discretion in the stop, search, and arrest of citizens, and the response that this provokes, constitutes part of this 'perpetual discussion' of legitimacy. One might think of the 1981 riots in Britain and the contested use of the 'sus' laws by the police, accused of targeting Afro-Caribbean young men;[28] or the rioting in France in 2005 amid protests of a racist police force and an immigrant underclass.

Tyler's work has focused on the manner and attitude of police and has found that if officers listen to citizens' accounts and treat them with respect, this provides a level of 'procedural fairness' that results in a greater acceptance of the legitimacy of the decisions of the police and courts (Tyler and Fagan 2008). But more fundamental than the manner of police-suspect encounters, is the decision to treat an individual as a suspect in the first place. Police power is characterized by the exercise of discretion in determining who to stop, search, arrest, detain, and charge and it is the choices that officers make in the exercise of these powers that will have a significant impact on what Bottoms and Tankebe call 'audience response' to claims to legitimacy. For example, in targeting certain groups in society to stop and search (i.e. young, Black men in the 1980s and 90s; young, Asian men in the 2000s), police actions have sometimes been perceived as racist and illegitimate.[29] In Beetham's (1991) terms, there is neither consent, nor a set of shared values and beliefs from those who constitute the audience whose response determines the legitimacy of the exercise of state power.

[27] See, for example, the miscarriages of justice in such cases as the Guildford Four and the Birmingham Six that led to the Royal Commission on Criminal Justice being established in 1991.

[28] See The Scarman Report (1981).

[29] See *Gillan and Quinton v. UK* [2010] ECHR 28, [84–5]; discussion in Office for Security and Counter-Terrorism, Equality Impact Assessment, January 2011, for review of s. 44 powers, available at: <www.parliament.uk/documents/impact-assessments/IA12-004H.pdf> accessed 24 July 2013.

To shift this analysis to the more specific context of counter-terrorism, the police powers under ss. 44 and 45 of the Terrorism Act 2000, allowing the stop and search of individuals against whom there was no criminal suspicion, were criticized widely as being too broad and providing no proper accountability. Crucially it was the *exercise* of these powers that was challenged as illegitimate by individuals and by the media, and was increasingly called into question by the government's own independent reviewer and, ultimately, the powers were ruled unlawful by the European Court of Human Rights (ECtHR). This demonstrates the complex way in which legitimacy is understood. Had the powers been exercised sparingly, they would no doubt have remained in force unchanged: the way that the police exercised these powers called into question their legitimacy and ultimately, their lawfulness.[30]

This 'dialogue' around legitimacy continues in the reform of both law and policy. The Home Secretary, Theresa May, in her foreword to the Review of Counter-Terrorism and Security Powers in 2011, wrote of the need to 'correct the imbalance that has developed between the state's security powers and civil liberties' and the review itself speaks of the 'intrusive' state and the 'indiscriminate use of stop and search'. The 'Prevent' strategy that underpinned much of counter-terrorism law and policy was also challenged later the same year on the basis that it confused the promotion of integration, with the prevention of terrorism.[31] Law and policy was no longer seen as legitimate even by the (new) power-holders.

THE LEGITIMACY OF EXTENDED POLICE POWERS

Turning now to more specific responses to terrorism, both Britain and France stress the importance of dealing with terrorism under the ordinary criminal law, emphasizing the credibility of a legal and judicial, rather than a political response. France has experienced the dangers of a specialist jurisdiction. During the Algerian conflict in the 1960s, a separate State Security Court (*Cour de sûreté de l'Etat*) was established, charged with investigating, prosecuting, and trying offences against the internal and external security of the state. Sitting in secret and composed partly of military officers, this was seen ultimately as a tool of political oppression and was dismantled in 1981 when Mitterrand took power.

But is this enough to guarantee legitimacy—the fact that the ordinary police investigate and those accused of terrorism offences are tried in the ordinary criminal courts? How far can we stretch criminal law and procedure before its credibility is

[30] Lord Carlile was critical of the exercise of these police powers, but did not wish to see them repealed. See Lord Carlile (2009: para. 150).

[31] The 'Prevent' strategy is one of four themes in the government's counter-terrorism strategy (CONTEST): Pursue (detecting, disrupting, investigating, and prosecuting terrorist threats at home and overseas); Prevent (preventing radicalization); Protect (assessing and reducing risk of terrorist attack); and Prepare (increasing resilience should there be a terrorist attack). See CONTEST: The United Kingdom's Strategy for Countering Terrorism (2011) Home Office, available at: <http://www.homeoffice.gov.uk/publications/counter-terrorism/counter-terrorism-strategy/?view=Standard&pubID=907671> accessed 24 July 2013.

undermined? In some instances, the legitimacy of the state response to terrorism is contested and has been tested out in the courts. And whilst the domestic judiciary has found no fault with the provisions, the ECtHR has found breaches of the European Convention on Human Rights (ECHR) and inadequate controls on the exercise of police discretion.

The extended UK police powers to stop and search without the need for any prior suspicion were unsuccessfully subjected to legal challenge in the High Court, Court of Appeal, and the House of Lords. Their legitimacy was accepted by the domestic courts. However, the ECtHR took a different view and the applicants were finally successful in their challenge in *Gillan and Quinton v. UK* (2010) 50 EHRR 45. Sections 44 and 45 of the Terrorism Act 2000 gave the police the power to stop vehicles and pedestrians at random and to search for articles that might be used in connection with terrorism, without the need for any grounds for suspecting the presence of such articles. This was preventive policing on a significant scale. An assistant chief constable or similar could authorize the exercise of this power within a specified area if it was considered 'expedient' for the prevention of acts of terrorism—as the ECtHR pointed out in *Gillan* (at [80]):

> 'Expedient' means no more than 'advantageous' or 'helpful'. There is no requirement at the authorisation stage that the stop and search power be considered 'necessary' and therefore no requirement of any assessment of the proportionality of the measure.

Because this power was exceptional in nature, authorizations lasted only 28 days. However, continuous authorizations were in place in the Metropolitan Police District from the moment the law came into force in February 2001, and despite hundreds of thousands of searches (Lord Carlile, the government's then independent reviewer of terrorism legislation, reported that there were between eight and ten thousand stops each month by early 2009[32]), no terrorist convictions resulted. Furthermore, areas with strikingly similar risk profiles did not use the powers in this way and Lord Carlile noted that existing ordinary police powers were found to be adequate in policing the G8 summit in Scotland in 2005.

There is also evidence that these powers were used disproportionately against Black and Asian people and there are ample examples of protestors and journalists being stopped and searched under the terrorist legislation.[33] However, because there was no requirement of reasonable suspicion, it was almost impossible to demonstrate that the power had been used improperly. The House of Lords considered there to be adequate legal controls on the police use of discretion, but the ECtHR disagreed and found (at para. 79) that: 'the safeguards provided by domestic law have not been demonstrated to constitute a real curb on the wide powers afforded the executive so as to offer the individual adequate protection against arbitrary interference.' The way that the police exercised these powers led the ECtHR to conclude that the state's response in enacting ss. 44 and 45 was not a legitimate one.

[32] Lord Carlile (2009).

[33] See e.g., Joint Committee on Human Rights '*Demonstrating respect for rights? A human rights approach to policing protest*', March 2009.

As a result, these powers have been modified under ss. 59–62 of the Protection of Freedoms Act 2012. Authorizations must be necessary (rather than expedient), will last for 14 days instead of 28, and searches will be for evidence that the person is a terrorist (rather than for articles that could be used in connection with terrorism). There is still no requirement of reasonable suspicion however. The number of searches in the year ending June 2011 decreased by 99 per cent—no doubt a result of changing political will as well as legislation.[34]

France has also extended police powers as a direct response to the perceived threat of terrorism. The main counter-terrorism statute was enacted in 1986, but this has been amended five times since 9/11, increasing powers to take preventive measures. For example, the 2006 legislation allowed (and even required) the use of video surveillance cameras in airports, train stations, on public transport, and wherever acts of terrorism may be carried out.

More significant are the greater investigative powers now provided to the police—not just for counter-terrorism, but more generally under the guise of targeting organized crime. In France, there is often a reciprocal relationship between the treatment of organized crime and drug trafficking and of terrorism; exceptions in one sphere, seamlessly applying to the other. In this way, legislation has extended and to some extent routinized the application of special measures designed to operate within the counter-terrorism field, to a wide range of other criminal activity. First, justified by the imperative of the fight against terrorism, wider police powers to search and survey individuals, their vehicles, and their homes were introduced in 2001 and 2003. Then, in 2004, the definition of terrorism was changed to sit within the wider notion of organized crime. In practice, this has widened police powers considerably as organized crime is defined in very broad terms: there are 18 types of offences in this category (Arts. 706–73 and 706–74 CPP) ranging from murder to theft, and they constitute organized, rather than ordinary crime when committed by 'any group formed or any association established for the preparation of one or more offences, characterized by one or more material acts' (Art. 132–71 *code pénal*, the French penal code). A group of boys who come together in order to steal another boy's bus pass would fall within this definition.

In order to combat terrorism and other forms of organized crime, the French police now enjoy wider powers to conduct identity checks; to conduct searches of vehicles and dwellings without the owner's consent; to engage in undercover surveillance by placing cameras in dwellings and in vehicles, and to infiltrate organizations; to intercept communications; and to interview witnesses and suspects abroad. Again, in the interests of fighting terrorism, the many databases held by the police and *gendarmes* have been formalized and centralized. The most recent legislation, passed at the end of December 2012, extends powers to access electronic communications for a further three years.[35]

[34] Home Office Statistical Bulletin, June 2012, *Operation of police powers under the Terrorism Act 2000 and subsequent legislation: arrests, outcomes and stops and searches.*

[35] Law No. 2012-1432 of 21 December 2012, concerning security and the fight against terrorism.

Police powers of pre-charge detention have also been expanded significantly in terrorism cases. In ordinary criminal cases in England and Wales, a suspect may be detained by the police without charge for a maximum of 36 hours and on the authority of a magistrate, for up to four days.[36] Terrorist suspects, however, can be held for much longer. There has been an astonishing willingness to restrict the kinds of due process protections otherwise considered essential when it comes to terrorism investigations. Terrorist suspects may be held for 14 days,[37] but until recently this was 28 days and there have been several attempts to extend this to 42 and even to 90 days.

As we have seen in relation to other police investigative powers, terrorism is often grouped with drug trafficking and organized crime in the justification of 'exceptional' procedures. This includes extending police detention and questioning for up to four days (instead of the normal 24 or 48 hours) and in delaying access to legal assistance, for 48 hours in organized crime cases and for 72 hours in terrorism and drugs trafficking.[38] Since 2006, terrorist suspects can be held by the police for a further two days (making six days in total) if there is a serious risk of an imminent terrorist attack, or if necessary for reasons of international cooperation.[39] However, more significantly, there is a different procedure in place for the investigation of serious offences in France and once referred to the *juge d'instruction* for investigation, terrorist suspects may be held in custody for up to three years before a decision whether to prosecute has been taken. The *juge* is free to question the suspect at any time during this period of detention while the investigation is ongoing. The treatment of suspects at the hands of the French counter-terrorism police has been criticized repeatedly by international bodies such as the European Committee for the Prevention of Torture and Inhuman or Degrading Treatment of Punishment. Suspects have been found to have been mistreated, subjected to very poor conditions and interrogated repeatedly for lengthy periods with inadequate breaks for sleep.[40]

In the UK, the legitimacy of such lengthy pre-charge detention has also been questioned and the repeated attempts to increase this to periods up to three months have given rise to concerns about the strategy of prevention and disruption, given that 'the criminal law has not traditionally been a preventive tool in the UK'.[41] It is perhaps telling that whilst Art. 5(1) ECHR makes clear that detention for the purposes of disruption or prevention is not permitted, in 2006, the Home Affairs Committee reported that this was in fact its primary use and suggested that preventive detention should be included as a statutory ground for detention. This was rejected by the Joint Committee on Human Rights (2006), which pointed out that this would require a derogation from Art. 5(1), something the Committee did not believe to be necessary.

This provides a prime example of the security and risk management driven approach to preventive forms of justice. There was no clear need to increase pre-charge detention,

[36] Sections 41–44 of the Police and Criminal Evidence Act 1984.

[37] Schedule 8 of the Terrorism Act 2000. [38] Art. 706–88 CPP. [39] Art. 706–88–1 CPP.

[40] European Committee for the Prevention of Torture and Inhuman or Degrading Treatment or Punishment (1998, 2001). The most recent report (2012) does not raise these concerns, but rather, issues of delays in allowing suspects their rights (e.g. the right to legal assistance or the right to have someone informed of their detention) in 'exceptional' circumstances.

[41] Joint Committee on Human Rights (2006) para. 12.

especially given that the charge threshold is evidence admissible at trial (rather than the usual higher threshold of requiring a realistic prospect of conviction), and the wide scope of acts preparatory to terrorism under s. 5 of the Terrorism Act 2006 allows for charge at the very earliest stages of preparation. The government case adopted a highly precautionary approach based on perceived risk and possibility; it asserted that there was 'the *risk* that, in the near future, it is *possible* that a serious terrorist suspect *may need* to be released because the police have insufficient time to bring a charge for a terrorist related offence' (emphasis added).

There continues to be no evidence of such a need. Of the 1,558 terrorist suspects detained since 11 September 2001, only 11 have been held for longer than 14 days.[42] Whilst there are annual variations, 63 per cent of those detained were held for less than two days—the time limit for standard cases. The government was promoting an exceptional crime control agenda and broadening the contours of criminal procedure, with no clear evidence of need. It was proposing an extended period of detention and questioning that the Joint Committee warned came dangerously close to preventive detention as prohibited under Art. 5(1) ECHR. The proposal also lacked the kinds of safeguards necessary to oversee the police exercise of such an extended power—i.e. proper judicial safeguards and an adversarial hearing for warrants for further detention—raising concerns about the procedure's compatibility with Art. 6 ECHR, concerning the right to a fair trial. The extension of detention beyond 28 days could not even be said to be a properly judicial procedure. Made on the order of the Home Secretary, it would be a decision of the executive.

In France too, the judicial corporatism that results from a small, closed circle of judges dealing with all aspects of terrorism investigations means that appeals fail to provide the necessary independent oversight and challenges to detention by the accused are rarely successful (see Hodgson 2006; Vienna Commission 2007).

THE LEGITIMACY OF PREVENTIVE CRIMINALIZATION

In counter-terrorism law and procedure, the emphasis is on a generalized policy of prevention and disruption, rather than the more traditional criminal law aims of repression and punishment, which generally require a more specifically identifiable harm. Offences are drafted in contingent terms—criminalizing the possession of information that is 'likely to be useful' to a person preparing an act of terrorism (s. 57 of the Terrorism Act 2000),[43] or articles possessed 'in circumstances which give rise to a

[42] Home Office *Operation of police powers under the Terrorism Act 2000 and subsequent legislation: Arrests, outcomes and stops and searches*, 15 December 2011, HOSB 19/11, Table 1.03. 517 suspects were charged, 906 released and 135 cautioned under non-terrorist legislation or dealt with under immigration or mental health legislation. 694 of these suspects were held for less than one day, a further 292 for up to two days, a further 411 for under 7 days and a further 150 for under 14 days.

[43] 'A person commits an offence if he possesses an article in circumstances which give rise to a reasonable suspicion that his possession is for a purpose connected with the commission, preparation or instigation of

reasonable suspicion' that possession is 'for a purpose connected with the commission, preparation, or instigation of acts of terrorism' (s. 58 of the Terrorism Act 2000).[44] These are serious offences with a maximum sentence of 15 and 10 years respectively.

These offences are extremely broad and lack the precision and clear definition that we expect and require of the criminal law. The 'audience response' to their legitimacy includes the response of the courts that must interpret and apply the offences. In relation to s. 57, what is meant by possession 'for a purpose connected with' the commission, preparation or instigation of an act of terrorism? How close must the connection be? Does possession of a plane ticket to Pakistan, where the defendant intends to carry out or instigate acts of terrorism, constitute an offence? What of the chequebook used to pay for the ticket? In *Z and others v. R* [2008] EWCA Crim 184, the Court of Appeal found (at [28]) the wording of s. 57 to be 'so imprecise as to give rise to uncertainty unless defined in a manner which constrains it.' The Court concluded (at [29]) that, 'if s. 57 is to have the certainty of meaning that the law requires, it must be interpreted in a way that requires a direct connection between the object possessed and the act of terrorism.' In what amounts to a judicial rewriting of the statute in more restricted terms, the Court said that '[t]he section should be interpreted as if it reads: A person commits an offence if he possesses an article in circumstances which give rise to a reasonable suspicion that *he intends it to be used for the purpose of* the commission, preparation or instigation of an act of terrorism.'[45]

Although the issue of the meaning of 'connected with' did not fail to be decided in the later case of *R v. J* [2009] UKHL 13, the Court's interpretation of s. 57 was called into question. The Court argued that in disproving the defence that possession was for a non-terrorist purpose, the Crown was not then required to prove beyond reasonable doubt that possession *was* for a terrorist purpose, as the defence had asserted in this case. It need only prove the elements of the offence (that possession gave rise to a reasonable suspicion of possession for a terrorist purpose); if a defence is raised, the Crown need only rebut that defence. Disproving the claim of possession for a non-terrorist purpose is different from proving a terrorist purpose.[46]

The wording of s. 58 is similarly problematic. The *actus reus* is remarkably all encompassing; almost anything is capable of being useful to terrorists—a London A-Z, or a map of the London underground. Context (and therefore interpretation and discretion) is everything.[47] Is it clear what kinds of activity are criminalized by these

an act of terrorism.' It should be noted that the Terrorism Act 2000 is based upon the Prevention of Terrorism (Temporary Provisions) Act 1989, which was targeted at terrorism related to 'the affairs of Northern Ireland' (s. 16A(2) of the 1989 Act).

[44] A person commits an offence if: (a) he collects or makes a record of information of a kind likely to be useful to a person committing or preparing an act of terrorism, or (b) he possesses a document or record containing information of that kind.

[45] In a further attempt to make sense of the operation of the statute (and despite the enactment of a separate offence of possessing propaganda with the intention of inducing acts of terrorism under s. 2(2)(f) of the Terrorism Act 2006) the Court concluded that possession of a document for the purpose of instigating an act of terrorism could also include possession for the purpose of inciting an act of terrorism.

[46] See, especially, [68].

[47] See also *Rowe v. R* [2007] EWCA Crim 635, which considered that data electronically stored on compact disc or computer hard drives is capable of being an article for the purposes of s. 57 of the Terrorism Act 2000. There is thus an overlap between ss. 57 and 58.

offences? In *K v. R* [2008] EWCA Crim 185, the Court of Appeal held that s. 58 material must be likely to provide practical assistance to a person committing or preparing an act of terrorism—simply encouraging the commission of an act of terrorism will not suffice. Secondly, the document itself must raise a reasonable suspicion that it is intended to be used to assist in the preparation or commission of an act of terrorism. A document innocuous on its face cannot be brought within the scope of s. 58 by reference to extrinsic evidence suggesting that it is intended to be used for a terrorist purpose. Thus, a London A-Z will not fall under this section, even if it is intended to be used by a terrorist to find her way to where she intends to carry out a terrorist act.

On the other hand, the House of Lords concluded in the later case of *R v. G* [2009] UKHL 13, that if material likely to be useful to a person committing or preparing an act of terrorism is collected or possessed by someone with no terrorist purpose at all, they will still be guilty of the offence. The Court considered that 'Parliament must have proceeded on the view that, in fighting something as dangerous and insidious as acts of terrorism, the law was justified in intervening... if the defendant's actual intention could not be established'. The balance, it went on, is the defence of reasonable excuse. *K v. R* interpreted reasonable excuse as meaning for a non-terrorist purpose, even if the purpose was to infringe some other provision of criminal or civil law. This was rejected in *R v. G*; the Court considered that any excuse must be objectively reasonable, otherwise, it reasoned, the word 'reasonable' was superfluous. In this case, the psychotic delusions of Mr G that led him to gather this material in order to 'wind up' prison officers whom he believed were whispering at his cell door each night was found to be (at [87]) '[o]n no view... a reasonable excuse for collecting and recording the information'. This places the onus on the accused to rebut a reasonable suspicion with an objectively reasonable excuse for the possession of the article or material.[48]

Under the Terrorism Act 2006, ss. 1 and 2 create offences of the encouragement of terrorism and the dissemination of terrorist publications (both punishable by up to seven years' imprisonment), described by some commentators as part of the 'new global McCarthyism'.[49] Like the Terrorism Act 2000 offences, these too have been criticized as being vague in their definition and scope, and an unnecessary extension of the current criminal prohibitions on incitement to violence (see further Hunt 2007). Although presented as the enactment of the Council of Europe Convention on the Prevention of Terrorism 2005, the offences as defined in the 2006 statute, go further, broadening the *mens rea* requirement and omitting the requirement that there must be danger that someone will be encouraged to commit an act of terrorism[50] (in order to guard against undue interference with freedom of expression, particularly in 'indirect encouragement' cases[51]). The Joint Committee on Human Rights concludes that the offence does not comply with the permitted restrictions to the right to freedom of expression under Art. 10 ECHR, as the 'glorification' requirement is too vague,

[48] For a comment on the case, see Hodgson and Tadros (2009).

[49] See e.g. Johnson (2005) and George Clooney's film on McCarthyism, 'Goodnight and Good Luck', (2005), which captures well the ease with which, within a climate of fear, a creeping enemy is created, despite the absence of hard fact or evidence.

[50] Terrorism Act 2006, s. 1(5)(b).

[51] See Art. 5 of the Council of Europe Convention on the Prevention of Terrorism 2005.

the definition of terrorism too broad, and the offence may be committed with no awareness that the defendant's statement is likely to encourage the commission of a terrorist act—objective recklessness will suffice.

Section 5 of the 2006 Act creates a new offence of 'acts preparatory to terrorism' (described by some as a conspiracy of one). This offence carries a maximum sentence of life imprisonment.

Section 5 of the Terrorism Act 2006 states:

(1) A person commits an offence, if with the intention of—
  (a) committing acts of terrorism, or
  (b) assisting another to commit such acts,
  he engages in any conduct in preparation for giving effect to his intention.
(2) It is irrelevant for the purposes of subsection (1) whether the intention and preparations relate to one or more particular acts of terrorism, acts of terrorism of a particular description or acts of terrorism generally.

Again, this is extremely broad and vague. The ordinary criminal law under the Criminal Attempts Act 1981, s. 1(1) defines an attempt as an act that is 'more than merely preparatory' and requires an intention to commit an offence.[52] This new offence criminalizes conduct in preparation for giving effect to an intention to commit or assist in acts of terrorism, that is, activity that is 'merely preparatory'. Thus, the prosecution must show that there is an intention to commit an act of terrorism or to assist another to do so, and some act that works towards giving effect to that intention. This criminalizes the individual at a very early stage. She may engage in some conduct towards giving effect to her intention, but what is meant by 'in preparation for giving effect' to an intention? How far towards 'giving effect' to the intention must it be? How is intention demonstrated, when by definition it is some way from being effected? What is the difference between an idea, a thought, a possible consideration, and an intention for the purposes of this Act? What is an act of terrorism? Is it any offence defined by the various pieces of terrorism legislation? The breadth of this offence appears to leave an unacceptable amount of discretion to the prosecutor.

This offence seems to be inspired by the French offence of *association des malfaiteurs*, described in government policy as the 'cornerstone' of the French legal response to terrorism (de Villepin 2006). Legislated in 1996, Art. 421-2-1 of the *code pénal* expands the criminal law's definition of acts of terrorism to include 'the participation in any group formed or association established with a view to the preparation, marked by one or more material actions, of any of the acts of terrorism provided for under the previous articles [of the criminal code]'—known as *association de malfaiteurs*.[53]

The investigation of terrorism offences in France is very different to that in England and Wales. Whilst the Crown Prosecution Service (CPS) are now organized in a

[52] Section 1(1) Criminal Attempts Act 1981: 'If, with intent to commit an offence to which this section applies, a person does an act which is more than merely preparatory to the commission of the offence, he is guilty of attempting to commit the offence.' See e.g., *Geddes* [1996] Crim LR 894 (CA).

[53] This is the single most important terrorist offence. Over 80 per cent of the 358 people imprisoned for terrorism offences in 2005 had been charged with *association des malfaiteurs* according to *Le Monde* in September 2005.

specialist unit and there is considerable cooperation with investigating officers, prosecutors have no pre-trial investigative role beyond one of advice. They have no originating powers of investigation, nor authority over the police.

As an inquisitorially rooted procedure, French criminal investigations are overseen by a judicial officer—in most cases the public prosecutor (*procureur*), but in the most serious cases, by the investigating judge (the *juge d'instruction*). As judicial officers, they are not seen as representing the prosecution case in the narrow sense, but as conducting a public interest oriented enquiry. As a result, defence safeguards are considered less necessary than in the more adversarial procedure in England and Wales. Until April 2011, all suspects held for police detention and questioning were allowed only a 30 minute consultation with a lawyer and were not informed of their right to silence. Since April 2011, lawyers are allowed to be present during the police interrogation (though they must not interrupt or pose questions) and the suspect is told of her right to silence. Terrorist suspects, however, can still have their access to legal assistance delayed for 72 hours.

French terrorist investigations are handled by a specialist group of *juges d'instruction* based in Paris. The *association de malfaiteurs* offence widened the scope of the *juges d'instruction's* powers significantly, allowing them to open investigations into those involved with terrorist organizations (within and outside France) before any terrorist act had taken place.[54] This offence pushes back the boundary of criminality, enabling the judge to act very much earlier when no act has been committed, but when the 'suspect' is perhaps buying materials, is in the very early stages of preparation towards a terrorist act, or is simply associating with a group established to prepare acts of terrorism—even when the judge is unable to identify a specific date or terrorist target to which these activities are linked.

Critics point to the risk of arbitrary law enforcement as offences aimed at prevention rather than simply suppression mean that the *magistrat* is able to determine that a lawful act is unlawful because of the alleged context in which it takes place—i.e. the context of intent to commit (unspecified acts of) terrorism. As counter-terrorism prosecutor Philippe Maitre explained, whilst an act may not be unlawful per se: 'The mere fact of having participated in an enterprise is punishable behaviour. When it comes to terrorism, the consequences are so serious that any behaviour that revolves around this objective is criminalized.'[55]

The vagueness of this definition seems questionable under Art. 7 of the ECHR. Such imprecision as to what kinds of behaviour will attract a criminal sanction will also affect the legitimate exercise of rights of association and expression. Present and former judges described to Human Rights Watch (2008: 23) the very tenuous connections

[54] The law is very flexible concerning territoriality. This offence applies to those within and outside France, and to targets within and outside France. See e.g. the arrest in June 2003 of Christian Ganczarski, a German national suspected by the French authorities of helping to organize the bombing of a synagogue in Djerba, Tunisia, killing 21 people. When the German authorities indicated that they lacked sufficient evidence to arrest him, the Saudi authorities deporting Ganczarski placed him on a flight via Paris, where he was arrested—the French claiming jurisdiction because French nationals were among the casualties in the Tunisia attack. Craig Whitlock, 'French push limits in fight on terrorism', *Washington Post Foreign Service*, 2 November 2004.

[55] Reported in Human Rights Watch (2008: 21–2).

between people that might amount to a network for this offence—friends, family members, or simply having a person's phone number. The evidence requirement is not high: those placed in custody during the investigation were: 'Young Frenchmen from the Magrheb, between 20 and 25 years old, who dreamed of finding an Islamic ideal. Small fry, just these young guys with posters of Bin Laden in their bedrooms.'

The *association des malfaiteurs* offence affords *magistrats* a very wide discretion to authorize sometimes mass arrests, on very weak grounds, simply as a preventive or disruptive measure, a strategy to 'destabilize the networks, and to undermine logistics. And it matters little if a good number of the accused are found to be innocent after spending one or two years in pre-trial detention' (see Bonelli 2005; Human Rights Watch 2008: 24–27).

Key to the judiciary's ability to act in this anticipatory manner is the close cooperation it enjoys with the intelligence services. Intelligence also plays a greater role in counter-terrorism criminal investigations in England and Wales, with resulting adjustments in approaches to intelligence-gathering and evidence-gathering. In France, the intelligence/evidence distinction is very much more fluid, raising concerns about the legitimacy of presenting as evidence information that is almost impossible to test at trial.[56]

THE LEGITIMATE USE OF INTELLIGENCE IN CRIMINAL INVESTIGATIONS

The use of intelligence in counter-terrorism operations in the UK has been more prominent during the last decade (see further Phythian 2005; Walker 2005). This is perhaps unsurprising given the rise in surveillance more generally, and in new technologies for gathering information in the prevention, investigation, and prosecution of serious crime.[57] However, it is not only in the prevention, disruption, investigation, and prosecution of terrorism activity that intelligence plays a role. Increasingly, it informs policy and law-making as pronouncements on the number of active terrorists and terrorist cells in Britain construct a (media bolstered) picture of the nature of the terrorist threat and therefore the nature of the necessary response. For example, immediately after the London bombings of July 2005, Scotland Yard estimated that around 200 British citizens and foreign nationals had travelled to Al Qa'eda training camps and then returned to the UK; intelligence officers put the figure at up to 3,000.[58]

In 2007, the day before the British Government announced its plans to increase the length of detention for terrorist suspects held for police questioning, the head of M15

[56] See discussion in Hodgson (2006).

[57] See e.g. the European Commission funded project SURVEILLE, which surveys these technologies as they operate across Europe; assesses their risks and benefits; and assesses the ethical and fundamental rights issues they raise, available at: <http://www.surveille.eu/index.php/about-surveille/> accessed 24 July 2013.

[58] J. Benetto, 'Predicted Bomb Attacks Reveal Intelligence Gaps on al-Qa'ida', *The Independent*, 8 July 2005.

announced that there were 2,000 active terrorists in Britain with a strategy of 'methodically and intentionally targeting young people and children in this country'.[59] Yet, we have no way of assessing the accuracy of such a statement, nor is it apparent that an increase in numbers requires a longer period of detention, as against for example, more officers. Care is needed in the handling of such information—as the fiasco over the claimed Iraqi weapons of mass destruction demonstrated. Intelligence may be collected in one context, but subsequently used and (mis)interpreted in another:

> In the best-known cases of intelligence failure, the most crucial mistakes have seldom been made by collectors of raw information, occasionally by professionals who produce finished analyses, but most often by the decision makers who consume the products of intelligence services... Intelligence failure is political and psychological more often than organizational (Betts 1978: 61, cited by Phythian 2005: 362).

In England and Wales, the evidentiary standards at trial, the adversarial nature of criminal procedure and the recognized right of the defence to interrogate the prosecution case, mean that intelligence cannot be treated as evidence in a criminal case.[60] In France, the use of intelligence as evidence poses fewer problems. The pre-trial judicial role, together with fewer evidential constraints, means that intelligence officers have been able to cooperate with judges as well as with police, and have gone on to subsume entirely the investigation and law enforcement function of the police in terrorism cases.

This arrangement dates back two decades. The domestic intelligence agency, the DST (*Direction de la Surveillance du Territoire*), began to work with *juges d'instruction* during the wave of Basque and Corsican separatist terrorist attacks in the 1990s. The terrorist branch of the ordinary judicial police were overstretched in terms of resources and this new arrangement allowed the judiciary direct access to intelligence officers who had until that point been under the jealously guarded authority of the interior minister. In 2008 the DST merged with the *Renseignements Généraux* (RG, the police general intelligence service) to form the *Direction Centrale du Renseignement Intérieur* (DCRI).[61]

The nature of the relationship is one of information flowing in both directions. If they feel that they have intelligence that justifies a judicial inquiry, the DST and now the DCRI, will go directly to the public prosecutor (the *procureur*) or *juge d'instruction*. If an *information* is opened,[62] prior intelligence gathered is part of what is termed an administrative investigation and so is not admissible as evidence, but it will form the basis on which judicial investigations will be carried out—searches, wire taps, interrogations, seizure of financial records, etc. Switching hats, as it were, acting in their capacity as judicial police, DCRI officers are then able to transform intelligence into

[59] Jonathon Evans, the head of M15 made this statement on Monday, 5 November 2007.

[60] Though more generally, see the Justice and Security Bill 2012–13.

[61] The other counter-terrorism police organization is the *Sous-direction Anti-terroriste de la Direction Centrale de la Police Judiciaire* (the Under-Direction of the central judicial police, created in 2006 and formerly the Anti-Terrorism National Division, DNAT).

[62] This is the process of transferring the investigation to the *juge d'instruction*.

evidence through the vehicle of the judicial investigation—what a number of *magistrats* describe as a process of 'judicialization'.[63]

The use of intelligence is claimed as the central strength of the French process of investigating terrorism. Former *juge d'instruction* Jean-Louis Bruguière, undoubtedly the most infamous of this specialist corps, describes the 'synergy' between the different actors working during the different procedural phases—police, intelligence, *parquet,* and *instruction*—and the permanent dialogue between *procureur* and *juge d'instruction*. Given the very sensitive nature of the material involved, the relationship between intelligence officers and *magistrats* (especially the *juges d'instruction*) is characterized by extremely high levels of trust, even greater than exists in police-*magistrat* dealings in ordinary investigations.[64] This is maintained institutionally by allowing *magistrats* to remain in the same post and to build up a body of expertise.

The knowledge and trust shared between judges and intelligence officers means that discussions take place and advice is sought prior to and beyond the official inquiry in a way that suggests the collapsing of the traditional divisions between the procedural phases of administrative and judicial inquiry. This is important when thinking about the legitimacy of the criminal process, which, as discussed earlier, is central to the state's response to terrorism. This arrangement elides the distinction between prevention-driven intelligence gathering and evidence-driven criminal repression. Intelligence feeds into and results out of judicial investigations. There is a symbiosis between the DCRI and the intelligence they can provide, and the wider powers they can enjoy when working with the *juge d'instruction*. This trust and cooperation is regarded as the strength of the system, enabling intelligence gathering and judicial inquiry to work together in ways that are of mutual benefit, but it also represents a potential weakness in the system.

There is a danger that the functional independence of the *parquet* and the *juge d'instruction* is eroded and that administrative and judicial powers overlap unduly, undermining the safeguards and systems of accountability underpinning each.[65] There are also dangers in the close working relationship between the *juge* and intelligence officers. This sharing of information, common formulation of policy, and decision making regarding whether and when to launch a judicial inquiry undoubtedly nurtures a shared expertise and trust, but it also risks undermining the independence of the *juge d'instruction*'s role if her perspective becomes that of the intelligence services. Given the level of trust that necessarily underpins their working relationship and the fact that the *juge d'instruction* will receive information from the DCRI that will never be 'judicialized', this unity of perspective cannot be ruled out. At its worst, this

[63] In 2006, I accompanied the Home Office on a trip to Paris to meet with *juges, procureurs,* and police involved with counter-terrorism investigations. It was suggested to us that this procedure made the DST (the predecessor to the DCRI) more responsible, as they could not blame another brigade or service if things went wrong.

[64] See Hodgson (2005) for a detailed study of the investigation and prosecution of crime in ordinary cases in France.

[65] Another limitation of this organization and strategy is that its effectiveness rests upon only a small number of people. For the same reason, there can often be long delays in investigations, especially where they require international cooperation and the translation of material.

runs the risk of the vehicle of the judicial inquiry simply empowering and legitimating what are essentially police and intelligence-driven investigations. This distorts the balance of power in the pre-trial phase and fails to guarantee sufficiently the reliability and credibility of evidence. This is of particular concern given the very small number of people exercising control over the production and evaluation of large amounts of information (much of it intelligence based), with very little outside control.[66] Rather than ensuring evidence of the highest quality in the investigation and prosecution of terrorism offences, the legitimacy of this process is called into question by the criticisms that the evidence is often weak and the dossier is held together by assumptions and suppositions, rather than any concrete proof. The 1999 FIDH (Federation of International Human Rights Leagues) Report (1999: 31–2) into the application of counter-terrorism laws in France noted in particular:

> ...the formulaic character of the interviews; the apparent and uncritical reliance on information provided by intelligence and police sources; the reluctance to take seriously evidence and explanations put forward by the defence and to accede to their requests to take action; the use of prejudicial but often unsubstantiated assertions and asides in the dossiers; and the mechanically negative responses to applications to bail.

These concerns were reiterated in the more recent study carried out by the organization Human Rights Watch. Defence lawyers reported that their requests for investigative measures were almost never granted and their ability to mount a defence was hampered by the involved and complex nature of the enquiries that make up the investigation. One lawyer described files as being built on 'an idea, a movement, and not on the accused. And then the defence becomes impossible' (Human Rights Watch 2008: 17). Another explained:

> There are 7.5 meters of case file, 78 volumes...325 kilos of paper. That represents 541 hours of reading time, in other words three and a half months. The lawyer's fee...is 450 euro. So when you do the math, I have the right to 75 cents an hour to guarantee his defence. And I didn't have two to three months to prepare my case like the prosecutor did, but one and a half months. The defence lawyer cannot do his job. (Human Rights Watch 2008: 17)

The *Chambre d'Instruction* provides some accountability but it reviews only the procedural legality of the *instruction*, the detention of those under investigation and the sufficiency of charges for the accused to be sent to trial; it does not delve into issues of fact or of strategy. Just as there is a small specialized corps of *procureurs* and *juges d'instruction*, so too there are three judges in the *Chambre d'Instruction* who deal with all terrorism cases.[67] Concerned to ensure the proper application of the law, these judges must base their ruling on what is contained within the dossier. As with other

[66] The Venice Commission (2007: 211–13) draw attention to the case hardening effects of this prolonged specialism and suggest restricting the time that judges can work in this area.

[67] Although they will also deal with other cases, these are the only judges to deal with terrorism cases. Judges in the *Chambre d'Instruction* are not entirely apart from their investigating colleagues and they will go to visit them in their offices.

forms of oversight and supervision in the French criminal process, this review is a paper one. It is exceptional that they would rule against the *juge d'instruction*, whether the challenge concerns detention, procedure, or the decision to send a person to trial (Hodgson 2006). And where a ruling has been made in the *Chambre d'Instruction*, the same issue cannot be raised again at trial. This has led to accusations of judicial corporatism, a common outlook fuelled further by the common and emotive goal of the 'war' or 'fight' against terrorism.

In theory, the defence has the right to challenge the intelligence through claims that it is not confirmed in the judicial inquiry. The officers can be questioned, but they are not required to answer. The defence may challenge the truth of the statement of evidence provided, but this is difficult when they have no information about who produced the intelligence or why. The only possibility is to provide an alternative account that challenges the one provided in the statement of evidence. Thus, the defence cannot challenge the inherent reliability of the statement by, for example, claiming that it was made by somebody who bears a grudge against them, or that the conversation immediately preceding that led in evidence alters the context and meaning of the words said—quite simply because they will know nothing of the identity of the intelligence subject.

Effectively, the inclusion of intelligence information in the dossier is an endorsement of its reliability by the *juge d'instruction*—just as a high degree of credibility attaches to other types of information regarded as the product of a judicially supervized investigation.[68] This is unrealistic: *magistrats* recognize that they are unable to determine the reliability of intelligence as they do not know the name of the informant, nor are they able to look behind the information. *Magistrats* rely upon professional trust, subsequent evidence obtained, and claims that it would not be in the interests of officers to provide unreliable information. This seems a weak basis on which to presume the credibility of information, especially where the source may be from outside France, in which case French officers are reliant upon the good faith of their foreign counterparts. The use of intelligence from countries where torture is common cannot therefore be identified or scrutinized. This raises serious concerns about the quality of the evidence before the trial court and the accused's right to a fair trial when the basis of evidence cannot be interrogated in the normal way. When established fair trial procedures are subordinated to security concerns, the legitimacy of the criminal process is undermined.

The use of intelligence is more circumscribed in England and Wales, not least because of the absence of any pre-trial judicial role and the limited involvement of even the CPS in counter-terrorism investigations. Some have argued that allowing intelligence obtained through intercept to be admissible as evidence would reduce the need for exceptional measures such as Terrorism Prevention and Investigation Measures (TPIMs) and their predecessor, the control order. With this in mind, the

[68] The Home Office's own report concluded that: 'In reality, the examining magistrate can never be fully confident about the validity of the information without having access to the methodology or the raw intelligence... However, in practice it is likely that any intelligence material admitted in court will have some form of impact on the outcome of a trial.'

Home Office considered adopting a version of the French approach, using a judge to conduct a pre-trial sift procedure. A small pilot of existing cases was run and the procedure was rejected as unsuitable. The study drew particular attention to the difficulty in expecting the jury to assess facts when they had no knowledge of the source of these 'facts'; the inability of even special advocates to cross-examine witnesses in order to probe the reliability of their evidence (a problem further exacerbated when the intelligence comes from outside Britain); and so the 'reliability gap' between intelligence and evidence. The study concluded that none of the intelligence material under consideration would have survived the pre-trial sift procedure as it was inherently incapable of being probed properly. Agents could have a range of motives for providing intelligence and even well-established agents could have been misled, or have intended to mislead, or both.

There can be no doubt that the wide powers of investigation and surveillance available to *magistrats* and police result in the production of valuable information in the investigation, prosecution, and prevention of terrorism in France. What, of course, is less clear is the price paid by citizens in terms of surrendering their privacy and even their liberty. The surveillance, detention, and questioning of individuals is an infringement of individual freedom which, even in cases as grave as suspected terrorism, can only be justified when based on good grounds. The extent to which individuals are subjected to speculative enquiry or effective targeting is unknown. Throughout the 1990s there were several high profile preventative round-ups or 'sweeps' (the word *rafle* was used, evoking rounding up of the Jews in German-occupied France) in which tens of people were arrested, detained, and questioned, with most then released.[69]

These operations are designed to disrupt activity and to gather general information that might be used in later enquiries and so might be considered a success, despite the feeble numbers subject to criminal investigation. There may be a high conviction rate of those brought to trial, but there are hundreds more detained and released after days, months, and even years in custody whilst investigations are ongoing.[70] It is difficult therefore, to make any judgement about the effectiveness of much of the investigative work. Most recently, a week after the death of Mohamed Merah, the man who shot and killed eight people in Toulouse, there have been arrests in the predominantly Muslim areas of a number of French cities. Some see this as a direct response to the Merah affair, designed to prevent his actions from inspiring others, whilst others see it as politically timed in the run-up to the presidential elections.

[69] In 1993, 88 people were interrogated, but only three were placed under investigation. In August 1994, after five French citizens were killed in Algeria, the then Interior Minister Charles Pasqua, ordered mass identity checks in sensitive neighbourhoods, resulting in the stopping and checking of more than 27,000 people in only two weeks (see Human Rights Watch 2007). In May 1998, 53 people were arrested in France as part of a Europe-wide operation aimed at dismantling dissident networks planning terrorist attacks during the World Cup. In fact, most were released within 48 hours. Raids on such a scale are less frequent, but there continue to be examples, such as the arrest of 165 people in the offices of the Iranian People's Mojahedin in 2003, of which only 17 were placed under formal investigation.

[70] One journalist reports that *Juge* Bruguière has ordered the arrest of over 500 people on suspicion of conspiracy in relation to terrorism. Craig Whitlock, 'French push limits in fight on terrorism', *Washington Post Foreign Service*, 2 November 2004.

THE LEGITIMACY OF SUPPLANTING LIBERTY WITH SECURITY

How are we to understand this? The balancing or contrasting of liberty with security is a common feature of current political discourse: the notion that more of one means less of the other. This is used to justify exceptional measures, the curtailing of freedoms and the attenuation of due process safeguards.

In the UK, the Joint Committee on Human Rights (2006: 13) rejects this approach:

> We reiterate the importance of not seeing liberty and security as being in an inverse relationship with each other...We agree with the view expressed by the European Commission for Democracy through Law (the Venice Commission) that 'State security and fundamental rights are not competitive values: they are each other's precondition'.

In the case that led to the discontinuance of indefinite detention in the high security Belmarsh prison and the establishment of the replacement regime of control orders, *A v. Secretary of State for the Home Department* [2004] UKHL 56 (at [97]), Lord Hoffman condemned this approach:

> The real threat to the life of the nation, in the sense of a people living in accordance with its traditional laws and political values, comes not from terrorism but from laws such as these. That is the true measure of what terrorism may achieve.

Despite external criticism of the way in which the balance is struck in French counter-terrorism investigations between the freedom of the citizen and the need to gather intelligence, as well as the heavy-handed tactics of judicial investigations,[71] criticism from within France seems thin on the ground. The value placed on collective security over that of individual freedom is frequently cited, strengthened by having suffered the waves of bombings in 1986 and 1995. Shapiro and Suzan (2003: 88) suggest that:

> [T]he French public is accustomed to and willing to tolerate a police bureaucracy that would certainly be viewed as invasive in the US, even taking into account the change in attitudes after the 9/11 attacks...there seems to be a consensus that the freedom to walk the street or to take the subway without fear of bombs lies at the base of all other civil liberties.

These two perspectives reflect the political debate around *sûreté* (inspired by the right of *habeas corpus*, the freedom from arbitrary arrest or detention, established in the 1789 *déclaration des droits de l'homme et du citoyen*) and the more contemporary theme championed by the Right—*sécurité*. The first article of the legislation passed on 18 March 2003, declares the right of *sécurité* as a fundamental right and one of the conditions for the exercise of individual and collective freedoms. But, this reframing of security as freedom is misleading. Counter-terrorism law and procedure is, of

[71] See e.g. the Council of Europe's Committee for the Prevention of Torture and Inhuman or Degrading Treatment or Punishment.

course, expressed in neutral terms, but it is not true to say that the liberties of all individuals are affected equally. As Dworkin (2002) puts it in relation to the changes in the US:

> ...almost none of us will be indefinitely detained for minor violations or offenses, or have our houses searched without our knowledge, or find ourselves brought before military tribunals on grave changes carrying the death penalty. Most of us pay almost nothing in personal freedom when such measures are used against those the President suspects of terrorism.[72]

When governments are acting reasonably, or 'we' are not the 'enemy', diminishing liberty may be perceived as less problematic. But diminishing liberty also diminishes our security in relation to the state (and it is questionable whether or not it increases our security against the threat of terrorism) by allowing for greater executive power. When the state defines 'us' as its new enemies, the liberty/security trade-off no longer appears legitimate.[73] As Cronin (2009: 6) has argued, terrorism has the potential to polarize populations and 'to compel states to undermine themselves through their responses'. The exercise of police discretion to use counter-terrorism powers against civil protestors and journalists, for example, is clearly illegitimate.

THE LEGITIMACY OF NON-CRIMINAL RESPONSES TO TERRORISM

The focus of this chapter, as part of a criminal justice collection, is on the state's response to terrorism through criminal law. But, we should also bear in mind the significant non-criminal context of intelligence-led preventive measures, as well as actions taken outside the rule of law. Guantánamo has been a dramatic and visible reminder of the state's ability to redefine what is legitimate action. But across the world there has been increased (and mandated) intelligence sharing;[74] the production of terrorist lists; secret and unlawful rendition; an erosion of the right to *non-refoulement* through the use of unenforceable diplomatic assurances; and a significant challenge to the primacy of a criminal justice response through the use of administrative counter-terrorism measures. As a recent European Parliament report (Pillay 2010: 3) puts it:

> ...the scale of the damage done to international human rights law, and to the practical protection of human rights, by the 'war on terror' should not be underestimated, and concerted efforts will be needed to reverse it.

[72] See also Waldron (2003).

[73] There are important related issues that I do not have the space to discuss here, including the problem of defining sections of our community as potential 'enemies' and the significance of power within society in challenging legitimacy.

[74] For example, the UN Security Council Resolution 1373 (2001); European Council Common Position of 27 December 2001 on Combating Terrorism.

In Britain, we have seen a series of administrative measures imposed, which place severe restrictions on the liberty of the individual, without the safeguards of the criminal law standard of proof and the due process protections of the trial process. Foreign nationals were first imprisoned in Belmarsh; this was replaced with the control order, a measure applicable to UK citizens as well as to foreign nationals; and these have most recently been modified slightly to the TPIM under s. 2 of the Temporary Prevention and Investigation Measures Act 2011.

Detentions in Belmarsh prison applied to foreign nationals suspected of international terrorist involvement[75] (and thus operated within civil immigration powers, rather than a criminal process framework[76]) who could not be deported because of the ill-treatment they were likely to suffer in their home country and could not be prosecuted because of the sensitive nature of the intelligence against them. The then House of Lords' decision in *A and others v. Secretary of State for the Home Department* [2004] UKHL 56, upheld the government's claim that there was sufficient public emergency to warrant derogation from Art. 5 ECHR, but the court went on to find that detention without trial was not a proportionate response. In its application only to deportable aliens it ignored the threat posed by British citizens, and as a 'prison with three walls', it allowed foreign terrorists to leave the jurisdiction and continue to be a security risk in plotting abroad.

The response was the establishment of control orders under the Prevention of Terrorism Act 2005. These orders were imposed by the Home Secretary in order to protect members of the public from a risk of terrorism, where there was either insufficient evidence for a criminal prosecution or the evidence was of such a sensitive nature that it might endanger operations or the lives of agents or informants. The order could be applied to a foreign or British citizen and depending on the stringency of its terms, may or may not require derogation. None of those issued relied upon derogation and the courts condoned confining controlees to their residence for up to 12 hours a day.[77] The current administration pledged to review control orders and the result has been the TPIM, a modified version of the control order.

A troubling aspect of these various non-criminal responses has been the procedure by which these various orders have been imposed. Evidence against those to be detained and who now have their liberty restricted in significant ways, is kept secret. As a result, a system of special advocates has been adopted, security cleared lawyers permitted to sec sensitive (closed) material, but not then able to discuss it with their

[75] They did not need to be affiliated to a proscribed organization, but they were required to pose a risk to national security.

[76] This was criticized as turning the Special Immigration Appeals Commission (SIAC): 'from a specialist immigration tribunal to a de facto counter-terrorism court... While the guarantees offered by SIAC's procedures were appropriate to its original civil function (reviewing deportation decisions on national security grounds), the use of the same tribunal to judicially review the Home Secretary's decision to indefinitely detain suspected terrorists has been inadequate to the task of protecting those detainees' rights to liberty.' JUSTICE evidence to Select Committee on Constitutional Affairs, Seventh Report (2005, at para. 33).

[77] *Secretary of State for the Home Department v. E and another* [2007] UKHL 47; *Secretary of State for the Home Department v. MB (FC) and others* [2007] UKHL 46.

'client', prohibiting any proper lawyer-client relationship. The controlee, and now the subject of a TPIM, must be given sufficient information about the allegations against them to give effective instructions to the special advocate,[78] but this is a low hurdle to jump. Special advocates also report an excessive tendency to keep material secret; in all cases they have found some closed material to be available from open sources. TPIMs and control orders look to be better than imprisonment, but it might be argued that the wholly inadequate system of special advocates provides only a fig leaf of legality, barely covering what is an objectionable procedure in which the Home Secretary need only have reasonable grounds for believing the individual to be or have been involved in terrorism related activity, and for the measure to be necessary to protect the public from a risk of terrorism.[79]

The use of intelligence by French *juges d'instruction* is far from ideal, but the TPIM regime is not a judicial order and does not require a criminal burden of proof. Special advocates cannot represent the controlee in any meaningful sense and so provide only the appearance of protection in a poor imitation of a hearing in which the accused is represented.

CONCLUSION

To conclude, this chapter suggests various ways in which we might understand the legitimacy of the state's response to terrorism: the scope of the criminal law in defining offences and moving towards preventive criminalization in both jurisdictions; the growing use of intelligence and the tensions in understanding this across different procedural traditions with different due process protections; the use of non-criminal measures in what might be properly considered the criminal sphere of deprivation of liberty; and finally, the exercise of police (and to a lesser extent prosecutorial) discretion in both jurisdictions in determining how to exercise increased powers. In all of this, the state must guard against excessive repression and a response that is perceived as lacking in legitimacy and so, becomes counter-productive. The Eminent Jurists Panel on Terrorism, Counter-terrorism, and Human Rights (2008: 4) sums up the opportunistic approach of states:

... ignoring lessons from the past, some states have allowed themselves to be rushed into hasty responses, introducing an array of measures which are undermining cherished values as well as the international legal framework carefully evolved over at least half a century. This is surely not the way to counter those whose actions seek to attack those same cherished values.

[78] *Secretary of State for the Home Department v. AF* (No 3) (2009) UKHL 28.

[79] Contrast the government assertion in the recent Green Paper that closed material procedures have been proven to work effectively and to deliver procedural justice, with the JCHR assessment that it 'is not capable of ensuring the substantial measure of procedural justice that is required' (JCHR 9th Report of 2009–10, HL 64, HC 395, para. 90).

REFERENCES

Altheide, D. L. (2006) 'The Mass Media, Crime and Terrorism', *Journal of International Criminal Justice* 4: 982–97.

Ashworth, A. and Zedner, L. (2012) 'Prevention and Criminalization: Justification and Limits', *New Criminal Law Review* 15(4): 542–71.

Beetham, D. (1991) *The Legitimation of Power*. Basingstoke: Macmillan.

Betts, R. K. (1978) 'Analysis, War and Decision: Why Intelligence Failure are Inevitable', *World Politics* 31(1): 61–89.

Bonelli, L. (2005) 'An "Anonymous and Faceless" Enemy. Intelligence, Exception and Suspicion after September 11, 2001' *Cultures and Conflicts* 58: 101–29.

Bottoms, A. and Tankebe, J. (2012) 'Beyond Procedural Justice: A Dialogic Approach to Legitimacy in Criminal Justice', *Journal of Criminal Law and Criminology* 102(1): 119–70.

Cahn, O. (2009) 'The Fight against Terrorism and Human Rights: The French Perspective' (pp. 467–503), in Wade, M. and Maljević, A. (eds) *A War on Terror? The European Stance on a New Threat, Changing Laws and Human Rights*. New York: Springer.

Carlile, Lord (2009) *Report on the Operation in 2008 of the Terrorism Act* 2000 *and of Part 1 of the Terrorism Act* 2006.

Coicaud, J-M. (2002) *Legitimacy and Politics*, Curtis, D.A. (trans). Cambridge: Cambridge University Press.

Cronin, A. (2009) *How Terrorism Ends*. Princeton and Oxford: Princeton University Press.

Dworkin, R. (2002) 'The Threat to Patriotism', *London Review of Books*, 28 February.

European Commission for Democracy through Law (Venice Commission) (2006–07) *Report on the Democratic Oversight of the Security Services*, study 388.

European Committee for the Prevention of Torture and Inhuman or Degrading Treatment or Punishment (1998) 'Rapport Au Gouvernement De La République Française Relatif À La Visite Effectuée Par Le Comité Européen Pour La Prévention De La Torture Et Des Peines Ou Traitements Inhumains Ou Dégradants (Cpt) En France Du 6 Au 18 Octobre 1996', Strasbourg.

European Committee for the Prevention of Torture and Inhuman or Degrading Treatment or Punishment (2001) 'Rapport Au Gouvernement De La République Française Relatif À La Visite En France Effectuée Par Le Comité Européen Pour La Prévention De La Torture Et Des Peines Ou Traitements Inhumains Ou Dégradants (Cpt) Du 14 Au 26 Mai 2000', Strasbourg.

European Committee for the Prevention of Torture and Inhuman or Degrading Treatment or Punishment (2012) 'Rapport Au Gouvernement De La République Française Relatif À La Visite En France Effectuée Par Le Comité Européen Pour La Prévention De La Torture Et Des Peines Ou Traitements Inhumains Ou Dégradants (Cpt) Du 28 Novembre Au 10 Décembre 2010', Strasbourg: CPT.

Galli, F. and Weyembergh, A. (eds) (2012) *Eu Counter-Terrorism Offences: What Impact on National Legislation and Case-Law?* Brussels: University of Brussels.

Hodgson, J. (2005) *French Criminal Justice: A Comparative Account of the Investigation and Prosecution of Crime in France*. Oxford: Hart Publishing.

Hodgson, J. (2006) *The Investigation and Prosecution of Terrorist Suspects in France*. Report for the Home Office. Available at: <http://papers.ssrn.com/sol3/papers.cfm?abstract_id=1321868> accessed 24 July 2013.

Hodgson, J. and Tadros, V. (2009) 'How to Make a Terrorist out of Nothing', *Modern Law Review* 72(6): 985–99.

HODGSON, J. and TADROS, V. (2013) 'The Impossibility of Defining Terrorism', *New Criminal Law Review* 16(3): 494–526.

Human Rights Watch (2007) *France. In the Name of Prevention: Insufficient Safeguards in National Security Removals*. Human Rights Watch, 6 June.

Human Rights Watch (2008) *Preempting Justice: Counterterrorism Laws and Procedures in France*. Human Rights Watch, 2 July.

HUNT, A. (2006) 'The Council of Europe Convention on the Prevention of Terrorism', *European Public Law* 12(4): 603–28.

HUNT, A. (2007) 'Criminal Prohibitions on Direct and Indirect Encouragement of Terrorism', *Criminal Law Review* 441–58.

JOHNSON, H. (2005) *The Age of Anxiety: McCarthyism to Terrorism*. Orlando: Harcourt.

Joint Committee on Human Rights (2006) *Counter-Terrorism Policy and Human Rights: Prosecution and Pre-Charge Detention* (twenty-fourth Report of Session 2005–06). London: The Stationery Office.

KOSTAKOPOULOU, D. (2008) 'How To Do Things With Security Post 9/11.' *Oxford Journal of Legal Studies* 28(2): 317–42.

MARRET, J. L. (2003) *Terrorisme: Les Stratégies de Communication* (Centre d'Etudes en Sciences Sociales de la Défense, Ministère de la Défense, Paris).

PHYTHIAN, M. (2005) 'Intelligence, Policy-making and the 7 July London Bombings' *Crime, Law and Social Change* 44: 361–85.

PILLAY, R. (2010) *Current Challenges Regarding Respect of Human Rights in the Fight against Terrorism* (briefing paper). Brussels: European Parliament, Directorate-General for External Policies.

SASSÒLI, M. (2006) 'Terrorism and War' *Journal of International Criminal Justice* 4: 959–81.

SCARMAN, The Rt Hon OBE (1981) 'Report to the Rt Hon William Whitelaw CH, MC, MP, Secretary of State for the Home Department, on the Brixton Disorders of 10–12 April 1981' ('The Scarman Report'). London: HMSO, November 1981.

SHAPIRO, J. and SUZAN, B. (2003) 'The French Experience of Counter-terrorism', *Survival* 45(1): 67–98.

TYLER, T. and FAGAN, J. (2008) 'Legitimacy and Cooperation: Why Do People Help the Police Fight Crime in Their Communities', *Ohio State Journal of Criminal Law* 6: 231–75.

VILLEPIN DE, D. (2006) *Prevailing Against Terrorism. White Paper on Domestic Security against Terrorism*. Paris: La documentation Française.

WADE, M. and MALJEVIC, A. (eds) (2010) *A War on Terror? The European Stance on a New Threat, Changing Laws and Human Rights Implications*. New York: Springer.

WALDRON, J. (2003) 'Security and Liberty: The Image of Balance', *Journal of Political Philosophy* 11(2): 191–210.

WALKER, C. (2005) 'Intelligence and Anti-Terrorism Legislation in the United Kingdom', *Crime, Law and Social Change* 44: 387–422.

WALKER, C. (2006) 'Clamping Down on Terrorism in the United Kingdom', *Journal of International Criminal Justice* 4: 1137–51.

10

'LEGITIMACY UNDER PRESSURE' IN HIGH SECURITY PRISONS

Alison Liebling[1]

Prisons are intensely relational and, some might say, political communities. Prisoners are powerfully alert to matters of justice and respect, or to matters of their own moral treatment, despite some lack of awareness of the implications of these sensitivities for their own morality and behaviour, and an uneven tendency to comprehend or articulate their experiences in abstract conceptual language.[2] They are persuasively articulate about the difference between 'right' and 'wrong' conduct by prison officers, the effects of staff indifference on their capacity to manage a prison sentence, and about why one prison is more 'decent' in its orientation to their condition and treatment than another. These are important and neglected issues, first placed on the agenda for prison sociology by Richard Sparks, Tony Bottoms, and Will Hay by their analysis in *Prisons and the Problem of Order*. Their 1995 paper, *Legitimacy and Order in Prisons* articulates the importance of:

> paying attention both to procedural and relational dimensions of prisons regimes; in other words, to the *recognition* of prisoners in terms both of their citizenship and their *ordinary humanity* (Sparks and Bottoms 1995: 59, emphasis added).

These terms—recognition, citizenship, and humanity—are of critical and growing importance in the study of prison life, as I shall argue in this chapter. The chapter outlines the findings from two detailed studies of a single high security prison (HMP Whitemoor) over two time periods, with some important methodological innovations and significant policy and political developments occurring in between. There

[1] I am deeply grateful to Helen Arnold and Christina Straub for research assistance on the second Whitemoor study, which we are developing together for publication as a book. I am also grateful to John Dunn for letting me use his terminology of 'legitimacy under pressure' (this volume) for my title. Helpful feedback and commentary on the early version of this paper delivered at the conference was received from Michael Spurr, John Dunn, and Richard Sparks in particular. Tony Bottoms and Bethany Schmidt provided detailed comments on a more developed version of the paper afterwards. I am most grateful for this constructive and stimulating dialogue.

[2] I propose that prisoners are more alert to and engaged in issues of the justness of their treatment than ordinary citizens, by the nature of their condition (see Dunn, this volume).

had never been any intention at the time of the first study to carry out a repeat study 12 years later, but such were the contrasts in the state of relationships in the prison that the overall project, of understanding life in maximum security prisons in England and Wales, has taken on a longitudinal character. Why has trust declined? Why are relationships distant? Is the long-term prison of 2009–11 less legitimate in the eyes of prisoners than the long-term prison of 1997–99? If so, what does this mean empirically, and why is it the case?

As some of the methods used in these projects also developed over time, the second study is arguably more accurately and carefully conceptualized and conducted than the first. This leaves some unanswered questions about 'Time 1'—was the quality of life at the prison really so much better than we found at 'Time 2'? But the main point of this chapter is to describe the current state of life and relationships in this high security prison with care and to consider the implications of our analysis. There is no question, in my mind, that new problems of legitimacy have arisen in high security settings, and that new theoretical resources are required to understand and evaluate the changing prison world.

TIME 1: AN EXPLORATORY STUDY OF STAFF-PRISONER RELATIONSHIPS IN A HIGH SECURITY PRISON

The first exploratory and ethnographic study of staff–prisoner relationships was conducted in 1997–99. It arose out of an unexpected research finding in another high security prison, relating to the introduction of a policy of incentives and earned privileges for prisoners, and in particular, to the use of discretion by prison officers (see generally, Liebling 2007; and Bottoms 2003). Prison officers had 'resorted to basic' (that is, placed prisoners on the most restricted level of privileges) on the wing where the least good relationships between staff and prisoners existed. They had used a new form of coercive or punitive power prematurely—failing to work through the kinds of skills being deployed elsewhere in the prison: talk, persuasion, and influence. Prisoners had responded in protest (causing significant damage and destruction, as well as injury); whereas on other wings, where relationships with staff were better, in all the 'right' ways (Liebling et al. 2010) power had 'flowed through' these relationships more effectively and prisoners had accepted a generally unwelcome policy change, because staff had 'sold it' to them, or persuaded them that it was both inevitable and in principle, reasonable (see Liebling 2000).

The first Whitemoor research project was very modestly funded, relatively unconstrained, and was a curiosity-driven project designed to learn as much as possible about the ways in which prison officers made decisions, used their authority, and policed prisoner behaviour (Liebling and Price 1999). It included an analysis of prisoners' relationships with each other, but this had not been the main focus of the research. The study tested the use of Appreciative Inquiry (AI)[3] with prison officers for the first time, to powerful effect, showing how prison officers worked at their best. The best officers were easily identifiable by prisoners and consistent with existing US research, they were neither too eager nor too unwilling to use their authority (see Muir 1977; Hepburn 1985). This study became the foundation of a book, *The Prison Officer* (Liebling and Price 2001; 2nd edn 2011), which outlines the central role of relationships, discretion and peacekeeping in the work of prison officers.

Whitemoor prison was arguably at a 'peak' in its professional history at that time because it was recovering from a dramatic set of escapes linked to under-enforcement of the rules (a distortion of the Radzinowicz notion of liberal-humanitarian: a liberal-permissive model of long-term imprisonment, no longer in fashion). The prison was extremely well resourced to manage this move away from under-enforcement towards auditable adherence to security requirements, under two consecutive highly competent and powerful Governors, who led the process of improvement with an explicit attentiveness to the quality of relationships between staff and prisoners. Both believed, and communicated to staff, that 'the higher the security quotient, the more relational "oil" is needed to smooth the flow' (senior manager, in Liebling and Price 2001). In general, prisoners were reasonably positive about the terms, tone and content of their time in the prison, and in particular their treatment by staff, considering the severity of their sentences:

> Relationships were described as 'quite close' and they were generally good humoured... Control clearly rested with staff, but there was a noticeable information flow with prisoners. Staff were physically present almost everywhere in the prison, but were relatively unobtrusive. They were often interested in group work, offending behaviour courses, and other constructive work with prisoners, and prided themselves on creating a 'pleasant atmosphere on the wing' (Liebling and Price 1999: 15).

Staff were highly professionally confident in the prison at 'Time 1'. Some finely graded trust was built up, or flowed, between staff and prisoners, as well as amongst prisoners, so that working knowledge about the characters, predictability, and reliability of others were in almost constant use, or under development, despite the risks being navigated by all.[4] We described the nature and quality of staff–prisoner relationships as generally 'good, but right'. These relationships provided a framework through which decisions were made: who got what job, who was unlocked on the wing if not working (against directives), who got placed on report, and how

[3] A largely *inductive* method aimed at in-depth imaginative conversation and the development of sensitizing concepts for further exploration. AI is concerned with lived experience, narrative, and meaning and includes an explicit use of *generative questions*. These are few in number, they generate emotion as well as experience, and they are based on real memories of specific experiences. The questions invite a deliberate focus on emotion and peak experiences, but negative experiences and accounts are not excluded in any way. See further Elliott (1999); Liebling et al. (1999); Liebling with Arnold (2004, ch. 3).

[4] It is important to note that trust can exist in the prison environment. As Sparks et al. note: '[Staff and prisoners] share the same physical and social space. They cannot sustain a state of submerged warfare all the time. They develop familiarities. They banter. There are acts of concern and kindness. It is a situation marked by contradictions' (Sparks et al. 1996: 196). See Liebling with Arnold 2004: 240–51.

difficult situations should be handled. This was not the 'favouritism' sometimes identified in poorer prisons with traditional cultures, but a form of 'risk-and-trust-based' decision making based on slowly acquired expertise about individual prisoners.

We wrote:

> Through relationships, prisoners (and officers) became individuals. Officers and prisoners sometimes knew truths about each other which others did not know (the bad mornings, the fiery tempers, the second girlfriend, the impending divorce, the parole rejection, and so on). Staff could use this information to deploy their authority more wisely and carefully with the complexities of their population in mind... In this aspect of their work, prison officers won our admiration (Liebling and Price 2001; 2nd edn 2011: 103).

The dynamics of prison life existed within a context of embedded relationships, particularly (but not exclusively) in long-term prisons, where staff often got to know prisoners well. Power flowed through these relationships, often in unseen ways, and in ways that combined power and authority with degrees of trust and respect. They influenced action, and importantly, generated either 'assent' or resistance and frustration. At their best, prison officers combined relationships with authority in ways that prisoners noticed, understood, and preferred. We have referred to this well-informed, 'recognitive' process of decision making elsewhere as 'dynamic authority'. This is a form of 'light presence' by staff in which their relationships with prisoners are used authentically and effectively to get through the day. Their power is held in reserve, so that prisoners feel cooperative rather than coerced (see Liebling 2011; Crewe et al., forthcoming; and Dunbar 1985, on the related concept of 'dynamic security'). Staff attitudes and approaches to their work were regarded as broadly legitimate at the time, on the whole, even if the material facilities and privileges on offer in the prison were not (Liebling and Price 1999; see also Sparks et al. 1996 on the comparable analysis of Albany prison in the 1980s). Prisoners had a stake in good working relationships too—prison officers were important gatekeepers, and it made prison life more bearable if there was 'a pleasant atmosphere on the wings'.

CAN PRISONS BE LEGITIMATE AT ALL?

We were, at the time of the first Whitemoor study, more concerned with depicting the shifting power bases upon which prison staff drew in their work, including a move away from 'reciprocal' and towards 'coercive' and 'expert' power (see Hepburn 1985), than we were with any analysis of the concept of legitimacy in practice per se. But our colleagues, Richard Sparks et al., had recently published their book, *Prisons and the Problem of Order*, and we were increasingly finding ourselves in conversations with the authors about whether, and to what extent, prisons could be 'legitimate'. Sparks had argued in an important 1994 article that matters of 'interior' legitimacy were highly relevant to, but not determinative of, the question of whether prisons could be legitimate. Exterior matters of structure, organization and population were significant too (Sparks 1994; Loader and Sparks, this volume). Their 1996 book focused mainly on these interior matters.

It was significant that the Sparks et al. book was written around the time of the publication of the Woolf Report, following a series of major disturbances in prisons in England and Wales (Woolf 1991). Woolf outlined 'something akin to a theory of legitimacy', as Sparks et al. argued (Sparks et al. 1996: 304). Sparks et al. proposed, following Woolf, that prisoners were more likely to assent to a regime perceived as (in shorthand) fair and relational than a regime that was restrictive, controlling, and somewhat over-policed. This seemed to be the case in practice. Long Lartin had been the only maximum security or 'dispersal' prison in England to be 'riot free'. It is important that Long Lartin embodied, in many ways, the clear vision of a 'liberal regime within a secure perimeter' recommended by Sir Leon Radzinowicz in 1968. His Committee's report set out the principles on which long-term imprisonment should be based, arguing that:

> The manner in which the prison service of this country meet the challenge of containing long-term prisoners in conditions that combine security and humanity will have a lasting effect on the service as a whole (ACPS 1968: 3).

Sparks et al. (1996) showed that different models of penal order could be identified, some of which were more sustainable and legitimate than others, but the authors were appropriately tentative about the extent to which any one model got the balance required between competing 'virtues' right. Better or more legitimate regimes allowed for some choice and self-determination, more dignity, hope for the future, and fostered a respectful interpersonal climate. They relied on social rather than simply on situational policing methods, and paid attention to the need for reasons to be provided for decision making. They were procedurally as well as interpersonally more fair. But they could sometimes be riskier places. Greater freedom and autonomy among prisoners, softer methods of policing, and 'permissiveness', brought with them opportunities for networks and power struggles to flourish. Their analysis set out, then, but did not set out to resolve, some of the tensions between freedom and safety, and organization and constraint, in prison. Their research was informed by the best available data at the time: observation, long interviews with staff and prisoners, and hospital records of injuries to prisoners. It provided a convincing case for, amongst other things, exploring the concept of prison quality (or legitimacy-in-practice)—including the state of its relationships and prisoners' perceptions of all aspects of their treatment—more closely and systematically.

My subsequent work, with others, aimed to develop a more precise understanding of the nature and quality of staff-prisoner relationships, and ways of assessing what came to be regarded (following the important and pioneering work of Moos, Toch, and others) as the 'moral and social climate' in prisons. Our research on measuring these aspects of the quality of prison life, over many years, has arguably empirically operationalized some of these critical but essentially qualitative aspects of the prison experience, in a grounded, interpretive way (a research approach I have recently called *ethnography-led measurement*). This has been achieved by talking at length with staff and prisoners about what matters to them most in prison (a form of 'strong evaluation',

Taylor 1985[5]), and also by talking together about how best to articulate and illustrate empirically what these important dimensions mean in practice (and then statistically testing these ideas; see Liebling with Arnold 2004). The highly structured quality of life survey to arise from this work is now used by the National Offender Management Service to assess the 'moral performance' or quality of life in every prison in England and Wales, as well as by members of the Cambridge Prisons Research Centre in ongoing research (see NOMS ACA 2011; Liebling et al. 2011). It has become known, in official circles, as the 'MQPL' survey (Measuring the Quality of Prison Life). It measures, amongst other things, prisoners' perceptions of their treatment by staff, the use of power and authority by staff, the opportunities for personal development in their prison, and levels of order, safety and well-being (see further Liebling et al. 2011). The study did not set out to operationalize or test legitimacy theory, but a structured dialogue with staff and prisoners led us in this direction. In retrospect, there are obvious reasons for this, given that (1) prisons have two 'castes' (Sykes 1958), those with and those without official power; (2) that legitimacy is essentially dialogic (Bottoms and Tankebe 2012 and this volume).

The survey was developed using the AI method (see n 3 earlier). This is a qualitative method borrowed from the field of organizational change that invites prisoners (or staff) to describe their best or peak experiences, and to embark on a deep conversation about their experience from that position. A set of 'dimensions that matter' were derived from open conversation about best and worst experiences in prison, what mattered most, and what the most important distinctions between prisons were.[6] Once identified, the dimensions became the starting point for a deeper set of questions about the prison experience.

Even in a culturally poor and disorganized prison, it is important to ask questions like, 'tell me about a time where you have been treated with respect in here? Who did this involve? Where was it? What happened? How did this make you feel?' These kinds of organized and directed conversations generate energy and emotion, and almost always stray into many worst experiences too, but they return to important and real experiences of 'when I felt like a human being'. Negative experiences can be 'reframed' in ways that affirm the underlying value being denied ('so what I hear you saying is that being treated with respect is very important to you?'). This kind of conversation often reveals or articulates the values underlying one's evaluation of one's treatment or experience. Charles Taylor's term, 'strong evaluation', best denotes this process, as it

[5] Charles Taylor's concept of strong evaluation denotes an authentic, illusion-free assessment of desires, and arises out of his argument that humans are beings to whom things matter, or have significance: that is, we distinguish between 'things that are recognised as having higher importance or worth and things which lack this or are of lesser value' (1985: 3). We can choose *between* desires. These qualitative evaluations are fundamental to what it is to be human. The evaluative process requires articulacy, or the use of terms, but once a strong evaluative language is acquired, it is possible to distinguish between our preferences in the light of who we want to be, and to rank 'goods'. There is always room for improvement in this process, and for re-evaluation. The important matters 'engage the whole self' (p. 42). 'Subject-referring feeling' is the mode of access to what matters most (p. 62). The vast majority of humans have this capacity for strong evaluation. I am arguing that a full AI exercise engages participants in precisely this kind of way.

[6] The dimensions to arise were: humanity, respect, staff-prisoner relationships, trust, support, safety, order, personal development, family contact, and well-being (Liebling with Arnold 2004).

draws on qualitative feeling and experience, and moves beyond superficial evaluation of material goods and services. It is a fast route to 'what matters' and an effective way of creating balanced, energized, and authentic conversation. These strong qualitative foundations formed the basis of a structured 'tick-box questionnaire'. Because of the methodology employed, and the close fit between the conversations embarked upon and the literature, the survey is empirical, conceptual, and normative. It has been refined and developed in several subsequent studies (see Liebling et al. 2011).

There are 21 dimensions in the most recent version of the survey arising from this work, each represented by a series of items or statements thought to reflect some aspect of the dimension in question. The dimensions include 'respect', 'staff-prisoner relationships', 'care for the vulnerable', 'staff professionalism', 'organization and consistency', 'policing and security', and 'personal development'. These dimensions reflect both relational and procedural aspects of the prison experience, and scoring well requires an appropriate balance to be struck between the 'security' and 'humanity' concerns expressed by Radzinowicz in his Report.

It may be stretching a point to argue that the MQPL survey can be used to 'model' prison legitimacy, but results arising from its use can certainly provide us with opportunities for detailed empirical explorations of important differences between prisons in these 'areas that matter', some links with outcomes (such as suicide, or levels of well-being), and some important changes over time. The results also confirm theoretically important relationships between dimensions, so that respect is highly correlated with fairness, which in turn is highly correlated with order, or 'the feeling that the prison environment is structured, stable, predictable and acceptable' (Liebling et al. 2005; Liebling with Arnold 2004: 281–96). This is a helpful empirical illustration of the Sparks et al. legitimacy and order thesis. It has been an important extension of the somewhat instrumental argument *for* legitimacy adopted by contemporary senior managers (see Loader and Sparks, this volume) that a more legitimate prison is not just more ordered, but it is a more psychologically survivable one (Liebling et al. 2005). Ben Crewe, Susie Hulley, and I have argued that order and safety *constitute,* or form part of, what prisoners think is legitimate (Crewe, Liebling, and Hulley, forthcoming) rather than being desirable outcomes per se (on a proposed distinction between what is *constitutive* of legitimacy and what *predicts* it, see Hough et al. this volume).

In *Prisons and their Moral Performance,* we argued that there are some complexities to prisoner evaluations of their quality of life in prison and that, for example, there can be too *much* trust as well as too little respect in prison, leading to breaches of boundaries and confusion or frustration among prisoners (or in the case of Doncaster prison, included in the study, to escapes; see Liebling with Arnold 2004: 435–42). We proposed (following the work of political theorist Valerie Braithwaite) that prisoners are 'moral dualists', favouring both respectful interpersonal treatment *and* safety and security, or harmony and security values (see Braithwaite 1994, 1998). Order without freedom is tyranny, and freedom without order is anarchy (so one unexpected finding from this overall research exercise is that prisoners, once engaged in these kinds of conversations, make rather good political theorists; see also McCleery 1968). This value balancing is an extremely difficult task to get right in a prison, and on many of these dimensions, the mean between 'excess and deficit' is extremely small (see Liebling with Arnold 2004: 436–42).

In less organized and 'professional' prisons, preoccupations with safety and survival dominate; opportunities are few, and negative emotional states are common. Prisoners retreat into their cells and avoid risk. In better, more legitimate, ordered and respectful prisons, prisoners describe having the psychological and emotional resources to think about the future, and more help or support is available. In more legitimate prison environments, a *feeling* of positive change is possible. More legitimate prisons, then, are more ordered, they are safer, prisoner well-being is higher and outcomes are likely to be better.

With this survey now routinely used in research, and with much conceptual refinement under our belts, we were invited back into Whitemoor.

TIME 2: AN EXPLORATORY STUDY OF STAFF-PRISONER RELATIONSHIPS IN A HIGH SECURITY PRISON TWELVE YEARS ON

The second study, conducted in 2009–10, had quite different origins from the first (although we insisted on curiosity as its main rationale) and was requested by the Home Office in light of an Inspectorate report suggesting poor and distant staff-prisoner relationships at the prison. Since the original study had found quite positive relationships at the establishment, this apparent decline was a matter of concern and interest. The population had changed, and there were some new official and media concerns about radicalization in the prison, which housed seven offenders convicted of terrorist offences. Close to forty per cent of the prisoners were Muslim—a dramatic increase since the first study (at which time the much lower figure was not even recorded)—but it was also significant that up to half of this number had converted to Islam whilst in prison.

The original request had been a high level proposal for a 'study of radicalization' in the prison, but following negotiations, a repeat of the original study of staff–prisoner relationships was proposed instead, as this would be more useful as well as scientifically more appropriate in finding out in a genuinely exploratory way what was going on in the prison. Other significant changes since the original study included the loss of two vulnerable prisoner units (a traditionally more compliant population; see for example, Sparks et al. 1996, ch. 6), the opening of a wing for dangerous and severely personality disordered prisoners, increases in the use of CCTV cameras, and some changing population demographics (e.g. higher numbers of Black and Minority Ethnic prisoners: an increase from 21 to 55 per cent) and sentence types (e.g. prisoners were serving longer and more indeterminate sentences).

Based on extensive observation and shadowing, the use of a dialogue group with a regular set of prisoners, and long, tape-recorded and fully transcribed interviews with 52 prisoners and 30 staff over a 12 month period in the prison, we reported a significant drop in trust, in the quality of staff–prisoner relationships, and in overall legitimacy at Whitemoor at 'Time 2' (Liebling et al. 2012). Newly long and indeterminate sentences, a political climate requiring no 'pampering' of prisoners, greater diversity in the population, an excessive emphasis on risk, and increasingly uncomfortable or less confident staff, seemed to have transformed the highly professional and reasonably legitimate prison we had described at 'Time 1' into a place where prisoners said things like:

> *This is not an honest prison. (Prisoner)*
> *There are lots of sad stories in here, and lost souls. You have to be mentally strong. I feel upset for people in here. It's not a happy place. (Prisoner)*
> *I [feel like] a casualty of politics. (Prisoner)*
> *They don't see you as a person. (Prisoner)*

Prisoners' lives 'on the street' had been violent and turbulent, the sentence was more often unexpected or unexpectedly long, compared to the first study, and the route out of prison seemed more difficult to navigate. In our regular dialogue group discussions, prisoners seemed more aware of, and willing to talk about, issues of class, discrimination, exclusion, and disadvantage, than the prisoners we had spoken to 12 years earlier. Their routes into prison felt less legitimate, as court procedures, and a changing political climate, as well as their disadvantages outside, seemed to have altered the balance of probabilities against them.

Once in prison, and through the extended period of 'shell shock' brought about by their extremely long tariffs or sentences, prisoners found that identity and meaning were hard to find in an environment in which creative activities were regarded as 'pampering', and relationships were fractured (see Liebling and Straub 2012). The important distinction between activities providing opportunities for meaning and development, and activities regarded as hedonistic and pleasurable, or self-indulgent, had been lost by officials concerned about negative media headlines (discussed later). Prisoners said:

> *You still feel you want to express yourself, but you can't in prison... so you don't know where you are. I have no idea any more where I am. (Prisoner)*
> *I'm a totally different person from when I first came to prison... I've lost my identity I think. (Prisoner)*
> *They don't see you as a person.* ***Interviewer:*** *What does it do to you, if you're not seen as a person?* ***Respondent:*** *It makes me ignore them. I blank them to their face. Simple as that... I'm not violent by nature but it makes me just want to give them a swift kick in the crotch, you know? So... here... It kind of makes you want to live up to... their impression. You think we're scum? Fine, we'll take it out on you. That sort of thing. And it stirs up the pot. It causes stress amongst other inmates and it's something we don't need 'cause... there's no way for us to get rid of it. (Prisoner)*

In-prison conversion to Islam was a new and highly complicated feature of life in the prison. Of our 52 interviewees, 12 of the 23 who described themselves as Muslim were in-prison converts. This level of interest in Islam fuelled fears among staff about the impact of housing convicted terrorist offenders holding extreme ideological views among impressionable and alienated young street fighters or drugs traders with little sense of belonging or identity and few constructive avenues for self-development in prison. Whilst 40 per cent of the population at Whitemoor were identified as Muslim, we discovered during the project that use of these categories was unreliable, and that some prisoners were identified as Muslim because they had been 'exploring' Islam, or attending Friday prayers. Fears about the risks of radicalization were well founded at one level (there was evidence from elsewhere that acts of terrorism could be linked to in-prison radicalization processes; see, e.g. Hamm 2012, 2013), but the legitimate way out of this potentially dangerous situation had not yet been imagined.

Alongside prisoner interest in Islam, there was also some evidence of coerced conversions, and some major incidents in the prison that looked, at least, as if they were to do with conflicts over faith. There was considerable fear and violence in the prison, and some new rivalries between prisoners, as well as mutual distancing from staff, which made the prison feel much less safe.

Staff seemed out of their depth, or culturally alienated by prisoners campaigning for pork-free kitchens, mid-regime prayer time, and foreign language literature: a situation reminiscent of Jacobs' American study of Stateville in the 1960s and 70s (1977). They were nervous of accusations of racism and discrimination, following a high-profile inquiry into the death of a young Asian prisoner at the hands of his White, racist cell-mate at another prison in 2000 (Keith 2006), and the demotion of a well-liked member of staff in their prison for racist language. Meanwhile, there were rumours that a member of staff in a high security prison might be beheaded, and evidence that one of the 2005 London bombers had been radicalized in prison (Hamm 2013). Staff were professionally anxious, and this led to retreat.

For prisoners in general, activities led by outside organizations had been curtailed (by a 'public acceptability test'[7]) and long-termers at the earliest stage in long sentences were not a priority for available courses. A 'risk climate' meant that routes into work, education, art, music, or other meaningful activities were more difficult, and getting downgraded from the highest security category seemed impossible. Prisoners were moved from cell to cell, in case relationships formed. We found it harder to gain entry to the prison, conduct our fieldwork, and request prisoner participation in our research-related activities. A re-organization of 'expertise' on prisoners away from the prison officer meant that the information flow had moved off the landings, onto computers and into the offices of specialists (a new form of soft, or 'biro-power'; see Crewe 2009). Interestingly, the most trusted people in the prison, by prisoners, were chaplains: their 'theology of the person' meant that normal human conversations could still go on. But chaplains were not considered by others in the prison to be experts on risk, so their view of prisoners on assessments was not sought. They too had become objects of suspicion. They might be susceptible to conditioning by prisoners, or they could themselves be a new source of radicalization, as their demographic profile (and preferred spoken language) changed to accommodate the growth in numbers of prisoners requiring access to Imams.

[7] A Prison Service Order placing new restrictions on the type of activities allowed in prisons was issued in 2009 following a series of media-driven inquiries into apparently unacceptable activities in prison (such as a comedy workshop, aimed at building self-esteem): 'Acceptable activities in prisons' (PSO 0500, issued 6 January 2009). These instructions were brought together by PSI 38/2010 and its accompanying guidance.

Prisoners felt invisible, except as objects of risk to those around them. They were aware of the high numbers of indeterminate sentence prisoners who had been recalled to prison, which added to their feeling of being a very long way from release. Their position—often within a few years of receiving a very long sentence, in the highest possible security category, deprived of meaningful relationships, and short of any means of progress—was beyond words. Imprisonment was far more than 'the physical deprivation of liberty'. In a risk-driven climate, it meant the deprivation of freedom of thought, action, and identity (see Liebling et al. 2011).

Prisoners joked with us about the lack of fairness or competence in risk assessment procedures:

> *I put my name down for a course, and my score went up!*

One prisoner had the wrong assessment form—he turned out to be in the wrong prison. He was neither confident nor experienced enough to do more than bring his Offender Assessment System (OASys) paperwork to our dialogue group to point out that he 'didn't have a four year old son or a wife, so what was all this about?' The other prisoners laughed at him, but they all acknowledged that this could happen to them. Scathing accounts were given of interactions with young, female psychologists, who 'sat in judgement' with 'all the power' and little understanding of 'my kind of life'. Prisoners felt 'unrecognized'. They were clear about what a good day felt like:

> *I would say good days are when you're treated as a human being, I suppose. Days when you are recognised as a person... as an individual... and treated like that, which can range from just somebody saying good morning to you... that sets up a good day, I suppose, and being spoken to equal footed. That, for me, is a good day. (Prisoner)*

Prisoners talked about the struggle to experience themselves as human in the face of widespread perceptions of dangerousness:

> ***I:** So what are the reasons why you interact with officers?* ***R:** To try and make them feel like we're human... Because they almost want to dehumanise man... you always get that vibe that 'he's a convict and he's dangerous.' I get that vibe a lot with them. (Prisoner)*
>
> *We're human beings at the end of the day, we're people. OK, some of us have done some very bad things, some of us have done some not quite so bad things, but that doesn't make us... we're still, you know, we still love and feel and have the same emotions as everybody else. (Prisoner)*

This is the opposite problem of the Doncaster value-balance dilemma described earlier, in which trust of prisoners reached risky proportions. In Whitemoor, the 'pursuit of security' (in Lucia Zedner's words, 2000)—a broad and dominant security orientation—had squeezed out relationships, humanity, trust, and in the eyes of prisoners, legitimacy. Whereas in 1999 'staff–prisoner relationships' were a 'project' that Governors and staff talked about (there was even a conference in the prison on the subject), in 2010 education and other staff, as well as prisoners, complained that if they were seen in conversation with individual prisoners for more than ten minutes, someone would 'submit a Security Information Report'. Relationships had shifted from 'glue' or 'oil', fundamental to the prison's functioning, to 'a risk'. A psychologist helpfully explained that 'we have to look at faith through a risk lens'. Imams making spiritual progress with confused converts to Islam were suspected of doing the opposite. No-one trusted anyone.

The problem was, as one mixed race prisoner put it, in his interview:

PRISONER: *I don't think a lot of people trust anyone, really.*
INTERVIEWER: *It feels like there's less trust now than there was when we first did the study ten years ago.*
PRISONER: *The best way to be able to feel that you can trust anyone in here is to be a Muslim.*
INTERVIEWER: *Eek.*
PRISONER: *Then you'll have... then you'll be able to... at least feel like you can trust people.*
INTERVIEWER: *Yeah?*
PRISONER: *Because it's so... it so unites... The teachings... of this Qu'ran are it promotes that kind of stuff, trusting each other... like I said, it's a proper temptation. When you look at it... from the outside, it's like the best thing in here, really ...*
INTERVIEWER: *Yeah?*
PRISONER: *Apart from the fact that it probably won't let you go home...* [both laugh]
INTERVIEWER: *But that makes it... that is really powerful, that... it's a kind of basic human need to feel trust somewhere ...*
PRISONER: *Yeah. And it is. It's the only place in the prison where there's lots of things. It's the only place in the prison where there's love, where there's trust, where there's real friendships, where there's any of them type of things. Loyalty, anything like that.*
INTERVIEWER: *But that means the Governor's problem is making sure those things exist elsewhere.*
PRISONER: *And that's what I was saying to you. There's no reward for us [those who resist]. There's no... you're just left out on your own... So you will always... see that as a kind of temptation.*

In relation to the chapter by Tony Bottoms and Justice Tankebe (this volume), we might say that, in their dialogues with prisoners, staff *didn't know their audience* any more. This made it difficult to operate in the skilled way they had operated before, making fine distinctions, giving prisoners a chance, and finding out more about them. There were still some 'professional-plus' officers, doing great work, but they tended to do this great work with familiar prisoners: White, Christian, older, or young vulnerable prisoners, who they could talk to and shape, in a direction they understood.

There were three main problems, then, in this new environment: (1) a young and somewhat disaffected prisoner population, shell shocked by long sentences and unable to find a direction or meaningful way through this sentence; (2) a complex and differentiated Muslim population, feeling poorly treated and regarded despite good faith-related provision, and (3) some new prisoner dynamics in which changing faith identities and practices had become a new 'no go area' in the prison—an opportunity for powerful leaders to push staff back, wield power in the prison, and challenge or unsettle staff authority. All of this led to fear among staff and prisoners, and some violence, and it felt like staff were professionally unclear, and insufficiently supported, in navigating their way through these new dynamics.

At Time 2, we were able to use the MQPL survey in addition to our other methods, with a random sample of 159 prisoners, and at an early stage in the research, to get a clear and detailed sense of how the prison was perceived. As all items are rated on a five point Likert scale, the scoring process means that 3 is the 'neutral' score: anything above it reflects an overall positive evaluation (the higher the better) and anything below reflects an overall negative score (the higher the better). This was in addition to the methods used in the previous study.

The only dimensions to score over 3 at Whitemoor, of 21, were 'policing and security' (at 3.29), safety (at a low 3.04), and 'drugs and exploitation' (at 3.06; see Table 10.1), meaning that prisoners felt staff were doing what they could to minimize the use of drugs and its effects in prison. Whilst it is often the case that prisoners in maximum security prisoners are inclined to evaluate their conditions more negatively than other prisoners on the whole (they are articulate, well aware of their entitlements, and acutely aware of changes and especially in-roads made to their quality of life over time), these figures are relatively as well as substantively low, and reflect the prison's new preoccupation with security over relationships: a change in the mission and tone of long-term prisons that had happened without explicit reasoning or awareness. These trends were supported by the qualitative data, and have been noted elsewhere (see, e.g. Drake 2012). The language of relationships and legitimacy had been replaced by the language of risk and public protection.

Muslim prisoners felt particularly aggrieved, a finding related to their distant and strained relationships with staff, and their heightened 'risk status' in the new political climate (see Table 10.1, and earlier discussion). But all prisoners were critical of their treatment, and of the state of relationships in the prison.

Non-Muslim prisoners agreed more strongly with the item: 'In this prison, you have to be in a group in order to get by' (31.4 per cent Christian prisoners agreed or strongly agreed compared to 17.4 Muslim prisoners), reflecting the stronger trend among Muslim prisoners towards affiliation and brotherhood, and the perception among other prisoners that this granted them power. Paradoxically, the stronger sense of brotherhood among Muslim prisoners was expressed in the survey, and in interviews, as a less anxious form of group solidarity. Non-Muslim prisoners described their gravitation towards a group as a strategy for survival in prison, a choice that was often laced with danger and ambivalence. They envied Muslim prisoners their strength in identity and numbers.

Muslim prisoners rated 'policing and security' slightly (but not significantly) higher than other prisoners, feeling that they were closely supervized and monitored by staff. Relationships both within and between these groups were complex and strained, however, and fear and violence in the prison were widespread (see Liebling and Arnold 2012). The most remarkable finding was the degree to which the prison—and relationships and opportunities within it—had declined in a relatively short period of time. The perceived legitimacy of the prison was low, prisoners expressed considerable anger and frustration, the concept of distributive (un)fairness in the community had appeared in the dialogue about the prison experience, access to risk reducing possibilities were constrained, and a 'political charge' could be felt among disaffected groups (see Hamm 2013).

Table 10.1 MQPL Dimension Results, 2010[8]

Category	Mean score All prisoners (N = 159)	Mean score Christian (N = 52)	Mean score Muslim (N = 50)
Harmony Dimensions			
Support on Entry into Prison	2.77	2.88	2.63
Respect/Courtesy	2.77	2.92	2.47*
Staff-Prisoner Relationships	2.61	2.68	2.24*
Humanity	2.54	2.76	2.27*
Decency	2.56	2.62	2.31*
Care for the Vulnerable	2.92	3.10	2.65
Help and Assistance	2.88	2.94	2.79
Professionalism Dimensions			
Staff Professionalism	2.67	3.02	2.49*
Bureaucratic Legitimacy	2.12	2.43	1.88
Organization and Consistency	2.51	2.63	2. 32*
Fairness	2.43	2.67	2.15*
Security Dimensions			
Policing and Security	3.29	3.26	3.38
Prisoner Safety	3.04	3.02	3.32
Drugs and Exploitation	3.07	2.83	3.20
Well-being and Development Dimensions			
Personal Development	2.66	2.73	2.47
Personal Autonomy	2.54	2.18	1.89
Well-being	2.39	2.35	2.23

DISCUSSION AND CONCLUSIONS

Whilst the English high security prison is not in any sense an exported 'supermax' prison (that is, a form of maximum security prison originating in the US and based on segregation, isolation, and intense surveillance), according to these observations, it has evolved and transformed in unexpected ways, some of which are recognizable in recent accounts of supermax custody (see, e.g. Rhodes 2004, 2007, and 2009) as well

[8] Muslim prisoners scored significantly lower than Christian (and other religious as well as non-religious groups, not reported here) on eight dimensions, asterisked in the Table: respect/courtesy, staff–prisoner relationships, humanity, decency, staff professionalism, fairness, and organization and consistency. An example of the scale of the difference is that 26.9 per cent Christian prisoners agreed or strongly agreed that 'Relationships between staff and prisoners in this prison are good', compared to 14.3 per cent Muslim prisoners. Neither figure is high. As these two religious groups were the highest declared affiliations, these are the only groups represented in this Table. Examples of items and percentages of all prisoners agreeing or strongly agreeing with each are available in Liebling et al. (2011).

as in accounts of long-term prisons in the US from two decades ago (Flanagan 1995). Prisoners describe 'an intensification of enclosure' (Rhodes 2009) relating to the length and nature of their sentences, the prominence of risk assessments, and the pressures they face in navigating and handling their circumstances in an environment at once still social and 'liberal' (in relation to each other), and yet also constraining, exclusionary, and potentially violent. Their relationships, with staff and other prisoners, are more distant, and the stakes feel high. The maximum security prison has become a 'contradictory terrain' (Rhodes 2009) in which meaning and hope are difficult to find, and yet 'progress' is expected on all sides. In the prohibition of creative and constructive activities that might permit psychological survival and growth (now known as 'pampering'), the concept of punishment is 'exploited' (Brown 2005) to the detriment of more civilized and humane forms of custody:

> [The supermax prison is] 'productive of what the philosopher Giorgio Agamben calls *bare life*. This term highlights the process of "stripping down" —of constituting the prisoner as nothing but his "bare", biological, dangerous life.' (Rhodes 2009: 194)

The problems described at Whitemoor at 'Time 2' felt like major problems of legitimacy. Prisoners were more frustrated and disturbed by the absence of trust, respect, and humanity they experienced in the new prison world, as well as more troubled by fear for their safety, than they had been at 'Time 1'. The survey results suggested very low scores on almost all of the dimensions that matter to prisoners.

There were also some new problems, not encountered so directly in other prisons research projects to date. Two new features of a legitimacy dialogue emerged from our analysis: the first is the concept of *recognition* and the second is related to *human flourishing* or *personal development*. I now consider these themes.

Social theorist Axel Honneth has described the foundations of recognition as based along three axes: love, respect, and esteem (Honneth 1995). Non-recognition (or misrecognition) of individuals along any of these axes is experienced as a harm or injustice which can lead to a greater struggle for recognition (see also van den Brink and Owens 2007). Sources of recognition (friendship, affirmation, activity, and relationships) were scarce in Whitemoor, and yet declarations of recognition (that is, risk assessments) were more prominent in its daily life and functioning. That they happened at a distance, and in non-transparent ways, was all the more offensive. There were two key areas where prisoners felt deeply unrecognized: in risk assessment procedures, as described earlier (this was true for all prisoners), and specifically, for Muslim prisoners, or those toying with Islam, in the pursuit of their faith.

Recognition may be a sub-dimension of respect: do you know who I am? Can you judge and assess me, or make predictions about me, knowing only what you know, and from a distance? A satisfactory conception of justice or legitimacy has to include a use of power that conceptualizes its recipients fully and accurately and treats them on that basis. When they become the objects of others' subjective fears, their own identities as well as their future freedoms are threatened. As Honneth argues, non-recognition, 'is experienced as a harm or injustice that, under favourable social conditions, will motivate a struggle for recognition'. What Honneth calls 'recognitive relations' of care, respect, and esteem, were absent at Whitemoor. When staff kept a distance and sent in

Security Information Reports stating, 'prisoner seen reading Qu'ran', they were undoing the relational glue that kept a prison flowing. Prisoners' integrity as moral agents depended on the availability of recognition: that is, on care or love, esteem, and respect. It was fascinating to us, the research team, that prisoners used the term 'love' regularly—describing its absence and the effects of this on their emotional and 'existential' states. Honneth argues that 'being a human being' requires relations of recognition.

The depiction of a decent prison officer described by prisoners reflected this:

'They talk to you. Like a human being'.

The second new dimension to arise was in the area of spiritual life or access to meaning: without access to educational, creative, or other meaningful activities (which had often been led by outside visitors to the establishment), or relationships with staff (including specialists) prison life was tortuous and without hope. Both prisoners and staff needed hope (see Bottoms 1990; and Armstrong 2013) in order to survive, or work effectively in support of long-term prisoners. Prisoners used the language of love, relationships, and meaning frequently to describe what was missing in their bleak environment (Liebling et al. 2011) and what they experienced as a lack of humanity (Liebling with Arnold 2004). Survival in prison was about more than fair procedures and respectful interpersonal treatment. It required opportunities to 'become', to develop potential, and to connect to others. This required trust. These aspects of human life are often missing in analyses of prison quality or desistance (but see Maruna 2004; and Shapland and Bottoms 2011), but they preoccupy prisoners as they search for sources of meaning and connection in an environment in which they have been morally excluded. Even without proximity to release, the need to grow, to stabilize or heal fragile identities, and imagine oneself in a better future state, through relationships and meaningful activities, is fundamental. Some prison laws (for example, in Germany) refer to a 'right to resocialization' that is consistent with human dignity. This includes 'the freedom to develop one's personality' (Lazarus, 2004: 40–45).

Trust had declined (from a small but important baseline) in the prison because of a complex constellation of general social factors best conceptualized as 'late modernity' (see e.g. Bottoms and Wiles 1996; Liebling and Lacey 2012),[9] and a set of more specific conditions arising from 9/11, 7/7, new risk technologies, changes to staffing and management, and a new prison population with multiple grievances, a sense of disenfranchisement, a need for identity (e.g. Nawaz 2012) and conflict with each other. Whilst its causes are many and varied, its consequences are stark and vivid. Humans 'cannot flourish without trust' (Hollis 1998: 4; see also Sztompka 1999). Armed with this

[9] 'The psychological 'habitus' of late modernity includes economic and ontological insecurity, resentment, powerlessness, anxiety, and lack of trust. These psychological changes are grounded in profound shifts not only in social culture but also in the organization of work and the structure of the economy since the collapse of Fordist production in the 1970s, and with it the disappearance of many manual or low skill jobs. As Jock Young has put the change, Britain has moved from an equilibrium of 'cultural exclusion but economic inclusion' to the opposite equilibrium of 'cultural inclusion but economic exclusion' (Young 1999). For the excluded, there is humiliation and disrespect, along with the sense of alienation which comes with relative deprivation in a world which prizes material success and purports to offer equal opportunity. Identities are fragile rather than fixed or grounded in 'turbo-charged' late capitalism. Solutions are found in fundamentalism, racism, hyper-masculinity, and denigration of 'the other'. (Liebling and Lacey 2012: 2)

information, the prison's new senior management team (and the High Security Estate more generally) are currently seeking to 'grow' some trust and meaning back, in whatever ways seem manageable, within the constraints of their 'public protection' purpose and 'public acceptability constraints'.[10] We hope to explore these efforts and their effects in a follow-up study.

The model we are developing in attempting to understand and measure the quality of prison life over time is conceptual and empirical, and an approximation to an operationalization of the emerging dialogue about legitimacy in prison (see Liebling et al. 2011). There will always be improvements and refinements to be made to our survey, its dimension structure, and to our concept of legitimacy: these are interactive processes, continually under review. There are important signs that higher scores on the existing measures lead to better outcomes (although this is highly complex in the case of the cause and measurement of reconviction outcomes). It is important to explore what else might need to be measured (for example, staff self-legitimacy, in Bottoms and Tankebe 2012) in order to take the operationalization of the concept of legitimacy in criminal justice further and to make sure it tests the theoretical arguments of others in this field. Our aim is to both trace the changing contours of the prison experience, at the same time as we learn to reflect this changing experience more accurately over time.

Our findings from the two studies summarized here suggest that it would be a serious mistake to design or operate high security prisons in ways that depart too radically from Radzinowicz's case for combining security with humanity, not least because the seeds of radicalization—an issue of 'profound socio-political complexity'—may lie, in part at least—in perceived illegitimate treatment. As Hamm argues:

> Research shows that Islam in prison poses a security threat only under certain conditions of confinement: In mismanaged understaffed and overcrowded maximum security prisons where offenders are radicalized through a process of one-on-one proselytizing by charismatic leaders. Otherwise Islam has a moderating effect on prisoners which plays an important role in prison security and rehabilitation (2013: 214; Hamm 2009, 2011).

Whilst Whitemoor was neither understaffed nor overcrowded, it had other characteristics of a 'failed state' prison at the time we returned to it, including unworkable policy demands, a relative absence of management presence, officer alienation and retreat and, for prisoners, a lack of purpose, safety, fairness, or opportunities for growth and meaning (see Useem and Goldstone 2002; and Hamm 2013 on the use of this term in prisons). Whether the 'best' prison environments ever allow human beings to 'flourish', or 'grow desirable virtues' (Annas 2011), remains to be determined. What is clear is that the direction of travel has been away from these possibilities, in long term prisons in particular. The 'legitimacy turn' (Tankebe 2013) in prisons and penal policy

[10] For example, an 'override' has been introduced into an otherwise austere benchmarking and specification process, whereby special consideration is given to the need for meaningful activities and access to education in the high security estate, despite the distance from release and the lack of an obvious 'resource justification'. More positively, chaplaincy teams from all backgrounds are being revitalized and encouraged to play a full role in the life of long-term and high security prisons. A research grant on 'Locating and building trust in high risk prison settings' has been awarded to the author and colleagues by the Economic and Social Research Council to investigate these efforts, and future developments, further.

came early, following the Woolf Report (Home Office 1991), and for political and financial reasons, currently seems to be in reverse.

Hollis argues, 'All errors in politics and morality are philosophical errors' (1998: 7). The changing form and nature of high security prisons represents a 'struggle over the nature of personhood' and the tension between 'bare life', and 'political life' (or citizenship). There is a logic underlying contemporary penal practice at the deep end of the system which is neo-liberal, risk averse, exclusionary, racialized (or religiously divided), cost constrained, and in contradiction to both rehabilitation and legitimacy. We should not turn a generation of prisoners, whatever the behavioural, attitudinal, and inter-group challenges they pose, into 'non-relational bodies'. Keeping the high security prison 'relational', if that is what we mean to do, ensuring the safety of staff and prisoners as well as prisoners' psychological survival, and providing support for the most positive manifestations of spiritual or personal development for prisoners in general, will require new and better strategies. Some trust must flow, and be 'placed intelligently' (O'Neill 2009), for a prison to work, and as an aid to both in-prison legitimacy, and risk management. When trust becomes only fragile, we lose the only social lubricant available to us (Hollis 1998).

Social scientists argue that the purpose of empirical social science is to take (often small) steps towards solving analytic puzzles about the social world: that by describing the social world accurately, we can change the conceptual landscape, offering new frameworks for interpretation and action, and sometimes a warning. It has been striking, in this study, that officials and senior managers have started to speak in a new language about long-term prisoners: a morally blind language that makes 'bare life' regimes easier to contemplate (Bauman and Donskis 2013; Rhodes 2009). The effects of this shift away from the language of humanity are potentially devastating, for prisoners and staff. Prison chaplains still use the language of 'sitting where they sit': a 'theology of the person' that makes blindness to the human soul, and how we should treat it, less possible. Unsurprisingly perhaps, prisoners in this study said they trusted chaplains, and revealed authentic feelings in their presence, more often than they did with others, including specialists tasked with assessing the risks they posed. A philosophical (or theological, or moral) language, of communion, dignity, dialogue, and love, was spoken by prisoners throughout this study, but in private, and without much confidence that others were receptive to or understood it. As Martin Buber argued:

> That peoples can no longer carry on authentic dialogue with one another is not only the most acute symptom of the pathology of our time, it is also that which most urgently makes a demand on us (Buber 1953).

REFERENCES

ANNAS, J. (2011) *Intelligent Virtue*. Oxford: Oxford University Press.

ARMSTRONG, R. (2013) *Life After Prison in America's Bible Belt: An Ethnography of Release From a Faith-Based Programme*, PhD Thesis, University of Cambridge: Institute of Criminology.

BAUMAN, Z. and DONSKIS, L. (2013) *Moral Blindness: The Loss of Sensitivity in Liquid Modernity.* Cambridge: Polity Press.

BOTTOMS, A. E. (1990) 'The Aims of Imprisonment', in D. Garland (ed) *Justice, Guilt and Forgiveness in the Penal System.* Edinburgh: University of Edinburgh, Centre for Theology and Public Issues, Occasional Paper No. 18.

BOTTOMS, A. E. (2003) 'Theoretical Reflections on the Evaluations of a Penal Policy Initiative', in Zedner, L. and Ashworth, A. (eds) *The Criminological Foundations of Penal Policy: Essays in Honour of Roger Hood.* Oxford: Oxford University Press: 107–198.

BOTTOMS, A. E. and TANKEBE, J. (2012) 'Beyond Procedural Justice: A Dialogic Approach to Legitimacy in Criminal Justice', *Journal of Criminal Law and Criminology*, 102(1): 119–70.

BOTTOMS, A. E. and TANKEBE, J. (this volume, ch 4).

BOTTOMS, A. E. and P. WILES (1996) 'Crime and Insecurity in the City', in Fijnaut, C. Goethals, J., Peters, T., and WALGRAVE, L. (eds) *Changes in Society, Crime and Criminal Justice in Europe*, Vol 1: *Crime and Insecurity in the City.* Antwerp: Kluwer Law International.

BRAITHWAITE, V. (1994) 'Beyond Rokeach's Equality-Freedom Model: Two Dimensional Values in a One Dimensional World', *Journal of Social Issues* 50: 67–94.

BRAITHWAITE, V. (1998) 'The Value Balance Model of Political Evaluations', *British Journal of Psychology* 89: 223–247.

BROWN, M. (2005) '"Setting the Conditions" for Abu Ghraib: The Prison Nation Abroad', *American Quarterly* 57: 973–97.

BUBER, M. (1953) 'Genuine Dialogue and the Possibilities for Peace', cited in Kramer, K. P. with Gawlick, M. (2003) *Martin Buber's I and Thou: Practicing Living Dialogue.* New York: Paulist Press.

CREWE, B. (2009) *The Prisoner Society: Power, Adaptation and Resistance in an English Prison.* Oxford: Clarendon.

CREWE, B., LIEBLING, A., and HULLEY, S. (forthcoming) 'Heavy/Light, Absent-Present: Re-thinking the "Weight" of Imprisonment', *British Journal of Sociology.*

DRAKE, D. (2012) *Prisons, Punishment and the Pursuit of Security.* Basingstoke, Hampshire: Palgrave Macmillan.

DUNBAR, I. (1986) *A Sense of Direction.* [Report] London: Home Office.

DUNN, J. (this volume, ch 1).

ELLIOTT, C. (1999) *Locating the Energy for Change: An Introduction to Appreciative Inquiry.* Winnipeg: International Institute for Sustainable Development.

FLANAGAN, T. J. (ed) (1995) *Long-Term Imprisonment: Policy, Science and Correctional Practice.* London: Sage Publishing.

HAMM, M. (2009) 'Prison Islam in the Age of Sacred Terror', *British Journal of Criminology* 49(5): 667–85.

HAMM, M. S. (2011) 'Prisoner Radicalization and Sacred Terrorism: A Life Course Perspective', in Rosenfeld, R., Quinet, K., and Garcia, C. (eds) 'Contemporary Issues in Criminological Theory and Research: The Role of Social Institutions—Papers from the American Society of Criminology 2010 Conference'. Wadsworth: Cengage Learning, USA: 173–204.

HAMM, M. S. (2012) 'Prisoner Radicalisation in the United States', *Prison Service Journal: Special Edition, Combating Extremism and Terrorism*, 203: 4–8.

HAMM, M. S. (2013) *The Spectacular Few: Prisoner Radicalization and the Evolving Terrorist Threat.* New York, NY: New York University Press.

HEPBURN, J. R. (1985) 'The Essence of Power in Coercive Organisations: a Study of Prison Guards', *Criminology* 23(1): 145–64.

HOLLIS, M. (1998) *Trust Within Reason.* Cambridge: Cambridge University Press.

Home Office (1991) 'Prison Disturbances 1990', The Woolf Report. London: HMSO.

Honneth, A. (1995) *The Struggle for Recognition: The Moral Grammar of Social Conflicts*, Anderson, J. (trans). Cambridge MA: Polity Press.

Hough, et al. (this volume, ch 16).

Keith, B. (2006) *The Zahid Mubarek Inquiry*. London: House of Commons/The Stationery Office.

Lazarus, L. (2004) *Contrasting Prisoners' Rights: A Comparative Examination of England and Germany*. Oxford: Oxford University Press.

Liebling, A. (2000) 'Prison Officers, Policing and the Use of Discretion', *Theoretical Criminology* 4(3): 333–57.

Liebling, A. (2007) 'Why Fairness Matters in Criminal Justice', in Padfield, N. (ed) *Who To Release? Parole, Fairness and Criminal Justice*. Cullompton, Devon: Willan Publishing: 63–71.

Liebling, A. (2011) 'Moral Performance, Inhuman and Degrading Treatment, and Prison Pain', *Punishment and Society* 13(5): 530–50.

Liebling, A with Arnold, H. (2004) *Prisons and their Moral Performance: A Study of Values, Quality and Prison Life*. Oxford: Clarendon Press.

Liebling, A. with Arnold, H. (2012) 'Social Relationships Between Prisoners in a Maximum Security Prison: Violence, Faith, and the Declining Nature of Trust', *Journal of Criminal Justice* 40(5): 413–24.

Liebling, A., Arnold, H., and Straub, C. (2012) *An Exploration of Staff-Prisoner Relationships at HMP Whitemoor: Twelve Years On*. London: National Offender Management Service.

Liebling, A., Crewe, B., Hulley, S., and McLean, C. (2010) *Values, Practices and Outcomes in Public and Private Sector Corrections*: Full Research Report ESRC End of Year Award Report, RES-062-23-0212. Swindon: ESRC.

Liebling, A., Durie, L., Stiles, A., and Tait, S. (2005) 'Revisiting Prison Suicide: The Role of Fairness and Distress', in Liebling, A. and Maruna, S. (eds) *The Effects of Imprisonment*. Cullompton, Devon: Willan Publishing: 209–31.

Liebling, A., Hulley, S., and Crewe, B. (2011), 'Conceptualising and Measuring the Quality of Prison Life', in Gadd, D., Karstedt, S., and Messner, S. (eds) *The Sage Handbook of Criminological Research Methods*. London: Sage.

Liebling, A. and Lacey, N. (2012) 'Late Modernity, Crime and Criminal Justice', written for British Academy Policy Study, *Crime, Punishment and the Prison* (in preparation).

Liebling, A. and Straub, C. (2012) 'Identity Challenges and the Risks of Radicalisation in High Security Prisons', *Prison Service Journal: Special Edition, Combating Extremism and Terrorism* 203: 15–22.

Liebling, A. and Price, D. (1999) *An Exploration of Staff-Prisoner Relationships at HMP Whitemoor*. Prison Service Research Report, No. 6: HMPS, London.

Liebling, A. and Price, D. (2001) *The Prison Officer*. Leyhill: Prison Service (and Waterside Press).

Liebling, A., Price, D., and Elliot, C. (1999) 'Appreciative Inquiry and Relationships in Prison', *Punishment and Society: The International Journal of Penology* 1(1): 71–98.

Liebling, A., Price, D., and Shefer, G. (2011) *The Prison Officer* (2nd edn). Cullompton, Devon: Willan Publishing.

Loader, and Sparks, R. (this volume, ch 6).

Maruna, S. (2004) 'What's Love Got To Do With It?', *Safer Society: Journal of Crime Reduction and Community Safety* 22: 12–14.

Moos, R. H. (1975) *Evaluating Correctional and Community Settings*. Wiley: New York.

MUIR, W. K. (1977) *Police: Streetcorner Politicians*. Chicago, IL: Chicago University Press.

NAWAZ, M. (2012) *Radical: My Journey from Islamist Extremism to a Democratic Awakening*. London: Ebury Publishing, WH Allen.

National Offender Management Service Audit and Corporate Assurance (NOMS ACA) (2011) Measuring the Quality of Prison Life.

O'NEILL, O. (2009) *Perverting Trust*. Ashby Lecture delivered on 15 May 2009.

RADZINOWICZ, L. (1968) *The Regime for Long-term Prisoners in Conditions of Maximum Security*, Report of the Advisory Council on the Penal System (Radzinowicz Report). London: HMSO.

RHODES, L. (2004) *Total Confinement: Madness and Reason in the Maximum Security Prison*. Berkeley, CA: University of California Press.

RHODES, L. (2007) 'Supermax as a Technology of Power', *Social Research* 74 (2): 547–56.

RHODES, L. (2009) 'Supermax Prisons and the Trajectory of Exception', in Sarat, A. (ed). *New Perspectives on Crime and Criminal Justice: Studies in Law, Politics and Society* 47: 193–218.

SHAPLAND, J. and BOTTOMS, A. (2011), 'Reflections on Social Values, Offending and Desistance Among Young Adult Recidivists', *Punishment & Society* 13(3): 256–82.

SPARKS, R. (1994) 'Can Prisons be Legitimate? Penal Politics, Privatization, and the Timeliness of an Old Idea', *British Journal of Criminology* 34 (5, special issue): 14–28.

SPARKS, R. and BOTTOMS, A. E. (1995) 'Legitimacy and Order in Prisons', *British Journal of Sociology* 46(1): 45–62.

SPARKS, R., BOTTOMS, A.E., and HAY, W. (1996) *Prisons and the Problem of Order*. Oxford: Clarendon Press.

SYKES, G. M. (1958) *The Society of Captives: A study of a Maximum Security Prison*. Princeton, NJ: Princeton University Press.

SZTOMPKA, P. (1999) *Trust: A Sociological Theory*. Cambridge, Cambridge University Press.

TANKEBE, J. (2013) 'Viewing Things Differently: The Dimensions of Public Perceptions of Police Legitimacy', *Criminology* 51(1): 103–35.

TAYLOR, C. (1985) 'What is Human Agency?', *Human Agency and Language: Philosophical Papers I*. Cambridge: Cambridge University Press: 15–44.

TOCH, H. (1982) 'Studying and Reducing Stress', in Johnson, R. and Toch, H. (eds) *The Pains of Imprisonment*. Beverly Hills, CA: Sage Publications.

TOCH, H. (1992) *Living in Prison: The Ecology of Survival*. New York, NY: The Free Press (first published 1977).

USEEM, B. and GOLDSTONE, J. A. (2002) 'Forging Social Order and its Breakdown: Riot and Reform in US Prisons', *American Sociological Review* 67: 499–525.

VAN DEN BRINK, D. and OWEN, D. (eds) (2007) *Recognition and Power: Axel Honneth and the Tradition of Critical Social Theory*. Cambridge: Cambridge University Press.

YOUNG, J. (1999) *The Exclusive Society*. London: Sage Publications.

ZEDNER, L. (2000) 'The Pursuit of Security', in Hope, T. and Sparks, R. (eds) *Crime, Risk and Insecurity*. London: Routledge: 200–14.

11

AN UNENVIABLE TASK: HOW FEDERAL COURTS LEGITIMIZED MASS INCARCERATION

Jonathan Simon

> [T]he new structure of penal power... can also lose its legitimacy when it breaches the boundaries of what is morally justifiable or when it loses consent for what it promises to do.
>
> (Pratt 2008: 365)

> However misguided and excessive were the harsh new criminal laws and determinate sentencing systems created thirty years ago, the justifying purposes of retribution, incapacitation, and deterrence still have moral and utilitarian purchase.
>
> (Weisberg and Petersilia 2010: 131)

INTRODUCTION: THE LEGITIMACY OF MASS INCARCERATION

Mass incarceration may be dying even in its global homeland the United States, where the latest government statistics show a second consecutive year of decline in the national prison and jail population (after 37 years of consecutive growth).[1] But even if the era of boundless prison growth is ending,[2] the legitimacy of incarcerating nearly one per cent of the adult population, many of them for offences involv-

[1] Bureau of Justice Statistics, Prisoners in 2011. The overall adult incarceration rate, a combination of jail inmates and prisoners over 18 compared to the equivalent population, reached its historic peak in 2010 at 960 per hundred thousand (nearly 1 per cent) and is now down to 937 per hundred thousand.

[2] Of course it may be premature to announce the passing of such an important penal phenomenon as mass incarceration, especially since this recent population decline has corresponded to a period of particularly severe recession that has seen state budgets (the key source of funding for US imprisonment) facing historic deficits.

ing little or no risk to other people, remains largely intact. This enduring legitimacy is a very real concern. So long as the prison population decline remains primarily a product of austerity and historically low crime, it will be easy for politicians, journalists, and interests of various sorts to revitalize mass incarceration as a project, either generally, or more likely against targeted demonized groups. Moreover, the broad damage done to both American society and democracy by a generation of 'governing through crime', is unlikely to be remediated by future governments unless a significant sense of moral wrongdoing is attached to mass incarceration. In short, real progress will require not just a gradual waning of mass incarceration, but a full-fledged crisis of legitimacy. This chapter examines one very important component of the overall legitimacy of mass incarceration in the US: the broad acceptance by the federal courts that widespread imprisonment was a rational and even necessary social policy, and offers an analysis of why that legitimacy may in fact be very vulnerable.

The problem of legitimacy and prisons has become a crucial framework for studying prisons, but primarily thus far at the micro level, in how prisoners and in some studies staff as well, view the legitimacy of the power arrayed around them in prisons (see Useem and Kimball 1989; Sparks 1994; Sparks and Bottoms 1995; Sparks et al. 1996; Carrabine 2005). This chapter applies the same considerations to a phenomenon of an admittedly very different scale and temporality (which presents problems of evidence and research to which I will return), the legitimacy of a whole penal system or regime; in this case mass incarceration in the United States since the 1980s.[3] We often presume that prison systems,[4] especially in wealthy democracies, are viewed as legitimate by both the legal elites (judges, legislators, and prosecutors) and the broader publics they can be said to serve. However, at certain moments, admittedly ones that scholars of punishment and society may be no better than anyone else at predicting,[5] the legitimacy of prisons to these audiences cannot be taken for granted. At such moments though, students of penal regimes at the macro level, may be able to productively ask many of the same kinds of questions about how penal legitimacy is created and sustained that empirical scholars have asked on the terrain of specific prisons

[3] Mass incarceration in the US has been marked by three features that distinguish it from other variations of carceral punishment since the Eighth Amendment: (1) a quantum shift upward in the long running level of incarceration in a particular society and, (2) by a transformation in the logic of prison sentencing toward incarcerating whole groups or categories of offenders without much individualized consideration. See David Garland, 'Introduction: The Meaning of Mass Imprisonment' (2001b: 3), (3) by the emergence of the 'warehouse' prison, a carceral penality in which custody alone replaces traditional activities like labour, education, religious training, or psychological treatment. See also, John Irwin (2004). It is an open question whether mass incarceration as such can be found outside the US in its full form, but its elements are widely distributed globally and some other states, England and Wales and the Netherlands among them, seem close to qualifying.

[4] We need not and should not presume that prison regimes and prison systems are contiguous. To be explicit I consider mass incarceration a distinctive style or logic that the prison system of a particular political unit (and thus individual prisons within it) might be said to draw in some degree or another. California's prison system has adopted mass incarceration about as completely as a system can, and thus I have to come to treat that system (at least through 2010 when a disruption of a profound sort occurred with the *Brown v. Plata* case). Other systems in the US and outside may be said to have elements of mass incarceration.

[5] Indeed our sociological theories may incline us to overestimate the stability of penal regimes because of stability in the underlying social structures we assume must anchor those regimes. See Philip Smith (2013: 114,115–16).

about how those prisons attain and how they can lose their legitimacy.[6] Sparks and Bottoms (1995: 47) set out a broad agenda for research on legitimacy inside prisons: 'To what extent is the legitimation of the prison's order possible? On what terms and conditions might it be sought? What are the consequences for penal politics of taking this idea seriously? What is legitimacy, anyway?'

To escape the dilemma that legitimacy exists until it does not, they and others have drawn on David Beetham's distinction between the question of whether any particular public actually believes in the legitimacy of an institution (or an entire constitutional system for that matter) and whether that institution can be said to be 'justified in terms of their beliefs' (Beetham 1991: 11, quoted in Sparks and Bottoms 1995: 48). Whether or not a system has legitimacy (or loses it) in the former sense, can only be determined after the fact (when it fails) or projected through the expensive (and highly problematic) instrument of a survey. But whether that system can be said to be 'justified in terms of their beliefs' is one on which we can, at least in principle, come to some agreement, and thus, albeit most imperfectly, infer some of the risk that the legitimacy of a penal system characterized by mass incarceration has of failing.

This chapter offers a view of the core beliefs around which the legitimacy of contemporary US prisons in federal courts may be said to be justified. Courts are of course only one audience for which the legitimacy of mass incarceration is important, but they are a very important one. No other institution receives as many complaints from prisoners, nor is as well placed in the American legal system to operate as a check on the populist punitiveness so often expressed through the length and conditions of imprisonment. Unlike their state counterparts, let alone legislators and executives, federal judges (at both the trial and appellate level, as well as the Supreme Court) have life-tenure, meaning they cannot be removed from their positions except for cause and by a burdensome process. Empowered by the Constitution to decide whether treatment complained of by inmates constitutes 'cruel and unusual punishment', and to order an end to conditions that do, federal courts have since the 1960s regularly intervened in state prison operations, ordering new procedures and sometimes whole new facilities (Feeley and Rubin 1998). While this pattern of court driven reforms has much diminished during the period of mass incarceration, the federal courts have been one of the few remaining American political institutions in which the issue of the legitimacy of imprisonment has been regularly raised at all during the long war on crime.[7] Should the courts reawaken on the issue of prisons, their advantages could drive a broader public and political revisiting of mass incarceration.

We will begin by looking closely at a 1979 appellate decision, *Spain v. Procunier*,[8] whose dramatic facts about the treatment of a small group of highly feared California

[6] In retrospect we can see moments when penal systems have lost their legitimacy and a major shift in penal forms and narratives occurs. See Garland (1985); Meranze (1996).

[7] While the legitimacy of imprisonment is often presumed in the political discourse of both the US and the UK, and Europe more generally, the existence of strong human rights organs in European Community and Union government bodies means that the legitimacy of imprisonment can be questioned and conditioned in the administrative state as in courts. In the US, courts alone have had to carry this burden and because of their unique political independence, mostly the federal courts.

[8] *Spain v. Procunier*, 600 F 2d 189, 193 (CA9 1979).

prisoners, cast prisoners nationwide and the tasks of imprisonment in a distinctive and alarming way; one that would later be used by the Supreme Court to anchor an extreme deference by courts toward prison managers. The *Spain* opinion offers a formula (the *Spain* formula hereinafter) which the Supreme Court would restate, is one that provides in extreme clarity the key elements behind the legitimacy of mass incarceration. At the end of the chapter we will look closely at a much more recent case, one from the Supreme Court, *Brown v. Plata*,[9] where equally dramatic facts, but this time about the entire California prison system's health care delivery system, offers the most significant opportunity in decades to recast the judicial understanding of contemporary prisons and place the legitimacy of mass incarceration squarely in question.

There are two important features of these cases that should be noted before we examine them more closely: one about the author of the opinions, and one about the penal system in which the two cases both arose.

First (and from a realist perspective none is more important), the jurist who wrote these texts with more than 30 years between them, Anthony Kennedy, now Justice Anthony Kennedy of the United States Supreme Court, has become the most important contemporary justice on the Supreme Court. Appointed by President Reagan as a reliable conservative with a moderate enough track record to get confirmed after Robert Bork, Kennedy has become the 'swing vote' on many issues. Moreover, in ways already apparent in his *Spain* opinion, as a member of the intermediate Justice Kennedy has long been particularly motivated by the idea of individual human dignity, a value that has been before and is becoming once again central to the meaning of the Eighth Amendment. If *Spain* has become a talisman expressing a confidence in prison no longer anchored in the facts, Justice Kennedy has unique access to the background presumptions that undergird that formula. Now far more clearly aware of the degrading effects of mass incarceration on prisoners and prison conditions, Justice Kennedy is in a unique position to set limits on populist penal policies when they conflict with regard for fundamental human dignity.[10]

Second, the cases in which the legal legitimacy of mass incarceration has been etched arise in California, once the most progressive and today perhaps the most degraded in the nation, and thus an extreme but revealing case of the larger burden of mass incarceration for the legitimacy of American government. Yet in these cases, California's often lurid factual circumstances are codified into national law where they have until recently encased mass incarceration policies in an armour of legitimacy. Furthermore, the broad significance that Justice Kennedy gave to dignity in interpreting the Eighth Amendment may have consequences for states that currently take comfort in being less overcrowded or medically unsound than California has been.

[9] 131 S.Ct. 1910 (2011) holding that chronic overcrowding prevented existing structural injunctions requiring extensive reforms of health care delivery in prisons from being accomplished and requiring the state to reduce the overall level of overcrowding to under 137 per cent of capacity within two years.

[10] Kennedy wrote the opinion striking down Life Without Parole (LWOP) sentences for juvenile non-homicide cases in *Graham v. Florida* (2010) 560 US 48 (2010) [130 S Ct 2011, No. 08-7412] and affirmed a lower court population reduction order against California's massively overcrowded prisons in *Brown v. Plata* (2011) 563 US ____ (2011), but he also just authored the opinion upholding routine body cavity searches in jail even for pre-trial detainees held on non-violent or drug crimes without particularized suspicion; *Florence v. Board of Chosen Freeholders of the County of Burlington*, 566 US ___ (2012), 132 S.Ct. 1510, No. 10-945.

A FORMULA TO LEGITIMIZE MASS INCARCERATION: *SPAIN V. PROCUNIER*

There are many obstacles to prisoners proceeding in US federal courts, all of which have gotten more difficult over time,[11] but the core challenge to any prisoner complaint, and thus the place where the primary legitimacy conditions of power or authority inside prisons is framed most clearly is the deference that courts are said to 'owe' prison administrators. During the era when federal courts were assertively reforming state prison systems, the prevailing tests for an Eighth Amendment violation was objective: Does the treatment of the prisoner, or the conditions in which they are being held, constitute 'cruel and unusual punishment?' This remained the case for prison condition cases until 1991 when the Supreme Court decided *Wilson v. Seiter*. In an opinion for a plurality of the Court, Justice Scalia dismissed the inmates' panoply of objective claims by holding that the court below had failed to consider whether the defendants acted intentionally, or with some culpable degree of awareness, creating, in effect, a criminal law like *mens rea* for establishing the violation of a civil right.

Three years later in *Farmer v. Brennan*, the Court made things worse by establishing by a clear majority vote, 'deliberate indifference', as required for any finding of Eighth Amendment violation based on treatment or conditions. Thus, even if prison officials were negligent in allowing prison conditions to degrade, or were unable to secure the funds to fix problems of which they were indeed aware, they would be insulated from a finding of constitutional violation. In explaining this extraordinary deference to prison officials, Justice Souter's majority opinion offered a talismanic expression of this deference:

> A prison official's duty under the Eighth Amendment is to ensure 'reasonable safety' . . . a standard that incorporates due regard for prison officials' '*unenviable task of keeping dangerous men in safe custody under humane conditions*', . . . Whether one puts it in terms of duty or deliberate indifference, prison officials who act reasonably cannot be found liable under the Cruel and Unusual Punishments Clause.[12]

The core language in this central bulwark against prisoner lawsuits is taken directly from Judge Kennedy's opinion in *Spain v. Procunier*. The last 13 words form a pithy rationale that has been quoted approvingly by federal courts in over 85 cases to grant to prison officials, in effect, immunity from violating the expectations of human dignity in prisons. *Spain v. Procunier* provides us, in eloquent brevity, with the core conditions in the United States for the legitimation of imprisonment in the era of mass incarceration.

Incorporating the language of current Supreme Court justices from cases decided while they sat on a lower court is standard practice in both briefs and in opinion writing. In upgrading Judge Kennedy's explanatory prose to constitutional significance,

[11] The Prison Litigation Reform Act of 1996 set limits to the kinds of relief that courts could grant federal prisoners. Supreme Court doctrine across a range of issues made establishing liability more difficult as well.

[12] *Spain v. Procunier*, 600 F 2d 189, 193 (CA9 1979); *Farmer v. Brennan*, 511 US 825, 845 (emphasis added).

Justice Souter may well have helped win Justice Kennedy's vote for the majority, but he also harnessed the simple but powerful clarity of its moral vision (i.e. prisons are moral when they have to keep dangerous men safe under humane conditions, and that is hard and difficult work). In this light especially, it is important to note the differences between the way this language was deployed in the two cases (*Spain* and *Farmer v. Brennan*) both textually and in the broader context.

Here is the way it appeared in full in the introductory paragraphs of an opinion largely upholding a district court's findings against state defendants in a prison case:

> The federal courts should use great restraint before issuing orders based on the finding that the state has followed unlawful procedures in discharging the unenviable task of keeping dangerous men in safe custody under humane conditions. *This said, it must also be remembered that enforcement of the Eighth Amendment is not always consistent with allowing complete deference to all administrative determinations by prison officials.* Whatever rights one may lose at the prison gates... the full protections of the Eighth Amendment most certainly remain in force. The whole point of the Amendment is to protect persons convicted of crimes. Eighth Amendment protections are not forfeited by one's prior acts. Mechanical deference to the findings of state prison officials in the context of the Eighth Amendment would reduce that provision to a nullity in precisely the context where it is most necessary. The ultimate duty of the federal court to order that conditions of state confinement be altered where necessary to eliminate cruel and unusual punishments is well established.[13]

For then Judge Kennedy, recognition of the unenviable task of state employees in operating prisons is only a nod before emphasizing that the Constitution requires courts to intervene despite their respect for that task. Moreover, following precedent in the Ninth Circuit, and in much of the country at that time, Judge Kennedy examined only the objective conditions, and not evidence of culpable intentions in upholding most of the district court's findings against the state.[14]

A second striking factor about *Spain v. Procunier* is that its protagonist, California prisoner Johnny Spain, was a leader of the revolutionary Black Panther party in California prisons, and a key participant in the single most violent prison incident in California correctional history; the 21 August 1971 takeover of San Quentin prison's 'Adjustment Center' led by fellow Black Panther George Jackson. At Attica a few weeks later false reports of the deliberate killing of prison officers helped generate a false social memory that also defamed prisoners as subhuman and helped underscore the necessity of mass incarceration to protect civilization (Thompson 2010: 704, 708). What happened that day remains deeply disputed despite being the subject of the most complicated criminal and civil litigation in the state's history, but it set the character of California's penal system ever since and, along with Attica, arguably helped remake the American penal imaginary. Spain, according to the testimony presented against him in court, was a chief deputy to Jackson, then a celebrated and vilified radical prisoner leader and author, who by most accounts initiated the takeover and freed

[13] *Spain v. Procunier*, 600 F 2d 189 at 193–4 (emphasis added).

[14] *Spain v. Procunier*, 600 F 2d 189 at 197.

Spain and the other prisoners. The facts are important to understanding the *Spain* formula as it has been used to pacify the American judiciary. I quote from the most complete version circulated in American case law, one from another case involving Spain (this time his criminal appeal) a few years later:

> On August 21, 1971, there was an outburst of deadly violence at the Adjustment Center [San Quentin's disciplinary space for isolating the most troubling or vulnerable prisoners under closer supervision]. George Jackson, also a member of the Black Panther Party, returned to the Adjustment Center after meeting with his lawyer, Stephen Bingham. When guards found a bullet clip on Jackson, Jackson removed a gun from under his wig and forced one of the guards present to open the cells of other prisoners. Many of the prisoners, including Spain, emerged from their cells. There was testimony that Spain played a role in binding guards and placing them in the cells where they subsequently were assaulted. He was seen approaching the guards with an earphone cord in his hands. The cord was of the type used to bind the guards. There also was testimony that at one point he held Jackson's gun, which was used to murder two of the guards.
>
> When an alarm was sounded, Jackson and Spain fled from the Adjustment Center, Jackson with a gun in his hand and Spain with some keys. Jackson was shot by guards and was killed instantly. Spain dove into some bushes where he was found hiding. When order was restored the aftermath of the violence was revealed: one officer had bled to death from a neck wound; two had been shot to death in the head; three others had their throats slashed, but survived; and two prisoners died of similar wounds. The Director of Corrections called the incident the worst in her eight years as Director.[15]

The facts of the Adjustment Center takeover, now invisible to even most legal readers of the *Spain* formula, were used in *Farmer v. Brennan* to establish a baseline of violence around which the dangerousness of prisoners and the security needs of prison regimes has been set. When federal courts quote the *Spain* formula about the 'unenviable task of keeping dangerous men', they are invoking George Jackson's ghost and memories of the most violent moments of recent American prison history. Just as importantly when they talk about holding such dangerous men 'safely' they are talking about the kinds of procedures that a traumatized California correctional staff felt necessary to impose on the most feared convicts in the system.

There is irony but also a real measure of how much degradation of prisoners this standard was prepared to tolerate in the facts of *Farmer v. Brennan* itself. Dee Farmer was an out, visible transsexual (an anatomical male living and presenting as a female), and quite at great risk from rape. Yet when federal authorities transferred him from the jail to a federal prison, they placed him in the general population. Farmer was raped and contracted HIV, an incurable chronic illness that untreated can become the fatal disease known as AIDS. The Supreme Court rejected the lower courts Eighth Amendment violation holding that the evidence must provide that the defendants were 'deliberately indifferent' regardless of how florid the facts. But whether it requires fact finding to determine whether federal authorities were 'deliberately indifferent' to

[15] *Spain v. Rushen*, 883 F 2d 712 (Ninth Circuit Court of Appeals (Cal), 1989).

Farmer's right to be treated like a human being or whether it is obvious, the important point is that Dee Farmer, incarcerated for credit card fraud, and thus no risk to any person, but in fact quite clearly at risk of terrible violence, is placed by the Supreme Court in the subject position of the 'dangerous men'.

There is a third striking feature of *Spain v. Procunier* that is especially ironic given its status as a foundation for an extremely deferential posture toward prison managers. Despite the fact that Johnny Spain was perhaps the most feared convict in California by prison officials and officers, the *Spain* decision upheld the most substantial parts of the district courts findings of Eighth Amendment violations by the state defendants and returned others for re-evaluation. Utilizing a lower threshold than it would be used to justify,[16] the *Spain* opinion was a ringing endorsement of the need for judicial oversight of the risk assessment of prison officials. In his final paragraph, Kennedy quoted from Justice William Brennan's powerful concurrence in *Furman v. George,* the Supreme Court's fragmented 1972 ruling striking down the death penalty as then practised in the United States:

> Underlying the Eighth Amendment is a fundamental premise that prisoners are not to be treated as less than human beings. Furman v. Georgia, 408 U.S. 238, 271-73, 92 S.Ct. 2726, 33 L.Ed.2d 346 (1972) (Brennan, J. concurring). The Amendment is phrased in general terms rather than specific ones so that while the underlying principle remains constant in its essentials, the precise standards by which we measure compliance with it do not... It follows that when confronting the question whether penal confinement in all its dimensions is consistent with the constitutional rule, the court's judgment must be informed by current and enlightened scientific opinion as to the conditions necessary to insure good physical and mental health for prisoners.[17]

By quoting Brennan, Judge Kennedy was signaling the depth of his interest in dignity as a constitutional value, and the degree to which it would carry him beyond the conventional left/right divide of constitutional politics in the 1980s.[18] In recent years the significance of dignity for Justice Kennedy in the context of criminal punishment has become apparent. In addition to *Brown v. Plata*, which will be discussed further, Kennedy has written majority opinions striking down the death penalty for juveniles and life without parole sentences for juveniles in non-homicide cases. Yet despite the emphasis on protecting the dignity of prisoners in *Spain v. Procunier*, the Supreme Court borrowed its formula to insulate prison officials in a case where the threat to the dignity of the prisoner was quite clear.

[16] Kennedy notes that 'wrongful intent' is not a necessary element on the part of prison officials to constitute cruel and unusual punishment. *Spain v. Procunier*, 600 F 2d 189, 200.

[17] *Spain v. Procunier*, 600 F 2d 189.

[18] At the time of Kennedy's nomination to the Supreme Court by President Reagan in 1987 he was considered a deeply conservative thinker, although more moderate than more controversial figures like Robert Bork. However, this strong language about prisoner's rights and citation to one of the most widely admired opinions of perhaps the most important liberal Supreme Court justice of the twentieth century may have been a telling early signal that he would emerge at the very centre of the Court. It is also noteworthy that Brennan's opinion is distinctive for its use of dignity language to explain the unconstitutionality of capital punishment; a minority view then even among the justices that voted to strike down existing capital laws, but one that anticipates the Human Rights approach to capital punishment in Europe.

DECODING THE *SPAIN* FORMULA

Time has now faded the collective memory of 21 August 1971, but the *Spain* formula transformed the very real but extraordinary violence of that day in California penal and political history into a timeless icon in our national legal consciousness and penal imaginary reflecting on ordinary prisoners in routine settings. Operating as a kind of 'talisman', that formula has helped pacify the federal judiciary during a period of time, the mid-1990s through the end of the past decade, when the project of mass incarceration was reaching its political high water mark and prisons were becoming markedly harsher environments. Each element of the *Spain* formula identifies a crucial anchor point for the legitimacy of mass incarceration. The function of a talisman is to lift meanings beyond the historical and to thus stabilize them against contradiction with changing social conditions. Only by bringing these elements back into a historically informed consciousness can the 'spell' be broken and the talisman restored to a piece of ordinary legal doctrine. With the real history of 21 August 1971 and the reaction to it in mind, we examine each of them in turn.

1. '... KEEPING DANGEROUS MEN ...'

As the facts of *Spain* remind us, the early 1970s was not only a period of declining confidence in the rehabilitative penology that had dominated state penal policies from the end of World War II, but also a high point of political violence in the US, both in prisons and outside. Violent protests and police violence against student protesters at Berkeley (1969) and Kent State University in Ohio (1970) seemed right in line with the Adjustment Center takeover and Attica. For many Americans, this politicized violence inside and outside the prison was assimilated to the overall growth of the murder threat, which had in fact more than doubled.

But while the distinctive violence of men like George Jackson and Johnny Spain (whether fairly attributed or not) was clear to the correctional officers and managers whose chaining of the 'San Quentin Six' would lead to the *Spain* case, the *Spain* formula transforms this into a categoric identification of all prisoners as dangerous (or potentially dangerous). This is not a regime of individualized knowledge and diagnosis that is prepared to tie the legitimacy of incarceration to diagnostic expertise and the individual danger posed by the prisoner. Instead it is the fact of felony that triggers a global assignment to a group whose presumed danger is defined by its most extreme examples. Much of the penal architecture and routine of mass incarceration to follow would be informed by this presumption and only make sense in light of it (like the massive Secure Housing Units in California that hold prisoners identified as gang members in more or less permanent isolation) (Reiter 2012).

The reasons for political violence in prisons in the 1970s are beyond the scope of our present enquiry, but whatever its meaning, as a baseline for the future of American incarceration it turned out to be a highly misleading moment of violence both in quantity and in quality. That is what the *Spain* formula helped turn it into however. The 1970s would resolve the direction of penal change in the US for the next three decades. The attitudes held by key players in shaping the penal field, whether prison officers, urban professionals, or the media would become frozen in time as a mass institutional expansion unfolded (see Page 2011; Garland 2001a).

2. '...IN SAFE CUSTODY...'

If keeping dangerous men in safe custody sounds commonsensical and reassuring, *Spain v. Procunier* is once again a revealing reminder of the extreme baselines of danger and security that California in this period set for courts. Johnny Spain and other prisoners involved in the 21 August 1971 events (known in the argot of the time as the 'San Quentin Six') were held from before their trial through the time of the civil litigation, more than four years, under conditions of extreme control. The hostage taking and attempted escape of that day had taken place in the Adjustment Center (AC), a part of San Quentin already devoted to the high security management of the most troublesome prisoners; a kind of supermax before there was a supermax (Shalev 2009).[19] Those who survived the onslaught launched within the prison against the AC takeover were returned to the same sector for the duration of their trials, the longest in California history. It was these conditions of confinement and treatment that was the subject of the civil rights lawsuit and the appeal taken in *Spain v. Procunier*:

> During their 4½ years of confinement in the AC... whether their destinations were in the prison or outside it, the plaintiffs were not allowed to leave the AC unless they were restrained by all of these devices: handcuffs; a waist chain or belt to which the cuffs were attached by a chain, hands in front of the prisoner; leg manacles, consisting of loops around each ankle connected by a chain; and a neck chain, consisting of a chain attached to the back of the waist chain and extending over one shoulder, across the neck, over the other shoulder and down the back. The neck chain could be pulled from the back to restrain or control a prisoner. Pain and sores resulted from the shackles being attached too tightly. While the prisoners remained outside of the AC, these restraining devices, including a neck chain, remained fastened for all out-of-cell movements and throughout visits with family, friends, or counsel, but, apparently, not during court proceedings.[20]

These security tactics would ultimately be abandoned by the state (in part because of the court orders in the *Spain* case), but only to be replaced by a larger scale and more systematic form of the same heightened level of fear and tolerance for violence and degradation against prisoners. During California's huge prison building surge in the mid-1980s California prison managers chose to build a supersized (1,000 bed capacity) supermax facility (Secured Housing Unit or SHU in California) as part of the new Pelican Bay State Prison complex, and to repurpose an existing 1,000 bed facility at Corcoran State Prison into a SHU unit at a time when they could have used those dollars to build any kind of prison they wanted to. Interviewed by criminologist Keramet

[19] Both involve near total isolation of presumably recalcitrant inmates, with the main difference being that supermax prisons are purpose built for such function and often hold many more prisoners for much longer than traditional disciplinary units.

[20] *Spain v. Procunier*, 600 F 2d 189, 196 (1979).

Reiter (2012: 106) more than two decades later these managers had no problem remembering the reason why they needed so many of the now controversial isolation units: 'we had eleven staff members murdered in 1971'.

As a whole, the taking of the AC and the tactics deployed afterwards inscribe an extraordinary level of danger and security in the fabric of the prison. When it comes to the general public this has meant a strong presumption that incarceration is the only really effective way to neutralize danger, and that community corrections, once highly touted, are largely unreliable for any purpose other than to extend the opportunity to incarcerate prisoners (Simon 2012b). It has also meant laws that channel discretion over the length of imprisonment to prosecutors, exemplified in the extreme by California's Three-Strikes Law (Zimring et al. 2003).

The facts of *Spain v. Procunier* are a window into the historically experienced crime fears in which many of the public policies that created and maintained mass incarceration were laid down. These emotions are forgotten, even to people who have lived through it, but provide an important clue as to why it is so hard to replace these policies with better and cheaper ways to accomplish the crime control goals of penal law. These form the implicit baseline against which alternatives to incarceration, like probation, even bulked up with electronic monitoring and quick sanctions, continue to seem inherently insufficient to many policy makers despite good evidence supporting them (Kleiman 2010).

3. '... UNDER HUMANE CONDITIONS ...'

Mass incarceration began in the late 1970s amidst a national wave of prison reform lawsuits that had transformed the Eighth Amendment's prohibition on 'cruel and unusual' punishments into an effective tool for prison reforms. Federal courts constitutionalized demands for adequate food, shelter, medical care, and equal access to those forms of rehabilitation or training made available (Feeley and Rubin 1998).[21] As prison populations began their nationwide upward pattern in the early 1980s, many states were either in the midst of prison construction required by courts enforcing modern correctional standards under the Eighth Amendment, or were considered to be compliant with those modern correctional standards aimed at sustaining a rehabilitation oriented prison regime.[22] Thus, as the era of mass incarceration began, judges easily assumed that state prisons either were or would soon be indeed decent and humane places to incapacitate the 'dangerous' while probably also rehabilitating them (a goal which remained part of the explicit promise of American corrections

[21] Courts were motivated by the contrast they discovered between mostly southern prison systems long accustomed to operating on the nineteenth-century basis of prison as involuntary servitude and the premises of modern correctionalism reflected in the Federal Bureau of Prisons and by national correctional accreditation agencies. As a result many of the most punitive states were pushed by judicial decrees to substantially improve the physical conditions and expanded their prison systems in the 1980s. Indeed, mass incarceration in many states was conditioned on satisfying court demands for more modern prisons. For the case of Arizona see, Lynch (2009).

[22] Feeley and Rubin (1998), noting that federal courts were facilitated in applying the Eighth Amendment to prison conditions by the apparent consensus on rehabilitation as the modern rationale for imprisonment and the federal government's lead in this respect.

even during the era of mass incarceration). Indeed in *Spain v. Procunier* the Court, otherwise quite critical of the treatment of the San Quentin Six, noted that the basic conditions of San Quentin prison where the complaining prisoners were held were decent and that their essential human needs had been satisfactorily met:

> The living conditions, sanitary facilities, and daily routine in the AC were described in detail by Judge Zirpoli. He concluded there was no serious deficiency concerning the physical structure and that medical, nutritional, and sanitary provisions for the prisoners were adequate. The plaintiffs did not appeal these findings relating to the AC.[23]

Spain, after all, dealt with California in the mid-1970s when it was still considered one of the most progressive penal systems in the world and at or near its lowest population. The court makes a point of revisiting this in its conclusion, going out of its way to suggest that the prison was mostly humane and only the conditions in the AC were problematic:

> In this case most of the prison practices challenged by the prisoners including provisions for food, medical care, and physical facilities, withstood challenge. [Omitting cites to numerous cases in which poor conditions were found in other states.] In part because these basic programs were sound, the trial court was in a position to properly focus its inquiry on certain specific aspects of the treatment in the adjustment center.[24]

These baseline presumptions about prison conditions, combined with the fact that the prisoners themselves were all healthy adults and facing terms that even at the extreme (in Johnny Spain's case 'life in prison'), under prevailing expectations of the late 1970s virtually assured release within a decade, made it easy to take the decency and humanity of prison conditions for granted.

BROWN V. PLATA: DELEGITIMIZING MASS INCARCERATION

Those who have sought to argue against mass incarceration policies over the past several decades, whether conscious of it or not, have been faced with a strong negative implicit bias shared by judges and other legal and political elites, the content of which is likely quite similar to the elements made explicit in the *Spain* formula. The factual context to all of these presumptions has, however, changed substantially, although in ways still largely invisible to legal elites as well as the public. With all the attention to our nationwide prison building boom during the 1980s and 1990s, both supporters and critics of mass incarceration alike often assumed that a growing number of prisoners were being incarcerated in modern facilities designed to deliver modern correctional standards, and that this portion would continue to go up even as the overall numbers in prison also grew. The initial growth of short prison sentences, associated with the war on drugs, helped mask the significant role that prolonged prison sen-

[23] *Spain v. Procunier*, 600 F 2d 189, at 192.

[24] *Spain v. Procunier*, 600 F 2d 189, at 200.

tences would have on the age of the prison population and on the numbers of prisoners doing time with chronic illnesses.

Only in the early years of the new century, as the nationwide crime decline cut the flow of first time felons to prisons and prison populations became more concentrated with prisoners on long sentences and those repeat players cycling back through prison on parole or probation violations, did the depth of the humanitarian challenge facing prisons begin to be visible, as for the first time, to courts and criminologists (Fleury-Steiner and Crowder 2008). The fact that mass incarceration policies are now rapidly moving from being unchallengeable to indefensible is testament to far more than the fiscal context that has made the costs of them politically harder to sell, or the drop in violent crime in most parts of the country (which have now stayed down or at least not gone up for nearly 20 years across good economic periods and bad), but rather the way all three of the core presumptions of the *Spain* formula have eroded substantially.

These new realities were made highly visible by the Supreme Court's 2011 decision in *Brown v. Plata*, upholding a massive prison population reduction order in California to assure better health care delivery.[25] The case was a consolidation of two major prison condition class actions. One had established that California's lack of adequate mental health care violated the Eighth Amendment.[26] A second established that California's lack of adequate medical care violated the Eighth Amendment.[27] The two cases were joined in 2009 on the theory that California's decade long period of hyper overcrowding (over 200 per cent of design capacity for over a decade) had made remedying the violations in the two cases impossible, and requesting the court to order California to reduce its population accordingly. A great deal of the focus of the remarkable three-judge court's order and opinion, issued in 2009 and upheld in totality by the close but deep Supreme Court majority, was devoted to showing that California's use of imprisonment did not in many cases add to public safety and that public safety could be improved by reducing reliance on prison. Much of the more than 200-page opinion was given over to outlining current criminological consensus on who does not need to be in prison.

In his majority opinion in *Brown v. Plata*, Justice Kennedy came full circle with *Spain v. Procunier*. In 1979 he had recognized the excessive security procedures of the AC as a contrast with the modern correctional standards and even progressive nature of California's overall prison system. In 2011, considering a challenge to prison health care involving every prisoner in California's massively extended prison that grew by more than 750 per cent in absolute numbers since 1977. Moved by the litigation's well documented evidence of prisoners suffering and dying from all manner of treatable medical conditions despite over a decade of court orders demanding remedies, Justice Kennedy did not shrink from using the word 'torture' to describe the effects of prison mismanagement on prisoners' bodies.

[25] *Brown v. Plata*, No. 09-1233.

[26] *Coleman v. Wilson*, 912 F Supp 1282 (E D Cal 1995) <http://rbgg.com/wp-content/uploads/Coleman-v-Wilson-912-F-Supp-1282-ED-Cal-1995.pdf> accessed 24 July 2013.

[27] *Plata v. Davis*, (N D Cal 2002, stipulated agreement) <http://www.clearinghouse.net/chDocs/public/PC-CA-0018-0005.pdf> accessed 24 July 2013.

In words that echo his conclusion in 1979's *Spain v. Procunier*, Justice Kennedy wrote in 2011:

> Prisoners retain the essence of human dignity inherent in all persons. Respect for that dignity animates the Eighth Amendment prohibition against cruel and unusual punishment. 'The basic concept underlying the Eighth Amendment is nothing less than the dignity of man.'[28]

Using strong, even harsh language, Justice Kennedy explicitly invoked a comparison between depriving prisoners of medical care and the practice of torture, and wrote that:

> Just as a prisoner may starve if not fed, he or she may suffer or die if not provided adequate medical care. A prison that deprives prisoners of basic sustenance, including adequate medical care, is incompatible with the concept of human dignity and has no place in civilized society.

Together these opening paragraphs make *Brown v. Plata* the strongest doctrinal case for prisoners' rights in decades (if not ever). In the intervening years, Justice Kennedy has become associated with a robust reading of dignity (Knowles 2009),[29] which is clearly in dialogue with the strong use of dignity by human rights courts like the European Court of Human Rights, as well as national courts like those of Germany, South Africa, and Israel.

In 2003, in a speech before the American Bar Association, and taking explicit note of the fact that he was in California giving the speech, Justice Kennedy drew national headlines with critical comments about American prisons rarely voiced by any US political leader:

> In California, even as we meet, this State alone keeps over 160,000 persons behind bars. In countries such as England, Italy, France, and Germany, the incarceration rate is about 1 in 1,000 persons. In the United States it is about 1 in 143 . . .[30]
>
> We must confront another reality. Nationwide, more than 40 percent of the prison population consists of African-American inmates. About 10 percent of African-American men in their mid-to-late 20s are behind bars. In some cities more than 50 percent of young African-American men are under the supervision of the criminal justice system.

Even more remarkably and largely unnoticed by the media at the time, Kennedy adverted in alarming terms to the qualitative aspects of American prisons, and the qualitative severity of its prison sentences. Kennedy cited legal scholar James Whitman's then recently published *Harsh Justice* (2003), a book that explicitly compares Europe and American prisons and finds American prisons stand out the degree to which they purposely degrade prisoners, something forbidden by human rights norms in Europe:

[28] *Brown v. Plata*, 131 S Ct 1910, 1928.

[29] Libertarians have read Justice Kennedy to embrace primarily a conservative/libertarian view that the state should never deprive you of your dignity, but it is far from clear that his strong reading of dignity is limited to a negative liberty view. In a penal setting, of course, the state actor is built in.

[30] <http://www.abanow.org/2003/08/speech-by-justice-anthony-kennedy-at-aba-annual-meeting/> accessed 24 July 2013.

> Professor Whitman concludes that the goal of the American corrections system is to degrade and demean the prisoner. That is a grave and serious charge. A purpose to degrade or demean individuals is not acceptable in a society founded on respect for the inalienable rights of the people. No public official should echo the sentiments of the Arizona sheriff who once said with great pride that he 'runs a very bad jail'.

Justice Kennedy implicitly invoked the role that the judiciary and legal system play in legitimizing mass incarceration when he turned to his lawyer audience and noted:

> It is no defense if our current prison system is more the product of neglect than of purpose. Out of sight, out of mind is an unacceptable excuse for a prison system that incarcerates over two million human beings in the United States. To that end, I hope it is not presumptuous of me to suggest that the American Bar Association should ask its President and the President-elect to instruct the appropriate committees to study these matters, and to help start a new public discussion about the prison system. It is the duty of the American people to begin that discussion at once.
>
> A decent and free society, founded in respect for the individual, ought not to run a system with a sign at the entrance for inmates saying, 'Abandon Hope, All Ye Who Enter Here'.[31]

But if Kennedy hoped his speech would jump start discussions among the legal and political elite he would be disappointed. He himself seemed unready to directly challenge mass incarceration, writing a majority opinion that very year upholding California's Three-Strikes law and seemingly endorsing California's extreme version of penal incapacitation.[32] In recent years Justice Kennedy has seemed increasingly ready to act through the Constitution to address the threat that American penal practices pose to human dignity. *Brown v. Plata* provided him with a fundamental test: would he endorse further judicial deference in the face of a state whose extreme incapacitation policies he had recently upheld, but whose continued inability to create constitutionally adequate health care in its prisons now confronted the court with powerful documented evidence of unnecessarily human suffering and death?

Importantly, Justice Kennedy upheld the three-judge court's order to reduce California's prison population by some 40,000 prisoners even in the face of the statutory requirement that the effect on public safety be given great weight. This order, which Justice Scalia in dissent called 'the most radical injunction issued by a court in our Nation's history', directly challenged the incapacitative logic behind mass incarceration; that prison, and only prison can provide public safety against criminals.[33] The population reduction plan was accepted as not only necessary to assure dignified conditions in prison, but compatible with maintaining or even improving public safety.

Brown v. Plata is an important victory for prisoners' rights, one that offers doctrinal hope of a much expanded Eighth Amendment protection against degrading conditions in prisons and an injunction that alone may be responsible for reversing mass incarceration in California. But read against the history of the *Spain* formula, we should also see in it an important step toward challenging the strong presumption of

[31] <http://www.abanow.org/2003/08/speech-by-justice-anthony-kennedy-at-aba-annual-meeting/> accessed 24 July 2013.

[32] *Ewing v. California*, 538 US 11 (2003).

[33] *Brown v. Plata*, 131 S.Ct. 1910, 1950.

legitimacy for mass incarceration policies that federal courts have largely accepted since *Farmer v. Brennan* created near immunity for states to ignore prison conditions. The picture of mass incarceration in *Brown* is one that speaks to each element of the *Spain* formula.

FROM DANGEROUS MEN TO EN-DANGERED MEN

Mass incarceration depends on the perception of a high and largely unchanging risk of crime posed by the average prisoner. A decade and a half of declining crime across the United States has now placed in question a generation of 'career criminal' criminological theories and anti-recidivism laws premised on an unchangeable risk. While some would claim mass incarceration is itself a cause of this crime decline, Franklin Zimring's (2007, 2011) close studies of the crime decline, and in particular New York City, the leading crime decline example in the world, documents that policing, not prison, seems to be the leading source of reduced crime. As policing improved in New York, the recidivism rate of prisoners went down significantly even as prison populations in New York were shrinking.

The presumptive dangerousness of prisoners is also being eroded by the increasing visibility of the demographic transformation of prisons that have accumulated an increasingly geriatric and chronically ill population. Judges in the era of *Spain v. Procunier* could assume that the overwhelming majority of prisoners were young men in the bloom of vigour and health. The portrait of prisoner health and prison health care documented for the Supreme Court is very different, with largely middle-aged men experiencing the degenerative injuries and the slow devastation of chronic illness like diabetes and high blood pressure in a prison system systematically unresponsive to medical needs. Prisoners are considered 'geriatric' by medical experts from age 55 because of the generally poor health in prisons. The number of geriatric prisoners has increased over 350 per cent in California in the past decade, and by 2030 one-third of state prison inmates will be geriatric (Williams et al. 2006). Studies have estimated that as many as 40 per cent of state prison inmates suffer from a chronic illness, including mental illness (Wilper et al. 2009).

The fact that many prisoners appear vulnerable and all too human is coalescing with a rebirth of criminological research emphasizing the role of life course events in mediating criminal offending, as well as studies of desistence from crime that emphasize opportunities for change. All of these point to a new understanding of prisoners as dynamic complex individual whose risks to the public and costs to incarcerate can change markedly over time. For elites this is clearly beginning to challenge the commitment to the 'new penology' of the 1990s with its pessimism about offenders and endorsement of long-term incapacitation strategies (Feeley and Simon 1992). To what extent that can also begin to change the popular penal imaginary is an open question.

UNSAFE CUSTODY

If the crime decline since the 1990s and the ageing of the prison population is beginning to make prisoners less dangerous, recent experience is also eroding confidence in penal incapacitation as a reliable means to protect public safety. Renewed attention to the fact that most state prison inmates are released with little in the way of planning or programming to aide with creating a law abiding life outside of prison has cast into doubt the assumption that warehousing prisoners is an unqualified gain for public safety. What is now called 'reentry' has become a gaping hole in the mass incarceration security model. The problem of prisoners with mental illness is an especially acute example of this since, for many of them, criminal behaviour is highly related to the lack of treatment both in prison and in the community.

Brown v. Plata did not order California to rely more on parole and probation, but the realignment plan, which the state has put in place to comply with the overcrowding limits the Court did endorse, has in fact re-emphasized sanctions. California political leaders have thus far said little about whether they actually endorse this as a sound public safety strategy, preferring to let the courts take the blame if there is a surge of violent crime. However the special three-judge court whose population reduction order was upheld in *Brown v. Plata* undertook hearings on the public safety issue and devoted much of its nearly 200-page opinion to summarizing the criminological evidence that mass incarceration in California was counterproductive to public safety, and that many California prisoners would pose less of a risk if they did frequently return to prison.[34]

While *Brown v. Plata* is quite limited in its direct legal impact, the questions it raises about the necessity of security may have wider reach if it liberates other courts to raise similar enquiries. The supermax prisons, total isolation units designed to help states manage the concentrations of criminal dangerousness in prisons created by mass incarceration premises and specifically to combat the alarming threat groups exemplified by the Black Panthers in the age of *Spain v. Procunier*, have come under increasingly negative scrutiny. In addition to questions about the cruelty of a regime that predictably makes some of its prisoners mentally ill, there are increasing doubts about the level of security these prisons provide.[35]

INHUMANE CONDITIONS

At the dawn of mass incarceration, courts considered prisons as generally progressive and well managed institutions organized to deliver rehabilitative services to prisoners held in safe and decent conditions. Today the courts and the public are confronting the fact that professional correctional standards and rehabilitative penology no longer assure a commitment to decent conditions. Chronic overcrowding, and the tendency of mass incarceration to select people with chronic illness (including mental illness) create the risk of humanitarian disaster in many state systems, as demonstrated by

[34] *Coleman v. Schwarzenegger*; *Plata v. Schwarzenegger*, Three-Judge Court, No. CIV S-90-0520 LKK JFM P, Opinion and Order, 4 August 2009, 6.

[35] Erica Goode, 'Fighting a drawn-out battle against solitary confinement', *The New York Times*, 30 March 2012, <http://www.nytimes.com/2012/03/31/us/battles-to-change-prison-policy-of-solitary-confinement.html?_r=2&hpw> accessed 24 July 2013. Recently California itself has issued a report suggesting its current policies for assigning prisoners to SHU prisons are overly rigid. See California Department of Corrections and Rehabilitation (2012).

California in *Brown v. Plata*, which involved medical and mental health care in the very same prison system that *Spain v. Procunier* had reviewed.

The Supreme Court was moved enough by the qualitative face of California prison conditions that they included three photographs documenting two distinctive features of California's version of mass incarceration. Two pictures depicted prison areas filled with hundreds of stacked metal beds (two and three tiered), in which California prisoners were often held for weeks or months awaiting transfer to a more normal (if overcrowded) cell. These pictures which depict hundreds of prisoners standing, sitting, and lying down right next to each other with no room for hygiene and privacy and no evidence of correctional officers portray the shear physical suffering involved in sustained imprisonment under such conditions.

The third picture was perhaps even more damning. A vertical cage, just big enough to hold a standing or crouching adult, fills the frame, standing in a hall, next to others. This cage, described in the picture as a 'dry cell', was used by California to hold prisoners experiencing such severe symptoms of mental illness that they were considered a high risk for suicide. The cell was intended to prevent suicide for prisoners under conditions of such high overcrowding that they could not be supervized or placed in a high security hospital bed for substantial time. Despite its benevolent purpose, the justices were clearly moved by the image, with Justice Breyer confronting California's lawyers with it during oral argument.

Many states and the federal government may have taken relief from the strong condemnation of California expressed in *Brown v. Plata* while imagining themselves much better suited to survive scrutiny. But the same trends of ageing, chronic illness, and poorly designed security oriented prisons challenge all the political units that embraced mass incarceration. The presumption that American prisons were humane and even progressive helped legitimize mass incarceration even where it was not safe to assume. If *Brown v. Plata* marks a shocked sense that even rich states like California harbour humanitarian nightmares in their prisons, it may go a long way toward encouraging a new wave of judicial action in the states.

CONCLUSION

> 'The...question is whether...the public imagination of the "convict" could ever be reshaped.'
>
> (Harcourt 2011)

Opponents of mass incarceration have worked to build up a powerful normative and empirical critique of mass incarceration in the US. In brief, this critique contends that US mass incarceration has been skewed heavily against working class men (and increasingly women) of colour and that the many negative externalities associated with incarceration therefore concentrate in communities already significantly disadvantaged by America's pervasive history of racial discrimination. To a remarkable degree the critique of mass incarceration has gained traction as doubts about our reliance on imprisonment are now being raised across the political spectrum (Simon 2012a). Indeed, it is precisely because mass incarceration is in many respects on the defensive that it is possible to wonder what its core legitimacy rests on and what might call that into question (Dzur 2011; Loader and Sparks 2010).

If the *Spain* formula is no longer an accurate portrait of the conditions that have underwritten the broad acceptance that mass incarceration has enjoyed as a legitimate penal policy and expression of democratic government, at least as far as the federal judiciary are concerned, that legitimacy now seems strikingly vulnerable. To put it back in Beetham's and Sparks and Bottoms' terms, the conditions under which prisons are 'justified in terms of their beliefs', where 'their' means the US federal judiciary, have changed significantly.

Of course to say it is so does not make it so. As a 'talisman', the *Spain* formula has enjoyed strong legal authority even as its factual predicates have been forgotten. What is needed is a clear message from the very top of the judiciary that prisoners will no longer be presumed to be dangerous men, that security demands will no longer trump the requirements of dignity, and that indecent conditions will not be tolerated even if incapacitation is the dominant or even sole purpose of punishment. *Brown v. Plata* represents, at best, only a partial signal of this sort.

If even a large part of this highly influential portion of the American legal elite, one with a unique power to intervene directly in prisons, turned decisively against mass incarceration, it would have broad and unforeseeable consequences. To an important degree the American judiciary, both federal and state have been complicit in normalizing mass incarceration despite the manifold objective ways in which it stands in stark contrast to the long history of incarceration in the United States. If courts begin to entertain more complaints against prisons[36] based on a reduction in the level of deference they accord to the legitimacy of prison affairs (and this is deference only partially controlled by the Supreme Court through legal formulas since district judges also decide on the facts which those legal standards are applied to), such claims will multiply rapidly and with them the effective cost of incarceration. This is especially true of the medical and mental health problems revealed by *Brown v. Plata*. With chronic illness rampant among state prison inmates, judicial scrutiny of correctional health care systems will be sector of problematization whose costs could ultimately run into the trillions of dollars if states do not find a way to reverse mass incarceration.

An expanded legal front to challenge imprisonment in US courts has the potential to drive change in the popular legitimacy of mass incarceration as well by transforming the context in which the public imagines prisoners. Already the appalling images reproduced by no less an authority than the Supreme Court in *Brown v. Plata*, images of humanitarian crisis inside California prisons, have become among the most widely viewed images of US prisoners. As Abu Ghraib demonstrated, fear-based popular support for wars on terror, do not necessarily authorize state actions that violate deeply

[36] This is especially true because the Prison Litigation Reform Act, 1996 (PLRA) had been intended to insulate states from federal court pressure, but the massive population order in *Brown* took place despite the PLRA.

held moral sensibilities. The humanitarian medical crisis brewing in US prisons has the potential to broadly delegitimize the expensive high security, low individual care prisons that many states built in the 1980s and 1990s under the thrall of mass incarceration.

REFERENCES

BEETHAM, D. (1991) *The Legitimation of Power*. Basingstoke: Macmillan.

California Department of Corrections and Rehabilitation (2012) 'Security, Threat Group Prevention, Identification and Management Strategy', available at: <https://s3.amazonaws.com/s3.documentcloud.org/documents/452638/cdcr-reforms-7-0.pdf> accessed 24 July 2013.

CARRABINE, E. (2005) 'Prison Riots, Social Order and the Problem of Legitimacy', *British Journal of Criminology* 45(6): 896–913.

DZUR, A.W. (2011) 'Restorative Justice and Democracy: Fostering Public Accountability for Criminal Justice', *Contemporary Justice Review* 14(4): 367–81.

FEELEY, M. and RUBIN, E. (1998) *Judicial Policy Making in the Modern State: How the Courts Reformed America's Prisons*. Cambridge: Cambridge University Press.

FEELEY, M. and SIMON, J. (1992) 'The New Penology: Notes on the Emerging Strategy of Corrections and its Implications', *Criminology* 30(4): 449–74.

FLEURY-STEINER, B. and CROWDER, C. (2008) *Dying Inside: The HIV/AIDs Unit at Limestone Prison*. Ann Arbor: University of Michigan Press.

GARLAND, D. (1985) *Punishment and Welfare: A History of Penal Strategies*. Aldershot: Gower.

GARLAND, D. (2001a) *The Culture of Control: Crime and Social Order in Contemporary Society*. Oxford: Clarendon.

GARLAND, D. (2001b) 'Introduction: The Meaning of Mass Imprisonment' (pp. 1–3), in Garland, D. (ed) *Mass Imprisonment: Social Causes and Consequences*. London: Sage.

HARCOURT, B. E. (2011) 'Reducing Mass Incarceration: Lessons from the Deinstitutionalization of Mental Hospitals in the 1960s', available at: <http://moritzlaw.osu.edu/osjcl/Articles/Volume9_1/Harcourt.pdf> accessed 24 July 2013.

IRWIN, J. (2004) *The Warehouse Prison: Disposal of the New Dangerous Class*. Los Angeles: Roxbury.

KLEIMAN, M. A. R. (2010) 'Toward Fewer Prisoners and Less Crime?', *Daedalus* 139(3): 115–23.

KNOWLES, H. J. (2009) *The Tie Goes to Freedom: Justice Anthony M. Kennedy on Liberty*. Plymouth: Rowman & Littlefield.

LOADER, I. and SPARKS, R. (2010) *Public Criminology?* New York: Routledge.

LYNCH, M. P. (2009) *Sunbelt Justice: Arizona and the Transformation of American Punishment*. Stanford: Stanford Law Books.

MERANZE, M. (1996) *Laboratories of Virtue: Punishment, Revolution, and Authority in Philadelphia, 1760–1835*. Chapel Hill: University of North Carolina Press.

PAGE, J. (2011) *The Toughest Beat: Politics, Punishment, and the Prison Officers Union in California*. Oxford: Oxford University Press.

PRATT, J. (2008) 'When Penal Populism Stops: Legitimacy, Scandal, and the Power to Punish in New Zealand', *Australian & New Zealand Journal of Criminology* 41(3): 364–83.

Reiter, K. (2012) *The Most Restrictive Alternative: The Origins, Functions, Control, and Ethical Implications of the Supermax Prison, 1976–2010*, Dissertation, University of California, Berkeley: JSP Program.

Shalev, S. (2009) *Supermax: Controlling Risk through Solitary Confinement*. Cullompton: Willan.

Simon, J. (2012a) 'Mass Incarceration: From Social Policy to Social Problem' (pp. 23–52), in Petersilia, J. and Reitz, K. (eds) *The Oxford Handbook of Sentencing and Corrections*. Oxford: Oxford University Press.

Simon, J. (2012b) 'Total Incapacitation: The Penal Imaginary and the Rise of an Extreme Penal Rationale in California in the 1970s' (pp. 15–38), in Malsch, M. and Duker, M. (eds) *Incapacitation: Trends and New Perspectives*. Farnham: Ashgate.

Smith, P. (2013) 'Punishment and Meaning: The Cultural Sociological Approach' (pp. 114–28), in Simon, J. and Sparks, R. (eds) *The Sage Handbook of Punishment and Society*. London: Sage.

Sparks, R. (1994) 'Can Prisons be Legitimate? Penal Politics, Privatization, and the Timeliness of an Old Idea', *British Journal of Criminology* 34(5): 14–28.

Sparks, R. and Bottoms, A. (1995) 'Legitimacy and Order in Prisons', *British Journal of Sociology* 46(1): 45–62.

Sparks, R., Bottoms, A., and Hay, W. (1996) *Prisons and the Problem of Order*. Oxford: Oxford University Press.

Thompson, H. A. (2010) 'Why Mass Incarceration Matters: Rethinking Crisis, Decline, and Transformation in Postwar American History', *Journal of American History* 97(3): 703–34.

Useem, B. and Kimball, P. (1989) *States of Siege: U.S. Prison Riots, 1971–1986*. Oxford: Oxford University Press.

Weisberg, R. and Petersilia, J. (2010) 'The Dangers of Pyrrhic Victories Against Mass Incarceration', *Daedalus* 139(3): 124–33.

Whitman, J. Q. (2003) *Harsh Justice: Criminal Punishment and the Widening Divide Between America and Europe*. Oxford: Oxford University Press.

Williams, B. A., Lindquist, K., Sudore, R. L., Strupp, H. M., Willmott, D. J., and Walter, L.C. (2006) 'Being Old and Doing Time: Functional Impairment and Adverse Experiences of Geriatric Female Prisoners', *Journal of the American Geriatrics Society* 54(4): 702–7.

Wilper, A. P., Woolhandler, S., Boyd, J. W., Lasser, K. E., McCormick, D., Bor, D. H., and Himmelstein, D. U. (2009) 'The Health and Health Care of American Prisoners: Results of a Nationwide Survey', *American Journal of Public Health* 99(4): 666–72.

Zimring, F. E. (2007) *The Great American Crime Decline*. New York: Oxford University Press.

Zimring, F. E. (2011) *The City that Became Safe: New York's Lessons for Urban Crime and its Control*. New York: Oxford University Press.

Zimring, F. E., Hawkins, G. and Kamin, S. (2003) *Punishment and Democracy: Three Strikes and You're Out in California*. Oxford: Oxford University Press.

12

THE SITUATED PRODUCTION OF LEGITIMACY: PERSPECTIVES FROM THE GLOBAL SOUTH

Andrew M. Jefferson

Countries emerging from war or from dictatorship represent situations where the stakes around legitimacy are particularly high and the foundations typically associated with discussions of legitimacy—a rational-legal, democratic state, for example—are absent, or under construction. Practices of establishment and construction and processes of critique and reform present a potent backdrop for a discussion of legitimacy. This chapter considers two empirical examples. The first—the case of *Omrie Golley*—reveals some of the dynamics operating beneath the surface of a state under (re)construction. The second—the case of Prisons Watch—illustrates the way legitimacy is a product of ongoing entangled encounters. Both cases demonstrate that legitimacy in such contexts is not merely dialogical or perpetually at stake but is in itself constitutive. The struggle for legitimacy is constitutive of relations between institutions and simultaneously constituted by those relations. This is a reading of legitimacy suggested by a social practice or 'relational theory of practice' (Lave 2011: 2) approach to social life. The chapter seeks to push our understanding of legitimacy as dialogical 'beyond procedural justice' (Bottoms and Tankebe 2012)—or even beyond Bottoms and Tankebe's critical reworking of the concept—by posing questions about how it is produced through entangled relations and practices.

The data drawn upon were collected primarily in Sierra Leone, initially during a period of seven months field work in 2006 and then during repeated shorter visits, most recently in August 2012. The initial study explored detention practices during and after the civil war. Subsequent visits have involved visits to local reform NGO's, initiation and supervision of studies (e.g. a qualitative assessment of prison climate in two prisons in eastern Sierra Leone) and an ongoing extensive study of the encounter between a reform agency and prisons. The chapter is divided into three main parts. After this introduction comes a short section justifying in theoretical terms why a relational take on legitimacy is worthwhile. Then we consider some perspectives on the relation between state and citizen-subject in sub-Saharan Africa generally, supplemented by some field-based reflections on Sierra Leone in particular. Then come the empirical examples and discussion, followed by some concluding remarks.

The substantive examples from Sierra Leone cannot be said to be representative of Africa as a whole. There are a number of factors—the exorbitant poverty, the particular history of the civil war, the very weak state structures and so on—which may make Sierra Leone rather atypical. Nevertheless, to the extent that other countries' underlying societal-political dynamics and recent histories resemble those of Sierra Leone I suspect some generalizability. Despite the preceding caveat I would expect the analytic orientation being proposed throughout this chapter to have purchase in other contexts, in spite of its localized exemplification.

TOWARDS A RELATIONAL PERSPECTIVE ON LEGITIMACY

Can we study legitimacy empirically? Is it a practice or a concept? These were questions raised at the Cambridge symposium in May 2012. Sparks, Bottoms, and Hay (1996) see legitimacy in relation to the social order of the prison as a conceptual tool, a way of making sense of the perennial problem of order. In such terms it is a concept which is dependent on the conditions of its own production. Because order is contingent and fragile so is our concept. To speak of the *situated production* of legitimacy is to speak of a constitutive process featuring a context (the situation) and an action or process (production). As suggested by the colon in the title of this chapter the analytic argument pursued here is a product of a dialectical relationship between theory and empirically-grounded observations or perspectives from the global south[1], more specifically from Sierra Leone in West Africa.

The nature and status of legitimacy as a concept and a practice is what is under the microscope. We will seek to analyse what legitimacy 'is' by looking at how it is created and operates in practice. Its essence (if a concept has essence) is, as it were, put under 'erasure.' The reader is invited to suspend preconceptions about what legitimacy might be and potentially re-imagine the concept as not merely 'beyond procedural justice' (Bottoms and Tankebe 2012) but beyond procedure all together, that is as more of an 'unfinished ideal' (Loader and Sparks, this volume). The ambition is to advance our conceptual understanding of legitimacy via field-based observations. Instead of thinking about legitimacy through the relatively static terms of power-holders and audiences—implying possession and imposition—this chapter rests on and explores the premise that legitimacy is best understood through analysis of its production in practice. This represents a turn towards understanding legitimacy as produced,

[1] The term global south requires a qualification. It is a term currently in vogue amongst anthropologists to refer to what is more commonly known as the developing world, previously the third world or sometimes the postcolony (Mbembe 2001). It is problematic in similar ways, carrying with it particular notions about a relationship between north and south.

mediated, and diffusely distributed[2] and not as something to be held or possessed, or intrinsic to a position or a status.

Sometimes, in the discourse of human rights practitioners[3] and popular political discourse, legitimacy is invoked as though it were a quantitative phenomenon—something one can have more or less of, something that some people or some governments have and some do not. Iris Marion Young's (1990) (anti- Rawlsian) discussions of both equality and justice share a common and instructive orientation. They de-privilege ideas about individual possession and societal distribution and instead foreground the structural and systemic causes and consequences of existing patterns. Like Geuss (2008) she directs our attention away from normative or ideal claims about how the world ought to be towards an analysis of the world 'as is'. The leaning is towards the facts of life rather than towards values for life.[4] Young's perspective gives support to the idea of an alternative relational approach focusing on production and generativity. A relational perspective focuses on the 'social structures and processes that produce distributions rather than on the distributions' (Young 1990: 18). Legitimacy is one way to order or make sense of distributions—of power, of justice, of resources, of recognition etc.—but it is also incumbent upon us to ask questions about the order or sense of legitimacy itself.

AGAINST/BEYOND BINARIES

To conceive of legitimacy as a relational phenomenon is to resist the tendency to think through binary oppositions.[5] This is easier said than done. As Lave (2011: 10–12) has pointed out binary thinking is a dominant feature of many 'epistemological frameworks' which even critical scholars (including herself) struggle to relinquish. It is part of our modernist heritage embedded in 'common-sense', and often 'semi-automatic', a kind of default position.[6] The language of audience and power-holders reveals such an orientation within dominant studies of legitimacy.

To speak of power-holders and audiences as Bottoms and Tankebe do (echoing others) is one way of articulating the relation between authorities and subordinates. Other versions include the relation between state and citizen, police and population,

[2] Here I am inspired by Deleuze and Guattari's (1980) notion of the rhizome suggesting non-hierarchical, non-linear connections and diffusions.

[3] Human rights are a polyvalent phenomena (Dembour 2010). In my experience, the version of human rights propagated according to sharply defined legal categories (external to practice) implies a view of legitimacy as an either/or notion. This may be stating it too strongly. Progressive human rights lawyers resist such characterizations. Nevertheless, the normative inclinations of the legal paradigm are rather widespread, informing, for example, practices such as the naming and shaming of violating states as though there were no shades of grey.

[4] On the fact-value distinction see Geuss (2008: 16) and Bottoms and Tankebe (2012: 130)

[5] Which, of course, are inherent to the legal paradigm which I am implicitly writing against.

[6] Speaking about the relation between state and society development scholar Christian Lund, whose work we will consider further later, notes that 'the binary opposition constitutes a profound mental template' (Lund 2006: 675).

guard and prisoner, torturer and the tortured, chief and chiefdom inhabitants, donor and recipient, or benefactor and beneficiary. This (clearly not exhaustive) list illustrates the variety of levels at which the fundamental relationship between authorities and subordinates plays out. In each of these relationships legitimacy is always at stake even as it is constituted. It is never fixed, not quite. It is under construction. A turn to the production of legitimacy implies a turn towards situated social practice, towards 'persons-in-practice' (Jefferson and Huniche 2009), towards a deeper consideration of the relationships themselves.

To speak of 'creating and sustaining' legitimacy would at first sight seem to resonate well with an orientation to generation and production but the elaboration of the issue reveals an all too one-sided orientation. Bottoms and Tankebe (2012) quote Tyler who writes that creating and sustaining is about 'what forms of social organization or what dynamics of authority are *viewed by* the members of particular social groups as being appropriate and hence legitimate the exercise of authority.' (Bottoms and Tankebe 2012: 124, my emphasis). Now, forms and dynamics might be equivalent to practices and relationships but privileging 'viewed by' is to neglect the dynamic practices through which legitimacy is lived. People may well view or consider authority as more or less legitimate and sometimes act accordingly. But perceptions are less important than actions. A simple rational-perceptual model is insufficient to account for the creation and sustenance of legitimacy, at least legitimacy as understood as categorically relational. As Bottoms and Tankebe themselves argue it is not within the domain of power-holders alone to cultivate legitimacy. It is dependent on 'some kind of *continuing relationship* between the power holder and the audience(s)' (Bottoms and Tankebe 2012: 129) It is this continuing relation to which we should pay empirical attention. In line with Bottoms and Tankebe's claim that 'legitimacy needs to be perceived as always *dialogic* and *relational* in character' and 'that legitimacy should not be viewed as a single transaction; it is more like a perpetual discussion' (2012: 129, original emphasis) the purpose of this chapter is to illustrate the organic, entangled nature of such perpetual discussions.

However, it is, on the face of it, not easy to conceive of legitimacy as relational in a manner that moves us beyond a simple binary and mechanistic connection because of the fundamental nature of the two parties—governed and governing; audience and power-holder; subject and state—that give it its intuitive meaning. The categories present themselves intuitively as counterpoints to one another. Our conceptual apparatus limits our perspective.

Others have pointed to the risks and consequences of binary thinking. Consider the following quote from Sally Falk Moore:

> A rule-focussed compliance/deviance approach reduces the colorful hurlyburly of social life and the dynamic logic it has for the actors to so arid a pair of pre-selected and pre-interpreted obedience categories, that understanding of what is actually going on on the ground may be blocked. (Moore 2000: 3).

This suggests that a perspective that primarily asks whether this or that regime is legitimate or not (especially based only on etic criteria, as epitomized by legal analysis or the 'axis of evil' paradigm of George W. Bush) risks limiting the terms of the debate so much that the point is missed.

Iris Marion Young also makes the point in strong terms:

> 'The irony of the logic of identity is that by seeking to reduce the differently similar to the same, it turns the merely different into the absolutely other... Not satisfied then to admit defeat in the face of difference, the logic of identity shoves difference into dichotomous hierarchical oppositions...' (Young 1990: 99).

Dividing the world of political order into legitimate or illegitimate—that is into categories we imagine are fixed and self-evident—runs the risk of posing different instantiations of governance as polar opposites rather than variations on a theme.

As is hopefully clear by now this chapter does not focus on who is legitimate and who is not but on how legitimacy is produced relationally. What is explored are examples of the binaries not opposing each other but making each other. It is the relationship—the constant generation and regeneration—that is significant for analysis. We will see how the figure of the traitor makes the state and how the state constructs the figure of the traitor and how il/legitimacy is generated dialectically in the process. We will see how the prison constructs the prison reform agency and how the reform agency shapes the prison and how legitimacy for both is established in the process as the relationship changes.

STATE AND CITIZEN-SUBJECTS IN AFRICA

Legitimacy is generally understood to have something to do with the relations between states and their subjects. The relation between states and subject-citizens in Africa has been studied widely (e.g. Mamdani (1996) on the citizen and the subject, and the bifurcated state; Mbembe (2001) on the subject and the neglect of the subject; Hansen and Stepputat (2001, 2005) on languages of the state and imagining the state; Bayart (1993) on the politics of the belly; Hyden (2006) on economy of affection; Chabal and Daloz (1999) on neo-patrimonialism, etc.). The extent to which the African state is 'a regulator of social life and a locus of territorial sovereignty and cultural legitimacy' (Hansen and Stepputat 2001: 1) and the extent to which African subjects are governed and defined in terms of power exuding from the state have been subjects of rich debate. Considered in the following paragraphs are some complimentary perspectives on legitimacy, authority, and the nature and dynamics of state–citizen relations in Africa. Subsequently, the concrete case of post war Sierra Leone is subject to analysis in the light of the framework presented.

Perhaps the most classic account of legitimacy in an African context is provided by A. Thomson (2000) in his book *An Introduction to African Politics*. Here legitimacy is defined as a psychological relationship that engenders a belief about the right to exercise public authority. Note three factors here: belief, right, and public authority (Thomson 2000: 99). Through Thomson's optic authority persuades rather than forces.

Thomson observes that immediately following independence 'it was legitimacy based on legal rational government... that was meant to underlie state authority'

(Thomson 2000: 99). The intention was that liberal democratic institutions would operate on behalf of the people through the impersonal actions of state officials. But these institutions were never strong. They had not been created through persuasion but through force and they did not last. The structures which made postcolonial states resemble Western Europe and North America were not robust and consolidated but skeletal and insubstantial. Modes of authority then emerged in many African countries based on a quite different logic, namely personal as opposed to impersonal rule. Political activity was highly centralized. The executive and often a single, charismatic figure within the executive came to dominate. Thomson argues that as the state became centralized government became neo-patrimonial. Centralization meant a collapsing of the idealized separation of powers. There were no checks and balances, and little accountability or genuine representation. As the executive developed a monopoly on power there was little real choice for the people. This resulted in, on the one hand, the neutralization of opposition, in some instances the creation of one party states and, on the other hand, the by-passing of legal-rational channels and the manipulation of power.

Immediately following independence the one party state model made considerable sense. Why, after all, should African politics be subject to the same logics as the western powers from whose grip they had just been liberated? Desires for unity and strong leadership fuelled the move towards centralized power as did the drive towards economic development (Thomson 2000: 103). The fading significance of the skeletal structures and the resultant lack of accountability encouraged, in Thomsons's words 'corruption and the formation of an exploitative bureaucratic bourgeoisie' (Thomson 2000: 104). Politics became subsumed by desire for personal gain. What are considered as the standard features of legal–rational governments—parliament, local government, laws etc.—became subordinated to the executive.[7]

Thomson's analysis does not imply that the colonial state collapsed into disorder and anarchy or that the emerging post-colonial state had no legitimacy but that a different type of order and legitimacy emerged. (See Thomson 2000: 107). Politics in Africa at this time was not pure patronage but a fusion. A rational–legal frame still existed but it was infused by informal relations and exchanges.[8] Through Thomson's lens political stability and order are created via 'vertical threads binding whole societies together' (Thomson 2000: 111). Weak institutions and exploitative political elites mean that legitimacy is generated not through the state apparatus but primarily via the distribution of resources through personal networks of obligation. This leads to an arbitrary quality to governance and to practices which to an external observer look like meddling or interference. The case of *Omrie Golley* which will be addressed later illustrates this.

[7] In Thomson's version of the legal–rational model of governance 'legitimacy is generated' (Thomson 2000:107) when 'institutional norms take precedence over personal whims'. The question is what happens to legitimacy in the absence of institutional norms?

[8] In the Africanist literature this arrangement is typically referred to as neopatrimonialism. DeGrassi (2008), in a review of this literature, cautions against making too broad claims about generalized African societies on the basis of too thin evidence, advocating for historical, empirical studies of the nuances of political life in African countries.

Thomson's analysis is useful to the extent that it unpacks some of the central general dynamics of authority's distribution and legitimacy's generation in Africa. What Thomson does not do is turn attention to the actual everyday practices which bring the governed and the governors together, that is to the substance of the relationship itself. We now consider how a perspective on the everyday can help us further our understanding of legitimacy.

Political philosopher and post-colonial scholar Achille Mbembe proposes a non-oppositional account of the relationship between the governed and the governors in the context of the African postcolony. Instead of oppositions, says Mbembe, 'the emphasis should be on the logic of "conviviality", on the dynamics of domesticity and familiarity, inscribing the dominant and the dominated within the same *episteme*' (2001: 110, original emphasis). Looking beyond binary categories he analyses the 'conviviality' integral to forms of authority. State and subject–citizens are bound to each other not only through ties of obligation and loyalty (Thomson's model) but also through performances and practices that are intimate, domestic, and proximal to the highest degree. 'The apparatus of state', he points out 'finds ways of getting into its subjects' most intimate spaces' (Mbembe 2001: 121). The display of the head of state in people's homes, offices, police stations, and on apparel are obvious examples. An authoritarian epistemology is thus reproduced in 'all the minor circumstances of everyday life' (Mbembe 2001: 128) and 'pretense (le simulacre) becomes the dominant modality of transactions between the state and society, or between rulers and those who are supposed to obey' (Mbembe 2001: 129).

As ought to be becoming clear, an argument can be made for looking even beyond the 'wider social science literatures' (Bottoms and Tankebe 2012: 119) in search of insights into the nature of legitimacy, for example to literature that concerns itself not merely with the global north but with the global south or even to ethnographic studies of legitimacy at work. The work of Utas (2012) is based upon such ethnographies. Utas points out that in Africa state and civil society are intimately interwoven and difficult at times to distinguish. Appearing often as only 'nominally sovereign' (Utas 2012: 3) African states are characterized by both horizontal and vertical 'structures of governance'. Such structures are suffused with ideas of the 'big man' and 'my man', occupying various structures of order and governance both formal and informal (though these distinctions are also often blurred). The notion of 'bigmanity' refers to the phenomenon of the single authoritative figure heading a network of informal power. In parallel, 'my-manism' implies the common practice of having a sponsor, someone one is obliged to, loyal to, someone who is simply 'my man' (Prisons Watch Sierra Leone, personal communication). It is worth emphasizing the *personal* aspect of personal rule. Even weak infrastructures have people associated with them. It may be unclear who has responsibility for what, the rationale may be opaque or even deliberately mystifying but the structures hang together, nevertheless, not because there are organizational rules or policies but because of complex and intimate but often not very transparent links between people.

Utas' main point is to warn of the dangers of failing to recognize that informal structures peopled by fractured groups headed by competing big men with diverse agendas are often the dominant form of political sociality in Africa (Utas 2012: 25–6).

Legitimacy here is formed not via formal structures but through contested, contingent alliances.

Another useful reference point in our discussion of legitimacy is Christian Lund's insightful work on twilight institutions (Lund, 2006). Complimenting Hansen and Stepputat's (2001, 2005) influential volumes on languages of the state which privilege actual practice with a focus on the state Lund et al. privilege the people in their analyses of the relations between authority and ordinary people. Lund argues pointedly against ignoring the process of the *formation* of public authority. He points out that Max Weber himself can be used to support a focus not merely on state-centred legitimacy via coercion but also on the substantive competitive activity of political authorities. The formation of public authority, says Lund 'takes place in day-to-day social encounters' (2006: 675) echoing Mbembe's orientation towards 'minor circumstances'.

Lund implies that given the fact that it is difficult to set boundaries around 'what is 'state' and what is not' (Lund 2006: 673) legitimacy is likely to be a concept with 'twilight' qualities. This means, to use Lund's language that 'the contours and features ... are hard to distinguish and discern'. Like Lave (2011) and Mbembe (2001), Lund's approach implies a deeply entangled and generative relationship. The processual or unfinished nature of legitimacy is also emphasized: 'legitimate authority is not necessarily legitimate authority for good but must be *vindicated and legitimated* through a broad array of social practices' (Lund 2006: 674, my emphasis). Legitimacy is not once and for all; it must be earned and earned over again. As Dunn puts it in this volume legitimacy ought to be seen as 'a permanent process of judgement, unevenly dispersed across a given population, and constantly shifting in valency'.

According to these scholars, then, legitimacy is not an abstract concept possessed by political science (or psychology for that matter[9]) but a living relationship produced in practice by states, societies, and persons under a variety of conditions. The scholars I have drawn on in previous paragraphs write about Africa. The orientation I have emphasized, transcending Weber's focus on legality, is consonant with the critiques put forward by Beetham (1991); Coicaud (2002) and other writers in this volume. In the following section I consider the broad conditions under which legitimacy is being generated in Sierra Leone before turning to examples of the minor circumstances of production.

ON SIERRA LEONE

How might we characterize state–subject relations in Sierra Leone? The lenses outlined earlier are illuminating. Real power rests with the political elites in Freetown,

[9] On the specific issue of legitimacy not being psychological, Beetham (1991), for instance, is sceptical of any effort to study legitimacy via public opinion because, as he puts it, the answer to the question of legitimacy of power cannot be found in the 'private recesses of people's minds' (p. 13). Thanks to Justice Tankebe for this observation.

not so much in the institutions and offices they are supposed to embody. Power is personal based on networks of grace and favour. William Reno (1995, 1998) has termed it a shadow state but skeletal might be an equally fitting adjective. The term skeletal alludes to the fact that institutions are weak and disconnected and supported and held together primarily with the assistance of donor agencies be these large or small.

The contemporary Sierra Leonean state can be characterized as skeletal and trifurcated.[10] Power and authority are distributed unevenly across politicians, state institutions, and external agencies, each representing a slightly different form of authority: personal/traditional; administrative and legitimating. The inter linkages between these forms of authority and the legitimacy generated through each creates the backdrop against which we must understand the unfolding dynamics of Sierra Leonean socio-political life.

What we see today is the co-existence of neo-patrimonial politics—obligations of kinship, commitment to personal rather than impersonal rule, opportunities for self-aggrandizement through official duties—and slowly strengthening rational legal models. The 'hurly-burly of social life' (Moore 2000) in the form of existing ties of loyalty and obligation and the 'minor circumstances' in which authority is exerted and recognized did not disappear with the arrival of development initiatives and internationally sponsored capacity-building projects. History did not start over when the war stopped. This is one of the mistakes, identified by Mbembe, of much scholarship on Africa, namely the failure to attribute a history to Africa and the concomitant failure to acknowledge meaning amid unfamiliar political forms and trajectories. Of course it is nonsense to imagine Africa as without history. It is through thinking about history (or 'time on the move', Mbembe 2001: 1)—more specifically about generative processes—that I believe we can most meaningfully think about legitimacy. Legitimacy is produced or generated through the minutae of political and societal interaction, through everyday encounters. We come now to the first of two cases which exemplify this point.

CASE I: THE (ALLEGED) TRAITOR AND THE STATE

Political elites in Sierra Leone have a lengthy history of meddling in the affairs of the judiciary to eliminate threats and for political gain. Even today the judiciary remains compromised in the eyes of many.

One striking (and paradoxical) case of the state trying to legitimate itself in the post war context—through interference rather than persuasion—is the *treason trial* of Omrie Golley, a former spokesman for the Revolutionary United Front (RUF), and one of the negotiators of the Lome peace accord on their behalf. He was arrested together with two co-accused in January 2006, after (by his own admission) initiating meetings, and distributing money and mobile telephones to former fighters. For over

[10] Cf Mamdani (1996) on the bifurcated (colonial) state in Africa where the split he emphasizes is between direct and indirect rule corresponding to colonial and native or centralized and delegated power.

12 months he was held in the central prison at Pademba Road, from his perspective what Amnesty International would call a prisoner of conscience, in the eyes of the state, a traitor, conspirator, and would be assassin. The charges levelled at him included plotting to overthrow the government and assassinate the vice-president, a figure he had formerly negotiated peace with.

A young British law student was following the case as part of his internship with one of the very few NGO's active in the field of legal reform and assistance. He articulated some of the ambivalence that the case immediately raised: if the case is fabricated then all diplomatic stops should be pulled out to have him freed but if he is foolish enough to be guilty and to have tried to disrupt the fragile post war peace and potentially reignite the conflict then he deserves all he might get. This was at least the gist of the student's attitude. The ambivalence expressed characterizes the doubts that accusations of treachery produce especially in the context of a poorly functioning judiciary. Accusations of treachery are no small matter. Treachery strikes at the heart of the state, even as accusations of treachery strike at the heart of the traitor. It is no accident that headlines 'Traitor arrested/Treason trial' etc. sell newspapers. The figure of the traitor (Thiranagama and Kelly 2010) is significant in contexts characterized by political in/stability, featuring histories of violently contested control, coups and countercoups, and where political side-swapping is endemic rather than occasional. The traitor as threat to the established order is a potent symbol of the fragility of state power and the ease with which power can change hands. State and media reactions to traitors—denunciation, condemnation and the blazing of headlines—illustrate the expressive and instrumental value of the figure of the traitor.

Accusations of treachery resonate in the populace. They are a call to take sides (similar to that of terrorism post 9/11). But the odds are stacked in favour of the accuser who holds the alleged traitor in prison and controls the account of his capture, at least in the first instance. In the *Golley* case he was not helped by the poor reputation of the rebels he had formerly acted as spokesperson for. His legitimacy was undermined as it were by his history of association. To those already inclined to paint the rebels as savages intent on rampant destruction the idea that their former spokesman might have been seeking to undermine the current relative stability would come as no surprise, even given his credentials as a well educated lawyer in possession of both British and Sierra Leonean citizenship, that is, as a kind of outsider–insider. Indeed in the popular imaginary these very assets may well have contributed to the possibility of his demonization. Was this not a man of privilege finally getting his comeuppance? The invocation to take sides implicit in the accusation, the loading of the dice in favour of the accusing state is a clear demonstration of the fact that the figure of the traitor is an important one in the process of state formation and legitimation and in the machinations of political power.

The prosecution team was led by the Attorney General who was also the Minister of Justice, a fact which already hints at a state of non-separation of powers and of the importance of the case to the government.

One incident at court provides a striking example of the state's meddling and the vulnerability of the accused citizen–subject. It was in late July already six months after Golley's initial arrest and incarceration. Golley and his two co-accused arrived in court in a truck escorted by a jeep with armed police on the back. They were escorted from the truck, not to the holding cells, but to the bench outside where prison officers and police typically congregate as they wait to perform their duties of escorting prisoners to and from court and ensuring they do not escape. Soon after the three accused were to be seen sitting in the public gallery of court number one. Prison officers were seated behind them and police guarded the exits at the back of the court. The following excerpt from my field notes tells us something about the whimsical, unpredictable nature of the encounter between the judiciary and the citizen–subject. It is at the level of such encounters that legitimacy is produced and sustained—or the reverse.

> After some time OG is instructed to accompany officers and they shift to the other court. No explanations. After a few moments waiting in the dock the three accused are moved downstairs to wait on the next landing down, keeping them out of sight, presumably some kind of security precaution, but also keeping them away from the public, from contact and reinforcing that their movements are at the whim of the escorting officers. Movements confused me. First one court, now the other, then they are removed from view. Is the Judge not in? Is it a good sign or a bad sign? I cannot read the signs. We are forced to wait, wait, wait. Time stands still. What does that mean? Is the waiting obscene or laughable? Vulgar or carnivalesque? In what ways is the relation between OG and the state at this point convivial? Perhaps in the shared space of the landing where accused and escorts wait together, a temporary cohabitation, in a limbo'ed location? (Field Note, 20 July 2006)

Let us pause from the field note for a moment to consider further what this vignette tells us about legitimacy. In my initial reflection I emphasized the way movements were controlled but apparently arbitrary, mystical to me and presumably to the accused, perhaps even to those who were escorting the accused. The accused were singled out for special treatment in that they occupied the places on the bench outside reserved for waiting officials rather than being subject to the indignities of the holding cells. But inside the court house they were moved indiscriminately from pillar to post ending up on the landing of the back stairs, hardly the prime location for the state's encounter with its 'enemy.'

The court appearance had been postponed previously due to the absence of a prison vehicle to bring the defendants to court but this absence had been publicized by the defence lawyer causing embarrassment to the Prisons Director so this time at least the presence of the accused was more or less guaranteed. The Judge however was absent, on vacation, we learned. Another Judge would adjudicate on his behalf but in the privacy of her chambers rather than in open court. The field notes continue the story:

> (The defence lawyer) stuffs his robe in a cloth bag dispensing with the accoutrements, attire and apparel of office to pursue justice behind the closed doors of the Judge's chamber. The rain fell heavily outside. The case for bail is heard behind closed doors in the Judge's chambers those present including the Director of Public Prosecutions (DPP), the defence lawyer and the three accused who sat on a sofa along one side of the room. (From my position outside the room) I did not glimpse the Judge. OG looked rather disinterested or perhaps more resigned. Time dragged. Time was

> consumed. (It was claimed later) that the DPP expressly instructed the Judge not to use her discretion in this case, given the absence of the presiding Judge in the matter, surely seeking to counter her independence. She did not even read the medical reports submitted on behalf of OG's claim for bail for health reasons. Judicial power is balanced in favour of the prosecution... Outside the Judge's chambers, the police and prison officers waited lackadaisically, one with a gun. He is official security for the DPP. When OG emerged with his legal entourage they became alert and led and followed him through the court towards the holding cells. To their surprise he turned suddenly walking the other way, saying he wanted to speak with his lawyer. One prison officer attempted to stop him. OG was upset and angry. He swung with an arm, almost pushing—indeed there was contact—to keep the officer at a distance, calling him *bobo* (boy) ordering him, in Krio, to sit down, but the officer protested this patronising treatment and stood his ground. OG seemed to question what right this officer had to stand in the way of him talking to his lawyer. But I sensed also that an outlet for his disappointment was also necessary. He sought the conflict, partly uncaring if it were to escalate. What does he have to lose? (There was) a brief angry exchange between them before a compromise was reached whereby OG and his defence lawyer sat down at the lawyer's benches and talked briefly, while I spoke with the co-defendants. They were clearly upset too. How much they had dared hope for I do not know. (Field Note, 20 July 2006)

Here again we have examples of the 'minor circumstances' through which legitimacy is being produced in the eyes and through the actions of the implicated actors. The Judge is absent, the DPP warns the replacement Judge (behind closed doors) not to act independently, procedures are circumvented, or at the very least postponed, reports are not read, co-defendants are ignored, and Omrie Golley ultimately challenges the authority of the state officials in his violent insistence on speaking with his lawyer as they pass through the court room. These encounters could be understood as procedural but it is a fluid, arbitrary, opaque kind of procedurality that characterizes the justice process on display here.

The case as a whole—from arrest to incarceration to eventual release—is instructive in relation to legitimacy's production in at least two ways. Firstly it allows us to think about how elimination of opponents through meddling in the judiciary can reveal the strength and weakness of the state. It had the power to arrest, imprison and have him tried and to withstand any pressure the international community or the British may have tried to bring to bear on them. But he was arrested because he posed a threat, real or imagined. The second way in which the case is instructive relates to the significance of upholding the façade of legitimacy. Procedures were followed even as they were subverted (e.g. evidence was collected and presented in court, though apparently fabricated after his arrest, a replacement Judge sat though her powers were effectively non-existent). Charges were laid; the man was imprisoned.

The unveiling of a traitor, accusations of treachery, and betrayal function to reinforce the sovereignty of the state as defined in opposition to its enemies and those who seek to threaten or undermine it. The figure of the traitor and the face of the state are inextricably linked. It is a parasitic relation, entwined and entangled, a relationship through which legitimacy is contested and thereby generated or subverted.

CASE II: THE ENTANGLEMENT OF REFORM AGENCY AND PRISON

Ethnographic encounters with prisons beyond the West[11] suggest that prisons are best characterized as relational institutions. A concept of entanglement has proved useful to describe them. Entanglement has emerged as a concept which initially made sense of the entwined quality of the relationship between prison staff and prisoners, and later between the prison and the neighbourhood. A further analytic move is to consider the relationship between reform agency and prison as similarly entangled. A close look at reform agencies reveals them to be dependent on the illegitimacy of those institutions they criticize and seek to transform. This is perhaps not surprising given their agenda to change and transform. Though there may be claims (explicit or implicit) to moral superiority, separation, independence, or autonomy, in empirical terms reform agencies are deeply entangled with the institutions they target for change.

In effect the field of prison reform is one of collaboration and confrontation between interlocking institutions. This calls for studies which address perpetrative institutions and intervening agencies in their own terms in practice but also in terms of each other, that is in terms of their entangled relationship. The point is the 'institutions' act on each other. Their respective characteristics and qualities are thus interdependent.[12]

Under a relational framework legitimacy is to be seen as simultaneously given or granted and earned and deserved. Bottoms and Tankebe (2012: 120) make an important step forward by attending to *claims and responses*. This can be further developed by paying attention to the production of legitimacy as power-holders and audiences actually interact. Examples of this can be seen later in the chapter in a discussion of some observed encounters between Prisons Watch—Sierra Leone (PWSL) and the Sierra Leonean Prison Service.

Central to the work of Prisons Watch is what they term 'monitoring.' Using a cohort of (sometimes salaried, sometimes volunteer) staff located across the country they perform what is essentially a watchdog function, observing and collecting data about who is detained in police stations and prisons and whether due process laws and best practices are followed and human rights legislation adhered to. Like many NGOs working to promote human rights in places of detention Prisons Watch write reports based on their observations. But it is what goes on behind the scenes, outside the purview of the general public (and not included in reports to donors) which is most striking about their work. During the last half decade Prisons Watch's position in relation to the Prison Authorities they seek to reform has gradually shifted from a position of confrontation and criticism to one of collaboration. This is not to say they have lost their critical edge. As their Director, with a charismatic but altogether integral rhetorical flourish, puts it 'we work with but not for the prisons service'. One justification

[11] On this matter see the work of members of the Global Prisons Research Network, available at:<http://www.gprnetwork.org> accessed 24 July 2013.

[12] This is the foundational assumption of the *Understanding Prison Reform* research project currently being undertaken by the author with partners in the Philippines, Kosovo, and Sierra Leone.

for working with the authorities rather than simply against them is contextual. The position of Sierra Leone close to the bottom of the UN's development index, the fragility of democracy, the disruption of the education system by the civil war, and the weakness of state institutions across the board leaves the justice sector under-resourced both in economic terms and in terms of the quality of personnel. In a recent interactive session with prison staff they themselves complained of being poorly trained and ill-equipped.

Another justification for occupying an insider position is that to some degree the voice of external critique is redundant. The Prison Service are all too aware of their structural weaknesses. They really don't need to have these pointed out repeatedly by, for example, organizations with epistemological bias but little epistemological basis (see Jefferson and Jensen 2009: 11). Naming and shaming is a strategy which will arguably achieve little since they are already ashamed and paralyzed as a result. Shame has produced passivity not innovation. Again this is not to say that Prisons Watch do not lobby and advocate for improvements. But their modus operandi is dialogical and practical. Through participation in forums and facilitation of interactive sessions (well-armed with documentation and irrefutable facts from their monitoring activities) they are able to speak authoritatively about human rights, norms and standards and at the same time listen to complaints and frustrations. Through provision of psycho-social and occasionally (when an acute need arises, for example) humanitarian assistance (mattresses, food etc.) they are centrally placed. They have credibility. They have legitimacy in the eyes of the authorities. This legitimacy is clearly not something they possess by virtue of being a rights-based NGO, or by virtue of them occupying some kind of moral high ground, or by reference to the norms and standards which they do acknowledge. It is a radically relational legitimacy. It is not given once for all. It is constantly at stake and has to be constantly nurtured as the following examples illustrate.[13]

During a courtesy call with Prisons Watch to Prison Head Quarters in August 2012 I witnessed a surprising intimacy between core Prisons Watch staff and HQ staff. The performance of hearty camaraderie, back-slapping, and humour was a joint practice which surely both revealed and created a sense of common purpose. Prisons Watch's strategy might be characterized as illocutionary. By acting 'as if' they have a common purpose the possibility of a common purpose is created. Objectively speaking the prisons are far from living up to human rights norms and standards. Prisons Watch *are* watching, keeping an eye on and holding the Prison Service accountable. Their monitoring activities *do* bring into the open problematic, even abusive and inhumane detention practices. But at the same time they might be said to 'suspend judgement' to give the authorities the benefit of the doubt.

Some would point to the inevitability of co-option, taking the previous description as evidence that reform efforts (however well-intentioned) always become subsumed

[13] Empirical observations in Africa seem to bring the relational elements into particularly sharp relief. But the situation presented here is not necessarily different from what one might observe between police/prisons and watchdog organizations in the West. It is an empirical question as to the degree to which watchdogs and those being watched are imagined or imagine themselves as distinct and separate or as engaged in an entangled, symbiotic relationship.

under the agenda of the state whose motives must be questioned.[14] But as we have seen, we—and Prisons Watch—are faced with a skeletal state, struggling to make some things work, neglecting others often at the beck and call of international agencies (and, if resources are provided, quite responsive to that call[15]). It is certainly true that PWSL do not fundamentally question the prison. They are not abolitionist. I am sympathetic to the calls of the neo-abolitionists to reduce the use of imprisonment and analytically I recognize the accuracy of the claim that reform efforts often fail to question the more deep-seated assumptions about punishment and criminal justice that justify the prison. Nevertheless, it seems incumbent to subject reform efforts to analysis and to do so via the lens of the entangled relationship. And it seems more than worthwhile to support local struggles to make incarceration tolerable for those subject to it—be this legitimately or not.

A second example is about escapes and their implications. Escapes are pretty much universally acknowledged as threatening the legitimacy of prisons. In the west (and east) African contexts fear of escape is one of the most significant motivating and anxiety producing factors for prison staff, not because escapes undermine the legitimacy of the Prison Service but because if found responsible individual officers lose their job and livelihoods.[16] In December 2010 there was a breakout (more accurately described as a 'walkout') from the Central Prison in Freetown which resulted in the more or less immediate suspension and later dismissal of the Director of Prisons, a figure who had been nurtured and generally seen as fairly progressive by the international justice sector reform agencies (since his time as Deputy). In the aftermath Prisons Watch were invited to sit on an *Investigation Committee* tasked with reporting on the incident which basically advocated for the re-instatement of the former director. This has however not happened and is not likely to. Instead Prisons Watch have been obliged to forge relationships with a new (at the time of writing still only Acting) Director much less well known or exposed to the international organizations, much less familiar with their discourse and initially at least much less inclined to look kindly on organizations like Prisons Watch seeking to encourage transparency and accountability. But they have forged new relationships, as 'uneasy bedfellows', which nevertheless seem to rest on a fragile form of trust and interdependence. The Acting Director seems to recognize some value in having a 'cordial' relationship with Prisons Watch. In turn, Prisons Watch recognize—or are perhaps resigned to the fact—that given the dynamics of personal rule discussed earlier they are obliged to nurture their relationship with the Acting Director.[17] Their search for a platform enhances his. Compromises

[14] A recent report by the Home Affairs Committee (UK) on the relationship between police forces and the Independent Police Complaint Commission makes interesting reading in this regard. <http://www.publications.parliament.uk/pa/cm201213/cmselect/cmhaff/494/494.pdf> accessed 24 July 2013.

[15] The Director of Advocaid—another organization committed to supporting prisoners in Sierra Leone, more specifically female prisoners—claimed that it is not lack of political will that is the problem; it is simply money.

[16] e.g. see Martin (2013).

[17] Actually to such a degree that they found it quite appropriate to propose (without warning in a joint meeting) that I could be a potential sponsor of a new project the Director had begun, namely a school for the children of prison staff. They have also sought to enlist the support of the US embassy in Freetown to facilitate and sponsor an exchange trip to the US for the Acting Director.

are made, some more real than others. In the light of the *Investigation Committee's* findings and recommendations, the upcoming—potentially volatile—elections and the fact that the position of Director of Prisons is to all intents and purposes a political appointment, means that Prisons Watch are operating in a political minefield. Cordial relations today can be hostile tomorrow. Relational legitimacy—or the legitimacy of an entangled relation—is contingent and uneasy.

A third example relates to the issue of multiple audiences or more accurately to multiple actors shifting between the role of power-holder and audience. The legitimacy of PWSL is enhanced in the eyes of some by their affiliation with a western NGO. In the eyes of others this might detract from their grassroots indigenous identity. The fact that this author has some credibility amongst some senior staff in the Prison Service based on research conducted independently of PWSL rubs off on them and adds legitimacy when we join forces. But when a colleague and I visited the prison with PWSL as representatives of an international NGO we were met with suspicion and a degree of hostility. Our presence created anxiety and defensiveness on the part of the Prison Service representative. Were we there to expose and embarrass them? Might our 'findings' result in them losing their jobs, their pensions, their livelihoods? Different positions, different alliances, and different political circumstances and timing all contribute to the generation of different perceptions of legitimacy. In one guise we were legitimate; in another not.

In this example we also see the distinction between audience and power-holder dissolve. We did not feel particularly powerful as we were confronted by the anxious and defensive commander. He was the 'big man' at that moment controlling our possibilities for access in a very real way. But clearly his fear of exposure and embarrassment did not leave him feeling very powerful either. Our delegation was his audience even as he was ours. Power, similarly, moved back and forth even as we interacted. Distinctions between formal and informal or structural and personal legitimacy also collapsed during this encounter based on previous histories. Legitimacy is never established in a vacuum. I had once spent a weekend in a rural village socializing with this particular commander and a colleague of his with whom I had developed a good relationship during the duration of my research. We had a (personal) history that operated beneath the surface even as we both performed our respective roles as commander of the prison on the one hand and NGO representative/prisons researcher on the other.

Pretence and performance seem to play crucial roles in the production of legitimacy.[18] It is about acting 'as if.' Roles are adopted and cast off not with abandon but with almost measured precision. Such performances are more like a dance than a display. There is no place for an audience merely observing. There are rather two (or more) players interacting, engaging, responding, each deeply dependent on the

[18] See Mbembe (2001: 129) for an interesting discussion of pretence or 'le simulacre' as a central characteristic of the relation between state and society in the postcolony. See also Comaroff and Comaroff (2006) on concepts of counterfeiting, shadows, and mimesis in relation to the production of law and disorder, again, in the postcolony.

other for clues and cues as how to interact appropriately and how to create and sustain legitimacy in each other's eyes.

These examples from Sierra Leone are intimate and particular. We cannot claim that legitimacy is produced this way in all contexts. What we might do is claim that a relational approach to legitimacy brings new practices and dynamics to our attention. What these accounts exemplify is that relations are entangled not distinct, that there is interdependence rather than independence, intimacy rather than alienation, proximity rather than distance. Or perhaps more accurately that these apparent binaries exist simultaneously and constitute each other in a manner which we might represent graphically as a relation of superimposition.

CONCLUSION: THE PRECARITY OF LEGITIMACY (LEARNING FROM THE SOUTH)

This chapter has taken as its point of departure Bottoms and Tankebe's claim that 'legitimacy needs to be perceived as always *dialogic* and *relational* in character' and 'that legitimacy should not be viewed as a single transaction; it is more like a perpetual discussion' (2012: 129, original emphasis). The purpose has been to illustrate the organic, entangled nature of such perpetual discussions (which in the terms of this chapter are perhaps best understood as relations and practices rather than discussions or transactions).

The cases from Sierra Leone and the insights of scholars of African society demonstrate that legitimacy can never be taken for granted. To concur, once again, with Bottoms and Tankebe it is certainly not the case that 'procedural fairness is the sole or central foundation of legitimacy in all societies at all stages of development' (Smith quoted by Bottoms and Tankebe 2012: 146). Indeed, we might do well to take issue with the idea of a foundation to legitimacy at all. From the perspective of this chapter legitimacy is rooted and grounded in everyday contingent encounters. Of course such encounters take place against a backdrop of sociopolitical dynamics which vary across societies. Roots, it is important to recognize, are not the same as foundations. Whereas a metaphor of foundations suggests a given, static basis, the metaphor of roots implies the production and generation, the creation and sustenance of legitimacy in all its precariousness.

The argument of this chapter draws on examples from the global south. I do not make a claim for an essential difference between legitimacy in the north and the south. In the early part of this chapter I claimed that legitimacy is dependent on the context of its production. It is in this regard that legitimacy in Sierra Leone might be distinct from legitimacy in the north, or in other African countries. If the arguments posed here are seen to have merit then it might be worthwhile to also turn the relational optic on to the everyday practices within which legitimacy is rooted and produced in modern neo-liberal states, to suspend our belief that we already know what legitimacy is, and to revisit existing debates taking seriously that '(W)ithin the dialogic framework, legitimacy is constantly in flux' (Bottoms and Tankebe 2012: 152) and can never be taken for granted.

REFERENCES

BAYART, J-F. (1993) *The State in Africa: The Politics of the Belly*. Longman: London.

BOTTOMS, A. and TANKEBE, J. (2012) 'Beyond Procedural Justice: A Dialogic Approach to Legitimacy in Criminal Justice', *Journal of Criminal Law and Criminology* 102(1): 119–170.

CHABAL, J. and DALOZ, J-P. (1999) *Africa Works: Disorder as Political Instrument*. James Currey. Oxford.

COMAROFF, J. and COMAROFF, J. (2006) *Law and Disorder in the Postcolony*. Chicago: University of Chicago Press.

DEGRASSI, A. (2008) '"Neopatrimonialism" and Agricultural Development in Africa: Contributions and Limitations of a Contested Concept', *African Studies Review* 51(3): 107–33.

DELEUZE, G. and GUATTARI, F. (1980). *A Thousand Plateaus* (trans). Brian Massumi: London and New York: Continuum (2004). *Capitalism and Schizophrenia*, vol 2 1972–1980. Trans of *Mille Plateaux*. Paris: Les Editions de Minuit.

DEMBOUR, M-B. (2010) 'What are Human Rights? Four Schools of Thought', *Human Rights Quarterly* 32(1): 1–20.

GEUSS, R. (2008) *Philosophy and Real Politics*. Princeton: Princeton University Press.

HANSEN, T. and STEPPUTAT, F. (2001) *States of Imagination. Ethnographic Explorations of the Post Colonial State*. Durham, London: Duke University Press.

HANSEN, T. and STEPPUTAT, F. (2005) *Sovereign Bodies. Citizens, Migrants and States in the Post Colonial World*. Princeton, NJ: Princeton University Press.

HYDEN, G. (2006) *African Politics in Comparative Perspective*. New York: Cambridge University Press.

JEFFERSON, A. M. and HUNICHE, L. (2009) '(Re)Searching for Persons in Practice: Field-Based Methods for Critical Psychological Practice Research', *Qualitative Research in Psychology* 6 (1 and 2): 12–27.

JEFFERSON, A. M. and JENSEN, S. (2009) (eds) *State Violence and Human Rights: State Officials in the South*. London: Routledge.

LAVE, J. (2011) *Apprenticeship in Critical Ethnographic Practice*. Chicago: University of Chicago Press.

LUND, C. (2006) 'Twilight Institutions: An Introduction', *Development and Change* 37(4): 673–84.

MAMDANI, M. (1996) *Citizen and Subject: Contemporary Africa and the Legacy of Late Colonialism*. Princeton University Press, Princeton.

MARTIN, T. (2013) *Embracing Human Rights. Governance and Transition in Ugandan Prisons*, PhD Thesis, Roskilde University.

MOORE, S.F. (2000) *Law As Process: An Anthropological Approach*. (2nd edn). Hamburg: LIT.

MBEMBE, A. (2001) *On the Postcolony*. Berkeley: University of California Press.

RENO, W. (1995) *Corruption and State Politics in Sierra Leone*. Cambridge: Cambridge University Press.

RENO, W. (1998) *Warlord Politics and African States*. London: Lynne Rienner Publishers.

Sparks, R, Bottoms, A. and Hay, W. (1996) *Prisons and the Problem of Order.* Clarendon Press, Oxford.

Thiranagama, S. and Kelly, T. (2010) *Traitors: Suspicion, Intimacy and the Ethics of State-Building.* Philadelphia: University of Pennsylvania Press.

Thomson, A. (2000) *An Introduction to African Politics.* London: Routledge.

Utas, M. (2012) 'Introduction: Bigmanity and Network Governance in Africa' in Utas M. (ed) *African Conflicts and Informal Power: Big Men and Networks.* London: Zed books.

Young, I. M. (1990) *Justice and the Politics of Difference.* Princeton, NJ: Princeton University Press.

13

LEGITIMACY AND THE DEVELOPMENT OF INTERNATIONAL STANDARDS FOR PUNISHMENT

Dirk van Zyl Smit[1]

In research on legitimacy and criminal justice relatively little attention has been paid to the international standards that seek to shape the implementation of punishment in national jurisdictions. Even less attention has been given to the process by which such standards are developed and the place of concerns about legitimacy in that process. Yet an understanding of the development of such standards is an essential precursor of a study of the substantive legitimacy of international standards for punishment. This chapter approaches the development of these standards by addressing a number of questions. What are these 'international standards of punishment'? What do we mean by legitimacy in this regard? What attention is paid to concerns about legitimacy in the process of developing international standards of punishment? And finally, what can we learn about legitimacy in instances where disputes arise about a particular standard?

The chapter does not focus directly on the question of how the legitimacy of international standards is reflected in national penal practices, except insofar as this feeds back into the legitimacy of their development. However, in the first instance, it finds that there is a large and clearly identifiable body of international punishment standards, whose legitimation can be examined. Secondly, the chapter sets out a range of ideas about how the role of legitimacy could be considered as a factor in the development of such standards. These ideas are derived from modern scholarship about the developmental factors that influence the legitimacy of international law, as well as from more general writings on social processes of legitimation. Thirdly, these ideas

[1] Thank you to Gráinne de Búrca, David Fraser, Steven Gardbaum, Jim Jacobs, János Kis, Alison Liebling, Lorna McGregor, Natalie Rea, Paul Roberts and Betine van Zyl Smit for their comments that enabled me develop my early ideas, initially expressed at the Cambridge conference, into a publishable paper. Thank you too to Alessandro Corda and Stuart Wallace for their research assistance.

are applied to examples of the evolution of specific international punishment standards, and it is shown that they have some power to explain how the legitimacy of such standards evolves. Fourthly, the closer examination of two particularly controversial court imposed standards suggests that how such standards are justified by the body that develops them can have a crucial impact on their acceptance. Finally, some brief and more general conclusions are drawn about the legitimacy of the corpus of international punishment standards.

INTERNATIONAL STANDARDS OF PUNISHMENT

What is meant by international standards of punishment? One place to start is the 2006 *Compendium of United Nations standards and norms on crime prevention and criminal justice* (United Nations Office on Drugs and Crime 2006). Its table of contents lists 55 standards. Of these, 23 relate to punishment. They are divided into five sections: treatment of prisoners, juvenile justice, alternatives to imprisonment and restorative justice, torture and other cruel, inhuman and degrading punishment, and capital punishment. Closer examination reveals some surprising inclusions and omissions. Some are what one may have expected. The very first standard listed is the well-known United Nations Standard Minimum Rules for the Treatment of Prisoners (UNSMR) (United Nations Congress on the Prevention of Crime and the Treatment of Offenders 1955), and the almost equally well known Tokyo Rules, the United Nations Standard Minimum Rules for Non-Custodial Measures (United Nations General Assembly 1990). But why are the Kampala Declaration on Prison Conditions in Africa (United Nations Economic and Social Council 1997) and the Arusha Declaration on Good Prison Practice (United Nations Economic and Social Council 1999) included in the *UN Compendium* and not, for example, the 2006 European Prison Rules (EPR) or any other of the Recommendations adopted by the Committee of Ministers of the Council of Europe? The formal answer is that all the standards in the *United Nations Compendium* were subsequently adopted in resolutions of major United Nations (UN) bodies: the General Assembly, the Economic and Social Council (ECOSOC), or the Human Rights Commission. This answer is interesting in itself, for these bodies lend some sort of imprimatur to the designated standards, which may have been the aim of those who had them included in this system.

What about standards that are not included in the *UN Nations Compendium*? I have already referred to the Recommendations of the Council of Europe as an example of such standards. They are conveniently contained in another compendium, *Penitentiary Questions: Council of Europe conventions, recommendations and resolutions* (Council of Europe 2009). The latest published version of this compendium, from 2009, includes 23 Recommendations on aspects of the implementation of punishment, all formally adopted by the Committee of Ministers of the Council of Europe. Of these, the 2006 EPR and the 1992 European Rules on Community Sanctions and Measures

(ERCSM) are perhaps the most significant—and interesting—European counterparts of the UN Rules I have mentioned.[2]

In other regions there are relatively fewer standards dealing directly with punishment. From Africa I have already referred to the Kampala and Arusha Declarations that were formally taken under the wing of the UN. And in the Americas we have *The Principles and Best Practices on the Protection of Persons Deprived of Liberty in the Americas* (Inter-American Commission on Human Rights 2008), which relate to a largely Latin-American human rights tradition (Burgorgue-Larsen 2011; Harris and Livingstone 1998; Buergenthal and Norris 1982).

Thus far we have focused on international standards on punishment clearly labelled as such. What they have in common is that they are adopted unanimously by the nation states of the world, or of particular regions of it, as rules or recommendations but that, legally speaking, their status, at adoption at least, is formally regarded in international law as not directly binding on the states that have adopted them.

There are, however, some punishment standards that are contained in international human rights treaties and that are therefore formally binding on the states that have ratified them.[3] Perhaps the clearest example of punishment standards in international treaties are the prohibitions on torture and other forms of cruel, inhuman or degrading punishment or treatment. Article 7 of the International Covenant on Civil and Political Rights (ICCPR) 1966, and Arts. 2 and 16 of the Convention against Torture 1984, at the international level, and Art. 3 of the European Convention on Human Rights (ECHR) 1950, Art. 5 of the American Convention on Human Rights 1969, Art. 5 of the African Charter of Human and Peoples' Rights 1981, all contain this prohibition in roughly the same words. In some conventions it is supplemented by a specific requirement that all persons deprived of their liberty shall be treated with respect for their dignity (Art. 10 of the ICCPR). Another, largely underdeveloped, standard for the implementation of punishment is the requirement in Art. 10(3) of the ICCPR that the 'the penitentiary system shall comprise treatment of prisoners the essential aim of which shall be their reformation or social rehabilitation'. Further provisions of the ICCPR and other treaties contain more general provisions that could be applied to the implementation of punishment too—rights to family life, freedom of expression, and even privacy, which prisoners may retain, for example—as well as safeguards against the imposition of retrospective punishments and other potential procedural abuses.

To convert these general rights into international punishment standards requires interpretation, and the international systems have set up a framework of institutions to do so. To take just two examples: The Human Rights Committee (HRC) pronounces on

[2] The focus of the European Compendium is more narrowly on the implementation of punishment than its United Nations counterpart. It does not include the Recommendation on Consistency in Sentencing that was adopted by the Committee of Ministers of the Council of Europe in 1992. For a discussion about international sentencing standards and what should be regarded as 'grossly disproportionate' in this context see van Zyl Smit and Ashworth (2004: 541–60). The interesting question of the legitimacy of such international sentencing standards is not pursued further in this chapter.

[3] This chapter focuses largely on adults but a similar analysis could be undertaken of standards for the punishment of children, starting with the Convention on the Rights of the Child 1989, which entered into force on 2 September 1990 and looking at its evolution and that of related secondary instruments, such as the Beijing Rules (United Nations General Assembly 1985).

the meaning of the ICCPR, and the European Court of Human Rights (ECtHR) does the same for the ECHR. These bodies set clear standards. A quick glance at a standard textbook, such as Nigel Rodley's *The Treatment of Prisoners under International Law* (2009) will show that the HRC has developed standards for the treatment of prisoners and indeed spelled out specifically what Art. 7 of the ICCPR requires as a minimum.

The ECtHR to an even greater extent has created clear and legally binding standards for punishment (van Zyl Smit and Snacken 2009). For example, Art. 3 means that corporal punishment imposed as punishment by the state on a juvenile is illegal: the ECtHR pronounced as early as 1978 in *Tyrer v. United Kingdom* (1978), and that is a binding standard—pronounced in the face of the solitary dissent from the UK judge who argued that the Convention did not deal directly with corporal punishment. Similarly, the procedural requirements for prison disciplinary processes (*Ezeh and Connors v. United Kingdom* 2003), or even the right of a prisoner to father children (*Dickson v. United Kingdom* 2007), have been turned into binding international standards by the court. And then there are prisoners' rights to vote, which are considered in the last part of the chapter.

There are also international standards about the death penalty. The treaty standards themselves are interesting. A person reading the ECHR cold, as it were, could be forgiven for thinking that Art. 2 makes it abundantly clear that that Convention explicitly allows the death penalty. However, as is well known there are two additional protocols to the ECHR: Protocol 6 that outlaws the death penalty in peace time and Protocol 13 that outlaws it also in times of war. Here clearly there has been a development of key international standards of punishment that requires explanation. Similarly, the carefully drafted Art. 6 of the ICCPR appears at least to tolerate the death penalty, admittedly with more restrictions than Art. 2 of the ECHR, but in this instance too, there is an Optional Protocol that enables states to express their binding commitment to the abolition of capital punishment.

Finally, this brief overview would be incomplete without reference to standards set by international bodies that are neither judicial nor the product of committees in which states negotiate rules or recommendations. What I have in mind are standards set by the CPT (the Committee for the Prevention of Torture) and the SPT (Subcommittee for the Prevention of Torture). The CPT is the pan-European inspectorate of detention. Since 1989 it has operated in terms of the European Convention on the Prevention of Torture and Inhuman and Degrading Punishment and Treatment 1987. As the preamble to this Convention explains, the drafters were:

> Convinced that the protection of persons deprived of their liberty against torture and inhuman or degrading treatment or punishment could be strengthened by *non-judicial* means of a preventive character based on visits (emphasis added).

Accordingly they adopted a Convention that sets no detailed standards but simply creates a treaty basis for a committee, the CPT, that:

> shall, by means of visits, examine the treatment of persons deprived of their liberty with a view to strengthening, if necessary, the protection of such persons from torture and from inhuman or degrading treatment or punishment (European Convention for the Prevention of Torture and Inhuman or Degrading Treatment or Punishment 1987: Art. 1).

From the beginning, however, the CPT had standard-setting ambitions. By making general statements in its annual reports, based on what it observed on its visits, on particular aspects of detention, and then combining these statements into a single document, it has produced (and publishes separately) the *CPT Standards* (European Committee for the Prevention of Torture and Inhuman or Degrading Treatment or Punishment 2011), which are a comprehensive set of standards directly applicable to how imprisonment and other forms of deprivation of liberty should be implemented in Europe.

The SPT, a newer international body that operates in terms of the Optional Protocol to the United Nations Convention against Torture (OPCAT) 2002, which came into force in 2009, has slightly different procedures. It not only inspects but also has to interact closely with national inspecting bodies through the so-called National Preventative Mechanisms (NPMs) that signatories are required to create. However, the SPT too is likely eventually to produce its own standards, which it will expect to be applied by all states that have ratified OPCAT (Murray, Steinerte, Evans, and Hallo de Wolf 2011).

LEGITIMACY IN THE ABSTRACT

Before I make some generalizations about the place of legitimacy in the development of these very diverse international standards for punishment, a word of warning: the notion that the legitimacy of such standards is open to question is not obvious to all participants. This is best explained by way of a brief conversation I had with a distinguished international lawyer who chairs one of the major international bodies that formulates standards on the implementation of punishment.

I reconstruct the informal conversation: Did he think the legitimacy of their standards raised questions, I asked? No, he replied, it did not, since their standard making authority was based on a treaty level instrument, which states chose freely to ratify. When the body he headed developed its own detailed standards, as its treaty base allowed it to do, it relied largely on the other standards and recommendations which, although not of treaty status themselves, had been endorsed by the same states that had ratified its founding instrument. The issue of legitimacy did not arise.

This approach is typical of how many international lawyers regard their field; they see specific legal authority of treaties and standards derived from them as being bolstered by a narrow, essentially Weberian notion of legitimacy based on the formal legal rationality of the process of elaborating the standards (Weber 1978). *Pacta sunt servanda* is taken literally and seriously. And while there may be debate about how international law is implemented at the national level (whether so-called monist or dualist conceptions are endorsed),[4] this is often not regarded by international lawyers

[4] The monist approach conceives international and national law as part of a single legal order. Under this view, international law is directly applicable within the national legal system and treaties come into force as soon as they are ratified. On the contrary, according to the dualist (or pluralist) approach national and international law are two different and separate systems of law, so a given country is required to pass domestic legislation implementing treaty obligations in order for those obligations to have legal force at the national level.

as a challenge to the legitimacy of the international standards themselves. Instead, it is seen as merely a practical matter for nation states to decide how they will give domestic effect to treaty based obligations, as well as to other standards of lesser legal status.

The reality, of course, is much more complex. International standards on punishment, as my cursory introductory overview has indicated, emerge from different international organizations in different ways and there are subtle and evolving gradations in their legal status. Even the process briefly described by my interlocutor hints at a *process of legitimation* in which a dynamic discourse is beginning to take place. It suggests a process in which information is already in other pre-existing standards and recommendations, which to some extent can be regarded as authoritative, and which are synthesized to create something new. However, we should not lose sight of the formal legal authority-equated-with-legitimacy strand as the single most direct source of legitimacy of all international punishment standards.

In fairness, it should also be acknowledged that academic international lawyers have noted that, as international law has moved away from being simply a body of law regulating the relationship between nation states and as it has come also to address the rights—indeed the human rights—of individuals, it has had to explain why it was moving towards protecting certain rights, and also why it was not protecting others. In other words, many international lawyers have recognized that formal legality is not enough: international law has to *legitimate* the standards it sets (Bodansky 2008). Justification is required of their content, of the process by which they are adopted, and indeed of whether they should be set at all.

In this regard my thinking has been influenced by the writings of the German-American international lawyer, Mathias Kumm, on the 'cosmopolitan turn' that the development of new international law has taken (Kumm 2009). This has implications also for its legitimacy. Kumm and others, building on the work of Thomas Franck (1990), have argued that international law has entered into an increasingly complicated legal landscape in which international human rights standards have to compete for legitimacy with national constitutional legal norms, particularly those that are enshrined in national constitutions. In this situation, the degree of legitimacy that the international norms achieve will depend not only on their formal adoption in authoritative international instruments in the way deemed appropriate by the rules of international law, that is, the formal principle of international legality, but also on a number of other requirements.

The three additional requirements that Kumm (2004) identifies in a seminal article on 'The Legitimacy of International Law' are: (1) compliance with the principle of subsidiarity in order to establish jurisdictional legitimacy; (2) adequate participation as a requirement of procedural legitimacy in the standard setting process and accountability by the standard setting body for its conclusions; and (3) the achievement of reasonable outcomes, what Kumm calls 'outcome legitimacy'. The legitimacy of standards set by international law, including those standards that relate to punishment, is sometimes attacked on the basis that they do not fully meet these requirements. It can be argued that standards for the implementation of punishment generally, or in a particular instance, should not be set at the international level but rather at the national level—and therefore infringe the principle of subsidiarity (a technical term of EU law but here used in a more general sense). It can also be argued that there may have been a democratic deficit in that participation in the setting of international standards on punishment and the accountability of the bodies that develop them further were inadequate. Finally, international standards can be, and are, attacked, in national parliaments and elsewhere, for failing to achieve reasonable outcomes: 'Too many rights for offenders and not enough being done for victims', the battle cries of popular punitivism, are certainly sometimes applied to international standards on punishment.

Fortunately, there are some rather direct rebuttals that can be made to the challenges posed by these three additional requirements: First, in respect of jurisdictional legitimacy it can be, and is, argued that protection of fundamental human rights should not always be denied by a concern with subsidiarity. To take two obvious examples: There is a strong case to be made for holding that genocide and torture are best prohibited internationally because individual states may be 'unable or unwilling'[5] to do so. Moreover, international human rights law may fill important gaps: that is, it may fulfil fundamental rights protecting functions that either cannot be or typically are not adequately performed at the national level (Gardbaum 2009: 252). This ensures that legal limits that may (or may not) be contained in national law on how states treat their nationals are extended to other populations. More widely, as Stephen Gardbaum explains:

> human rights law has [not only] helped to make individuals subjects of international law, it also renders states the objects of legitimate scrutiny and action by other states as well as by international and nongovernmental organizations (Gardbaum 2009:254).

Secondly, on the question of the participation necessary for procedural legitimacy, it can be observed that in the setting of international standards there is often a degree of interaction between three key groups. First there are scientific 'experts', who bring their specialist knowledge to the creation of such standards. Foucault (1977; 1980), amongst others, has noted that such knowledge may itself be a source of power that impacts directly on any action taken in its name (Schrader and Denskus 2010: 29–54). A second group of players is comprised of representatives of non-governmental organizations (NGOs), who stress the importance of significant values. Studies of standards set in diverse areas, some admittedly far removed from the implementation of punishment, have suggested that NGO involvement has a crucial legitimizing role in international standard setting (Peters, Koechlin, Förster and Zinkernagel 2009; Hachez and Wouters 2011). In the third instance, there are national diplomats, who represent their citizens in international fora, while bringing to bear their own 'official' knowledge on the setting of international standards. While scrutiny by a democratically elected parliament is important, it may plausibly be suggested that an active role for national legislatures in the development of such standards is not essential to their overall legitimacy.

[5] This phrase is adopted from Art. 17(1)(a) of the Rome Statute of the International Criminal Court 1998.

This point has been powerfully advanced by Jens Steffek (2003) in his reflections on legitimacy beyond the nation state.[6] Steffek, who draws on elements of both Weber's theory of legal rationality as a source of legitimacy (Weber 1978) and Habermas's idea of legitimation through justificatory discourse (Habermas 1992), argues that standards developed by an international organization can enjoy considerable legitimacy, even in the absence of direct democratic approval, if the overall goals, principles, and procedures of such an organization are broadly accepted.

Related to the question of participation is the growing awareness within international law that its overall scope, as well as the status of some of its specific rules, can, in practice, be expanded by granting additional legal recognition to settled 'custom'. What this means to international lawyers is that a 'general practice accepted as law' merits elevated status.[7] To the lawyers the interpretation of these words is a highly technical question. There is much debate about when a 'practice' is sufficiently general, and what 'accepted by law' means. For our purposes, however, it is interesting not least because acceptance in this sense allows consideration as sources of international law also of the general principles of law that are recognized by 'civilized nations' (Art. 38(1)(b) of Statute of the International Court of Justice 1945), as well as of the judgments of international and other courts and of the 'teachings' of legal experts in a particular area (Art. 38(1)(c) of the Statute of the International Court of Justice 1945; Shaw 2011: 112–113). In other words, internal to international law is already a process that resembles the justificatory discourse on which Habermas places so much emphasis.

In addition, even stronger recognition is given in international law to norms that can be described as *jus cogens*. Again the detailed controversies amongst international lawyers about what is meant by *jus cogens* need not concern us—it is best understood as referring to those strictly binding norms that are part of general international law and accepted by the community of states as a whole (Shaw 2011: 123–128).[8] The prohibitions of genocide or piracy may be examples. Of particular relevance in the context of this chapter is whether the prohibition of torture, also when it becomes part of the implementation of judicially imposed punishment, may be so regarded. This gives particular salience to debates about what is meant by torture and whether associated prohibitions on cruel, inhuman or degrading punishment should be given the same high legitimacy, *jus cogens* status, as the prohibition on torture, when discussing the standards punishment should meet.

Thirdly, the legitimacy of outcomes can be justified both by defending the reasonableness of the substantive outcomes directly, that is by arguing that an internationally recognized standard is inherently desirable, as well as by referring back to the other standards of legitimacy. On the latter defence Kumm (2004: 927) explains:

[6] See also more broadly Steffek and Hahn (2010).

[7] Article 38(1) of the Statute of the International Court of Justice includes 'international custom as evidence of a general practice accepted as law' as one of the sources of international law. This Statute is the accepted point of departure for analyses of the sources of international law: See, for example, Shaw (2011:69–71).

[8] Acceptance in this sense does not imply that in practice the legal norm is never breached, rather that such breaches are routinely condemned in principle.

> Where jurisdictional legitimacy weighs in favour of international law and international procedures were adequate, there is a strong presumption that a national community's assessment of the substantive outcome is an inappropriate ground for questioning the legitimacy of international law.

Indirectly, challenges to legitimacy can be addressed, perhaps even more effectively, by a sophisticated understanding of how international law, and, for our purposes, of how international standards on punishment, are developed. In this regard Kumm draws attention to the complex way in which binding 'constitutional' norms generally are developed in the modern world, whether they are eventually articulated at the national or the international level. In reality, there is considerable interaction—a dialogue, if you like—between those directly involved in developing and adopting international standards and other actors, both at the international and the national levels. Expressed differently, key standards are being developed in an increasingly 'cosmopolitan' process, which arguably has a broadly positive impact on their eventual legitimacy, even though the process itself may be subject to challenge.

Finally, although this chapter is largely concerned with the normative aspects of legitimacy, it should be emphasized, with David Beetham (1991), that legitimation inevitably has an empirical dimension too. Evidence of the perception that international standards have been consented to and accepted as legitimate, by national penal policy makers for example, is therefore to be considered as a factor in understanding their further development.[9]

LEGITIMACY IN THE PROCESS OF DEVELOPING INTERNATIONAL STANDARDS OF PUNISHMENT

How have some of the key instruments described in the preceding section been developed and how has this influenced their legitimacy? Let us begin with examples of the standards contained in the compendia of the UN and the Council of Europe.

(a) United Nations Standard Minimum Rules for the Treatment of Prisoners (UNSMR)

The oldest and best known of these is undoubtedly the United Nations Standard Minimum Rules for the Treatment of Prisoners (UNSMR), which was adopted at the very first UN Congress on the Prevention of Crime in 1955 and given the further imprimatur of the Economic and Social Council (ECOSOC) in 1957 and, with less enthusiasm than the Congress might have liked, by the General Assembly of the UN in 1971 (Clark 1995: 135). Since then the Rules have remained unchanged, with the exception of the addition of a single Rule, approved by ECOSOC in 1977, which extended their scope to persons arrested and imprisoned without charge (previously it had only applied to awaiting trial and sentenced prisoners).

A closer examination of the early history of the UNSMR reveals that it is much more complex than this brief description, which emphasizes its adoption by senior

[9] For an application of Beetham's distinction between normative and empirical legitimacy to this area, see Snacken (2013: 50–70).

(and arguably, legitimacy-conferring) UN bodies, such as ECOSOC and the General Assembly, would suggest. The idea that there should be international prison standards had its roots in the scientific conferences of criminologists and penologists of the late nineteenth and early twentieth centuries. Already in 1926 the International Penological and Penitentiary Council (IPPC)—as Sir Leon Radzinowicz (1999), an early participant in its work, has pointed out, the IPPC too had an interesting mixture of governmental and expert members—had begun drafting a set of standard minimum rules for the treatment of prisoners, and in 1934 the IPPC draft received the endorsement of the League of Nations (Clifford 1972: 232–236).

The result was that when the UN began its standard setting role in the 1950s, key legitimating steps had already been taken. An established body of knowledge, legitimated by the 'scientific knowledge' of the experts involved in its creation on what the minimum standards should be in this area had been established.

Equally important was that a dialogue had begun between the purveyors of this penological expertise and the makers of international law. The initial link between the IPPC and the League of Nations provided a foundation for this dialogue on which the UN could build by providing a forum for its continuation. This forum was provided by the First United Nations Congress on Crime Prevention and Criminal Justice in Geneva in 1955 which allowed for a similar mixture of official and 'expert' knowledge (Radzinowicz 1999: 390), and at which UN member states could assent to the first international standard on an aspect of the implementation of punishment.

A notable feature of the UNSMR is that its legal status was initially very limited. The Rules themselves adopt an almost apologetic tone. The preliminary comments to the UNSMR indicate that they:

> are not intended to describe in detail a model system of penal institutions. They seek only, on the basis of the general consensus of contemporary thought and the essential elements of the most adequate systems of today, to set out what is generally accepted as being good principle and practice in the treatment of prisoners and the management of institutions.

This is not the wording of a binding treaty and international lawyers of the time would have had no difficulty denying that the UNSMR was an instrument of any legal significance, a self-limiting reassurance that undoubtedly initially made it easier for diverse states to accede to it. However, since then the legal standing of the UNSMR has increased greatly. This has been primarily due to the use that has been made of the Rules by bodies such as the Human Rights Committee in giving content to the treaty based prohibition on cruel, inhuman or degrading punishments that is contained in Art. 7 of the ICCPR. Thus Rodley is able to quote several references to specific rules in the UNSMR pertaining to diverse issues ranging from cell size to use of dark cells and handcuffs as punishment, which the HRC now regard as direct legal obligations of states (Rodley and Pollard 2009: 386). It has even been suggested the UNSMR 'have entered the corpus of general customary human rights law' (Clark 1995: 99).

Indirectly enhanced legal authority produces a virtuous circle of reinforcement. NGOs and governments alike have relied on the UNSMR as a framework for reform proposals, and national courts too, have quoted them as indicators of what is acceptable at an international level.

Although NGOs played a relatively small part in the initial drafting process, recently they have more deliberately sought to boost the legitimacy of the UNSMR. One way in which this has been done has been by way of the commentaries that do not attempt to alter the UNSMR but seek to make it more useful, thus indirectly contributing to its legitimacy by promoting its acceptance as a valuable instrument. Thus in the early 1990s the NGO, Penal Reform International, developed a detailed commentary on the UNSMR entitled *Making Standards Work* (Penal Reform International (2001). The idea was for the government of the Netherlands to present it to the 9th Congress in Cairo in 1995 for formal adoption. In the event even this was blocked, primarily by the USA, who wanted to deny it even this small additional imprimatur.

It is worth also considering further attempts to develop the UNSMR, for not only is the presentation of the Rules overly apologetic, but their substance is somewhat dated. One obvious strategy would be to enact the UNSMR or similar Rules in the form of a binding Convention to which states could accede. This was proposed at the 1970 Congress and again in 1990. However, on both occasions the initiative was defeated with arguments of the time-is-not-yet-ripe type (Clark 1995: 134–6, 165–7, 248–9).

At the 12th Congress in 2010 another attempt was made. Professor Manfred Nowak, then the UN Special Rapporteur on Torture, made a dramatic plea for such a binding Convention (Nowak 2010). Although this too was rebuffed, it did result in the resolution requesting the Commission on Crime Prevention and Criminal Justice (the body that has responsibility for these matters between congresses) to take further steps to modernize and thus increase the impact of the existing UN Rules on prisons (United Nations General Assembly 2010).

Two reasons can be highlighted in explaining why this initiative had some traction while so many before it had failed. First, there is Nowak's personal influence. He combined the role of the purveyor of expert knowledge with that of the moral entrepreneur as rule creator.[10] Both expert knowledge and charismatic authority are recognized sources of legitimacy—and in the appropriate setting they operate well in combination.

Secondly, the adoption by the Congress and subsequently by the General Assembly (2011) of the United Nations Rules for the Treatment of Women Prisoners and Non-custodial Measures for Women Offenders (the Bangkok Rules) was of considerable significance. These Rules are actually a gloss on the UNSMR. They create new rules that refer back systematically to the UNSMR and in the process indicate the detailed developments that would make the UNSMR fully suitable for women prisoners in the twenty-first century. The success of the Bangkok Rules may be attributable to their ability to draw on the legitimacy that development of women's rights has accumulated in modern international human rights law: no state would want to be seen to oppose them and thus present themselves as being 'against women' (Tiefenbrun 2012;

[10] See the classic description by Howard S. Becker of a moral entrepreneur as either a rule creator or a rule enforcer: (Becker 1963) Becker characterizes the former as a crusading reformer, who is profoundly disturbed by some evil and who is often driven by humanitarian concerns. This model seems to fit the role played by Nowak as a distinguished human rights lawyer (rather than a criminal justice expert), who sought to highlight iniquities that he had seen in many prisons around the world by calling for a binding treaty that would eliminate them.

Peters and Wolper 1995). However the Bangkok Rules were undoubtedly also significant as a practical indication that development of the UNSMR could be possible within the UN framework.

These interventions have opened the way to amendment of the UNSMR themselves. They led to the General Assembly adopting a resolution in December 2010 the preamble of which:

> Notes with appreciation the decision to establish an open-ended intergovernmental expert group to exchange information... on the revision of existing United Nations standard minimum rules for the treatment of prisoners so that they reflect recent advances in correctional science and best practices, with a view to making recommendations to the Commission on Crime Prevention and Criminal Justice. (United Nations General Assembly 2010a: para. 8)

What this meant, notwithstanding the guarded wording of the resolution, was that there was an opportunity to update the UNSMR for the first time for more than 50 years. A first group of experts nearly missed the opportunity, by suggesting that the time might still not be ripe as a review process could lead to a weakening of the Rules and that a commentary on the existing Rules would suffice (United Nations Office on Drugs and Crime 2011). However, in October 2011 a second NGO-led group at an expert meeting in Vienna managed to get onto the agenda the idea that key rules in the UNSMR needed revision.

And this has remained the position. A more formal Expert Group of mostly government members developed the idea further and it was formally recommended by the United Nations Crime Commission (2012) at its meeting in Vienna in April 2012, together with a guarantee that the existing UNSMR would not be weakened. This in turn led to the formal resolution on the UNSMR, which was unanimously adopted, first by ECOSOC on 26 July 2012 (United Nations Economic and Social Council 2012), and subsequently by the General Assembly on 20 December 2012 (United Nations General Assembly 2012). It is fascinating to observe the indications in the text of the resolution about how acutely conscious the word-careful drafters were of the need to legitimate this development. A few illustrations: the resolution refers back to longstanding concern of the UN for the humanization of criminal justice and the protection of human rights, thus situating this development in the context of earlier United Nations standard setting that already enjoys a high degree of legitimation. It emphasizes the part played by the 12th Congress in requiring such developments. It reiterates that the existing UNSMR 'have stood the test of time and that they remain the universally acknowledged minimum standards for the detention of prisoners' (United Nations General Assembly 2012: para. 1). Nevertheless, the resolution acknowledges the role of the Bangkok Rules for the treatment of women in already modifying the UNSMR, and reviews in some detail the role that prior expert committees have played in pushing for change. Finally, it recognizes the need for some provisions of the Standard Minimum Rules for the Treatment of Prisoners to be reviewed so that the Rules 'reflect the latest advances in correctional science and good practices' (para. 5); lists the proposed changes; and then goes on to propose a cautious course of action for achieving this circumscribed objective (para. 6). Time will tell whether this process finally succeeds in bringing about substantive change, but the process itself is clearly well underway.[11]

(b) European Prison Rules

Similar analyses could be undertaken of the perceived need to legitimate the development of other bodies of rules that have already been adopted. Consider, for example, the passage of the most recent version of the European Prison Rules (EPR). Here too individual expert consultants (who deliberately produce 'appropriate knowledge' that could be applied to rules) and an expert committee, the Penological Council of the Council of Europe (PCCP) interacted with the government dominated European Committee on Crime Problems (CDPC) (van Zyl Smit and Snacken 2009: 35).

There were also differences between the processes of development of the UNSMR and the EPR, which arguably relate directly to the greater legitimacy of the latter. In the production of the EPR it was possible by reference to bring into the creative dialogue a wealth of judgments of the ECtHR which had interpreted the ECHR and set standards that could be reflected in the EPR. With these references came not only legal substance but also a legitimacy dividend, by association with the premier regional human rights tribunal in the world.[12] Also important was the overt support for the new EPR from the CPT as a body and the direct incorporation of some CPT standards in the EPR (van Zyl Smit and Snacken 2009: 36). CPT standards have the advantage of having been developed inductively as a response to the observed shortcomings of prison practice in the countries visited by the CPT, which lends weight to this 'scientific' way of creating new knowledge (Morgan and Evans 2001; Murdoch 2006). Indeed, Kicker and Möstl (2012) argue explicitly that the legitimacy of standards set by bodies such as the CPT is increased by their being developed by independent experts. Moreover, the CPT itself enjoys considerable recognition, both because of its own treaty status and in acknowledgement of the impact of its work in all Council of Europe countries.

The EPR, as it emerged in 2006, were far more tightly drafted than the 1955 UNSMR. For one, it is introduced by a clear set of emphatic general principles that arguably were already regarded as legitimate in international human rights law. 'All persons deprived of their liberty shall be treated with respect for their human rights', reads Principle 1. 'Restrictions placed on persons deprived of their liberty shall be the minimum necessary and proportionate to the legitimate objective for which they are imposed', reads Principle 3. This is more the language of a treaty, although, like the UNSMR, the EPR was not supposed to be a formally binding instrument.

In reality, the status and legal authority of the 2006 EPR have been reinforced even more quickly than that of the UNSMR was after its adoption. Not only does the CPT often quote the EPR in its national reports, but the ECtHR also cites them in its

[11] A further meeting of the Intergovernmental Expert Group continued this process in Buenos Aires in December 2012. For details see <https://www.unodc.org/documents/justice-and-prison-reform/EGM-Uploads/final_report_2nd_IEGM.pdf> accessed 10 February 2013.

[12] On the legitimacy of the ECtHR generally see, from the perspective of empirical political science, Cali, Koch, and Bruch (2011); from the perspective of a former president of the Court, see Costa (2011).

judgments, both on issues of principle and in order to give very specific instructions.[13] Take, as a single example amongst many, the decision of the ECtHR in the case of *Gülmez v. Turkey* (2008). It turned on whether the disciplinary process in Turkish prisons met the procedural requirements of Art. 6 of the ECHR. The Court ruled that it did not. It then went on to instruct the Turkish government to reform its systems and to do so in the light of the specific requirements for prison disciplinary procedure set out in the EPR. For practical purposes, the EPR was treated as binding and the Turkish government was formally ordered to comply.

The growing legal stature of the EPR in the six years since its adoption seems clear. Less certain is what this means for the long-term legitimacy of the EPR and for the adoption of similar standards. On the one hand, there are empirical indications of the growing legitimacy of the EPR in the member states of the Council of Europe (Council of Europe 2011). A survey conducted by the Council of Europe has provided evidence of their widespread impact: 24 of the 31 states that answered the relevant question in the survey replied that they had reviewed their national legislation in the light of the EPR. Most described measures to implement the Rules: these ranged from training courses based on the EPR in 29 countries to detailed changes in practices. The Russian Federation reported, for example, that as a result of the EPR it was allowing the children of female prisoners to be held with their mothers and was granting extended familial visits to prisoners. This survey is itself an example of an international body seeking to increase the legitimacy of a particular standard by producing evidence of its impact in practice.

On the other hand, there is the danger that the increasing legal authority granted to the EPR may make states somewhat reluctant to accept provisions in future recommendations, which, while framed as policy guidelines, might later be reinterpreted as binding legal requirements. In this regard it is significant that the CDPC, as the key political body in the Council of Europe standard-setting process in this area, has changed its procedures to ensure that the states are involved at an earlier stage in the development of recommendations. The 'expert' PCCP has recently been required to follow the instructions of the CDPC more closely and to involve member states more fully in the process of developing recommendations.[14]

(c) Rules on Community Sanctions

More briefly for reasons of space: A similar analysis to that of the UNSMR and the EPR could be undertaken of the major UN and European instruments dealing with non-custodial punishment. They too emerged from a long process of expert international

[13] A survey undertaken by the author reveals that the EPR were cited by the CPT in 37 of its reports between 2008 and August 2012. In some reports more than one rule is cited: there are 88 such references in all. The CPT used the Rules in its reports to states parties to indicate how they should improve their prison practices. The EPR were also cited with approval by the ECtHR in 110 of its judgments between 2008 and August 2012. In these cases reference was made 751 times to various rules, as in several cases more than one rule was cited.

[14] See, for example, the decision of the Bureau of the European Committee on Crime Problems (CDPC) at The Hague, 20–21 October 2011 (cdpc-bu/docs 2011/cdpc-bu (2011) 7—e) <http://www.coe.int/t/dghl/standardsetting/cdpc/Bureau%20documents/CDPC-BU(2011)7%20-%20e%20-%20%20_list%20of%20decisions.pdf> accessed 2 December 2012.

gestation that goes back to the late nineteenth century, and similar steps were taken to ensure the legitimacy of the processes that led to their immediate creation.[15] The difference that I would highlight is that international tribunals have played a relatively small role in their further legitimization. However, in the European case at least, the CEP (the European Probation organization), an ambitious European NGO with strong links to probation practitioners, has used these recommendations to establish the legitimacy of probation across Europe—and to strengthen its own position in the process.[16]

(d) The Death Penalty

A rich analysis could also be undertaken of the emergence and continued impact of international standards relating to the death penalty. Although fuller consideration is not possible here, it is worth noting that, as in the case of community sanctions, NGOs have played a particularly important role, particularly in Europe and South and Central America, in the consolidation of the abolitionist sentiments into binding international punishment standards (Hood and Hoyle 2008). Moreover, the prohibition of the death penalty has been legitimated in Europe to such an extent that it has become symbolic of a shared European identity (Girling 2006: 69–82; Zimring 2003), even in the United Kingdom where doubts are often expressed about the extent to which the country shares values with other European countries.[17]

Countries of the former Soviet bloc that wished to join European institutions after 1990 were required to commit to abolition of the death penalty before being admitted into the European club (van Zyl Smit and Snacken 2009: 25).This notion of opposition to the death penalty as part of a shared European identity has also encouraged the European Union, acting collectively on behalf of its members to enter into dialogue with non-European countries on this issue. Sometimes this cosmopolitan dialogue has contributed to remarkable results, exemplified by the decision of the US Supreme Court to abolish the death penalty for juveniles after taking into account international standards in a case in which the EU intervened directly (*Roper v. Simmons* 2005).

DISPUTED LEGITIMACY

What has been described thus far are various processes in which legitimacy has gradually been built up during the creation of particular standards, and this has continued after the formal adoption of such standards through their growing recognition by high status institutions other than those directly responsible for their creation. But what about instances where the legitimacy of new standards has been disputed, even as they

[15] For a comprehensive overview of this history, see Morgenstern (2002).

[16] This is particularly true in the case of the most recent of these instruments, the 2010 Council of Europe Probation Rules: see van Zyl Smit (2012: 191–208).

[17] See, for example, the comment of the former British Prime Minister Tony Blair in the course of a speech where he otherwise stressed the similarities between the views of the US and the UK: 'I'm not saying America does not make mistakes; does not in its insularity of thinking sometimes seem obstinate to the concerns of the rest of the world. American political culture, for example on the death penalty, is different from European culture, and in Britain, in this respect at least, our culture is more European.' (Blair 2004).

were being developed? Thus, for example, the decision of the US Supreme Court to refer to international standards that prohibit the imposition of the death penalty on juveniles was not without controversy. Indeed, the turn to international standards has been subjected to extensive criticism in the US and critics of the judgment have sought to portray the use of international and comparative law as a weakness rather than a strength of the judgment. This position in turn has been disputed, most subtly by Jeremy Waldron (2012), who argues that sophisticated legal systems can engage with international legal standards without losing their own identity as long as they carefully examine their communalities and the arguments based upon them.

In instances where standards are disputed, it seems to me that the justificatory discourse, to which Habermas refers, becomes particularly important, for it can lead not only to the development of substantive standards but also to the mutual reinforcement of the legitimacy of the institutions developing those standards. However, this outcome is by no means inevitable. This can be illustrated by two contrasting examples of controversial punishment-related standards, both developed (in the sense of expanded or extended) by the ECtHR.

(a) The ECtHR and Preventive Detention[18]

The first example concerns a direct challenge to whether something is punishment at all and therefore should be bound by an international standard. There is a well-known international rule that punishment should not be imposed retrospectively. In Europe it is spelt out by Art. 7 of the ECHR. Germany has a similar rule in its own constitution. However in that country it has long been possible for a court to impose additional preventive detention on offenders who had committed serious offences. More recently the length of the period for which such detention could be imposed was extended, and this was applied retrospectively. The number of persons subject to preventive detention increased sharply.

An offender, M, who initially would have been released after a maximum of ten years after his sentence had this term extended indefinitely on grounds of continued dangerousness. He sought relief from the German Federal Constitutional Court (FCC), arguing that his right to be free of retrospective punishment was being infringed. The FCC declined to assist him, holding that his continued detention, even though it flowed from a conviction, was a 'measure' not a punishment and therefore not governed by the German constitutional provision preventing retrospective criminal punishments.

M took his case to Strasbourg. Although the ECtHR recognized that the judgment of the FCC had been 'thoroughly reasoned' (*M v. Germany* 2009: 27), it disagreed with the conclusion. In deciding whether something was a punishment or not, the ECtHR could not be bound by the label attached to conduct by the law of a particular state party. The ECtHR regarded M's continued detention as a punishment and therefore extended the application of the standards of the ECHR, which meant in this case the

[18] For a fuller account of the sequence of events described here, including references to the legal details of the judgments and the underlying statutes, see Drenkhahn, Morgenstern and van Zyl Smit (2012); Peters (2012).

'punishment' of additional preventive detention could not be imposed retrospectively (and if it were imposed this could only be done in compliance with due process requirements set by the ECHR to safeguard unwarranted loss of liberty).

Thus were sown the seeds of a crisis about an international (European) standard for punishment developed by the ECtHR. The German FCC enjoys very high national legitimacy ratings,[19] and German politicians and the popular German press were outraged that an outside body could deign to overrule 'their' Court.[20] The German government attempted a legislative compromise, but this failed to go to the heart of the matter. The whole question of the constitutional status of preventive detention again came before the German FCC, where the German Minister of Justice personally argued the matter. She pointed out that in German law the judgments of the ECtHR had a status only equivalent to ordinary legislation. She also claimed that the German way of dealing with the most dangerous offenders through preventive detention was not only fair, but inherently superior to regarding it as punishment, for the discretionary targeting of the 'really dangerous' led to fewer people being detained than would have been the case in penal systems that imposed longer sentences on all serious offenders so as to ensure the continued detention of the most dangerous.

How should the German FCC have responded? It could simply have taken an unbending stance and stuck to its recent precedent. However, it chose not to do so and upheld the challenge that M had originally made to the constitutionality of the legislation that had led to his continued detention—although not on quite the grounds that those in M's position may have expected.

What the German Court did was to say that the German Basic Law should always be interpreted in a way that was sympathetic to international law (*völkerrechtsfreundlich*). Where international law developed, as the ECtHR had done by an extended application of the ECHR in this case, the German FCC should reconsider its own jurisprudence. The German Court now conceded, not only that preventive detention led to significant loss of liberty, but also that M had a 'legitimate expectation' that he would not be detained beyond the date set in legislation. Even if this preventive detention was not a punishment (and the German Court did *not* accept the analysis of the ECtHR in this regard and therefore did *not* apply the specific German constitutional prohibition of retrospective punishment) the more general principles of the German constitution required that someone in the position of M should not have their liberty taken away, except in extreme circumstances of very clearly established, serious danger to the public. Moreover, if such detention were imposed, it would have to be done under conditions that clearly distinguished it from imprisonment.

[19] For relatively early studies, see Gibson, Caldeira and Baird (1998: 343–57); Vanberg (2000: 333–53). This trend has grown stronger. A recent 'You Gov' poll reported in the newspaper, *Die Zeit*, reveals that 40 per cent of the population has great or very great confidence in the FCC, while only 14 per cent have such confidence in the German Federal Government: Schlieben (2012). A poll in *Frankfurter Algemeine Zeitung* of 21 August 2012 found an overall confidence rating of 75 per cent in the FCC as compared to a rating of 38 per cent for the German Federal Government: Köcher (2012).

[20] The Bavarian Minister of Justice declared the ECtHR decision 'a fiasco', while her colleague in Lower Saxony announced that he would seek to prevent any releases taking place: Von Hipp and Rosenbach (2010). When a person formerly held in preventive detention but released as a result of the judgment of the ECtHR, committed a further offence the newspaper *Welt am Sonntag* was quick to blame the ECtHR: Stolt (2011).

Leaving aside technical issues, the real impact of this judgment will be, I suspect, fewer preventive detainees held in better conditions in Germany and increased legitimacy of international regulation in this difficult area. Certainly most public reaction to the verdict of the FCC was broadly positive in Germany, even if it meant that some preventive detainees would be released.[21] What is interesting for our purpose is how this result was reached in a very sophisticated interaction between two tribunals—tribunals which both proceeded from (empirically established) bases of legitimacy. The interaction was respectful of different points of departure. Nevertheless, it seems to have resulted in an outcome where a normative standard, the restriction of indeterminate detention of offenders beyond what would be justified by their offences, unless they continued demonstrably to be highly dangerous, has been established.

(b) The ECtHR and prisoners' right to vote

Of course, such dialogue does not always run so smoothly. My second and final example is prisoners' right to vote. Here too the ECtHR, in the case of *Hirst v. United Kingdom (No.2)* (2005), created a standard for the implementation of punishment by interpreting other provisions in its foundational treaty, in this instance Art. 3 of Protocol No.1 which deals with the democratic process. In some ways its judgment was exemplary: it sought to legitimate its views by spreading its net widely—for example, by undertaking comparative analysis not only in Europe, but also of the key Canadian decision on this topic (*Sauvé v. Canada* 2002) and even a post-Apartheid South African case (*August and another v. Electoral Commission and others* 1999). The judgment also made clear that it was not ordering the United Kingdom to give all sentenced prisoners the vote. It was simply ruling that a blanket ban was contrary to the ECHR, whilst emphasizing also that the United Kingdom retained wide discretion on when and under what circumstances it could deny some serving prisoners the vote.

The majority ran into trouble, however, when it suggested that only limited weight should be attached to the position adopted by the UK legislature. It came to this conclusion because it found that, although there had been recent legislation allowing unsentenced prisoners to vote, there had not been 'any substantive debate by members of the legislature on the continued justification in light of modern day penal policy and of current human rights standards for maintaining such a general restriction on the right of [sentenced] prisoners to vote' (*Hirst v. United Kingdom (No.2)* 2005: 79). This was an unfortunate and fundamentally unnecessary argument, for there was a principled way in which the Court could have dealt with the whole issue without relying on the ostensible shortcomings of the British legislative process: It could simply have pointed out, as Judges Tulkens and Zagrebelsky did in their exemplary joint concurring opinion, that:

> [t]here are no practical reasons for denying prisoners the right to vote (remand prisoners do vote) and prisoners in general continue to enjoy the fundamental rights guaranteed by the Convention, except for the right to liberty. As to the right to vote there is no

[21] See, for example, *Die Zeit*, which commented positively on the resourceful (*listenreiche*) way in which the FCC achieved an acceptable compromise that built upon the judgment of the Strasbourg Court (Kreuzer (2011)).

room in the Convention for the old idea of 'civic death' that lies behind the ban on convicted prisoners' voting.

A principled and fully reasoned human rights argument of this kind, if fully adopted by the majority, would have avoided what the two judges admit in the same opinion is a 'difficult and slippery terrain'—a terrain 'in which two sources of legitimacy meet, the Court on the one hand and the national parliament on the other' (*Hirst v. United Kingdom (No.2)* 2005, Tulkens and Zagrebelsky concurring).

These concurring reflections, cast explicitly in the language of legitimacy, were prophetic. Successive British governments delayed implementing the decision in *Hirst*.[22] More than five years after the ECtHR had handed down its judgment, a parliamentary vote in the British House of Commons sought directly to undermine the legitimacy of the substantive decision of the ECtHR by declaring in a formal motion that, while it accepted the UK's Treaty obligations, it supported the current situation where no sentenced prisoner is permitted to vote (Hansard, HC Debates, vol 539, col 493, 10 February 2011).

In a recent article in *Public Law* Danny Nicol contends that it was acceptable for Parliament to adopt this motion, as a legitimate expression of the parliamentary sovereignty and the separation of powers (Nicol 2011).[23] That latter part of Nicol's proposition is of course true, as far as it goes. What becomes apparent though, when one reads the debate closely, is that supporters of the motion, which was carried by 234 votes to 22, did not deal seriously with the substantive issue, that is, with why prisoners should or should not vote. Most of them simply reacted like the Prime Minister, who had previously said that the thought of allowing prisoners to vote made him feel 'physically ill' (Little 2010). Substantive arguments about the appropriate standard for determining the civil rights of prisoners provoked nothing more than gut reaction, devoid of rational rebuttal.

The supporters of the motion did not make a serious attempt to come up with any solution that would enable, as their resolution had promised, the United Kingdom to fulfil its treaty obligations as required by the principle of legality. Habermas has argued that, for bare legality to be legitimated, citizens have to foster it by what he calls *demokratische Sittlichkeit*, (loosely, the ethical spirit of democracy) (Habermas 1994: 678). This requires, Habermas has explained, that political actors do not simply express their personal feelings but rather engage collectively with the process of understanding what binding legal rules mean and how they should be interpreted within a wider liberal democratic framework. However, the supporters of the motion in the House of Commons felt entitled by the perceived slight to British parliamentary sovereignty to abandon the broader democratic spirit by refusing to engage in a rational process of discussion and debate. They did not enter into a dialogue that considered carefully the substantive reasoning of the ECtHR on prisoners' right to vote. Nor did they explore

[22] There is a large literature on this tortuous process and the litigation it has involved, which at the time of writing, October 2012, is still to run its full course. A good and impartial overview is to be found in the Parliamentary Briefing Papers: White (2012).

[23] For perceptive accounts of how the ECtHR misunderstood the constitutional significance of Parliament in the UK and the reasons that it may give for coming to certain decisions, see Lewis (2006); Murray (2012).

the considerable scope for accommodating their policy preference within the wide discretion that the ECtHR judgment allowed them.

The opponents of the motion were more nuanced. Some parliamentarians argued directly for the right to vote of some or all sentenced prisoners (Hansard, HC Debates, vol 539, cols 543–546, 10 February 2011). Others said that, although they were opposed to giving sentenced prisoners this right, it was more important for the UK to fulfil its international obligations (Hansard, HC Debates, vol 539, col 555, 10 February 2011): the legality—*pacta sunt servanda*—argument again. However, this argument was much unfortunately weakened in this instance by the ECtHR's constitutionally insensitive criticisms of the role of the British parliament, which made it much harder for would-be defenders of the *Hirst* judgment to articulate either form of support for it.

These two examples show that the process of developing and legitimating international standards for punishment is not a one-way street. Objections can be raised against standards by challenging the legitimacy of those who make them and the arguments that are put forward to justify them. However, what these two contrasting examples show is that just how the setting of standards is presented can make a big difference to their legitimacy. To quote Mathias Kumm again:

> When citizens in a constitutional democracy comply with legitimate international law, citizens are not compromising constitutional principles. Instead they are complying with the demands of principle that underlie the best interpretation of the liberal constitutional tradition they are part of (Kumm 2004: 928).

What is necessary, of course, is to persuade sceptics that what is being done forms part of the relevant constitutional tradition and that it is really the best available interpretation of it. In this regard, the importance of normative coherence in international standards for punishment cannot be overestimated and the dangers of an insensitive portrayal of national procedures are clear. Tactical errors in this regard can undermine the legitimacy not only of a specific standard but also of the standard-setting institutions, in this instance the ECtHR.[24]

CONCLUSION

If one believes that there may be some virtue in the development of international standards for punishment, one should not be too pessimistic about the potential legitimacy of regulating punishment by means of such standards. An enormous range and

[24] See the rather plaintive article by Sir Nicolas Bratza (2012), the outgoing president of the ECtHR, in which he comments on the historical commitment of the UK both to human rights in general and to the ECHR but notes that it was 'frustrating and disappointing to see that, largely because of a single judgment concerning the right to vote of some categories of convicted prisoners, the [ECtHR] has become a sort of hate figure, not just in the popular press, but also in the sound bites of politicians, some of them senior, and, even more disturbingly, judges—again some of them senior'. On the same day that Bratza's article appeared the Prime Minister announced that the government, contrary to what the Attorney-General had suggested, would not support sentenced prisoners being given the vote: Wintour and Sparrow (2012).

variety of standards of punishment has been developed internationally in the last 50 years—particularly in Europe, but also elsewhere.

This development has been brought about by states acting together through their official representatives, in concert with experts and, in some instances, NGOs. Those who have developed these standards have tried to legitimate them by using as effectively as possible the legal and other conceptual tools described in this chapter, as well as by making empirical claims about their efficacy. At times different arguments have been addressed to different audiences. Development has not been a 'one off' process, as many standards have evolved further after their initial adoption, and in the course of such evolutionary processes additional sources of legitimacy have been invoked.

This chapter shows also that international penal standards derived further support and legitimacy from the imprimatur given to them by courts and tribunals. Admittedly, these bodies have not always been equally effective in the ways that they have sought to increase the legitimacy of their judgments by following particular lines of argument, as the prisoners' vote imbroglio indicates. It is noteworthy, though, that perceptive members of the judiciary, such as judges Tulkens and Zagrebelsky in the *Hirst* case, have thought clearly about the efficacy of the jurisprudence of international courts and tried to shape the justifications for their decisions to take into account potential political challenges to their legitimacy. Such cases are probably the exception: more often than not, courts and tribunals have been successful in contributing to a degree of legitimacy for the international standards of punishment that would have been unthinkable at the time they were adopted.

A study of the legitimacy of criminal justice standards cannot focus only on reactions to them when they are eventually implemented in practice. This book seeks to go beyond such a narrow view of legitimacy. It must recognize that standards bring with them varying degrees of initial legitimacy, which are established in the complex process of their development. In explaining that interactions between key international actors are a crucial part of this developmental process, this chapter has highlighted a dimension that is often overlooked. As international standards multiply and become more prominent in national penal systems, and as the exigencies of globalization make references to international standards more frequent, it will become ever more important to understand the international dimension of the legitimation of these standards.

REFERENCES

BECKER, H. (1963) *Outsiders: Studies in the Sociology of Deviance*. New York: The Free Press.

BEETHAM, D. (1991) *The Legitimation of Power*. Atlantic Highlands NJ: Humanities Press International.

BLAIR, T. (2004) *Prime Minister's Speech*, 15 November 2004, Guildhall London, available at: <http://217.154.230.218/NR/rdonlyres/23B6E38C-DC30-48D8-BAC3-E256351AF119/0/MC%20_SP_lmbanquetblair_04.pdf> accessed 16 August 2012.

BODANSKY, D. (2008) 'The Concept of Legitimacy in International Law', in Wolfrum, R., and Röben, V. (eds) *Legitimacy in International Law*. Berlin: Springer. 309–17.

BRATZA, N. (2012) 'Why Does the Notion of Human Rights Get Such a Bad Press in Britain?', *The Independent*, 24 October, available at: <http://www.independent.co.uk/voices/comment/why-does-the-notion-of-human-rights-get-such-a-bad-press-in-britain-8225045.html> accessed 30 November 2012.

BUERGENTHAL, T. and NORRIS, R. (1982) *Human Rights: The Inter-American System*. New York: Oceana Publications.

BURGORGUE-LARSEN, L. (2011) *The Inter-American Court of Human Rights: Case Law and Commentary*. Oxford: Oxford University Press.

ÇALI, B., KOCH, A., and BRUCH, N. (2011) *The Legitimacy of the European Court of Human Rights: The View From The Ground*. London: UCL.

CLARK, R. (1995) *The United Nations Crime Prevention and Criminal Justice Program: Formulation of Standards and Efforts at their Implementation*. Philadelphia: University of Pennsylvania Press.

CLIFFORD, W. (1972) 'The Standard Minimum Rules for the Treatment of Prisoners' *American Society of International Law Proceedings* 66: 232–6.

Council of Europe (2011) 'Report Presented to the 16th Conference of Directors of Prison Administration: Summary of the Replies Given to the Questionnaire Regarding the Implementation of the Most Recent Council of Europe Standards Related to the Treatment of Offenders while in Custody as well as in the Community', Strasbourg: Council of Europe.

COSTA, J. P. (2011) 'On the Legitimacy of the European Court of Human Rights' Judgments' *European Constitutional Law Review* 7: 173–83.

Council of Europe (2009) Penitentiary Questions: Council of Europe conventions, *recommendations and resolutions*. Strasbourg: Council of Europe.

DRENKHAHN, K., MORGENSTERN, C., and VAN ZYL SMIT, D. (2012) 'What is in a Name? Preventive Detention in Germany in the Shadow of European Human Rights Law' *Criminal Law Review* 167–87.

European Committee for the Prevention of Torture and Inhuman or Degrading Treatment or Punishment (2011) *CPT standards*. Strasbourg: Council of Europe. CPT/Inf/E (2002) 1—Rev. 2011.

FOUCAULT, M. (1977) *Discipline and Punish: The Birth of the Prison (Part 3)*, Sheridan, A. (trans). Harmondsworth: Penguin.

FOUCAULT, M. (1980) *Power/Knowledge: Selected Interviews and Other Writings, 1972–1977*. New York: Pantheon Books.

FRANCK, T. (1990) *The Power of Legitimacy Among Nations*. New York: Oxford University Press.

GARDBAUM, S. (2009) 'Human Rights and International Constitutionalism' (pp. 233–55), in Dunoff, J. and Trachtman, P. (eds) *Ruling the World? Constitutionalism, International Law and Global Governance*. Cambridge: Cambridge University Press.

GIBSON, J., CALDEIRA, G'., and BAIRD, V. (1998) 'On the Legitimacy of National High Courts' *American Political Science Review* 92: 343–57.

GIRLING, E. (2006) 'European Identity, Penal Sensibilities and Communities of Sentiment' (pp. 69–82), in Armstrong, S. and McAra, L. (eds) *Perspectives on Punishment: The Contours of Control*. Oxford: Oxford University Press.

HABERMAS, J. (1992) *Faktizität und Geltung: Beiträge zur Diskurstheorie des Rechts und des demokratischen Rechtsstaats*. Frankfurt: Suhrkamp.

HABERMAS, J. (1994) *Nachwort in Faktizität und Geltung: Beiträge zur Diskurstheorie des Rechts und des demokratischen Rechtsstaats*. Frankfurt: Suhrkamp.

Hachez, N. and Wouters J. (2011) 'A Glimpse at the Democratic Legitimacy of Private Standards: Assessing the Public Accountability of GlobalG.A.P' 14 *Journal of Economic Law* 677–710.

Hansard, HC Debates, vol 539, cols 493–586, 10 February 2011, *Voting by Prisoners*.

Harris, D. J., and Livingstone, S. (1998) *The Inter-American Human Rights System*. Oxford: Clarendon Press.

Hood, R. and Hoyle C. (2008) *The Death Penalty: A Worldwide Perspective*. Oxford: Oxford University Press.

Kicker, R. and Möstl M. (2012) *Standard-Setting Through Monitoring: The Role of Council of Europe Expert Bodies in the Development of Human Rights*. Strasbourg: Council of Europe.

Köcher, R. (2012) 'Das Bollwerk', *Frankfurter Allgemeine Zeitung*, 21 August, available at: <http://www.faz.net/aktuell/politik/inland/bundesverfassungsgericht-das-bollwerk-11863396.html> accessed 24 October 2012.

Kreuzer, A. (2011) 'Karlsruhe zwingt die Regierung zum Umbruch', *Zeit Online*, 11 May, available at: <http://www.zeit.de/politik/deutschland/2011-05/sicherungsverwahrung-verfassungsgericht-kommentar> accessed 30 November 2012.

Kumm, M. (2004) 'The Legitimacy of International Law: A Constitutionalist Framework of Analysis', *European Journal of International Law* 15: 908–31.

Kumm, M. (2009) 'The Cosmopolitan Turn in Constitutionalism: On the Relationship between Constitutionalism in and Beyond the State' in Dunoff, J., and Trachtman, P. (eds) *Ruling the World? Constitutionalism, International Law and Global Governance*. Cambridge: Cambridge University Press.

Lewis, T. (2006) 'Difficult and Slippery Terrain': Hansard, Human Rights and *Hirst v UK*', *Public Law* 209–18.

Little, A. (2010) 'PM: Giving Prisoners Vote Makes Me Feel Sick' *Daily Express*, 4 November 2010 available at: <http://www.express.co.uk/posts/view/209397/PM-Giving-prisoners-vote-makes-me-feel-sick> accessed 2 December 2012.

Morgan, R. and Evans, M. (2001) *Combating Torture in Europe*. Strasbourg: Council of Europe.

Morgenstern, C. (2002) *Internationale Mindeststandards für ambulante Strafe und Maßnahmen*. Mönchengladbach: Forum Verlag Godesberg.

Murdoch, J. (2006) *The Treatment of Prisoners: European Standards*. Strasbourg: Council of Europe.

Murray, R., Steinerte, E., Evans, M., and Hallo De Wolf, A. (2011) *The Optional Protocol to the UN Convention Against Torture*. Oxford: Oxford University Press.

Murray, C. (2012) 'A Perfect Storm: Parliament and Prisoner Disenfranchisement' *Parliamentary Affairs* 66: 1–29.

Nicol, D. (2011) 'Legitimacy of the Commons Debate on Prisoner Voting', *Public Law* 681–91.

Nowak, M. (2010) *Speech on Crime Prevention and Criminal Justice*, 12 April 2010, Salvador Brazil, available at: <http://www.un.org/webcast/crime2010/plenary/statements/12nowak_en.pdf> accessed 30 November 2012.

Penal Reform International (1995) *Making Standards Work: An International Handbook on Good Prison Practice*. London: Astron Printers Ltd.

Penal Reform International (2001) *Making Standards Work: An International Handbook on Good Prison Practice* (2nd edn), London: Astron Printers Ltd.

Peters, A., Koechlin, L., Förster, T., and Zinkernagel F. (2009) *Non-State Actors as Standard Setters*. Cambridge: Cambridge University Press.

Peters, B. (2012) 'Germany's Dialogue with Strasbourg: Extrapolating the Bundesverfassungsgericht's Relationship with the European Court of Human Rights in the Preventive Detention Decision', 13 *German Law Journal* 757–72.

Peters, J., and Wolper, A. (1995) *Women's Rights, Human Rights: International Feminist Perspectives*. London: Routledge.

Radzinowicz, L. (1999) *Adventures in Criminology*. London: Routledge.

Rodley, N. and Pollard, M. (2009) *The Treatment of Prisoners under International Law* (3rd edn), Oxford: Oxford University Press.

Rosenbach, M. and Von Hipp, D. (2010) 'Plötzliche Freiheit', Der Spiegel, 17 May, available at: <http://www.spiegel.de/spiegel/print/d-70500967.html> accessed 30 November 2010.

Schlieben, M. (2012) 'Großes Vertrauen in Karlsruhe, wenig in die Regierung', Zeit Online, 9 July, available at: <http://pdf.zeit.de/politik/deutschland/2012-07/umfrage-institutionen-karlsruhe.pdf> accessed 23 October 2012.

Schrader, L. and Denskus, T., (2010) 'The Debate of NGOs' Legitimacy: What we can Learn from the Classics?' (pp. 29–54), in Steffek, J. and Hahn, K. (eds) *Evaluating Transnational NGOs: Legitimacy, Accountability, and Representation*. Basingstoke: Palgrave Macmillan.

Shaw, M. (2011) *International Law*. Cambridge: Cambridge University Press.

Snacken, S. (2013) 'Legitimacy of Penal Policies: Punishment Between Normative and Empirical Legitimacy' (pp. 50–70), in Crawford, A., and Hucklesby, A. (eds) *Legitimacy and Compliance in Criminal Justice*, London: Routledge.

Steffek, J. (2003) 'The Legitimation of International Governance: A Discourse Approach', *European Journal of International Relations* 9: 249–73.

Steffek, J. and Hahn, K. (eds) (2010) *Evaluating Transnational NGOs: Legitimacy, Accountability, Representation*. Basingstoke: Palgrave Macmillan.

Stolt, R. (2011) 'Wer schützt unsere Kinder?', Die Welt, 24 July, available at: <http://www.welt.de/print/wams/nrw/article13504459/Wer-schuetzt-unsere-Kinder.html> accessed 26 October 2012.

Tiefenbrun, S. W. (2012) *Women's International and Comparative Human Rights*. Durham: Carolina Academic Press.

United Nations Office on Drugs and Crime (2006) *Compendium of United Nations Standards and Norms in Crime Prevention and Criminal Justice*. New York: United Nations.

United Nations Office on Drugs and Crime (2011) *Report on the High Level Expert Group Meeting on the United Nations Standard Minimum Rules for the Treatment of Prisoners Held in Santo Domingo from 3 to 5 August 2011*. Vienna: United Nations Office On Drugs and Crime.

United Nations General Assembly (2012). Resolution on the Standard Minimum Rules for the Treatment of Prisoners adopted on 20 December 2012 (A/RES/67/188).

Vanberg, G. (2000) 'Establishing Judicial Independence in West Germany: The Impact of Opinion Leadership and the Separation of Powers', *Comparative Politics* 32: 333–53.

Van Zyl Smit, D. (2012) 'Non-custodial sanctions and European human rights law', in Roberts, J., and Zedner, L. (eds) *Principles and Values in Criminal Law and Criminal Justice: Essays in honour of Andrew Ashworth*. Oxford: Oxford University Press, 191–208.

Van Zyl Smit, D. and Ashworth, A. (2004) 'Disproportionate Sentences as Human Rights Violations', *Modern Law Review* 67: 541–60.

Van Zyl Smit, D. and Snacken, S. (2009) *Principles of European Prison Law and Policy: Penology and Human Rights*. Oxford: Oxford University Press.

Waldron, J. (2012) *'Partly Laws Common to All Mankind' Foreign Laws in American Courts*. London: Yale University Press.

Weber, M. (1978) *Economy and Society: An Outline of Interpretive Sociology*, Roth, G., Wittich, C., and Fischoff, E. (trans). Berkeley: University of California Press.

White, I. (2012) *Prisoners' voting rights updated 26 September 2012*, SN/PC/01764, London: House of Commons available at: <http://www.parliament.uk/briefing-papers/SN01764> accessed 26 October 2012.

Wintour, P. and Sparrow, A. (2012) 'I Won't Give Prisoners The Vote, Says David Cameron', *Guardian Online*, 24 October, available at: <http://www.guardian.co.uk/society/2012/oct/24/prisoners-vote-david-cameron> accessed 26 October 2012.

Zimring, F. (2003) *The Contradictions of American Capital Punishment*. New York: Oxford University Press.

INTERNATIONAL TREATIES

African Charter on Human and Peoples' Rights, 27 June 1981, 21 ILM 58 (1982) (entered into force 21 October 1986).

American Convention on Human Rights, 22 November 1969, OASTS 36 (entered into force 18 July 1978).

Convention Against Torture and Other Cruel, Inhuman or Degrading Treatment or Punishment, 10 December 1984, 1465 UNTS 85 (entered into force 26 June 1987).

Convention for the Protection of Human Rights and Fundamental Freedoms, 4 November 1950, ETS 5 (entered into force 3 September 1953).

Convention on the Rights of the Child, 20 November 1989, 1577 UNTS 3 (entered into force 15 January 1992).

European Convention for the Prevention of Torture and Inhuman or Degrading Treatment or Punishment, 26 November 1987, ETS 126 (entered into force 1 February 1989).

International Covenant on Civil and Political Rights, 16 December 1966, 999 UNTS 171 (entered into force 23 March 1976).

Optional Protocol to the Convention against Torture and other Cruel, Inhuman or Degrading Treatment or Punishment, 18 December 2002, A/RES/57/199 (entered into force 22 June 2006).

OTHER INTERNATIONAL AND REGIONAL INSTRUMENTS

Inter-American Commission on Human Rights (2008) *Principles and Best Practices on the Protection of Persons Deprived of Liberty in the Americas*, 3–14 March 2008, OEA/Ser/L/V/II.131 doc. 26.

Recommendation No. R (92) 16 of the Committee of Ministers to Member States on the European Rules on Community Sanctions and Measures adopted by the Committee of Ministers on 19 October 1992 at the 482nd meeting of the Ministers' Deputies.

Recommendation No. R (92) 17 of the Committee of Ministers to Member States on the European Rules on Consistency in Sentencing adopted by the Committee of Ministers on 19 October 1992 at the 482nd meeting of the Ministers' Deputies.

Recommendation Rec (2006) 2 of the Committee of Ministers to member states on the European Prison Rules adopted by the Committee of Ministers on 11 January 2006 at the 952nd meeting of the Ministers' Deputies.

Recommendation CM/Rec (2010) 2 of the Committee of Ministers to member states on the Council of Europe Probation Rules adopted by the Committee of Ministers on 20 January 2010 at the 1075th meeting of the Ministers' Deputies.

United Nations Congress on the Prevention of Crime and the Treatment of Offenders *Standard Minimum Rules for the Treatment of Prisoners* 30 August 1955, UN Doc A/CONF/611, annex I

United Nations Economic and Social Council (1957) ECOSOC Resolution 663 C (XXIV) of 31 July 1957 on the *Standard Minimum Rules for the Treatment of Prisoners.*

United Nations Economic and Social Council (1977) ECOSOC Res 2076 (LXII) of 13 May 1977 on the *Standard Minimum Rules for the Treatment of Prisoners.*

United Nations Crime Commission (2012) *Standard Minimum Rules for the Treatment of Prisoners: draft resolution*, 23 April 2012 E/CN.15/2012/L.4/Rev.1.

United Nations Economic and Social Council (1997) *Kampala Declaration on Prison Conditions in Africa*, 30 April 1997, E/CN.15/1997/L.18.

United Nations Economic and Social Council (1999) *Arusha Declaration on Good Prison Practice*, ECOSOC Res 1999/27 annex (1999).

United Nations Economic and Social Council (2012) *Standard Minimum Rules for the Treatment of Prisoners*, 26 July 2012, E/RES/2012/13.

United Nations General Assembly (1985) *Standard Minimum Rules for the Administration of Juvenile Justice (Beijing Rules)*, 29 November 1985, A/RES/40/33, annex.

United Nations General Assembly (1990) *Standard Minimum Rules for Non-Custodial Measures ('The Tokyo Rules')* 14 December 1990, A/RES/45/110 (1990).

United Nations General Assembly (2010) *Salvador Declaration on Comprehensive Strategies for Global Challenges: Crime Prevention and Criminal Justice Systems and Their Development in a Changing World*, 21 December 2010, A/RES/65/230 (2010) annex GA Res 65/230.

United Nations General Assembly (2010a) *Human rights in the administration of justice*, 1 April 2011, A/RES/65/213.

United Nations General Assembly (2011) *United Nations Rules for the Treatment of Women Prisoners and Non-custodial Measures for Women Offenders ('The Bangkok Rules')*, 16 March 2011, AIRES/65/229.

CASES

August and another v. Electoral Commission and others CCT 8/99, 1999 (3) SA 1 (CC).

Dickson v. United Kingdom (2008) 46 EHRR 41, [GC] 4 December 2007 (44362/04).

Ezeh and Connors v. United Kingdom (2004) 39 EHRR 1, [GC] 9 October 2003 (39665/98; 40086/98)

Gülmez v. Turkey, 20 May 2008 (16330/02).

Hirst v. United Kingdom (No. 2) (2006) 42 EHRR 41, [GC] 6 October 2005 (74025/01).

M. v. Germany (2010) 51 EHRR 41, 17 December 2009 (19359/04).

Roper v. Simmons 543 US 551 (2005).

Sauvé v. Canada (Chief Electoral Officer) 2002 SCC 68 (SC).

Tyrer v. United Kingdom (1979–80) 2 EHRR 1, 25 April 1978 (5856/72).

14

DIALOGUE AND DIALECTIC: POLICE LEGITIMACY AND THE NEW PROFESSIONALISM

Peter Neyroud and Lawrence Sherman

Police legitimacy depends on a continuing dialectic between the *contradictory* demands of the many audiences of police practice (Sherman 1998a), which is central to the problem of order (Wrong 1995). The contradictory and multi-centric character of these demands is inherent in the nature of the police task, often seen as preserving liberty while reducing liberty. In this context, police legitimacy may be established not just on the basis of effectiveness under the rule of law, but on demonstrated police mastery of a *complex body of knowledge generated by scientific methods of testing and analysis* (Sherman 2011). By visibly presenting that knowledge, the new police professionalism offers the potential for managing the dialectic between more and less liberty with evidence about the optimal balance between the two. Yet the mere development or existence of such evidence alone cannot achieve this goal. Only by proactively cultivating a dialogue with police audiences (Bottoms and Tankebe 2012) can police leaders explain the evidence for police decisions, and use the idea of police competence for its effectiveness as a central basis of public perceptions of policing as legitimate.

THESIS

Our thesis is that twenty-first century policing can only sustain its legitimacy by a visible demonstration of its mastery of a complex body of knowledge that assures police effectiveness. That knowledge must be seen as the basis of the fundamental *competence* of the police to manage, if not solve, the problem of order: the 'pacification of violent strife among men and the secure establishment of cooperative social relations' (Wrong 1994: 36)—a problem so fundamental it is apparently shared by all primates (Flack, et al. 2006). What makes this problem distinctive among twenty-first century humans is not just the scale of the group size that must be policed—such as 330 million Americans or 1.2 billion Indians—but rather the unprecedented complexity of their communications and transportation patterns. Every time we get on an aeroplane or make an internet purchase with a credit card, we know we are subject to attack from predators we have never seen or met, who may live on another continent. Surely no primates before us have faced such complexity.

The new complexity of the old problem of order has made police look less effective against challenges both old and new. The success of terrorists in London in 2007 was reportedly met by retribution against a ringleader from Birmingham who was killed in Pakistan by a US missile launched from a drone (*The Telegraph*, 1 May 2012). Many will remember the London murders; few will ever know of the retribution. That is a far cry from a Hue and Cry, in which police visibly lead a successful capture of a threat to public safety. Similarly, the use of hand-held communication devices has created enormous complexity in the management of disorder in London, for which centuries of police experience provides little guidance.

There has also been an intensification of the demand for security within local neighbourhoods. A recent manifestation of this in the UK was the Coalition government's proposal that the police would have to respond to a collective requirement for action against crime and disorder from five households. In 1998, a Labour government passed legislation obliging police to deal with crime in whole local authority areas. By 2012, the major parties were competing to identify the smallest unit of accountability to hold police to account.

The rising complexity of the core police task of harm prevention intensifies the dialectic between competing demands for police to do more—and less—to prevent crime (Sherman 1998a). A dialectic of this kind is defined as a 'conflict of opposites through which change takes place, sometimes by resolving the opposites and creating new ones' (Sherman 1998a: 433). The intensity of dialectic may be defined as the level of resistance to compromise among those at each pole of a dimension of conflict. This resistance may grow more extreme as the absolute number of issues increases. The question of how much liberty police need to take from some citizens to guarantee liberty for most citizens is no longer, for example, just a matter of how horses are used in riot control; it now goes to the question of every email exchange we have, and every website we visit. While technology changes not only our behaviour but the capacity of others to monitor it, we all suffer future shock and anger at the disorienting pace of change. Authorities are always convenient targets for anger (Muir 1977), and police are the most convenient authority to blame.

In the face of the rising intensity of the dialectic between those who want more intrusive policing and those who want less, one solution is apparent. That solution is both the reality and appearance of greater complexity in the nature of policing itself. Complex policing is not just a useful tool for solving complex problems of order (Sherman 1998b). It is also a useful symbol for reassuring a future-shocked society. That reassurance rests on a claim that the police are competent enough to meet these challenges effectively. Like oncologists trained in the latest techniques for choosing cancer treatment methods based on analysing tumour DNA, police must be seen to be competent in choosing the most effective and up-to-date methods for preventing attacks on such events as the London Olympics. But the achievement and use of complex knowledge of solutions to public order problems cannot be seen as autodidactic. No oncologist would claim to be self-taught, or taught by other 'experienced' oncologists who were largely self-taught. Neither can police—without risking a loss of their legitimacy.

Our thesis, in other words, is that *police leadership, and eventually all police officers, must be taught and certified as knowledgeable by the same kinds of institutions as those for other professions: universities and Royal Colleges (or professional learned societies).* The dizzying growth of knowledge and information makes democracies require shorthand signals of competence. The rise of professions has not just been conspiracy against the laity (George Bernard Shaw 1908), but an incredibly successful way of improving the competence level—on average—of people performing complex tasks. The fact that all professionals are not perfect, or that regulation of professions regularly exposes incompetence and venality does not alter that success. Who among us would not want highly trained (and certified) engineers designing our aeroplanes? Who would want amateur dentists pulling our teeth? Or self-trained chemists colouring our food? It is only by creating monopolies of the competent that we can achieve the highest levels of health and safety in the history of the world.

Instinctive public understanding of the importance of police competence is found on both sides of the dialectic between more and less policing. Both sides appeal to this instinct when they say (on the left) that the best defence of liberty is the incompetence of the police, or (on the right) that police have been 'handcuffed' by court decisions limiting their tactics to obtain evidence against suspects. Yet in the past 40 years, the dialogue has rapidly shifted from traditional cops-and-robbers contests to allegations of 'omni-shambles' in occasional failures to stop serial killers, terrorists, paedophiles, and drug gangs, as well as the longstanding problems of domestic violence, burglary, and armoured car heists.

Thus the contemporary dialogue within and between police audiences (Bottoms and Tankebe 2012) seems to have been intensifying its contradictions (Sherman 1998a). Our thesis is that the escape from this tightening noose around police legitimacy can be found in a partnership between police and universities, of the kind described by observers from Vollmer (1936) to Sherman (2011). The core idea of this partnership is to create a profession modelled on the truly oldest professions (not occupations): the clergy, the lawyers and the doctors, followed by engineers, accountants, and other occupations using 'high knowledge' (Sherman 2013): the application of complex decision-making frameworks to an ever-changing body of facts, as distinct from the mere memorization and application of a set of clear rules. Each of the professions using 'high knowledge' is founded on a self-regulating civil society whose first duty is to set standards for what its members must know. By using democratic methods to determine and measure that knowledge, these professional bodies govern both admissions to (and continuation of) practice in the profession.

This category of 'high knowledge' occupations, in contrast to a previous generation's definition of professionalism, does not rely on mere *competence* to define its unique character. Many occupations are competent and highly skilled, from driving a taxicab in London to wiring a skyscraper. But such competence does not generally require the application of a complex analytic framework with an ever-growing body of knowledge. It is only by embracing and claiming to employ 'high knowledge' that the police can sustain their legitimacy in an intensifying dialectic.

This thesis embraces the 'new' police professionalism (Stone and Travis 2011) as something far more useful than bureaucracy and internal control, but rather a strategy for making *knowledge* based on empirical research a central test for fitness to wield the state's monopoly on the legitimate use of force (Weber 1947). The complex body of knowledge associated with universities would then provide both substance and symbol to the steadily growing competence of police professionals to meet increasingly complex challenges.

Like all theses in dialectics, our thesis must engage its anti-thesis, whether or not there is any prospect of a synthesis. The antithesis to our thesis is found not just in any form of dialogue (Bottoms and Tankebe 2012), but in a dialectic between critics of police 'centrists' from both left and right.

ANTI-THESIS

Neither critical scholars nor classic libertarians have many good things to say about government institutions. Their thesis is essentially that *appointed officials cannot be trusted to do the right thing on behalf of the public interest, so they should receive as little power as possible.* The only thing worse than a dumb police officer, in this sense, is a smart one: someone who knows how, like a 'Yes Minister' civil servant, to manipulate the powers of government to serve the interests of officials rather than the public. This thesis of both right and left has become the anti-thesis underlying most of the criticisms of the anti-professionalization camps.

Professionalism, as Chan et al. (2003) have pointed out, is often a 'rhetorical device used by occupational groups to legitimate their power and authority' (p. 5). Manning (1977) has argued that the police are no exception to this strategy: they have used professionalism in the past as a means of keeping their 'clientele' at a distance, unifying the diverse interests within their occupation—particularly the distinct interests of Chiefs and frontline—thereby securing power and authority. Manning's arguments and the concerns raised by Sklansky (2011) about the 'persistent pull of police professionalism' highlight the potentially negative impacts of a new interest in police professionalism. Neyroud (2011) and Stone and Travis (2011) suggest a more positive future, in which professionalism is a strategy for improving policing, its ethical focus and its delivery. Unsurprisingly, Chan et al. (2003) has asserted that the nature, value, and effect of police professionalism are 'disputed'.

The debate about police professionalism has a long history. It was a key topic at the first national police convention in St Louis, Missouri, in 1871, where the Chairman exhorted the 112 delegates to 'make more perfect the police regulations of the whole land' (Vila and Morris 1999: 43). It was a key part of Theodore Roosevelt's 'American Ideals' at the turn of the 20th century (Berman 1987). At the same period in England and Wales, there was the emergence of what Emsley (2009) has called the 'professional consciousness', which manifested itself in the growth of police-specific professional journals and campaigns for more collective action to improve police living conditions and status.

These early flowerings of professionalism were primarily concerned with the identity and working conditions of the new occupation of policing. The middle of the twentieth century saw more focus on the development of a philosophy and practice of police professionalism, both of which can be seen in the work of August Vollmer and his protégé Orlando W. Wilson. Goldstein (1990) summarized the so-called 'professional model' that emerged from their work: its core ideas centred on a better bureaucratic machine, improved technology and investment in better educational standards for the personnel. Vollmer (1936) also placed a high value on policing as a moral calling—a true, priest-like 'vocation' with an ethical foundation. This was reflected in the 1957 Law Enforcement Code of Ethics in the US, which focused strongly on encouraging the police to act lawfully and impartially.

These early flowerings of a rhetoric of professionalism were admirable ideas, perhaps, but not based on the 'high knowledge' claims of the classic of professions. The rhetoric claimed the virtue of the self-governing 'operational independence' enjoyed by most classical professions, without requiring that the knowledge come first as a precondition of independence rather than as a result. As a response to a century of political interference and exploitation of police power for personal profit, it was hardly illogical. Yet it may have confused the police themselves over the extent to which the legitimacy of their independence from politics could survive their independence from universities.

The British model of Post War police professionalism was more focused on institutional change than the Vollmer–Wilson model in the US. Sir Frank Newsam, the Permanent Secretary at the Home Office, led a process of reform centred on enhancing the educational basis of the occupation. In the White Paper 'Higher Training for the Police Service of England and Wales' (Home Office 1947), a new National Police Staff College was conceived. Its remit was to raise the standards of senior leadership—even the title 'Staff College' made explicit links with the military staff colleges whose focus was the training of officers. The British model also asserted a professional separation from the citizen.

The successes of the mid-twentieth century professionalization movement in building better police forces and improving the training of leaders did not spare it from a harsh judgement from later generations. Goldstein (1990) subsequently criticized the 'professional model' for its internal focus. More centrally to our thesis, he criticized it for interpreting the route to impartiality as one that distanced the police not just from political influence but also from communities. Sklansky (2011) characterized the original professional model as 'thoroughly discredited' and argued that it emphasized the 'thin blue line' mentality of a small elite group of experts fighting crime against the odds. He suggested that it encouraged tactics of aggressive law enforcement, which contributed to poor relationships with black communities. Stone and Travis (2011), in their arguments for a 'new professionalism', substantially agreed with Goldstein and Sklansky. They argued that the old model was a 'distorted view of professionalism' which emphasized top-down management and 'assembly line techniques' rather than professional discretion, whilst the 'Three Rs' strategies it supported—random patrol, rapid response to 911 calls, and reactive investigations—had failed to control crime. Moreover, as Williams and Murphy (1990) observed, many police leaders infused their 'professionalism' with racism.

The British system, focused as it was on the training of middle and senior managers, also illustrated one other aspect of the early professional model: it was over focused on the senior leadership of the organization. As the title of Reiner's (1978) study of frontline police showed, the 'blue-coated worker' had only been slightly affected by the professional aspirations of the senior ranks. Indeed, the educational standards required for recruits remained stubbornly unchanged into the twenty-first century (Winsor 2012).

This critique of what has long been called the 'professional model' suggests a rather bleak picture of the prospects for police professionalism. Kleinig (1996) was no more optimistic. In outlining the ethics of policing, he suggested that professionalism should be distinguished from the process of professionalization. The latter was a 'process in which some purveyors of a service organize themselves to be the primary or recognized providers of that service' and do so through means such as 'certification, continuing education and the promulgation of a code of ethics' (p. 44). If successful in gaining recognition, then the occupation may 'acquire the status of a profession' (p. 45). Kleinig went on to identify the 'contours of a profession' and compare the police against it. He concluded that there were three substantial obstacles to the police achieving a full professional status. Firstly, the paramilitary nature of the organization was in tension with the autonomy and discretion characteristic of a professional. Like Goldstein (1990), he also questioned whether policing had a definable body of knowledge or the commitment to invest in acquiring it and embedding it in practice. Finally, he pointed out the obvious problems with the police, particularly in the light of their primacy in the use of force, regulating themselves like other professions.

Yet in setting out a critique of the old police professional model, Goldstein (1990) also provided the basis of a new one. The problem-solving model that he proposed was designed to shift police officers to a more 'creative, customized' model of practice, within a decentralized structure in which the frontline officer would be assigned greater autonomy and discretion (Roberg, Crank, and Kuykendall 2000: 378).

Goldstein's pessimism about developing a body of knowledge unique to policing also proved to be unwarranted. In contrast to Kleinig's assessment, the last 30 years have seen a substantial change in the knowledge base of policing. The UK, for example, has seen the development of professional 'doctrine' and significant investment in raising the standards and accreditation of knowledge for crime investigators (Neyroud, 2011). In the USA, Sherman et al.'s (1997) work on 'what works?', Skogan and Frydl's National Research Council report (2004), the Matrix of evidence based practice (Lum et al. 2011) and the work of the Campbell Crime and Justice group have, amongst others, provided a complex body of knowledge about the evidence on effective policing practices. They have also implicitly suggested that the application of such techniques requires a radical reconsideration of the education, training and development of police officers.

SYNTHESIS: A NEW PROFESSIONALISM?

Our synthesis is that any proposal for a new professionalism that fails to invoke empirical and quantitative knowledge is doomed to failure as a basis for legitimating police practice. Building on the admirable emphasis Goldstein provided for obtaining better *results* of policing, the American proposals for a new professionalism have walked right into a UK power struggle. The heart of this struggle lies between elected and professional police leaders contesting the basis for deciding *how* to obtain best results. The anti-evidence rhetoric of Harvard scholars offering 'craft experience' as the core of better police results (e.g. Sparrow 2011) allows any politician with experience in other walks of life to claim even better experiential knowledge of how to solve community problems. It is only by invoking the classic structure of a profession that police can sustain their judicial independence.

Imagine the scene when King James I said he would sit as a judge in a Crown Court—literally 'his' court. The response of the Lord Chief Justice, Sir Edward Coke, was this:

> the King in his own person cannot adjudge any case, either criminall...or betwixt party and party...but this ought to be determined and adjudged in some Court of Justice, according to the Law and Custom of England....Then the King said, that he thought the Law was founded upon reason, and that he and others had reason, as well as the Judges: To which it was answered by me, that true it was, that God had endowed his Majesty with excellent Science, and great endowments of nature; but his Majesty was not learned in the Lawes of his Realm of England, and causes which concern the life, or inheritance, or goods, or fortunes of his Subjects; they are not to be decided by naturall reason but by the artificiall reason and judgment of Law, which Law is an act which requires long study and experience, before that a man can attain to the cognizance of it; And that the Law was the Golden metwand and measure to try the Causes of the Subjects; and which protected his Majesty in safety and peace. (12 Co Rep 63, 63–5)

In other words, we could say that not even the King can practise law until he has passed his bar examination! The fact that King James I later dismissed Lord Justice Coke reflects the repeated failure of the Stuarts to understand the legitimation of governmental power based on claims to worldly knowledge. It is exactly the principle Lord Chief Justice Coke evoked that supports our proposed synthesis of a new professionalism based on high knowledge.

The starting point for Stone and Travis' proposal for a 'new police professionalism' is Goldstein's vision of problem-oriented, community-based policing. Their paper was prepared for the Harvard Session on Policing and Public Safety, which brought together US, Australian, and UK police officials, academics and US government representatives. It was written in a US context of financial pressures on US police departments' budgets for community policing approaches (Gascon and Fogelsong 2010). A lack of money appeared to be forcing police departments to consider a 'retreat to the core'—effectively the old professional model based around emergency response and reactive response.

Instead of the 'retreat to the core', Stone and Travis (2011) argued for 'new police professionalism' based around four propositions: accountability (particularly democratic accountability); legitimacy; innovation; national coherence. Stone and Travis suggest that the police have become considerably more accountable since the 'old' professional era, partly in reaction to the perceived insularity and some of the problems of the old era. They cite Tyler's work (2007) in support of placing legitimacy in the centre of their model. Responding to the financial pressures, they suggest that police need to make innovation a key plank of their profession. Moreover, given the need to avoid duplication and the challenge of cross-jurisdictional crime, they conclude by advocating greater national coherence.

Note what they did not say. They did not say what method should be used to produce or evaluate innovations. They did not say what the basis for 'coherence' should be: opinions or evidence. In short, they said nothing about the complexity of policing requiring more specialized knowledge than rudimentary understanding of the law. The underlying assumption is that policing is a craft requiring smart people, not a science requiring long study. Their model ignores the historic role of high knowledge in gaining the trust of a lay population utterly dependent on the power of the profession, however accountable or coherent it may be. This lacuna could thus guarantee that their model would never achieve the legitimacy it seeks.

This lacuna stems directly from the 'illusion of validity' that practitioners gain from extensive experience in trying to solve problems (Kahneman 2011). Unless practitioners are actually given feedback for the results of their work, it is unlikely that high levels of skill can develop (Sherman 1984, 2013). The idea that 'fast thinking' by police can ever replace 'slow thinking' by research and development sciences is itself an insult to the complexity of policing. It also plays right into the trap set by those who wish to undermine the rule of law in favour of populist democracy. That is why the craft conception of policing has been losing appeal in the UK, where police have long been immune to populist politics in ways that US police leaders would find unimaginable.

Thus in the very different context in England and Wales in 2010, when Neyroud was commissioned by the Home Secretary to consider the future of police leadership and training, he turned away from a craft model of policing in favour of police-led science (Weisburd and Neyroud 2011). Writing in the light of a major programme of reform by the Conservative-Liberal Democrat Coalition (Home Office 2010), Neyroud was asked how to raise standards while cutting budgets. The government's reforms, which were accompanied by 20 per cent cuts to operational budgets, were framed around three main themes: (1) a major reconfiguration of local accountability by the replacement of local police authority boards with a single, directly elected Police and Crime Commissioner (PCC); (2) significant institutional change at the national level that reduced the role of chief constables in governing police infrastructure, and (3) radical reviews of police officer and police staff appointments, 'remunerations and conditions' (Winsor 2011 and 2012).

The Neyroud Review (2011) said that policing should increasingly require graduate education as a qualification for leadership, with all superintendents and above holding master's degrees at the time of their appointment. In this single statement, he parted company with the Harvard view of a new professionalism, and drew a line in the sand for the Cambridge view that police legitimacy depends on advanced education on *crime and policing* for police leaders (and not just business, finance, or public policy in general).

Although Neyroud drew directly on Stone and Travis' framework for his emphasis on democratic accountability—a central plank of police reform—and national coherence, he provided a far more evidence-based framework for the kind of knowledge that should guide police practice. The national coherence idea appeared to be an important counter-balance to the localization of British policing inherent in creating PCCs. But accountability, in Neyroud's view, should be based not on the untested opinions of those who inspect or investigate the police, but rather on the facts of each case in light of the best and most relevant research evidence.

Whether a police decision not to arrest a domestic violence suspect was the cause of a subsequent domestic murder, for example, should not (in this view) be a matter of assumptions by those holding police accountable. Rather, Her Majesty's Inspectorate of Constabulary (HMIC) and the Independent Police Complaint Commission (IPCC) should themselves be held to account based upon empirical research showing no relationship between arrest and subsequent homicide (Sherman and Strang 1996).Thus Neyroud went well beyond Stone and Travis in seeking to operationalize the 'new professionalism' in extensive detail. His Review successfully proposed the setting up of a new 'Police Professional Body' (PPB) to give institutional shape to the new police profession—echoing Newsam's creation of the first National Police College at Bramshill with the far more powerful College of Policing created in 2012. The framework for the college adopted most of Neyroud's recommendations that it should be responsible for the registration, accreditation, and qualifications of police personnel (officers and unsworn staff), their training and development and their national practice standards. The college also embodies the Neyroud Review's proposal for a whole police service professional body. The college is to be independent from government, but accountable through nominated board members. Its agenda includes a major overhaul of the pre-qualification for joining and qualifications to become frontline and senior managers and a new emphasis on continuous professional development. Finally, the college, is drawing on Shepherd (2003),Weisburd and Neyroud (2011) and Sherman (2011), in reshaping police training and development on partnerships with Higher Education.

As the government's response to the Neyroud Review showed in its summary of consultation responses (Home Office 2011), the proposals stirred up a considerable debate. Just as Chan et al. (2003) had asserted, police professionalism is contested territory. Some respondents described raising educational thresholds and qualification standards as creating a risk of excluding those who had practical experience but no formal qualifications. The debate about educational qualifications was given further exposure in the subsequent second report of the Winsor Review (2012). Both Neyroud and Winsor linked their arguments in favour of raising the educational standards to the greater technical complexity and demands of the modern police role. As Winsor pointed out, the reality of the competition for places in policing in the UK had already raised the standards close to his proposed threshold.

In both the UK and USA, there is, therefore, an important debate about the extent, nature, and opportunity for professionalization of the police. In the UK, that debate has centred on a major programme of institutional change by a government not seen as friendly to police. In the US the debate has been more philosophical. The two came together at the 2013 Jerry Lee Symposium on Capitol Hill, when heads of various US bodies for peace officer standards and training met with the CEO and two directors of the UK's new College of Policing. Their consensus on the importance of promoting evidence-based practice in police training and standards marked a notable shift from earlier discourse. It even included preliminary discussions of a kind of international qualification accrediting knowledge of what works in policing. In both countries, proponents of change have placed legitimacy firmly at the centre of their approach. What remains for this chapter to suggest is the relationship of these visions of professionalisms to the concepts of dialogue with audiences that are themselves in dialectical struggles.

DIALOGUE AND DIALECTIC

The synthesis we propose between those who want more policing, those who want less, and those who want both is this: *liberal democracies should use the rules of scientific evidence to help decide how much harm can be prevented by certain kinds of policing, and whether the diverse costs of that policing are justified.* The definitions of both harms and costs for this synthesis are highly contestable. But that is not a bad thing. It is the contest, in fact, that can make police legitimate in the light of knowledge.

The dialogue between police and their audiences rarely includes well-established facts. Even in the UK, police officers appear on news media without reliable statistics, sometimes even guessing (by admission) but using great self-confidence to argue their point. In this respect they differ very little from politicians. But until they do, their legitimacy is arguably threatened.

What Bottoms and Tankebe (2012) propose suggests that police must make knowledge and evidence part of the 'dialogic' process between the claims to legitimacy by the police as a 'power-holders' and the response by 'audiences.'

In developing their analysis Bottoms and Tankebe start from Beetham and Coicaud's threefold conceptualization of audience legitimacy: legality, shared values, and consent. None of these three concepts are simple in their application to policing. Each conceals tensions, which we propose to illustrate by discussing them in the context of the new professionalism within the UK police reform programme. The creation of a new professional institutional structure seems to be most relevant to discussion against 'power-holder' legitimacy, given that the Professional Body was explicitly designed as the 'the professional guardian of the quality of policing' (Neyroud 2011: 11). On other hand, the key components of the new professionalism, including the commitment to democratic accountability and an innovatory, evidence based approach seem to have a strong relationship with the 'audience'.

On the face of it, legality should be the most straightforward of the concepts to apply to policing. As Meares and Neyroud have put it:

> Police are creatures of law. That law authorizes, circumscribes and shapes police activity is what distinguishes police from vigilantes. Police compliance with the law is one of the most important aspects of democratic society. The public expects police officers to enforce laws fairly according to law and rules that limit their power. The very existence of these rules justify the claim that police are a rule-bound institution engaged in the pursuit of justice and protection of individual liberties as well as the battles against crime (2012: 1)

Yet the pursuit of legal compliance can, as Scarman (1982) described it, conflict with the maintenance of order—if sections of the community perceive that police powers have been used with partiality. The old professionalism was criticized for just such an adherence to the rules and falling back on the 'legal valence' (Meares and Neyroud 2012) to justify police actions. Legality, we would suggest, like effectiveness, is a necessary condition for legitimacy, but not a sufficient basis for sustaining it.

As Neyroud (2011) demonstrated, almost all police training regimes in the US and UK place law at the core of the police curriculum. *Blackstone's Police Manuals* (2013) are a living testimony to an older model of professionalism, which has roots going back to 1829. Yet police have been taught law the way electricians have been taught wiring diagrams, or the way taxicab drivers have been taught to memorize the map of London. There is little attention in either the manuals or the curriculum to the process of implementing the law or the most effective strategies for enforcement with minimal use of force. Despite the central place of 'the public interest' in the lawful exercise of police discretion, police are taught nothing about evidence on whether police tactics prevent or tragically increase crime and harm. Law and legality are disconnected from impact and outcome.

A new police knowledge-on-more-than-law, or what we might call knowledge on-how-to-achieve-outcomes, has blossomed in the last half century (Skogan and Frydl 2004). This knowledge has barely percolated into most police agencies, let alone into the public or political forums of police policy debates. The only way to make this knowledge visible is for police themselves to articulate it. No matter how many academic journal articles or newspaper columns professors may write, it is only police leadership which can be the voice of professional knowledge. Until police leaders themselves adopt the stance of using knowledge produced in partnership with universities, few citizens will believe that such knowledge even exists. If such knowledge is available, citizens might think, why wouldn't the police want to use it?

The internal dialectic: organizational legitimacy and the new professionalism. There is one further aspect of the 'audience' that Bottoms and Tankebe do not specifically address and which may be particularly important in the success of the approach we are advocating. That audience is police themselves, in relation to their perceptions of whether their employers promote 'organizational justice.' In a recent study of the impact of such perceptions on police officers, Wolfe and Piquero (2011) have analysed a survey on police misconduct with a random sample of 483 police officers employed in the Philadelphia Police Department. Their results indicate that 'officers who view their agency as fair and just in managerial practices are less likely to adhere to the code of silence or believe that police corruption in pursuit of a noble cause is justified' (p. 332).

This finding from a police agency builds on prior evidence of a strong association between organizational justice and the behaviours of employees in many kinds of organizations. Two substantial meta-analyses (Cohen-Charash and Spector 2001; Colquitt et al. 2001) have shown that the application of the three key elements of organizational justice—procedural, distributive, and interactional—by supervisors and managers is associated with positive outcomes such as improved service and productivity. Wolfe and Piquero concluded 'organizational justice is a promising framework to understand police misconduct and may help guide police administrators in the implementation of effective management strategies to reduce the incidence of the behavior' (p. 332).

A forthcoming study by Bradford and Myhill looked more closely at the relationship between the procedurally fair policies and the implementation of fair police conduct towards the public. They show that internal organizational justice had a strong association with positive officer attitudes to the citizen. They suggest that the application of organizational justice may be critical to the 'operational change culture' to 'effect the change in the habitus of operational police officers that has remained elusive thus far' (p. 15). Their study provides further support for the role of a professional body embracing all ranks and roles in a policing model in which the professional institution takes ownership not only of professional standards of practice, but also the development of leaders and managers, whose attention to internal organizational fairness appears to be critical to making progress with external organizational legitimacy.

We would go beyond these conclusions to suggest that employer legitimacy is an essential encouragement for the autonomous professional discretion founded on research evidence. Legitimacy of research within police agencies is both central to our approach and potentially linked with better outcomes. In one experiment, for example, the organization provided substantial education to the experimenting officers in the evidence based practice underpinning the approach. Officers were transported to Cambridge to take part in an intensive briefing in preparation for the trial, with clear support from their senior managers. The briefing covered a large body of research on factors promoting offender desistance from criminal careers. In applying this research, the officers exhibited a high degree of bold experimentation with conditions of diverting offenders from prosecution, including the use of restorative justice to resolve an assault on their own colleagues. An external review (Neyroud and Slothower 2013) identified a high degree of dialogue between officers about their application of the research evidence to a new research project applying prior evidence.

Let us connect this point to our dialectic and synthesis. We suggest that police legitimacy based on knowledge requires that officers feel supported by their senior managers to experiment with police practices. Confidence in the legitimacy of experiments themselves may well, in turn, be a significant component of their own perceived authority to negotiate successfully with offenders. The production of new knowledge to achieve better outcomes may, in these circumstances, be best deployed in an organization in which organizational justice and professionalism are central to the ethos. Legitimacy based on knowledge therefore replaces the old rules of a paramilitary force with new rules of professionalism based on high knowledge.

Once police leaders understand this and promote the existence of such knowledge, they can create a new partnership with universities. Widespread publicity about new knowledge in policing can promote public understanding of what police do and how difficult policing is. Public acceptance of tough decisions may also be more forthcoming. If there is an issue of how many days suspected terrorists may be detained, for example, police leaders might discuss the research rather than their own opinions. Judges write opinions. Surgeons do research. Police practice is much more like surgery than judging. The fact that police engage in knowledge-based dialogue with its diverse audiences, however, does not mean that a consensus across those audiences can ever be reached. A dialectical audience will respond differentially to police proposals or practices based on complex evidence. Nothing will ever be neat and tidy about a dialogic process of creating legitimacy, either with or without dialectic. But the dialectic makes the messiness clearer in the sense that there will be predictable fault lines of public opinion that police can try to straddle—or ignore, strategically. However, as police communicate across the social chasms of liberal democracies, they can become more open and transparent around knowledge. They can be accountable to knowledge, and not just to power, as the key principle for making the right decision. They can use more cost-benefit estimation, trying to raise the level of discussion from intuitive Systems I thinking to a more effortful and accurate form of Systems II (Kahneman, 2011). It is just this use of dispassionate analysis that has been the basis for the increasing civility of the modern world (Elias, 1994; Pinker, 2011). The spread of education has preceded the decline of mortality rates and over-population across the world. We may not be at the end of history. But we must certainly all support a growth of knowledge and the legitimacy of its use.

REFERENCES

Berman, J. S. (1987) *Police Administration and Progressive Reform: Theodore Roosevelt as Police Commissioner of New York.* New York: Greenwood Press.

Connor, P., Johnston, D., Hutton, G., and McKinnon, G. (eds) (2012) *Blackstone's Police Manuals.* Oxford: Oxford University Press.

Bottoms, A. E. and Tankebe, J. (2012) 'Beyond Procedural Justice: A Dialogic Approach to Legitimacy in Criminal Justice', *Journal of Criminal Law and Criminology* 102(1): 119–70.

Chan, J. B., Devery, C., and Doran, S. (2003). *Fair Cop: Learning the Art of Policing.* Toronto: University of Toronto Press.

Cohen-Charash, Y. and Spector, P. E. (2001) 'The Role of Justice in Organizations: A Meta-Analysis', *Organizational Behaviour and Human Decision Processes* 86(2): 278–321.

Colquitt, J. A., Conlon, D. E., Wesson, M. J., Porter, C., and Ng, K. Y. (2001) 'Justice at the Millennium: A Meta-Analytic Review of 25 years of Organizational Justice Research', *Journal of Applied Psychology* 86(3): 425–45.

Elias, N. (1994) *The Civilizing Process: Sociogenetic and Psychogenetic Investigations*. Oxford: Basil Blackwell.

Emsley, C. (2009) *The Great British Bobby: a History of British Policing from the 18th Century to the Present*. London: Quercus.

Flack, J. C., Girvan, M., de Waal, F. B. M., and Krabauer, D. C. (2006) 'Policing Stabilizes Construction of Social Niches in Primates', *Nature* 439: 426–9.

Gascon, G. and Fogelsong, T. (2010) 'Making Policing More Affordable: Managing Costs and Measuring Value in Policing', *New Perspectives in Policing*. Washington, DC: National Institute of Justice.

Goldstein, H. (1990) *Problem-Oriented Policing*. New York: McGraw-Hill.

Home Office (1947) *Higher Training for Police Service in England and Wales*. London: HMSO, Cm. 7070.

Home Office (2010) *Policing in the 21st Century: Reconnecting Police and the People*. London: HMSO, Cm. 7925.

Home Office (2011) *Peter Neyroud's Review of Police Leadership and Training: Summary of Consultation*. London: Home Office.

Kahneman, D. (2011) *Thinking, Fast and Slow*. London: Allen Lane.

Kleinig, J. (1996) *The Ethics of Policing*. Cambridge: Cambridge University Press.

Lum, C., Koper, C. S., and Telep, C. W. (2011) 'The Evidence Based Policing Matrix', *Journal of Experimental Criminology* 7(1): 3–26.

Manning, P. K. (1977) *Police Work: The Social Organization of Policing*. Cambridge, MA: MIT Press.

Meares, T. and Neyroud, P. W. (2012) 'Rightful Policing', unpublished paper presented to the Harvard Executive Session on Policing and Public Safety.

Muir, W. K. (1977) *Police: Streetcorner Politicians*. Chicago: University of Chicago Press.

Neyroud, P. W. (2011) *A Review of Police Training and Leadership*. London: Home Office.

Neyroud, P. W. and Slothower, M. (2013) 'Operation Turning Point: Interim Report on a Randomised Trial in Birmingham, UK', unpublished report for West Midlands Police.

Pinker, S. (2011) *The Better Angels of Our Nature: the Decline of Violence in History and its causes*. London: Allen Lane.

Reiner, R. (1978) *The Blue Coated Worker*. Cambridge: Cambridge University Press.

Roberg, R., Crank, J., and Kuykendall, J. (2000) *Police and Society*. Los Angeles: Roxbury Publishing Company.

Scarman, Lord (1982) *The Report into the Brixton Riots*. Harmondsworth: Penguin.

Shaw, G. B. (1908) 'The Doctor's Dilemma', in Bernard Shaw's *Collected Plays with Their Prefaces*. London: Bodley Head.

Shepherd, J. (2003) 'Explaining Feast or Famine in Randomised Controlled Trials: Medical Science and Criminology Compared', *Evaluation Review* 27(3): 290–315.

Sherman, L. W. (1984) 'Experiments in Police Discretion: Scientific Boon or Dangerous Knowledge?' *Law and Contemporary Problems* 47(4): 61–81.

Sherman, L. W. (1998a) 1998 'American Policing.' (pp. 429–56), in Tonry, M. (ed) *The 1998 Handbook of Crime and Punishment*. NY: Oxford University Press.

Sherman, L. W. (1998b) *Evidence-Based Policing*. Washington, DC: Police Foundation. Ideas in American Policing Series available at: <http://www.policefoundation.org> accessed 20 May 2013.

Sherman, L. W. (2011) 'Professional Policing and Liberal Democracy' Benjamin Franklin Medal Lecture, 1 November. London: Royal |Society for the Promotion of the Arts, Manufactures and Commerce available at: <http://www.thersa.org/events/audio-and-past-events/> accessed 20 May 2013.

SHERMAN, L. W. (2013) 'The Rise of Evidence-Based Policing, 1975–2025: Targeting, Testing and Tracking' in Tonry, M. (ed) *Crime and Justice*, vol 42. Chicago: University of Chicago Press (forthcoming).

SHERMAN, L. W., GOTTFREDSON, D., MACKENZIE, D., ECK, J., REUTER, P., and BUSHWAY, S. (1997) *Preventing Crime: What Works, What doesn't, What's Promising*. Washington, DC: National Institute of Justice.

SHERMAN, L. W. and STRANG, H. (1996) 'Policing Domestic Violence: The Problem-Solving Paradigm.' Canberra: Australian National University, Research School of Social Sciences available at: <http://www.aic.gov.au/criminal_justice_system/rjustice/rise/sherman-strang.html> accessed May 2013.

SKLANSKY, D. (2011) 'The Persistent Pull of Police Professionalism', *New Perspectives in Policing*, available at: <http://ssrn.com/abstract=1788463> accessed 24 July 2013.

SKOGAN, W. and FRYDL, K. (eds) (2004) *Fairness and Effectiveness in Policing: the evidence*. Washington, DC: National Academies Press.

SPARROW, M. K. (2011) 'Governing Science', *New Perspectives in Policing*. Washington DC: National Institute of Justice.

STONE, C. and TRAVIS, J. (2011) 'Towards a New Professionalism in Policing'. *New Perspectives in Policing*, available at: <https://www.ncjrs.gov/App/Publications/abstract.aspx?ID+254446> accessed 20 May 2013.

VILA, B. and MORRIS, C. (1999) *The Role of Police in American Society*. Westport, Connecticut: Greenwood Press.

VOLLMER, A. (1936) *The Police and Modern Society*. Montclair NJ: Patterson-Smith.

WEBER, M. (1947) *The Theory of Social and Economic Organization*, Henderson, A. M. and Talcott Parsons (trans). Introduction by Talcott Parsons. New York: Free Press.

WEISBURD, D. and NEYROUD, P. W. (2011) 'Police Science: A New Paradigm', *New Perspectives in Policing*. Washington DC: National Institute of Justice.

WILLIAMS, H. and MURPHY, P. (1990) 'The Evolving Strategy of Police: A Minority View', *Perspectives on Policing*. Washington DC: National Institute of Justice.

WINSOR, T. P. (2011) *Independent Review of Police Officer and Staff Remuneration and Conditions: Interim Report*. London: Home Office.

WINSOR, T. P. (2012) *Independent Review of Police Officer and Staff Remuneration and Conditions*. London: HMSO, Cm. 8325.

WOLFE, S. E. and PIQUERO, A. R. (2011) 'Organizational Justice and Police Misconduct', *Criminal Justice and Behavior* 38: (4) 332–53.

WRONG, D. H. (1994). *The Problem of Order: What Unites and Divides Society*. New York: The Free Press.

WRONG, D. H. (1995) *Power: its Forms, Bases, and Uses*. New Brunswick: Transaction Publishers.

15

DOES LOW LEGITIMACY CAUSE CRIME? A REVIEW OF THE EVIDENCE

Manuel Eisner and Amy Nivette

Some scholars argue that legitimacy (i.e. the right to rule) should be at the core of criminology as the science of rule making, rule breaking, and rule enforcement (Bottoms & Tankebe 2012; LaFree 1998; Tyler 1990). The claim is that legitimacy is a crucial theoretical construct for understanding the link between social order and crime, for explaining the motivations behind compliance with the law, and in bridging the gap between macro and micro explanations of crime. This chapter reviews the empirical literature on whether legitimacy predicts crime. Findings suggest a weak effect in the predicted direction. However, we also identify a number of limitations that future research should address. They include: (1) more consistent operationalization of legitimacy, (2) better statistical control for potential confounding factors, (3) tests for alternative assumptions of the causal order between legitimacy and crime, (4) integration of macro- and micro-level research, and (5) more cross-cultural comparison.

LEGITIMACY OF THE STATE AND RULE BREAKING

In December 1988, while still in prison, *Nelson Mandela* wrote a memorandum in preparation for a meeting with the then President of South Africa, P.A. Botha. In the document Mandela outlined the view of the ANC on violence:

> The organisation has no vested interest in violence. It abhors any action which may cause loss of life, destruction of property and misery to the people. It has worked long and patiently for a South Africa of common values and for an undivided and peaceful non-racial state. But we consider the armed struggle a legitimate form of self-defence against a morally repugnant system of government which will not allow even peaceful form of protest.

The quote captures a core argument of freedom fighters and revolutionaries around the world: A state that is repressive and corrupt has no moral authority and loses the exclusive right to use coercive force. Violence hence becomes a legitimate means for self-defence, and for achieving liberty, independence or equality.

But is there also a link between the legitimacy of the state and the more mundane refusals to comply with its rules such as shoplifting, burglary, or homicide? The fourteenth-century artist *Ambrogio Lorenzetti* certainly thought so. In 1340 he painted the famous Allegories of Good and Bad Government in the town hall of Siena so that the city council would be reminded of the consequences of its actions (Rubinstein 1958): Under a good and legitimate government, the paintings explain, there is peace, people obey the law, and trade and the economy prospers. Under a bad and illegitimate government, in contrast, one can see innocent people being arrested, homicides being committed, and economic life coming to a standstill.

Contemporary research suggests that Lorenzetti was up to something important. Thus, a growing number of studies show a substantial correlation between political legitimacy and levels of rule-breaking behaviour: In societies where the state and its institutions are felt to lack legitimacy the citizens are less likely to comply with the rules laid down in the law. Potentially this means that criminology has to consider the question raised by *John Locke* much more seriously: Namely under what conditions are the members of a society obliged to comply with a state's laws? As is well known, Locke's answer was that an obligation to obey only exists if authority is based on legitimacy, which it gains through the free consent by those subjected to an institution (Locke 1988 [1689]). *A legitimate authority is one that is 'justified in claiming the right to hold power over other citizens'* (Bottoms and Tankebe 2012: 124). But how strong is the evidence for legitimacy as an explanation of compliance and crime? What are the limitations of current research? And how could the evidence be strengthened?

A REVIEW OF THE EVIDENCE

Evidence on the presumed effect of legitimacy on crime comes from two research traditions: One is macro-level research on the factors that explain variation in levels of crime and violence over time and between nations, regions or neighbourhoods (e.g. LaFree 1998). The other is micro-level research on the extent to which an individual's willingness to comply with rules is affected by the perceived legitimacy of those who make and enforce these rules (e.g. Tyler 1990). These two traditions have had limited contact and we discuss them in separate sections.

We do not claim to have found all relevant studies, but we believe we cover the major work in the area. Also, we exclusively consider studies that examine actual compliant, norm-breaking, or criminal behaviour as the outcome. We ignore work that examines the effects of legitimacy on norms, behaviour intentions, or beliefs.

MACRO-LEVEL RESEARCH

In comparison to other indicators such as urbanism or social inequality rather few studies have considered the legitimacy of the state as a predictor of macro-level variation in levels of crime (Nivette, 2011). While understandable from a practical point of view—measures of legitimacy are far more difficult to obtain than measures of GDP or the proportion of young people—the almost complete neglect of variables related to the state's 'right to rule' has no justification in criminological theory. Enlightenment theorists like *Jeremy Bentham* (2007 [1781]) and *Cesare Beccaria* (1764) agreed that compliance with the law and cooperation amongst free citizens rested less on the harshness of punishment than on the rightness of the laws, the fairness of the judges, and the swiftness of the legal bureaucracy—in other words: on a law-bound state that creates the very conditions under which citizens are prepared to self-regulate their behaviour.

But amongst empirical criminologists the idea that legitimacy could explain macro-level variation in crime only gained some prominence in the late 1990s. In '*Losing Legitimacy*' LaFree (1998) argued that three key social institutions—the family, the economy, and the state—motivate citizens to abide by the rules, participate in social control, and obey the law. When these social institutions are seen as unfair, useless, or corrupt, they lose legitimacy and subsequently the ability to maintain social control. LaFree (1998) tested these arguments using post-World War II crime data in the United States. He measured legitimacy in a number of ways: by distrust in government and collective action or protest (political legitimacy), inflation and income inequality (economic legitimacy), and ideological challenges and structural change in the form of divorce rate and female-headed households, respectively (legitimacy of the family). LaFree found a positive bivariate relationship between these forms of institutional illegitimacy and violent crime, and that these effects were particularly strong for African Americans. He concluded that legitimacy was first lost in political and family institutions during the 1960s and 1970s, and that the crisis then spilled over into economic institutions, leading to the deterioration of social control and an increase in crime.

Eisner (2001) and Roth (2009) examined large-scale variation in homicide rates over several centuries in Europe and the United States. Both concluded that neither economic development nor the rise in the coercive power of the state could model the long-term decline in homicide since the sixteenth century. Rather, it seems that on both sides of the Atlantic change in the legitimacy of the political and social order was a major force behind change in the likelihood that men would fight each other in public space.[1] Roth distinguished four aspects of legitimacy: the belief that government is stable and that its legal and judicial institutions are unbiased and will redress wrongs and protect lives and property; a feeling of trust in government and the officials who

[1] Elijah Anderson (1999) documented this in his ethnographic study of poor, urban residents in the United States. Residents alienated from police and society developed a 'code of the streets' to regulate status, public space, and social behaviours, including the use of violence.

run it, and a belief in their legitimacy; patriotism, empathy, and fellow feeling arising from racial, religious, or political solidarity; and the belief that the social hierarchy is legitimate, that one's position in society is or can be satisfactory and that one can command the respect of others without resorting to violence. These constructs are certainly difficult to measure over long periods of time but in a recent paper Roth (2012) has proposed ways to tackle this problem.

Other macro-level research has examined the link between legitimacy and crime cross-sectionally by considering variation between states. For example, Chamlin and Cochran (2006) have asked whether citizens are more likely to comply with social institutions if these institutions are perceived to function according to justifiable universalistic rules. They argued that states perceived as serving the interests of a few and allowing economic success based on ascribed rather than meritocratic principles would lose legitimacy and hence experience more violence. Moreover, they hypothesized that the perceived lack of legitimacy is the mechanism that accounts for the well-known link between economic inequality and homicide rates. They tested this hypothesis using a sample of 33 countries. Legitimacy was measured by two questions from the *World Values Survey*: 'people in [this] country are poor because society treats them unfairly' (economic legitimacy) and 'the government is run to further the interests of social elites rather than for the benefit of all' (political legitimacy) (p. 239).[2] Contrary to their hypothesis they found no direct effect of lacking economic or political legitimacy on homicide, and they found no empirical support for the idea that perceived lack of legitimacy can account for the effect of inequality on homicide rates. However, there was some evidence suggesting that in the subgroup of highly modernized countries a low level of political and economic legitimacy is associated with higher homicide rates.

In a recent cross-national study Nivette and Eisner (2013) extended the analysis to a much larger sample, using a broader measure of legitimacy. They relied on Gilley's (2009) indicator of legitimate political power, which combines three components initially proposed by Beetham (1991): the *moral rightfulness* of laws and rules as seen by those subject to a power; *legality* in the sense of the conformity of power with the laws; and *consent* by those who are subject to those in power. Items included in this indicator are: evaluation of state respect for human rights, confidence in police and civil society (legality); satisfaction with democratic development, evaluation of the political system, use of violence in protest (justification); voter turnout and payment of quasi-voluntary taxes (consent).

Control variables considered in their models included income inequality, infant mortality rate, female labour force participation, young male population, population growth, GDP per capita, and a Latin American dummy variable. The findings supported the idea that political legitimacy is negatively related to homicide rates (see also Nivette 2012, on political legitimacy and homicide in Europe). In their sample of

[2] Arguably, these measures are limited in that they only capture perceptions about the distributive fairness of economic and political resources. While distributive justice in an important aspect of legitimacy (Beetham 1991), overall legitimacy is the product of many parts: procedural justice, distributive justice, effectiveness, legality, and behavioural consent (Tankebe 2013).

$N = 65$ countries the bivariate correlation between Gilley's measure of legitimacy and homicide was $r = -.51$, and in the multi-variate analysis the standardized effect of legitimacy on homicide rates was $\beta = -.34$.

The link between legitimacy and crime has also been examined at the level of neighbourhoods. In this research strand scholars have mainly focused on *legal cynicism* as a measure for the lack of legitimacy, following a study by Sampson and Bartusch (1998). Sampson and Bartusch (1998) interpreted legal cynicism as a form of anomie in which individuals perceive that the criminal justice system is unjust or illegitimate, and so legal norms are weak and not binding. Developing this argument further Kirk and Papachristos (2011) argued that sub-cultures of cynical attitudes towards the law 'frame' situations in such a way that violence is more likely. This is in line with evidence that violence is higher in neighbourhoods where the criminal justice system is perceived to be unfair, ineffective, and lacking legality (Kane 2005; Kubrin and Weitzer 2003).

In the first neighbourhood-level study on the effects of police legitimacy on violent crime Kane (2005) analysed panel data for 74 New York precincts from 1975 to 1996. He examined whether compromised police legitimacy can cause more violence by discouraging citizens from cooperating with the police, and hence encouraging the use of violent self-help (Black 1983). The study did not measure police legitimacy directly, but relied on measures of police misconduct and over-policing (i.e. 'aggressive' policing) as proxies. Precincts were divided into three categories based on their level of structural disadvantage: 'low', 'high', and 'extreme'. The study found that the first indicator of compromised police legitimacy, namely police misconduct, was related to more violent crime in neighbourhoods with 'high' and 'extreme' disadvantage. Over-policing was significantly related to high violent crime only in extremely disadvantaged neighbourhoods. In precincts with low disadvantage, however, police misconduct and aggressive policing had no effect on violence. Kane (2005) argued that this is likely because these more resourceful communities address misconduct through official means of accountability.

More recently Kirk and Papachristos (2011) examined the effects of legal cynicism on violent crime in Chicago, Illinois. They argue that legal cynicism is an adaptation to structural disadvantage, and that cynical attitudes discourage citizens from building social ties and therefore reduce collective efficacy. Their sample, drawn from the *Project on Human Development in Chicago Neighborhoods* from 1994–1995, was composed of 343 neighbourhood clusters in which 8,782 residents were surveyed. Legal cynicism was measured with three items: (1) 'laws are made to be broken', (2) 'the police are not doing a good job in preventing crime in this neighborhood', and (3) 'the police are not able to maintain order on the streets and sidewalks in the neighborhood' (p. 1207). The authors also accounted for a range of neighbourhood-level covariates, including collective efficacy, concentrated poverty, immigrant concentration, residential stability, proportion of youth, spatial effects, and tolerance of deviance. They found that in neighbourhoods where residents were more cynical towards the law, homicide was higher ($r = .49$) (Kirk and Papachristos 2011). They also found that cynicism partially explains the link between poverty and homicide, and that cynicism discourages participation in neighbourhood social control (i.e. collective efficacy).

Further, examining the residual change in homicide from the 1990s to the early 2000s (i.e. any changes not in line with the overall decline), high legal cynicism partially explained why homicide persisted in certain neighbourhoods when city-wide poverty and homicide declined.

In sum, the neighbourhood-level studies suggest that a police force or legal system that is considered illegitimate can create cultural adaptations that favour the use of violence to resolve conflicts, particularly in disadvantaged communities, where social and political capital are already weak.

INDIVIDUAL-LEVEL RESEARCH

Individual-level research on the effects of legitimacy on crime is shaped by the pioneering work of *Tom Tyler* and colleagues (e.g. Sunshine & Tyler 2003; Tyler 1990, 2006). Tyler argues that there exist two strategies to seek compliance with the law. The first uses coercion and the threat of punishment. It tries to increase the costs of rule breaking and assumes rational actors. This strategy is, Tyler argues, largely ineffective. The second approach relies on self-regulation, i.e. the abstention from crimes due to internalized constraints. To be activated, self-regulation requires a motivational basis—a good reason to develop and use internal constraints. The most important such basis is legitimacy—which Tyler (2009: 313) defines as 'the feeling of responsibility and obligation to follow the law, to accept the decisions of legal authorities, and to cooperate with and help legal authorities to do their jobs'. Tyler links this subjective sense of legitimacy to the actual performance of the criminal justice system: If the legal authorities effectively manage problems, resolve conflicts, behave in a fair and transparent way, and treat citizens with dignity and courtesy—in short: if they are governed by *procedural justice*—they are more likely to be seen as legitimate, hence making self-regulated abstinence from transgressions more likely.

Empirical research inspired by Tyler rarely refers to crime or delinquency as dependent variables. Its most common outcome is 'compliance', which is generally operationalized as the absence of norm-breaking. Thus, a typical item asks respondents how often they 'follow the rule of *not* taking inexpensive items from stores without paying' (Sunshine & Tyler, 2003). Such items are really inversely worded delinquency items. Asking whether legitimacy increases compliance with the law is therefore equivalent to asking whether the lack of legitimacy leads to more crime.

Over the past 25 years various empirical studies have examined the extent to which legitimacy predicts delinquent rule breaking, respectively compliance with the law.

Two panel studies have examined the effects of legitimacy on compliance (Tyler 2006). The first study was conducted in 1985 in Chicago (Tyler 1990). It entailed 1,575 participants in wave 1, of whom 804 could be re-interviewed a year later. In that study the perceived legitimacy of the police or the courts in wave 2 was found to have a weak significant effect ($\beta = .11$, $p < .05$) on the level of compliance also measured in wave 2 when compliance in wave 1 was controlled.

The second study (Fagan and Piquero 2007) investigated the short-term effects of legitimacy and legal cynicism on a sample of 1,355 adolescent offenders recently convicted of a serious felony offense in Philadelphia, PA and Phoenix, AZ. The participants were interviewed shortly after adjudication in court and re-interviewed in six-month intervals for two years. Legitimacy was measured based on Tyler's (1990) items, and legal cynicism was measured based on Sampson and Bartusch's (1998) scale. The authors also included a range of cognitive (e.g. perceived rewards of crime), psychological (e.g. mental health), and prior offending (e.g. court history) variables in the statistical analyses. Controlling for these factors, legitimacy only weakly predicted trajectories of self-reported offending (total offending: $b = -0.031$, $p < .10$; aggression (e.g. physical violence): $b = -0.034$, $p < .10$; property crime (e.g. theft, burglary): $b = -0.034$, $p < .10$). Legal cynicism was only predictive of total self-reported offending ($b = 0.027$, $p < .01$).

Furthermore, Sunshine and Tyler (2003) reported results from two cross-sectional studies. The first was based on a telephone survey amongst a general population sample of 586 respondents aged 19 to 88 in New York City. Legitimacy was operationalized via a 19-item questionnaire that included measures of the obligation to obey the legal authorities, the extent of trust in the police, and the feeling people had about the New York Police Department. Compliance was measured with a 7-item inverted delinquency scale (e.g. 'not take items without paying'). Results suggested that after controlling for demographic variables and risk estimates legitimacy had a significant association with compliance ($\beta = .22$). However, the model only accounted for a very small proportion (9 per cent) of the variance in delinquency/compliance. The second study (Sunshine & Tyler 2003: 528ff) was also based on telephone interviews and included a community sample of 1,653 respondents in New York City. The instruments for measuring legitimacy and compliance were similar to those used in the first study. In that study legitimacy ($\beta = .14$) was again found to be a significant predictor of compliance. But as in the first study only a small amount of variation in compliance was accounted for by the model ($R^2 = 8$ per cent).

The small proportion (i.e. less than 10 per cent) of explained variance in these two studies merits attention. It suggests that important covariates of delinquency/compliance were not included in the models. This in turn means that the effect of legitimacy on compliance may have been overestimated because of unmeasured shared covariates.

Two recent studies have examined the impact of potential confounds. Reisig, Wolfe, and Holtfreter (2011) examined the extent to which legitimacy and legal cynicism remain predictors of offending once variation in *self-control* was taken into account. This is important because aspects of low self-control such as self-centredness and short-sightedness could influence the perceived legitimacy of criminal justice agencies as well as the likelihood of delinquency. The authors used cross-sectional survey data from a convenience sample of 626 students at Arizona State University. They first showed that legitimacy and legal cynicism should be considered different constructs. Also, initial bivariate relationships with delinquency were in the expected direction but with a stronger association for legal cynicism ($r = .36$) than for legitimacy ($r = -.16$). Finally, the findings suggest that self-control considerably attenuates the effects of legitimacy and legal cynicism on delinquency. But legal cynicism remained a more important predictor of offending ($\beta = .247$, $p < .01$) than legitimacy, which only barely reached statistical significance ($\beta = -.087$, $p < .05$).

The second study examined whether legitimacy still predicts general offending (e.g. shoplifting) and traffic offences when respondents' *morality*—i.e. the perception that it was morally wrong to break the law—is statistically controlled (Jackson et al. 2012). It was based on a representative sample of 937 respondents aged 16 and over in England and Wales. The authors found that once morality was included in the model, *legitimacy* only had a marginal effect on general offending. Moreover, the 'obligation to obey the police' was entirely unrelated to offending, while effects in the expected direction were found for the 'obligation to obey the law' ($\beta = -.20$, $p < .05$) and the 'moral alignment with the police' ($\beta = -.23$, $p < .01$). Furthermore, legitimacy measures turned out to be completely unrelated to compliance with traffic laws, once the perceived wrongfulness of traffic offenses was taken into consideration.

Fagan and Tyler (2005) examined effects of legitimacy on delinquency amongst children and adolescents. The study used a sample of 215 respondents at ages 10 to 16 drawn from two racially and socio-economically contrasting neighbourhoods in New York City. It distinguished three domains of legal socialization, namely *legitimacy*, *legal cynicism*, and *moral disengagement*. In this study legitimacy was operationalized as the respondent's perception of fairness and equity of legal actors in their contacts with citizens, including both police contacts and court processing (e.g. 'overall, the police are honest', see Fagan and Tyler 2005: 228). An offending variety score based on 30 items was used to measure compliance/delinquency. In a multiple regression that controlled for, amongst others, violent exposure, delinquent peers and low self-control, the study found that legitimacy was a significant but modest predictor of delinquency with a standardized effect of $\beta = -.13$, $p < .01$).[3] The two other components of legal socialization, namely legal cynicism and moral disengagement failed to predict delinquency.

Two studies explored compliance in the domain of white collar crimes: Murphy (2005) examined whether the lacking legitimacy of the tax authorities predicted whether people pay taxes. Legitimacy was measured with two subscales, namely the legitimacy of the tax office and the obligation to obey. Compliance was also measured by two different subscales, namely an attitudinal component (psychological resistance to paying taxes) and engagement in actual acts of tax evasion. The study found that a lack of legitimacy was a highly significant predictor of the psychological resistance to paying taxes ($\beta = -.25$). In contrast, it did not predict actual acts of tax evasion (Murphy 2005: 575). In the second study Murphy used panel data to predict change in levels of 'resistance' and 'tax evasion'. The study confirmed the findings from the first cross-sectional study: legitimacy at t_0 predicted change in resistance from t_0 to t_1, but it had no effect on levels of actual tax evasion.

[3] Standardized coefficient calculated by us, based on unstandardized coefficients and standard deviations in Fagan and Tyler 2005: 235 and 237).

Tyler and Blader (2005) examined the role of legitimacy in shaping compliance with rules amongst 540 employees of a large financial services institution. In that study legitimacy had a small but significant effect on self-reported rule breaking ($\beta = -.10$). In a second study reported in the same paper Tyler and Blader examined 4,430 employees from a wide range of occupational backgrounds. In that study legitimacy was predictive of *self-reported* rule-breaking ($\beta = -.26$), but not predictive of *supervisor-assessed* compliance with rules ($\beta = -.01$).

Only one study used police records to measure crime. Tyler et al. (2007) examined a sample of 415 Australian adults who had been arrested for drunk driving and participated in a restorative justice experiment. They found that participants who viewed the law as more legitimate were less likely to be rearrested (Tyler et al. 2007: 567). While the measurement of crime via police records is a strength of this study, the legitimacy of the law was operationalized by two questions that appear to measure anticipated compliance itself rather than legitimacy in the sense defined by Tyler ('The conference/court case will keep you from breaking the law in the future,' and 'What happened in the conference/court case will encourage you to obey the law in the future.'). It is therefore perhaps not so surprising that respondents who thought that the criminal justice experience would keep them from re-offending actually did re-offend less frequently.

In a unique study, Papachristos et al. (2012) examined the role of social networks, gang membership, and legitimacy in relation to gun carrying and fighting in a sample of 141 randomly-selected residents of Chicago that were either on parole or probation. They measured legitimacy using four items: 'I feel that I should accept the decisions made by legal authorities,' 'People should obey the law even if it goes against what they think is right,' 'The law represents the values of people in power rather than the values of people like me,' and 'People in power use the law to try and control people like me' (2012: 417). In addition, they included perceived risk of detection and punishment (deterrence), general perceptions of police and prosecutors (e.g. 'Most police treat people with respect'), and the number, closeness, and types (e.g. criminal vs. legitimate) of social ties the respondent had. They found that offenders who saw the legal system as legitimate were significantly less likely to report carrying a gun ($b = -1.537$, $p < .05$), however perceptions of legitimacy were not significantly related to self-reported fighting in the last six months ($b = -0.581$, n.s.).

To our knowledge, only one paper has yet looked into the psychological mechanisms through which legitimacy may affect compliance. Murphy and Tyler (2008) examined whether anger, respectively happiness mediate the effect of procedural justice on subsequent compliance. The study used longitudinal survey data collected in two real-life contexts, namely a taxation dispute ($N = 652$) and compliance at the workplace ($N = 2{,}366$). They showed that perceptions of procedural justice influence people's emotions. In particular, a sense of procedural justice or injustice at t_1 was found to be linked to greater happiness, respectively anger at t_2. These emotions, in turn, influenced whether actors would or would not comply with authority decisions and rules.

LIMITATIONS

An impressive amount of work has tested the hypothesis that legitimacy increases compliance and reduces rule breaking. Studies have included different populations, various settings, and diverse outcomes. All studies find a substantial significant relationship in the predicted direction when considering simple bivariate associations. In multivariate models the effects of legitimacy tend to be smaller and several studies find no effects of legitimacy after controlling for other predictors. In studies that use individual-level data the net effect sizes reported in multivariate models are in the small to modest range ($\beta = .10 - .20$). For aggregate level studies the findings are too varied to arrive at an overall conclusion, although the robust effect of legitimacy on homicide in the cross-national study by Nivette and Eisner (2013) is encouraging. However, several limitations of extant research make it difficult to draw firm conclusions on whether lacking legitimacy effectively causes an increase in crime and delinquency.

OPERATIONALIZING LEGITIMACY

First, conclusions about the effect of legitimacy on crime are hampered by the high variability in how legitimacy is defined and measured.

We illustrate the problem with individual-level research. In one of the core statements of legitimacy theory Tyler argues that the core of legitimacy is an internalized sense of the *obligation to obey* (Tyler 2003: 309). But he suggests that legitimacy can also be measured in terms of *confidence in the police* (e.g. 'I feel proud of the Chicago police'), positive feelings about, respectively *identification with the police*, and the *lack of legal cynicism* (Tyler, 2003: 310).

However, there is considerable variation in how legitimacy has effectively been operationalized empirically. For example, the legitimacy measure in Sunshine and Tyler (2003) comprised the sub-dimensions of *obligation to obey* and *confidence in the police*, but not *legal cynicism*. *Confidence in criminal justice actors* was also the core of the legitimacy measure used by Piquero et al. (2005: 279), but the items hardly addressed the component of the obligation to obey. Fagan and Tyler (2005), in contrast, operationalized legitimacy through items that measure the *perceived fairness and equity of legal actors*. And in the Canberra drinking and driving experiment, finally, legitimacy was measured with two items that ask respondents about their future *likelihood* to comply with the law, a question that only indirectly bears on the *obligation* to obey (Tyler et al. 2007: 582).

In micro-level research alone legitimacy has hence been variously operationalized through items that tap on the obligation to obey, the perceived fairness of legal actors, or the future likelihood of complying with the law. But the measures become even more motley when one considers macro-level indicators. Chamlin and Cochran (2006) used survey items on perceptions of fairness as legitimacy indicators; Nivette and Eisner (2012) used a composite score that includes items on trust, evaluations of performance, confidence in institutions, as well as measures of consenting behaviours (i.e. voting), while LaFree (1998) used a range of variables such as 'trust in the government', inequality, or collective action—some of which (e.g. 'trust') might contribute to the legitimacy of a government, while others (e.g. protest movements) are likely to result from its lack of legitimacy.

Although it is possible that all these approaches measure the same underlying construct, we along with a number of other scholars (see Kaina 2008; Reisig et al. 2011; Tankebe 2009, 2013) believe that this is unlikely. For instance, Kaina (2008) explicitly rejects the notion that *trust*, *legitimacy*, and the *obligation to obey* are part of one underlying construct. She argues that trust is based on prior institutional performance, and consists of expectations about the future, whereas legitimacy is based on one's own moral principles. Obligation, or 'decision acceptance' as she calls it, is not part of legitimacy because it 'can also be attributed to other causes such as habits or utilitarian calculations' (p. 513). It seems that different theoretical approaches to legitimacy, such as the differences between the approach suggested by Bottoms and Tankebe (2012), Kaina (2008) and that proposed by Tyler (1990), would require different operationalizations, which in turn might lead to different conclusions about the extent to which legitimacy predicts crime or compliance with the law.

LACK OF CONTROL FOR CONFOUNDS

A second limitation is the restricted extent to which research has adequately considered potential confounds, i.e. variables that affect both the perceived legitimacy of the criminal justice system *and* rule-breaking behaviour. Failure to do so can result in inflated estimates of the hypothesized causal link between legitimacy and crime.

The possibility that the association between legitimacy and crime is at least partly due to shared factors is raised by the handful of studies that have considered personality characteristics such as self-control (Reisig at al., 2011 Fagan and Tyler 2005) or morality (Jackson et al. 2012) as control variables. In these studies the effects of legitimacy were greatly attenuated once personality characteristics were taken into consideration. In part, legitimacy and crime are hence correlated because people with poor self-control and low moral beliefs are both less likely to perceive the police as legitimate and more likely to commit crimes. But other personality characteristics, which have not yet been examined, may be responsible for additional parts of the association between legitimacy and crime. For example, individual characteristics such as high risk-seeking or low empathy might also predict a reduced belief in the legitimacy of the police and an increased likelihood of offending.

However, the list of potential confounds that have only been partially considered does not end with personality characteristics. For example, experiences of personal victimization (e.g. child abuse or bullying victimization) might have a negative impact on the perceived legitimacy of the authorities and at the same time also increase the likelihood of future offending. But while this seems a plausible developmental mechanism, we are not aware of any studies on legitimacy that include victimization in their models.

ATTENTION TO REVERSE CAUSAL ORDER

The problem of partial control for potential confounds is linked to the issue of causal order. Throughout the reviewed literature researchers test a causal order whereby legitimacy makes people comply with the law, not the other way around. However, this causal order is often assumed rather than demonstrated, and the observed correlations between legitimacy and crime could often stem from causal mechanisms in the opposite direction.

For example, one of the convincing findings presented by LaFree (1998) on the effects of 'losing legitimacy' was the strong association between change in the extent to which Americans distrusted the government and levels of homicide rates after World War II. In Figure 15.1 we reproduce these data, extending the original series until 2010. For the period 1948 to 1995 the two series are very highly correlated (r = .90), as LaFree (1998) observed. But the parallel movement is open to two opposite interpretations: In line with the legitimacy framework it is possible that change in the legitimacy of the political system drove crime rates up and down. However, it is equally plausible that the boom periods of crime were seen as evidence of the state's failure to control crime, and that this nourished people's distrust in whether the government works for the good of the country. Moreover, starting in about 2000 the positive correlation between distrust in the government and crime breaks down entirely: While homicide—along with virtually all other types of crime—continued to decline over the past 12 years or so, distrust in the national government rose continuously and was back to levels as high as those last seen in the early 1990s.

A similar problem bedevils the micro link between legitimacy and compliance. In particular, the transgression of rules (i.e. crimes) is likely to reduce subsequent beliefs in the obligation to comply and the legitimacy of the police. For example, the work by Sykes and Matza (1957) on neutralization techniques and Bandura's work on moral disengagement (Bandura 1990) suggests that people who break moral rules develop inner excuses and justifications that make the transgression look more favourable (Barriga and Gibbs 1996; Maruna and Copes 2005; Ribeaud and Eisner 2010). These justifications may develop before and/or after deviant activity in an attempt to rationalize the act: 'disapproval flowing from internalized norms and conforming others in the social environment is neutralized, turned back, or deflected in advance' (Sykes and Matza 1957: 666–7). Several of these justification techniques directly relate to the obligation to obey and the perceived trustworthiness of the police. For example, it is easier to self-excuse past harmful behaviour if one condemns the condemner (e.g. the police only serve the powerful), morally justifies the detrimental acts (e.g. theft is merely informal redistribution of wealth) and makes advantageous comparisons with the behaviour of others (e.g. in a world of injustice my own theft doesn't really count). This tradition of theoretical and empirical thinking has as yet only found limited impact on legitimacy research. However, causal pathways in both directions can be plausibly constructed, and should be equally tested empirically.

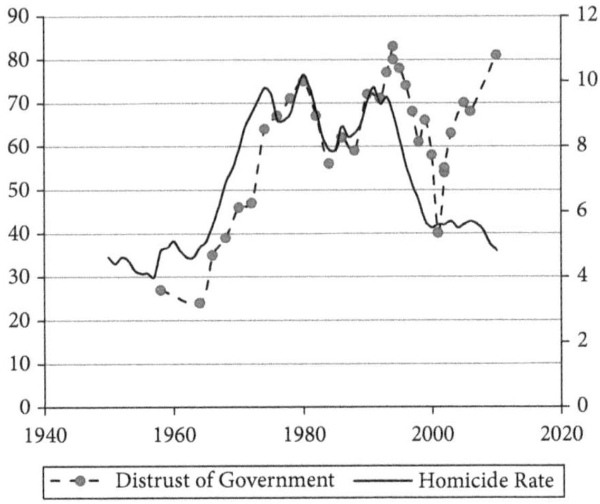

Figure 15.1 Government Illegitimacy and Homicide Rate in the United States, 1948–2010[4]

LACKING INTEGRATION OF MACRO AND MICRO LEVEL PERSPECTIVES

The link between legitimacy and crime has been examined both at the micro-level of individuals and the macro levels of states or neighbourhoods. However, little has yet been done to integrate both perspectives. In the macro-level tradition legitimacy is conceptualized in a broad sense as the overall authority of those with power to impose rules and to request compliance. This can include parents, teachers, politicians, managers or any other person or institution that somehow imposes constraints on the interactions between humans (Trinkner et al. 2012). In the micro-level tradition, in contrast, legitimacy is generally addressed much more narrowly as something that relates to the quality of everyday interactions between citizens and police and the criminal justice system. Tyler (2011: 257) for instance argues that, 'from a legitimacy perspective, every encounter that the public have with the police, the courts and the law should be treated as a socializing experience that builds or undermines legitimacy. Each contact is a "teachable moment" in which people learn about the law and legal authorities.'

The difference between these two perspectives has important implications. In the criminal justice view of legitimacy crime can be kept low if the police and the courts operate fairly and effectively, no matter how the rest of society is organized. In the broader view of legitimacy, more common amongst researchers working in the macro perspective, the legitimacy of the social order matters, and the police and the judiciary only constitute one amongst other agents that produce and request legitimacy.

[4] *Source*: Trust in Government: *The American National Election Studies, Trust in the Federal Government, 1958–2008, % trusting only 'some of the time' and 'never'*. <http://www.electionstudies.org/nesguide/toptable/tab5a_1.htm>. Homicide: Bureau of Justice Statistics.

We find that focusing on one level of analysis inhibits a full understanding of how individuals interact with state institutions, structural characteristics, and (sub-) cultural environments to develop a sense of legitimacy. Multilevel models in particular can highlight the role of institutions—economic, political, family, welfare, education, criminal justice—in maintaining order by embedding individuals in obligations, instilling non-violent moralities, constructing social interactions based on trust and reciprocity, and overall encouraging obedience to authority and a willingness to cooperate as agents of informal social control (LaFree 1998; Karstedt 2010; Tyler 2004).

Integrating macro- and micro-level perspectives can also tell us how the effects of legitimacy differ across and within groups (e.g. ethnicities, neighbourhoods, social classes, police districts, countries). On the one hand, state policies, scandals, and failures should impact the collective perception of the state's ability and moral right to rule. On the other hand, there is evidence to believe that changes in legitimacy only have an effect on individuals that are the most 'socially distant' or 'disengaged' from society (Murphy and Cherney 2012). If we incorporate both contextual and individual background characteristics, we can sort out the more 'permanent' effects of legitimacy that develop over the life course among certain sub-groups from reactive effects to unfair situations that could occur across various populations.

LACK OF CROSS-CULTURAL EVIDENCE

Most studies reviewed here were conducted either in the United States or the United Kingdom. Even among the macro-level comparative evidence studies tend to focus on European or western, developed societies. This lack of cross-cultural evidence has two related implications for the study of legitimacy and crime: (1) we do not know if the theoretical model of legitimacy is relevant outside the western, democratic state-building tradition and (2) as such, we do not know whether the effects of illegitimacy are the same in totalitarian, underdeveloped, conflict-ridden, or newly democratizing states. Some models, such as Beetham's (1991) 'legitimacy-in-context' and Bottoms and Tankebe's (2012) dialogical model, do not make assumptions about the actions, norms, and behaviours involved in the legitimation process, and therefore have some cross-cultural flexibility. Others, such as Buchanan's (2002) democracy model and Tyler's (1990) procedural justice model, argue for necessary and fundamental criteria for legitimation.

Research conducted outside Europe hints at the likelihood of different cross-cultural models of legitimacy. In Ghana, Tankebe (2009) found that utilitarian criteria were more important in explaining cooperative behaviours than procedural justice. He attributes this association to the division between authority stemming from the traditional and ethnic realms and authority stemming from imported state structures. In postcolonial African societies, moral obligations to obey are grounded in traditional social structures, whereas criminal justice institutions may elicit only instrumental compliance. Whether or not this argument is generalizable to other postcolonial societies has yet to be seen, but Tankebe's point is that the role of the police are not necessarily a 'moral authority' across all societies, contexts and eras, and so we cannot assume that legitimacy and procedural justice will lead to more law-abiding behaviours in all contexts.

CONCLUSION AND OUTLOOK

Legitimacy is a central construct for criminology. It addresses important questions about the link between individual offending, the bases for cooperation and compliance, the functioning of the justice system, and the wider foundations of a political and social order. The argument that individuals break the law not because of the likelihood and costs of punishment, personality characteristics, or opportunities, but due to feelings about the rightfulness of law, the authority of those who represent it, and an inner sense of obligation to obey has made criminologists rethink traditional models of crime and offending. If true, it has important implications for crime-reduction strategies.

This review suggests that the empirical evidence in support of legitimacy as a theoretical construct that explains crime is promising. Bivariate correlations between measures of legitimacy and crime, respectively compliance, tend to be substantial while results from multivariate analyses show a more mixed picture with sometimes very small effects of legitimacy on crime. We believe that progress along several lines is needed to clarify the nature of the link between legitimacy and crime.

First, conclusions about the effects of legitimacy on crime are hampered by inconsistent operationalization and measurement. This is true both within the micro- and the macro-traditions of legitimacy research, but also in respect of the link between these two research strands. Partly, differences in operationalization reflect different theoretical approaches, but even within any one strand of theoretical thinking we found more variety than would be desirable. We therefore believe that progress could be made by examining, for example, the relationship between more objective and subjective measures of legitimacy, by comparative psychometric analyses of the various scales that are presently interpreted as measures of legitimacy, and by careful examination of the delineation between measures of legitimacy and related constructs such as, for example, procedural justice, good governance, and trust.

Second, we believe that in order to gain wider acceptance as an explanation of crime and rule breaking legitimacy theory must be tested in competition with the major existing criminological theories and established empirical risk-factors. It would be hugely important, for example, to clarify theoretically whether legitimation theory contradicts, extends, or ignores criminological theories such as social control theory (Hirschi 1969), neutralization theory (Sykes and Matza 1957), or strain theory (Agnew 1992). And it would be pivotal for future tests of the effects of legitimacy on crime that core constructs of potentially competing explanatory models (e.g. self-control, morality) are included.

Third, we believe that more empirical tests using longitudinal data are essential, both at the micro and at the macro level. Theory suggests that the legitimation process has a feedback loop between the state and citizens, but this has not been empirically examined. The example of trust and homicide in the United States showed that legitimacy might be a reaction to the state's failure to control crime rather than a cause of crime. On the individual level, we must examine the effects of victimization or perpetration of criminal acts on perceptions of legitimacy and future behaviours, because it is possible that delegitimization occurs as a result of moral neutralization.

Finally, we believe that legitimacy cannot be reduced to either individual beliefs in the obligation to obey or macro-level indicators of good governance. In our view researchers must therefore pay more attention to how legitimacy operates and interacts between different levels of analysis. Part of this involves linking observed characteristics of the state (e.g. corruption, violence, ineffectiveness) with individual beliefs about the state, but this also means investigating links between legitimacy and other sociological constructs (e.g. poverty, neighbourhood characteristics, immigrant concentration).

REFERENCES

AGNEW, R. (1992) 'Foundation for a General Strain Theory of Crime and Delinquency', *Criminology* 30(1): 47–87.

ANDERSON, E. (1999) *Code of the Street: Decency, Violence, and the Moral Life of the Inner City.* New York: W.W. Norton & Company.

BANDURA, A. (1990) 'Mechanisms of Moral Disengagement' in Reich, W. (ed) *Origins of Terrorism: Psychologies, Ideologies, Theologies, States of Mind.* Cambridge: Cambridge University Press.

BARRIGA, A. Q. and GIBBS, J. C. (1996) 'Measuring Cognitive Distortion in Antisocial Youth: Development and Preliminary Validation of the "How I Think" Questionnaire', *Aggressive Behavior* 22(5): 333–43.

BECCARIA, C. (1764) *Dei delitti e delle penne.*

BEETHAM, D. (1991) *The Legitimation of Power.* Atlantic Highlands: Humanities Press International.

BENTHAM, J. (2007 [1781]) *An Introduction to the Principles of Morals and Legislation.* Oxford: Clarendon Press.

BLACK, D. (1983) 'Crime as Social Control', *American Sociological Review* 48(1): 34–45.

BOTTOMS, A. and TANKEBE, J. (2012) 'Beyond Procedural Justice: A Dialogic Approach to Legitimacy in Criminal Justice', *Journal of Criminal Law and Criminology* 102(1): 119–70.

BUCHANAN, A. (2002) 'Political Legitimacy and Democracy', *Ethics* 112(4): 689–719.

CHAMLIN, M. B. and COCHRAN, J. K. (2006) 'Economic Inequality, Legitimacy, and Cross-National Homicide Rates', *Homicide Studies* 10(4): 231–52.

EISNER, M. (2001) 'Modernization, Self-Control and Lethal Violence—The Long-Term Dynamics of European Homicide Rates in Theoretical Perspective', *British Journal of Criminology* 41(4): 618–48.

FAGAN, J. and PIQUERO, A. R. (2007) 'Rational Choice and Developmental Influences on Recidivism Among Adolescent Felony Offenders', *Journal of Empirical Legal Studies* 4(4): 715–48.

FAGAN, J. and TYLER, T. (2005) 'Legal Socialization of Children and Adolescents', *Social Justice Research* 18(3): 217–41.

Gilley, B. (2009) *The Right to Rule; How States Win and Lose Legitimacy*. New York: Columbia University Press.

Hirschi, T. (1969) *Causes of Delinquency*. Berkeley: University of California Press.

Jackson, J., Bradford, B., Hough, M., Myhill, A., Quinton, P., and Tyler, T. R. (2012) 'Why do People Comply with the Law? Legitimacy and the Influence of Legal Institutions', *British Journal of Criminology* 52(6): 1051–71.

Kaina, V. (2008) 'Legitimacy, Trust and Procedural Fairness: Remarks on Marcia Grimes' Study', *European Journal of Political Research* 47(4): 510–21.

Kane, R. J. (2005) 'Compromised Police Legitimacy as a Predictor of Violent Crime in Structurally Disadvantaged Communities', *Criminology* 43(2): 469–98.

Karstedt, S. (2010) 'New Institutionalism in Criminology: Approaches, Theories and Themes' (pp. 337–59) in McLaughlin, E. and Newburn, T. (eds) *The Sage Handbook of Criminological Theory*. London: Sage.

Kirk, D. S., and Papachristos, A. V. (2011) 'Cultural Mechanisms and the Persistence of Neighborhood Violence', *American Journal of Sociology* 116(4): 1190–233.

Kubrin, C. E., and Weitzer, R. (2003) 'Retaliatory Homicide: Concentrated Disadvantage and Neighborhood Culture', *Social Problems* 50(2): 157–80.

LaFree, G. D. (1998) *Loosing Legitimacy; Street Crime and the Decline of Social Institutions in America*. Boulder: Westview.

Locke, J. (1988 [1689]) *Two Treatises of Government*, P. Laslett (ed). Cambridge: Cambridge University Press.

Loeber, R. and Farrington, D. P. (eds) (1998) *Serious and Violent Offenders; Risk Factors and Successful Interventions*. Thousand Oaks: Sage.

Loeber, R. and Farrington, D. P. (2001). 'Young Children who Commit Crime: Epidemiology, Developmental Origins, Risk Factors, Early Interventions, and Policy Implications', *Development and Psychopathology* 12(04): 737–62.

Lösel, F. and Farrington, D. P. (2012) 'Direct Protective and Buffering Protective Factors in the Development of Youth Violence', *American Journal of Preventive Medicine* 43(2): S8–S23.

Maruna, S., and Copes, H. (2005) 'Excuses, Excuses: What Have We Learned from Five Decades of Neutralization Research', *Crime and Justice*, 32: 221–320.

Murphy, K. (2005) 'Regulating More Effectively: The Relationship Between Procedural Justice, Legitimacy, and Tax Non-compliance', *Journal of Law and Society* 32(4): 562–89.

Murphy, K. and Cherney, A. (2012) 'Understanding Cooperation with the Police in a Diverse Society', *British Journal of Criminology* 52(1): 181–201.

Murphy, K. and Tyler, T. R. (2008) 'Procedural Justice and Compliance Behaviour: the Mediating Role of Emotions', *European Journal of Social Psychology* 38(4): 652–68.

Murray, J., Farrington, D. P., and Eisner, M. (2009) 'Drawing Conclusions about Causes from Systematic Reviews of Risk Factors: The Cambridge Quality Checklist', *Journal of Experimental Criminology* 5(1): 1–23.

Nivette, A. E. (2011) 'Cross-National Predictors of Homicide: A Meta-Analysis', *Homicide Studies* 15(2): 103–31.

Nivette, A. E. (2012) 'Spatial Patterns of Homicide and Political Legitimacy in Europe', *International Journal of Comparative and Applied Criminal Justice* 36(3): 155–71.

Nivette, A. E., and Eisner, M. (2013) 'Do Legitimate Polities Have Fewer Homicides? A Cross-National Analysis', *Homicide Studies* 17(1): 3–26.

Papachristos, A.V., Meares, T. L., and Fagan, J. (2012) 'Why Do Criminals Obey the Law? The Influence of Legitimacy and Social Networks on Active Gun Offenders', *Journal of Criminal Law and Criminology* 102(2): 397–440.

PIQUERO, A., FAGAN, J., MULVEY, E. P., STEINBERG, L., and ODGERS, C. (2005) 'Developmental Trajectories of Legal Socialization Among Serious Adolescent Offenders', *Journal of Criminal Law and Criminology* 96(1): 267–98.

REISIG, M. D., WOLFE, S. E., and HOLTFRETER, K. (2011) 'Legal Cynicism, Legitimacy, and Criminal Offending: The Nonconfounding Effect of Low Self-Control', *Criminal Justice and Behavior* 38(12): 1265–79.

RIBEAUD, D., and EISNER, M. (2010) 'Are Moral Disengagement, Neutralization Techniques, and Self-Serving Cognitive Distortions the Same? Developing a Unified Scale of Moral Neutralization of Aggression', *International Journal of Conflict and Violence* 4(2): 298–315.

ROTH, R. (2009) *American Homicide*. Cambridge, MA: Belknap Press.

ROTH, R. (2012) 'Measuring Feelings and Beliefs that May Facilitate (or Deter) Homicide', *Homicide Studies* 16(2): 197–216.

RUBINSTEIN, N. (1958) 'Political Ideas in Sienese Art: The Frescoes by Ambrogio Lorenzetti and Taddeo di Bartolo in the Palazzo Pubblico', *Journal of the Warburg and Courtauld Institutes* 21(3/4): 179–207.

SAMPSON, R. J. and BARTUSCH, D. J. (1998) 'Legal Cynicism and (Subcultural?) Tolerance of Deviance: The Neighborhood Context of Racial Differences', *Law and Society Review* 32(4): 777–804.

SUNSHINE, J., and TYLER, T. R. (2003) 'The Role of Procedural Justice and Legitimacy in Shaping Public Support for Policing', *Law and Society Review* 37(3): 513–48.

SYKES, G., and MATZA, D. (1957) 'Techniques of Neutralization: A Theory of Delinquency', *American Journal of Sociology* 22: 664–70.

TANKEBE, J. (2009) 'Public Cooperation with the Police in Ghana: Does Procedural Justice Matter?' *Criminology* 47(4): 1265–93.

TANKEBE, J. (2013) 'Viewing Things Differently: The Dimensions of Public Perceptions of Police Legitimacy', *Criminology* 51(1): 103–35.

TRINKNER, R., COHN, E. S., REBELLON, C. J., and VAN GUNDY, K. (2012) 'Don't Trust Anyone Over 30: Parental Legitimacy as a Mediator Between Parenting Style and Changes in Delinquent Behavior Over Time', *Journal of Adolescence* 35(1): 119–32.

TYLER, T. R. (1990) *Why People Obey the Law*. New Haven: Yale University Press.

TYLER, T. R. (2003) 'Procedural Justice, Legitimacy, and the Effective Rule of Law', *Crime and Justice* 30: 283–357.

TYLER, T. R. (2004) 'Enhancing Police Legitimacy. The Annals of the American Academy of Political and Social Science' 593: 84–99.

TYLER, T. R. (2006) 'Psychological Perspectives on Legitimacy and Legitimation', *Annual Review of Psychology* 57: 375–400.

TYLER, T. R. (2009) 'Legitimacy and Criminal Justice: The Benefits of Self-Regulation', *Ohio State Journal of Criminal Law* 7(1): 307–59.

TYLER, T. R. (2011) 'Trust and Legitimacy: Policing in the USA and Europe', *European Journal of Criminology* 8(4): 254–66.

TYLER, T. R., and Blader, S. L. (2005) 'Can Businesses Effectively Regulate Employee Conduct? The Antecedents of Rule following in Work Settings', *The Academy of Management Journal* 48(6): 1143–58.

TYLER, T. R., SHERMAN, L., STRANG, H., BARNES, G. C., and WOODS, D. (2007) 'Reintegrative Shaming, Procedural Justice, and Recidivism: The Engagement of Offenders' Psychological Mechanisms in the Canberra RISE Drinking-and-Driving Experiment', *Law and Society Review* 41(3): 553–86.

16

LEGITIMACY, TRUST, AND COMPLIANCE: AN EMPIRICAL TEST OF PROCEDURAL JUSTICE THEORY USING THE EUROPEAN SOCIAL SURVEY

Mike Hough, Jonathan Jackson, and Ben Bradford

INTRODUCTION

This chapter presents findings from a large-scale empirical test of procedural justice theory, which we (and colleagues) designed using the fifth European Social Survey. The chapter first of all locates concerns about institutional legitimacy within a broader framework of 'compliance theories'. It then sets out its definitional stall in an attempt to clarify what is meant by the 'slippery' concept of legitimacy and how the term is used in different contexts. Then, in testing various hypotheses on procedural justice, we employ a tripartite definition of empirical (i.e. perceived) legitimacy. We define empirical legitimacy as the recognition and justification of the right to exercise power and influence, with influence mostly of the normative (rather than instrumental) variety, and importantly our tripartite notions of consent, moral alignment, and legality accord with some well-established social psychological mechanisms of identification and internalization.

INSTITUTIONAL LEGITIMACY AND COMPLIANCE THEORIES

Compliance theories have been well classified by Bottoms (2002), who proposed that there are four categories of explanation for compliance with authority in general, and with the criminal law in particular. These are:

- prudential or self-interested calculations about the potential costs and benefits of punishment, which take into account the risks and costs of punishment;
- normative considerations about the 'rights and wrongs' of non-compliance;
- the impact of obstructive strategies, such as locking up offenders to prevent their reoffending, and locking up the targets of criminal attention, literally or metaphorically; and,
- habit.

This chapter is concerned neither with obstructive (incapacitative) explanations nor with habit—though the latter is arguably the best explanation for why so many of us break the law so infrequently, and one that is much ignored by criminologists.[1] Both these explanations are in a sense secondary because they presuppose, respectively, that something led to offending at such a level or rate that imprisonment was needed, or else created the habit of compliance with the law. Our focus is whether normative explanations for compliance—and in particular those that appeal to the legitimacy of institutions of justice (Tyler 2006a, 2006b, 2011a, 2011b)—are fuller and more satisfactory than those that simply invoke the rational calculations of *homo economicus*.

The last two decades have seen an exponential increase of interest within criminology in issues of institutional legitimacy and normative compliance. Properly speaking this is a rediscovery, as the intellectual origins can be traced back readily to Durkheimian and especially Weberian thinking about the roots of social order. On the one hand, there has been renewed interest over the last two decades in the relationship between crime and 'political economy' (see Reiner 2007; Cavadino and Dignan 2006, 2013), which has traced the connections between the social distribution of wealth and attachment to—or detachment from—social norms. The emergence of neo-liberal economic policies is obviously implicated in this trend. Theories of institutional anomie (see Messner and Rosenfeld 2001, 2010) serve as good examples of this line of thought, whereby rapid transitions towards the values of free-market economies are thought to unbalance and weaken traditional normative systems of social control. More generally, the idea that high levels of income inequality fuel crime is almost a criminological truism, with a long sociological pedigree—even if the evidence is less conclusive than some would expect (see van Dijk 2013, for a critique).

On the other hand, there are compliance theories about the effect on societal norms of the institutions of formal social control, such as the work of Robinson and Darley, and that of Tyler. Thus, Robinson and Darley argue that if the law's potential for building a moral consensus is to be exploited, judicial outcomes, and especially court sentences, must be aligned at least to some degree with public sentiments (Robinson and Darley 1997, 2004; Robinson 2012). Their 'intuitive justice' arguments are partly retributivist in nature (that the least indefensible way of making judgements about relative offence gravity is by reference to public opinion) and partly consequentialist (that judicial decision making needs to keep in step with public opinion if it is to command legitimacy). This second leg of their argument is about the role of *outcome justice* (or distributive justice) in securing the legitimacy of the institutions of justice, and the courts in particular.

[1] A notable exception being the work of Wikström (e.g. Wikström et al. 2012).

Tyler and colleagues (e.g. Sunshine and Tyler 2003; Tyler and Fagan 2008; Kirk et al. 2012; Huq et al. 2011a, 2011b; Tyler et al. 2010; Tyler et al. 2007; Tyler and Wakslak 2004) have developed a parallel set of consequentialist arguments, based on the role of procedural rather than outcome justice in shaping institutional legitimacy. This body of work emphasizes the need for justice institutions to pursue fair and respectful *processes*—in contrast to *outcomes*—as the surest strategies for building trust in justice, and thus institutional legitimacy and compliance with the law. This is the central hypothesis in procedural justice theory. Some elaborations of procedural justice theory (e.g. Jackson et al. 2012a, 2012b; European Social Survey 2012; Hough et al. 2013) propose that procedural justice and 'moral alignment' are the most critical factors in fostering or retaining institutional legitimacy, albeit with felt obligation and consent to legal authority also playing a role.

Stated at their most general level—that winning 'hearts and minds' is central to the effective use of authority—these consequentialist arguments about securing compliance through strategies of institutional legitimation are ones that have enjoyed political currency, with varying degrees of saliency, for many years. Thus in the UK, community policing enjoyed a vogue in the 1979s and 1980s (see Alderson 1984). The same basic ideas were reintroduced as 'Reassurance Policing' and 'Neighbourhood Policing' in the first decade of this century. However, politicians have tended not to articulate the rationales for these policing styles with any precision, and when they have done so, they have usually appealed to ideas about a partnership between the police and 'the law abiding majority' which would yield public cooperation in the 'fight against crime'. Very little has been made of the fact that legitimate institutions can command not only public cooperation but also compliance with the law—probably because few politicians are rash enough to suggest to their electorate that those who vote them into power are anything but law-abiding.

The two broad families of compliance theory—with their different emphasis on securing social justice and a fair system of justice—are obviously compatible. Social justice and fairness in the justice system are both likely to be preconditions for a well-regulated society. However, only the second family carries direct implications for policy and practice within criminal justice. Many criminologists would like to see the crime-preventive dividend of a fairer distribution of income and wealth, but for ministers of justice and for senior justice officials, these arguments are at best subsidiary to ones about what they should do in the 'here and now' of improving systems of justice. Policies to achieve social justice are probably best justified in their own terms, and not in terms of their spin-off benefits for crime control.

THEORIES OF COMPLIANCE AND THEIR POLITICAL CONTEXT

The sorts of compliance theories just discussed—whether relating to social justice or institutional justice—are quite subtle. Two sorts of pressures have emerged over the last two decades in the politics of developed industrialized countries that tend to stifle or at least occlude these ideas. The first such trend is the diminished role of the 'technocratic expert' in social policy, and a greater responsiveness to the voice of the public (see Giddens 1991). This trend has been particularly marked in countries such as the UK and the US with adversarial political systems, on the one hand, and attachment to neo-liberal market principles on the other, though similar processes can be observed in other countries (see Cavadino and Dignan 2013; Lappi-Seppala 2013; Sack and Schlepper 2013). Many commentators have associated this increased responsiveness with populist punitiveness (Bottoms 1995) or penal populism (e.g., Pratt 2007; Roberts et al. 2002).

The second trend has been the development of a 'small state' style of governance in which politicians specify the *outcomes* required of state institutions such as the police, usually in the form of numerical targets, but leave the detail of the *processes* to local agencies. These principles of 'New Public Management' (NPM) are often applied in parallel with processes of 'marketization'—where private sector companies compete for contracts to provide public services—and consumer choice, where service recipients can exercise control over the services they receive (see Hood 1991).

In combination, the increased weight given by politicians to the public voice and the increased uptake of forms of governance through numerical target-setting have squeezed out subtlety from political discourse about crime and justice. Politicians increasingly tend to adopt a crude and simple instrumental discourse about 'the war on crime' in which weapons of deterrence and incapacitation are deployed against 'criminals' on behalf of the 'law abiding majority'. They have found themselves trapped in this discourse partly because they judge that this is the only one that will be favourably received by the media and, behind them, the electorate; and equally, the logic of NPM has driven politicians to adopt simple numerical targets that are built around crime and detection statistics.

Whether these trends towards over-simplification of policy are structural—in the sense of being an inherent feature of politics in late-modernity—remains to be seen. There are clear signs, in the UK at least, of a retreat from the worst excesses of NPM, as well as frequent calls for more mature and less adversarial forms of politics. It is as yet unclear as to whether this will create more political space for the development of effective strategies for building the legitimacy of institutions of justice and thus securing normative compliance. There is some room for optimism, in that procedural justice theory is developing traction in the US, where the over-reliance on mass incarceration is increasingly seen as unaffordable and counterproductive.[2] There may thus be emerging what Tankebe (2013) has dubbed a *legitimacy turn*.

DEFINING INSTITUTIONAL LEGITIMACY

We have suggested that theories of normative compliance with the law have ebbed and flowed. Ideas about institutional legitimacy tended to get submerged in political—and

[2] Much of the pressure for reform comes from the Republican right. See <http://www.rightoncrime.com> accessed 24 July 2013.

criminological—debate in the 1990s, and only now seem to be resurfacing.[3] If the concept of legitimacy has only recently re-emerged as a key one in Anglophone criminology, political philosophers have devoted considerable energy to its analysis, showing how social institutions need legitimacy if they are to develop, operate, and reproduce themselves effectively (Easton 1965).

One of the things that emerged most clearly at the conference leading to this book was that legitimacy is a 'slippery' concept to handle. Generally speaking, legitimacy is the right to rule and the recognition by the ruled of that right (Sternberger 1968; Beetham 1991; Coicaud 2002; Tyler 2006a; Bottoms and Tankebe 2012). However, Hinsch (2008, 2010) has made a much quoted distinction between normative (or objective) legitimacy and empirical (or subjective) legitimacy. Legitimacy is, on the one hand, a normatively laden term used by political philosophers to describe whether states (or state institutions) meet certain desirable standards. In political debate we naturally and properly want to make value judgements about the extent to which regimes (or institutions within regimes) exercise legitimate authority, judged against external or 'objective' criteria.

On the other hand, the term is also used in a less value-laden way, to describe whether, 'as a matter of fact', those who are subject to authority confer legitimacy on that authority (Hinsch 2010). The distinction is a real one, because one can envisage the possibility of regimes that enjoy substantial popular support—which can thus be said to enjoy 'empirical legitimacy'—whilst totally failing to meet basic standards of 'normative legitimacy'. Nazi Germany and the Khmer Rouge government are obvious examples, at least in their early periods. Whilst the distinction between normative and empirical legitimacy is an important one, it is often forgotten or ignored in academic and political discussion.

NORMATIVE LEGITIMACY

A normative concept of legitimacy sets out some 'objective' criteria against which the legitimacy of an authority or institution might be judged (Hinsch 2008). Normative legitimacy refers to whether the actions of authorities meet certain substantive requirements (usually of justice and rationality) for which objective evidence can be adduced. Legitimacy is here a property of organizational performance and institutional structure. It is conferred by or grounded in things that the justice system does, and in the objective relationships between system and citizen (such as those indicated by a freedom from arbitrary arrest). This 'system-conferred' legitimacy can be usefully measured by national-level statistics concerning efficiency, accountability, legality and so forth.

A normative conception of legitimacy has to justify selection of the specific criteria against which legitimacy is to be judged and this needs careful consideration. Because both empirical and normative legitimacy are needed if a fully

[3] See Hough (2007), for an account of the way in which both criminal policy and criminology allowed the concept to disappear from usage in the 1990s in the United Kingdom—with the exception of Northern Ireland.

rounded picture of the legitimacy of legal authorities is to be forthcoming (Bottoms and Tankebe 2012), they need to refer to the same 'thing'. Thus, both concepts require a shared theoretical grounding, otherwise comparison across the two would become impossible. Note, however, that the aim here is not to 'validate' the empirical by recourse to the normative; rather the purpose is to triangulate data in order to achieve a more accurate assessment of the legitimacy of a particular justice system.

What, then, should this theoretical grounding be? In a broadly Weberian framework, legitimacy is located in public acceptance of the right of an institution—such as the justice system—to wield power and define behaviour. Here there one might be tempted to apply just one criterion of normative legitimacy for the justice system: that people within the society consent willingly to its power and authority, for example they feel an obligation to obey the rules it embodies and enforces. Legitimacy might thus be indicated by some aggregate measure of citizen consent to the role and authority of criminal justice agencies. Here, the notions of empirical and normative legitimacy overlap.

Few, however, would be willing to accept this as a sufficient criterion of normative legitimacy, not least because it says so little about the form and nature of the social arrangements to which citizens are acquiescing. A broader definition is needed—one that captures not just expressed consent, but also a wider recognition of the right of the justice system to wield power (Beetham 1991). Here, legitimacy also resides in the extent to which justice institutions operate according to certain moral and ethical standards (according to accepted and justifiable standards of justice, rationality, accountability, and transparency), while also working under the rule of law. This requires recourse to a broad yet deep definition of legality, whereby the system of law in question was consistent with conventions relating to human rights: a regime that had legislated to remove protections of due process, for example, might be observing legality in its own terms, without meeting internationally recognized standards of legality. Under such conditions, its claim to be legitimate in Hinsch's normative sense would be in doubt.

An observer looking at criminal justice systems across Europe, for example, would judge the standing of these systems by drawing upon data addressing such substantive requirements: a justice system is legitimate when it meets certain standards of effectiveness, fairness, accountability, rule of law, and so forth (using national-level statistics concerning efficiency, accountability, legality, etc.). Conversely, *empirical legitimacy* is found when and where individuals believe that the criminal justice system is legitimate. For example, we might then claim that the police are legitimate when the police find approval among the policed, when individuals commit themselves to the normative and inferential consequences of their beliefs and approval (in that, for example, they are more likely to cooperate with legal authorities and comply with the law, because they believe that to do so is to meet the expectations of legitimate authority). Yet, according to a normative account of legitimacy such a claim might well be premature. People acting within a system may see institutions as legitimate, and act accordingly, but if a certain set of substantive requirements are not met by the system, then the observer sitting outside it would not accept the truth (or validity) of people's beliefs (Hinsch 2010: 42).[4]

EMPIRICAL LEGITIMACY

Social scientists have also been concerned with the measurement of empirical legitimacy, to assess whether the governed experience authority as legitimate, and more recently whether power-holders feel that they have an entitlement to command. This is a different enterprise from a normative assessment of an institution's success in meeting criteria of legitimacy as defined earlier. While one would expect to see *some degree* of correlation across jurisdictions between political scientists' assessments of normative legitimacy and measures of empirical legitimacy, there are good reasons for thinking that for cultural and historical reasons populations will differ in their orientation to authority, even when there is no objective difference in the quality of this authority.

Empirical legitimacy is a relational concept (see Bottoms and Tankebe 2012), in which the governed recognize an obligation to obey power-holders, believe that power-holders act according to appropriate normative and ethical frameworks, and believe that power-holders act under the rule of law (and the power-holders have a reciprocal sense of entitlement to command). In the survey work discussed later in the chapter using the European Social Survey (Jackson et al. 2011; European Social Survey 2011, 2012; Hough et al. 2013), we have conceptualized empirical legitimacy as having three sub-components—obligation to obey, legality, and moral alignment—and have constructed scales to measure each of these three components.[5] This definition follows Beetham (1991) in arguing that an authority has legitimacy when three preconditions are met:[6]

(1) The 'governed' offer their willing consent to defer to the authority;[7]
(2) And this consent is grounded:
   (a) on the authority's conformity to standards of legality (acting according to the law); and
   (b) on a degree of 'moral alignment' between power-holder and the governed, reflected in shared moral values.

[4] Positive public consent to the power of legal authorities may constitute an important overlap between empirical and normative legitimacy. In a departure from Hinsch (2010)—who sees empirical and normative legitimacy as conceptually distinct—aggregate levels of felt obligation may contribute to a normative account (in that we want to estimate levels of public consent at the national population of level), but that consent of the population needs to be bolstered by other aspects of normative legitimacy. In doing so we might draw on the notion that aggregate measures of public opinion—for example—are not reducible to individual beliefs or propensities, but represent social facts in and of themselves.

[5] We were concerned with measuring the legitimacy of both police and courts, and had separate measures for each institution.

[6] This is a somewhat broader definition than that used by Tyler, at least in his early work, which tended to equate perceived legitimacy with deference to authority.

[7] Note that a sense of public consent and felt obligation constitute, in our framework, both empirical and normative legitimacy, albeit at different levels of aggregation. At the individual level, consent and felt obligation operates as empirical legitimacy, in that it authorizes power-holders and generates a corresponding duty to obey. At the national level (or system level), some aggregate of expressed public consent and felt obligation operates as normative legitimacy, combining with national/system data on accountability, transparency, efficiency, and lawfulness.

According to this definition, legitimacy is not simply signified by a positive duty to obey authority and a perception of that authority's entitlement to command. The second and third pre-conditions of empirical legitimacy—legality and moral alignment—ensure that the obligation to obey is built on a combination of legality and the moral validity of institutions of justice. Legitimacy is thus defined as an additive function of all three components. To say that the police are legitimate, for example, is to say that people feel a positive duty to obey the instructions of police officers, feel aligned with the moral values of the police as an institution, and believe that it acts according to the rule of law. While some variation in individual—and indeed aggregate—'scores' on these variables is to be expected, significant shortfalls in any one set of opinions or propensities might lead us to infer that the institution involved suffers from some sort of legitimacy deficit.

Tankebe (2013: 12), examining police legitimacy, has taken a slightly different approach, proposing that the concept of legitimacy is constituted by four sub-components: namely, public perceptions of procedural fairness, distributive fairness (or outcome justice), effectiveness, and lawfulness (or legality). Perceived lawfulness reflects the belief that the police act legally, while perceived procedural fairness, distributive fairness, and effectiveness are conceived of as shared values that create a normative justifiability of police power, in that these '... shared beliefs and values specify and institutionalize the rightful source of power and define the qualities appropriate to the assumption and exercise of that power'.

Thus we define legitimacy as felt obligation, moral alignment, and perceived lawfulness, while Tankebe defines legitimacy as perceived effectiveness, procedural fairness, distributive fairness, and lawfulness. We measure shared values by asking individuals whether they believe that the police share their *moral* values; by contrast Tankebe measures shared values by asking individuals whether they believe that the police are effective (would the police turn up quickly in an emergency?) and fair (would the police treat one with respect and dignity?).

These are differences in conceptual rather than empirical analysis, in that we have set different boundaries to the concept of legitimacy. Expecting the police to turn up quickly in emergencies (and assuming that the police treat people with fairness and dignity) seems to us to be closer to the psychological state of trust than it is to the psychological state of legitimacy. Trust is believing that the police have the right intentions and are competent to do what they are tasked to do; legitimacy is recognizing and justifying police power and authority. But empirically there is—unsurprisingly—little difference between us. Our work has found that Tankebe's components of procedural fairness, distributive fairness, and effectiveness are certainly *predictive* of empirical legitimacy, as we have measured it, even if we do not regard them as *constitutive* of legitimacy.[8] We end up drawing similar conclusions about the relationships between trust, legitimacy, and compliance, and make similar recommendations for policy.

In other words, we would regard fairness and effectiveness as preconditions of empirical legitimacy, without positing a conceptual correspondence between fairness and effectiveness, on the one hand, and legitimacy on the other. Thus, we treat

[8] We may, of course, be using the term 'constitutive' in different ways. We would agree that perceptions of effectiveness, for example, are likely to build or consolidate perceived legitimacy, and to this extent it is constitutive of it; but the concept of legitimacy has a contingent rather than logical relationship with perceived effectiveness.

people's perceptions of the effectiveness and fairness of the police as trustworthy judgements, and we make a conceptual distinction between trust and legitimacy. But we would agree on the need to measure these factors and to identify their relative importance as 'drivers' of legitimacy. By way of contribution to the debate, we return, later in the chapter, to some comparisons of the two different definitions of empirical legitimacy.

THE EUROPEAN SOCIAL SURVEY: AN EMPIRICAL TEST OF PROCEDURAL JUSTICE THEORY

There is now a reasonable and rapidly growing body of evidence in support of procedural justice theory (see Tyler et al. 2007; Tyler 2011a, 2011b; Bradford et al. 2009; Jackson et al. 2012a, 2012b, 2013; Hough et al. 2010; Bradford et al. 2013). This research has established the various linkages between trust in the police, police legitimacy, and consent to the rule of law that are posited by the theory. In essence:

- If legal authorities, such as the police, are seen by the public to be unfair and disrespectful, this damages trust in them;
- Low trust in legal authorities reduces their legitimacy in the eyes of the public;
- The less that institutions of justice are seen as legitimate, the less the public will defer to their authority;
- And this will reduce public commitment to the rule of law and preparedness to help the police and the courts.

Different studies have identified variations in the drivers of police legitimacy. Tyler's US work has stressed the importance of the *style of* police contact: treating people fairly, respectfully, and giving them a voice. He has suggested that factors of this sort have primacy over public perceptions of distributive justice (or outcome fairness) on the one hand, and perceptions of competence or effectiveness on the other, as shapers of legitimacy. We and colleagues had the opportunity in 2008 and 2009 to develop a suite of questions for the fifth European Social Survey to see to what extent the US evidence was replicated in a large number of European countries (see Hough and Sato 2011).

The European Social Survey (ESS) is an academically-driven social survey designed to chart and explain the interaction between Europe's changing institutions and the attitudes, beliefs, and behaviour patterns of its diverse populations. The ESS was established in 2001 and fieldwork for the fifth sweep was conducted in late 2010. A central coordinating team runs the survey, and is funded by the European Commission. Each participating country covers the costs of employing its own country coordinator, translating the questionnaire, and commissioning fieldwork. Although not all countries achieve this, the aspiration is that countries should have probability samples of the adult (15 plus) population, with high response rates, interviewed face-to-face using CAPI (computer assisted personal interviewing). The survey is recognized currently to be one of the highest quality cross-European surveys. The questionnaire comprises an invariant core of questions asked of all respondents in each round, and a series of rotating modules which are included in only some rounds. Academics are invited to bid for space on the questionnaire in each round. Fieldwork for Round 5 of the ESS was done in 2010/11; 28 countries took part (some of which were 'European' in only quite a loose sense); and a dataset on 26 countries became available for academic analysis in early 2012, comprising 52,041 interviews.

The module on 'trust in justice' that we developed comprised 45 questions, which took around 20 minutes to administer. The dataset included other relevant questions on topics such as personal and political trust, fear of crime and victim experience, as well as demographics. We thus had access to a very significant resource for criminological research.

Our part of the questionnaire was designed from the outset as a theory-testing project[9] about the ways that different dimensions of public trust in justice related to the perceived legitimacy of justice institutions and public cooperation and compliance. As in Tyler and Huo's (2002) work, we hypothesized a set of 'classic' procedural justice relationships between: fair and respectful treatment on the part of justice officials; a consequent sense of the legitimacy of institutions of justice on the part of the public; resulting in greater preparedness to cooperate with the police and the courts; and to comply with the law. As in Tyler's research, we expected to find that public trust in the fairness of justice officials would be a stronger predictor of perceived legitimacy than trust in effectiveness and competence. The most significant way in which we developed procedural justice theory was to operationalize the concept of moral alignment between the public and the institution as of justice. In other words, we set out to test empirically a version of procedural justice theory that combined elements of Tyler's work with that of Beetham. The key constructs that we set out to measure in the module are set out in Box 16.1.

In presenting selected results here we have grouped countries into types, drawing on classifications used by Cavadino and Dignan (2006, 2013) and Seppi-Lappala (2011): Neo-liberal; Conservative corporatist; Social democratic corporatist; Southern European; Post-communist; and Israel.

VARIATIONS IN TRUST AND LEGITIMACY ACROSS COUNTRY

In presenting findings, we first present some 'league tables' for questions which we subsequently incorporated into scales measuring variously: trust in effectiveness; trust in procedural fairness; trust in distributive fairness; felt obligation to obey the police; moral alignment with the police; and perceived legality of police action. In each figure, countries are grouped according to our six-category scheme and are ordered within each category from low levels of trust to high levels of trust.

Figure 16.1 shows one of three items used to measure trust in police effectiveness. The question asked respondents how quickly the police would arrive if a violent crime occurred near their home, using an 11-point scale. There was limited variation across

[9] See <http://www.europeansocialsurvey.org/index.php?option=com_docman&task=cat_view&gid=145&Itemid=80> (accessed 24 July 2013) for a comprehensive guide to the module.

Box 16.1 Some of the key concepts measured in the Trust in Justice module of ESS Round 5

a. Trust in justice institutions
   i. Trust in police effectiveness
   ii. Trust in police procedural fairness
   iii. Trust in police distributive fairness
   iv. Trust in court effectiveness
   v. Trust in court procedural fairness
   vi. Trust in court distributive fairness

b. Perceived legitimacy
   vii. Consent to police authority (a sense of obligation to obey the police)
   viii. Consent to court authority (a sense of obligation to defer to the authority of the courts
   ix. Moral alignment with the police
   x. Moral alignment with the courts
   xi. The perceived legality of the police
   xii. The perceived legality of court officials

c. Willingness to cooperate with the police and courts
   xiii. Preparedness to report crimes to the police
   xiv. Preparedness to identify suspect to the police
   xv. Preparedness to act as a juror in court

d. Compliance with the law: self-report measures of law-breaking over the past 5 years

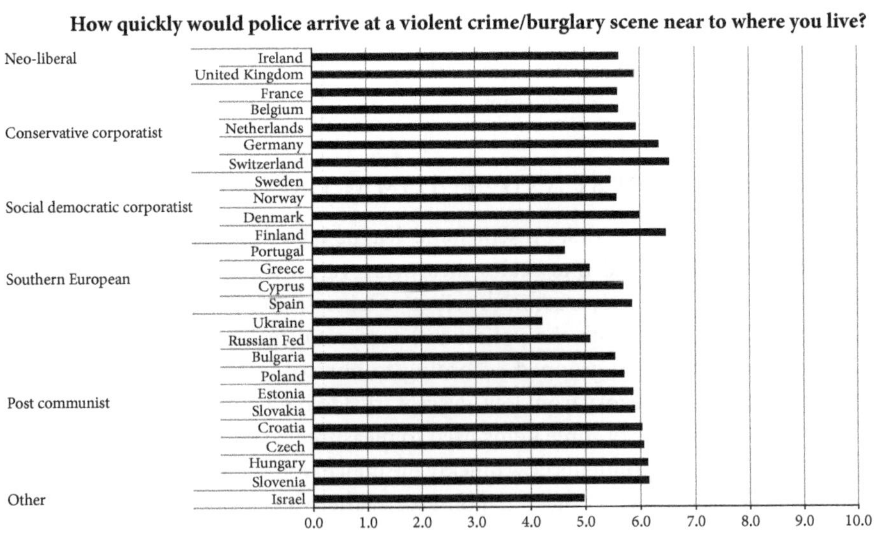

Figure 16.1 Trust in police effectiveness, by country

Question: 'If a violent crime or house burglary were to occur near to where you live and the police were called, how slowly or quickly do you think they would arrive at the scene?' (11-point scale running from slow to quick.)

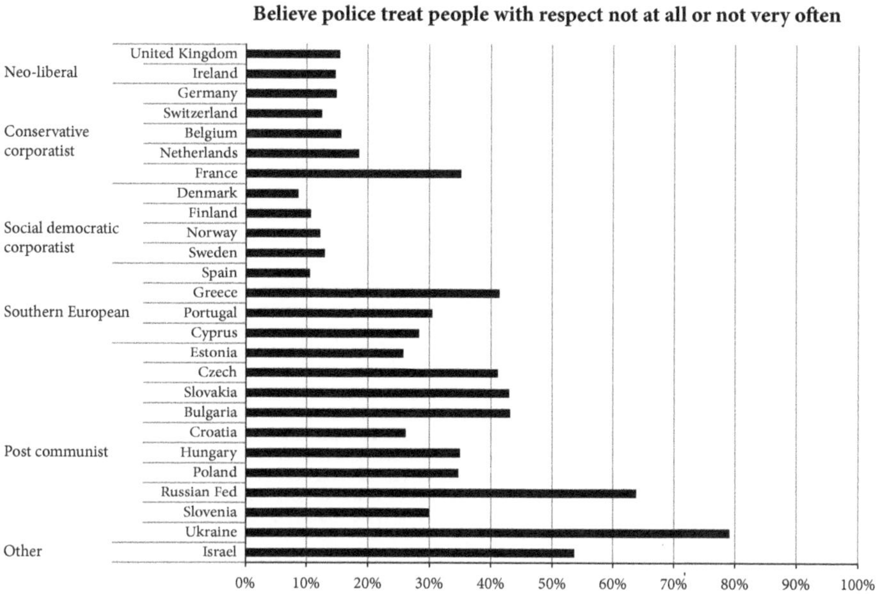

Figure 16.2 Trust in police fairness

Question: 'Based on what you have heard or your own experience how often would you say the police generally treat people in [country] with respect?' (4-point scale, not at all often, not very often, or, very often.)

the 26 countries, with means ranging from 6.5 (Switzerland, with the highest mean) and 4.2 (Ukraine). Despite stereotypes of Scandinavian or northern European efficiency and southern or eastern European tardiness, it seems that Europeans have broadly equivalent beliefs and expectations about the ability of the police to turn up promptly when needed.

Figure 16.2 shows responses to an item about the procedural fairness of the police. We asked respondents how often the police treat people fairly, with responses ranging from 'very often' to 'often' to 'not very often' and 'not at all often'. Figure 16.2 plots the proportion of people who say either 'not at all/not very often' (as opposed to 'often or very often'). Ukraine, the Russian Federation, and Israel have the least positive views on how the police treat people, while Denmark, Finland, Norway, and Spain have the most positive views.

In contrast to the picture in relation to trust in police effectiveness, we find here significant variation across the different *groups* of countries. Trust in the fairness of the police is highest in the social democratic Scandinavian countries, followed by the neo-liberal fringe of UK and Ireland, and the conservative corporatist states. Trust in police fairness then declines as we move south and east, to what appears to be exceptionally low levels in the Russian Federation, Ukraine, and Israel.

What about trust in distributive fairness? Figure 16.3 shows the proportion of people who think that when dealing with victims of crime, the police treat poor people worse than rich people. The countries least trusting of the police in this regard are Ukraine, Greece, the Russian Federation, Slovakia, and Israel. Netherlands, Denmark,

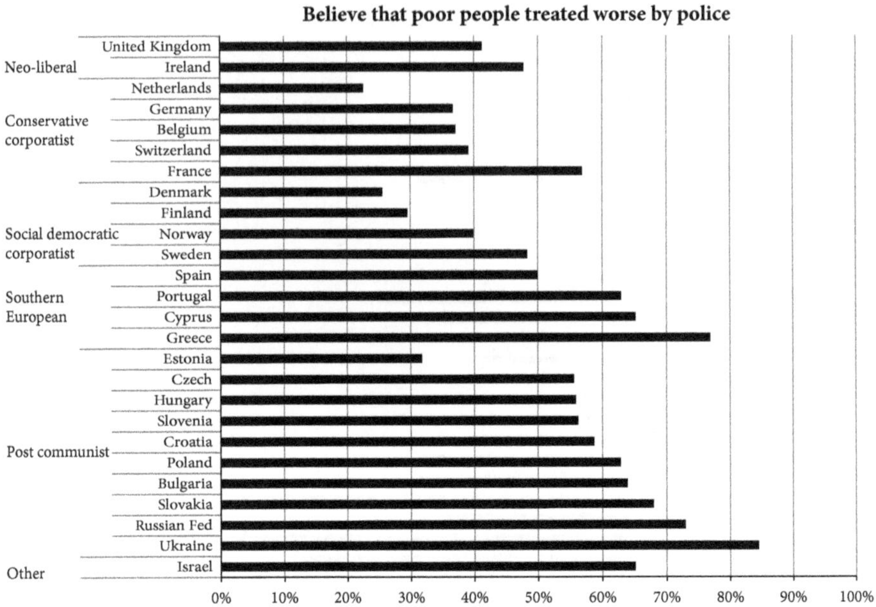

Figure 16.3 Trust in police distributive fairness, by country

Question: 'When victims report crimes, do you think the police treat rich people worse, poor people worse, or are rich and poor treated equally? Choose your answer from this card.' (3-point scale: Rich people treated worse, Poor people treated worse, Rich and poor treated equally.)

Finland, and Estonia score relatively well. Variation here appears less closely correlated with country type, although, in general, perceptions of distributive fairness are worse in the southern European and post-communist states and more favourable in the social democratic, conservative corporatist, and neo-liberal countries.

The next three figures present findings for items contributing to scales for each of our three sub-components of empirical legitimacy. Figure 16.4 presents findings for a question measuring respondents' sense of obligation to obey the police. Scores are highest in Denmark, Finland, Sweden, and Cyprus, and lowest in the Russian Federation, Ukraine, and Slovenia.

Our second dimension of police legitimacy is moral alignment. We have argued that for the policed to regard power-holders as having legitimate authority, their sense of obligation to obey must flow at least in part from a sense of moral alignment—or a belief that its power is normatively justified. We measured the justification of police authority using questions such as 'The police generally have the same sense of right and wrong as I do'. These items are assumed to indicate whether or not people believe the police are policing according to a shared vision of appropriate social order.

Figure 16.5 shows levels of agreement with the statement 'The police have the same sense of right and wrong as I do'. We see that moral alignment is highest in Denmark, France, Sweden, and Norway, and lowest in Estonia, Cyprus, Poland, and the Russian Federation. The pattern here is broadly similar to that in relation to felt obligation, and citizens of northern and western European countries generally felt more morally

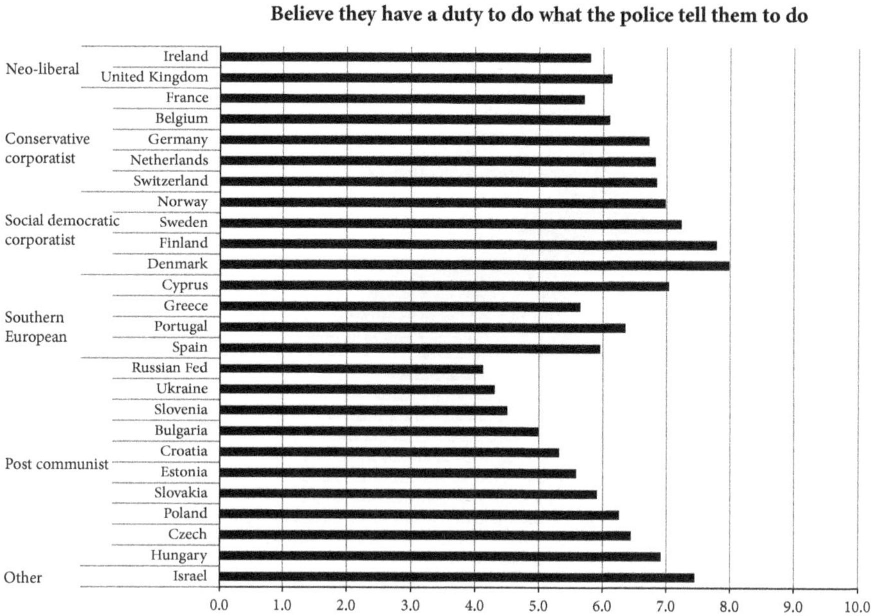

Figure 16.4 Felt obligation to obey the police, by country

Question: 'To what extent is it your duty to do what the police tell you even if you don't understand or agree with the reasons?' (11-point scale, running from 'not at all' to 'completely'.)

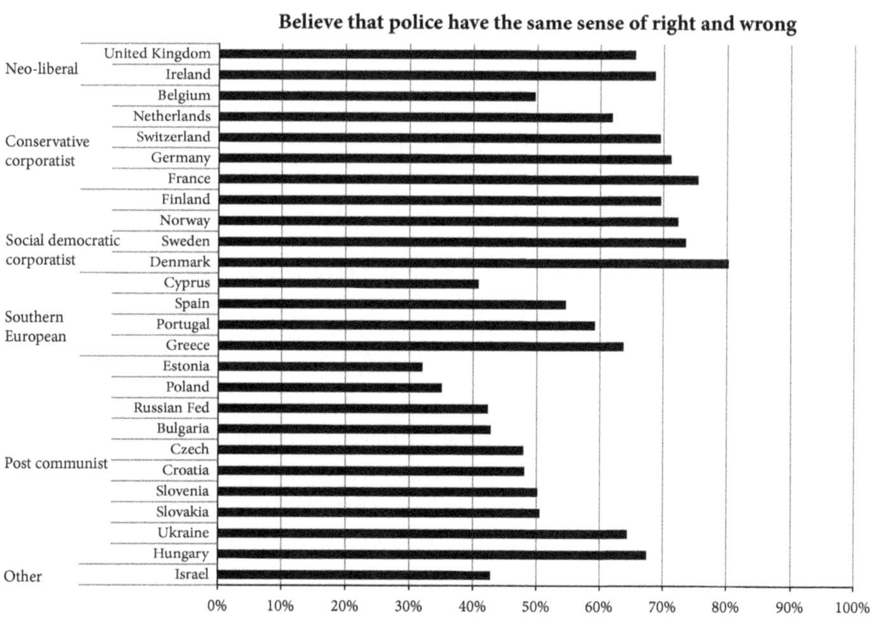

Figure 16.5 Moral alignment with the police, by country

Question: 'The police generally have the same sense of right and wrong as I do.' (Five point scale, running from 'completely agree' to 'completely disagree'.)

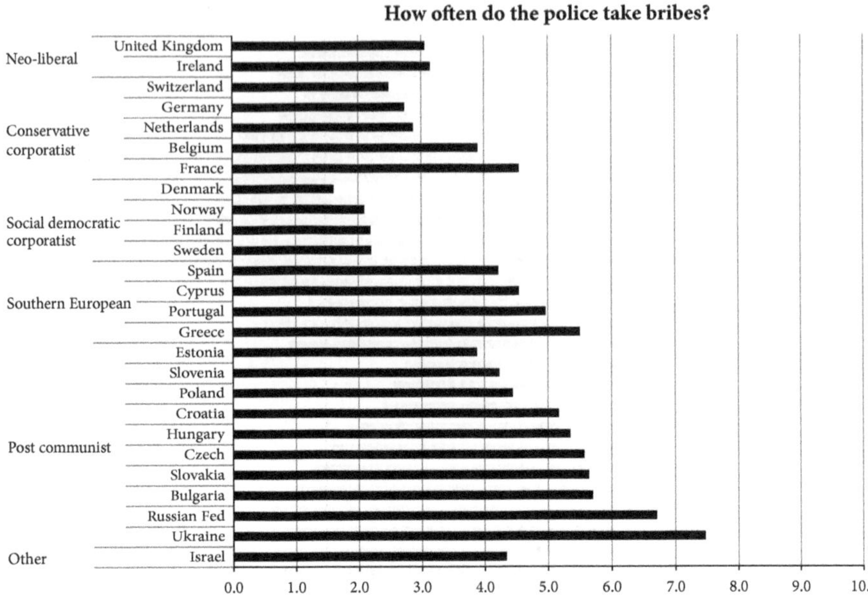

Figure 16.6 Perceived legality of police action, by country

Question: 'How often would you say that the police in [country] take bribes?' (11-point scale where 0 is never and 10 is always.)

aligned with their police, while scores on this measure were generally lower in the post-communist east.

The final sub-component of police legitimacy is the perceived legality of their actions. For the police to have the right to rule, they must not abuse their power by acting above the rule of law. Figure 16.6 shows how often people think the police take bribes. We see that police bribe-taking is seen to be lowest in Denmark, Finland, Norway, and Sweden, and highest in the Ukraine, the Russian Federation, Bulgaria, and Slovakia. There is again significant variation by country type. Perceptions of police corruption were most favourable in the social democratic Scandinavian states and least favourable in the Southern European and post-communist countries.

THE PREDICTORS OF POLICE LEGITIMACY

As described in the previous section, procedural justice theories maintain that trust in institutions—and particularly trust in their fairness—is predictive of the legitimacy granted to them by those they govern. The next three figures present the correlations between public trust in police effectiveness, procedural fairness, and distributive fairness, on the one hand, and the three components of legitimacy—felt obligation, moral alignment, and perceived legality—on the other. In line with the general predictions of the procedural justice model, we expect that trust in the fairness of the police will be the most important predictor of legitimacy across most if not all of the countries included in the analysis. If this is indeed the case, such a finding would seem to have significant policy implications for European criminal justice policy—particularly if, in the same countries, the legitimacy of the police can at a later date be linked to cooperation and compliance.

We used latent variable techniques to generate measures of trust and legitimacy that are more accurate and reliable than the single-item indicators used earlier (see Jackson et al. 2011). Moreover we tested the model—linking trust in police effectiveness, procedural fairness, and distributive fairness to obligation, moral alignment, and perceived legality—separately for each country. This means that we estimate conditional correlations between the different dimensions of trust and legitimacy in each country.

Taking each component of legitimacy in turn we find, first, that trust in police procedural justice is the strongest and most consistent predictor of felt obligation to obey. This association was positive and statistically significant in all 26 countries. Trust in police effectiveness and distributive fairness were much less consistent predictors of obligation to obey, although in some countries—notably the UK—there were significant and substantively large associations between trust in effectiveness and this component of legitimacy. This finding from the ESS therefore stands in contrast to other UK studies which have found only weak correlations between trust in police effectiveness and legitimacy (e.g. Jackson et al. 2012a, 2012b).

Trust in police procedural fairness was also the most important predictor of the second component of legitimacy, 'moral alignment'. This association was positive in all countries, although it generally seemed to be smaller in magnitude than the link between procedural justice and felt obligation. The associations between trust in police effectiveness and distributive fairness and moral alignment were again both weaker and less consistent.

The picture changes as we turn to the legality component of legitimacy (measured by beliefs about corruption). While trust in police effectiveness and procedural justice are only weak and inconsistent predictors of this component of legitimacy, there appears to be stronger associations between trust in distributive justice and perceptions of corruption. Precisely why this might be is at this stage unclear: one interpretation might be that people perceive corruption as enabling or entailing an unfair distribution of resources or outcomes.

Taken together, these results seem to support our original hypotheses. Across the 26 countries included in the analysis, trust in police procedural justice was the strongest and/or most consistent predictor of legitimacy. Yet, trust in effectiveness and distributive justice was also important in some countries, and particularly in relation to the legality component of legitimacy. The empirical legitimacy of the police across Europe appears to be strongly founded in trust in the procedural fairness of its behaviour but, unsurprisingly, other factors are also in play and, in any particular context, may attain major importance.

These findings are summarized in Figures 16.7, 8, and 9. These show how the three dimensions of trust in the police (trust in police effectiveness, trust in their procedural fairness, and trust in their distributive fairness) are related, respectively to the three dimensions of perceived legitimacy (perceived obligation to obey, perceived moral alignment, and perceived legality). For each country the strength of the relationship is indicated by the positioning of the dot on a scale which has positive and minus values. The position on the scale indicates the 'effect size' of the conditional correlation

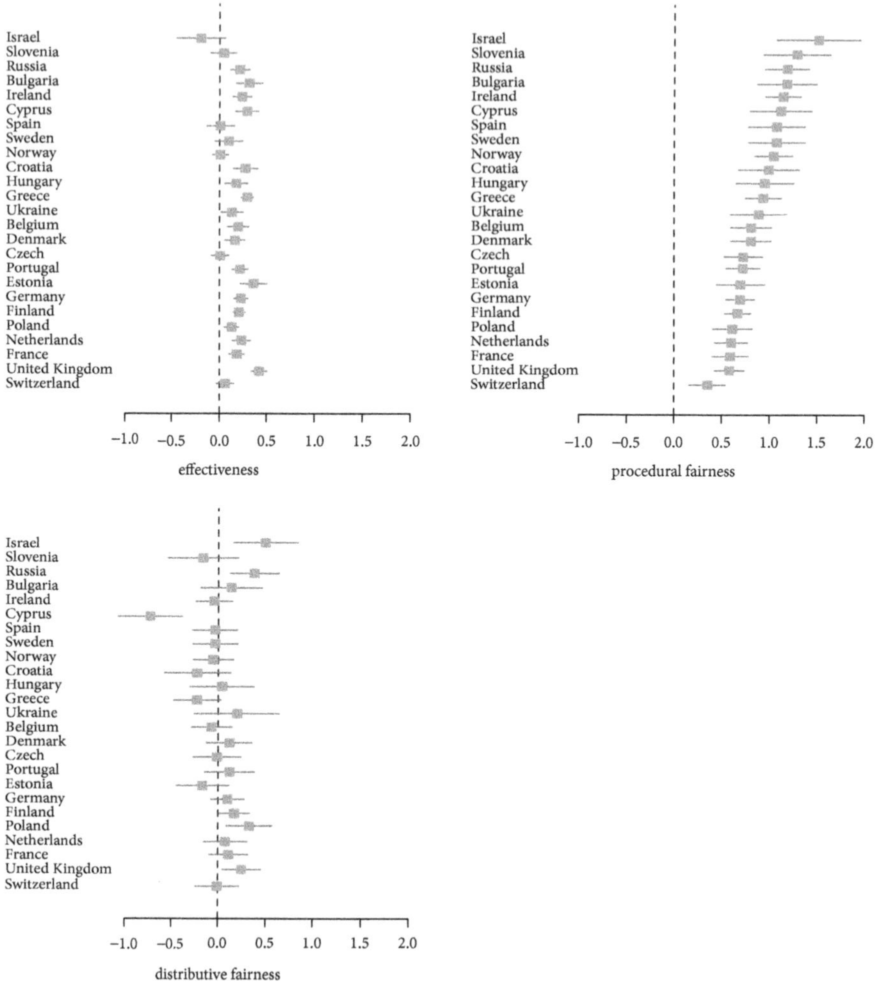

Figure 16.7 Relationships between forms of trust in the police and perceived obligation to obey

between variables in our structural equation models. High positive scores mean strong positive correlations, and high negative scores mean strong negative correlations. The 'arms' spreading out from each dot indicate confidence intervals in our estimates of effect size. (In other words, the true effect size could lie anywhere between the 'stretch' of the two arms.) Where the value of zero falls within the confidence intervals, the relationship is not statistically significant.

THE CONSEQUENCES OF LEGITIMACY: COMPLIANCE AND COOPERATION

At the time of writing, we had not yet completed a full analysis across all ESS countries of the relationships between empirical legitimacy on the one hand, and

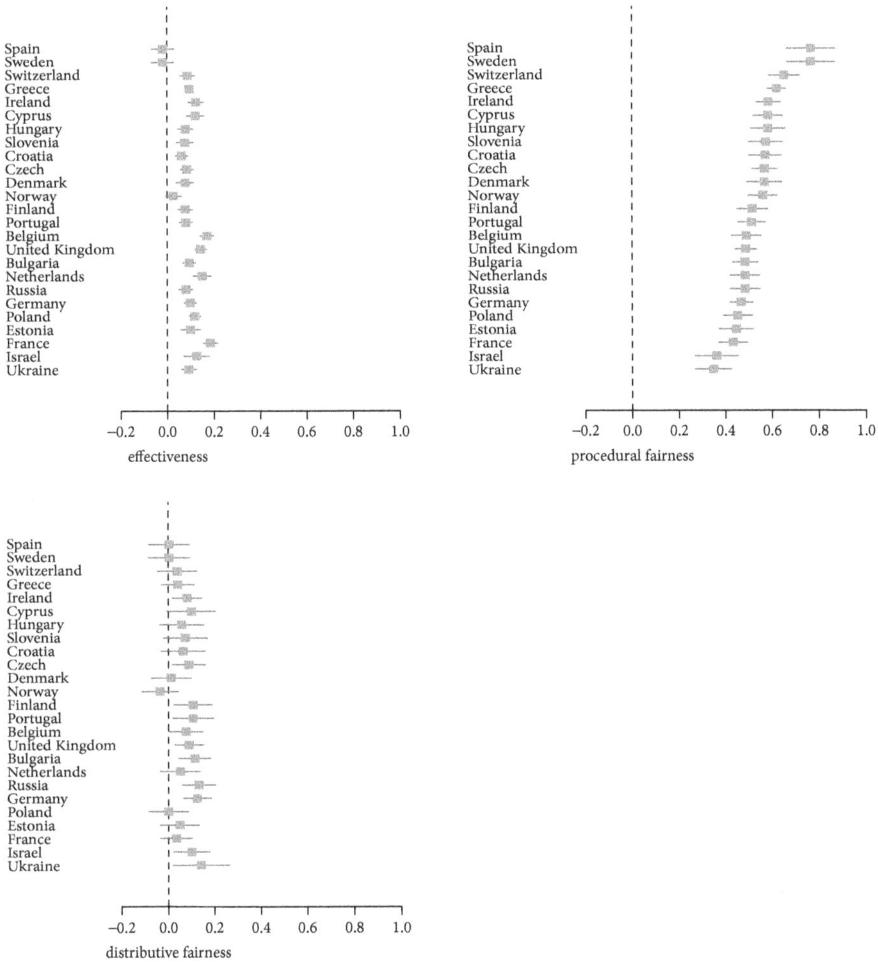

Figure 16.8 Relationships between forms of trust in the police and perceived moral alignment with the police

compliance with the law and cooperation with justice, on the other. Analysis in progress shows that moral alignment is a strong predictor of cooperation with justice across all countries, whilst perceived obligation to obey is predictive in only some. Analysis of the links between empirical legitimacy and compliance with the law has been complicated by weak measures of self-reported offending, and is ongoing, but we have conducted analysis of the UK dataset, examining compliance and cooperation respectively (see European Social Survey 2012 for more details). Next, we extend these models to include distributive fairness and perceived legality (while also combining felt obligation to obey the police and law). Figures 16.10 and 11 summarize the findings.

Moving from left to right, Figure 16.10 shows first the relationships between measures of trust and legitimacy; it then shows relationships between perceived police

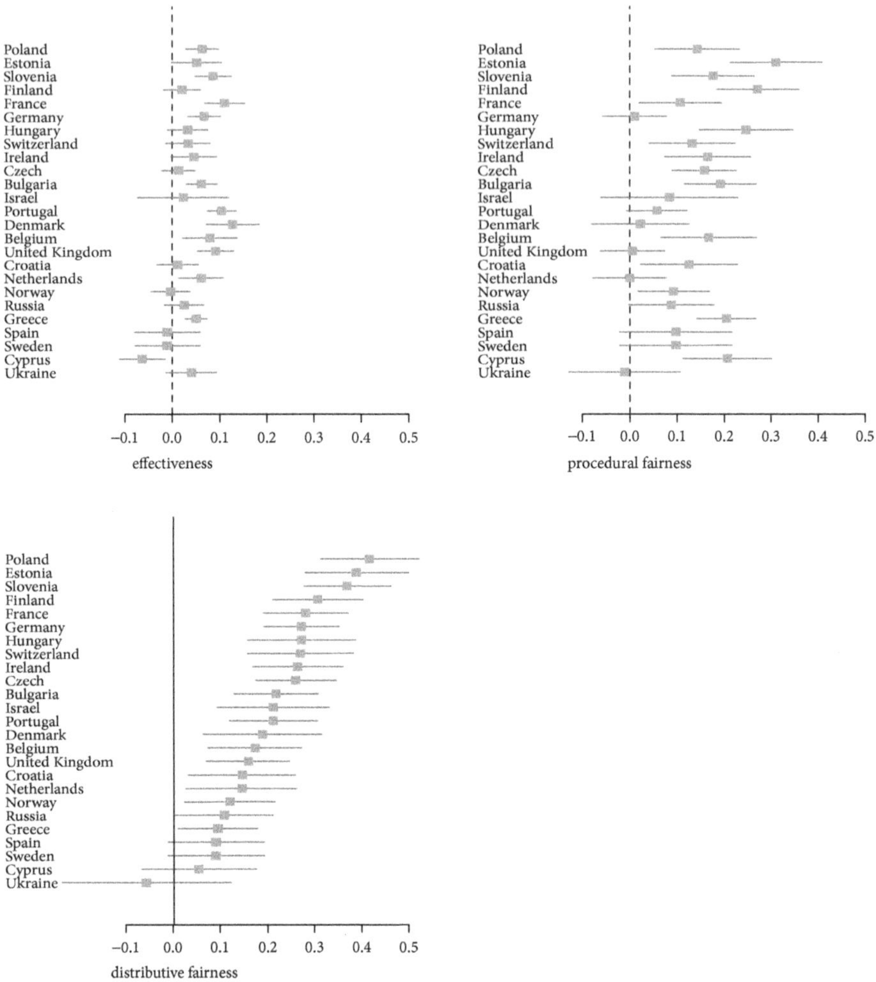

Figure 16.9 Relationships between forms of trust in the police and perceived legality

legitimacy, risk of sanction, and offending behaviour. This analytical approach allows us to examine a number of potentially competing pathways to compliance (see Jackson et al. 2012b). Looking at the relationships between our three different forms of trust and our three different components of legitimacy, these are statistically significant for all except the one between trust in effectiveness and perceived legality. Trust in procedural justice has strong or very strong relationships with all three components of legitimacy.

Looking at the predictors of compliance with the law (or offending behaviour), we see that four are significant. The first is the pathway of *instrumental compliance*. This is where an individual responds in a self-interested way to policing, whether to gain a reward or to avoid punishment. Finding some small evidence for this pathway, the indirect effect of trust in police effectiveness— via the perceived risk of getting caught— on buying stolen goods is statistically significant (albeit with a substantively small effect

Structural equation modeling with categorical indicator and probit regression for committing crime (Mplus 5.2).
Measurement models not shown for visual ease.
Perceived risk of sanction is allowed to co-vary with felt obligation, moral alignment with the police, perceived lawfulness and personal morality.
All latent variables are regressed onto gender and age.
Felt obligation and perceived lawfulness also allowed to co-vary (r=.08).
Chi-square 749, df96, $p<.0005$. CFI 0.925, TLI 0.967, RMSEA 0.053.
* p <.05. ** p <.01. *** p <.001.

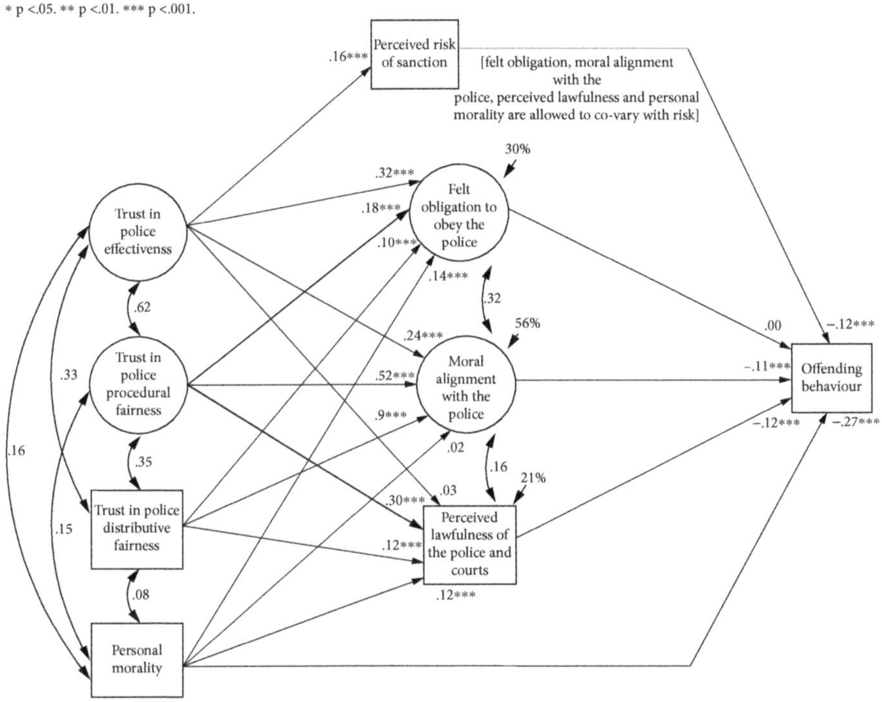

Figure 16.10 Why do people comply with the law?[10]

size). Believing that the police are effective (in controlling and deterring criminals and turning up generally in cases of emergency) and believing that one is likely to get caught is associated with a lower likelihood of admitting to buying stolen goods.

The second pathway is the *morality of the act*. Here the effect is relatively strong. People who think it is wrong to buy stolen goods also tend to report not having bought stolen goods (probably because they haven't, but possibly also because they do not like reporting things that they think are immoral). They refrain from behaving in a certain way—even if that act was suddenly made *legal* or they would benefit personally—because their moral principles lead them to comply.

The third significant pathway is *moral alignment with the police*. People who feel aligned with the values of the police tend to have a relatively low expected chance of buying stolen goods. Controlling for their sense of obligation to obey the law and police, their perception of the risk of getting caught, and their feelings about the morality of the act, moral alignment with the police plausibly generates a sense of social identification with the police; identification with the police as a source of moral values may then generate role and expectation involvement, with a corresponding

[10] *Source*: European Social Survey Round Five (2010), UK data.

need to meet the expectations of that role (the 'law-abiding citizen'). Adjusting for specific assessments of morality and sanction, they believe that the police represent appropriate normative and ethical frameworks. People who identify with the police are intrinsically motivated to work towards group welfare; the group is integrated with their self-concept (Blader and Tyler 2009); so they are more likely to act in ways that accord with the larger group (e.g. obey the law).

The fourth significant pathway is *perceived lawfulness of the police and criminal courts*. People who believe that police officers and judges take bribes are also more likely to have bought stolen goods. This effect is separate to both that of obligation and of moral alignment.

Figure 16.11 presents a similar structural equation model for cooperation with the police.[11] It addresses the question why some people are more prepared than others to cooperate with the police, in providing information, provide witness statements and evidence in court. Studies in the US and elsewhere (e.g. Sunshine and Tyler 2003; Murphy et al. 2009; Kochel 2012; Gau et al. 2012; Bradford et al. 2013; Mazerolle et al. 2013) have consistently found that trust in the procedural fairness of the police is far more important in explaining variation in cooperation than trust in the effectiveness of the police.

Figure 16.11 shows various correlations between trust in effectiveness, trust in procedural and distributive fairness, legitimacy, and readiness to cooperate. Trust in the police is correlated with legitimacy, as in Figure 16.10, and there is a particularly strong relationship between trust in police fairness and moral alignment with the police (people seem to identify with the police as a moral authority when they believe that they wield their power in fair ways; moral alignment seems to some degree to be based upon the values that the police express and project when wielding their power and authority). Finally, all three aspects of legitimacy are significant predictors of willingness to cooperate with the police.

USING TANKEBE'S (2013) DEFINITION OF LEGITIMACY WITH ESS DATA

As mentioned earlier, Tankebe defines legitimacy as perceived effectiveness, procedural fairness, distributive fairness, and lawfulness. This definition can be applied using the ESS data. Figure 16.12 shows the findings, focusing this time on compliance with the law. The four dimensions of legitimacy are on the left, alongside personal morality. The model then places felt obligation to obey the police and the law in the middle, and offending behaviour on the right. In Tankebe's framework, felt obligation is an outcome of legitimacy not a constituent of legitimacy, since people can feel obligated to obey the police not only because they believe that the police have a positive right to dictate appropriate behaviour, but also out of 'fear, a sense of powerlessness or pragmatic acquiescence' (Tankebe 2013: 5).

[11] The fit of the model is good according to the approximate *fit* statistics, although not according to exact fit statistics: Chi-square 706, degrees of freedom 150, and $p<.001$; CFI .98, TLI .98, and RMSEA .04.

Structural equation modeling using Mplus 5.2.
Measurement models not presented for visual ease. Standardized coefficients.
All variables are regressed onto gender and age.
Felt obligation and perceived lawfulness also allowed to co-vary (r=.10).
Chi-square 474, df 58, p<.0005. CFI 0.946 TLI 0.979; RMSEA 0.055.
* p <.05. ** p <.01. *** p <.001.

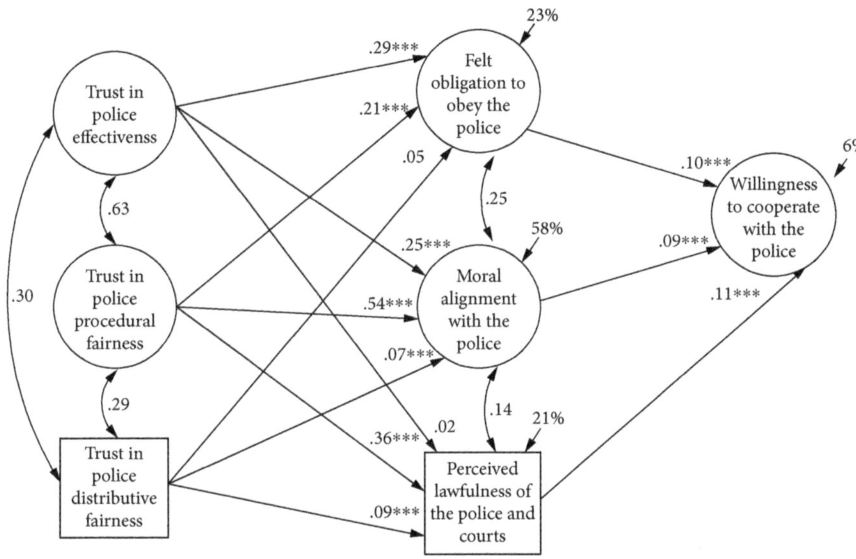

Figure 16.11 Why do people cooperate with the police?[12]

The findings indicate that personal morality is the biggest predictor of offending behaviour, with perceived risk of sanction and perceived lawfulness as smaller but still statistically significant predictors. We would ask, here, though, what are the mechanisms linking legitimacy to offending behaviour? In terms of the link between police lawfulness and offending, the mechanism is presumably the same as that described earlier. In the case of the other components of legitimacy as described by Tankebe, the potential mechanisms are less clear.[13] But, in any case, perceived effectiveness, procedural fairness, and distributive fairness are not significant predictors of offending, adjusting for the other predictors in the model.[14] It appears that the concept

[12] *Source*: European Social Survey Round Five (2010), UK data.

[13] One could suggest, for example, that based on the group engagement model of procedural justice, when people feel the police act in a procedurally fair way their identification with the group the police represent (the nation or state) is strengthened, and they are thus more likely to follow the rules (laws) of this group. This would not, however, be an argument about legitimacy in this sense outlined here, but about the dynamics of intra-group processes (albeit that these are closely related to legitimacy concerns).

[14] In the fitted model represented in Figure 16.10, trust in police procedural fairness had a statistically and substantively significant effect on offending behaviour via moral alignment. But in the model using Tankebe's (2013) definition of legitimacy there was no statistically (nor substantively) significant direct (or indirect) effect from procedural fairness on offending behaviour. Further analysis revealed that this was mostly because one is controlling for the effect of perceived police effectiveness on offending behaviour, with procedural fairness and effectiveness highly correlated.

Structural equation modeling with categorical indicators and probit regression for committing crime (Mplus 5.2).
Measurement models not shown for visual ease.
Perceived risk of sanction is allowed to co-vary with felt obligation, perceived lawfulness and personal morality.
All latent variables are regressed onto gender and age.
Felt obligation and perceived lawfulness also allowed to co-vary (r=.08).
Chi-square 642, df 68, *p*<.0005. CFI 0.900 TLI 0.937; RMSEA 0.059.
* p <.05. ** p <.01. *** p <.001.

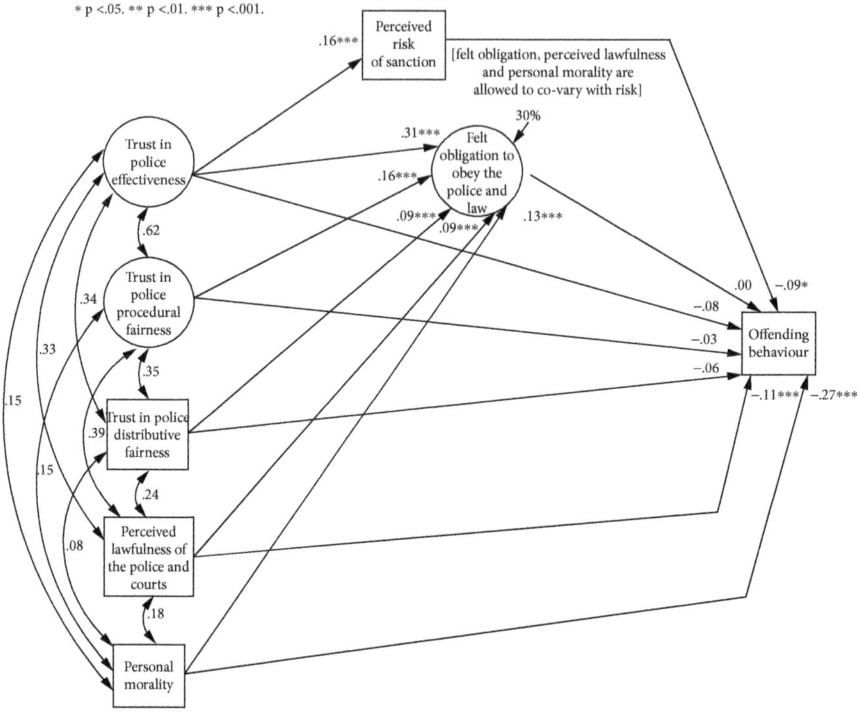

Figure 16.12 Why do people comply with the law? Applying Tankebe's (2013) definition

of moral alignment with the police, absent from Tankebe's definition of legitimacy, is both a predictor of self-reported offending and the bridge that links trust in police procedural fairness, and indeed effectiveness, with offending: it is, we would claim, a key aspect of legitimacy that represents citizen's sense that the police share their values (that they believe that the police are justified in holding power because the police are operating according to acceptable normative and ethical frameworks). This in turn promotes social identification with the police and activates a reciprocal role relationship that encourages law-abiding behaviour.

We ran a similar model to identify predictors of public cooperation with the police using Tankebe's definition of legitimacy. In this, three out of the four of Tankebe's dimensions of legitimacy predict cooperation (as does felt obligation to obey the police and law). The biggest factor is perceived procedural fairness, and distributive fairness was not statistically significant. Whilst there may be differences between our ESS analysis and Tankebe's approach to conceptual analysis, our key empirical findings on cooperation are compatible.

LESSONS FROM THE ESS FOR EUROPEAN POLICY

Whilst analysis continues, our work to date has shown that trust in the police is an important factor in shaping people's sense of police legitimacy, and trust in police fairness is the crucial dimension across Europe. And in one jurisdiction where analysis has been carried out, the hypothesized relationships between empirical legitimacy, compliance, and cooperation emerge as strongly significant. We have established, convincingly we hope, that there is strong empirical support for central aspects of 'procedural justice' theory. The findings presented here show clear and strong relationships between dimensions of trust in the police, and dimensions of perceived police legitimacy. Of particular importance is the strong relationship between trust in fairness and dimensions of perceived legitimacy. The clear policy lesson here is that any strategies to build a sense of police legitimacy in the eyes of the public needs to focus on procedural fairness. Fair and respectful treatment of the public by the police seems likely to be the fastest route to improved legitimacy, from the perspective of the policed.

REFERENCES

ALDERSON, J. (1984) *Law and Disorder*. London: Hamish Hamilton.

BEETHAM, D. (1991) *The Legitimation of Power*. London: Macmillan.

BLADER, S. and TYLER, T. R. (2009) 'Testing and Expanding the Group Engagement Model', *Journal of Applied Psychology* 94: 445–64.

BOTTOMS, A. (1995) 'The Philosophy and Politics of Punishment and Sentencing', in Clarkson, C. and Morgan, R. (eds) *The Politics of Sentencing Reform*. Oxford: Clarendon Press.

BOTTOMS, A. (2002) 'Compliance and Community Penalties' (pp. 87–116), in Bottoms, A., Gelsthorpe, L., and Rex, S., *Community Penalties: Change and Challenges*. Cullompton: Willan.

BOTTOMS, A. and TANKEBE, J. (2012) 'Beyond Procedural Justice: A Dialogic Approach to Legitimacy in Criminal Justice', *Journal of Criminal Law and Criminology* 102(1): 119–70.

BRADFORD, B., JACKSON, J., and STANKO, E. (2009) 'Contact and Confidence: Revisiting the Impact of Public Encounters with the Police', *Policing and Society* 19: 20–46.

BRADFORD, B., HUQ, A., JACKSON, J,. and ROBERTS, B. (2013) 'What Price Fairness When Security is at Stake? Police Legitimacy in South Africa', *Regulation and Governance*, doi: 10.1111/rego.12012.

CAVADINO, M. and DIGNAN, J. (2006) *Penal Systems. A Comparative Approach*. London: Sage Publications.

CAVADINO, M. and DIGNAN, J. (2013) *Political Economy and Legal Systems*, in Body-Gendrot, S., Lévy, R., Hough, M., Snacken, S., and Kerezsi, K. (eds) *The Routledge Handbook of European Criminology*. London: Routledge.

COICAUD, J-M. (2002) *Legitimacy and Politics*. Cambridge: Cambridge University Press.

EASTON, D. (1965) *A Framework for Political Analysis*. Englewood Cliffs: Prentice-Hall.

European Social Survey (2011) 'Trust in Justice: Topline Findings from the European Social Survey', *ESS Topline Results Series Issue 1*. By Jackson, J., Hough, M., Bradford, B., Pooler, T. M., Hohl, K., and Kuha, J.

European Social Survey (2012) 'Policing by Consent: Understanding the Dynamics of Police Power and Legitimacy', *ESS Country Specific Topline Results Series Issue 1 (UK)*. By Jackson, J., Hough, M., Bradford, B., Hohl, K., and Kuha, J.

Gau, J. M., Corsaro, N., Stewart, E. A. and Brunson, R. K. (2012) 'Examining Macro-Level Impacts on Procedural Justice and Police Legitimacy', *Journal of Criminal Justice* 40: 333–43.

Giddens, A. (1991) *The Consequences of Modernity.* Cambridge: Polity Press.

Hinsch, W. (2008) 'Legitimacy and Justice', in Kuhnelt, J. (ed) *Political Legitimation without Morality?* London: Springer.

Hinsch, W. (2010) 'Justice, Legitimacy, and Constitutional Rights', *Critical Review of International Social and Political Philosophy* 13(1): 39–54.

Hood, C. (1991) 'A Public Management for all Seasons', *Public Administration* 69(1): 3–19.

Hough, M. (2007) 'Policing, New Public Management and Legitimacy', in Tyler, T. (ed) *Legitimacy and Criminal Justice.* New York: Russell Sage Foundation.

Hough, M., Jackson, J., Bradford, B., Myhill, A., and Quinton, P. (2010) 'Procedural Justice, Trust and Institutional Legitimacy', *Policing: A Journal of Policy and Practice* 4(3): 203–10.

Hough, M. and Sato, M. (eds) (2011) *Trust In Justice: Why it is Important for Criminal Policy, and how it can be Measured: Final Report of the Euro-Justis project.* Helsinki: HEUNI.

Hough, M., Jackson, J., and Bradford, B. (2013 forthcoming) 'Trust in Justice and the Legitimacy of Legal authorities: Topline Findings from a European Comparative Study' in Body-Gendrot, S., Hough, M., Levy, R., Kerezsi, K., and Snacken, S., (eds) *The Routledge Handbook of European Criminology*. London: Routledge.

Huq, A. Z., Tyler, T. R. and Schulhofer, S. J. (2011a) 'How do the Purposes and Targets of Policing Influence the Basis of Public Cooperation with Law Enforcement?', *Psychology, Public Policy and the Law* 17(3): 419–50.

Huq, A. Z., Tyler, T. R. and Schulhofer, S. J. (2011b) 'Mechanisms for Eliciting Cooperation in Counterterrorism Policing: A Study of British Muslims', *Journal of Empirical Legal Studies* 8(4): 728–61.

Jackson, J., Bradford, B., Hough, M., Kuha, J., Stares, S. R., Widdop, S., Fitzgerald, R., Yordanova, M., and Galev, T. (2011) 'Developing European Indicators of Trust in Justice', *European Journal of Criminology* 8: 267–85.

Jackson, J., Bradford, B., Stanko, E. A., and Hohl, K. (2012a) *Just Authority? Trust in the Police in England and Wales.* London: Routledge.

Jackson, J., Bradford, B., Hough, M., Myhill, A., Quinton, P., and Tyler, T. R. (2012b) 'Why do People Comply with the Law? Legitimacy and the Influence of Legal Institutions', *British Journal of Criminology* 52(6): 1051–71.

Jackson, J., Huq, A., Bradford, B., and Tyler, T. R. (2013) 'Monopolizing Force? Police Legitimacy and Public Attitudes towards the Acceptability of Violence', *Psychology, Public Policy and Law.*

Kirk, D. S., Papachristos, A. V., Fagan, J., and Tyler, T. R. (2012) 'The Paradox of Law Enforcement in Immigrant Communities: Does Tough Immigration Enforcement Undermine Public Safety?', *The Annals of the American Academy of Political and Social Science* 641: 79–98.

Kochel, T. R. (2012) 'Can Police Legitimacy Promote Collective Efficacy?', *Justice Quarterly* 29(3): 384–419.

Lappi-Seppälä, T. (2013) 'Imprisonment and Penal Demands: Exploring the Dimensions and Drivers of Systematic and Attitudinal Punitivity' in Body-Gendrot, S., Hough, M., Levy, R. Kerezsi, K., and Snacken, S. (eds) *The Routledge Handbook of European Criminology.* London: Routledge.

MAZEROLLE, L., ANTROBUS, E., BENNETT, S., and TYLER, T. (2013) 'Shaping Citizen Perceptions of Police Legitimacy: A Randomised Field Trial of Procedural Justice', *Criminology* 51(1): 33–63.

MESSNER, S. and ROSENFELD, R. (2001) 'An Institutional-Anomie Theory of Crime', in Paternoster, R. and Bachman, R. (eds) *Explaining Criminals and Crime*. Los Angeles: Roxbury.

MESSNER, S. and ROSENFELD, R. (2010) 'Institutional-Anomie Theory: A Macro-Sociological Explanation of Crime', in Krohn, A. J. L. and Hall, G. P. (eds) *Handbook on Crime and Deviance*. New York: Springer.

MURPHY, K., TYLER T. R., and CURTIS, A. (2009) 'Nurturing Regulatory Compliance: Is Procedural Justice Effective When People Question the Legitimacy of the Law?', *Regulation and Governance* 3(1): 1–26.

PRATT, J. (2007) *Penal Populism*. Milton Park, Abingdon: Routledge.

REINER, R. (2007) *Law and Order: An Honest Citizen's Guide to Crime Control*. Cambridge: Polity Press.

ROBINSON, P. H. (2012) 'Criminalisation Tensions: Empirical Desert, Changing Norms, and Rape Reform', in Duff, R. A., Farmer, L., Marshall, S. E., and Tadros, V. (eds) *The Structures of the Criminal Law*. Oxford: Oxford University Press.

ROBINSON, R. H. and DARLEY, J. M. (1997) 'The Utility of Desert', *Northwestern University Law Review* 91: 453–99.

ROBINSON, P. H. and DARLEY, J. M. (2004) 'Does Criminal Law Deter? A Behavioural Science Investigation', *Oxford Journal of Legal Studies* 24: 173–205.

SACK, F. and SCHLEPPER, C. (2013) 'Changing Definitions of the Criminal Law in Germany in Late Modernity', in Body-Gendrot, S., Lévy, R., Hough, M., Snacken, S., and Kerezsi, K. (eds) *The Routledge Handbook of European Criminology*. London: Routledge.

STERNBERGER, D. (1968) 'Legitimacy' (p. 244), in D. L. Sills (ed) *International Encyclopedia of the Social Sciences* (vol 9). New York: Macmillan Company.

SUNSHINE, J. and TYLER, T. (2003) 'The Role of Procedural Justice and Legitimacy in Public Support for Policing', *Law and Society Review* 37(3): 513–48.

TANKEBE, J. (2013) 'Viewing Things Differently: The Dimensions of Public Perceptions of Legitimacy.' *Criminology* 51(1): 103–135.

TYLER, T. R. (2006a) 'Psychological Perspectives on Legitimacy and Legitimation', *Annual Review of Psychology* 57: 375–400.

TYLER, T. R. (2006b) *Why People Obey the Law*. Princeton: Princeton University Press.

TYLER, T. R. (2011a) *Why People Cooperate: The Role of Social Motivations*. Princeton: Princeton University Press.

TYLER, T. R. (2011b) 'Trust and Legitimacy: Policing in the USA and Europe', *European Journal of Criminology* 8: 254–66.

TYLER, T. R. and FAGAN, J. (2008) 'Legitimacy and Coöperation: Why do People help the Police Fight Crime in their Communities?', *Ohio State Journal of Criminal Law* 6: 231–75.

TYLER, T. R. and HUO, Y. J. (2002) *Trust in the Law: Encouraging Public Cooperation with the Police and Courts*. New York: Russell-Sage Foundation.

TYLER, T. R., SHERMAN, L., STRANG, H., BARNES, G. C., and WOODS, D. (2007) 'Reintegrative Shaming, Procedural Justice, and Recidivism: The Engagement of Offender's Psychological Mechanisms in the Canberra Rise Drinking-and-Driving Experiment', *Law and Society Review* 41(3): 553–86.

TYLER, T. R., SCHULHOFER, S. J., and HUQ, A. Z. (2010) 'Legitimacy and Deterrence Effects in Counter-Terrorism Policing: A Study of Muslim Americans', *Law and Society Review* 44(2): 365–401.

Tyler, T. R. and Wakslak, C. J. (2004) 'Profiling and Police Legitimacy: Procedural Justice, Attributions of Motive, and Acceptance of Police Authority', *Criminology* 42: 253–82.

van Dijk, J. (2013) 'It Is Not Just The Economy: Explaining Post World War II Crime Trends in the Western World', in Body-Gendrot, S., Hough, M., Levy, R., Kerezsi, K., and Snacken, S. (eds) *The Routledge Handbook of European Criminology*. London: Routledge.

Wikström, P. O. H., Oberwittler, D., Trieber, K. and Hardie, B. (2012) *Breaking Rules: The Social and Situational Dynamics of Young People's Crime*. Oxford: Oxford University Press.

INDEX